Sun Performance and Tuning

Java and the Internet

Adrian Cockcroft

with Richard Pettit

Sun Microsystems Press
A Prentice Hall Title

≡

Editorial/production supervision: *Joe Czerwinski*
Copyeditor: *Mary Lou Nohr*
Cover photo: *Tim Wren — CAR Magazine, EMAP Publications Ltd., London*
Manufacturing manager: *Alexis R. Heydt*
Marketing manager: *Stephen Solomon*
Acquisitions editor: *Gregory G. Doench*
Sun Microsystems Press publisher: *Rachel Borden*

10 9 8 7 6 5 4 3 2 1

ISBN: 0-13-095249-4

About the Cover: The cover shows a 1992 Porsche 911 Carrera 4. There is a special analogy between the development over the years of the Porsche 911 and the UNIX® operating system. Both were created in the 1960s, in a form which is recognizably the same as the current product. Both have been revised and developed continuously since they were created—they have grown larger and much more powerful. Both represent the latest and best technology applied to a product that has endured despite its quirks—both are exceptional high-performance tools. Guess how I spent most of the royalties from the first edition?

SunSoft Press
A Prentice Hall Title

Contents

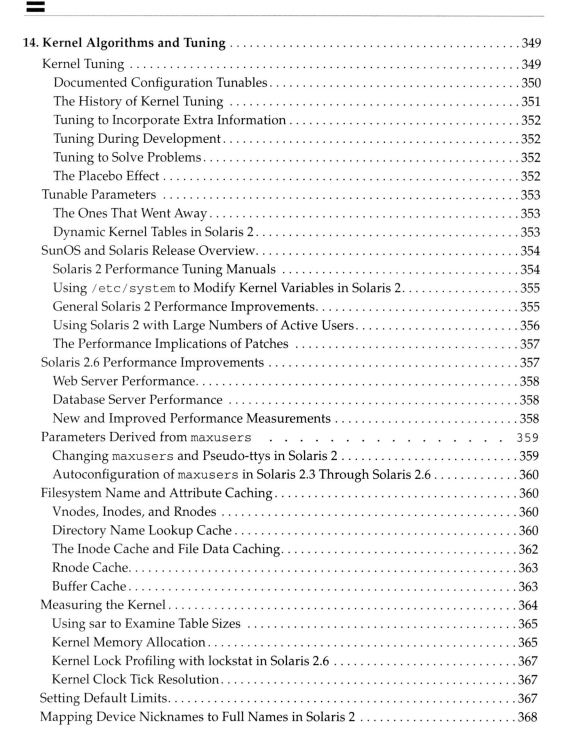

List of Figures

List of Tables

Acknowledgments

Thanks to my family, Linda, Oliver, Camilla and our labrador Tyla, for keeping me rooted in the *real* world and making sure I get some excercise.

This book is dedicated to Sun's Systems Engineers worldwide; the people who have to deal with configuration, performance, and tuning issues on a daily basis.

Special thanks to Brian Wong, Richard McDougall, Don Devitt, Rachael Fish, Enrique Vargas, David Deeths, Graham Hazel, Steven Gan, Christian Demeure, Jim Mauro, Phil Harman, David Pinnington, Mike Bennett, Charles Alexander and Mark Connelly for their technical input and support, and Mary Lou Nohr, Rachel Borden, and Greg Doench for their help in reviewing and producing this book.

Richard Pettit shared my frustration with the inflexibility of performance tools, and had the vision to create and develop the SE Performance Toolkit. This has given me a very powerful and productive vehicle for developing and testing ideas, and I invited him to join me as co-author of this edition, to describe the toolkit and the interfaces used to construct performance tools.

All the engineers at Sun who work on designing high performance hardware and tuning Solaris deserve a special mention for their advice, and all the performance improvements and measurements they devise for each successive release. In particular Ashok Singhal, Michel Cekleov, George Cameron, Chaitanya Tikku, Todd Clayton, Allan Packer, Jim Skeen, and John Lipinski in SMCC; Marc Tremblay in Sun Microelectronics, and Steve Parker, Mukesh Kacker, Jerry Chu, Bruce Curtis, Jim Litchfield, Jeff Bonwick, Bryan Cantrill, Kevin Clarke, Roger Faulkner, Tim Marsland, Michael Sebrée, Yousef Khalidi, Bart Smaalders, and Wolfgang Thaler in SunSoft.

My father Nick Cockcroft, at the University of Hertfordshire in the UK, gave me my first contacts with computers while I was at school in the early 1970s. I first used UNIX in the Physics Department Lab at The City University, London. While working for Cambridge Consultants Ltd., I became the UNIX systems administrator at one of the first Sun user sites in the UK. Brian Wong was instrumental in both bringing me to work with him in the USA in 1993, and my return to telework from the UK in 1996. I would like to thank all of them for their major contributions to getting me where I am today.

— *Adrian Cockcroft*

Preface

This book consists of everything I have learned over the years about performance and tuning. It includes a structured approach, opinions, heuristics, and references. It contains documentation of the *behavior* of systems, with recommendations that are often needed but that are rarely available. I cover all of the Solaris™ operating system releases up to Solaris 2.6, and major Sun® products up to the beginning of 1998.

This second edition of *Sun Performance And Tuning* has doubled in size, and almost all the content is new. I have been writing a monthly performance question and answer column for *SunWorld Online* magazine at *http://www.sun.com/sunworldonline*, and many of those columns have been updated and incorporated into this book. You should read my column regularly to keep up to date with developments that postdate publication of this book.

During the three years since first publication, the Internet transitioned from a useful tool to a major part of the computer business, and the Java™ phenomenon arrived. This is both a subject for discussion—hence the new subtitle for this edition—and a resource for obtaining detailed and up-to-date information. I have also worked closely with Richard Pettit over the last few years to develop the SE Performance Toolkit, and this edition contains detailed documentation written by Richard on the toolkit, and the performance interfaces provided by Solaris. We decided not to include it with the book on a CD-ROM, as it is easy to download the latest release over the Internet. The SE3.0 release is available from http://www.sun.com/sun-on-net/performance/se3, and my January 1998 SunWorld Online column is an FAQ for SE.

This book is aimed both at developers who want to design for performance and need a central reference to better understand Sun machines, and at system administrators who have a Sun machine running applications and want to understand and improve overall performance.

This book covers an incredibly complex and fast-changing topic. I have tried to organize it in a useful manner with the most important information up front in each chapter and many cross-references. A book like this can never truly be complete and finished, but it has to be frozen at some point so it can be published!

How This Book Is Organized

This book is intended to be read sequentially, as it tries to cover the most significant and most common performance problems first. You can use it as a reference work by following the many cross-references that link related topics.

Chapter 1, "Quick Tips and Recipes," is for those of you who need results *now* and don't have time to read the whole book first.

Chapter 2, "Performance Management," covers the methods and tools used to manage performance.

Chapter 3, "Performance Measurement," tells you what kind of things to measure and how to decide whether your efforts at tuning have made any difference to the system performance.

Chapter 4, "Internet Servers," contains an introduction to TCP/IP and offers guidelines on tuning and sizing web servers and proxy caching web servers.

Chapter 5, "Java Application Servers," contains a complete sizing guide for serving the new class of Network Computer client systems based on Java.

Chapter 6, "Source Code Optimization," is aimed primarily at developers and end users who have access to the source code of the application being tuned. It covers Java performance and 64 bit issues.

Chapter 7, "Applications," tells you how to find out what an off-the-shelf application is doing and discusses changes in the execution environment.

Chapter 8, "Disks," investigates the performance characteristics of disk subsystems and describes how to monitor and tune them.

Chapter 9, "Networks," contains Sun-specific information on network hardware and performance issues.

Chapter 10, "Processors," looks at how to decide whether you have enough CPU power for your workload. The chapter also provides a high-level description of the interactions between multiprocessor machines and Unix®.

Chapter 11, "System Architectures," looks at the way uniprocessor and multiprocessor SPARC® systems are put together.

Chapter 12, "Caches," looks at how caches work in principle, with examples of hardware and kernel based caching mechanisms.

Chapter 13, "RAM and Virtual Memory," explains how the paging algorithm works and where memory flows to and from in the system.

Chapter 14, "Kernel Algorithms and Tuning," provides an insight into the algorithms and tunable parameters of the Solaris 2 kernel.

Chapter 15, "Metric Collection Interfaces," describes the interfaces to Solaris and how to code to them to get at performance information.

Chapter 16, "The SymbEL Example Tools," documents the example tools that are provided with the SE performance toolkit.

Chapter 17, "The SymbEL Language," contains the complete user manual and descriptions of how to use this freely available performance toolkit.

Appendix A, "Tunables Quick Reference," turns the advice given elsewhere into tunable values summarized in table form.

Appendix B, "References," contains a long list of sources of further information, with a description of what is of interest in each document.

Related Books

I have tried to avoid duplicating the techniques and content covered by my colleague Brian Wong in his book *Configuration and Capacity Planning for Solaris Servers*, Sun Press, 1996. There is some natural overlap, but it is best to treat the two books as a matched pair. Brian covers in great detail the techniques required to decide on an initial configuration and has far more information on system and storage architectures than I do.

During the summer of 1997, I presented a week long "Practical Performance Methods" class with Dr. Neil Gunther as part of the Stanford University Western Institute of Computer Science (WICS) summer seminar program. Neil's material is covered in his book, *The Practical Performance Analyst*, McGraw-Hill, 1998. Neil takes the most advanced techniques of performance analysis and modeling and relates them to real-world situations in a way that you can use directly to solve problems. For updates on his work and future seminars, visit http://members.aol.com/CoDynamo/Home.htm.

Typographic Changes and Symbols

The following table describes the type changes and symbols used in this book.

Table PR-1 Typographic Conventions

Typeface or Symbol	Description	Example
`AaBbCc123`	The names of commands, files, and directories; on-screen computer output	Edit your `.login` file. Use `ls -a` to list all files. `system%` You have mail.
`AaBbCc123`	What you type, contrasted with on-screen computer output	`system%` **`su`** `password:`
AaBbCc123	Command-line placeholder: replace with a real name or value	To delete a file, type `rm` *filename*.
AaBbCc123	Book titles, new words or terms, or words to be emphasized	Read Chapter 6 in *User's Guide*. These are called *class* options. You *must* be root to do this.

Code samples are included in boxes and may display the following:

`%`	Unix C-shell prompt	`system%`
`#`	Superuser prompt, either shell	`system#`

Sun Performance and Tuning

Quick Tips and Recipes <span></span>1

This book presents too much detail for you to absorb quickly, so, to start you off, I'll first list a few recurring situations and frequently asked questions I have encountered, with references to the rest of the book for in-depth detail. If you are new to Solaris, some of these tips may be confusing. You can follow the cross-references to get a deeper explanation, or read on and return to the tips later.

For situations where you have no idea where to begin, I have also outlined a "cold start" procedure that should help you focus on problem areas. That section is followed by some performance-oriented configuration recipes for common system types.

Quick Reference for Common Tuning Tips

This list focuses primarily, but not exclusively, on servers running Solaris 2. It should help you decide whether you have overloaded the disks, network, available RAM, or CPUs.

The system will usually have a disk bottleneck.

In nearly every case the most serious bottleneck is an overloaded or slow disk. Use `iostat -xn 30`[1] to look for disks that are more than 5 percent busy and have average response times of more than 30 ms. The response time is mislabeled `svc_t`; it is the time between a user process issuing a read and the read completing (for example), so it is often in the critical path for user response times. If many other processes are accessing one disk, a queue can form, and response times of over 1000 ms (not a misprint, over one second!) can occur as you wait to get to the front of the queue. With careful configuration and a disk array controller that includes nonvolatile RAM (NVRAM), you can keep average response time under 10 ms. See "Load Monitoring and Balancing" on page 75 for more details.

Increasing the inode cache size may help reduce the number of disk I/Os required to manage file systems; see "The Inode Cache and File Data Caching" on page 362. If you have a large memory configuration, the inode cache will already be big enough.

---

1. The –xn option is Solaris 2.6 specific; use –x in previous releases.

Keep checking `iostat -xn 30` as tuning progresses. When a bottleneck is removed, the system may start to run faster, and as more work is done, some other disk will overload. At some point, you may need to stripe file systems and tablespaces over multiple disks.

Disks that contain UFS file systems will show high average service times when they are idle. This is caused by short bursts of updates from the filesystem flushing process described in "Idle Disks and Long Service Times" on page 186. *This effect can safely be ignored*, hence the 5% busy threshold mentioned above.

Poor NFS response times may be hard to see.

Waiting for a network-mounted file system to respond is not counted in the same way as waiting for a local disk. The system will appear to be idle when it is really in a network I/O wait state. Use `nfsstat -m` or (if you are running Solaris 2.6) `iostat -xn` to find out which NFS® server is likely to be the problem, go to it, and check its disk performance. You should look at the NFS operation mix with `nfsstat` on both the client and server and, if writes are common or the server's disk is too busy, configure a Prestoserve or NVRAM at the server. A 10-Mbit Ethernet will be overloaded very easily; the network should be replaced with 100-Mbit Ethernet, preferably in switched full-duplex mode. See the *SMCC NFS Server Performance and Tuning Guide* on the Solaris SMCC Hardware AnswerBook® CD, or look for it on http://docs.sun.com.

Avoid the common `vmstat` misconceptions.

When you look at `vmstat`, *please* don't waste time worrying about where all the RAM has gone. After a while, the free list will stabilize at around 3% of the total memory configured[2]. The system stops bothering to reclaim memory above this level, even when you aren't running anything. See "Understanding vmstat and sar Output" on page 320. You can also ignore the third "w" column, which is a count of how many *idle* processes are currently swapped out. Of course, you must also remember to ignore the first line output by `vmstat`.

```
% vmstat 5
 procs     memory            page            disk          faults      cpu
 r b w   swap  free  re mf pi po fr de sr f0 s0 s1 s5   in   sy  cs us sy id
 0 0 0   9760 16208   0  4  6  2  5  0  0 141 35 19 149  898  99  6  2 92
 0 0 12 212672 1776   0  1  3  0  0  0  0   1  0  0 105  140  50  0  0 99
```

---

2. The actual level depends on the version of the operating system you are running; it may be fixed at a megabyte or less.

Don't panic when you see page-ins and page-outs in **vmstat**.

These activities are normal since all filesystem I/O is done by means of the paging process. Hundreds or thousands of kilobytes paged in and paged out are not a cause for concern, just a sign that the system is working hard.

Use page scanner "sr" activity as your RAM shortage indicator.

When you really are short of memory, the scanner will be running continuously at a high rate (over 200 pages/second averaged over 30 seconds). If it runs in separated high-level bursts and you are running Solaris 2.5 or earlier, make sure you have a recent kernel patch installed—an updated paging algorithm in Solaris 2.5.1 was back-ported to previous releases. See "Understanding vmstat and sar Output" on page 320.

Look for a long run queue (**vmstat procs r**).

If the run queue or load average is more than four times the number of CPUs, then processes end up waiting too long for a slice of CPU time. This waiting can increase the interactive response time seen by users. Add more CPU power to the system (see "Monitoring Processors" on page 229).

Look for processes blocked waiting for I/O (**vmstat procs b**).

A blocked process is a sign of a disk bottleneck. If the number of blocked processes approaches or exceeds the number in the run queue, tune your disk subsystem. Whenever there are any blocked processes, *all CPU idle time is treated as wait for I/O time!* The vmstat command correctly includes wait for I/O in its idle value, but it can be viewed with iostat or sar. If you are running database batch jobs, you should expect to have some blocked processes, but you can increase batch throughput by removing disk bottlenecks.

Check for CPU system time dominating user time.

If there is more system time than user time and the machine is not an NFS server, you may have a problem. NFS service is entirely inside the kernel, so system time will normally dominate on an NFS server. To find out the source of system calls, see "Tracing Applications" on page 155. To look for high interrupt rates and excessive mutex contention, see "Use of mpstat to Monitor Interrupts and Mutexes" on page 236.

1

Watch out for processes that hog the CPU.

Processes sometimes fail in a way that consumes an entire CPU. This type of failure can make the machine seem sluggish. Watch for processes that are accumulating CPU time rapidly when you don't think they should be. Use ps or see "pea.se" on page 488. If you find that the system process fsflush is using a lot of CPU power, see the description of the kernel variables "tune_t_fsflushr and autoup" on page 339.

Cold Start Procedure

I see a lot of questions from users or administrators who have decided that they have a performance problem but don't know where to start or what information to provide when they ask for help. I have seen email from people who just say "my system is slow" and give no additional information at all. I have also seen 10-megabyte email messages with 20 attachments containing days of vmstat, sar, and iostat reports, but with no indication of what application the machine is supposed to be running. In this section, I'll lead you through the initial questions that need to be answered. This may be enough to get you on the right track to solving the problem yourself, and it will make it easier to ask for help effectively.

1. **What is the business function of the system?**
   What is the system used for? What is its primary application? It could be a file server, database server, end-user CAD workstation, internet server, embedded control system.

2. **Who and where are the users?**
   How many users are there, how do they use the system, what kind of work patterns do they have? They might be a classroom full of students, people browsing the Internet from home, data entry clerks, development engineers, real-time data feeds, batch jobs. Are the end users directly connected? From what kind of device?

3. **Who says there is a performance problem, and what is slow?**
   Are the end users complaining, or do you have some objective business measure like batch jobs not completing quickly enough? If there are no complaints, then you should be measuring business-oriented throughput and response times, together with system utilization levels. Don't waste time worrying about obscure kernel measurements. If you have established a baseline of utilization, business throughput, and response times, then it is obvious when there is a problem because the response time will have increased, and that is what drives user perceptions of performance. It is useful to have real measures of response times or a way to derive them. You may get only subjective measures—"it feels sluggish today"—or have to use a stopwatch to time things. See "Collecting Measurements" on page 48.

4. What is the system configuration?

How many machines are involved, what is the CPU, memory, network, and disk setup, what version of Solaris is running, what relevant patches are loaded? A good description of a system might be something like this: an Ultra2/2200, with 512 MB, one 100-Mbit switched duplex Ethernet, two internal 2-GB disks with six external 4-GB disks on their own controller, running Solaris 2.5.1 with the latest kernel, network device, and TCP patches.

5. What application software is in use?

If the system is just running Solaris services, which ones are most significant? If it is an NFS server, is it running NFS V2 or NFS V3 (this depends mostly upon the NFS clients). If it is a web server, is it running Sun's SWS, Netscape, or Apache (and which version)? If it is a database server, which database is it, and are the database tables running on raw disk or in filesystem tables? Has a database vendor specialist checked that the database is configured for good performance and indexed correctly?

6. What are the busy processes on the system doing?

A system becomes busy by running application processes; the most important thing to look at is which processes are busy, who started them, how much CPU they are using, how much memory they are using, how long they have been running. If you may have a lot of short-lived processes, the only way to catch their usage is to use system accounting; see "Using Accounting to Monitor the Workload" on page 48. For long-lived processes, you can use the ps command or a tool such as top, proctool, or symon; see "Sun Symon" on page 35. A simple and effective summary is to use the old Berkeley version of ps to get a top ten listing, as shown in Figure 1-1. On a large system, there may be a lot more than ten busy processes, so get all that are using significant amounts of CPU so that you have captured 90% or more of the CPU consumption by processes.

Figure 1-1   Example Listing the Busiest Processes on a System

```
% /usr/ucb/ps uaxw | head
USER        PID %CPU %MEM    SZ  RSS TT         S    START   TIME COMMAND
adrianc    2431 17.9 22.63857628568 ?          S    Oct 13   7:38 maker
adrianc     666  3.0 14.913073618848 console   R    Oct 02 12:28 /usr/openwin/bin/X :0
root       6268  0.2  0.9 1120 1072 pts/4      O 17:00:29  0:00 /usr/ucb/ps uaxw
adrianc    2936  0.1  1.8 3672 2248 ??         S    Oct 14  0:04 /usr/openwin/bin/cmdtool
root          3  0.1  0.0    0    0 ?          S    Oct 02  2:17 fsflush
root          0  0.0  0.0    0    0 ?          T    Oct 02  0:00 sched
root          1  0.0  0.1 1664  136 ?          S    Oct 02  0:00 /etc/init -
root          2  0.0  0.0    0    0 ?          S    Oct 02  0:00 pageout
root         93  0.0  0.2 1392  216 ?          S    Oct 02  0:00 /usr/sbin/in.routed -q
```

Unfortunately, some of the numbers above run together: the %MEM field shows the RSS as a percentage of total memory. SZ shows the size of the process virtual address space; for X servers this size includes a memory-mapped frame buffer, and in this case, for a Creator3D the frame buffer address space adds over 100 megabytes to the total. For normal processes, a large SZ indicates a large swap space usage. The RSS column shows the amount of RAM mapped to that process, including RAM shared with other processes. In this case, PID 2431 has an SZ of 38576 Kbytes and RSS of 28568 Kbytes, 22.6% of the available memory on this 128-Mbyte Ultra. The X server has an SZ of 130736 Kbytes and an RSS of 18848 Kbytes.

7. What are the CPU and disk utilization levels?

How busy is the CPU overall, what's the proportion of user and system CPU time, how busy are the disks, which ones have the highest load? All this information can be seen with `iostat -xc` (`iostat -xPnce` in Solaris 2.6—think of "expense" to remember the new options). Don't collect more than 100 samples, strip out all the idle disks, and set your recording interval to match the time span you need to instrument. For a 24-hour day, 15-minute intervals are fine. For a 10-minute period when the system is busy, 10-second intervals are fine. The shorter the time interval, the more "noisy" the data will be because the peaks are not smoothed out over time. Gathering both a long-term and a short-term peak view helps highlight the problem areas. One way to collect this data is to use the SE toolkit—a script I wrote, called `virtual_adrian.s`, (See "The SymbEL Language" on page 505, and "virtual_adrian.se and /etc/rc2.d/S90va_monitor" on page 498.) writes out to a text-based log whenever it sees part of the system (a disk or whatever) that seems to be slow or overloaded.

8. What is making the disks busy?

If the whole disk subsystem is idle, then you can skip this question. The per-process data does not tell you which disks the processes are accessing. Use the `df` command to list mounted file systems, and use `showmount` to show which ones are exported from an NFS server; then, figure out how the applications are installed to work out which disks are being hit and where raw database tables are located. The `swap -l` command lists swap file locations; watch these carefully in the `iostat` data because they all become very busy with paging activity when there is a memory shortage.

9. What is the network name service configuration?

If the machine is responding slowly but does not seem to be at all busy, it may be waiting for some other system to respond to a request. A surprising number of problems can be caused by badly configured name services. Check `/etc/nsswitch.conf` and `/etc/resolv.conf` to see if DNS, NIS, or NIS+ is in use. Make sure the name servers are all running and responding quickly. Also check that the system is properly routing over the network.

10. How much network activity is there?

You need to look at the packet rate on each interface, the NFS client and server operation rates, and the TCP connection rate, throughput, and retransmission rate. One way is to run this twice, separated by a defined time interval.

```
% netstat -i; nfsstat; netstat -s
```

Another way is to use the SE toolkit's nx.se script that monitors the interfaces and TCP data along the lines of iostat -x.

```
% se nx.se 10
Current tcp RtoMin is 200, interval 10, start Thu Oct 16 16:52:33 1997
Name  Ipkt/s Opkt/s  Err/s  Coll% NoCP/s Defr/s  tcpIn  tcpOut Conn/s %Retran
hme0   212.0  426.9   0.00   0.00   0.00   0.00      65  593435   0.00    0.00
hme0   176.1  352.6   0.00   0.00   0.00   0.00      53  490379   0.00    0.00
```

11. Is there enough memory?

When an application starts up or grows or reads files, it takes memory from the free list. When the free list gets down to a few megabytes, the kernel decides which files and processes to steal memory from, to replenish the free list. It decides by scanning pages, looking for ones that haven't been used recently and paging out their contents so that the memory can be put on the free list. *If there is no scanning, then you definitely have enough memory.* If there is a lot of scanning and the swap disks are busy at the same time, you need more memory. If the swap disks are more than 50% busy, you should make swap files or partitions on other disks to spread the load and improve performance while waiting for more RAM to be delivered. You can use vmstat or sar -g to look at the paging system, or virtual_adrian.se will watch it for you, using the technique described in "RAM Rule" on page 456.

12. What changed recently and what is on the way?

It is always useful to know what was changed. You might have added a lot more users, or some event might have caused higher user activity than usual. You might have upgraded an application to add features or installed a newer version. Other systems may have been added to the network. Configuration changes or hardware "upgrades" can sometimes impact performance if they are not configured properly. You might have added a hardware RAID controller but forgotten to enable its nonvolatile RAM for fast write capability. It is also useful to know what might happen in the future. How much extra capacity might be needed for the next bunch of additional users or new applications?

Configuration and Tuning Recipes

The rest of this book gives you the information you need in order to understand a lot about how SPARC systems running Solaris work and about the basic principles involved in performance and tuning. Probably all you really want right now is to be told what to do or what to buy and how to set it up. This section just tells you *what* to do, with references to the rest of the book if you want to find out *why*. If you decide that you want to vary the recipes and do something different, you should really read the rest of the book first! For much more information on configuration issues, you should definitely get a copy of the book *Configuration and Capacity Planning for Solaris Servers*, by Brian Wong *(Sun Press)*.

The intention behind these recipes is to provide situation-oriented advice, which gathers together information about how to use a system rather than focusing on a particular subsystem in a generic sense.

Single-User Desktop Workstation Recipe

Local Disks and NFS Mounts

My recommended configuration is to NFS-mount home, mail, and applications programs directories from one or more workgroup servers. Configure a single, local disk to have two partitions, one for the operating system and one for swap space. It is easy to overload a single swap disk, so if you have more than one local disk, split any swap partitions or files evenly across all the disks (keep one clear for cachefs if necessary; see below).

Swap Space

Most application vendors can tell you how much swap space their application needs. If you have no idea how much swap space you will need, configure at least 128 Mbytes of virtual memory to start with. It's easy to add more later, so don't go overboard. With Solaris 2, the swap partition should be sized to top up the RAM size to get to the amount of virtual memory that you need[3]; e.g., 96-Mbyte swap with 32-Mbyte RAM, 64-Mbyte swap with 64-Mbyte RAM, no swap partition at all with 128 or more Mbytes of RAM. If your application vendor says a Solaris 2 application needs 64 Mbytes of RAM and 256 Mbytes of swap, this adds up to 320 Mbytes of virtual memory. You could configure 128 Mbytes of RAM and 192 Mbytes of swap instead. If you run out of swap space, make a swap file (I put them in /swap) or add more RAM. Older systems tend to run smaller

---

3. See "Virtual Memory Address Space Segments" on page 325 for a description of the unique Solaris 2 swap system.

applications, so they can get away with less virtual memory space. Later systems running the Common Desktop Environment (CDE) window system will need a lot more virtual memory space than systems running OpenWindows™.

File Systems and Upgrades

Make the rest of the disk into one big root partition that includes /usr, /opt, /var, and /swap. The main reason for doing this is to pool all the free space so that you can easily use upgrade or install to move up to the next OS release without running out of space in one of the partitions. It also prevents /var from overflowing and makes it easy to have a /swap directory to hold extra swap files if they are needed. In Solaris 2, /tmp uses the RAM-based tmpfs by default; the mount /tmp command should be uncommented in /etc/rc.local to enable it for SunOS 4.X.

Solaris 2 systems should be automatically installed from a JumpStart™ install server that includes a post-install script to set up all the local customizations. Since the disk can be restored by means of JumpStart and contains no local users files, it is never necessary to back it up over the network. A JumpStart install is much less frequent than a network backup, so its use aids good performance of the network. A useful tip to free up disk space for upgrades is to remove any swap files before you run the upgrade, then re-create the swap file afterwards.

```
# swap -d /swap/swapfile
# rm /swap/swapfile
comment out the swapfile in /etc/vfstab
shutdown and run the upgrade
# mkfile 100M /swap/swapfile
# swap -a /swap/swapfile
add the swapfile back into /etc/vfstab
```

Applications and Cachefs

If possible, NFS-mount the applications read-only to avoid the write-back of file access times, which is unwanted overhead. Configure the cache file system for all application code mount points. First, make /cache, then mount all the application directories, using the same cache. If you use large applications, check the application file sizes; if anything you access often is over 3 Mbytes, increase the *maxfilesize* parameter for the cache with cfsadmin.

Do not use cachefs for mail directories. It might be useful for home directories if most files are read rather than written—try it with and without to see. Cache loads when a large file is read for the first time can overload the disk. If there is more than one disk on the system, then don't put any cache on the same disk as any swap space. Swap and cache are often both busy at the same time when a new application is started. The cache works best for files that don't change often and are read many times by the NFS client.

If your application is very data-intensive, reading and writing large files (as often occurs with EDA, MCAD, and Earth Resources applications), you are likely to need an FDDI or 100-Mbit Fast Ethernet interface. If large files are written out a lot, avoid cachefs for that file system. Figure 1-2 shows how to set up and use cachefs.

Figure 1-2   Setting up Cachefs and Checking for Large Files

```
# cfsadmin -c /cache
# find /net/apphost/export/appdir -size +3000k -ls
105849 3408 -rwxr-xr-x  1 root       bin        3474324 Mar   1 13:16
/net/apphost/export/appdir/SUNWwabi/bin/wabiprog
# cfsadmin -u -o maxfilesize=4 /cache
cfsadmin: list cache FS information
    maxblocks       90%
    minblocks        0%
    threshblocks    85%
    maxfiles        90%
    minfiles         0%
    threshfiles     85%
    maxfilesize     4MB
# mount -F cachefs -o backfstype=nfs,cachedir=/cache apphost:/export/appdir
/usr/appdir
```

Example Filesystem Table

The filesystem mount table shown in Figure 1-3 is for a system with a single local disk. Application program code is mounted read-only from *apphost*, using cachefs. Mail is mounted from *mailhost*. Home directories are automounted and so do not appear in this table. This system has a swap partition, and an additional swap file has been added. Direct automount mappings can be used to mount applications (including the cachefs options) and mail.

Figure 1-3   Sample /etc/vfstab for Workstation Recipe

#device	device	mount	FS	fsck	mount	mount
#to mount	to fsck	point	type	pass	at boot	options
/proc	–	/proc	proc	–	no	–
fd	–	/dev/fd	fd	–	no	–
swap	–	/tmp	tmpfs	–	yes	–
/dev/dsk/c0t3d0s0	/dev/rdsk/c0t3d0s0	/	ufs	1	no	–
/dev/dsk/c0t3d0s1		–	swap	–	no	–

Figure 1-3   Sample `/etc/vfstab` *for Workstation Recipe*

#device	device	mount	FS	fsck	mount	mount
#to mount	to fsck	point	type	pass	at boot	options
/swap/swapfile	-	-	swap	-	no	-
apphost:/usr/dist	/cache	/usr/dist	cachefs	3	yes	ro,backfstype=nfs,cachedir=/cache
mailhost:/var/mail	-	/var/mail	nfs	-	yes	rw,bg

Kernel Tuning

Since this setup is the most common, Solaris is already well tuned for it, so you don't need to set anything.

Workgroup Server Recipe

Workgroup servers provide reliable file storage and email and printer support at a departmental level. In a Unix environment, NFS file services are provided; in a PC environment, Microsoft SMB, Novell NetWare, and Apple file service protocols need to be supported, commonly using Syntax TotalNet or Samba to provide the service. It has also become common to provide web services on the home file server, so that it also acts as a home page server for the users and the projects associated with the department. Network Computers such as Sun's JavaStation™ need a boot server and backend application support that can be combined with the other functions of a workgroup server. If a sophisticated proxy caching web server hierarchy is implemented across the enterprise, then the workgroup server may also be the first-level cache.

This sounds like a complex mixture, but over the last few years, individual system performance has increased and several functions have coalesced into a single system. Solaris has several advantages over Windows NT-based workgroup servers in this respect. The stability and availability requirements of a server increase as more and more users and services depend upon it, and Solaris is far more robust than NT. Solaris can also be reconfigured and tuned without requiring rebooting, whereas almost every change to an NT server requires a reboot that adds to the downtime. NT has also picked up a bad reputation for poor performance when several workloads are run together on a system. Solaris not only time-shares many competing workloads effectively, it also scales up to far larger systems, so more work can be combined into a single system. Taking all this into account, a typical new Solaris workgroup server installation is likely to replace several diverse existing servers. Administrative and installation simplicity is important, the hardware can be configured to be resilient to common failures, and Solaris is well tested and reliable, so a single server is appropriate. The complexity and rigorous procedures needed to run a high-availability cluster will rule it out for all but the biggest installations.

Workload Mixture

File service is going to be the largest component of the workload. The basic Solaris email services are efficient enough to support many hundreds of users, and by the use of Solstice™ Internet Mail Server (SIMS), tens of thousands of users can be hosted on a single machine, so a workgroup environment will not stress the email system. The web server load will also be light, with occasional short bursts of activity.

NFS requests will always run in the kernel at a higher priority than that of user-level programs, so a saturated NFS server is unlikely to provide high performance for other uses. However, NFS is now so efficient and system performance is so high that it is, in practice, impossible to saturate even a small server. Serving PC-oriented protocols by using Samba is less efficient than NFS but is still comparable to a dedicated PC file server. A uniprocessor UltraSPARC™ server can saturate a 100-Mbit network with HTTP, NFS and/or SMB traffic if there is enough demand from the clients.

RAM Requirements

Dedicated file and mail servers do not need much RAM. The kernel will be configured to be a little larger than normal, but the main, active user program will be `sendmail`. The rest of RAM is a cache for the file systems. Unix-based NFS clients do a great deal of caching, so they don't usually ask for the same data more than once. Home directories and mail files are specific to a single user, so there will not often be multiple reads of the same data from different machines. Anything that is constantly reread from the server by multiple workstations is a prime candidate for setting up with cachefs on the clients.

NFS clients that are PCs running MS-Windows™ or MacOS™ put much less load on an NFS server than a Unix client does, but they require fast response times for short bursts of activity and do little caching themselves. It may be worth having extra memory on the server to try and cache requests to common files.

Allow 16 Mbytes of RAM for the kernel, printing, and other Solaris daemons, then 64 Mbytes for each fully loaded FDDI or 100-Mbit Ethernet being served.

Write Acceleration

The problem of making writes go fast on file servers merits special consideration. As an example, consider a single NFS write. The server must update the inode block containing the last modified time, the indirect block (and possibly a double indirect block), and the data block itself. The inodes and indirect blocks may not be near the data block, so three or four random seeks may be required on the same disk before the server can confirm that the data is safely written. To accelerate this process, all the filesystem metadata writes (inodes and indirect blocks) are quickly logged somewhere as a sequential stream.

The log is not read back very often because the original data is still in memory and it is eventually flushed to its proper location. If the system crashes, the data in memory is lost, and on reboot, the log is read to quickly restore the filesystem state.

There are several ways to implement the log.

- The oldest implementation is a nonvolatile memory board known as a Prestoserve™ that intercepts synchronous filesystem writes. These boards are still available for use in small systems, but the SBus device driver can only handle systems that have a single SBus, so large servers are not supported.

- The SPARCstation™ 10, 20, SPARCserver™ 1000, and SPARCcenter™ 2000 systems accept a special nonvolatile memory SIMM (NVSIMM) that uses a Prestoserve driver. A problem with this solution is that the data is stored inside a system, so if it is configured as a dual-failover, high-availability system, the logged data cannot be accessed when failover occurs. However, it is the fastest option for a single system.

- The current generation of Ultra Enterprise server products does not have an NVSIMM option, and all the newest machines have a PCIbus rather than an SBus. The log is stored in the disk subsystem so it can be shared in an HA setup. The disk subsystem could include a controller with its own NVRAM (remember to enable fast writes on the SPARCstorage™ Array and similar products), or at the low end, a dedicated log disk should be used with a product such as Solstice DiskSuite™. The log disk can be used to accelerate several file systems, but it should be completely dedicated to its job, with no distractions and a small partition (no more than 100 Mbytes) to make sure that the disk heads never have to seek more than a few cylinders.

- The current 7200rpm disks have very high sequential data rates of about 10 Mbytes/s and handle logging well. You just have to ignore the unused few gigabytes of data space: *don't make a file system on it.*

The recommended disk configuration is to have a single, large, root partition like the workstation recipe with the exception of the /var directories. /var/mail should be on a separate disk partition because it needs to be accelerated. Mail programs on the NFS clients rewrite the entire mail file when the user saves changes; the time this rewrite takes is very noticeable, and a log disk or Prestoserve speeds it up a great deal. The /var file system should be big enough to hold a lot of mail (several megabytes per user account). You will need space in /var/spool for outgoing mail and printer jobs (at least 10 or 20 megabytes, sometimes much more). Home directories should be striped over several disks and configured with a log disk.

Network Configurations

A typical setup for a commercial workgroup is based on a 100-Mbit connection from a server to a network switch that feeds multiple, independent 10-Mbit networks with client PCs or Network Computers. Engineering workstations should be using 100-Mbit client connections in a switched full-duplex network infrastructure. Don't skimp on network bandwidth if you care about performance—an Ultra 1/170 is fast enough to saturate a 100-Mbit connection. The server may need to use multiple 100-Mbit networks to feed all its clients. High bandwidth connections may be done by trunking, where the Quadruple Fast Ethernet (QFE) card aggregates its ports to behave like a 400-Mbit duplex connection.

An upcoming option is gigabit Ethernet. Sun's initial product is a switch that takes a gigabit connection from a server and feeds multiple switched 100-Mbit ports to its clients. Some high-end sites are using 155-Mbit ATM cards in the client systems and 622-Mbit cards from the server to an ATM switch, or back-to-back ATM622 cards to provide a high bandwidth link between a pair of servers. A benefit of ATM is that the default maximum IP packet size is 9 Kbytes when used as a LAN. This is far more efficient that the 1500 byte packets used by ethernet, but is only effective if there is an ATM connection all the way from the server to the clients.

CPU Loading for NFS Servers

A SuperSPARC™ can handle four or five 10-Mbit Ethernets. Each fully loaded 100-Mbit Ethernet or FDDI should have two SuperSPARC processors or one UltraSPARC to handle the network, NFS protocol, and disk I/O load.

Disk Configurations

Since an NFS lookup or read can involve two trips over the network from the client as well as a disk I/O, getting good perceived performance from the server requires a low latency disk subsystem that averages better than 40 ms service time. Use Solstice DiskSuite or SPARCstorage Manager (VxVM) to stripe file systems so that the load is evenly balanced across as many independent disks as possible. You will get six times better performance from a stripe of six 4.3-Gbyte disks than you will get from one 23-Gbyte disk. For good performance, configure four to six disks in the stripe for each loaded 100-Mbit network. The data-intensive clients that need faster networks tend to do more sequential accesses and so get more throughput from the disks than the typical random access load. The logging file system supported by Solstice DiskSuite is especially useful with multi-gigabyte file systems because it avoids a time-consuming, full filesystem check.

Setting the Number of NFS Threads

In SunOS™ 4.X, each NFS daemon appears as a separate process, although the NFS daemons do all their work in the kernel. In Solaris 2, a single NFS daemon process and a number of kernel threads do basically the same job. Configure two threads per active client machine, or 32 per Ethernet. The default of 16 is suitable only for casual NFS use, and there is little overhead from having several hundred threads, even on a low-end server. Since kernel threads all use the same context, there is little thread switch overhead in either SunOS 4 or Solaris 2.

For example, a server with two Ethernets running SunOS 4 would need `nfsd 64` to be set in `/etc/rc.local` and, when running Solaris 2, would need `/usr/lib/nfs/nfsd -a 64` to be set in the file `/etc/init.d/nfs.server` (which is hardlinked to `/etc/rc3.d/S15nfs.server`).

Kernel Tuning

NFS servers don't often need a lot of RAM but do need large, name lookup caches, which are sized automatically, based on the RAM size in Solaris 2. The two main changes recommended are to make the inode and directory name lookup caches have at least 8,000 entries. See "Vnodes, Inodes, and Rnodes" on page 360 for more details.

The default size of both caches in Solaris 2 will be (RAM-2)*17+90. For a 64-Mbyte system, this size works out at 1144. If you have more than 512 Mbytes of RAM, the cache is big enough (see Figure 1-4).

Figure 1-4   Sample `/etc/system` *Kernel Tuning Parameters for a 128-Mbyte Solaris 2 NFS Server*

```
set ncsize=8000 for NFS servers with under 512 MB RAM
set ufs:ufs_ninode=8000for NFS servers with under 512 MB RAM
```

Database Server Recipe

I am not a database specialist. You should refer to the many good books on database performance tuning for each of the main database vendors. Here, I'll give some general recommendations on system considerations that apply to most databases.

Workload Mixture

System performance scales to much higher levels than most databases require. Whereas in the past we would recommend that a separate system be used for each database, it is now more common to consolidate several workloads onto a single, large system. With a greater dependency on a smaller number of systems, configuring for high availability is more important. Failover and parallel database clusters are becoming much more common.

The two main categories of database usage are online transaction processing, such as order entry typified by the TPC-C benchmark, and complex analytical queries made against a data warehouse, as typified by the TPC-D benchmark. Take the time to read the detailed reports of tested configurations that are available on the TPC web site at http://www.tpc.org. A lot of effort goes into setting up very high performance configurations for those tests, and you can copy some of the techniques yourself.

RAM Requirements

Database servers need a lot of RAM. Each database and application vendor should provide detailed guidelines on how to configure the system. If you have no other guidance, I will suggest a starting point that has been used with Oracle®. For the database back end, allow 64 Mbytes of RAM for the kernel, Solaris daemons, and database backend processes. Then, allow another 2 Mbytes for each user if time-shared, or 512 Kbytes per user on a pure back end. Finally, add memory for the shared global area.

Log -Based and Direct I/O File Systems

Use the log-based UFS file system supported by Solstice DiskSuite if your database tables must be stored in UFS file systems rather than on raw disk. Oracle, Informix, and Sybase work best with raw disk, but other databases such as Ingres and Progress have to use file systems. With Solaris 2.6 there is a direct I/O option that can be used to provide raw access to a file in the file system. This option is not as good as raw but can greatly reduce memory demands.

Network Loading for Database Servers

The network activity caused by SQL is so application dependent that it is hard to give general guidelines. You will need to do some work with the snoop command or a network analyzer on a live system to work out the load. Some applications may work well over a dial-up modem, whereas others will need 100-Mbit networks or may only work well when the client and server are on the same machine.

CPU Loading

CPU loading cannot be estimated easily; any guidelines provided in this book would lead to a mixture of overconfigured and underconfigured systems. Database sizing involves too many variables and is outside the scope of this book. I recommend that you read Brian Wong's book *Configuration and Capacity Planning for Solaris Servers*, which covers the subject in depth. Sizing data for common application and database combinations is being generated within Sun for use by systems engineers and resellers. Database vendors often place restrictions on the publication of performance-related information about their products.

Disk Configurations

Getting good, perceived performance from the server requires a low-latency disk subsystem. For good write latency, NVRAM is normally configured in the disk controller subsystem. Use Solstice DiskSuite, SPARCstorage Manager or a hardware RAID system such as Sun's RSM2000 to stripe file systems so that the load is evenly balanced across as many independent disks as possible. You will get six times better performance from a stripe of six 4.3-Gbyte disks than you will from one 23-Gbyte disk. Extremely large disk configurations are now common, and several thousand disks may be connected to a single system. Make sure you are familiar with the new iostat options in Solaris 2.6, described in "Output Formats and Options for iostat" on page 183. You can now get an inventory of the disk configuration and look for error counts on a drive-by-drive basis.

Setting the Shared Memory Size

Shared memory size is often set too small. On a database using raw disks, the size needs to be set higher than on a system with UFS. The effect of UFS is to provide additional data buffering and a duplicate copy of the data in shared memory. This improves read performance and can help sequential table scan rates when UFS prefetching is more aggressive than the database's own prefetching. The drawback is that more RAM and CPU time is used. When running raw, you can choose to run with less caching and use less RAM, or you can go for higher performance by using a much bigger shared memory area and similar total RAM usage. As a first approximation, use half of your total main memory as shared memory, then measure the database to see if it is oversized or too small and adjust as necessary.

Kernel Tuning

Databases tend to use lots of shared memory and semaphore settings. These do not affect performance; as long as shared memory and semaphore settings are big enough, the programs will run. Each database vendor supplies its own guidelines. See "tune_t_fsflushr and autoup" on page 339 for advice on tuning the fsflush daemon. Figure 1-5 presents an example.

Figure 1-5   Example /etc/system Entries for a Database Server

```
* example shared memory settings needed for database
set shmsys:shminfo_shmmax=268435456
set shmsys:shminfo_shmmni=512
set shmsys:shminfo_shmseg=150
```

```
set semsys:seminfo_semmap=350
set semsys:seminfo_semmni=350
set semsys:seminfo_semmns=1000
set semsys:seminfo_semmnu=700
set semsys:seminfo_semume=100
* keep fsflush from hogging a CPU
set autoup=240
```

Multiuser Server with ASCII or X Terminals Recipe

There is little difference in kind between dumb ASCII terminals, proprietary graphics terminals connected over serial ports, IBM 3270 terminals connected over SNA, and X terminals. The terminal understands a fixed, low-level display protocol and has varying amounts of built-in functionality, but all application processing is done on time-shared multiuser servers.

What's the Difference between Client/Server and Time-shared Configurations?

The term *client/server* is sometimes used to describe a time-shared system with X terminals. Personally, I don't like this use of the term because I think it is misleading. The primary extra capability of an X terminal over other types of terminals is that it can make direct connections to many servers at the same time. As an example, consider upgrading a time-shared server by replacing ASCII terminals with X terminals running the same application in a terminal emulator window. There is still no separate client processing going on. An upgrade to client/server would be to have users running part or all of the application on a SPARCstation or PC on their desk, with an application-specific protocol linking them to a database or an NFS server back end.

Performance Is Usually a Problem on Time-shared Systems

From a performance point of view, time-shared systems are usually a source of problems. Part of the problem is that Unix assumes that its users will be well behaved and has few ways to deal with users or programs that intentionally or accidentally take an unfair share of the system. It is sometimes known as a *Denial-of-Service Attack* when a user tries to consume all the CPU, RAM, disk space[4], swap space, or overflow kernel tables. Even unintentional overload can cause serious problems. Instead, if you can configure a client/server system where users get their own SPARCstation or PC to use and abuse, then it is much harder for one user to affect the performance for the rest of the user community.

---

4. If this is a problem, then you can use the standard BSD Unix disk quotas system in Solaris.

The Softway ShareII resource management system has been ported to Solaris 2. This product was developed to solve the problem by allocating fair shares of system resources to users and groups of users. See http://www.softway.com.au for more details.

Another problem occurs when applications that were developed for use on high-end SPARCstations are installed on a server and used via X terminals. If the application runs well on a low-powered machine like a SPARCstation 5, then sharing a more powerful machine makes sense. If the application is normally used on an Ultra 2, then don't expect many copies to run simultaneously on an X-terminal server.

X terminals work very well in a general office environment where most users spend a small proportion of their time actually working at the X terminal. X terminals don't work well if all the users are active all the time. Try to avoid configuring data entry or telephone sales sweatshops or student classrooms full of X terminals; the backend system needed to support them will often be large and expensive or seriously underpowered. Some software licensing practices can make a single, large system with X terminals cheaper than lots of smaller systems. Hopefully, more software vendors will convert to floating per-user licenses for software.

There is a large movement in the industry to replace all kinds of terminals with Network Computers running Java, so old-style terminals are beginning to die out.

Internet and Java Server Recipes

The whole subject of Internet and intranet web servers, proxy caching web servers, and servers for Java-based applications is covered in detail in Chapter 4, "Internet Servers," and Chapter 5, "Java Application Servers." The simplest sizing recipe is based on two key things. The first is that the minimum baseline for good web server performance is Solaris 2.6 and an up-to-date, efficient web server. The second is that given efficient software, it will be easy to saturate your network, so base all your system sizing on how much network traffic your switches, backbones, and wide-area links can handle.

Performance Management <span></span>

Do performance problems sneak up on you? If you find yourself working late or dropping other work to fix urgent performance problems, perhaps it's time to start managing the performance of your computer systems in a proactive way. *Manage performance or it will manage you!*

What Is Performance Management?

Performance Management is the measurement, analysis, optimization, and procurement of computing resources to provide an agreed-upon level of service to the organization and its end users. These computing resources could be CPU, memory, disk, network, and application related. It is a complete proactive process, far removed from the crisis-driven tuning and upgrading that seem so common.

Financial Management Scenario

The principles and benefits of managing resources should be familiar to everyone. A good analogy is financial management, so consider this scenario. A large department in a company is given responsibility to do some work. It also negotiates a capital budget, a staffing level, and an expenses budget for a time period. The expectation is that the work will be done in that time period and the budget will be consumed. The financial managers in the department will set up a plan of how the money will be spent, monitor progress against the plan, and set up controls to approve each expenditure. The outcome could go one of three ways:

1. If there are no plan and no effective controls, staff members will grab as much budget as they can to ensure that their own piece of work will be well funded. At some point, all the money will have gone. Some of the staff will have no funding; others will be conducting extensive field trials in the Bahamas! In the end, the work will not be completed because large parts of it were underfunded.

2. If management does its job right, it will balance and pace the funding so that staff are constrained but all have enough to get the job done. A contingency reserve is used to help out jobs that are lagging, and the work is completed on time and within budget.

To achieve this dream, a detailed plan is needed up front that contains good estimates of the resources needed and predicts several possible worst-case situations that may need to be avoided. The extra management work required is part of the plan.

3. If management is overzealous, it may spend too much time planning and replanning. All the budget is consumed by layers of managers and administrators who micromanage the staff and demand frequent status reports. The administrative overhead involved in spending any of the budget costs more than the items being purchased. Progress is so slow that the work has barely started by the time it should have ended.

I'm sure that you recognize each of these situations. The first one is common in startup companies. It is also has a close analogy with computer system performance management in areas where performance management is a relatively new technology, such as networks of Unix systems and PCs. The second situation is the ideal target, just enough management to keep control without a lot of overhead. The third situation is typical of long-established companies and government departments. Scott Adams' Dilbert works in a place like this! This third situation is analogous to computer performance management in some mainframe installations; management overhead prevents changes from occurring and can consume a lot of the system.

Computer System Performance Analogies

The analogy with financial management works with a finer level of detail as well.

The workload, or the work to be performed, is the key thing to be managed. It may be people, or processes running on the computer, but you need to have some regular measure of how much work is being done and what resources are being consumed to do it. The Unix system accounting reports are a simple way to get this data, but application-specific measurements like orders entered, or HTTP operations per hour, are also needed.

Money used can be divided into capital budgets and expenses. The equivalent of a capital budget and staff headcount is system capacity such as RAM, swap space, filesystem space and database tablespace. These are consumed once in large chunks by each workload when it starts up. The equivalent of an expense budget is CPU usage, network traffic, and disk I/O rates. These are consumed at a variable rate that depends upon how quickly work is being done. There is a maximum available rate that the combined workloads cannot exceed.

If you don't have enough capital budget or staff, then you can't support all the workloads at the same time. For the computer scenario, rather than buy a bigger computer that could run everything at once, you might set up a batch queue so that workloads take turns using a resource.

If you have no expense controls, then you cannot prevent important workloads from being crowded out by low-priority work. The concept of allocating priorities and shares of the CPU and network resources on a per-workload basis is largely unknown in the PC and Unix worlds. It is the default way that work is done in the mainframe world, and a financial manager could not operate without expense controls. A big part of the work required to bring a Unix system into a performance management regime is to set up a way to measure and control the workloads running on a system. A common but inflexible approach is to put each workload on its own machine, then size each machine separately. In cases where a single machine runs multiple workloads, then you can use a share-based scheduler (see ShareII on page 19) or binding workloads to sets of CPUs (see `psrset` on page 229). Charging users for the resources they consume will also tend to have a useful but indirect effect on the consumption of each workload.

Performance management, like financial management, starts by setting up processes to guide the managers. It involves planning for the future, then measuring progress against the plan and reporting the current status. You should start by thinking about the financial management systems that you use every day, then try to develop similar kinds of systems for performance management. When you have to explain to your own management what you are trying to do, you may find that they have a better understanding of finance than computers, and this analogy may be helpful. For example, the Accounting department has a financial management software package to manage its general ledger of income and expense. Perhaps you should have a software package to help manage the performance of your computer systems?

So, performance management involves setting objectives, measuring progress, obtaining resources, and negotiating with other managers.

Performance Management Cost Justification

Performance management has been developed as a discipline over the last twenty years or more. In the mainframe world, systems are so expensive that the payback from tuning the system or making the right upgrade could be justified simply by the direct cost saving in the computing budget. Now that client/server systems are extending computerization and replacing mainframes, the hardware costs are far lower. It is becoming even more important to quantify the indirect value to the business of a computer system.

For example, an upgrade that enables an increase in throughput of an order entry system would be worth a lot in business terms. You could choose one of several different cheap hardware upgrades or spend time and money analyzing the system. After installation of several upgrades, one after another, the months go by and performance is actually worse than before! Finally, you analyze the system and find that a database configuration change coupled with an upgrade that you hadn't thought of gives you a huge speedup that you could have implemented months ago. The value of a few months of improved order entry throughput turns out to be many times the cost of the analysis and upgrades. I didn't have to invent this example—I have seen this situation many times!

Whenever cost justification is involved, you must try to look at the bigger picture of the service that the system provides to your organization.

The Life Cycle of Performance Management

Performance management starts with an understanding of the business. The reason why a computer system exists may seem obvious, but if you state the role of the system clearly, you can identify performance problems caused by extra work. Users often run extra applications on a system that are not part of its business role. Educating the users or threatening to restrict their freedom can keep a system working within its limits.

One technique I used when I was a system administrator was to pin up various accounting summaries by a printer. While waiting for printouts, users would read who and what was hogging the CPU time, disk space, and printer consumables. Peer pressure was enough to keep things in check.

An important part of performance management is to know the level of service required by the business and the current performance in business terms. You gain this knowledge by collecting and processing performance metrics from several sources, thus providing a baseline when a problem occurs in the future. By analyzing the metrics, you determine the probable cause and the severity of a problem. A corrective action plan describes the required changes, and, finally, the change can be implemented.

To determine if the corrective action has helped, you go back to understanding the new performance and service level by collecting and analyzing the metrics.

You could also be more proactive before a problem occurs by trying to predict the performance and service level in anticipation of a change, for example, a change in business requirements, user load, applications, or hardware.

The main stages of performance management can be broadly classified as:

1. Obtain business requirements.

2. Collect, monitor, and understand performance metrics.

3. Analyze, identify, and publicize performance problems.

4. Set objectives and implement changes.

5. Forecast or project the effect of changes.

After Step 4 is done, you go back to Step 2 to see if the implemented plan has achieved the objective. Typically, in order to achieve Step 2 and Step 3, you use a performance management tool of some kind.

In real life, the steps to performance management are not as clearly defined as those stated here. However, this classification provides the basic foundation upon which most performance management is built.

Performance Tools Provided in Solaris 2

In the Solaris 2 operating system environment, performance-related tools and utilities are provided as part of the operating system.

- `vmstat`, `iostat`, `sar`, `mpstat`, `perfmeter`, `netstat`, `nfsstat`, `ps`, etc.
- Symon is provided on SPARC servers since Solaris 2.5.1

Also, freely available tools provide performance-related information.

- `top`—a curses-based `ps` that shows the top few processes
- `proctool`—a GUI-based tool that greatly extends the "top" concept
- `memtool`—a GUI-based tool that tracks down memory usage by file and process
- the SE performance toolkit
- the packet shell for TCP network analysis and visualization

You can use these tools to obtain performance metrics that enable you to isolate performance problems and tune overall system performance. However, the usefulness of these tools depends heavily on your knowledge and experience. It is difficult to get a business-oriented overview of the system at the application level, and in a networked environment, monitoring multiple nodes and correlating and logging the data is difficult. You can set up `sar` on each system to log some utilization information, but this utility does not capture network activity.

Further, the experience level of the *average* Unix administrator is *decreasing over time* because of the wide adoption of Unix servers and workstations in commercial environments and the lower costs of ownership expected of these systems. At the same time, an administrator is now required to perform more tasks as well as handle a larger number of users and systems.

Commercial performance management software products provide more functionality than do the bundled tools. Many vendors provide performance management solutions ranging from monitoring a single system to predicting the performance of a complex multivendor network.

Performance Management Products

Many products help automate the processes of performance management, but there is a difference between the promise of the glossy brochure and the reality of a product. It is also hard to compare tools which have overlapping functionality across a wide spectrum of uses. To research this subject and write an initial report, Steven Gan from the Sun Singapore field office was seconded to work with me for five weeks during 1994. I initiated the study, provided guidance, and edited the resulting white paper. This section is based upon an updated summary of the paper.

We selected some major vendors and invited them to provide an evaluation copy of their software. Those vendors who supplied software in time to be evaluated assisted in the installation and testing of their products and, in some cases, indicated their future plans for the product. The products evaluated covered a wide range of both price and functionality. Comparisons made in this study were intended to show the range of functions available, so that users could make their own decision on what they need. Since the initial study, some products have ceased to exist, new ones have appeared, and the remainder have changed significantly.

I have extensive hands-on experience with several products and also provide reference information on products that I have not evaluated. The state of the art in performance management in 1994 indicated that it was an immature market. Many vendors produced brand-new products or added major extensions to existing products. Now in 1997, the market is more mature. Large organizations tend to standardize on a particular vendor and deploy a related set of products across their organization. This leads to a two-tier market, with a few large vendors handling many big distributed installations, and smaller vendors holding on to a specialized niche.

Performance Management Terminology and Functions

In the industry, vendors commonly use a number of terms to describe their performance management products: Performance Monitoring, Historical Trend Analysis, Performance Tuning, Troubleshooting, Performance Analysis, Performance Forecast, Capacity Planning, Performance Assurance, and so forth. To compare the various products from these vendors, we defined four categories to include this variety of terms:

- Collection—Referred to as data capture, logging, or storage of performance data
- Monitoring—Known as viewing or display of snapshot data
- Trend Analysis—Viewing historical data and projecting a trend into the future
- Forecast—Sometimes known as predicting, modeling, or capacity planning

Each product implements a different subset, so I'll start with a generic view of what this class of products does, then get to the specifics of which product actually does what.

Collect

Collection of performance data is done by reading the kernel statistics interfaces. It may also involve reading per-process information. The measurements are then stored with timestamps onto disk. In some cases, data is sent over the network to a centralized store. Some tools use specialized additional sources of information such as network packet analysis or use a custom kernel module. Other tools run standard system utilities like sar, vmstat, or ps, and parse the output. This is more portable, but far less efficient, and the values obtained are less accurate.

Monitor and Understand

You typically need a graphical user interface to display the collected data, in real-time snapshot or historical form. There is usually a choice of graph formats. It is useful if graphs are lined up so that different measures can be correlated in time.

The real-time data display allows you to troubleshoot performance bottlenecks with the use of thresholds and alarms to pinpoint the specific area. The historical data display allows you to study the long-term trend and helps identify potential problems in advance.

Analyze, Identify, and Isolate

The most common techniques used for real-time snapshot data are alarms or events generated based on a threshold. The usefulness of the default alarms and the flexibility of the alarm setup in a real-life environment is one of the differentiating factors for the vendor.

However, for trend analysis based on historical data, no particular technique is currently used by the vendors to assist you to identify or isolate potential and growing problems.

Forecast or Project

Typically, in order to forecast performance levels, one or more data modeling techniques are employed.

- Rules of thumb
- Linear programming
- Network queueing model
- Discrete simulation
- Workload benchmark

For details of these techniques, see *The Practical Performance Analyst* by Neil Gunther, published by McGraw-Hill.

Another important aspect of Forecast or Project is the ability of the product to allow you to ask "What If" questions. You can then determine the performance impact before making a change. There are two basic categories of these questions:

1. Set Change, Predict Performance Level

   You ask questions like "What if I upgrade the CPU?" or "What if I increase the number of users?" or "What if I add more memory?" and let the product predict for you the expected performance level. The performance level would be expressed in terms of throughput or response time for the work being performed and the utilization level of the system's CPUs and disks.

   This category of question allows you to determine if you should perform the actions, by predicting the impact on the system first. The BGS Best/1 product, for example, has this capability.

   If you have already decided on a performance target and you are trying to find out what kind of changes will bring about the required result, you will have to use trial-and-error methods and ask many "What-If" questions.

2. Set Performance Level, Suggest Change Required

   Here, you first determine the performance level that you want to achieve, such as a certain throughput or response time of an application, then you ask questions like, "What if I want a form's update response time to drop from 8 seconds to 4 seconds?" or "What if I don't mind that the time it takes to produce a report increases from 8 minutes to 12 minutes?" and so on. Then, let the product predict the performance impact and suggest to you what kind of changes you need to make in order to achieve them.

   The second approach is more intuitive, as we are used to setting an objective and carrying out an action plan to achieve that objective.

   This approach does not require trial-and-error and so is easier to use than the earlier type of "What-If" questions. There may be several possible actions to reach a given objective, so heuristics and cost metrics need to be applied to prioritize them. Unfortunately, I don't know of any products that can do this.

With either type of "What-If" question, you have a very powerful tool to investigate many dimensions of performance level and computing resources before actually making any change to the system.

Set Objectives and Implement

Although some vendors seem to be working toward providing the set objective category, no vendor products have yet demonstrated this functionality for Unix. It's up to you to pick your own objectives and figure out how to get there.

Product Overview

Table 2-1 lists some performance management software products in alphabetical order by company name and shows which basic functions they cover.

Table 2-1   Performance Management Software Products

Products	Collect	Monitor	Trend	Forecast
AIM SharpShooter	No longer sold			
Amdahl OpenTune/ AUMA	Yes	Yes	No	No
BGS Best/1 for UNIX	Yes	Yes	Yes	Yes
BMC Patrol	Yes	Yes	No	No
Resolute Software RAPS	Yes	Yes	Yes	No
Compuware Ecotools	Yes	Yes	No	No
Datametrics	Yes	Yes	No	No
HP GlancePlus	No	Yes	No	No
HP MeasureWare	Yes	Yes	Yes	No
Landmark PerformanceWorks	Yes	Yes	Yes	Yes
Metron Athene/UNIX	Yes	No	Yes	Yes
SAS IT Service View (CPE)	No	No	Yes	Yes
SES Workbench/Strategizer	No	No	Yes	Yes
Sun Symon 1.4	No	Yes	No	No
TeamQuest Baseline	Yes	Yes	Yes	Yes

This table lists products that I think are interesting. I have omitted network management tools such as SunNet Manager and HP OpenView as they serve a different set of needs with only a minor overlap into performance management. The categorization is based upon my own opinion of their functionality, not the vendors' claims. For example, anyone who can draw a graph over time claims he can do trending, but I want to see some support for fitting a curve to a trend and hitting a threshold in the future or evaluating alternative future growth scenarios.

2

Product Evaluations

I'm going to give my biased opinion of these products. I don't have much hands-on experience with some of them. In most cases, that is because I don't find it useful for my own personal situation and I don't have time to try everything that comes along. Products are evaluated in alphabetical order.

AIM SharpShooter

This product was a favorite of mine because it was easy to use and solved a hard problem very well. It was the best performance monitor for NFS servers, but it was discontinued at the end of 1996, some time after Network General acquired AIM Technology. One possible reason why the product did not take off in the market is that for a long time it ran only on Sun machines, and despite ports to Auspex and SGI, it never managed to get enough market coverage or break out of its reputation as an NFS-specific tool.

Amdahl OpenTune/OpenWatch AUMA

The main claim to fame of this product is that it is based on the X/Open Universal Measurement Architecture (UMA) standard. The idea of UMA is that multiple tools from multiple vendors can share the same collected data. The problem is that Amdahl is the only company making a UMA-based product. A secondary problem is that the version of UMA on which Amdahl based its product predates the final standard (described in "The X/Open Universal Measurement Architecture Standard" on page 372) and there are changes to the interfaces and datapool definitions in the final standard. The OpenTune tool itself is a data browser with some good party tricks like moving seamlessly from current data to historical data, but it does not support complex rule-based alerts and requires an expert for setup. OpenWatch tracks multiple machines, using OpenTune to drill down on problems.

While the tool is quite usable and does the job of monitoring systems and databases, it has not had a big impact on the performance tools market, and Amdahl remains a minor player.

More details can be found at http://www.amdahl.com.

BGS Best/1 for Unix and BestView

BGS is a well-established company that builds only performance tools. It has pioneered the use of performance modeling, starting off on mainframes 20 years ago and launching a Unix-based product in 1993. There are two sides to the product, a real-time performance monitor that covers the same ground as many other products, and a performance analysis and prediction tool that is the market leader at the high end. BGS is growing fast and rapidly adding functionality to its range of tools for the mainframe, minicomputer (VAX and AS/400), Unix (most vendors), and PC (NT and OS/2) platforms. Their breadth of coverage puts them into a market category where large corporations standardize on a vendor and install tools right across the enterprise. The downside of this functionality is that the entry-level cost is at the high end of the scale, both financially and in the time and training required to use a modeling tool effectively.

I have developed a close working relationship with BGS developers, assisting with information they needed for their initial port to Solaris and beta testing new versions of Best/1. I have found the tool to be particularly useful for filling in the configuration matrix in a sizing guide. You can collect and analyze one benchmark run, then use prediction to estimate the performance of other hardware configurations and workload mixes. I have not used this tool in a production environment to monitor systems over the long term, but it not only has the features required to do this, it has the ability to set up and automate the entire process of generating regular reports that include modeling of alternative future scenarios.

The tool has a Motif-based GUI that works well enough, but which I think could be much easier to use. The initial configuration of the tool can be daunting. BGS is working to make configuration simpler, and in large installations, training and consultancy support mask this problem. Best/1 for Unix exports data into a PC-based Visualizer performance database that also pulls in data from all other types of system that BGS has tools for. If you have a PC on your desk, this is OK, but for Unix-oriented people like me, it is annoying to have to switch between systems to view all the data. Visualizer can automatically generate reports that can be browsed via the Web.

In summary, if you have experience of the way capacity planning is done in the mainframe world and want to merge this knowledge with Unix-based system and database performance monitoring, this tool does the job. If you are coming from a typical Unix system administrator background or are looking for low-priced monitoring tools, you may not be able to justify the investment needed to work out how to make good use of this product.

BestView is a different kind of product that breaks down network usage on a per-workload basis by collecting routing information from SNMP and RMON probes. It does conversational analysis to figure out which clients are causing network traffic on which network segments to get to their servers.

BGS is at http://www.bgs.com.

BMC Patrol

BMC is another market leader with a background in mainframe markets, but with a very different focus than that of BGS. Patrol is a distributed *application management* system. Performance management is only part of the problem to be solved; keeping applications up and running and collecting application-specific measurements is just as important to

Patrol. The product has a good underlying architecture that scales well in large distributed installations, with multiple data storage points and management consoles. Like BGS, BMC monitors by evaluating rules in a local agent on each node; however, BMC's rules are more complex, and its predefined *Knowledge Modules* understand how to manage everything from an Oracle Financials database to a Netscape web server. I think this is the right approach, but Patrol is often criticized for imposing a larger load on the system being managed than do other tools. Their collection strategy is to run a standard system utility, such as vmstat, and parse the output, which is less efficient than reading the kernel directly. Patrol data can be viewed with a web browser, and Patrol integrates closely with many of the network and system management tools. Patrol does not include trending and prediction tools, however.

If your systems administrators, network operators, database administrators, and application developers all work together and want a common toolset, then BMC Patrol is a very good choice.

BMC is at http://www.bmc.com.

Compuware EcoTools and EcoSCOPE

Compuware is another mainframe company that has moved to add a Unix- and NT-oriented product set over the last few years. EcoTools focuses on database performance monitoring and management. It competes mainly with BMC Patrol in this area. Its application coverage is less broad than that of Patrol, but it has good configuration management and security features, and it may be preferred by database administrators. Performance management is again a small part of the functionality, and it has no trending or prediction capability.

EcoSCOPE is a network workload analysis package based on SNMP and RMON; it is similar in some ways to the BGS BestView product.

Compuware is at http://www.compuware.com.

Datametrics ViewPoint

ViewPoint has a Windows PC as its console and collects data from a very large number of different systems. The focus is on a high level of coverage in a diverse environment, rather than on in-depth analysis and platform-specific details. It performs alert-based monitoring and has an analysis and report generation capability that includes statistical correlation analysis. Datametrics comes from a Unisys mainframe background.

Datametrics is at http://www.datametrics.com.

HP GlancePlus and MeasureWare

GlancePlus is a single-system GUI monitor that originated on HP-UX and has been ported to several other vendors. It is cheap, easy to use, and provides a good view of what is going on the server, but it doesn't provide long-term storage of data. It runs as a single, monolithic process, using remote X display for viewing from a desktop system, so the load on the server can be quite high. In a Sun-based environment, the Solstice Symon product (which is provided free with servers) has similar functionality but separates the GUI from the data collector. If you want the same simple and easy-to-use tool on servers from several vendors, then GlancePlus is a good choice.

MeasureWare used to be called PCS—performance collection system. It provides long-term storage of collected data from systems, applications, networks, and databases. The data can be fed to a tool called PerfView, which provides trend analysis, fitting a line to a historical graph that extends into the future. A new feature that HP has pioneered is the instrumentation and analysis of end-to-end response time, using a proposed standard interface called ARM. Many other vendors (including Sun) are working to implement and promote the ARM standard so that applications are instrumented to generate the required data.

One criticism of the HP tools is that they collect more data and run better on the HP-UX platform than they do on Sun or IBM systems. This is what you would expect—HP builds the tool to take advantage of special features of HP-UX and takes a more generic approach to features of other platforms.

HP has also worked to make the PCS data formats into a common interchange format for other tools such as SAS. This common format is useful because it allows you to analyze data in alternative ways without adding to the collection overhead. In a mixed environment with a lot of HP equipment, the HP tools are a good choice.

HP's performance tools division is at http://www.hp.com/openview/rpm/.

Landmark Systems Corporation PerformanceWorks

Landmark started off with a range of mainframe-based tools and added Unix tools to its product line in the early 1990s. Landmark generally competes with BMC and BGS for large-scale installations at major corporations.

This product was once known as TMON for Unix (The MONitor), but it now integrates well into a mixed Unix and Windows NT environment. The GUI is available for both Motif and Windows and can monitor Sun, HP, and IBM Unix servers as well as NT, including database servers. As well as monitoring, Landmark provides an Analyzer that does trending and correlation and recently added a modeling package called Predictor as an option on the Windows version of the product. A lot of work has gone into the GUI, which looks good and is easier to use than most. The Motif and Windows GUIs are very similar.

Landmark would be a good choice in a mixed Unix and NT environment because the product integrates them well from either side. In comparison, BGS does have tools for Unix and NT, but they have quite different functionality and interfaces when run on either desktop.

Landmark is at http://www.landmark.com.

Metron Athene/UNIX

Metron is one of the few companies to have a performance modeling capability. The tool is completely Windows based, with a slick, easy-to-use GUI. The data collection side is relatively weak, however, as Metron basically uses `sar` and `ps` commands to get information, along with Unix system accounting data. Compared to BGS Best/1, the data collected is less comprehensive and has higher overhead, although Metron does use accounting data, which is ignored by Best/1. The tool contains some powerful data trending and statistics functions and a queueing model solver, called Planner, that is similar to Best/1 Predict but is less detailed because it has less information to work with.

Metron is at http://www.metron.co.uk.

Resolute Software—RAPS

Resolute Software is a small company with a relatively new product. It is designed to compete in the application management space with BMC Patrol. RAPS uses very efficient data collectors and has an advanced distributed storage architecture and a good GUI. An interesting thing about the product is that my co-author Rich Pettit, who built the SE toolkit while he was at Sun, thought that the product and company was so good that he now works for Resolute and is architecting RAPS. He aims to take maximum advantage of the features of Solaris 2. The ruleset that RAPS uses is based on a superset of the rules I published in my original `virtual_adrian.se` script, but the product is a full, distributed, multiplatform tool. Sometimes, people ask us if we have any plans for a fully supported version of the SE toolkit that runs on other platforms as well as on Sun machines, and this is as close as you will get.

Resolute Software is at http://www.resolute.com.

SAS IT Service Vision (CPE)

SAS has a wide range of statistical analysis products. SAS/CPE has been used to process computer performance data for many years in both mainframe and Unix environments. It has a much more sophisticated performance database than do other products, with a very wide range of analysis, reporting, and modeling functions. It is often used in conjunction with performance monitoring products from other vendors to provide a capacity planning, performance prediction, and reporting capability.

More information can be obtained from http://www.sas.com/vision/itservice/.

SES Workbench and Strategizer

SES Workbench is a well-established performance simulation tool. This simulation is very different from the analytical performance modeling done by BGS Predict and others (which work by solving a set of equations). With a simulator, you create a model of the components in your system, then drive it with input load levels and wait for the simulation to stabilize over time. Running a simulation is far more resource intensive than analytical modeling in both setup time and CPU time. If you have a well-constructed simulation, you do get much more information than is available from an analytical model. SES/Workbench runs on Unix and is being ported to NT.

To make it easier to construct models of computer systems and networks, SES/Strategizer is preconfigured with high-level components that match common system types in some detail. It still needs a lot of experience to make good use of the tool, but it is a lot quicker to construct a model. SES/Strategizer runs only on Windows NT.

SES is at http://www.ses.com.

Sun Symon

Symon was developed by the server division of Sun to provide a graphical user interface to its server products. It is deliberately very hardware specific, and it covers functionality that generic tools from other vendors do not address. In particular, it contains a detailed knowledge of the configuration of a system and identifies low-level faults, such as correctable memory and disk errors, or high temperature levels that may lead to downtime if they are not identified and acted upon. Symon has a configuration browser that contains full-color images of system components as well as a simple hierarchy view.

The GUI monitors only a single system at a time but is a distributed application. A data collection process is all that runs on the server. An event monitor process runs on a separate machine and looks for problems. In the event of system downtime, the event monitor can raise the alarm even if the GUI is not in use. The Motif GUI can be installed on a separate desktop system. As a performance management tool, Symon is equivalent to HP's GlancePlus product in that it does not store long-term data (a rolling 2-hour history is available) but it does graph all the usual performance data. Its configurable alert capability has many predefined rules and can pass SNMP traps to a network management package; it also has an event log viewer.

Symon can monitor any of Sun's UltraSPARC-based systems and the previous generation of servers such as the SPARCserver 1000 and SPARCcenter 2000. It is supported only on server configurations, but since the Ultra 1 and Ultra 2 workstations are the basis for the Enterprise 150 and Enterprise 2, it works on them just as well (the graphical view of an E150 appears if you use it on an Ultra 1, however).

The latest release can be downloaded over the Internet from http://sunsolve.sun.com/sunsolve/symon/. For more information on Symon, go to http://www.sun.com/products-n-solutions/hw/servers/symon.html. At that address, you can also view a demo of a future version of Symon that will have a Java-based user interface. Symon's initial capabilities were limited so that it could be developed in a short time. Feedback from users is guiding development of a much extended product, with the same hardware-oriented focus.

TeamQuest Baseline

TeamQuest Baseline is another tool that has been developed by a mainframe-oriented vendor. It supports Unix, including Cray and Convex supercomputer versions, NT, and Unisys mainframes, and collects data from the operating system (including accounting logs) and databases. A nice feature of the product is that it can be driven from a web browser interface as well as from Motif. It is a well-thought-out tool, with better than average analysis tools and a performance modeling option, but it does not seem to have much market presence. I think it deserves to be evaluated against products from Landmark and BGS.

Teamquest is at http://www.teamquest.com. It offers a demonstration of its Web browser-based interface that is a live copy of the system with some inputs disabled, and you can try it out directly over the net.

Thoughts on the Future

The performance tools market is evolving, and a few trends are visible. Vendors are figuring out what their competition does that customers like, and they are implementing it themselves. This strategy leads toward a similar common set of functionality but does not help interoperability. In general, data collected by an agent from one vendor cannot be used by an analysis and display system from another vendor. This reality leads to hard choices when it would be nice to combine the best of two tools. The UMA standard attempts to solve this problem, but it does not have enough support from the tools vendors and has ended up as a Unix-oriented standard, just when users want to include Windows NT in their environments. The full standard is also more complex than most existing solutions. I worked on UMA to improve the data definitions, and that part of the standard is covered in more detail later in this book.

User interfaces are one area where performance tools vendors are in a mess. Some vendors support Windows only, others have separate Unix and Windows products, and many have to support a wide range of Unix releases to get market coverage. There is now a good solution to this problem that several vendors are already working toward. By using a web browser as the user interface, with static HTML for reporting and Java applets for active parts of the GUI, a common interface works across all the platforms. With some care, and by testing on both Netscape Navigator and Microsoft Explorer browsers, they can greatly reduce the amount of time and effort required to port and support the GUI.

Finally, there is an increasing interest in performance modeling in the Unix marketplace. Because Unix systems are now so large and are deployed in such mission-critical applications, the effort required to build and use performance models is very worthwhile. Modeling is a common technique in the mainframe market, and now that many high-end Unix systems are actually far bigger than the mainframes they are replacing, the same performance management techniques need to be applied.

Performance Measurement 3≡

In some cases, it is obvious that there is a performance problem; when it is fixed, there may be a noticeable improvement and your job is finished. It is much more common for performance tuning to consist of many small cumulative steps. Some of the steps may reduce performance overall or make one part of the system faster at the expense of another part of the system

Problems can arise when it is necessary to quantify the changes or to measure minor performance changes in complex systems. If the aim of the work is to improve the performance in a well-defined benchmark, such as one of the SPEC or TPC measures, then the measurement can be well defined. In real life, it may be necessary to design a controlled set of experiments to measure performance on the system being worked on.

The analysis of test results can be used to produce sizing or performance models. A method for producing a configuration and sizing guide for multiuser systems is described at the end of this chapter.

The normal situation, illustrated in Figure 3-1, is that you have a computer system with a particular configuration and an application workload running on that system. You then measure the performance, analyze the results, and make changes to the configuration.

Figure 3-1   A Conceptual Model of Performance

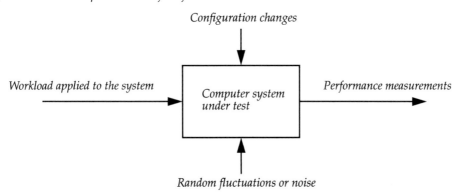

In many cases, no measurements at all are taken until there is some sign of a problem. It is important to collect a background level of information at all times so you can see what changed when a problem occurs. If you just collect performance measurements, you still

have three unknown quantities. You need to keep careful records of configuration changes and to monitor the workload levels as well. That leaves the random fluctuations, and they can be averaged out over time or correlated with time of day and the calendar. This averaging is why you need to collect over a long period.

The Workload

The workload is actually one of the hardest things to deal with. In some cases, you can have total control, for example, when running a single CPU-bound application with fixed input data. In other cases, the workload is totally beyond your control, for example, on a timesharing server with many users running different applications.

The workload selection is also your weakest point if someone wants to challenge the results you are claiming credit for. If you didn't spend a lot of time researching your workload, then you have no comeback to a critic who says, "That's all very well, but in real life the applications aren't used like that, and you have measured and tuned the wrong things." It is much harder for someone to dismiss a detailed, written justification of the workload you have used. For this reason, it is worth writing up the workload and circulating the workload justification to interested parties before you start to collect data. You are likely to get valuable review feedback that will help you target your efforts more precisely.

Fixed Workloads

The biggest problem with a fixed workload is that because you have total control, you yourself have to make decisions that can affect the results you get. In real situations, the same program is usually run with different input data each time it is used. You must make sure that the input data you use is somehow representative of the kinds of data for which you want to optimize the system performance. It is worth spending a lot of time investigating the typical usage of an application by your user base. If you don't investigate, then your carefully tuned optimizations may not have the desired effect.

Random Workloads

Random workloads are in some ways easier to deal with. If you can't control the workload, you don't have to spend so much time investigating it. Instead, you have to spend more time analyzing the measured results to separate out the random fluctuations from the effect of your tuning. Some fluctuations will occur, depending on the time of day or whether a departmental staff meeting is in progress or whether a particular project team is trying to meet a delivery deadline.

In some cases where you have a very large number of users, the average behavior of the users is very predictable. This is the case for Internet web servers, where the daily load levels follow a regular pattern. The pattern is disturbed only by events that reach a large number of people, such as new content on the web server, a major news event, or a popular TV program!

Managed Workloads

An increasing number of tools can be used to capture, encapsulate, and drive a workload into your test system from another computer. The workload can either be captured from a live session or constructed manually. These tools can be divided into two categories. *Journalling*-based tools capture the user input only and simply attempt to replay it at a fixed speed. They blindly continue even if something unexpected happens or the system responds more slowly than during capture, and they cannot be programmed to react appropriately to variable responses from the system being tested. *Emulator*-based tools pattern-match the received responses to ensure that the system is still on track, measure response times, and decide when the next input is due. These are sophisticated and expensive tools, so they are not for the casual user. They allow complex workloads to be run reliably and repeatedly and are normally used to produce system sizing information or capacity planning guides. Traditionally, these tools have worked with ASCII text applications on directly connected lines or telnet over Ethernet, but they have been extended to work with client/server database protocols and HTML. The main vendors are PurePerformix Inc., with Empower™; Performance Awareness Corp, with PreVue™; and Mercury, with LoadRunner™. These tools are often known as RTE systems, for Remote Terminal Emulator. In "Emulating NC-Based Users" on page 112, I describe how to emulate Java applications that use arbitrary client/server protocols.

Workload Characterization

If your workload consists of multiple users or individual components all running together, then it can be very useful to run each component separately (if possible) and measure the utilization profile over time. A plot of the CPU, disk, and network activity will show you when the peak load occurs and whether the load is even or peaks with idle time in between. Capacity planning tools, like the Best/1™ product from BGS Inc., sample the resource usage of each process on the system to measure the profile over time. Best/1 helps you create user classes and transaction classes, then combines them into workloads. This information is fed into a queuing model that can be used to predict the behavior of the system under various conditions. The most common uses are to see what would happen to response times if more users were added to the system and to predict the effect of hardware upgrades.

Configuration Changes

There is a tendency to make a bunch of small changes at one time, in the hope that they will have a big effect on the system. What is needed instead is a systematic approach that gives you the results you need to decide which changes are making a significant difference and which changes can be ignored.

There are always too many possibilities. To illustrate, in Table 3-1 I tabulated some possible configuration factors from the subsequent chapters of this book. The important thing is to clearly identify the factors you wish to vary and then to pick a small number of levels that span the usable range for the factor.

Table 3-1   Example Configuration Factors and Levels

Factor	Example Levels for the Factor
Algorithm design	Bubblesort, shellsort, quicksort
Compiler flags	Debug, base optimization (`-O`), high optimization (`-fast`)
I/O library	`stdio.h`, direct unbuffered read/write, mmap, asynchronous I/O
Filesystem type	Some subset of: NFS, ufs, tmpfs, raw disk, cachefs, logfs, VxFS
Application version	Compare new and old releases of the application
User count	Vary the number of simultaneously active users of the machine
Database shared mem	Minimum default, 100 MB, 500 MB
Database parameters	Defaults, simple DB tuning guide changes, database guru fixes
OS version	Compare several releases of the operating system
Kernel buffer sizes	Defaults, minimum sizes, extra large sizes
Paging parameters	Defaults, reduced values
Cache configuration	On-chip + external 1 MB, on-chip + external 4 MB
Memory size	Subset of 16 MB, 32 MB, 64 MB, 128 MB, 256 MB, 512 MB, 1 GB, 2 GB
Disk type	535 MB, 1.05 GB, 2.1 GB, 2.9 GB, SPARCstorage Array
Disk configuration	4 striped, 8 individual, 6 mirrored, RAID5, etc.
CPU type	microSPARC, microSPARC II, SuperSPARC, UltraSPARC
CPU clock rate	Subset of 167 MHz, 200 MHz, 250 MHz, 300 MHz, 600 MHz, etc.
CPU count	Subset of 1, 2, 4, 6, 8, 10, 12, 16, 20, 32, 48, 64
Backplane type	83-MHz UPA, 100-MHz UPA, 83-MHz GigaPlane, 83-MHz Crossbar
Network type	Ethernet, Token Ring, FDDI, 100BaseT, Switched, Duplex, Gigabit, ATM
NetWork protocol	TCP/IP, UDP/IP, PPP, NFS, SMB, HTTP, etc.
Network count	1, 2, 3, 4, etc.

The best way to approach a large-scale set of tests is to perform an initial small set of tests with just two levels for each factor. Raj Jain, in *The Art of Computer Systems Performance Analysis*, describes a sophisticated statistical technique that drastically reduces the number of tests required to work out the factors that make a significant difference and those that can be ignored. To fully measure every combination of six different factors with four levels for each factor would take $4^6 = 4096$ separate measurements. Reducing to two levels for each factor brings this number down to $2^6 = 64$ separate measurements. Using the statistical methods to analyze the results, you carefully pick certain combinations of levels to measure and do the analysis on only seven measurements to find out which factors can be ignored for a more complete set of tests.

One extra benefit of doing a small preliminary test is that you start analyzing the results sooner than you would if you did all the measurements in one session. Since you will often find some bug in your measurement methods, you have a chance to fix it before you spend a lot longer taking bad measurements. It is common for a large proportion of the measured data to be useless for some reason, even in the best-designed experiments.

Measurement Types and Relationships

The fundamental types are throughput, response time, queue length, and utilization. Nearly all the measurements you can make fit into one of these categories. You can perform a simple mental check whenever you are collecting a set of measurements to make sure that you are collecting at least one of each type. You do not have the complete picture and can easily be misled if you don't have a complete set of measurements available to you. In some cases, given some of these measures or some related measures, you can calculate the complete set.

It is important to remember that it is the *steady state average* throughput, response time, queue length, and utilization that are being measured. The most common source of confusion when dealing with the mathematics of queueing comes from forgetting that everything is always worked out as an average.

Fundamental Types

Throughput is the amount of work that is completed in a given amount of time. The transactions per second (TPS) measures quoted for databases are one example. Do not confuse *throughput* with *bandwidth*. Bandwidth is typically the peak, possible speed ignoring any overhead. *Maximum throughput* is how much work you can actually get done at 100 percent utilization.

- A Fast SCSI bus rated at 10.0 Mbytes/s *bandwidth* has a *maximum throughput* of about 7.5 Mbytes/s when you take the SCSI protocol overhead into account. A Fast Wide SCSI bus rated at 20.0 Mbytes/s has a maximum throughput of about 16 Mbytes/s.

- The MBus used on the SPARCstation 10 and the XDBus™ used on the SPARCserver 1000 both have the same bandwidth of 320 Mbytes/s. Assuming a typical mix of transaction types, the throughput of the MBus is about 100 Mbytes/s, and the throughput of the XDBus is about 250 Mbytes/s. The large variation is due to a totally different protocol on each bus. The MBus is not good for throughput, but it does have substantially less latency than that of the XDBus.

- The throughput of a disk is reported as both reads and writes per second, and Kbytes read and written per second by `iostat`.

Response time is a measure of the time that the user has to wait for some work to complete. When measured by an RTE system, this can be as fine as the time taken to echo characters being typed, or it can be the time taken for a database transaction to complete for that particular user. Latency is the same thing, but this term is more often used when a protocol is being discussed. The BGS Best/1 performance modeling tool measures the CPU consumption of a process over time. The elapsed time taken to consume a fixed amount of CPU time can be defined as the response time. If the system is overloaded, that process will slow down and accumulate CPU time more slowly, and Best/1 reports that increase in response time.

Think time is a measure of how long the user waits before starting another operation. A high think time reduces throughput and utilization.

Service time is the time taken to process the request once it has reached the front of the queue. At low utilization levels, the queue is empty, so the response time is the same as the service time. Service time can be calculated as the utilization divided by the throughput. The measure that `iostat` calls `svc_t` is actually the response time of the disk, not the service time, if the right terminology is used.

Queue length is the number of requests that are waiting for service. A long queue increases the response time but does not affect the service time. Queue length can be calculated as the throughput times the response time.

Utilization is a measure of how much of the computer's resources were used to do the work. It is the busy time as a proportion of the total time.

To illustrate these measurements, we can use some sample `iostat` output, shown in Figure 3-2, to check the formulas and derive what is missing.

Figure 3-2   Example `iostat -x` Disk Statistics

```
extended disk statistics
disk      r/s  w/s   Kr/s   Kw/s wait actv  svc_t  %w  %b
sd1       0.6 14.6    2.0  220.8  0.0  0.7   43.9   0  16
```

For `sd1`, the throughput is `r/s+w/s`, which is 15.2. The total queue length is `wait+actv`, which is 0.7; disk utilization is `%b`, which is 16% or 0.16.

$$DiskServiceTime = \frac{DiskUtilization}{Throughput} = \frac{0.16}{15.2} = 0.011 = 11ms$$

$$TotalResponseTime = \frac{TotalQueueLength}{Throughput} = \frac{0.7}{15.2} = 0.046 = 46ms$$

The queue length needs to be reported more precisely than 0.7 to get an exact result. Working backward, the queue length should be 0.67 if the throughput and response times given are accurate. It is clear that iostat is reporting the response time of an I/O request as svc_t. The service time of the disk itself (which is what the disk makers quote) is 11 ms in this case.

Remembering that these times are averages and that the mathematics assumes an exponential distribution of service times, we can estimate response percentiles.

- 80 percent of response times occur in less than the *average response* x 5 / 3.
- 90 percent of response times occur in less than the *average response* x 7 / 3.
- 95 percent of response times occur in less than the *average response* x 9 / 3 (or x 3).

So, if you are dealing with a requirement that involves the 95th percentile response time, you can estimate that this is about three times the average response time.

Multiuser System Response Time

If a particular configuration of a multiuser system is tested with an RTE, then the test can be repeated under controlled conditions with different load levels or user counts. The throughput, response time, and utilization can be measured at each load level and plotted. The resulting set of plots normally takes one of the forms shown in Figure 3-3.

Figure 3-3   Saturation Points and the Relationship Between Performance Measures

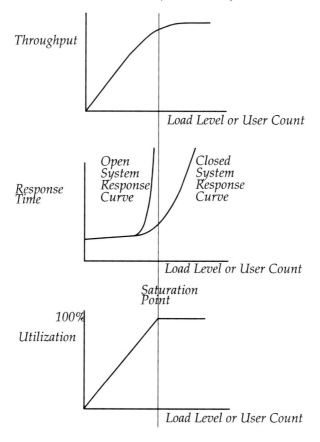

If several users run a job at once, then the utilization level will be higher, the response time will be similar, and the throughput will have increased. At some point as users are added, the utilization approaches 100 percent and the user jobs must wait in a queue before they can continue. Utilization is a generic term. In practice, the CPU usage level is the most common utilization measure, although it is also common for the initial bottleneck in the system to be an overloaded disk drive with high utilization.

As shown in Figure 3-3, once we reach 100 percent utilization, throughput stops increasing and the response time starts to climb. This is the saturation point of the system. If still more users are added, the overhead of managing long queues and switching between users takes an increasingly large proportion of the CPU, the system CPU time climbs, the user CPU time drops, and the throughput drops with it.

I have shown two generic curves for response time. They represent two different cases. The *open system* response time curve occurs when you have a very large number of potential users, such as on an Internet-connected web server. The *closed system* response time curve occurs when you have a finite number of users, such as a database order entry system, and the users have a think time. The queuing equations are shown in Figure 3-4.:

Figure 3-4   Response Time Equations

$$OpenResponse = \frac{ServiceTime}{1 - Utilization}$$

$$ClosedResponse = \frac{NumUsers}{Throughput} - ThinkTime = \frac{NumUsers \times ServiceTime}{Utilization} - ThinkTime$$

In an open system, if you consider a web server running SPECweb96, the response time at low load levels and low utilization over a LAN is about 5 ms, so that value provides an estimate of the base-level service time for one operation when there is no queue to delay it. As CPU utilization reaches 50% (0.5 in the equation), the response time should double to 10 ms. At 90% busy, the response time will be 50 ms. If you ever reach 100% busy, you will be getting more incoming requests than you can complete, so the queue grows to be infinitely long and the system responds infinitely slowly. In the real world, you get a TCP connection time-out after many seconds of waiting.

In a closed system, users are either thinking or waiting. As the system saturates, more users are waiting and fewer are thinking. Ultimately, they are all waiting, so there are no more users left to increase the load. This is why response time increases gradually and the system does not come to a complete halt under a heavy load. For example, with one user completing a transaction every ten seconds (throughput = 0.1) and thinking for nine seconds, each transaction must have a response time of one second. One hundred users with a throughput of eight transactions per second would give a response time of 4.5 seconds.

The ideal situation is to always run under the 90 percent utilization level, with a very stable workload. In practice, most machines have a widely fluctuating workload and spend most of the time at a low utilization level. When a peak load occurs, it may exceed the saturation point; what happens at saturation can make a big difference to the perceived performance of the system.

At saturation, the response time increases. The goal should be to have a steady increase over a wide load range; that way, users find that the system gradually seems to slow down, and they tend to reduce their demand on the system. If the response time increases sharply over a short load range, users find that the system suddenly stops responding with little advance warning, and they will complain about poor performance.

When you are installing a new system or tuning an existing one, deliberately drive it into a saturated state. If you then carefully tune the performance under excessive load, you may be able to get a gradual response degradation curve. This result may mean that the system begins to slow down a little earlier than before, which acts as a warning to the users. Be aware that if a system is tuned so that every resource hits 100 percent utilization at the same time, you will have a very fast degradation at the saturation point.

Collecting Measurements

According to Heisenberg's Principle, one cannot measure something without also affecting it in some way. When you measure the performance of a system, be aware of the effect that your measurement tools may have. Fortunately, most of the data collection utilities have a negligible impact on the system. A sar, vmstat, or iostat collecting data at 5-second intervals is not going to make a noticeable difference. Collecting a system call trace of an active process is an example of the kind of high-speed data collection that should be used with care.

Using Accounting to Monitor the Workload

If you have access to a group of end users over a long period of time, then enable the Unix system accounting logs. The logs can be useful on a network of workstations as well as on a single time-shared server. From them, you can identify how often programs run, how much CPU time, disk I/O, and memory each program uses, and what the work patterns throughout the week look like. To enable accounting to start immediately, enter the three commands shown at the start of Figure 3-5.

Figure 3-5   How to Start Up System Accounting in Solaris 2

```
# ln /etc/init.d/acct /etc/rc0.d/K22acct
# ln /etc/init.d/acct /etc/rc2.d/S22acct
# /etc/init.d/acct start
Starting process accounting
# crontab -l adm
#ident   "@(#)adm      1.5     92/07/14 SMI"   /* SVr4.0 1.2   */
#min    hour    day     month   weekday
0       *       *       *       *          /usr/lib/acct/ckpacct
```

30	2	*	*	*	/usr/lib/acct/runacct 2> \
	/var/adm/acct/nite/fd2log				
30	9	*	*	5	/usr/lib/acct/monacct

Check out the section "Administering Security, Performance, and Accounting in Solaris 2" in the *Solaris System Administration AnswerBook* and see the `acctcom` command. Some `crontab` entries must also be added to summarize and checkpoint the accounting logs. Collecting and checkpointing the accounting data itself puts *no additional load* onto the system. Accounting data is always collected by the kernel, so the only decision is whether to throw it away when the process exits or to write a 40-byte record to the accounting file. The summary scripts that run once a day or once a week can have a noticeable effect, so they should be scheduled to run out-of-hours. The most useful summary can be found in `/var/adm/acct/sum/rprtMMDD` and in `/var/adm/acct/fiscal/fiscrptMM`, where MM is the month and DD is the day. This is the data provided for each user:

LOGIN UID	NAME	CPU (MINS) PRIME	NPRIME	KCORE-MINS PRIME	NPRIME	CONNECT (MINS) PRIME	NPRIME	DISK NPRIME	# OF BLOCKS	# OF PROCS	# DISK SESSSAMPLES	FEE
0	TOTAL	83	235	865222	2446566	3994	10638	0	1062	14	0	0
0	root	58	165	687100	1945493	0	0	0	63	0	0	0
9506	adrianc	6	18	134523	381188	3994	10638	0	366	14	0	0

The data provided for each command includes some indication of process size as well as the CPU usage.

COMMAND NAME	NUMBER CMDS	TOTAL KCOREMIN	TOTAL CPU-MIN	TOTAL REAL-MIN	MEAN SIZE-K	MEAN CPU-MIN	HOG FACTOR	CHARS TRNSFD	BLOCKS READ
TOTALS	26800	177210.42	37.02	76549.92	4786.86	0.00	0.00	3120715200	4633
netscape	3	91875.33	6.33	10471.48	14523.83	2.11	0.00	683552768	6
mailtool	7	29960.85	2.99	19144.39	10018.68	0.43	0.00	525712736	15
symon	5	13687.47	1.26	52.80	10861.63	0.25	0.02	19416320	6
sh	3947	7840.11	4.90	5650.93	1599.53	0.00	0.00	3404445	9

TOTAL COMMAND SUMMARY

3

Collecting Long-Term System Utilization Data

Collect overall system utilization data on all the machines you deal with as a matter of course. For Solaris 2, this process is already set up and just needs to be uncommented from the crontab file for the sys user. Figure 3-6 illustrates a crontab collection for long-term use.

Figure 3-6   crontab Entry for Long-Term sar Data Collection

```
# crontab -l sys
#ident"@(#)sys1.592/07/14 SMI"/* SVr4.0 1.2*/
#
# The sys crontab should be used to do performance collection. See cron
# and performance manual pages for details on startup.
#
0 * * * 0-6 /usr/lib/sa/sa1
20,40 8-17 * * 1-5 /usr/lib/sa/sa1
5 18 * * 1-5 /usr/lib/sa/sa2 -s 8:00 -e 18:01 -i 1200 -A
```

The Solaris 2 utilization log consists of a sar binary log file taken at 20-minute intervals throughout the day and saved in /var/adm/sa/saXX, where XX is the day of the month. sar collects a utilization profile for an entire month. Save the monthly records for future comparison.

When a performance-related problem occurs, it is far easier to identify the source of the problem if you have measurements from a time when the problem was not present. Remember that the real-life user workload is likely to increase over time. If you are trying to justify to a manager the purchase of an upgrade, that manager will find it hard to dismiss a plot showing a long-term utilization trend.

Percollator—A Customizable Data Collector

I wrote an "se" script called percollator.se (see "The SE Toolkit Web Server Performance Collator, percollator.se" on page 88), which stands for Performance Collator but is also a Java coffee reference (it has a Java-based graphical browser). The script aims mainly to log the performance of web servers and proxy servers, but it can be customized to log anything. It gathers data from many sources, including application log files and also includes a summary of the state of the system, using the same rules as the virtual_adrian.se script.

Processing and Analyzing the Measurements

Processing and analyzing the measured results of a set of experiments is an open-ended activity. Collected data is often simply processed into averages and tabulated or plotted. I'm sure that even with the best of intentions, the postprocessing and analysis of results could often be described as cursory. Part of the problem is a lack of tools and techniques, so I will explore some simple methods and give examples of the kind of advanced results that can be obtained by use of a good statistics package like SAS/CPE™ or S-PLUS™.

Generating Averages with **sar**

If you have the automatic utilization log enabled, then the default for a sar command is to print out the log for the day with an average at the end. Whenever sar is used to read a sar log file, you can specify start and end times, and sar will produce an average.

See "Understanding vmstat and sar Output" on page 320 for more details. sar records all the information that the more familiar iostat and vmstat commands report, as well as many other useful measurements. Its major flaws are that it does not store any network-related information, so a supplemental netstat output log may be needed, and its output formats do not show all the collected data.

You can use an awk script[1] to pick out the information of interest from sar, and you can combine data from several measurements into a table like the one shown in Figure 3-7. This table shows how the CPU and disk utilization vary with increasing number of users on a complex, RTE-driven, database workload that has a large batch processing component.

Figure 3-7   Example Data from sar *Averages Tabulated with* awk

users	cpu.usr	cpu.sys	cpu.wio	cpu.idl	disk.sd32	disk.sd33
16	58	19	22	1	9	62
32	73	24	3	0	14	37
48	72	26	2	0	15	34
64	74	26	0	0	15	12
96	70	28	1	0	11	50
128	70	30	0	0	10	17
160	58	42	0	0	7	9

Using the Results Generated by an Emulator System

Emulator systems run a program to emulate each user. This program uses a script of commands and responses and includes defined operation sequences (sometimes known as user functions). Each user program writes a log of every command and response that has the function start and end points with accurate timestamps embedded in it. After a mixture of these programs has been run as a workload, special postprocessing commands extract the named functions and timestamps. Reports can then be generated for a

---

1. Details of this script are left as an exercise for the reader, but the Solaris head, tail, cut, and paste commands may also be useful.

particular start and end time during the test (which should match the start and end time used for the `sar` utilization averages). The report lists the number of times each named function completed in the specified time interval and the maximum, minimum, mean, and standard deviation of the time taken.

The number of functions completed in the time interval is a throughput measure, and the average time taken is a latency measure. This measure, together with the `sar`-based utilization information, affords a good basis for further analysis.

If a set of results is taken with varying numbers of users, then the measurements will often have the form shown in Figure 3-3 on page 46.

Obtaining Results on a Live System

If you are monitoring a live system with real users, then you will need to find a way of quantifying the throughput. Response times are very hard to obtain on a live system, but in many cases, they can be inferred from the throughput and utilization measures. To find a throughput measure, look at the system accounting reports to see if a key application program that is associated with the users uses a significant amount of CPU or I/O. You can also look at the typical execution times for the program, and it may be possible to derive a throughput measure either from the number of times the program executed or from the total amount of CPU time or I/O consumed by that program in a given time. Database applications are somewhat easier because you can usually identify how many transactions of a given type have occurred in a given time period and use this as the throughput measure.

Whereas a managed workload using an RTE may process data over a time period measured in minutes, a real-life workload will often need measurement periods measured in hours or days. If users log in only once each day and use a single instance of an application throughout the day, then the daily CPU usage for that application could be extracted from the accounting logs each night, by means of `awk`, as a throughput measure.

Analyzing the Results

The analysis required depends on the situation. If you are conducting a sizing or capacity planning study, then many results for different configurations of the system can be combined into a sizing model. If you are monitoring a live system and trying to identify where the next bottleneck will occur, then you need to build a model of changes in the system over time.

Producing a Sizing Model

I will briefly describe a method that has worked well for sizing multiuser workloads, using the Performix Empower RTE and the StatSci S-PLUS statistical modeling package.

The tabular data on utilization, throughput, and response time at varying user counts was produced for each system configuration that was tested. A system was set up with a particular disk, memory, and CPU configuration, and then a series of measurements was made with increasing numbers of users. At the high user counts, the system was pushed well into an overloaded state for some configurations. Configuration changes were made by varying the number of CPUs[2], changing the disk setup, and changing the amount of think time in the workload scripts.

To repeat our experience: First, plot the data to make sure that it looks "clean." Next, estimate the saturation point for each configuration in terms of users. Then, fit a straight line from the origin through the first few points of the throughput data. This line represents the region where the system is underused; the only constraint on throughput is the think time of the users (the rate at which they ask the system to do work for them). Draw another straight horizontal line from the point of peak throughput; the intersection of the two lines is defined as the saturation point and projected down to produce a user count. Figure 3-8 illustrates the technique.

Figure 3-8   Finding the Saturation Point

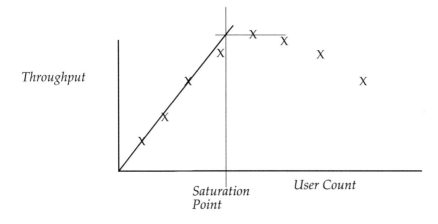

---

2. This can be done programmatically; see "CPU Control Commands — `psrinfo`, `psradm`, and `psrset`" on page 229.

We found this measure to be very stable, and it didn't fluctuate much when we repeated the measurements on the same configuration, whereas the position of the peak throughput varied much more. The measure has the additional benefit of not requiring measurements of response time, so it can be used in situations where the response time measurement cannot be obtained.

You can characterize each test by its saturation point measured in number of users, the peak throughput level, the utilization levels of the various parts of the system at the measured saturation point, and the configuration factors used for the test. The response time at this point should always be good, so it does not need to be included.

Store the test results in S-PLUS as a *data frame* for modeling. S-PLUS can calculate a model that produces a set of coefficients relating the configuration factors to the saturation point. Each coefficient is used for one level of the factor; for example, in an ideal world, the CPU coefficients might be 0.5 for two CPUs, 1.0 for four CPUs, and 2.0 for eight CPUs (see Figure 3-9). When we used the model to predict results, the values predicted by this model were within a few user values of the measured results across the entire range. The residual errors were small, and we obtained a good fit for the model. A similar formula for predicting the peak throughput can also be obtained.

Figure 3-9   Model Formula and Coefficients Produced for System Sizing

$$Users \;=\; Intercept \times \begin{bmatrix} Timeshare \\ ClientServer \end{bmatrix} \times \begin{bmatrix} 2CPU \\ 4CPU \\ 6CPU \\ 8CPU \end{bmatrix} \times \begin{bmatrix} ShortThink \\ MediumThink \\ LongThink \end{bmatrix}$$

In the formula shown in Figure 3-9, a coefficient is produced for each value shown. To get the saturation point value in users for a particular combination, the coefficients for that combination are multiplied, for example, Intercept × Timeshare × 6CPU × MediumThink.

A useful aspect of this method is that the statistics package maintains information on the variance of each coefficient, and when the formula is used to predict the value of a saturation point, the standard deviation of that prediction is also calculated. The tests used to calculate the model represent a sparse subset of the complete configuration space (i.e., to save time, not every possible combination of configuration options was tested). So, if a group of related predictions is calculated to have a large standard deviation, then more tests can be performed in the region of that group, and the model can be regenerated with reduced variance.

The statisticians among you may be curious about the method used to produce a multiplicative model equation, when the standard techniques work with additive models. There are two ways to handle this in S-PLUS. One way is to take logarithms of the data before calculating the additive model, then use exponents to regenerate the coefficients. A more sophisticated method is to use the generalized linear model with a Poisson link function, which sounds complicated but is actually easier to use. (It took me a while to work out that this was the right thing to do, since S-PLUS has hundreds of possible modeling options!). This model has the property that the variance of the result is proportional to its value, so the error in a 10-user prediction might be 1 user, while for a 200-user prediction, the error might be 20 users.

Looking for Trends

Take many short samples of utilization data (like the hourly `sar` measures) and plot them to produce a distribution curve or histogram over a longer period (perhaps weekly). That way, you count the number of hours per week that utilization was in a certain range and, as time goes on, you can compare the weekly distribution plots to see if there is an increase in the number of hours per week at high utilization levels. Do this for CPU run queue size, for each disk's service time, and for the page scan rate[3].

Further Reading

The Practical Performance Analyst by Neil Gunther, McGraw-Hill, 1997, provides an easy-to-follow guide to the parts of performance modeling and queuing theory that you really need to know.

The Art of Computer Systems Performance Analysis by Raj Jain provides comprehensive coverage of techniques for experimental design, measurement, simulation, and performance modeling.

Statistical Models In S by John M. Chambers and Trevor J. Hastie is quite specific to the S-PLUS statistics package, but it gives an excellent insight into the range of techniques available in modern statistics and how the combination of statistics and numerical modeling can be used to make sense of data.

---

3. A high scan rate indicates a memory shortage; see "Understanding vmstat and sar Output" on page 320.

Internet Servers 4

Solaris is often used to provide network services. In this chapter, I describe the performance characteristics of some common types of Internet and intranet servers, web servers, and web proxy servers. The next chapter extends this discussion to cover the characteristics and sizing of servers for Java-based applications. A foundation for this discussion is the Transmission Control Protocol, TCP, so that is where we start.

Introduction to TCP

The TCP Internet Protocol (TCP/IP), described in RFC793, is simple in concept, but the reality of making it work reliably in a wide range of conditions adds a lot more complexity. There are a large number of protocol counters that can be viewed with netstat -s, but only a small number of them are of general interest. There is a set of tunable values that can be obtained and set by means of the ndd command.

The netstat -s command lists several protocols, but here I just show the TCP data that is reported by Solaris 2.6.

```
TCP tcpRtoAlgorithm      =       4tcpRtoMin        =     200
    tcpRtoMax            =240000tcpMaxConn         =      -1
    tcpActiveOpens       = 99968tcpPassiveOpens    = 42383
    tcpAttemptFails      = 26522tcpEstabResets     =     363
    tcpCurrEstab         =      78tcpOutSegs        =14443181
    tcpOutDataSegs       =11374607tcpOutDataBytes    =2916877934
    tcpRetransSegs       = 84092tcpRetransBytes     =43663829
    tcpOutAck            =3041562tcpOutAckDelayed    =899607
    tcpOutUrg            =      42tcpOutWinUpdate    = 17850
    tcpOutWinProbe       =     632tcpOutControl      =314162
    tcpOutRsts           = 27554tcpOutFastRetrans   = 24631
    tcpInSegs            =13952067
    tcpInAckSegs         =9102057tcpInAckBytes       =2916262961
    tcpInDupAck          =353041tcpInAckUnsent      =       0
    tcpInInorderSegs     =10659334tcpInInorderBytes   =1955569952
    tcpInUnorderSegs     = 24921tcpInUnorderBytes   =7497810
    tcpInDupSegs         = 37258tcpInDupBytes       =15618525
    tcpInPartDupSegs     =     384tcpInPartDupBytes  =201980
    tcpInPastWinSegs     =       0tcpInPastWinBytes  =       0
```

```
tcpInWinProbe        =    871tcpInWinUpdate      =    605
tcpInClosed          =    524tcpRttNoUpdate      = 54130
tcpRttUpdate         =8940231tcpTimRetrans        = 71271
tcpTimRetransDrop    =     18tcpTimKeepalive     =   1266
tcpTimKeepaliveProbe=    373tcpTimKeepaliveDrop =      5
tcpListenDrop        =      0tcpListenDropQ0      =      0
tcpHalfOpenDrop      =      0
```

To make sense of this list and to pick out the data of interest, let's start with a simplified description of TCP and relate this description to the data reported by `netstat -s`.

TCP is a reliable, connection-oriented protocol. You first have to establish a connection between two machines, then send data, making sure it gets there safely, then shut down the connection. At any point, there will be some number of connections in each of these states. It's rather like making a telephone call—dialing, talking, then hanging up. The common alternative to TCP is UDP, which is much more like the postal service. You send a packet and hope that it gets there. UDP has no congestion or retransmission support but has about the same per-packet overhead. TCP controls the transmission rate so that it matches the ability of the network and the receiver to consume packets. It is self-monitoring and self-tuning on a per-connection and per-correspondent basis.

Connections

Some connections are opened by your system as it calls out to another machine; conversely, other connections are opened as a result of another machine calling in. Again, this is just like a phone call, where you could be making the call or receiving the call. Once the call is established, it is symmetric; both sides can send and receive data as they wish, and either side can terminate the connection. The outgoing calls you make are called *active opens*, and you decide whom to call and why. An outgoing remote login or web browser request causes an active open. The incoming calls are called *passive opens*; they occur without any activity on your part—you just have to have a program running that is waiting to "pick up the phone." For example, an HTTP server listens on port 80 for any incoming requests. Two counters keep track of how many of each type have occurred.

```
    tcpActiveOpens       = 99968tcpPassiveOpens      = 42383
```

You should keep track of the rate at which opens occur. The fundamental performance limit of many web servers is the rate at which they can perform the passive open. Systems can run at hundreds (with Solaris 2.5.1) to thousands (with Solaris 2.6) of connections per second. If you need more, split the load over multiple systems. A concentrated program of kernel tuning pushed the Solaris 2.6 rate into the range of thousands of connections per second per system by making the relevant code paths scale well on multiprocessor systems.

Each connection may last a few milliseconds (for a web server on a local LAN running a benchmark), many seconds or minutes (for a large transfer on a slow Internet connection), or essentially forever (for rlogin/telnet sessions). Each established connection will use up a process or a thread in your system. The number of currently established connections is reported by `netstat` as:

```
tcpCurrEstab          =     78
```

During connection setup, there is a three-way handshake sequence. This sequence can take a while because several round-trip delays between the two systems will occur. There is a limit on the number of connections in this state for each listening application (known as the listen queue), and for connection-intensive workloads on high latency networks (you guessed it —Internet web servers), the limit may be too low. The default before Solaris 2.5 was 5, and the maximum was 32. Since Solaris 2.5, the default is 32 and the maximum is 1024. In Solaris 2.5.1, an extra counter, called `tcpListenDrop`, was added to the `netstat -s` TCP output. It counts the number of times that a connection was dropped because of a full listen queue. If you see non-zero values of `tcpListenDrop`, you can increase the size of the queue by changing applications to call the `listen(3n)` routine with a higher backlog. The maximum backlog is set by the ndd tunable `tcp_conn_req_max` in older releases and will also be increased by installing the latest TCP patch. (Tuning is discussed later in this chapter.)

The initial handshake consists of an incoming packet with only its SYN (synchronize sequence numbers) flag set. The server makes an entry in its listen queue and sends a packet that not only acknowledges the first packet but also includes its own SYN to synchronize the sequence number in the opposite direction. The next packet from the client acknowledges the second SYN, and the connection-handling code schedules the server process to return from the `accept(3n)` call and move the connection from the listen queue to the active connection list.

If the client only sends a SYN packet and never completes the connection by acknowledging the second SYN, then it will eventually time out and be discarded from the listen queue by the server. This feature is exploited by a denial of service attack, where a server is flooded with SYN packets by a special program that generates SYN packets that have nonexistent source addresses. This attack causes the listen queue to become completely full. New connections can get through only as old ones are discarded from the queue, and a web server will stop or slow to a crawl.

TCP/IP Patches and the Listen Queue Fix

The latest Solaris 2.5 and 2.5.1 TCP and IP patches solve this problem and are incorporated in Solaris 2.6. The fix was first included in revision 12 of the Solaris 2.5.1 TCP patch. The TCP patch number is 103582 for SPARC/Solaris 2.5.1, 103581 for

Intel/Solaris 2.5.1, and the IP patch number is 103630 for SPARC/Solaris 2.5.1, 103631 for Intel/Solaris 2.5.1. The change reduces problems caused by SYN flood denial of service attacks. There are now two separate queues of partially complete connections instead of one, and two new tunables replace `tcp_conn_req_max`, which no longer exists. There are also two new counters shown by `netstat -s`.

tcpListenDrop	=	0tcpListenDropQ0	=	0
tcpHalfOpenDrop	=	0		

The two new tunable values are `tcp_conn_req_max_q` (default value 128), which is the maximum allowed backlog of completed connections waiting to return from an accept call as soon as the right process gets some CPU time, and `tcp_conn_req_max_q0` (default value 1024), which is the maximum number of connections with handshake incomplete. A SYN flood attack could affect only the incomplete queue, and valid connections can still get through. The `tcpHalfOpenDrop` counter is incremented only if a dubious connection is being discarded, so it indicates that a SYN flood attack is likely to have caused the connection being dropped. The new values are high enough not to need tuning in normal use of a web server.

The TCP Slow Start Algorithm and Congestion Window Problems

At the start of a connection, it is not clear how much bandwidth is available or what the round-trip latency is. It may be possible to estimate the round-trip latency from previous transfers on the same route, but if all connections are very short, this information is not reliable enough to be used. To avoid flooding a slow network, TCP implements a slow start algorithm by limiting the number of packets it sends until it has had an acknowledgment. This limit is known as the congestion window, and there have been problems due to bugs in several implementations of TCP that cause an extra delay to occur at the start of each connection. The TCP standard says the initial congestion window should be one packet, and that number is doubled each time an acknowledgment is received. Doubling gives an exponential ramp-up, but for very short connections that are typical of HTTP servers, there may be only a handful of packets to send. There are two defects in other TCP implementations that interact badly with Solaris' *correct* TCP implementation, and a workaround has been provided in Solaris.

One defect is that most other TCP implementations count the last acknowledgment of the connection setup and double the congestion window to 2 before they start sending data packets. This behavior can be enabled on Solaris 2.6, and on Solaris 2.5.1 with TCP patch revision 15 and later, by changing the tunable `tcp_slow_start_initial` from 1 to 2. The result is slightly faster transmission of small amounts of data on unsaturated networks. Of greater importance, however, is that this behavior also masks a defect in the Microsoft TCP implementation that is used in Windows NT4 and Windows 95. If you send one packet to these systems at the start of a connection, they do not immediately acknowledge receipt, causing an additional startup delay of a fraction of a second. If you send them two packets, they acknowledge immediately. In the same situation, sending one packet to Solaris causes an immediate acknowledgment.

The result of this problem is that benchmark performance between Windows clients and Solaris servers over a high-speed network is impacted. Higher response times than normal will be seen in LAN-based web benchmarks. In the real world, there is often a high-latency wide-area network separating the systems, and the clients are on low-speed links such as modem connections. The extra delay prevents this problem from occurring, so there is no performance impact. The problem affects only the first exchange of packets, so large transfers and long-lived connections are not noticeably affected, either.

Most TCP implementations already start with a congestion window of 2, and the standard is expected to be changed to allow 2 as the initial value. Changing the Solaris default of 1 to 2 is advisable, and a future patch or release of Solaris is likely to make 2 the default.

TCP Data Transfer

For many network servers, the first performance bottleneck is the amount of network bandwidth available. With up-to-date software, almost any system can saturate a 10-Mbit Ethernet, even with web traffic. The current generation of UltraSPARC-based systems can easily saturate a 100-Mbit network. We can look at the access logs to see how much data is being sent, but that information does not include the protocol overhead or the incoming requests. We can get a better idea of the traffic levels by looking at the TCP throughput counters. The outgoing data is divided into segments, with each segment corresponding to an Ethernet packet. Delivery of a segment is acknowledged by the other end. If no acknowledgment is received, the segment is retransmitted. To decide whether the segment has been lost or is just taking a long time, a complex, adaptive time-out scheme is used. Both ends are working the same way, so as well as sending data segments, they send acknowledgment segments for the data they receive. Here are the output counters reported by netstat. They are 32-bit values, so they soon wrap around. It is best to take the difference of two readings taken over a time interval that is short enough to avoid the possibility of counter wrapping.

```
tcpOutSegs        = 80370
tcpOutDataSegs    = 57395      tcpOutDataBytes    =9854298
tcpRetransSegs    =  4826      tcpRetransBytes    =644526
tcpOutAck         = 23486
```

The total number of segments (tcpOutSegs) is mostly made up of tcpOutDataSegs and tcpOutAck, although the numbers don't add up exactly. The protocol is more complex than I have described it here. There is the overhead of a TCP/IP header for every segment. On Ethernet this overhead is increased by the Ethernet encapsulation, the minimum size (64 bytes) of an Ethernet packet (which is enough to hold the IP and TCP headers and 6 bytes of data), and the 9.6 ms (at 10 Mbits) minimum interpacket gap, equivalent to another 12 bytes. You could calculate from all this an approximation to the actual bit-rate due to TCP on an Ethernet, but you can't figure out all the other protocols, so it's probably not worth it. I generally just watch the `tcpOutDataBytes` value and use `tcpRetransBytes` to calculate a retransmission percentage. Problems with the retransmission algorithm have been fixed in the latest kernel patches for Solaris 2.4 through 2.5.1. If you see more than 30% retransmissions, make sure you have the patch. If you still see high retransmissions with the latest patch, you may have some bad network hardware or a congested route that is dropping packets.

The maximum TCP segment size is negotiated on a per-connection basis. For local LAN-based connections, the maximum is usually 1,460 bytes. I have observed that most connections over the Internet to *www.sun.com* use 576 bytes, which is less efficient. The protocol overhead for 1460-byte packets is about 5%; for 576-byte packets, it is about 12%. Inasmuch as many additional small packets are also sent to carry acknowledgments, the actual protocol overhead is worse than this. The retransmission rate over a LAN is usually near zero, but the Internet seems to vary between 5% and 20%, depending upon traffic conditions at the time. The overhead for sending bulk TCP data can therefore vary from about 5% to 30% or more. If you are close to saturating an Ethernet, there is even more inefficiency coming from high collision rates and low-level Ethernet retransmissions.

On the receiving side, there are no retransmissions to worry about. The incoming data segments may arrive in the wrong order in some circumstances, so there are two counters, one for in-order and one for out-of-order. You might regard out-of-order data as a sign of routing problems, but I'm not sure what you could do about it. The total incoming data rate is given by these counters:

```
tcpInInorderSegs    = 63348     tcpInInorderBytes   =20318851
tcpInUnorderSegs    =     0     tcpInUnorderBytes   =       0
tcpInDupSegs        = 37258     tcpInDupBytes       =15618525
tcpInPartDupSegs    =   384     tcpInPartDupBytes   =201980
```

The counters for duplicated data indicate another problem that may occur. Incoming segments may be duplicated when an acknowledgment is lost or delayed and the other end retransmits a segment that actually arrived correctly the first time. This situation can be a sign that the remote systems are retransmitting too quickly and the remote systems may need to be tuned or patched.

Network Data Transfer

At the lowest level, we can look at the total number of bytes sent and received on each network interface. This number includes all protocols and is divided into normal, broadcast, and multicast counters. Every interface is different, and older versions of Solaris do not provide these counters. The Solaris 2.5.1 patches for the "le" (103903-03) and "hme" (104212-04) interfaces do include the counters, and they are incorporated in Solaris 2.6. These counters can be accessed with SNMP or can be read from the `kstat` interface as described in "The Solaris 2 "kstat" Interface" on page 387.

The new counters added were:

- `rbytes, obytes`—read and output byte counts
- `multircv, multixmt`—multicast receive and transmit byte counts
- `brdcstrcv, brdcstxmt`—broadcast byte counts
- `norcvbuf, noxmtbuf`—buffer allocation failure counts

An undocumented option to `netstat` dumps out all the kernel statistics; you can use the command `netstat -k [interface]` to look at the full raw data for each interface. In older releases of Solaris, the interface cannot be specified.

```
% netstat -k le0
le0:
ipackets 0 ierrors 0 opackets 0 oerrors 5 collisions 0
defer 0 framing 0 crc 0 oflo 0 uflo 0 missed 0 late_collisions 0
retry_error 0 nocarrier 2 inits 11 notmds 0 notbufs 0 norbufs 0
nocanput 0 allocbfail 0 rbytes 0 obytes 0 multircv 0 multixmt 0
brdcstrcv 0 brdcstxmt 5 norcvbuf 0 noxmtbuf 0
```

An unfortunate by-product of this change is that a spelling mistake was corrected in the metrics for "le"; the metric "framming" was replaced by "framing." Not many tools look at all the metrics, but the SE toolkit does, and if patch 103903-03 is loaded, an old SE script that looks at the network and finds an "le" interface fails immediately. The fix for SE version 2.5.0.2 is to edit the file `/opt/RICHPse/include/kstat.se` and correct the spelling change in the `ks_le_network` definition. SE version 3.0 and later detect whether the patch is loaded and use the new counters and new spelling.

TCP Flow Control

TCP has a way to control the flow of data between the two systems. The receiving system tells the sender how much data it will accept (known as the receive window). The sender will never send more segments than will fit into the advertised window. When the receiver acknowledges some data, a new window is sent as part of the acknowledgment. The receiver normally moves the window on by the size of the data being acknowledged.

If for some reason the program that is reading the data stops and the receiver runs out of buffer space, the receiver will still acknowledge segments but will not advance the window. This situation pauses the transfer.

The size of the window varies. I have observed windows of anything from 512 bytes to 48 Kbytes in transfers from *www.sun.com* to the many and varied systems out there running web browsers. The window size should always be at least four times the maximum segment size. SunOS 4 defaults to 4 Kbytes, and Solaris 2 defaults to 8 Kbytes. Making the default larger will, in general, use up more RAM, especially if you have a lot of connections to handle. For most systems that run browsers, however, there are few connections, and a larger default may well help data flow more smoothly over the Internet.

The size of the window that you need depends on the *bandwidth-delay product*. This is the speed at which your connection can run multiplied by the time it takes to send a data segment out and receive the acknowledge back. You can get some idea of latencies by using the /usr/sbin/ping -s command, although some machines may hide behind firewalls that only allow web traffic.

If your system is on a 10-Mbit Ethernet, you should find a latency of about 1 ms; the bandwidth is about 1 Mbyte/s, so the product is 1 Kbyte. From this calculation, you can see that the default window of 8 Kbytes is enough for LANs connected through routers as long as the latency stays below 8 ms. At 100 Mbit/s Fast Ethernet or FDDI, the latency is less than 1 ms and the bandwidth is about 10 Mbytes/s. The product is thus less than 10 Kbytes. This result explains why only small gains (if anything) are to be made by increasing the default window size on local connections over 100-Mbit networks. Old, busy, or slow systems that take longer to turn around a reply may benefit more from a larger window.

If your system is on a 28.8-Kbit modem, you need to take into account the size of the packet. At 3 Kbytes/s, a 1500-byte packet takes 500 ms to transfer, while an acknowledgment or a ping of 64 bytes will take about 20 ms. If you are connecting over the Internet, you may have to add several seconds to the total. If we assume 3 seconds and 3 Kbytes/s, the product is 9 Kbytes. If you are lucky enough to have a high-speed connection to the Internet, your bandwidth is much higher but the latency is not much better—you only save the local transfer delay of a few hundred milliseconds. In this case, you may find that an 8-Kbyte window is too small and that you can get better throughput with a 32-Kbyte window.

The TCP window needs to be increased on the receiving end. It is on the client systems with browsers that a change needs to be made, and there is not a lot that can be done on the web server. For very high speed connections, it may help a bit to increase the default transmit buffer size.

Sometimes, a high-speed connection also has high latency, for example, over a satellite link. This connection may require windows much larger than the normal maximum of 64 Kbytes. A TCP window scale option (RFC1323) allows the window size to be multiplied by a power of 2 up to a gigabyte. The option is available as a consulting special in older releases of Solaris and is included in releases starting with Solaris 2.6.

TCP Parameter Tuning

Network tuning is performed by means of the ndd(1) command. Changes are used by new connections immediately—a huge improvement on most other operating systems where a kernel rebuild or reboot is necessary for a change to take effect. If you monitor the TCP counters directly (using a tool like the SE toolkit script nx.se), then you can see the effect of a change as it happens. To retain changes after a reboot, place an ndd command in the file /etc/rc2.d/S69inet.

The complete list of tunable values can be obtained as shown. I have edited the output to show only the tunables I'm going to discuss. The other values should never be changed on a production system.

```
# ndd /dev/tcp
name to get/set ? ?
tcp_close_wait_interval     (read and write)
tcp_conn_req_max_q          (read and write)
tcp_conn_req_max_q0         (read and write)
tcp_xmit_hiwat              (read and write)
tcp_recv_hiwat              (read and write)
tcp_slow_start_initial      (read and write)
```

Tuning the Close Wait Interval and TCP Connection Hash Table Size

When a TCP connection is closed by a web server, it remembers the connection for a few minutes to make sure it can identify any leftover packets in transit over the network from clients related to that connection. The TCP standard defines this interval as twice the maximum lifetime of a TCP packet. Not all implementations use the same value—some use 60 or 120 seconds—and Solaris 2 follows the letter of the standard and sets the value to 240 seconds. The actual value is set as 240,000 ms, using ndd.

When high connection rates occur, a large backlog of TCP connections builds up. For example, at 100 connections/s, 24,000 connections will be in the backlog. Locating a TCP data structure in the kernel can become inefficient, and the server will slow down. One way to work around this problem is to reduce tcp_close_wait_interval. For SPECweb96 tests, the run rules let you set the interval to 60 seconds. Don't set the interval to less than this. In Solaris 2.6, two changes solve the connection backlog problem. First, the connection hash table size can be increased to make lookups more efficient, and, second, the code that removes connections from the list has been streamlined. The connection hash table size can be set only once, at boot time; it defaults to 256, and for SPECweb96 tests, it is set to 262144. It must be a power of 2, somewhere between those two figures, and is set in /etc/system, for example,

```
set tcp:tcp_conn_hash_size=8192
```

You can change the close wait interval at any time by using ndd, for example,

```
# /usr/sbin/ndd -set /dev/tcp tcp_close_wait_interval 60000
```

Tuning the Listen Queue

To adjust the old-style listen queue, adjust the parameter tcp_conn_req_max. You can do this interactively or as an inline command. The latest listen queue algorithm does not need tuning. It is preferable to add the latest TCP/IP patches to Solaris 2.5.1 or to upgrade to Solaris 2.6 where this tunable is obsolete.

```
# /usr/sbin/ndd -set /dev/tcp tcp_conn_req_max 1024
```

Tuning the TCP Window Size

The transmit buffer and receive window are controlled by tcp_xmit_hiwat and tcp_recv_hiwat. If you aren't concerned about using up extra memory, you can set them both to 32 Kbytes by using:

```
# /usr/sbin/ndd -set /dev/tcp tcp_xmit_hiwat 32768
# /usr/sbin/ndd -set /dev/tcp tcp_recv_hiwat 32768
```

If you set them to 65536 or more with Solaris 2.6, you trigger the TCP window scale option (RFC1323).

Tuning TCP Slow Start

As I describe in "The TCP Slow Start Algorithm and Congestion Window Problems" on page 60, increase the initial value of the slow start counter from 1 to 2.

```
# /usr/sbin/ndd -set /dev/tcp tcp_slow_start_initial 2
```

Features of the Solaris Internet Server Supplement

The Solaris Internet server supplement was released at the end of 1996. Solaris 2.5.1 was used as the baseline, and some TCP features that were later released as part of Solaris 2.6 were folded into the supplement. This kernel was provided as part of the Netra 3.1

internet server bundle. Now that Solaris 2.6 is available, 2.5.1/ISS is obsolete, and anyone using it should upgrade. The 2.5.1/ISS release was well tested as an Internet server but was not tested for general-purpose applications. There are also some complex patch issues because normal Solaris 2.5.1 kernel patches will not apply to 2.5.1/ISS.

TCP Monitoring with the SE Toolkit

The SE toolkit, described later, is a C-based interpreter that has built-in interfaces that can read and write any kernel data. It has been available for free download over the Internet since 1995. As well as the more conventional kvm and kstat interfaces, the SE toolkit has a mib interface to all the network data, so mib$tcp gets you the entire TCP data structure that netstat -s shows. The toolkit also has an ndd interface, so, for example, reading or writing to ndd$tcp.tcp_xmit_hiwat is the same as using the ndd command.

Predefined code calculates per-second rates that are shown by several SE scripts. A TCP rule also watches over the counters, looking at their behavior. The rule, which is a new feature of SE version 3.0, watches the retransmission rate, the listen queue, incoming connections to invalid ports, and outgoing attempts that fail.

One SE user took advantage of these toolkit features to write a GUI-based tool that both monitors TCP data and enables you to tune some TCP parameters by using sliders if you run the tool as root. The tcp_monitor.se tool, shown in Figure 4-1, is provided with the current version of SE. The SE toolkit also includes a convenient way to obtain per-second rates for all the key metrics, and a TCP rule watches for common problems like high retransmission rates and listen queue overflows.

One thing we discovered when reading TCP data is that the data-collection mechanism locks TCP as far as new connections are concerned so that all the parameters are a consistent snapshot. If you are already saturating TCP on a Solaris 2.5.1 system, you may find that running netstat -s takes several seconds and hurts web server throughput. Some work was done in Solaris 2.5.1/ISS to reduce this effect, and performance fixes solve this problem for Solaris 2.6.

Further Reading

If you want to know how TCP *really* works (I tried to keep it simple), I recommend *TCP/IP Illustrated Volume I - The Protocols* by W. Richard Stevens, Addison Wesley, 1994. Appendix E of that book covers the meaning of the ndd options for Solaris 2.2. An updated Appendix E to cover Solaris 2.5.1 is available from Stevens' web site: http://www.kohala.com/~rstevens/tcpipiv1.html.

As with any set of tuning parameters, you can easily mess up your system if you get carried away. Please take care: don't tweak production systems unless you are certain you have a problem, and make sure you have studied *TCP/IP Illustrated* really carefully.

Figure 4-1   The TCP Monitor Program

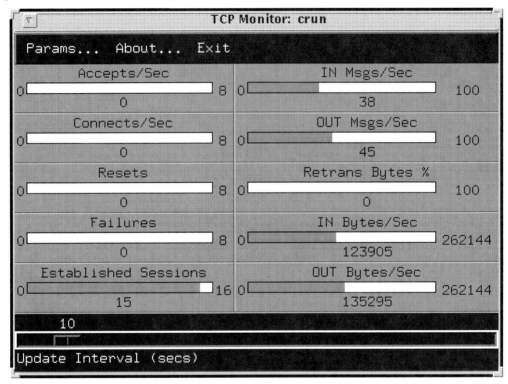

TCP Transfer Characteristics for Web Servers

TCP transfers can be classified into a number of recognizable, characteristic sequences that can determine problems. A tool for visualizing the sequences makes this classification a lot easier to do. Examples of some common sequences seen on web servers illustrate the characteristics. The tool is available as a free download from the Internet, and I'll illustrate how you can use it to see things that you can't figure out from a snoop listing or packet analyzer. The Packet Shell is available at http://playground.sun.com/psh/, and it includes a tcp.analysis tool written by Steve Parker of SunSoft. The basic tool is a language called the packet shell (psh) that understands protocols like TCP/IP over Ethernet. By coupling the tcl/tk toolkit and a simple X-based plotting utility, Parker constructed a GUI-based tool.

The `tcp.analysis` tool reads a `snoop` or `tcpdump` file, sorts the packets into TCP sequences, and lets you pick one to graph. A screenshot is shown Figure 4-2. The data shown on each line starts with the source IP address and port number, then the destination IP address and port number. The total number of bytes in the sequence and the number of segments (Ethernet packets) are followed by the TCP sequence numbers and any flags seen in the sequence. If there is a SYN, then you have captured the start of a sequence in the `snoop` file.

Figure 4-2   The `tcp.analysis` Program

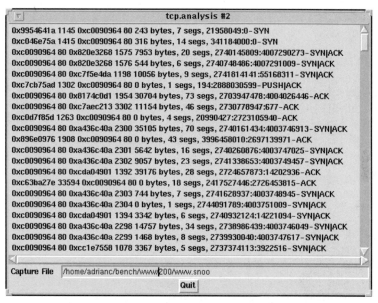

Collecting a **snoop** Sequence

You must have superuser permissions to run `snoop`. You should also be careful about the security of traffic on your network, and don't provide read permission for others on collected `snoop` files. You can cut down the size of a `snoop` file by truncating saved packets to 128 bytes. This size allows capture of most higher-level protocol headers (like HTTP and NFS). If you just want the TCP header, truncate collection to 54 bytes. The `tcp.analysis` tool slows down if there are too many packets in the file. I would suggest 1,000 packets on a lightly loaded network and no more than 10,000 on a busy one. If possible, collect using a separate system that has no traffic of its own to get in the way and no other jobs running to steal CPU time. If you have to, you can collect on an active server as long as there is some spare CPU time. If the collecting system is too busy, you may drop some packets.

You must also avoid generating more packets with snoop. Don't write the output file over NFS, and don't run snoop from an rlogin session over the same network without redirecting the stderr output to /dev/null. I always write the output to /tmp because it is memory based. You can either monitor every packet that goes by or use snoop's filtering capabilities to look for a particular host or protocol. While it is running, snoop counts out the packets to stderr.

```
# snoop -s 128 -c 1000 -o /tmp/test.snoop
Using device /dev/le (promiscuous mode)
1000
#
```

I collected some snoop data on web servers, both on the Internet and on a local, high-speed connection to see if the data was random or if it could be characterized into common sequences. In looking through the data, I and engineers from SunSoft's Internet Engineering Group found about ten different-looking plots overall and gave up after everything else we looked at matched one of the categories. The results are explained in the next section, with example plots taken from the tool.

Tiny HTTP Transfer Characteristics

Figure 4-3 shows an HTTP GET incoming request and acknowledgment packets on the left, and the matching response on the right.

Figure 4-3   HTTP GET Incoming Request and Outgoing Response

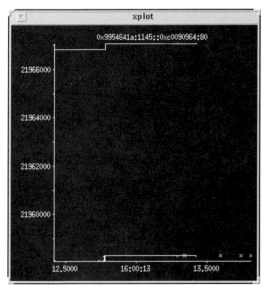
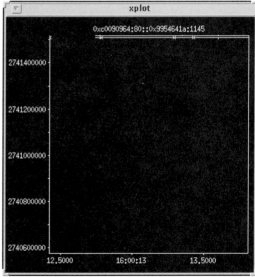

The trace shows the sequence number on the y axis, and time along the x axis. The upper line is the advertised receive window, the lower line is the acknowledged data. In this case, they are 8 Kbytes apart, which is the default for Solaris 2. This trace shows the Solaris server receiving on port 80 and a remote client sending on port 1145. The server gets a 243-byte incoming GET request marked by a vertical bar with arrows at each end. It then gets acknowledgments for the data it is sending; these are shown in another graph. The request is acknowledged immediately, and the received data line and the advertised window both step up by the segment size like a staircase.

The outgoing HTTP GET response is the reverse direction on ports 1145 and 80; the last packet sent had a zero sequence number, so the plot is bunched up at the top.

I use the left mouse button to zoom in by rubber-banding the parallel lines at the top until they fill the view. The upper line is the HTTP client's receive window, and the lower line shows what the client has acknowledged. The vertical bars show three packets. If you mess up the zooming in, you can zoom back out by clicking the left mouse button outside the drawing area (e.g., by the axes labels).

Next, I zoomed in on the packets, as shown in Figure 4-4. You can see that the first packet is 200 bytes or so; this is the HTTP header being returned, and it occurs twice with the same sequence number about 500 ms apart as it is retransmitted. The second packet is about 300 bytes of data; it is sent after the first packet has been acknowledged, and you can see the received data window step up at that point. When you finish looking at the graph, use the right mouse button to kill it.

Figure 4-4   Zoom In Twice on HTTP GET Response

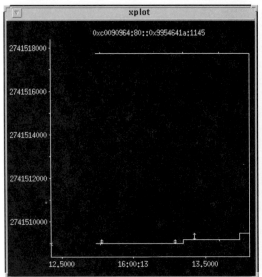
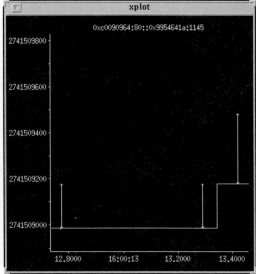

Medium-Sized HTTP Transfer with Retransmit Congestion

This connection is typical of the kind of transfer that occurs in the presence of retransmit bugs and the minimum retransmit timer default of 200 ms. The bugs are present in the original release of Solaris 2.5.1 but were fixed by patches soon afterward and backported to older releases. The request shown on the left of Figure 4-5 just shows more acknowledgments than last time.

Figure 4-5   HTTP Request and Response with Retransmit Congestion

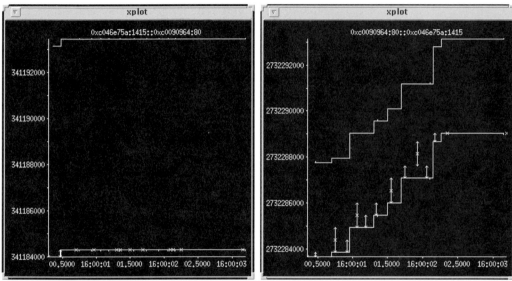

The response on the right of Figure 4-5 shows that almost everything is retransmitted twice. The server first sends a short header packet, which arrives, so next time the server sends two packets back-to-back. It doesn't receive an acknowledgment in time, so it resends the first of the two packets. Just after that, the acknowledgment for the pair comes in. The server sends two more back-to-back packets, retransmits the first one, then gets an acknowledgment for the first one only, and so retransmits the second one. The next attempt gets both back-to-back packets there in one attempt. It probably hasn't processed the incoming acknowledgment before it sends the next single packet. So, when it sees the acknowledgment, it sends two more packets, then retransmits the first one before getting an acknowledgment for all three at one time. The last packet sent is a short one. There is a delay at the client before the connection shutdown is acknowledged.

Zooming in on the first retransmit, we get the result shown in Figure 4-6. The acknowledgment comes in, and there is a short delay before the pair of output packets appears on the wire. After 200 ms, the first packet is retransmitted, and it gets to the wire a little quicker, appearing just under 200 ms after the first one. About 40 ms later, the acknowledgment for the first pair arrives. Note that the packets are about 1,500 bytes long.

Figure 4-6   HTTP Response Retransmission

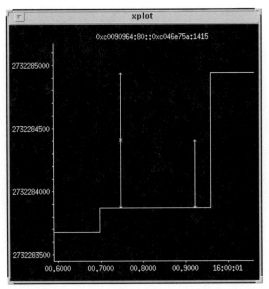

A Clean Transfer to a Buggy TCP Client

This transfer goes well, but the client machine does nasty things with the TCP window by closing it down at the end and sending a reset packet. The reset packet contains a zero window value. The zero window value displays as higher than the sequence number, which is over the 2-Gbyte mark. The plotting routine treats the sequence number as negative and compresses the axes so the data appears as ticks along the bottom. To correct the display, zoom in on the x axis until you see the data as shown on the left side of Figure 4-7. The window size is about 24 Kbytes, and the packets are about 500 bytes. TCP ramps up the transfer nicely, sending larger and larger packet clusters until it finishes. The server then waits for the client to finish processing and acknowledge the end of the connection. The client then illegally shrinks the TCP window it is advertising before the connection eventually clears, and the client sends a reset.

Zooming in again on the data transfer, you see the sequence shown on the right side of Figure 4-7. The client is turning around acknowledgments in about 100 ms, so there are no retransmits.

Figure 4-7   Clean Transfer to Buggy TCP Client

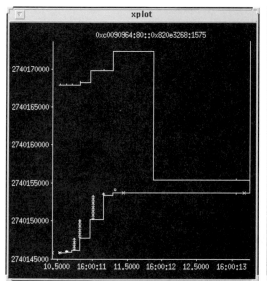 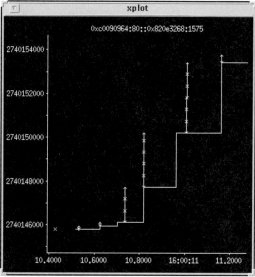

Small Window-Limited Transfers

The left side of Figure 4-8 shows a long, slow transfer where the client advertises a 3-Kbyte window and 500 byte packets are used. You can see that despite long delays between packets there is no retransmission. The transfer starts off behind the window, then catches up; then, for the second half of the transfer, as soon as the window opens up, a packet is sent. Packets at the end of the transfer seem to be missing, although the acknowledgments must be present. I think this trace is truncated by the 10-second snoop collection period I used.

The right side of Figure 4-8 has a 2-Kbyte window, but we are trying to send 1500-byte packets. The server is forced to issue a 500-byte packet after each 1500-byte packet, then it stops until the window is reopened. The client system is badly misconfigured. Eight Kbytes are really a minimum window size for a low-speed, high latency network.

Figure 4-8   Two Separate Window-Limited Transfers

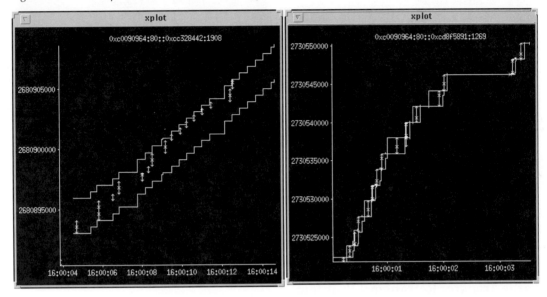

Tail End of Large Transfer with Window Close

The left side of Figure 4-9 shows a 30704-byte transfer of 73 segments; it starts before the snoop collection period. The window size starts at approximately 11 Kbytes, drops to 4 Kbytes, and briefly closes completely before opening up to 11 Kbytes again as the connection goes through another slow start sequence and a few retransmits. The client closes the window to zero at the end (illegal but not problematic TCP behavior).

The window closed in the middle because the client was processing the data that had been sent but had not emptied its buffers. The window close is the mechanism used by TCP for flow control. When a window-close event happens, it is a sign that the client side needs to be faster or have a bigger input buffer.

The right side of Figure 4-9 shows another similar transfer of 35 Kbytes in 70 packets. Both these transfers have chosen a maximum transfer size of about 500 bytes.

Figure 4-9   Large Transfers with Window-Close Flow Control

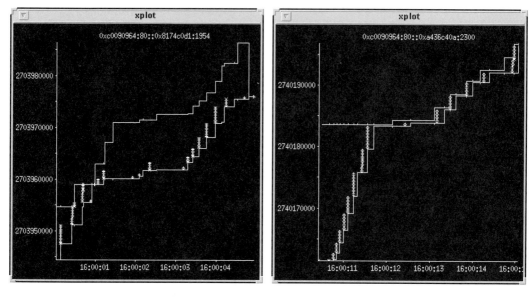

Large Transfer Retransmit Problems

Another long sequence of packets, shown on the left side of Figure 4-10, uses 46 segments to transfer 11,154 bytes. One problem is that the maximum transfer size appears to be 256 bytes, which is very inefficient and a sign of a badly configured router or client. The server also seems to be suffering from a lot of lost and retransmitted data. An odd effect occurs on the server. Look just before the 16:00:05 mark, where a packet appears below the lower line.

Zoom in on the offending packet, as shown on the right side of Figure 4-10, to see that this is a case of the packet being queued for transmission, then being delayed long enough for the acknowledgment to arrive before the packet is sent. It occurs for two packets here. Other transfers, interleaved with this one, cause the delay, and the "le" interface tends to make this problem worse by giving much higher priority to incoming packets.

Another, separate, example is shown at the bottom of Figure 4-10. I zoomed in already on this sequence, as the six reset packets at the end extend the y axis too far. It shows many retransmit attempts, caused by a very lossy route for this connection that is dropping a lot of packets.

Figure 4-10 Retransmission Problems with Large Transfers

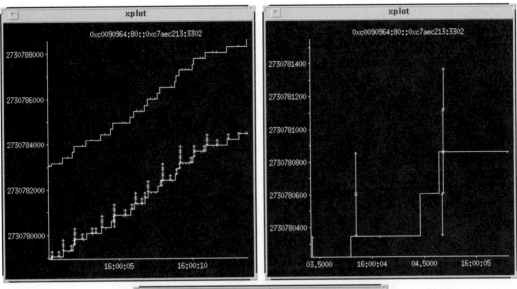

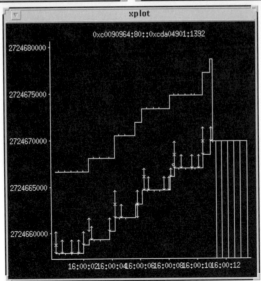

Increased Minimum Retransmit Time-out

To work around high retransmissions, increase the minimum retransmit time-out. Doing so has unpleasant side effects, so make sure your TCP patch is up to date and don't experiment with the default time-out. Delay caused by an increased time-out can be seen on the left of Figure 4-11. This is a normal transfer, but the server drops a packet. It then stalls for 1500 ms before it retransmits the packet, showing the penalty that occurs when the retransmit timer is increased. The time-out is a compromise between too many unnecessary retransmits and long service times for lossy transfers.

Retransmission avoided by increased time-out is shown on the right of Figure 4-11. The acknowledgments are returning after about 500 ms for most of the packets in this transfer. The server avoids retransmitting and becoming stuck in the congested mode by waiting a little longer for the first packet, then continues the transfer by sending two large packets. The tail end of this plot is cut off by the end of the snoop capture.

Figure 4-11   Increased Minimum Retransmit Time-out

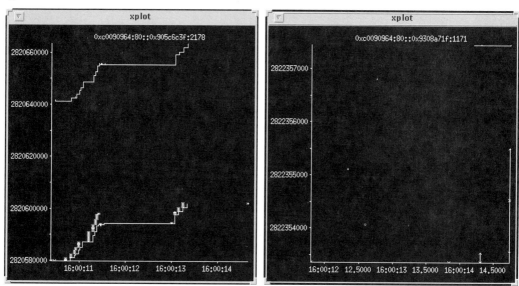

HTTP Persistent Connection Sequences

The plots have so far been based on one connection per HTTP request, using a Netscape 1.12 server. The following plots were taken using Netscape 2.0 server, which supports persistent connections, part of the HTTP 1.1 standard and also known as HTTP keepalive. In this case, after each request, the connection is held open, ready for additional requests. The request and response sequences for two requests are shown in Figure 4-12.

Two small responses are shown; the header goes out and is followed by a single packet.

Figure 4-12 Transfers Using HTTP Persistent Connections

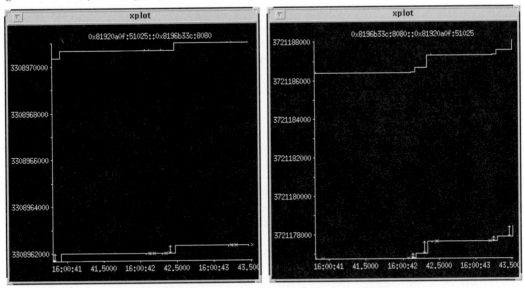

The high bandwidth transfer in Figure 4-13 shows the response only for two small transfers followed by a large one, over a high-speed network from a proxy server.

Figure 4-13 High Bandwidth Persistent Connection Transfers

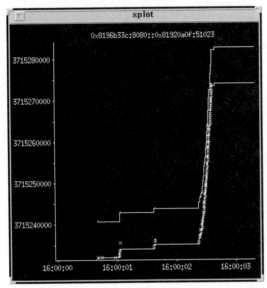

4

Additional TCP Sequences

We looked at many more HTTP sequences, and everything we saw looked like one of the above categories. If you look at other protocols, you may be able to discover problems such as inefficient block sizes or lack of pipelining. It is also clear when an increase in TCP window size is going to make a difference. In the case of a web server, the input traffic is small, but web clients and proxy servers can sometimes benefit from larger receive windows.

Internet Web Server Sizing

A web server provides data to browsers by means of the hypertext transfer protocol, HTTP. This protocol runs on top of a TCP connection.

What is important from a performance point of view is the size of the data transfer. The content type does not matter: the load on the server is the same whether the data being transferred is an HTML page, a GIF image, or a Java class.

The most important issue is that normally a complete TCP connection is set up and destroyed as part of each transfer. This cycle increases the response time and stresses TCP in ways that it was not really designed to handle. It has been said that HTTP is an abuse of TCP!

The most common operation by far in the protocol is GET; each request is tagged with the revision of the protocol, normally HTTP 1.0 or HTTP 1.1. The response contains a MIME type header and the data itself. MIME is the Multimedia Internet Mail Extensions standard, which was originally created so that email attachments of many different types could be identified.

The protocol does not contain the name of the server; the TCP connection to that server is opened specially, so the protocol is a single-shot operation between one client and one server.

An optimization (HTTP 1.1 persistent connections) keeps the connection open for perhaps five requests or until a time-out expires. This optimization assumes the client will get several small things from the same server. The optimization is not allowed for SPECweb96 benchmark results and is not supported by the old Netscape 1.12 server code. It is supported by Netscape 2.0 and later servers and most other recent servers. Recent clients, including all versions of Netscape Navigator and Microsoft Internet Explorer, also implement this option. My measurements on *www.sun.com* indicate that about 25% of all HTTP operations reuse a connection. You can measure reuse as the difference between the incoming TCP connection rate and the HTTP operation rate.

Modern clients also open several simultaneous connections, often to the same server, to improve response time by overlapping transfers. This practice reduces the benefit of HTTP 1.1 persistent connections because there is less work for each individual connection to do.

How Many Users?

Basing sizing on the number of users can lead to oversizing a system. Most users are idle almost all the time. Even when a user is active, say, loading many class files for a Java application or a large number of GIF images on a complex web page, the average rate during the load is 1 httpop/s or less, even for a high-speed browser over Fast Ethernet (Netscape on an Ultra 1). Peak rates of up to 5–10 ops/s can occur but are not sustained for more than a few seconds. Over a wide-area network, the rate will be much lower.

How Many Operations Per Day and Per Second?

Given an estimate of the requirement in terms of operations rather than users, you can use some simple calculations to size a system. I'll run through an example calculation based on 5 million httpops/day. This number represents a very busy server that can comfortably be handled by a high-performance uniprocessor (Ultra 1 class) with a reasonable amount of headroom. In absolute terms, only a few sites in the world are this busy.

The server needs to support short-term peak rates that are much higher than the average daily rate suggests.

5M/day = 58/s, but allow 3x peak = 175/s

Allow 10 KB/op = 1750 KB/s peak data rate

Allow TCP and network overhead 30% = 2275 KB/s

18 Mbits/s network bandwidth needed by this server

This calculation doesn't include email, news, ftp, outgoing HTTP requests from this site to other sites, etc. A system running at this data rate needs more than a 10-Mbit local network connection. If it is feeding the Internet, the site will need a T3 (45-Mbit) connection.

Network Capacity for HTTP

So, how many SPECweb96 httpops/s can a network support in theory? A theoretical maximum level can be calculated, but there is always some protocol overhead as well. Some network media, like Ethernets, cannot be driven flat out because collisions cause extra congestion and overhead. The peak level shown in Table 4-1 is a realistic maximum, taking various kinds of overhead into account and rounding down.

Table 4-1   Network Capacity for SPECweb96 HTTP Traffic

Network Connection	Bandwidth (bits/s)	Peak httpops/s
28.8K modem	28.8K	0.25
56K modem	56K	0.4
ISDN 1 BRI	64K	0.5
ISDN 2 BRI	128K	1
T1	1.5M	10
Ethernet	10M	60
T3	45M	300
Fast Ethernet	100M	500
Full Duplex Fast Ethernet	100M+100M	700
FDDI	100M	600
ATM (OC3)	155M+155M	900
ATM (OC12)	622M+622M	3500
Gigabit Ethernet	1000M+1000M	5000?

You can use this table to make sure your estimates make sense. For example, if you expect to drive 200 httpops/s into a system that is connected via a 10-Mbit Ethernet, you will not succeed. If you have 100 users connected via 28.8-Kbyte modems, they cannot generate more than 25 httpops/s even if they are all active at the same time. If your average transfer size is larger or smaller than the SPECweb96 average of about 13 Kbytes, then you can scale the above table appropriately. In some cases, network connections are full duplex; this is a common option for Fast Ethernet and is the way ATM works. Since almost all the traffic is going out of the server, the main benefit is with Ethernet because the incoming requests and acknowledgments no longer collide with outgoing data.

HTTP-Only Server Performance

If your server does nothing but send static pages of data, Java applets, and images, you can base the size on a single 167 MHz UltraSPARC running Solaris 2.6 for each 100-Mbit network. If your server does more, then see the next section and configure extra capacity. You can use a smaller system if you are driving a slower network, using faster server code, or running a later release of Solaris. You can scale up the processor speed and the number of processors if you have a larger network to drive or if you have additional workloads.

A single, high-end uniprocessor running Solaris 2.6 can drive a full 45-Mbit T3 or 100-Mbit Ethernet with typical transfer sizes. Scalability with Solaris 2.6 is almost linear up to four processors, as the SPECweb96 results for the Enterprise 450 server demonstrate (see Table 4-2).

Table 4-2   SPECweb96 Performance Results

Solaris	Web server	System	CPU	Network type	Network speed	SPECweb96 httpops/s
2.5.1/ISS	Netscape	Ultra2/2200	2x200 MHz	Ethernet	2x100 Mbit	626
2.6	SWS	E450	1x300 MHz	ATM	1x622 Mbit	884
2.6	SWS	Ultra2/2300	2x300 MHz	ATM	2x622 Mbit	1488
2.6	SWS	E450	2x300 MHz	ATM	1x622 Mbit	1628
2.6beta	SWS	E3000	6x250 MHz	Ethernet	5x100 Mbit	2535
2.6	SWS	E450	4x300 MHz	ATM	2x622 Mbit	2905
2.6beta	Netscape	E4000	8x250 MHz	Ethernet	5x100 Mbit	2796
2.6beta	SWS	E4000	10x250MHz	ATM, Enet	2x622+3x100	3746

Spare network capacity is configured for benchmarks, partly to prevent capacity from being a bottleneck and sometimes because device driver code scales better with several network interfaces on the same machine. One reason ATM is faster than Ethernet in this benchmark is that it is normally configured with a 9-Kbyte maximum segment size rather than the 1.5-Kbyte segments used on Ethernet. A larger proportion of the transfers occurs in a single segment. The combination of a faster memory system and a more efficient PCIbus ATM622 card used in the E450 provides higher performance than does the Ultra 2/2300 using the same CPU modules. The Solaris 2.6 beta results were released much earlier than the E450 results and do not have all the optimizations of the final release of Solaris 2.6.

Additional Web Server Workloads

Secure connections using SSL, search engines, ftp serving, dynamic content, serving multiple audio or video stream serving, and database backends that generate dynamic pages are now common. They cause a significant extra load that is not included in the SPECweb96 rating, although the SPECweb98 benchmark does include more server-side processing.

The server may have to parse the data it sends, looking for conditional HTML, run JavaScript™ on the server, or start up server-side Java applications. It may also provide a boot service for Network Computers

These applications may need an enterprise server with many CPUs and striped high-performance disk subsystem if they run at high operation rates.

Disk Capacity and HTTP Access Patterns

Most SPECweb96 results are posted with 512 Mbytes to 2 Gbytes of RAM. The entire data set is cached to avoid disk latency, but this caching is unrealistic for most sites. It is better to assume uncached random read accesses. Each http operation matches a random disk read, but each individual transfer is slow, so there are no fast sequential reads. You can approximate this case by taking the 8-Kbyte random read rate for each disk. Typical disks sustain about 100 ops/s flat out; as a sizing guideline, halve that number and allow 50 httpops per disk, which is about 400 Kbytes/s. Stripe disks together until you have enough to saturate your network.

RAM Requirements

Operating system overhead could be 8–32 Mbytes (more if you run a local window system). The OS takes more megabytes if you have more RAM because it needs to keep track of the RAM, and some kernel tables scale as RAM is added. If you also start a window system, you will need a lot more RAM than if you run the system as a pure "server" with dumb serial console. As the system goes faster, a large backlog of TCP connections is retained, as described in "Tuning the Close Wait Interval and TCP Connection Hash Table Size" on page 65. At 580 bytes per connection, this backlog can add up to several tens of megabytes when the system is running at hundreds of connections per second and a TIME_WAIT state of 1 to 4 minutes.

The system shares code for server processes. Once-off memory usage is typically 1–2 Mbytes per application. Don't forget the search engine and the cgi-bin utilities perl, sh, awk, grep, etc. You also have to allow memory for each instance of a process. Each concurrently active TCP connection needs some memory for data buffers.

Each different program you run has a sharable component (the code and shared libraries) and an unshared component (the stack and heap private to each instance of the program).

The application's executable size on disk gives an estimate of the sharable component. The private resident size is hard to measure; special instrumentation showed that Netscape 1.12 used 440 Kbytes per process. One hundred processes are typical for a busy server, so this is 44 Mbytes. Netscape 2.0 defaults to four multithreaded processes, with up to 32 threads per process. When the server was idle, each process seemed to be about 1 megabyte; when the server was busy, the size grew to 10–20 megabytes. Common pages are cached in RAM by Netscape 2.0, further increasing the size.

Search engines are quite large, averaging 3 Mbytes per search on *www.sun.com*. Searches tend to occur singly, so there is less sharing, although a busy site may have several simultaneous searches. The search activity may also cause the search data to displace other files from the filesystem cache.

The file cache occupies its own dedicated memory space on some operating systems and uses up all otherwise unused space on others (notably SVR4 and SunOS/Solaris). This memory is reclaimed for other uses on a not recently used (NRU) basis. "Not recent" tends to be a few minutes unless the system is seriously short of RAM, when it drops to a few seconds.

RAM Usage—How Many Instances?

There are two cases to consider: short-duration connections over a LAN are the kind generated by SPECweb96, and long-duration connections are typical over the Internet. You need a thread, or a process, and a data buffer for each concurrent connection.

With a high-speed LAN, the round-trip time is typically under 1 ms. SPECweb96 benchmarks or LAN HTTP transfers take 10 ms in total, so even at high connection rates, few connections are concurrent and a small amount of memory is needed for server instances. From basic queueing theory, the throughput times the average response time gives you the average queue length. For example:

500 ops/s @ 10ms/op = 5 instances required on average

Large transfers hold on to a connection longer, but with each client system on a 100-Mbit/s network, several hundred kilobytes can be transferred in a few tens of milliseconds. It is clear that benchmarks must use large memory just for a file cache. Disk transfer times of 20 ms or so will have a big impact on performance, so as much data as possible is cached in RAM.

Round-trip times on the Internet are often measured in seconds and vary by seconds from one packet to the next. Each connection includes several round trips during setup and shutdown, as well as the time taken to transfer the data (often at a peak rate of a few hundred bytes/s to a few kilobytes/s) and the time taken to retransmit dropped segments.

To serve a long latency load, you must be able to dedicate a process or a thread to the connection for a long period of time. Connections over the Internet to end users on 28.8-Kbyte modems typically take longer than a second for a round trip. Internet or WAN transfers take several (or many) seconds to complete, so even at low connection rates many transfers are concurrent. A large memory is needed for server instances. For example,

500 ops/s @ 2s/op = 1000 instances required on average

Since each file transfer runs so slowly, the time taken to get the data from disk (20 ms or so) is lost in the propagation delay (several seconds), and it is not worth having a big file cache in RAM. The bulk of memory usage will be used to provide per-instance stack space and data buffers.

HTTP Size Mixes and Benchmarks

A web server receives a mixture of large and small requests. Most requests are small, but there are enough large ones that the average is quite high. Use the mean size for network capacity calculations, but remember that small operations dominate.

The average transfer size on *www.sun.com* was 8 Kbytes for the month of February 1996; the next month a free download of the Java WorkShop code was made available from the server. This 10-MByte file transferred in a single operation but took minutes to hours to transfer. The TCP data rate and packet rate more than doubled, and the httpop rate increased a little.

There are two common web server benchmarks: Webstone and SPECweb96.

Webstone was invented by Silicon Graphics and made freely available. Webstone results are uncontrolled, with no "run rules." There are several versions of the benchmark and several variations on the workload. Published Webstone results are meaningless because they cannot credibly be compared. The benchmark code itself can be useful as a starting point for customized testing.

SPECweb96 has strict run rules, tuning disclosure rules, and a standard mix—just like the SPECsfs LADDIS NFS benchmark. Results are available at http://www.specbench.org. SPECweb96 is modeled on an ISP serving many home directories. About 5.1 Mbytes of content are allocated per directory, and the number of directories scales up as the load level is increased. About 460 Mbytes are needed for a 400 ops/s run. The formula is:

number_of_directories = 0.5 + 10 * sqrt(httpops/5).

In comparison, Webstone uses a few fixed files of varying size, and they are normally completely cached in 20 Mbytes or so of RAM. When the size of the operations increases, the operations take longer; so, with a larger average size, expect fewer operations/s if you are constrained by network bandwidth. With a bigger file set than you have RAM to cache, performance reduces and disks can become the bottleneck.

The SPECweb96 size mix consists of a distribution with 35% up to 1 Kbyte, 50% up to 10 Kbytes, 14% up to 100 Kbytes, and 1% up to 1 Mbyte. It is important to monitor your own size mix because not only will it vary from the SPECweb96 mix, it will change throughout the day and vary whenever the content is updated.

HTTP Performance Measurement

Servers maintain an access log, with one line for each http operation. Each line contains a date stamp and the size of the transfer, among other things. You can obtain the operation rate by counting the number of lines in a given time window, and you can obtain the size distribution from the log. Sizes can range from zero to several megabytes.

Since accesses can take a long time (seconds to minutes or more), the data rate cannot be calculated from the log file. Most systems have TCP counters that can be sampled to obtain the data rates, connection rates, and retransmission rates. (See "TCP Monitoring with the SE Toolkit" on page 67.)

The most common problem is network bandwidth. Sometimes, the local Ethernet may be overloaded, but more likely the WAN or Internet bandwidth is used up by this system and other systems and applications. Adding CPUs will help HTTP only if you are running Solaris 2.6 or later (but does help other workload components). In most other operating systems and earlier Solaris releases, the TCP connection setup code is largely single threaded, and this code dominates HTTP's CPU usage. The TCP bulk data transfer code is already well threaded in Solaris 2, and as the transfer size increases, the protocol becomes more efficient. Very few protocols are as connection intensive as HTTP, and the common implementations of TCP/IP were designed on the assumption that connections were relatively infrequent.

HTTP is a new protocol, and implementations have changed rapidly over the last few years. If your server code or OS patch revision is more than a year old, it is obsolete. You need to keep up with the latest code because the learning curve and rate of change is very high. Upgrading a system from an NCSA 1.3 server (late 1994) to Netscape FastTrack (mid-1996) should make the system about *ten times* faster. Running Solaris 2.6 on a small multiprocessor server (mid-1997) should make it ten times faster still. That is a 100-fold speedup in less than three years, from 20 to 200 to 2,000 httpop/s. Larger multiprocessor servers are already pushing 4,000 httpops/s, and I predict that over 10,000 httpops/s is achievable during 1998. The SPECweb96 benchmark is too simplistic and will soon be superseded by SPECweb98. SPECweb98 includes persistent connections and dynamic content, it is much more complex, and it puts a far higher load on the server. The TCP stack is less of a bottleneck.

Operating system updates take a year or more to go through development and test. The latest revisions now contain bug fixes and tuning specifically aimed at web server workloads.

Web Server Performance Management

Few commercial products manage web server applications and manage both performance and availability. BMC Patrol Knowledge Module for Internet Servers is an application management tool that covers web servers, including specifically the Netscape Enterprise Server, as well as DNS, mail, ftp, and other services that are often found together. It concentrates on monitoring performance and looks for problems that might cause downtime. BMC has also built a Java-based browser front end for the Patrol product. See http://www.bmc.com. Resolute Software[1] focuses its RAPS product on application performance management, has efficient collectors, detailed network protocol monitoring, and a web server monitoring module. See http://www.resolute.com.

The SE Toolkit Web Server Performance Collator, `percollator.se`

There are several sources of information from which data needs to be collected. It is most convenient if a single tool collects from them so that they have a single measurement interval. The sources do the following:

- Count HTTP operation rates from the access log file
- Parse size distribution, operation type from the access log entries
- Read TCP data rates, retransmissions, and connection rates from the "`mib`" interface
- Obtain network interface packet rates, collisions from the "`kstat`" interface
- Read CPU and disk utilization levels from `kstat`
- Run performance monitoring rules and log the status

I use short-term sample intervals (5 seconds) for HTTP measurements and longer reporting intervals (5 minutes) to measure everything else, and I log the results. I wrote a customizable SE script that does this job for both normal and proxy web servers. See also "pea.se" on page 488.

---

1. My co-author Rich Pettit works for Resolute Software.

A monitoring tool can track the entries in a log file by reading lines from it until end-of-file, then sleeping for a few seconds, then reading again. The number of lines read in the interval is the operation completion rate. Note that we don't normally know when the operation started, and it may be running a long time. Other data like operation size and operation type (read, write, run script, etc.) can be extracted from the log.

There are a huge number of protocol counters; the only ones worth collecting long term are the data rates for TCP. Compare these data rates with the available wide-area network bandwidth to see when you are network-capacity limited. This is the most significant bottleneck. Retransmissions are caused by a mixture of true packet loss, which varies but is normally in the 5% to 20% range for the Internet. Impatient TCP implementations that don't wait long enough cause higher retransmissions and should be tuned or patched.

The local network connection can be a problem when serving intranets and may also be a bottleneck if too many Internet servers are grouped together. Carefully watch collision rates on 10-Mbit networks. On 100-Mbit networks, they are less likely to be a problem, so don't worry about collision rates too much.

With typical network latency measured in seconds, disk latency is not an issue. As long as there is enough spare capacity to service requests, disk performance is not likely to be a major issue for HTTP service. Search engines can cause higher disk loads, and if search performance becomes a problem (unlikely unless you are running a major search site), you may need to pay more attention to disk tuning.

Processing Collected Data

The `percollator.se` script stores a daily performance log file as a regular ASCII table with column headings for easy manipulation. It is in a very wide format, so it is best to read it into a spreadsheet or statistics package. I recommend that you copy it from the server at midnight, along with the access logs. A Java applet that processes and graphs these files is available with the SE toolkit; see "GPercollator Java Browser" on page 492.

Real-World HTTP Rate Changes over Time

The graphs shown in Figure 4-14 are derived from observations at *www.sun.com*. They are typical of the load on a commercial internet site being used to provide marketing and product information. Other types of sites should construct their own versions of these graphs.

Figure 4-14   Workload Patterns

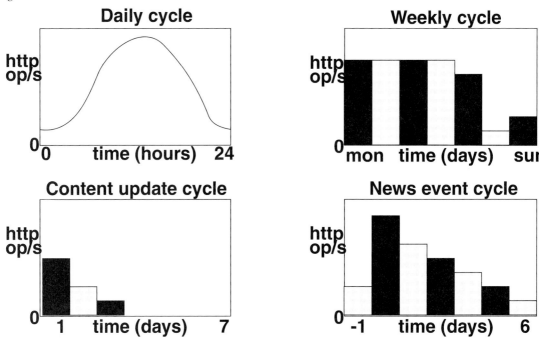

The first graph shows the load varying during the day. The load depends upon the audience, but for *www.sun.com*, it peaks during working hours for the western USA time zone. The eastern USA brings the level up earlier in the day, and Europe and Japan keep it going through the night. Other sites that serve users at home may peak in the early evening. There is such a high concentration of Internet users on the U.S. West Coast that sites in other time zones still see a bias of activity to that zone.

The second graph shows a weekly cycle. The Monday through Thursday pattern is constant, Friday is quieter because it is already Saturday in the Asia/Pacific time zones. Saturday is the only day when it is weekend everywhere in the world. Sunday is a bit higher because it is already Monday in the Asia/Pacific time zones, i.e., global load is displaced from Friday to Sunday for a system located on the U.S. West Coast.

The third graph shows the effect of updating the content on the web server. On *www.sun.com*, updating occurs about once a month: a new home page image and new articles are put out. Internet search engines like Infoseek run a "robot" over the new content to index it, end users get to expect new content, and word-of-mouth creates a small and short boost in the load over a few days. A spoof home page on April 1, 1996, caused the load on *www.sun.com* to double to a record level for that one day! Radical changes in content (like providing large downloadable files) permanently change the workload mix.

The fourth graph shows what happens for a major product launch or news event. There is an increased load before the event, as news leaks out and people check out the site, looking for details. On the day the news breaks, there is a big boost (an extra 30% to 50% load is typical), which decays over a period of about a week.

Superimposed on all of these graphs is a slow growth in load caused by the increase in population of the Internet itself.

Load Curve for a Week

The graph in Figure 4-15 shows Friday March 1, through the following Thursday. Friday was a content update day, but some of the extra load was postponed until Sunday/Monday. The graph shows the sustained 5-minute interval average operation rate with a little smoothing.

Figure 4-15 Load on www.sun.com for the First Week in March 1996

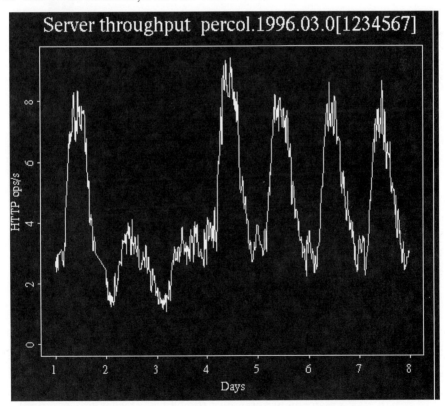

HTTP Load over a Month

The bar graph in Figure 4-16 shows the same data as in the previous plot but summarizes each day into an overall average rate for the day, the peak 5-minute period, and the peak 5-second period.

Figure 4-16   HTTP Load over a Month

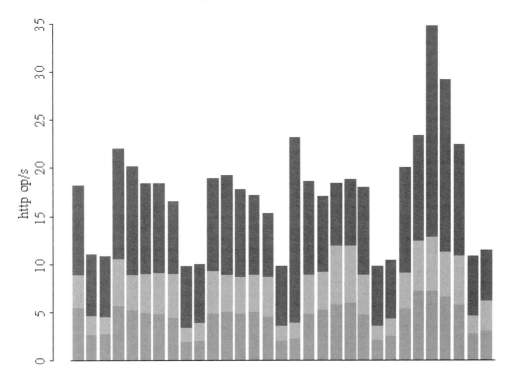

The first seven bars correspond to the plot in Figure 4-15, and the graph continues throughout the whole month. Weekends are clearly visible.

The peak at the end of the month corresponds to a product launch. The launch was "trailered" well in advance, and increased activity can be seen leading up to the launch day itself. (Launch was a major new version of the Netra internet server range). There is also a seasonal variation through the year.

The sustained rate shown is typically between 5 and 8 ops/s; multiplied by 24*3600, this rate results in 430,000 to 700,000 ops/day.

The peak daily rate is around 20 ops/s, rising to 35 at its highest. The characteristic of the load is that the peak is about 3 to 4 times the sustained average. The trough is about one-third of the sustained average. The overall dynamic range is about 10:1.

Proxy Web Caching Servers

A caching web server acts as an invisible intermediary between a client browser and the servers that provide content. It cuts down on overall network traffic and provides administrative control over web traffic routing. Performance requirements are quite different from those for a regular web server. After discussing the issues, I'll look at several extra metrics that need to be collected and analyzed.

There are two different classes of caching proxy web server. They are used in small- to medium-sized installations to implement companywide intranets. They are also used in very large installations to provide country-level caching and filtering on the Internet. In both cases, the primary goal is to reduce wide-area web traffic by caching commonly used data closer to the end users. In common usage for small-to-medium intranet sites is the Netscape Proxy Cache Version 2.5. Sun has been using it to provide web service infrastructure for their internal wide-area network, and I'll concentrate on it in this section. Medium-to-large scale sites need to use a clustered proxy system such as Squid or the Harvest cache. I'll highlight the advantages of the clustered proxy, but I have more direct experience with Netscape 2.5 at the moment.

We should start by remembering the caching principle of temporal and spacial locality. In the case of a web cache, cacheable objects are always separate and are always read in their entirety with no prefetching. The only spacial locality you get is that several requests may go to the same server, and you may see a benefit from HTTP 1.1 persistent connections. Since the client browser always talks to the same cache, this optimization is quite beneficial. The web cache mostly works by using temporal locality. If cached items are read more than once in a reasonably short time interval, the cache will work well. If every user reads completely different pages, the cache will just get in the way. If the same user rereads the same pages, that browser will cache the pages on the client, so the server cache won't be used effectively.

Not all web content is cacheable. Some of the busiest traffic is dynamic in nature, and caching it would prevent the browser from seeing an update.

Cache Effectiveness

The caches I have looked at have a cache hit rate of about 20% to 30%, with only 60% of the data being cacheable. That figure does not take into account the size of each access—just the total number of accesses. Each cache transaction takes a while to complete and adds significant latency to the connection time. In other words, the cache slows down the end users significantly, and only a small proportion of the data read is supplied from the cache. There is also a "funneling" effect because all the users go through the cache regardless of their final destination. This redirection can increase network load at a local level because accesses to local web servers will normally go via the cache, causing two trips over the local net rather than one.

The other big problem is that the cache is a single point of failure, with every user depending upon its presence. I've drawn some diagrams (see Figure 4-17) to show the difference. Remember that there are a large number of client systems, at several sites. I've shown only one proxy cache, at a remote site. The subject of how many caches and where to site them is discussed later.

Figure 4-17 Direct Web Service Without Proxy Cache

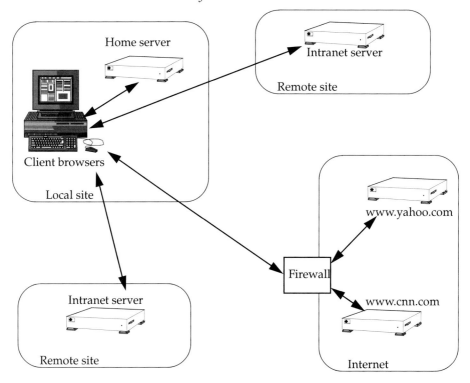

The direct web service allows the browser to contact web servers directly whenever possible. This contact may involve a firewall proxy that does not provide caching to get out to the public Internet.

In contrast, when a proxy is introduced, all the browsers connect to the proxy by default. An exception can be made for named systems and domains that may be accessed more efficiently via a direct connection.

Figure 4-18 Indirect Web Service

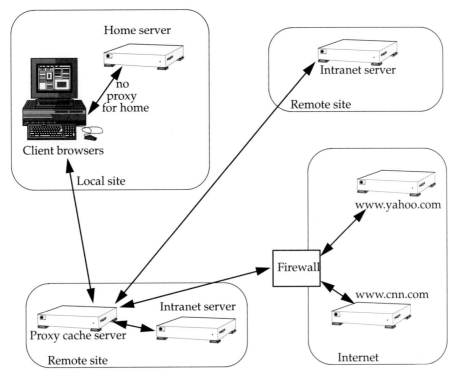

Caching for Administrative Control

The reduction in wide-area network traffic from a 20%–30% hit rate is worth having, especially since wide-area links are expensive and may be saturated at peak times.

The real reason to set up a proxy cache intranet infrastructure is the administrative control that you get. Security is a big problem, and one approach is to set up the firewall gateways to the Internet so that they will route web traffic only to and from the proxy caches. The proxy caches can make intelligent routing decisions. For example, Sun has connections to the Internet in Europe and the USA. If a user in Europe accesses an Internet web site in Europe, that access is routed via the local connection. When an access is made to a site in the USA, a choice can be made. The route could go to the USA over Sun's private network to the USA-based gateway, or it could go directly to the Internet in Europe and find its own way to the USA. The second option reduces the load on expensive private transatlantic links, but the first option can be used as a fallback if the European connection goes down.

Restricted routing also forces every end user who wishes to get out to the Internet to do so via a proxy cache. The cache can make routing and filtering decisions, and logs every access with the URL and the client IP address (which is usually sufficient to identify the end user). If the corporate policy is "Internet access is provided for business use only during business hours," then employees who clog up the networks with non-business traffic can be identified. It is probably sufficient to make it known to the employees that their activity is being logged and that they can be traced. Posting an analysis of the most visited sites during working hours for everyone to look at would probably have a sobering effect! Filtering can be added to deny access to popular but unwelcome sites.

The point I am making is that you have a limited amount of expensive wide-area network capacity. There is a strong tendency for end users to consume all the capacity that you provide. Using gentle peer pressure to keep the usage productive seems reasonable and can radically improve the performance of your network for real business use.

Client Web Browser Configuration

Netscape Navigator has several network setup options. One option is to read its configuration from a given URL. This approach allows centralized setup of the binding to a proxy cache, but end users can reconfigure their browser themselves. One extra option is a list of sites that are accessed directly, bypassing the proxy cache. If there are web servers that are "closer" to the end user than the proxy cache, then it is much better to go directly to such a server, which may include the user's home page server. In Figure 4-18, this route is shown as an arrow marked "no proxy for home."

The browser also has several megabytes of local cache, so individual users cache their own frequently visited sites. The shared proxy cache benefits only groups of users who all visit the same sites.

Clustered Proxy Cache Architectures

The Netscape 2.5 proxy cache is an extension of a conventional web server. It is used singly, and although it can be used in a hierarchy of caches, there is no optimization between the caches. An alternative is a clustered cache. Basic research has resulted in two common implementations. The Harvest Cache was the original development and is now a commercial product. The Squid cache is a spin-off that is freely available and is the basis for some commercial products, including Sun's own proxy cache product. Squid is in use at the biggest cache installations that I'm aware of, caching traffic at country level for very large Internet Service Providers.

Clustered caches use an intercache protocol (ICP) to talk among themselves and form an explicit hierarchy of siblings and parents. If the load would overwhelm a single machine or high availability is important, multiple systems are configured as siblings. Each sibling stores data in its cache but also uses the ICP to search the other siblings' caches. The net result: The effective cache size is that of all the siblings combined, the hit rate is improved, and it doesn't matter which sibling a client visits. The parent-child relationships also form a more efficient hierarchy because the ICP-based connections are much more efficient than individual HTTP transfers. ICP connections are kept open, and transfers have lower latency.

As shown in Figure 4-19, the home server now also doubles as the first level in the hierarchy. It caches from some sites directly and uses a larger parent cache for others and for Internet connections. The parent handles traffic from a large number of clients at many sites. It uses dual systems running as siblings for high availability and for splitting the load. It also uses ICP to talk to an upgraded firewall that acts as a first-level cache for the Internet. Since ICP-based traffic has much lower latency than HTTP traffic, more levels of the cache hierarchy can be used without slowing down the end user. There is also a benefit when making routing decisions because ICP carries the full domain name of the host with it and saves a lot of DNS lookups that often occur in an HTTP-based hierarchy.

The clustered approach is a little more complex to set up and maintain. It also requires coordination between administrators at widely separated sites. The simpler HTTP-based caches are all independent entities and so may be easier to administer. As wide-area network speeds increase and individual server performance also increases, there is less need to build a hierarchy. It's horses-for-courses, and you can start with one, then change the software to try the other approach to see which works best for you.

Figure 4-19   Clustered Web Cache Service

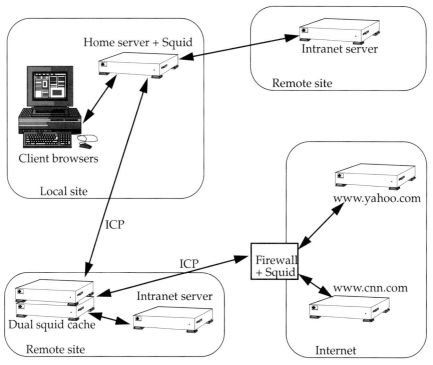

Configuring and Monitoring the Netscape 2.5 Proxy Cache

I've been collecting data and monitoring load levels on a Netscape 2.5 proxy cache that has been serving most of Sun UK's 1,000 or so employees for a while. It is situated at the largest site, so some users have LAN-based access speeds. There are several other sites in the UK though, running over 500-Kbit frame relay links to the central site. There are also a number of users connected over 128-Kbit ISDN and 28.8-Kbit dial-up connections.

The access log contains the same data that a normal web server log contains, but several additional values are logged. Netscape supports two extended formats and also allows a custom format to be specified. The format in use at Sun is a fairly complete custom log format. The format string looks like this:

```
%Ses->client.ip% - %Req->vars.pauth-user% [%SYSDATE%] "%Req->reqpb.proxy-request%"
%Req->srvhdrs.status% %Req->vars.p2c-cl% %Req->vars.remote-status% %Req->vars.r2p-cl%
%Req->headers.content-length% %Req->vars.p2r-cl% %Req->vars.c2p-hl% %Req->vars.p2c-hl%
%Req->vars.p2r-hl% %Req->vars.r2p-hl% %Req->vars.xfer-time% %Req->vars.actual-route%
%Req->vars.cli-status% %Req->vars.svr-status% %Req->vars.cch-status%
[%Req->vars.xfer-time-total%  %Req->vars.xfer-time-dns%  %Req->vars.xfer-time-iwait%
%Req->vars.xfer-time-fwait%] %Req->srvhdrs.clf-status%
```

The breakdown, with examples is shown in Table 4-1.

Table 4-1   Netscape Proxy Custom Log Format Specification

Format String Entry	Meaning	Example Values
1. Ses->client.ip	client hostname	129.156.123.32
2. -	-	-
3. Req->vars.pauth-user	authentication	-
4. [SYSDATE]	system date	[19/Jun/1997:13:21:12
5.	time zone	+0100]
6. "Req->reqpb.proxy-request"	request	"GET
7.	URL	http://host.domain/page.html
8.	protocol	HTTP/1.0"
9. Req->srvhdrs.status	status to client	200
10. Req->vars.p2c-cl	length to client	4177 (bytes)
11. Req->vars.remote-status	status from server	200
12. Req->vars.r2p-cl	length from server	4177 (bytes)
13. Req->headers.content-length	length from client	- (used for outgoing POST messages)
14. Req->vars.p2r-cl	length to server	- (used for outgoing POST messages)
15. Req->vars.c2p-hl	client header req	339 (bytes)
16. Req->vars.p2c-hl	proxy header resp	271 (bytes)
17. Req->vars.p2r-hl	proxy header req	379 (bytes)
18. Req->vars.r2p-hl	server header resp	271 (bytes)
19. Req->vars.xfer-time	transfer total secs	5
20. Req->vars.actual-route	route	- DIRECT PROXY(host:port) SOCKS
21. Req->vars.cli-status	client finish status	- = not started, FIN = OK INTR = interrupted/terminated
22. Req->vars.svr-status	server finish status	- FIN INTR TIMEOUT
23. Req->vars.cch-status	cache finish status	WRITTEN REFRESHED ERROR NO-CHECK UP-TO-DATE HOST-NOT-AVAILABLE CL-MISMATCH DO-NOT-CACHE NON-CACHEABLE

Table 4-1   Netscape Proxy Custom Log Format Specification (Continued)

Format String Entry	Meaning	Example Values
24. Req->vars.xfer-time-total	total transfer secs	[4.988
25. Req->vars.xfer-time-dns	dns lookup	0.000
26. Req->vars.xfer-time-iwait	initial wait	4.802
27. Req->vars.xfer-time-fwait	full wait	4.980]
28. Req->srvhdrs.clf-status	yet another status	200

The interesting data to extract is the mixture of possible cache outcomes that determines whether it is a cache hit or not, the routing information, and the transfer time. I extended my `percollator.se` script to parse this log format and summarize the data.

I extract field number 20, the route. I count all the entries that go to PROXY or SOCKS and report the percentage that are indirect. This is the percentage that gets routed to the Internet, rather than being DIRECT references to other servers in the corporate intranet or incomplete transfers marked with a "-".

I extract field number 23, the cache finish status, and divide the operations into four categories. The NO-CHECK and UP-TO-DATE states are cache hits. The WRITTEN, REFRESHED, and CL-MISMATCH states are misses that cause cache writes. The DO-NOT-CACHE and NON-CACHEABLE states are uncacheable, and anything else is an error or incomplete transfer. I work out the percentages for the first three and record them.

I extract field number 24, the total transfer time. This field is a higher-resolution version of field 19, with millisecond rather than second resolution. I work out the average transfer time, but since the transfer size varies from zero to several megabytes, I also work out the average transfer time for each of the size ranges for which I record the mix. The mix in my latest `percollator.se` code is based upon the SPECweb96 size boundaries of up to 1 Kbyte, 1 Kbyte up to 10 Kbytes, 10 Kbytes up to 100 Kbytes, 100 Kbytes up to 1 Mbyte, and over 1 Mbyte. I end up with the percentage of ops and the average transfer time in each size range.

Observed Results in Practice

On a fairly quiet weekday, 280,000 accesses went via this cache, and 56% of the accesses went out to the Internet. The cache breakdown was this: 34% of the accesses hit in the cache, 16% missed and caused a cache write, 49% of the accesses were not cacheable, and 1% ended in some kind of error. A week's worth of data showed that the indirect and cache hit rates vary by 5% to 10% from day to day.

The transfer time averages about 2.3 seconds. The problem with this figure is that it includes a small number of very large or very slow transfers. The average for transfers up to 1 Kbyte was 1.8 seconds; for 1–10 Kbytes, it was 2.5 seconds; for 10–100 Kbytes, it was 6 seconds; for 100 Kbytes–1 Mbyte, it was 40 seconds; and for over 1 Mbyte, it was 188 seconds. Within each of these size bands, connections are taking place over everything from 100-Mbit Ethernet to 28.8-Kbit modems, so it's hard to tell how much impact the cache is having.

Transfer Time Versus Size Distribution

I also took 10,000 accesses, and after removing all zero content length and zero time transfers, I plotted size against transfer time, using log-log axes. The result shows that transfer time is not very dependent upon size until the size gets into the 10–100 Kbyte region, as you can see in Figure 4-20.

Figure 4-20 Log-Log Plot of Response Time Versus Size

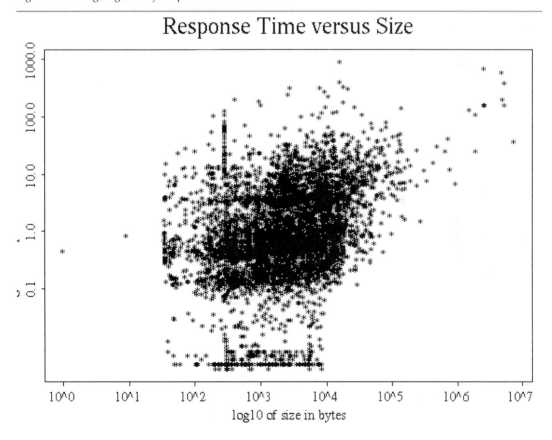

This plot shows bands of transfer times that depend upon the user location. A lot of users are locally connected, but others are operating over slower networks. The transfer time includes the time spent waiting for the remote server to respond, so although it does not represent the extra time imposed by the cache, it actually gives a reasonable summary of the response time that users are experiencing with their browsers. This information is useful because you can collect it at a central point rather than attempting to measure the response time at an individual user site.

In this case, the server is not responding as well as it might. Its disks are a bit too busy at times, and HTTP 1.1 persistent connections are temporarily disabled because of problems interacting with the Internet gateway proxy. You should make a plot like this that summarizes a day or a week of data and look for changes in the plot over time. The data can also be viewed as a probability density histogram, as shown in Figure 4-21.

Figure 4-21 Perspective Log-Log Plot of Response Time Versus Size Distribution

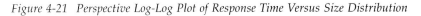

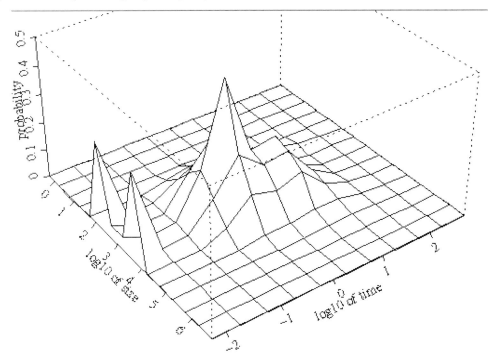

This plot shows that the most probable response is at about 0.5 seconds and 1 Kbyte. Remember that the average response time is 2.3 seconds on this data. It is clear that the average does not tell the whole story.

Hardware Configuration Issues for a Proxy Cache

The biggest difference between a normal web server and a proxy cache is that there is a significant amount of writing cache contents to disk with a proxy cache. There is also a higher CPU load per operation, but the CPU is rarely the bottleneck. The ideal configuration for a high-end proxy cache would use a disk array with nonvolatile RAM for fast writes. More typical cache systems are smaller and use a handful of disks. The effect of the NVRAM can be obtained from a transaction log, and this log should reside on a dedicated disk if you want good performance.

I'll assume you have something like an Ultra 1 or Ultra 2 desktop server with two internal disks and an external multipack containing four to twelve disks (preferably on its own SCSI bus). You put all the operating system, swap space, and web server code on the first internal disk and use Solstice DiskSuite 4.1 to stripe the external disks together with a 128-Kbyte interlace. To make writes go fast, you take the second internal disk and make a single 100-Mbyte partition on it into the transaction log, then combine the stripe and the log into a logging file system. The key is that the transaction log is small, and the disk heads are always moving over it in very short seeks, doing sequential writes to the log. Resist the temptation to make a mounted file system on the remainder of the log disk because the extra-long seeks will hurt log performance. Instead, take the attitude that the disk is 100% occupied from a service-time performance point of view, even if it has spare storage and throughput capacity.

A single log can be used by several different file systems, but it doesn't need to be any bigger than 100 Mbytes. If you do share the log disk with other activity, it is still better than no log at all, but you will get much worse service times than are possible with a dedicated log disk. Figure 4-22 shows the situation where the log is sharing the system disk with everything else.

Figure 4-22 Example `iostat` *Results on a Proxy Cache with Logging File System*

disk	r/s	w/s	Kr/s	Kw/s	wait	actv	svc_t	%w	%b	us	sy	wt	id
						extended disk statistics					cpu		
md0	6.1	5.3	34.8	14.2	0.0	0.4	35.5	0	15	4	4	8	83
md1	4.6	6.8	22.8	23.4	0.0	0.3	24.8	0	10				
sd0	0.4	0.9	3.2	16.7	0.0	0.0	12.4	0	2				
sd17	0.9	1.4	4.9	3.6	0.0	0.1	31.9	0	4				
sd18	2.0	1.2	10.4	3.0	0.0	0.1	28.0	0	6				
sd32	1.6	0.9	10.1	1.0	0.0	0.1	31.8	0	5				
sd33	1.6	1.8	9.4	6.6	0.0	0.2	47.6	0	7				

Solstice DiskSuite 4.1 shows its metadisks in `iostat` automatically. In this case, `sd0` is the system and log disk. `sd17`, `sd18`, `sd32`, and `sd33` are the stripe disks. `md0` is the stripe, and `md1` is the log accelerated stripe that is actually mounted.

You can see that the system/log disk is averaging a 12.4 ms response time, and since most of the synchronous writes are logged, this is the effective response time seen by proxy cache writes. The mounted logging file system `md1` has a service time of 24.8 ms for its reads and writes. The `md0` stripe and the individual disks are higher than that. Overall, this is OK, but the load level is low. As the system gets busier, the combined system/log disk becomes a bottleneck with slow service times.

Java Application Servers

Java is a hot topic in the computer industry today. It has quickly become ubiquitous and its multiplatform portability is extremely valuable to anyone who has to deal with many types of computer system. Java has now spawned a new class of desktop client system known as a Network Computer or NC. Most NCs have to find ways to access preexisting applications, but a whole new class of "100% Pure Java™" applications are being developed to run on NCs and on any other Java-enabled system.

The deliberately restricted capabilities of the initial generation of NCs force considerable functionality to be centralized on a server system and accessed over the network. There is, however, a great deal of freedom to vary the amount of functionality on the server versus the client, and individual applications draw the boundary in many ways.

The natural question that arises is "What kind of server and network load will I get for a given population of NCs?" The short answer is—as always—"It depends...." I was given the task of writing a guide to try and provide a better answer. At the time (mid-1996), there wasn't much real data to go on, so I adopted a two-track strategy. I used some basic analysis to make comparisons with other client/server configurations and investigated the few existing applications to explore the range of client/server activity. Together with generic information on web server sizing, this study formed the initial sizing guide for the launch of Sun's JavaStation NC in October 1996.

At the same time, plans were laid for a more in-depth analysis that would coincide with the initial deliveries of systems to the early adopters of the technology during 1997. Sun is itself installing 3,000 JavaStations for internal use in this time frame, and this project helped justify the full-time assignment of an internal systems development engineer, Christian Demeure, to work on the project with me. The project was completed in September 1997 and is the basis of this chapter and an updated sizing guide.

Java Overview and Terminology

Herein is a quick tour through the relevant parts of the technology. If you want to learn more, there are many books on Java, and the latest information is available at http://java.sun.com. My own favorite introductory text is *Just Java*, by Peter Van der Linden, Sun Microsystems Press and Prentice Hall.

5

What Is Java?

There are a lot of possible definitions of Java, so here is my attempt to sum up the key features.

Java is designed to solve the problems of constructing secure, distributed, portable, object-oriented applications.

Java Security

There are two ways to build a secure system that is also network-aware. One way is to start with an existing insecure system, remove insecure features, and add new safe features. This preserves investment in existing systems, but it has problems in practice. The problem is that a compromise is made, which is not a very secure solution, yet it is different enough from existing practice to frustrate application developers. The reuse of existing insecure development practices and tools pushes the compromise away from a secure solution.

The second way to build a secure system is to start from scratch and build security in at every stage, as Java does. The system excludes insecure operations, so all the developers and tools must use the techniques of programming in a secure environment as their default.

Applet Security

A Java program can be designed to run as a stand-alone application in the conventional sense. However, a new alternative, known as an *applet*, is designed to run under the control of a web browser. The applet is downloaded automatically when the browser visits a web page, so security is a big issue. The applet executes under very severe restrictions. By default, the only system to which it can make a network connection is the server from which it was downloaded. It cannot read or write files on the system running the browser, and the only permitted I/O is keyboard and mouse input and graphical output within a window on the screen. To prevent a rogue applet from making arbitrary calls into the system, the Java language does not allow the programmer to call the OS or manipulate addresses directly. The generated code from a Java program could be modified to make illegal references, but at the time it is loaded, all the code is inspected and illegal calls and references are rejected. To be able to perform these checks, the generated code contains far more semantic information than does normal machine code. It uses a special-purpose instruction set known as *Java bytecode* that is interpreted by a *Java Virtual Machine* (JVM). Digital signature techniques will allow *signed* trusted applets to access any other system directly over the network and to perform local file I/O, but trusted Java applets will be the exception, not the rule. It will always be safer to be suspicious and restrictive by default.

Java Portability and Efficiency

Every computer system that wishes to run a compiled Java program needs to have a JVM interpreter ported to it. At this time, it seems that a JVM is now available for every kind of system, from home computers to mainframes. It is even starting to appear in embedded applications, like web-enabled TV sets and combination Cellphone/Pocket-computers. It is also provided as an integral part of the current releases of many operating systems including Windows, MacOS, and Solaris.

One of the key attractions for developers is that Java code is compiled once and can then run on any kind of system. This feature drastically decreases the cost of supporting many versions of a product and increases the size of the market that can use the product.

Code optimization can be performed by the JVM, and the runtime efficiency of Java code is increasing rapidly over time as vendors compete to have the fastest implementation. CPU designers are also optimizing their hardware to run Java. Sun Microelectronics (an operating company of Sun Microsystems) has developed a range of CPUs that run the most common Java bytecodes directly, thus avoiding most of the overhead of the JVM.

Distribution and Installation

When an application is installed on a large number of end-user desktop systems, a number of problems arise. The main problem is the cost and time taken to do the installation. A secondary problem is version maintenance and distribution of bug fixes. The solution provided by Java is to use the web browser as a common host environment for applets. Each applet is downloaded on demand as it is used, so no special installation is required for each user. The latest version is always used. Caching can be employed to avoid reloading commonly used applets. A *conditional get* is used by the browser to download the new version only if it is newer than the one already in the cache. Large applets can be provided as a number of separate "class" files, so minor changes would cause only the changed classes to be reloaded. For more efficient loading, a combined file called a Java Archive (JAR) file can be produced that contains a number of compressed classes to be loaded as a unit.

Distributed Java Applications

A Java applet cannot read or write files at the desktop, and it can communicate only with the server from which it was downloaded. So how can a Java-based word processor save your files? And how can a Java-based SNA3270 terminal emulator connect to a mainframe? The answer is that a server-side *helper* process is used. This process must be authenticated, so a user name and password must be provided. An NC asks for these at login time so they can be provided to a local server automatically. A PC running a browser, or an NC accessing a server that is outside its administrative domain, will need to provide the user name and password at the time the application is started.

Once the helper process is running on the server, it has all the normal capabilities of any program and it can be written in any language. If the helper process is itself written as a stand-alone Java application (as opposed to an applet), then it will be portable to any kind of server that can run Java.

The helper process can provide extra compute power for an applet. It can contain the core of an application that has been ported to Java by merely rewriting the GUI as an applet. It can hold large amounts of data, using the virtual memory capabilities of the server to run applications that are too large to fit in the limited memory of a PC or NC. It can open network connections to other systems using different protocols. It can provide an SQL gateway for database access. All these uses put a load on the Java application server and on the network and were evaluated as part of the sizing project.

Client/Server Comparisons

One reason that the name World Wide Web came into use is that the client-to-server relationships form a tangled web that spans wide-area networks. Other computing architectures are normally structured as a star or tree configuration, with each user ultimately connected to a single backend server that is situated locally.

A Java client often has a local server, either at the Internet Service Provider (ISP) or in corporate environments at the department, building, domain, or site level. A vendor-independent NC boot process is being defined. However, for the first release of the JavaStation client, a Sun JavaServer™ is needed to provide boot services and network information services (NIS). The server also provides home directory service and may run the server-side components of Java applications. If the Java client is a Windows PC, Macintosh, or Unix workstation with a local web browser, then there is no need for a network boot process or local JavaServer.

The local server may also act as a proxy cache, retaining copies of frequently requested data, and may provide a gateway through a firewall for security. Local servers may also provide a Usenet news feed and the user's mail box. Mail is not sent directly to the client inasmuch as the client may be powered down or disconnected and may not have regular backups. The mail server provides a reliable mail destination.

In operation, the Java client accesses information and Java applications in a location-independent manner from systems throughout the intranet and Internet. In contrast, most other computing architectures tie the client system to a local server and are optimized for continuous, low-latency communications between the client and the server.

Client/Server Characteristics

The characteristics of each class of client/server relationship can be displayed by a *dumbbell* diagram consisting of two connected spheres. The size of the client sphere indicates the complexity of the client system. The size of the server sphere indicates the complexity of the server code required per client. The width of the connecting arrow indicates the relative bandwidth required, and the length of the arrow indicates the latency that can be tolerated. A short, thick arrow indicates a low-latency, high-bandwidth connection, as to a local Ethernet. A long, thin arrow indicates the ability to work over low-speed, wide-area networks. The user actions that require interactive response (like selecting an item from a menu or scrolling through a list) may involve the client only or include the server as well. This interaction is shown with one or more round-trip arrows. Figure 5-1 illustrates these conventions.

Figure 5-1   Dumbbell Diagram for Java Computing Architecture

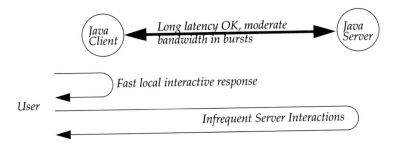

Java Computing Clients

Java clients tolerate high latencies because user GUI interaction is done locally and the HTTP protocol is optimized for Internet-style latencies. The bandwidth needed is moderate in bursts while the Java client is booting over the net or loading applications, but the net is mostly idle. Web and boot services and Java application backend support put a very small load on servers and networks in most cases. More complex backend applications involve CORBA object servers or databases and may include a third tier of backend server.

Dumb Terminal Clients

IBM 3270 terminal clients operate as block-mode character devices, passing whole lines or screenfuls of text in one operation. This operation is low bandwidth and can tolerate fairly high latency. More of the application load resides on the server, and server interactions are more frequent than with a Java frontend GUI. Dumb terminal "VT220"-style clients echo every character back and forth and so need lower latency than do 3270-

style clients. Where there is a requirement to interface with legacy applications, a terminal emulator written in Java can provide access. Once loaded, the terminal emulator has bandwidth and latency requirements similar to those of a real terminal. OpenConnect Systems Inc.'s WebConnect terminal emulator provides 3270, 5250, and VT220 terminal emulation for Java and puts a very low load on the network and Java server. Figure 5-2 illustrates a dumbbell diagram for dumb terminals.

Figure 5-2   Dumbbell Diagrams for Dumb Terminals

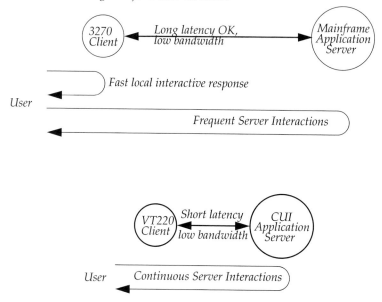

Fat Clients: PCs and Workstations

Fat client PC and Unix workstation clients that have local OS disks combined with a shared file server get most of their needs met locally, so they can tolerate moderate bandwidth and latency and put a small load on a file server. PC clients include those running Windows 95 or Windows NT and Macintoshes. Diskless workstations need a short latency and high bandwidth connection, but NFS service is efficient enough to require only a small server in most cases.

The network bandwidth required by a typical networked PC is expected to be comparable to that of a JavaStation. However, this statement covers a wide range of possibilities.

A PC or Unix workstation loading a web browser over the network from a file server actually generates about 50 per cent more network traffic than does an NC booting! With Solaris, this traffic can be reduced by use of the cachefs file system. Sun's latest NFS support package for PCs (Solaris PC Client) includes cachefs functionality as well. Figure 5-3 illustrates the configurations for fat clients.

Figure 5-3   Dumbbell Diagrams for Fat Clients

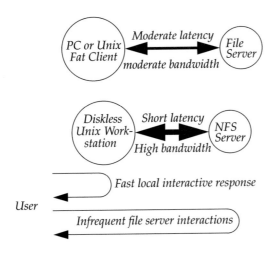

X-Terminal Clients

X terminals run complex GUI code on the server and display it on the desktop; these activities often require very powerful servers with large amounts of RAM when many users are active and require low-latency, high-bandwidth networks for the GUI to be responsive (see Figure 5-4).

There is a superficial similarity between a JavaStation and an X terminal. The key difference is that an X terminal is not programmable. Complex window system features like scrollbars are implemented in the GUI code that runs on the server, with mouse movements and low-level drawing operations passing over the network. In contrast, a

JavaStation loads a Java class that implements the scrollbar or other complex GUI feature in a single operation. It then loads the data to be scrolled, and the user can then browse the data locally, with no further network interactions.

Figure 5-4   Dumbbell Diagrams for X-Terminal Clients

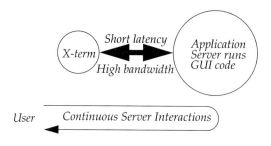

Emulating NC-Based Users

In the past, tools emulated dumb terminal-based users by opening a telnet session to a server and from a process that simulates the user. More recently, these tools have been extended to capture client/server traffic at the SQL level between PCs and database servers. They have also attempted to capture and replay X-terminal traffic (without much success), and the very latest versions can capture and replay simple HTML traffic from web browsers to web servers. We investigated tools such as Pure Performix Empower, Performance Awareness PreVue, and Mercury WebRunner in early 1997. None of them could capture and replay a Java applet that was connected to a backend process via an arbitrary protocol.

Java-Based Testing Tool

The breakthrough came when we discovered a Java-based testing tool, called JavaStar, developed by a spin-off, called SunTest, from Sun's research labs (see http://www.suntest.com). This tool can capture and replay any pure Java application. It is itself written in Java, and it captures the user's timed actions as a script that is also in Java. We found that it could capture and replay complete sessions by controlling the HotJava™ browser (which is in itself a Java application) running on a Unix workstation. The sessions included browsing through web pages, starting and operating applets, and using complete Java applications that include a backend server component.

NC Emulation Using JavaStar

The HotJava browser is a pure Java application. A customized version also forms the core of the user interface to the JavaOS™ used by NCs such as Sun's JavaStation, so running a copy under Unix is as close as we can get to emulation of an NC.

JavaStar is oriented to the problems of automated testing of Java programs by developers. One feature added to support this testing is a command-line interface that allows the testing to be run from a Unix makefile or script as part of an automated build and regression test setup. This includes an "invisible" option, which suppresses all graphical display. The test results are logged, and parameters can be passed into the script. This option is just what is needed to emulate an NC! By collecting and parameterizing a series of user sequences, we can build a workload mix that can be replicated to any number of users and that does not need any graphical display.

Problems and Restrictions

Unfortunately, in order to "fake out" a program that still thinks it is talking to an X display, JavaStar needs to connect to an X server to provide the right responses. Even though the application is invisible, it is still connected. This case limits the number of sessions to about 50 because there is a limit to the number of X connections that can be made to a single X server. We also found some applications that worked when displayed normally but that did not run reliably in invisible mode. To avoid the need for invisible mode and to run with a higher number of sessions, Christian obtained a copy of the generic X11R6 server. He ran it in a "null X server" mode, where it ran without connecting to screen or keyboard devices. He could then run 50 copies of JavaStar per null X server, all on a large multiprocessor system that has no graphical display. A total of several hundred sessions can be emulated with this technique, although the CPU and memory required to run a lot of emulations quickly saturated a single, large E6000 server. A large number of machines can work together to emulate as many sessions as their combined capacity allows.

Each emulated user runs its own HotJava browser under the control of a copy of JavaStar, with a parameterized workload that has been modified to loop continuously through a sequence of actions and to use randomized think time delays.

Some programs were written to automate the startup of a workload mix of distributed emulated users and to process the resulting log files to measure the user response times and number of operations completed.

There are a few restrictions to be dealt with. Because it redefines the enveloping Java classes to take control of an application's user interactions, JavaStar can only control applications built with the same version of Java that JavaStar is built with. Our initial tests with an old Java 1.0.2-based alpha release of HotJava and an early version of JavaStar worked quite well. The full version of JavaStar is based on Java 1.1, so we had to convert to use HotJava 1.0 (which uses Java 1.1 and is the version included in Solaris 2.6).

Emulation System Loads

Emulation uses a substantial amount of memory (several megabytes per user) and CPU power. The amount of think time in the workload is the key to overall CPU usage. With a simple applet, about 20 to 50 emulated users per CPU could be sustained. With more complex applications and realistic think times, this number decreased to about 10 to 15 users. In most of our tests, each CPU was a 167 MHz UltraSPARC with 512-Kbyte cache. Faster CPUs can emulate proportionally more users; a few tests on a 300 MHz UltraSPARC with a 2-Mbyte cache approximately doubled the number of users per CPU. Under extreme load, the emulation is still reliable—it just slows down. Correct behavior under load is a very useful feature. You cannot take it for granted, and I have previously found that careful tuning was needed to make scripts run reliably under load in telnet-based scenarios. I have also found out the hard way that it is often impossible to make X-terminal emulation scenarios run reliably under load because the X protocol sequences become nondeterministic as the relative speed of the client and server changes. Overall, it seems that the JavaStar approach is robust and deterministic.

Network Load Emulation

One effect of the emulation is that network traffic is serialized out of the single interface of the emulation system. This serialization has different characteristics from a large population of NCs all transmitting in parallel and colliding with each other. The effect can be mitigated by use of multiple emulation systems to generate the load. Multiple emulation may also be necessary in cases where a single, large, multiprocessor server is not available for use as an emulation system.

Measuring and Predicting the Server Load with BGS Best/1

We used the Best/1 performance analysis and prediction tools from BGS Systems Inc. (See http://www.bgs.com) to collect data on the server during each test. This tool measures the average resources used by each process on the system over time. In the analysis phase, we identified the users and server processes that were involved in each test to form a workload definition. We could then predict the performance and utilization of that workload with a different number of users or assuming a different CPU and memory configuration. Best/1 uses a queuing model, and it takes into account paging rates and memory requirements of each process to produce estimates that seem to be reasonable in practice. Multithreaded server processes that handle work from multiple clients are more difficult to model; in this case, varying user count predictions are made by varying the throughput of the process to get CPU usage. Memory usage is predicted by watching the process size with zero, one, and many users and interpolating by hand.

Sizing Tests and Results

A range of applications were put through the test process to produce results that can be used as examples. To start with, the boot sequence was examined in detail.

Boot Sequence Analysis

A simple measurement is the activity during a JavaStation boot to the point where it presents a login screen. This activity involves the transfer of about 4 Mbytes of data using a total of about 4,000 packets in about 40 seconds. Apart from a small number of various kinds of name service lookups, the bulk of the traffic consists of a TFTP bootstrap of 158 Kbytes, followed by an NFS transfer of the 4-Mbyte JavaOS 1.0 image, using 8-Kbyte NFS V2 reads over UDP. JavaStations that can store a copy of JavaOS in a nonvolatile "flash PROM" are being developed. They will download the full 4-Mybte image only if a different version is seen on the server, further reducing network loads. Note that subsequent versions of JavaOS may be a different size or use different protocol options. Some other vendors use TFTP to download the entire boot image to their NC.

The login process takes about ten seconds, and including name service password lookups and a load of the default home page takes only 60 packets.

Booting Storms

One NC booting on its own is not going to be a problem. The problems arise when a large population of NCs boot at the same time. Synchronization may occur at certain times of the day if the users are working regular shifts. Another synchronization point occurs after a building-level power cut. The server and network may have uninterruptable power services, but users' desktop machines will not. Ideally, the NC should stay powered down until a user toggles the power switch, to spread out the startup times when building power is restored.

The bottleneck will be the network infrastructure. Since each boot takes 40 seconds to move about 4 Mbytes (500 NFS reads), an average rate of 100 Kbytes/s (12.5 NFS read/s) is needed. A 10baseT network can support about 8 to 10 simultaneous boots before boot time increases significantly (this number was tried in practice). A 100baseT server connection feeding 10 or more switched 10baseT segments could support 80 to 100 simultaneous boots. This adds up to 1,000 to 1,250 NFS read/s. All reads are of the same 4-Mbyte file, which will be cached in RAM at the server, so there is no need for a high-performance disk subsystem.

The SPEC LADDIS NFS server benchmark uses a mix that contains a lot of reads and writes. Overall, continuous reads of the same data are likely to be a lighter CPU load than the LADDIS mix, so we can take the LADDIS rating for a server as an overestimate for the CPU power needed during the JavaStation boot process. The LADDIS rating for a uniprocessor UltraSPARC system is over 2,000 NFSops/s, so a rough sizing estimate would be that one UltraSPARC CPU can saturate one 100baseT network for a 100-client booting storm. A high-end Sun NFS server can sustain 10,000 to 30,000 NFSops, so given enough network capacity (a few gigabit Ethernet interfaces, perhaps) it seems possible to configure for even an extreme booting storm with several thousand JavaStations all booting at the same instant and finishing in a time window of a few minutes.

In reality, this scenario should be considered an extreme situation. Every time you double the boot-time window, you halve the load. Every time you segment your population by using multiple Java servers, you also reduce the load. A more realistic aim might be to boot all the users in a 5-minute period. A single 10baseT connection would support about 50 JavaStations, and a 100baseT connection to an entry-level UltraSPARC system would support about 500 JavaStations.

NFS Workstation Browser Startup Comparisons

A Solaris system can be configured similarly to a JavaStation, with a single copy of a browser loaded from a central location so the Solaris system can be updated simply.

The network load for a minimal CDE user login and startup of an NFS-mounted copy of the Netscape browser on a Solaris desktop system added up to about 6,000 packets in about 20 seconds on a SPARCstation 5 over 10baseT. This does not include booting Solaris, but it is 50 percent more packets than a JavaStation boot process and twice as long as a JavaStation login on basically similar hardware.

By comparison, Netscape and Solaris use more network capacity than do HotJava and JavaOS, but Solaris can drive the network at higher rates for large transfers. Replacing Solaris desktops that use mainly browser-based applications with JavaStations is not likely to require any upgrades to internal networks. The large roll-out of JavaStations for internal use at Sun seems to support this position.

If PCs are also configured to load shared applications from a file server, I would expect to see a similar result.

HotJava Views

An alternative to the normal boot into a browser, HotJava Views™ combines the browser with a set of default office desktop applications that are loaded as part of a slightly larger boot image (about 5 Mbytes). The applications provided are:

- HotJava browser
- Email reader using the IMAP4 protocol
- Calendar viewer
- Card index style name/address database

The server components include email support via an IMAP4 mail server. The calendar manager daemon is a standard part of Solaris.

We do not yet have a version of HotJava Views that is built with the Java 1.1 libraries and runs on Solaris, so we cannot control it with JavaStar to do any testing. We estimate that the load will be dominated by the IMAP4 mail server. Mail server sizing is already being done by the Solstice Internet Mail Server group.

Simple HTML Web Browsing and Java Applets

There is no server load from a simple applet once it has been downloaded to the browser. This makes applets somewhat uninteresting for this study. The performance of servers for download of static web pages is measured by the SPECweb96 benchmark. Static pages contain HTML, images, and Java applets, among other file types. The SPEC benchmark results can be found at http://www.specbench.org.

Dynamic web pages are not measured by SPECweb96; they involve customized server processing for each user to generate a web page. A simple example is a cgi-bin script that displays the result of a search query. The updated SPECweb98 benchmark should include some dynamic web page processing when it is released.

All the following workloads include some web server activity as the Java client code is downloaded from the Java server. The activity level of the web server is so low that it did not add a significant CPU load in any of the tests. The web server does use perhaps up to 10 Mbytes of RAM, and this value is included in the RAM sizing.

Applix Anyware

Applix Anyware consists of an office suite of tools, including a spreadsheet, word processor, presentation package, mail client, and database access system. It has a Java front end, but the application code that performs calculations and does operations like generating a graph are performed by a server-side process for each user and sent to the client. The network and server load is significant if many users are active at once or real-time data feeds are in use. The workload is more like an X terminal in concept, although a large proportion of the GUI has been loaded into the Java client. For example, scrolling around a large spreadsheet on a JavaStation does not involve any network traffic or server load, but it would generate a lot of traffic and server load on an X terminal. Recalculating the spreadsheet or resizing a graph uses the JavaServer and network. The trade-off that Applix has made is to rewrite the GUI portion of an existing application.

This approach provides JavaStation users with a very complete and highly functional product with a very short time-to-market. Rewriting the whole product in Java would take a lot longer and be far less functional in the short term.

The workload script lasts about 30 minutes. It starts in the word processor, entering a page of text and performing six intermediate saves. The spreadsheet is used next, entering 5 columns and 50 rows of data, computing the average for each column and performing four intermediate saves. Entering new data is likely to be much more server intensive than browsing existing data, so we think this is quite a heavy load. The server used was an E6000 with 15 x 167 MHz CPUs and 1 Gbyte of RAM on a 100-Mbit network. We were RAM-limited to running about 100 sessions, the CPU load was 21% of a single CPU, and the main disk activity came from paging at the 100-user level. We collected the load with Best/1 and predicted additional results. If we assume that only 25% of users are active, a single processor system could handle a total of 400 connected sessions if it had almost 4 Gbytes of RAM. Each user needs about 10 megabytes to avoid paging delays when users start to use the system again after a long idle period. Table 5-1 summarizes our results; Figure 5-5 illustrates the configuration.

Table 5-1   Applix Anyware Emulation Sizing

Active Users	Inactive Users	CPU	Network	RAM
100 measured	0	1.5% of 18 x 167 MHz	1.8% of 100 Mbit	1 GB
50 predicted	0	11% of 1 x 167 MHz	0.9% of 100 Mbit	0.5 GB
100 predicted	300 predicted	21% of 1 x 167 MHz	1.8% of 100 Mbit	4 GB

Figure 5-5   Applix Anyware Configuration

VT220 Terminal Emulation

The Digital VT220 is a common type of ASCII terminal that is often used to provide basic login services to Unix systems. For a JavaStation, the VT220 provides a command-line interface that can be connected over the network to any Unix server.

Open Connect Inc.'s VT220 emulator was configured on a uniprocessor 167 MHz UltraSPARC system. Each user starts up the emulator and logs in to a third system. The user then spends about five minutes running various commands that display text output;

then the user loops back and runs the commands again. The third system was used so that we measured only the character traffic load and had both incoming and outgoing network connections on the Java server.

The OpenConnect server is a single process that serves a large number (hundreds) of clients. This arrangement is far more efficient than having a process for each user. If high-end scalability is an issue, several server processes can be started to handle high connection counts. The server started off at 3.5 Mbytes for a single user and added about 1 Mbyte for every eight additional users. The test system was overconfigured with 192 Mbytes of RAM—a base level of 64 Mbytes for a small setup and 128 Mbytes for even a very large number of clients is enough.

We had a 7-user demonstration license for the emulator, so we tested seven concurrent scripts and collected the per-process activity, using the BGS Best/1 performance modeling package. A single Unix process handles the server activity for all the users, and with seven active users, total CPU usage was 3.14% (including some measurement overhead, etc.). Using Best/1 to predict the load for 300 users raised the CPU usage to 49%. 10baseT Ethernet usage was 0.5% at 7 users and would be about 20% at 300 users.

Remember that not all users may be active. If we assume that a lot of users leave their terminal emulator idle for long periods of time, then we need only allow RAM for them. Table 5-2 summarizes our results, and Figure 5-6 illustrates the configuration.

Table 5-2   VT220 Terminal Emulation Sizing

Active Users	Inactive Users	CPU	Network	RAM
7 measured	0	3% of Ultra 167 MHz	0.5% of 10 Mbit	192 MB
50 predicted	0	10% of Ultra 167 MHz	3.6% of 10 Mbit	64 MB
100 predicted	0	18% of Ultra 167 MHz	7.2% of 10 Mbit	70 MB
300 predicted	0	49% of Ultra 167 MHz	20.0% of 10 Mbit	100 MB
50 predicted	500	10% of Ultra 167 MHz	3.6% of 10 Mbit	128 MB

Figure 5-6   OpenConnect VT220 Emulation

≣ 5

3270 Terminal Emulation

The IBM3270 is a block-mode IBM mainframe terminal.

Open Connect Inc.'s 3270 emulator was configured on a uniprocessor 167 MHz UltraSPARC system. Each user starts up the emulator and logs into a mainframe system. The mainframe we used has its own TCP/IP to SNA gateway, but it would also be possible to configure SNA3270 protocol support on the JavaServer for direct native connection to a mainframe. Users spend about five minutes running various commands that display text output, then they loop back and run the commands again. The commands used were `DISPR 100`, which displays 100 test screens, and `FLIST`, which displays a list of available files and shows the contents of three of them. We suspect this may be a higher than normal text throughput rate.

We had a 7-user demonstration license for the emulator, so we tested seven concurrent scripts and collected the per-process activity by using the BGS Best/1 performance modeling package. A single Unix process handles the server activity for all the users, and with seven active users, total CPU usage was 6.5% (including some measurement overhead, etc.).

Remember that not all users may be active. If we assume that a lot of users leave their terminal emulator idle for long periods of time, then we need only allow RAM for them. Table 5-3 summarizes our results; Figure 5-7 illustrates the configuration.

Table 5-3   3270 Terminal Emulation Sizing

Active Users	Inactive Users	CPU	Network	RAM
7 measured	0	6.5% of Ultra 167 MHz	2.0% of 10 Mbit	192 MB
50 predicted	0	37% of Ultra 167 MHz	14.3% of 10 Mbit	64 MB
100 predicted	0	61% of Ultra 200 MHz	28.6% of 10 Mbit	70 MB
300 predicted	0	62% of Ultra 4x167 MHz	8.5% of 100 Mbit	100 MB
50 predicted	500 predicted	37% of Ultra 167 MHz	14.3% of 10 Mbit	128 MB

Figure 5-7   OpenConnect 3270 Emulation

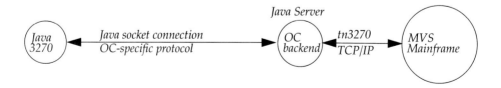

Corel Office for Java

Corel Office contains several well-known applications that have been ported to run in the Java environment, including the WordPerfect word processor. This is a client-side-oriented application plus file services on the server. It runs very efficiently with little network or server-side load (much less than that for Applix). It does capture and replay in our test environment, but Corel is currently rewriting it, so there is little point testing the current version in any detail.

Custom RDBMS Clients

Sun internal applications for sales forecasting, order entry, travel expenses management, customer support, and others are being migrated to Java. We encouraged the developers to use JavaStar as part of their development testing process. When we came to perform sizing tests, there was no need to debug use with JavaStar, and some usage workloads were already available. However, there is a significant difference between functionality tests and performance tests. Functionality tests aim for high coverage of the options in the application and run with no think time. Performance tests are weighted by expected usage patterns and contain realistic amounts of randomized think time.

Sun Sales Forecasting Application

This application was tested in the late stages of development. It will be used by the Sun sales force to forecast opportunities for business and manage their "pipeline" over time. There is also a sales management interface to summarize the total revenue stream. The interface is based on Java 1.1 and uses the Java Remote Method Invocation (RMI) interface to make calls from the applet to a server application written in Java. Two server processes, a Java RMI registry and a multithreaded application server, handle all the clients (and use most of the CPU required). The server also runs a Sybase 11 database that uses the JDBC™ (Java database with connectivity) interface to communicate with the Java application server process. The database and RMI registry each account for about 15 percent of the total CPU load. The database could be located on a separate system if required. A single server will be used to support a large geographic region, so most local sales offices will be communicating over a wide-area network. The total number of concurrently connected users could be quite high, but few of them are expected to be active at the same time. Figure 5-8 illustrates the configuration.

Figure 5-8   Sun Sales Forecast Application

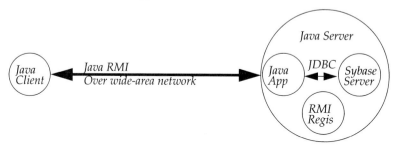

We ran a 10-user test using a dual 200 MHz Ultra 2 as the server, collected the results with BGS Best/1, and did a basic analysis of the load so that we could predict some larger configurations. The server had 256 Mbytes of RAM and eight 4.2-Gbyte disks. The total number of sessions we could start was limited by the application setup available at the time. The disk usage was very low, and the network usage is extremely low. The use of high-level RMI calls instead of JDBC or the more traditional SQL interfaces over the network seems to minimize network activity. Sybase was configured to use about 100 Mbytes of RAM and did not grow when users were added; the RMI registry took 5 Mbytes and increased by 0.5 Mbytes for 10 users. The application process took 6 Mbytes and also increased by about 0.5 MBytes for 10 users. Best/1 decided that about 200 Mbytes of RAM were in use overall at 10 users. Table 5-4 summarizes the results.

Table 5-4   Sun Forecast Emulation Sizing

Active Users	Inactive Users	CPU	Network	RAM
10 measured	0	14% of 2 x 200 MHz	0.2% of 10 Mbit	200 MB
50 predicted	0	68% of 2 x 200 MHz	1.6% of 10 Mbit	250 MB
100 predicted	0	56% of 6 x 167 MHz	3.2% of 10 Mbit	300 MB
10 predicted	90 predicted	24% of 1 x 200 MHz	0.2% of 10 Mbit	300 MB

When predicting larger systems, we aimed to keep the CPU queue length and the Best/1 response time estimate low to allow for peaks in the load. These criteria resulted in configurations where the overall CPU was about half used. More testing on a much larger system is needed to establish whether the high-end predictions are reasonable and at what point Sybase memory usage should be increased, but the prediction gives us a first guess at the size of system to put together for a larger test.

With only 10 percent of the users active at a time, a uniprocessor system would handle 100 connected users if configured with enough RAM to avoid page-in delays when each user begins to use the system again.

X-Terminal Emulation

For access to existing Unix-based tools, there are two approaches. One approach is to use a combined X-terminal and NC product; the other is to use a Java-based X emulator. Many of the existing X-terminal manufacturers have converted their products to NCs by adding Java capability to their existing system, thus providing the highest performance for an X-dominated workload. For occasional X usage during a transition to a completely Java-based environment, the Graphon RapidX package enables a Java-based system to view an X Window System inside an applet. The X applications connect to a process on the Java server. A special, lightweight protocol is then used to display the X session on the Java client system. The X-session process uses a lot of CPU power and memory on the Java server, and early versions are quite slow on the Java client. Network usage is less than that for a normal X-terminal session as long as the application being used is also resident on the Java server.

We have not found a way to capture and replay sessions in this environment. There is little point because the sizing is fundamentally equivalent to X-terminal server sizing.

Windows PC Applications

The approach taken is to provide a Windows NT-based server on the network and to run multiple user sessions on it, with display redirected to a Java-based client applet. Insignia Solutions provides a product called NTrigue.

In this case, we felt that measuring the performance of an NT system running multiple copies of PC applications fell outside the scope of our JavaServer sizing project and our own personal expertise. We will leave this as an exercise for others to work on since it can be measured by means of a non-Java client.

Overall Sizing Estimates

Two basic questions first must be answered to narrow the range for each situation to a manageable number of options.

What are users' work patterns?

- Random or intermittent activity like office work is a *light* load.

- Continuous or synchronized activity generates the highest load. Shift work, tele-sales or student classrooms are examples.

What applications run server-side code?

- Booting, static web pages, and simple applets are a very light server load but generate the largest network loadings.

- Server-side gateways like an SNA gateway for 3270 terminals are light. A single server process supports many users, and RAM requirements are reasonably small.

- Applications using server-side code, e.g., Applix Anyware, need little CPU, but each user needs several megabytes of RAM to keep the user's own server-side process from being paged out.

- Databases may cause high loads in any environment; however, the additional overhead of supporting Java frontend applications is small, and the network load can be less than a more conventional application.

Conclusion

We established a reliable method of capturing Java-based application workloads and used it to reliably and repeatably simulate large numbers of Java-based NCs.

We also established the range of expected performance impact from NCs, and the bad news is that it is a very wide range. The good news is that a large proportion of workloads have a very low impact on networks and servers. The exceptions can be identified by answers to a few key questions.

- How much of the application runs on the server?

- How often does the applet interact with the server?

- How much network data is transferred in each interaction?

Source Code Optimization 6

This chapter is aimed at software developers. It covers instrumenting and tuning Java programs; 64 bit development issues; linking with libraries; and optimizing compiler options.

Java Tuning

There is a good paper on Java that includes a lot of performance tuning information at http://www.sun.com/solaris/java/wp-java/, and I have found a very useful web site with up-to-date performance and optimization information at http://www.cs.cmu.edu/~jch/java/optimization.html. A Java percollator graphing program that I'm tuning includes a useful class to help measure Java performance. I've tried out the profiler feature of Java WorkShop 2.0 on it.

Almost two years ago, I figured out Java far enough to put together a very simple performance graphing applet, and during summer 1997, I helped a student intern rewrite and extend it. The result is a much more useful tool that runs as both an applet and as an application and browses the files generated by my percollator script for monitoring web server performance. When graphing large amounts of data, the program can slow down, so I added code to time critical operations and report a summary. Since that is a useful code fragment in itself, that's where I'll start.

The Metrognome Class

I wanted a simple object that measured a time interval multiple times, then generated a summary of the results. The name is a joke, as it's a kind of small, helpful personalized metronome. The main design idea was to create a separate object that had a simple collection interface but which could be upgraded and extended without changing the interface. That way, a program using the `Metrognome` class could be instrumented in more detail by just replacing the class. No recompilation or interface changes should be necessary.

You construct a Metrognome by giving it a text label that identifies it.

```
Metrognome redrawTimer = new Metrognome("Display redraw");
```

At some point in the code, let's say during the paint method that redraws the display, we call the start method then call the stop method.

```
paint() {
  redrawTimer.start();
  // lots of display update code
  redrawTimer.stop();
}
```

The Metrognome class will collect the duration of all these display updates. Somewhere else in the code we need to have a way to show the results. The getSummary method returns a String that can be displayed in a GUI, written on exit to the Java console, or whatever else you like. Some individual performance data can also be read from the Metrognome and displayed, but it is easy to update the contents of the String if a more sophisticated Metrognome is used.

The summary string shows the label, count, and min/mean/max times in seconds.

```
"Display redraw: count= 5  Latency(s) min= 0.017  mean= 0.029  max= 0.041"
```

Figure 6-1   Code for the Metrognome Class

```
//  Metrognome.java  - the 'g' was Adrian's idea, not mine

import java.lang.*;
import java.util.*;
import java.text.*;

public class Metrognome extends Object {
    private String label;
    private long total_time;
    private long begin_time;
    private long count;
    private long min;
    private long max;

    public Metrognome(String lb) {
      label = new String(lb);
      begin_time = 0;
      count = 0;
      total_time = 0;
      min = 0;
      max = 0;
    }

    public void start() {
      if (begin_time == 0) {
```

```
      begin_time = new Date().getTime();
    }
  }

  public void stop() {
    long diff;
    if (begin_time != 0) {
      diff = (new Date().getTime() - begin_time);
      if (count == 0 || min > diff) min = diff;
      if (max < diff) max = diff;
      total_time += diff;
      begin_time = 0;
      count++;
    }
  }

  public double getMeanLatency() {
    if (count == 0) {
      return 0.0;
    } else {
      return ((total_time / 1000.0) / count);
    }
  }

  public long getCount() {
    return count;
  }

  public long getTotalTime() {
    return total_time;
  }

  public String getSummary() {
    DecimalFormat df = new DecimalFormat("0.0##");
    return label + ": count= " + count + "   latency(s) min= " +
      df.format(min/1000.0) + "   mean= " + df.format(getMeanLatency()) +
      "   max= " + df.format(max/1000.0);
  }
}
```

As usual, I have more ideas than time to implement them. Some possibilities for extending the Metrognome class without changing the interface to the rest of the program might include these actions:

- Accumulate time buckets to produce a histogram of the time distribution.
- Log a timestamped record to a buffer on each start.
- Update the record on each stop with the duration.

- Log the records somewhere.
- Make all the Metrognomes share one big buffer—you would need to apply access locking.
- Wait until a few times have been counted, then compare against the mean and deviation to report on abnormally large delays.
- Open an RMI connection to report back to a central data collection server.

Java Tuning and Java Virtual Machines

One of the nice things about Java is that investment levels are very high. That is, everyone is competing to provide the fastest Java Virtual Machine, and speeds are increasing all the time. This can trap the unwary. Things that are slow in one release can suddenly become fast in the next one. You must be very careful not to write unnatural code just for the sake of short-term performance gains. The introduction of first-generation Just In Time (JIT) compilers has made loops go much faster, but JIT compilers do not speed up method invocations very much, and since a whole class is compiled before it is run, startup time is increased and gets worse as optimization levels rise. As more JIT-based optimizations are perfected, more language features will be accelerated. Sun is working on an incremental compiler technology, known as HotSpot™, which uses a run-time profile of the code to decide which classes and methods to compile. It has quite different performance characteristics than those of a JIT, with a faster startup time and better directed optimization.

On Solaris, there are several versions of Java. Java is upward compatible, but if you use recent features, you cannot go back and run the code on earlier releases. The Java 1.0 specification and its support classes were found to need improvements in some areas. Java 1.1 was based on a lot of user feedback and takes code from several vendors, not just Sun, to provide a much more robust and usable standard that should remain stable for much longer than 1.0.

GPercollator Performance and Size Issues

The GPercollator GUI is shown in Figure 16-22 on page 493. The tool can append many days of data from separate URLs and can display several colored traces of different metrics. The two operations that we timed using Metrognomes in GPercollator are the graphical display update and the data load from URL operation. At present, they seem to run reasonably quickly, but as the amount of data on the display increases, the update slows down. One display option, triggered by an Info button, shows credits, the version, and the Metrognome summaries.

The most CPU-intensive operation is loading a new day's data. Each file contains about 280 rows and 20 to 30 columns of data, mostly numeric. Processing the file is tricky and inefficient, taking up to a second of CPU time. I tried to use the StreamTokenizer, but it doesn't behave the way I want it to when processing numbers. I store the result in a class called a `DataFrame` that contains a Vector of Vectors, which can cope with the variation in type from one column to another. Some data starts with a numeral but is really a string, like the local timezone timestamp: "08:35:20". The `StreamTokenizer` breaks this numeral into two tokens if you let it interpret the number. We force it to pick off space-delimited strings and to check that the whole token is a valid number before converting the data, using `Double(String)`. This conversion operation is inefficient; a comment in the code for the `Double` class points this out. The `StreamTokenizer` contains its own code for parsing numbers, which seems like wasteful duplication but it is much faster. I'm hoping that the performance of `Double(String)` will be fixed for me one day.

The other area of concern is the size of the program. It can load many days' worth of data and then show up to 16 differently colored plot lines on the graph. The process size on Solaris when `GPercollator` is run as an application can reach well over 10 Mbytes. The code size is under 50 Kbytes, but it does require the additional Java WorkShop™ GUI class library `visualrt.zip`, which is about 600 Kbytes. To save downloading this library dynamically each time you start an applet, you can grab a copy and put it on your local `CLASSPATH`. The main memory hog is the array of DataFrames, each containing a Vector of Vectors of Doubles or Strings. I'd like to make it a Vector of arrays of double where possible but haven't yet figured out how. I do trim the Vectors down to size once I have finished reading the file. I tried to find a tool that could pinpoint the memory usage of each object but only found people that agreed with me that it would be a good idea to build one.

The Java WorkShop Performance Analyzer

My summer intern, Graham Hazel, wrote the new Graphical percollator browser (`GPercollator`) with a lot of feedback and a few code fixes from me. You can run it from http://www.sun.com/sun-on-net/www.sun.com/gpercol, and you can also get a tar file of the code from that location. We built `GPercollator` using Java WorkShop 2.0 as the development tool and GUI builder. One feature of Java WorkShop is that it provides a simple menu option that starts the program or applet along with a performance profiler. After the program exits, the profile is loaded and you can see which methods took longest to run. You can also see and traverse the call hierarchy.

When we first tried this, our top routine was an iso8859 character conversion method. Initially, we didn't see it because the profiler shows only your own code. When we looked at the system library code as well, we could see the problem. When we tracked it down, we realized that we were processing the input data without buffering it first. This is a common mistake, and when we wrapped a buffer around the input stream, the processing went a lot faster and that routine dropped way down the list. We also compiled the application with debug turned on to start with, and when we changed to invoke the optimizer, the individual class sizes dropped and we got a reasonable speedup on our classes. Overall performance is dominated by the provided system classes, so the biggest gains come from using the libraries more effectively.

Java WorkShop Profiler Display Examples

I compiled the code with debug and used the old-style input stream methods. This technique is deprecated in Java1.1 but is based on old code I wrote using Java1.0. I started it up as an applet from Java WorkShop, using the profiler button. The tool automatically loaded a data file, and I reloaded it another four times so that the load time would dominate the tool startup time. The initial profile shown in Figure 6-2 does not include system routines.

Figure 6-2   Debug Profile Without System Routines (Times in ms)

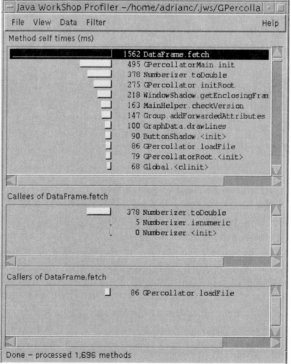

When the system routines are shown, as in Figure 6-3, the top one is the idle time routine
`Object.wait`. Next comes the stream tokenizer, using about 15 seconds of CPU. The
first routine of my own code, `DataFrame.fetch`, is about 1.5 seconds. Input goes via a
`BufferedInputStream`.

Figure 6-3   Debug Profile with System Routines (Times in ms)

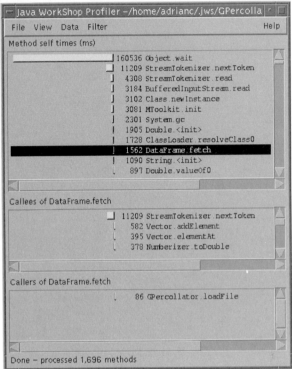

The code is now brought up to date by adding an `InputStreamReader` between the
input stream and the `StreamTokenizer` rather than a `BufferedInputStream`.

```
InputStreamReader is = new InputStreamReader(url.openStream());
StreamTokenizer st = new StreamTokenizer(is);
```

This is part of the improved internationalization of Java1.1. Spot the deliberate mistake—there are now about 200 seconds of overhead with 104 seconds in `ByteToChar8859_1.convert` on its own. It needs a buffer!

Figure 6-4   Debug Profile Times with Unbuffered Input

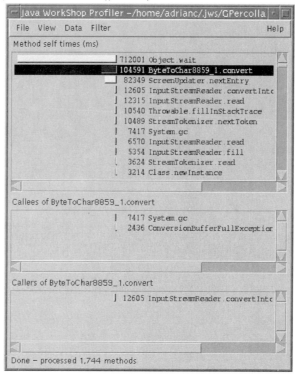

Buffering increases the size of the chunk of data being processed by each method invocation, thus reducing the overall overhead. The new code wraps a `BufferedReader` around the input.

```
BufferedReader br = new BufferedReader(new InputStreamReader(url.openStream()));
StreamTokenizer st = new StreamTokenizer(br);
```

This buffering reduces the overhead to about the same level as the original code, as you can see in Figure 6-5.

Figure 6-5   Debug Profile Times with Java1.1 BufferedReader

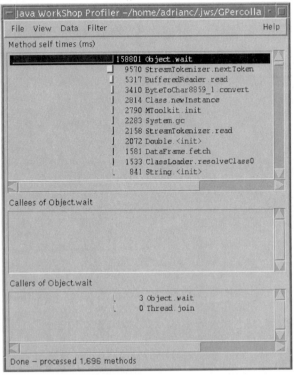

The next step is to turn off the debug compilation flag and turn on the optimizer. The total size of the compiled classes is 54 Kbytes when compiled with debug and 46 Kbytes when compiled with -O.

When the code is run without the profiler with debug code, the average time taken to do a load operation, as measured by Metrognome, is 0.775 seconds. This is a lot faster than the profiled time of 5.47 seconds, so there is quite a large profiler overhead. This result justifies using techniques like the Metrognome class to instrument your own code. When the code was optimized, overall performance did not increase much, but since most of the time is spent in system routines, this performance is not really surprising. If we look at the profile of the optimized code in Figure 6-6, excluding system time, the DataFrame.fetch routine is a lot faster, but that only amounts to a reduction from 1.5

seconds to 1.0 seconds, as the total CPU for five fetch operations. To tune the code further, I need to work on making more efficient use of the system functions. Here is the optimized profile for my own code.

Figure 6-6   Optimized Profile Times

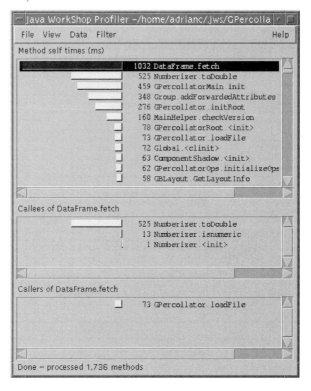

So far, I have managed to build a program that is fast enough to be useful but bigger than I would like. It's a useful test bed for me as I learn more about tuning Java code to make it smaller and faster. The subject is not covered much in the many books on Java, but SunSoft Press is planning a book on Java Performance, by Achut Reddy of the Java WorkShop development team.

When Does "64 Bits" Mean More Performance?

There has recently been a lot of talk about 64-bit systems. There are also claims that 64-bits are faster than 32-bits, and some of the fastest CPUs have 64-bit capability. Can you take advantage of 64-bit operations to make applications run faster? There have been several occasions over the last few years where systems have been marketed as "64 bit," so what is the difference this time?

There is a lot of confusion surrounding this issue. Part of the problem is that it is not always clear what the term "64 bit" is referring to. I'll start with a generic statement of the difference between 32-bit and 64-bit operations. We can then look at the many ways in which "64 bitness" has been applied over the years.

Note – 64-bit operations provide more *capacity* than do 32-bit operations. If you are performing operations that use more than 32 bits, then these operations can be performed with several 32-bit operations or a reduced number of 64-bit operations. If you are performing operations that fit within 32 bits, then they will run on a 64-bit system at the same speed—or sometimes more slowly.

There are two ways to increase computer performance. You can increase the clock rate, and you can increase the amount of work done in each clock cycle. Over the years, microprocessors have steadily increased their clock rates. To do more work per cycle, they have also increased the width of their internal and external buses, arithmetic operations, and memory addresses. Over the last few years of microprocessor evolution, arithmetic operations moved to 64 bits first. Internal and external buses went to 64 bits at the same time or soon afterward. We are now in the final phase, as all the major microprocessor architectures are adding 64-bit addressing capability.

It is important to consider the software implications of the move to 64 bits. In the case of the width of an internal or external bus, no software changes are required. In the case of arithmetic operations, most computer languages already support a full range of 32-bit and 64-bit arithmetic options. If some of the implicit defaults change (such as the size of an int or long in C), then some work is required to port code. In the case of changes in addressing, the implication is a major rewrite of the operating system code, and any applications that use the increased addressing capability will need some work.

SPARC and Solaris Versions

Older SPARC CPUs implement the 32-bit version 8 definition of the architecture. This implementation includes microSPARC™ I, microSPARC II, HyperSPARC™, SuperSPARC, and SuperSPARC II. The very oldest SPARC CPUs rely on the operating system to emulate any missing features so that they can still run SPARC V8 code. Sun's UltraSPARC, and Hal Computer Systems' SPARC64 are the first two 64-bit SPARC V9 implementations. Since SPARC V9 is a full superset of V8 for user mode applications, V8 code runs perfectly well on these new CPUs. In this case, the terms 32 bit and 64 bit refer to the size of the linear address space that can be manipulated directly by the CPU. To take advantage of any SPARC V9 features, the application has to be specially recompiled and will no longer run on SPARC V8 systems. An intermediate specification is known as

V8plus. It is a minor 32 bit upgrade to V8 that includes some of the extended features that are part of V9. Solaris 2.5 through 2.6 support V8plus mode for UltraSPARC-specific code. Additional support for SPARC V9 is due in the next major Solaris release.

64-bit Floating-Point Arithmetic

Floating-point arithmetic is defined by the IEEE 754 standard for almost all systems. The standard includes 32-bit single precision and 64-bit double precision data types. For many years, single precision operations were faster than double precision. This changed when first supercomputers, then microprocessors implemented 64-bit floating point in a single cycle. Since both 32-bit and 64-bit operations take the same time, this was the first opportunity for marketing departments to talk about 64 bitness. It is common for Fortran programmers to assume that a 64-bit system is one where double precision floating point runs at full speed.

The SuperSPARC, HyperSPARC, and UltraSPARC processors all contain floating-point units that can perform double precision multiply and add operations at the same rate as single precision. They can all be counted as full-speed, 64-bit arithmetic processors. The older SPARC CPUs and microSPARC I and II all take longer to perform double precision operations. One of the first microprocessors to be *marketed* as 64 bit, on the basis of arithmetic operations, was the Intel i860 in the early 1990's.

SPARC defines 32 floating-point registers. SPARC V8 defines these as single precision registers. For 64-bit operations, the registers pair up, so there are only 16 double precision floating-point registers. SPARC V8plus and V9 define all the registers to be capable of operating in single, double, or a SPARC V8-compatible paired mode. You get 32 double precision registers in SPARC V9 mode.

In summary: Full-speed, 64-bit, floating-point arithmetic has been available since SuperSPARC shipped in 1992. A full set of 64-bit floating-point registers is available in V8plus mode on UltraSPARC.

64-bit Integer Arithmetic

The C language is usually defined to have `integer` and `long` as 32-bit values on 32-bit systems. To provide for 64-bit arithmetic, an extension to ANSI C creates the 64-bit `long long` type. Some CPU architectures have no support for 64-bit integer operations and use several 32-bit instructions to implement each 64-bit operation. The SPARC architecture has always provided support for 64-bit integers, using pairs of 32-bit registers. Older SPARC chips take many cycles to execute the instructions, but SuperSPARC, HyperSPARC, and UltraSPARC can all efficiently implement 64-bit load store, add, subtract and shift operations.

SPARC V8 defines the integer registers to be 32 bit. In SPARC V9, all the registers support 32-bit, 64-bit and a V8-compatible paired mode. UltraSPARC supports some 64-bit integer operations in V8plus mode and can accelerate 64-bit integer multiplies and divides. A problem is that the data is passed in V8-compatible, paired 32-bit registers, it has to be moved to 64-bit V9 registers to do the multiply, then moved back, so there will be some benefit to integer arithmetic from V9 mode.

In summary: Fast 64-bit integer arithmetic has been available since SuperSPARC shipped in 1992. Integer multiplication and divide is accelerated by V8plus and will be accelerated further by V9.

The Size of `int` and `long`

In an unprecedented display of common sense, the major players in the industry have made some decisions about a 64 bit version of the Unix programming interface. The most basic decision revolves around the question of the size of `int` and `long` when pointers are 64 bits. The agreement is to leave `int` as 32 bits but to make `long` 64 bits. This decision is in line with systems that have been shipping for some time from SGI and Digital. You can prepare your code in advance by always using `long` types to perform pointer arithmetic and avoiding `int`. This approach is known as the LP64 option: `long` and `pointer` types are 64 bit, and `int` remains 32 bit. Correctly written code is portable between ILP32 and LP64 modes without the need to use any conditional compilation options.

Internal Buses or Datapaths

The internal buses that route data inside the CPU are also known as datapaths. If a datapath is only 32-bits wide, then all 64-bit-wide data will take two cycles to transfer. As you might guess, the same CPUs that can perform 64-bit floating-point and integer operations in one clock cycle also have 64-bit internal datapaths, namely, SuperSPARC, HyperSPARC, and UltraSPARC. The wide datapath connects the registers, the arithmetic units, and the load/store unit. Since these CPUs are also superscalar, they can execute several instructions in a single clock cycle.

The permitted combinations of instructions are complex to explain, so I'll just provide one example. In SuperSPARC, the integer register file can accept one 64-bit result or two 32-bit results in each clock cycle. For example, two 32-bit integer adds could be processed—or a single 64-bit integer load. Even though a single 64-bit operation takes the same length of time as a single 32-bit operation, the CPU can sustain twice as many 32-bit operations in the same time period.

6

External Buses and Caches

Data has to get in and out of the CPU somehow. On the way, it gets stored in caches that speed up repeated access to the same data and accesses to adjacent data items in the same cache block. For some applications, the ability to move a lot of data very quickly is the most important performance measure. The width of the cache memory and the buses that connect to caches and to main memory are usually 64 bits and as much as 128 or 256 bits in some CPUs. Does this make these CPUs into something that can be called a 64-, 128-, or 256-bit CPU? Apparently, Solbourne thought so in 1991 when it launched its own SPARC chip design, marketing it as the first 64-bit SPARC chip! In fact, it was the first SPARC chip that had a 64-bit-wide cache and memory interface and was similar in performance to a 33 MHz microSPARC.

All of the microSPARC, SuperSPARC, HyperSPARC, and UltraSPARC designs have caches and main memory interfaces that are at least 64 bits wide. The SuperSPARC on-chip instruction cache uses a 128-bit-wide datapath to load four instructions into the CPU in each cycle. The SuperSPARC and HyperSPARC access memory over the MBus, a 64-bit-wide system interconnect. The MBus-based systems use 144-bit-wide memory SIMMS to provide 128 bits of data plus error correction. It takes two data transfer cycles to pass the data from the SIMM over the MBus to the CPU. For UltraSPARC system designs, the 128-bit interface from the UltraSPARC chip connects to its external cache and continues to a main memory system that provides 256 or 512 bits of data per cycle.

In summary: External interfaces and caches are already at least 64 bits wide. The fastest designs are wider still.

64-bit Addressing

The latest development is 64-bit addressing. Pointers and addresses go from 32-bit quantities to 64-bit quantities. Naturally, the marketing departments are in full swing, and everyone is touting his high-performance, 64-bit capabilities as the solution to the world's problems. In fact, the performance improvements in UltraSPARC and other 64 bit processors come *despite* the 64-bit address support, not because of it!

If we go back to my generic statement at the beginning of this section, you get a performance improvement only when you go from 32 bit to 64 bit if you are exceeding the capacity of 32 bits. In the case of addresses, this implies that you can expect a performance improvement if you are trying to address more than 4 Gbytes of RAM. There is also a downside from the increase in size of every pointer and address. Applications embed many addresses and pointers in code and data. When they all double in size, the application grows, reducing cache hit rates and increasing memory demands. It seems that you can expect a small decrease in performance for everyday applications.

One benchmark that benefits from 64-bit addressing is the TPC-C OLTP database test. High-end results are already using almost 4 Gbytes of RAM for the shared memory database buffer pool. You can expect that as vendors move to 64-bit addressing and can configure more than 4 Gbytes of shared memory, even higher TCP-C results will be posted. This expectation has little relevance to most production systems and is not an issue for the TPC-D Data Warehouse database test, which can use many private data areas and a much smaller shared memory space.

A Hundred Times Faster? Nothing to Scream About!

How does this discussion square up with those Digital advertisements that claimed their computer was 100 times faster because of the use of 64 bits? On page 89 of the July/August 1995 issue of Oracle Magazine (http://www.oramag.com) is a description of the tests that Digital performed. I'll try to briefly summarize what the article says about the "100 times faster" figure.

The comparison was performed by running two tests on the same uniprocessor Digital Alpha 8400 system. That is, both the slow and the 100-times-faster results were measured on a 64-bit machine running a 64-bit Unix implementation. The performance differences were obtained with two configurations of an Oracle "data warehouse style" database running scans, index builds, and queries on each configuration. Of several operations that were evaluated, the slowest was 3 times faster, and the fastest was a five-way join that was 107 times faster.

The special features of the configuration were that the database contained about 6 Gbytes of data, and the system was configured with two different database buffer memory and database block sizes. The slow configuration had 128 Mbytes of shared buffer memory and 2 Kbytes database blocks. The fast configuration had 8.5 Gbytes of shared buffer memory and 32 Kbytes database blocks. For the fast tests, the entire database was loaded into RAM, and for the slow tests, lots of disk I/O in small blocks was performed.

So, what does this have to do with 64 bits versus 32 bits? The performance difference is what you would expect to find, comparing RAM speeds with disk speeds. They greatly magnified the performance difference by using a database small enough to fit in memory on the fast configuration, and only 128 Mbytes of shared buffer memory and smaller blocks on the slow configuration.

To redress the balance, a more realistic test should have a database that is much larger than 6 Gbytes. A few hundred gigabytes is more like the kind of data warehouse that would justify buying a big system. Six Gbytes is no more than a "data shoebox"; it would fit on a single disk drive. The comparison should be performed with the same 32-Kbyte database block size for both tests, and a 3.5-Gbyte shared buffer, not a 128-Mbyte shared buffer, for the "32 bit" configuration. In this updated comparison, I would not be surprised if both configurations became CPU and disk bound, in which case they would both run at essentially the same speed.

At Sun we ran some similar tests, using an E6000 with 16 Gbytes of RAM. We found that we could use UFS filesystem caching to hold a 10-Gbyte database in RAM, for a speedup using OLTP transactions of 350 times faster than a small memory configuration. This did not require any 64-bit address support.

How Does a 32-bit System Handle More Than 4 Gbytes of RAM?

It may have occurred to some of you that Sun currently ships SPARC/Solaris systems than can be configured with more than 4 Gbytes of RAM. How can this be? The answer is that the SuperSPARC memory management unit maps a 32-bit virtual address to a 36-bit physical address, and the UltraSPARC memory management unit maps a 32-bit virtual address to a 44-bit physical address. While any one process can only access 4 Gbytes, the rest of memory is available to other processes and also acts as a filesystem cache. UltraSPARC systems also have a separate 4-Gbyte address space just for the kernel.

The Sun SPARCcenter 2000 supports 5 Gbytes of RAM, and the Cray CS6400 supports 16 Gbytes of RAM. The Sun E6000 supports 30 Gbytes of RAM, and the E10000 supports 64 Gbytes of RAM. It would be possible to make database tables in file system, and to cache up to 64 Gbytes of files in memory on an E10000. There is some overhead mapping data from the filesystem cache to the shared database buffer area, but nowhere near the overhead of disk access.

The Bottom Line

So, where does this leave us on the issue of performance through having 64 bits? In the cases that affect a large number of applications, there is plenty of support for high-performance 64-bit operations in SuperSPARC and HyperSPARC. The performance improvements that UltraSPARC brings are due to its higher clock rate, wider memory interface, and other changes. The full, 64 bit SPARC V9 architecture has an advantage over the intermediate 32 bit V8plus specification because the integer registers can handle 64-bit integer arithmetic more efficiently.

There are a small number of applications that can use 64-bit addresses to access more than 4 Gbytes of RAM to improve performance. There should be good, application source code portability across the 64-bit addressed implementations of several Unix variants.

Most vendors have released details of their 64 bit CPU architecture and have announced or shipped 64 bit implementations. The marketing of 64 bitness is now moving to software considerations like operating system support and application programming interfaces.

The next major release of Solaris will have the *option* of running with a 64-bit address enabled kernel on UltraSPARC systems. In this mode:

- Both 32 bit and 64 bit environments are supported simultaneously for user programs.

- All 32 bit user-level applications will run unchanged. There is complete backward compatibility with applications that run under Solaris 2.6. The majority of the system-supplied commands and utilities will still be running in the 32 bit environment.

- All device drivers will need to be remade to handle 64-bit addresses. Existing device drivers will only work in a 32-bit kernel.

- New 64-bit applications will link to additional 64-bit versions of the supplied system libraries. A 64-bit application cannot link with a 32-bit library.

- The `file` command can be used to identify binaries or libraries.

```
% file /bin/ls
/bin/ls: ELF 32-bit MSB executable SPARC Version 1, dynamically linked, stripped
```

If you are a developer of device drivers and libraries, you should talk to Sun about early access and ISV support programs for the upcoming release, as other users will be dependent upon device and library support.

The white paper, *64-bit Computing in Solaris,* is available at http://www.sun.com/solaris/wp-64bit.

Linker Options and Tuning

Dynamic linking is the default for Solaris 2. It has several advantages and, in many cases, better performance than static linking.

I'll start by explaining how static and dynamic linking operate so that you understand the difference. I'll explain why dynamic linking is preferred, then I'll look at using dynamic linking to improve application performance. The difference between interfaces and implementations is a crucial distinction to make.

- **Interfaces** — Interfaces are designed to stay the same over many releases of the product. That way, users or programmers have time to figure out how to use the interface.

- **Implementations** — The implementation hides behind the interface and does the actual work. Bug fixes, performance enhancements, and underlying hardware differences are handled by changes in the implementation. There are often changes from one release of the product to the next, or even from one system to another running the same software release.

6

Static Linking

Static linking is the traditional method used to combine an application program with the parts of various library routines that it uses. The linker is given your compiled code, containing many unresolved references to library routines. It also gets *archive* libraries (for example, /usr/lib/libm.a) containing each library routine as a separate module. The linker keeps working until there are no more unresolved references and references, then writes out a single file that combines your code and a jumbled-up mixture of modules containing parts of several libraries. The library routines make system calls directly, so a statically linked application is built to work with the kernel's system call interface.

Archive libraries are built with the ar command, and, in older versions of Unix, the libraries had to be processed by ranlib to create an index of the contents for random access to the modules. In Solaris 2, ranlib is not needed; ar does the job properly in the first place. Sun had so many people ask "Where's ranlib?" that in Solaris 2.5, it was put back as a script that does nothing! It acts as a placebo for portable makefiles that expect to find it on every system.

The main problem with static linking is that the kernel system call interface is in itself a dynamic binding, but it is too low level. Once upon a time, the kernel interface defined the boundary between applications and the system. The architecture of the system is now based on abstractions more sophisticated than the kernel system call interface. For example, name service lookups use a different dynamic library for each type of server (files, NIS, NIS+, DNS), and this library is linked to the application at run time.

Performance problems with static linking arise in three areas. The RAM that is wasted by duplicating the same library code in every statically linked process can be very significant. For example, if all the window system tools were statically linked, several tens of megabytes of RAM would be wasted for a typical user and the user would be slowed down a lot by paging. The second problem is that the statically linked program contains a subset of the library routines and they are jumbled up. The library cannot be tuned as a whole to put routines that call each other onto the same memory page. The whole application could be tuned this way, but very few developers take the trouble. The third performance problem is that subsequent versions of the operating system contain better tuned and debugged library routines or routines that enable new functionality. Static linking locks in the old slow or buggy routines and prevents access to the new functionality.

There are a few ways that static linking may be faster. Calls into the library routines have a little less overhead if they are linked together directly, and startup time is reduced because there is no need to locate and load the dynamic libraries. The address space of the process is simpler, so fork(2) can duplicate it more quickly. The static layout of the code also makes run times for small benchmarks more deterministic, so that when the same benchmark is run several times, there will be less variation in the run times. These speedups tend to be larger on small utilities or toy benchmarks, and much less significant for large complex applications.

Dynamic Linking

When the linker builds a dynamically linked application, it resolves all the references to library routines but does not copy the code into the executable. When you consider the number of commands provided with Solaris, it is clear that the reduced size of each executable file is saving a lot of disk space. The linker adds startup code to load the required libraries at run time, and each library call goes through a jump table. The first time a routine is actually called, the jump table is patched to point at the library routine. For subsequent calls, the only overhead is the indirect reference. You can see the libraries that a command depends upon by using the `ldd` command. Shared object libraries have a '.so' suffix and a version number.

```
% ldd /bin/grep
    libintl.so.1 => /usr/lib/libintl.so.1
    libc.so.1 => /usr/lib/libc.so.1
    libw.so.1 => /usr/lib/libw.so.1
    libdl.so.1 => /usr/lib/libdl.so.1
```

These libraries include the main system interface library (`libc.so`), the dynamic linking library (`libdl.so`), wide-character support (`libw.so`), and internationalization support (`libintl.so`). This support raises another good reason to use dynamic linking: statically linked programs may not be able to take advantage of extended internationalization and localization features.

Many of the libraries supplied with Solaris 2 have been carefully laid out so that their internal intercalling patterns tend to reference the minimum possible number of pages. This reference procedure reduces the working-set size for a library and contributes to a significant speedup on small memory systems. A lot of effort has been put into the OpenWindows and CDE window system libraries to make them smaller and faster.

Solaris 1 Compatibility

Many Solaris 1/SunOS 4 applications can be run on Solaris 2 in a binary compatibility mode. A very similar dynamic linking mechanism is also the default in Solaris 1. Dynamically linked Solaris 1 applications link through specially modified libraries on Solaris 2 that provide the best compatibility and the widest access to the new features of the system. Statically linked Solaris 1 applications can run on Solaris 2.3 and later releases by dynamically creating a new kernel system call layer for the process. This solution is a bit slower; moreover, the applications cannot access some of the features of Solaris 2.

There are more problems with access to files that have changed formats, and the applications can only make name lookups via the old name services. Solaris 2.5 adds the capability of running some mixed-mode Solaris 1 applications that are partly dynamic and partly statically linked.

Mixed-Mode Linking

Mixed-mode linking can also be used with Solaris 2 applications. I don't mean the case where you are building an application out of your own archive libraries. Where there is a choice of both archive and shared libraries to link to, the linker will default to use the shared one. You can force some libraries to be statically linked, but you should always dynamically link to the basic system interface libraries and name service lookup library.

Interposition and Profiling

It is possible to interpose an extra layer of library between the application and its regular dynamically linked library. This layer can be used to instrument applications at the library interface. You build a new shared library containing only the routines you wish to interpose upon, then set the LD_PRELOAD environment variable to indicate the library and run your application. Interposition is disabled for setuid programs to prevent security problems.

Internally at Sun, two applications have made heavy use of interposition. One application instruments and tunes the use of graphics libraries by real applications. The other helps automate testing by making sure that use of standard APIs by applications does actually conform to those standards. The API tester is available as a free, unsupported tool from the http://opcom.sun.ca web site.

The LD_PROFILE option allows a gprof format summary of the usage of a library to be generated and accumulated over multiple command invocations. That way, the combined use of a shared library can be measured directly. See the ld(1) manual page for more details. LD_PROFILE is available in Solaris 2.5 and later releases. A new extension in Solaris 2.6 is the sotruss(1) command, which traces calls to shared libraries.

Dynamic Performance Improvements in Solaris 2.5

Several new features of Solaris 2.5 libraries provide a significant performance boost over earlier releases. Dynamically linked applications transparently get these speedups. The standard recommendation is to build applications on the oldest Solaris release that you wish to run on. If you statically link, you miss out on these improvements.

The libraries dynamically figure out whether the SPARC CPU in use has integer multiply and divide support. This support is present in all recent machines but is not available in the old SPARCstation IPX and SPARCstation 2. The new library routines use the instructions if they are there and calculate the result the old way if not. You no longer have to choose whether to run fast or to run optimally on every old SPARC system.

Parts of the standard I/O library (`stdio`) were tuned. This tuning also helps some I/O-intensive Fortran programs.

For UltraSPARC-based systems, a special "platform specific" version of some library routines is interposed over the standard routines. These provide a hardware speedup that triples the performance of `bcopy`, `bzero`, `memcopy`, and `memset` operations. The speedup is transparent as long as the application is dynamically linked.

Dynamic linking is the only way to go. Sun was an early adopter of this technology, but every other vendor now offers shared libraries in some form. Banish static linking from your makefiles and figure out how to take best advantage of the technology.

SunSoft Official Position on Linking Options

by Rob Gingell, SunSoft Chief Scientist.

Using the default linker options provides several important properties:

- **Portability** — Options that aren't universally available are used.

- **Insulation** — By using the default configurations of libraries that are dynamically linked, you are insulated from bugs or limitations in the implementation which would otherwise become part of your program.

- **Evolution** — Related to insulation, the evolution of the shared library implementation may provide to your application performance other benefits which become available simply by running the extant application against the new libraries.

- **Quality** — The dynamic implementation of a library, with its single configuration of modules and capability for being manipulated independent of any application, yields better testing and ultimately better quality. Although any bug fixes found in a dynamic version are also applied to the static implementation, such fixes are not available to application programs without reconstruction of the application. And, the essentially arbitrary combinations of modules possible with archive libraries are not exhaustively tested by us or any other vendor—the combinatorics are simply too vast.

- **Stability** — A property of dynamic linking is that it creates an expression of dependencies between software modules. These dependencies are expressed in terms of the interfaces through which they interact rather than an (often very temporal) relationship based on the status and behavior of the implementation. These relationships can, through emerging tools, be validated in both their static and dynamic behaviors. Thus, a level of application portability higher than one currently enjoys is assured without the need for constant retesting as the implementation behavior changes.

UltraSPARC Compiler Tuning

Compilers have a huge variety of options. Some should be used as a matter of course, some give a big speedup if used correctly, and others can get you into trouble. What are the implications of using the UltraSPARC-specific options, and which options make the most difference to performance?

The answer depends upon your situation. If you are a software vendor, your main concern is likely to be portability and testing costs. With a careful choice of options, you can support a large proportion of the Solaris installed base with very good performance. If you are an end user with source code and some CPU intensive applications that take a long time to run, you may be more interested in getting the very best possible performance from the particular system you have.

Applications are what sells computers. In recognition of this fact, Sun designs its systems to be compatible with preexisting applications. Sun is also concerned about the costs a software vendor incurs to support an application on Solaris. The key is to provide the opportunity for the largest possible volume of sales for a single version of an application.

The installed base of Solaris on SPARC is now between one and two million units. This installed base is not uniform however, as it consists of many different SPARC implementations and operating system releases. It is possible to build applications that work on all these systems, but it is easy to inadvertently build in a dependency on a particular implementation or release.

This section tells you what you can depend upon for maximum coverage of the installed base. It indicates several ways that you can optimize for a particular implementation without becoming incompatible with all the others. It also describes opportunities to optimize further, where performance or functionality may justify production of an implementation-specific version of the product.

Solaris 2.5 contains support for hardware implementations based on the UltraSPARC processor. UltraSPARC is based on an extended SPARC Version 9 instruction set and is completely upward compatible with the installed base of SPARC Version 8 applications. The new Ultra Systems Architecture requires its own specific "sun4u" kernel, as do the previous "sun4m" MBus-based desktop systems and "sun4d" XDBus-based server systems. Correctly written device drivers will work with all these kernels.

Although end users may be concerned about the implications of the new features provided by UltraSPARC, they will find that it operates as just another SPARC chip. If their applications work on microSPARC-, SuperSPARC-, and HyperSPARC-based systems, then they will also work on UltraSPARC. End users may find that over time some application developers will produce versions that are specifically optimized for UltraSPARC.

Some vendors may wish to balance the work required to optimize for UltraSPARC and the likely benefits. A trade-off between several compatibility, performance, and functionality issues can be made. I'm going to clarify the issues and recommend a course of action to follow that allows incremental benefits to be investigated over time.

An Incremental Plan for UltraSPARC Optimization

There are several steps to take; each step should usually be completed before the next step is attempted. After each step is complete, you have the option to productize the application, taking advantage of whatever benefits have been obtained so far. I'll briefly describe the steps, then cover each step in detail.

1. Test and support the existing application on UltraSPARC hardware.

All user mode applications will work. Correctly written device drivers will also work. You should see a substantial performance boost over previous generation SPARC systems.

2. Design for portability.

Review the interfaces that your application depends upon, and review the assumptions you have made about the implementation. Move to portable standard interfaces where possible, and isolate implementation-specific interfaces and code into a replaceable module if possible.

3. Make sure the application uses dynamic linking.

Solaris 2.5 and subsequent releases contain platform-specific, tuned versions of some shared library routines. They are automatically used by dynamically linked programs to transparently optimize for an implementation but will not be used by statically linked programs.

4. Migrate your application to at least SPARCompiler™ 4.0 Release.

You can do this step independently of the OS and hardware testing, but it is a necessary precursor to optimization for UltraSPARC. With no special, platform-specific options, a "generic" binary is produced that will run reasonably well on any SPARC system.

5. Optimize code scheduling for UltraSPARC by using SPARCompilers 4.0.

The optimal sequences of instructions for UltraSPARC can be generated using the same SPARC instructions that current systems use. This is the option that Sun recommends to application developers to try out. Compare the performance of this binary with the one produced at the end of Step 4, both on UltraSPARC machines and any older machines that comprise a significant segment of your user base.

Note – The following optimizations are not backward compatible, and software vendors are *strongly discouraged* from using them. They are intended primarily for end users in the imaging and high-performance computing markets.

---

6. Build an UltraSPARC-only application.

Using the all-out UltraSPARC compile options, you get access to the 32-bit subset of the SPARC V9 instruction set and you double the number of double precision, floating-point registers available. Many programs will see no improvement. A few Fortran programs speed up a great deal. Determine if the benefit of any extra performance outweighs the cost of maintaining two binaries (one for UltraSPARC and one for older machines).

7. Build a VIS instruction set-enabled, device-specific module.

Applications that already implement a device-specific driver module mechanism for access to graphics and imaging accelerators can build a module by using the VIS instruction set extensions. Determine if the benefit of any extra performance outweighs the cost of maintaining an UltraSPARC-specific module or using the standard VIS-optimized XGL and XIL libraries.

Running the Existing Application on UltraSPARC Hardware

All user-mode applications that work on *older* SPARC systems running Solaris 2.5 or later will also work on an UltraSPARC system. Applications that depend upon the kernel architecture may need minor changes or a recompile. If in the past you needed to take into account the difference in kernel architecture between a SPARCstation 2 (sun4c), SPARCstation 20 (sun4m), and a SPARCserver 2000 (sun4d), you may need to be aware of the new features of the UltraSPARC kernel (sun4u).

Comparing Performance

You should collect performance data to compare against older hardware. There is a wide range of speedups for existing unmodified code running on UltraSPARC. A rough guideline for integer applications is that an average speedup is the ratio of clock rate of the SuperSPARC and UltraSPARC CPUs tested (use % **/usr/sbin/psrinfo -v** to check the clock rates). For floating-point applications, the speedup is a bit larger. This ratio does not apply for microSPARC and HyperSPARC. If you get less than you would expect, you may be disk, RAM, or network limited. There are also a few programs that fit entirely in the 1- to 2-Mbyte SuperSPARC cache and don't fit in a 512-Kbyte UltraSPARC cache. If you compare systems with the same sized caches or increase the cache size on UltraSPARC, results will be more predictable. If you get more speedup than you would expect, then you may have been memory bandwidth limited on the older MBus-based machines.

Processor -Specific Dynamic Libraries

Solaris 2.5 and later releases contain platform-specific versions of some library routines. They are automatically used by dynamically linked programs.

The UltraSPARC versions take advantage of VIS instructions for high-speed block move and graphics operations. If you static link to libc, you will not take advantage of the platform-specific versions. When used with Creator graphics, the X server, XGL, and XIL libraries have all been accelerated by means of VIS instruction set extensions and the Creator frame buffer device driver.

Solaris 2.5 libraries automatically use the integer multiply and divide instructions on any platform that has them. This use allows generic binaries to be built for the oldest SPARC Version 7 CPUs (e.g., SPARCstation 2) but to take advantage of the instructions implemented in SPARC Version 8 and subsequent CPUs (e.g., SuperSPARC and UltraSPARC). In Solaris 2.5.1, some additional optimizations use UltraSPARC-specific instructions, for example, to multiply the 64-bit long long type.

The UltraSPARC-specific VIS block move instruction performs a 64-byte transfer that is both cache coherent and nonpolluting. This feature is used by the platform-specific libc bcopy, bzero, memcpy, memmove, memset, memcmp operations. The term "nonpolluting" refers to the fact that data that is moved is not cached. After copying a 1-Mbyte block of data, the CPU cache still holds its original contents, unlike the case with other designs that would have overwritten the cache with the data being moved. On a 168 MHz Ultra 1/170E, large memory-to-memory data moves occur at over 170 Mbytes/s, limited by the 350-Mbyte/s throughput of the single Ultra 1/170 memory bank. Memory-to-Creator frame buffer moves occur at 300 Mbyte/s, limited by the processor interface throughput of 600 Mbyte/s. Faster UltraSPARC systems have even higher data rates. A move involves a read and a write of the data, which is why the data is moved at half the throughput. These operations are about five times faster than a typical SuperSPARC-based system. The Ultra Enterprise Server systems have more memory banks and sustain aggregate rates of 2.5 Gbytes/s on the E6000, and 10.4 Gbytes/s on the E10000.

Migrating Your Application to at Least SPARCompilers 4.2

You can migrate your application independently of the OS and hardware testing, but it is a necessary precursor to optimization for UltraSPARC. SPARCompilers 4.2 improves performance on all platforms by perhaps 10%–30% for CPU-intensive applications. There may be issues with old code written in C++ because the language is evolving; it changes from one release of the compiler to the next, as the compiler tracks the language standard. If you are already using SPARCompilers 3.0 you should have few, if any, problems.

To support the maximum proportion of the installed base, Sun recommends that applications be compiled on the oldest practical release of Solaris. SPARCompilers 4.2 is fully supported on Solaris 2.3 and 2.4, and all code generation options, including UltraSPARC-specific ones, can be used on older releases.

Application vendors who want to ship one binary product for all SPARC Solaris 2 systems and who want the best performance possible on older systems should use the generic compiler options. The options are stated explicitly in Figure 6-7 for clarity. The level of optimization set by x03 generates small, efficient code for general-purpose use. The xdepend option tells the compiler to perform full dependency analysis; it increases compile time (which is why it is not done by default) but can give up to a 40% performance boost in some cases. Try with and without xdepend to quantify the difference on your application. The compiler defaults to xchip=generic xarch=generic; these options tell the compiler that you want to run reasonably well on all SPARC processors. Adding the options to your makefile, even though they are defaults, makes it clear that this is what you are trying to do.

Figure 6-7   Recommended Compiler Options to Optimize for All SPARC Systems

```
cc -x03 -xdepend -xchip=generic -xarch=generic *.c
f77 -x03 -xdepend -xchip=generic -xarch=generic *.f
```

For the C compiler, the commonly used -O option defaults to -x02. The extra optimization invoked by -x03 is only problematic in device driver code that does not declare memory mapped device registers as volatile. The Fortran compiler already maps -O to -x03.

Optimizing Code Scheduling for UltraSPARC

The optimal *sequences* of instructions for UltraSPARC can be generated by means of the same SPARC instructions that current systems use.

To understand what I mean by this statement, let's take the analogy of an Englishman talking to an American. If the Englishman speaks normally, the American will be able to understand what is being said, probably with a little extra effort (and the comment "I *do* love your accent..."). If the Englishman tries harder and says exactly the same words with an American accent, they may be more easily digested, but other English people listening in will still understand them. The equivalent of full optimization would be to talk in an American accent, with American vocabulary, phrasing and colloquialisms (let's touch base before we go the whole nine yards, y'all). The words mostly look familiar but only make sense to other Englishmen familiar with American culture.

The sequencing level of optimization avoids using anything that cannot be understood by older SPARC chips, but instructions are put in the most optimal sequence for fast execution on UltraSPARC.

Compare the performance of this binary with the one produced in the previous stage, both on UltraSPARC machines and any older machines that constitute a significant segment of your customer base. Performance on UltraSPARC platforms can show a marked improvement. The xchip=ultra option puts instructions in the most efficient order for execution by UltraSPARC. The xarch=generic option is the default, but it is good to explicitly state your intentions. The generic option tells the compiler to use only instructions that are implemented in all SPARC processors.

Figure 6-8   Recommended Compiler Options to Optimize for UltraSPARC

```
cc -xO3 -xdepend -xchip=ultra -xarch=generic *.c
f77 -xO3 -xdepend -xchip=ultra -xarch=generic *.f
```

These options are intended to be realistic and safe settings for use on large applications. Higher performance can be obtained from more aggressive optimizations if assumptions can be made about numerical stability and the code "lints" cleanly.

The Implications of Nonportable Optimizations

Up to this point, the generated code will run on any SPARC system. The implications and trade-off implicit in following the above recommendations are that a single copy of your application will be portable across all SPARC-based environments. The performance and capability of the CPU will be maximized by the run-time environment, but some performance benefits unique to specific implementations may not be available.

The subsequent optimizations are not backward compatible, and software vendors are *strongly discouraged* from using them unless they are *only* interested in running on UltraSPARC-based systems.

There may be cases in which tuning an application to a specific processor or specific system platform is worth more to you than losing generality and portability. If you use UltraSPARC-specific compiler options, you should be aware that you will either need to create a different binary or continue to support an existing one, to run on older systems.

Building an UltraSPARC-Only Application

The primary interest in UltraSPARC-specific code comes from Fortran end users in the high-performance computing (HPC) marketplace. It is common for HPC end users to have access to the source code of their applications and to be interested in reducing the very long run times associated with large simulation and modeling computations by any means available. There is also relatively less interest in running the code on older, slower SPARC systems. The commonly used SPECfp95 benchmarks contain several examples of this kind of application.

There are also situations where the UltraSPARC system is embedded in a product manufactured by an OEM. Since there is complete control over the hardware and the software combination, it is possible to optimize the two very closely together without concern for backward compatibility.

Using the all-out UltraSPARC compile options, you get access to the 32 bit subset of the SPARC V9 instruction set, and you increase the number of double precision, floating-point registers from 16 to 32. This combination of V8 and V9 is known as the V8plus specification; it is enabled with the –xarch=v8plus compiler option. No source code changes will be required, but the code will no longer run on older systems. You can identify the binaries by using the file command.

```
% f77 -o prog -fast -xO4 -depend -xchip=ultra -xarch=v8plus *.f
% file prog
prog:        ELF 32-bit MSB executable SPARC32PLUS Version 1, V8+ Required,
dynamically linked, not stripped
```

Compare the performance of this binary with one using –xarch=v8 instead of –xarch=v8plus. Determine if the benefit of any extra performance outweighs the cost of maintaining two binaries.

You can expect a speedup from –xarch=v8plus if your code is double precision, vectorizable, and the compiler can unroll do loops. A large number of temporary variables need to be stored in registers in the unrolled loop to hide load-use latencies. A version of the Linpack DP1000 benchmark went 70% faster with this option, which is the most you can expect. Single precision code shows no speedup because there are already 32 single precision registers. The performance improvement obtained by the above options with –xarch=v8 and –xarch=v8plus on each component of SPECfp92 varied from 0% in several cases to a best case of 29%. The geometric mean increased by 11%. It is rare for one loop to dominate an application, so a mixture of accelerated and unaccelerated loops gives rise to a varying overall speedup. The potential for speedup increases with the highest optimization levels and should increase over time as the compiler improves its optimization strategies.

I have not seen a significant speedup on typical C code. In general, don't waste time trying xarch=v8plus with the C compiler.

The compiler's code generator has many more options. The ones I have described are the ones that usually make a significant difference. In a few cases, I have found that profile feedback can be useful as well. The highest level of optimization is now -xO5, and it should only ever be used in conjunction with a collected profile so the code generator knows which loops to optimize aggressively. You simply compile with xO4 and xprofile=collect, run the program, then recompile with xO5 and xprofile=use. This is easy to set up on small benchmarks but is more tricky with a large application.

Numerical Computation Issues

Floating-point arithmetic suffers from rounding errors and denormalization (when very small differences occur), and results can vary if you change the order of evaluation in an expression. The IEEE 754 standard ensures that all systems which comply fully with the standard get exactly the same result when they use the same evaluation order. It does add overhead, and it is not used on older architectures such as the IBM S390 mainframe, the Digital VAX, and the Cray supercomputer. If you perform the same calculation on all of these systems, you will get results that are different. Algorithms that have high numerical stability produce very similar results; poor algorithms can produce wildly variable results. By default, the Sun compiler is very conservative and sticks to IEEE 754. You can configure IEEE 754 rounding modes and other options.

If you are working with code that is known to be numerically stable and produces good results on a Cray, VAX, mainframe, *and* IEEE 754-based system, then you can run faster by turning off some of the expensive IEEE 754 features, using the fsimple and fnonstd options. The fsimple option tells the compiler that you want it to assume that simple mathematical transformations are valid, and fnonstd turns off rounding and underflow checks. The Sun compiler manual set comes with a *Numerical Computation Guide*, which explains these issues in much more detail.

Building a VIS Instruction Set-Enabled, Device-Specific Module

Going back to my analogy, if the Englishman and the American start to talk in dense industry jargon, full of acronyms, no one else will have a clue what they are discussing, but the communication can be very efficient. The UltraSPARC processor implements an extension to the SPARC V9 instruction set that is dedicated to imaging and graphical operations that is a bit like talking in jargon—it is highly nonportable.

Some applications already have device-specific modules that provide access to accelerators for imaging and graphics operations. These modules can code directly to the VIS instruction set. For pixel-based operations, the VIS instructions operate on four or more pixels at a time. This approach translates into a four times speedup for large filtering, convolution, and table lookup operations. Several developers are reporting this kind of gain over the base-level UltraSPARC performance for applications like photographic image manipulation and medical image processing. For the first time, MPEG2 video and audio stream decoding can be performed at full speed and resolution with no add-on hardware. The best way to access VIS is via the standard graphics (XGL) and imaging (XIL) libraries, which are optimized to automatically take advantage of the available CPU and framebuffer hardware.

Sun MicroElectronics has created a VIS developers kit and several libraries of routines that implement common algorithms and is promoting the use of VIS for specialized new-media applications.The libraries are available from http://www.sun.com/sparc.

Summary

The implication of following Sun's general recommendations is that a single copy of your application will be portable across all SPARC-based environments. The inherent performance and capability of the processor will be maximized by the run-time environment, but some performance benefits unique to specific implementations may not be available to your application.

A white paper on compiler optimization techniques, called *UltraComputing: How to Achieve Peak Performance from Solaris Applications*, is available at http://www.sun.com/solaris/wp-ultracomputing/ultracomputing.pdf.

Applications

This chapter discusses the ways by which a user running an application on a Sun machine can control or monitor on a program-by-program basis.

Tools for Applications

When you don't have the source code for an application, you must use special tools to figure out what the application is really doing.

Tracing Applications

Applications make frequent calls into the operating system, both to shared libraries and to the kernel via system calls. System call tracing has been a feature of Solaris for a long time, and in Solaris 2.6 a new capability allows tracing and profiling of the shared library interface as well.

Tracing System Calls With `truss`

The Solaris 2 `truss` command has many features not found in the original SunOS 4 `trace` command. It can trace child processes, and it can count and time system calls and signals. Other options allow named system calls to be excluded or focused on, and data structures can be printed out in full. Here is an excerpt showing a fragment of `truss` output with the `-v` option to set verbose mode for data structures, and an example of `truss  -c` showing the system call counts.

```
% truss -v all cp NewDocument Tuning
execve("/usr/bin/cp", 0xEFFFFB28, 0xEFFFFB38)  argc = 3
open("/usr/lib/libintl.so.1", O_RDONLY, 035737561304) = 3
mmap(0x00000000, 4096, PROT_READ, MAP_SHARED, 3, 0) = 0xEF7B0000
fstat(3, 0xEFFFF768)= 0
    d=0x0080001E i=29585 m=0100755 l=1  u=2      g=2      sz=14512
    at = Apr 27 11:30:14 PDT 1993   [ 735935414 ]
    mt = Mar 12 18:35:36 PST 1993   [ 731990136 ]
    ct = Mar 29 11:49:11 PST 1993   [ 733434551 ]
    bsz=8192  blks=30    fs=ufs
....
```

```
% truss -c cp NewDocument Tuning
syscall       seconds    calls  errors
_exit           .00        1
write           .00        1
open            .00       10       4
close           .01        7
creat           .01        1
chmod           .01        1
stat            .02        2       1
lseek           .00        1
fstat           .00        4
execve          .00        1
mmap            .01       18
munmap          .00        9
memcntl         .01        1
                ----      ---     ---
sys totals:     .07       57       5
usr time:       .02
elapsed:        .43
```

An especially powerful technique is to log all the file open, close, directory lookup, read, and write calls to a file, then figure out what parts of the system the application is accessing. A trivial example is shown in Figure 7-1.

Figure 7-1   Example Using `truss` to Track Process File Usage

```
% truss -o /tmp/ls.truss -topen,close,read,write,getdents ls / >/dev/null
% more /tmp/ls.truss
open("/dev/zero", O_RDONLY)                          = 3
open("/usr/lib/libw.so.1", O_RDONLY)                 = 4
close(4)                                             = 0
open("/usr/lib/libintl.so.1", O_RDONLY)              = 4
close(4)                                             = 0
open("/usr/lib/libc.so.1", O_RDONLY)                 = 4
close(4)                                             = 0
open("/usr/lib/libdl.so.1", O_RDONLY)                = 4
close(4)                                             = 0
open("/usr/platform/SUNW,Ultra-2/lib/libc_psr.so.1", O_RDONLY) = 4
close(4)                                             = 0
close(3)                                             = 0
open("/", O_RDONLY|O_NDELAY)                         = 3
getdents(3, 0x0002D110, 1048)                        = 888
getdents(3, 0x0002D110, 1048)                        = 0
close(3)                                             = 0
write(1, " T T _ D B", 5)                            = 5
write(1, "\n b i n\n c d r o m\n c".., 251)          = 251
```

Tracing Shared Library Calls With `sotruss`

The dynamic linker has many new features. Read the `ld(1)` manual page for details. Two features that help with performance tuning are tracing and profiling. The Solaris 2.6 and later `sotruss` command is similar in use to the `truss` command and can be told which calls you are interested in monitoring. Library calls are, however, much more frequent than system calls and can easily generate too much output.

Profiling Shared Libraries with `LD_PROFILE`

The `LD_PROFILE` profiling option was new in Solaris 2.5. It allows the usage of a shared library to be recorded and accumulated from multiple commands. This data has been used to tune window system libraries and `libc.so`, which is used by every command in the system. Profiling is enabled by setting the `LD_PROFILE` environment variable to the name of the library you wish to profile. By default, profile data accumulates in `/var/tmp`, but the value of `LD_PROFILE_OUTPUT`, if it has one, can be used to set an alternative directory. As for a normal profile, `gprof` is used to process the data. Unlike the case for a normal profile, no special compiler options are needed, and it can be used on any program.

For all these utilities, security is maintained by limiting their use on set-uid programs to the root user and searching for libraries only in the standard directories.

Timing

The C shell has a built-in `time` command that is used during benchmarking or tuning to see how a particular process is running. In Solaris 2, the shell does not compute all this data, so the last six values are always zero.

```
% time man madvise
...
0.1u 0.5s 0:03 21% 0+0k 0+0io 0pf+0w
%
```

In this case, 0.1 seconds of user CPU and 0.5 seconds of system CPU were used in 3 seconds elapsed time, which accounted for 21% of the CPU. Solaris 2 has a `timex` command that uses system accounting records to summarize process activity, but the command works only if accounting is enabled. See the manual pages for more details.

Process Monitoring Tools

Processes are monitored and controlled via the /proc interface. In addition to the familiar ps command, a set of example programs is described in the proc(1) manual page, including ptree, which prints out the process hierarchy, and ptime, which provides accurate and high-resolution process timing.

```
% /usr/proc/bin/ptime man madvise
real        1.695
user        0.005
sys         0.009
```

Note the difference in user and system time. I first ran this command a very long time ago on one of the early SPARC machines and, using time, recorded the output. The measurement above using ptime was taken on a 300 MHz UltraSPARC, and by this measurement, the CPU resources used to view the manual page have decreased by a factor of 43, from 0.6 seconds to 0.014 seconds. If you use the csh built-in time command, you get zero CPU usage for this measurement on the fast system because there is not enough resolution to see anything under 0.1 seconds.

The ptime command uses microstate accounting to get the high-resolution measurement. It obtains but fails to print out many other useful measurements. Naturally, this can be fixed by writing a script in SE to get the missing data and show it all. The script is described in "msacct.se" on page 485, and it shows that many process states are being measured. Microstate accounting itself is described in "Network Protocol (MIB) Statistics via Streams" on page 403. The msacct.se command is given a process ID to monitor and produces the output shown in Figure 7-2.

Figure 7-2   Example Display from msacct.se

```
% se msacct.se 354
Elapsed time        3:29:26.344   Current time Tue May 23 01:54:57 1995
User CPU time           5.003     System call time          1.170
System trap time        0.004     Text pfault sleep         0.245
Data pfault sleep       0.000     Kernel pfault sleep       0.000
User lock sleep         0.000     Other sleep time       9:09.717
Wait for CPU time       1.596     Stopped time              0.000
```

The Effect of Underlying Filesystem Type

Some programs are predominantly I/O intensive or may open and close many temporary files. SunOS has a wide range of filesystem types, and the directory used by the program could be placed onto one of the following types.

Unix File System (UFS)

The standard file system on disk drives is the Unix File System, which in SunOS 4.1 and on is the Berkeley Fat Fast File system. Files that are read stay in RAM until a RAM shortage reuses the pages for something else. Files that are written are sent out to disk as described in "Disk Writes and the UFS Write Throttle" on page 172, but the file stays in RAM until the pages are reused for something else. There is no special buffer cache allocation, unlike other Berkeley-derived versions of Unix. SunOS4 and SVR4 both use the whole of memory to cache pages of code, data, or I/O. The more RAM there is, the better the effective I/O throughput is.

UFS with Transaction Logging

The combination of Solaris 2.4 and Online: DiskSuite™ 3.0 or later releases supports a new option to standard UFS. Synchronous writes and directory updates are written sequentially to a transaction log that can be on a different device. The effect is similar to the Prestoserve, nonvolatile RAM cache, but the transaction log device can be shared with another system in a dual-host, failover configuration. The filesystem check with fsck requires that only the log is read, so very large file systems are checked in a few seconds.

Tmpfs

Tmpfs is a RAM disk filesystem type. Files that are written are never put out to disk as long as some RAM is available to keep them in memory. If there is a RAM shortage, then the pages are stored in the swap space. The most common way to use this filesystem type in SunOS 4.X is to uncomment the line in /etc/rc.local for mount /tmp. The /tmp directory is accelerated with tmpfs by default in Solaris 2.

One side effect of this feature is that the free swap space can be seen by means of df. The tmpfs file system limits itself to prevent using up all the swap space on a system.

```
% df /tmp
Filesystem          kbytes    used   avail capacity  Mounted on
swap                 15044     808   14236     5%     /tmp
```

The NFS Distributed Computing File System

NFS is a networked file system coming from a disk on a remote machine. It tends to have reasonable read performance but can be poor for writes and is slow for file locking. Some programs that do a lot of locking run very slowly on NFS-mounted file systems.

Cachefs

New since Solaris 2.3 is the cachefs filesystem type. It uses a fast file system to overlay accesses to a slower file system. The most useful way to use cachefs is to mount, via a local UFS disk cache, NFS file systems that are mostly read-only. The first time a file is accessed, blocks of it are copied to the local UFS disk. Subsequent accesses check the NFS attributes to see if the file has changed, and if not, the local disk is used. Any writes to the cachefs file system are written through to the underlying files by default, although there are several options that can be used in special cases for better performance. Another good use for cachefs is to speed up accesses to slow devices like magneto-optical disks and CD-ROMs.

When there is a central server that holds application binaries, these binaries can be cached on demand at client workstations. This practice reduces the server and network load and improves response times. See the `cfsadmin` manual page for more details. Solaris 2.5 includes the `cachefsstat`(1M) command to report cache hit rate measures.

Caution – Cachefs should not be used to cache-shared, NFS-mounted mail directories and can slow down access to write-intensive home directories.

Veritas VxFS File System

Veritas provides the VxFS file system for resale by Sun and other vendors. Compared to UFS, it has several useful features. UFS itself has some features (like disk quotas) that were not in early releases of VxFS, but VxFS is now a complete superset of all the functions of UFS.

VxFS is an *extent-based* file system, which is completely different from UFS, an *indirect, block-based* file system. The difference is most noticeable for large files. An indirect block-based file system breaks the file into 8-Kbyte blocks that can be spread all over the disk. Additional 8-Kbyte indirect blocks keep track of the location of the data blocks. For files of over a few Mbytes, double indirect blocks are needed to keep track of the location of the indirect blocks. If you try to read a UFS file sequentially at high speed, the system has to keep seeking to pick up indirect blocks and scattered data blocks. This seek procedure limits the maximum sequential read rate to about 30 Mbytes/s, even with the fastest CPU and disk performance.

In contrast, VxFS keeps track of data by using extents. Each extent contains a starting point and a size. If a 2-Gbyte file is written to an empty disk, it can be allocated as a single 2-Gbyte extent. There are no indirect blocks, and a sequential read of the file reads an extent record, then reads data for the complete extent. In November 1996, Sun published a benchmark result, using VxFS on an E6000 system, where a single file was read at a sustained rate of about 1 Gbyte/s. The downside of large extents is that they fragment the disk. After lots of files have been created and deleted, it could be difficult to allocate a large file efficiently. Veritas provides tools with VxFS that de-fragment the data in a file system by moving and merging extents.

The second advanced feature provided is snapshot backup. If you want a consistent online backup of a file system without stopping applications that are writing new data, you tell VxFS to snapshot the state of the file system at that point. Any new data or deletions are handled separately. You can back up the snapshot, freeing the snapshot later when the backup is done and recovering the extra disk space used by the snapshot.

Direct I/O Access

In some cases, applications that access very large files do not want them buffered by the normal filesystem code. They can run better with raw disk access. Raw access can be administratively inconvenient because the raw disk partitions are hard to keep track of. The simplest fix for this situation is to use a volume management GUI such as the Veritas VxVM to label and keep track of raw disk space. A need for many small raw files could still be inconvenient, so options are provided for direct I/O access, unbuffered accesses to a file in a normal file system. The VxFS extent is closer in its on-disk layout to raw, so the direct I/O option is reasonably fast. A limitation is that the VxFS extent can only be used for block-aligned reads and writes. The VxFS file system can be used with Solaris 2.5.1.

UFS `directio` is a new feature in Solaris 2.6; see `mount_ufs`(1M). UFS still suffers from indirect blocks and fragmented data placement, so `directio` access is less efficient than raw. A useful feature is that `directio` reverts automatically to buffer any unaligned access to an 8-Kbyte disk block, allowing a mixture of direct and buffered accesses to the same file.

Customizing the Execution Environment

The execution environment is largely controlled by the shell. There is a command which can be used to constrain a program that is hogging too many resources. For `csh` the command is `limit`; for `sh` and `ksh` the command is `ulimit`. A default set of Solaris 2 resource limits is shown in Table 7-1.

Users can increase limits up to the hard system limit. The superuser can set higher limits. The limits on *data size* and *stack size* are 2 Gbytes on recent machines with the SPARC Reference MMU but are limited to 512 Mbytes and 256 Mbytes respectively by the sun4c MMU used in the SPARCstation 1 and 2 families of machines.

Table 7-1   Resource Limits

Resource Name	Soft User Limit	Hard System Limit
cputime	unlimited	unlimited
filesize	unlimited	unlimited
datasize	524280–2097148 Kbytes	524280–2097148 Kbytes
stacksize	8192 Kbytes	261120–2097148 Kbytes
coredumpsize	unlimited	unlimited
descriptors	64	1024
memorysize (virtual)	unlimited	unlimited

In Solaris 2.6, you can increase the `datasize` to almost 4 Gbytes. The `memorysize` parameter limits the size of the virtual address space, not the real usage of RAM, and can be useful to prevent programs that leak from consuming all the swap space.

Useful changes to the defaults are those made to prevent core dumps from happening when they aren't wanted:

```
% limit coredumpsize 0
```

To run programs that use vast amounts of stack space:

```
% limit stacksize unlimited
```

File Descriptor Limits

To run programs that need to open more than 64 files at a time, you must increase the file descriptor limit. The safest way to run such a program is to start it from a script that sets the soft user limit higher or to use the `setrlimit` call to increase the limit in the code:

```
% limit descriptors 256
```

The maximum number of descriptors in SunOS 4.X is 256. This maximum was increased to 1024 in Solaris 2, although the standard I/O package still handles only 256. The definition of FILE in `/usr/include/stdio.h` has only a single byte to record the underlying file descriptor index. This data structure is so embedded in the code base that it cannot be increased without breaking binary compatibility for existing applications. Raw file descriptors are used for socket-based programs, and they can use file descriptors above the `stdio.h` limit. Problems occur in mixed applications when stdio tries to open a file when sockets have consumed all the low-numbered descriptors. This situation can occur if the name service is invoked late in a program, as the `nsswitch.conf` file is read via stdio.

At higher levels, additional problems occur. The `select`(3C) system call uses a bitfield with 1024 bits to track which file descriptor is being selected. It cannot handle more than 1,024 file descriptors and cannot be extended without breaking binary compatibility. Some system library routines still use `select`, including some X Window System routines. The official solution is to use the underlying `poll`(2) system call instead. This call avoids the bitfield issue and can be used with many thousands of open files. It is a very bad idea to increase the default limits for a program unless you know that it is safe. Programs should increase limits themselves by using `setrlimit`. If the programs run as root, they can increase the hard limit as well as implement daemons which need thousands of connections.

The only opportunity to increase these limits comes with the imminent 64-bit address space ABI. It marks a clean break with the past, so some of the underlying implementation limits in Solaris can be fixed at the same time as 64-bit address support is added. The implications are discussed in "When Does "64 Bits" Mean More Performance?" on page 134.

Databases and Configurable Applications

Examples of configurable applications include relational databases, such as Oracle, Ingres, Informix, and Sybase, that have large numbers of configuration parameters and an SQL-based configuration language. Many CAD systems and Geographical Information systems also have sophisticated configuration and extension languages. This section concentrates on the Sun-specific database issues at a superficial level; the subject of database tuning is beyond the scope of this book.

Hire an Expert!

For serious tuning, you either need to read all the manuals cover-to-cover and attend training courses or hire an expert for the day. The black box mentality of using the system exactly the way it came off the tape, with all parameters set to default values, will get you going, but there is no point in tuning the rest of the system if it spends 90 percent of its time inside a poorly configured database. Experienced database consultants will have seen most problems before. They know what to look for and are likely to get quick results. Hire them, closely watch what they do, and learn as much as you can from them.

7

Basic Tuning Ideas

Several times I have discovered database installations that have not even started basic tuning, so some basic recommendations on the first things to try may be useful. They apply to most database systems in principle, but I will use Oracle as an example, as I have watched over the shoulders of a few Oracle consultants in my time.

Increasing Buffer Sizes

Oracle uses an area of shared memory to cache data from the database so that all Oracle processes can access the cache. In old releases, the cache defaults to about 400 Kbytes, but it can be increased to be bigger than the entire data set if needed. I recommend that you increase it to at least 20%, and perhaps as much as 50% of the total RAM in a dedicated database server if you are using raw disk space to hold the database tables. There are ways of looking at the cache hit rate within Oracle, so increase the size until the hit rate stops improving or until the rest of the system starts showing signs of memory shortage. Avoiding unnecessary random disk I/O is one of the keys to database tuning.

Solaris 2 implements a feature called *intimate shared memory* by which the virtual address mappings are shared as well as the physical memory pages. ISM makes virtual memory operations and context switching more efficient when very large, shared memory areas are used. In Solaris 2, ISM is enabled by the application when it attaches to the shared memory region. Oracle 7 and Sybase System 10 and later releases both enable ISM automatically by setting the SHM_SHARE_MMU flag in the shmat(2) call. In Solaris 2.6 on UltraSPARC systems, the shared memory segment is mapped by use of large (4 Mbyte) pages of contiguous RAM rather than many more individual 8-Kbyte pages. This mapping scheme greatly reduces memory management unit overhead and saves on CPU system time.

Using Raw Disk Rather Than File Systems

During installation, you should create several empty disk partitions or stripes, spread across as many different disks and controllers as possible (but avoiding slices zero and two). You can then change the raw devices to be owned by Oracle (do this by using the VxVM GUI if you created stripes) and, when installing Oracle, specify the raw devices rather than files in the file system to hold the system, redo logs, rollback, temp, index, and data table spaces.

File systems incur more CPU overhead than do raw devices and can be much slower for writes due to inode and indirect block updates. Two or three blocks in widely spaced parts of the disk must be written to maintain the file system, whereas only one block needs to be written on a raw partition. Oracle normally uses 2 Kbytes as its I/O size, and the file system uses 8 Kbytes, so each 2-Kbyte read is always rounded up to 8 Kbytes, and each 2 Kbyte write causes an 8-Kbyte read, 2-Kbyte insert and 8-Kbyte write sequence. You can avoid this excess by configuring an 8-Kbyte basic block size for Oracle, but this solution wastes memory and increases the amount of I/O done while reading the small items that are most common in the database. The data will be held in the Oracle SGA as well as in the main memory filesystem cache, thus wasting RAM. Improvements in the range of 10%–25% or more in database performance and reductions in RAM requirements have been reported after a move from file systems to raw partitions. A synchronous write accelerator, see "Disk Write Caching" on page 173, should be used with databases to act as a database log file accelerator.

If you persist in wanting to run in the file system, three tricks may help you get back some of the performance. The first trick is to turn on the "sticky bit" for database files. This makes the inode updates for the file asynchronous and is completely safe because the file is preallocated to a fixed size. This trick is used by swap files; if you look at files created with `mkfile` by the root user, they always have the sticky bit set.

```
# chmod +t table
# ls -l table
-rw------T   1 oracle dba 104857600 Nov 30 22:01 table
```

The second trick is to use the direct I/O option discussed in "Direct I/O Access" on page 161. This option at least avoids the memory double buffering overhead. The third trick is to configure the temporary tablespace to be raw; there is often a large amount of traffic to and from the temporary tablespace, and, by its nature, it doesn't need to be backed up and it can be re-created whenever the database starts up.

Fast Raw Backups

You can back up small databases by copying the data from the raw partition to a file system. Often, it is important to have a short downtime for database backups, and a disk-to-disk transfer is much faster than a backup to tape. Compressing the data as it is copied can save on disk space but is very CPU intensive; I recommend compressing the data if you have a high-end multiprocessor machine. For example,

```
# dd if=/dev/rsd1d bs=56k | compress > /home/data/dump_rsd1d.Z
```

Balance the Load over All the Disks

The log files should be on a separate disk from the data. This separation is particularly important for databases that have a lot of update activity. It also helps to put indexes and temporary tablespace on their own disks or to split the database tables over as many disks as possible. The operating system disk is often lightly used, and on a very small two-disk system, I would put the log files on the system disk and put the rest on its own disk. To balance I/O over a larger number of disks, stripe them together by using Veritas VxVM, Solstice DiskSuite, or a hardware RAID controller. Also see "Disk Load Monitoring" on page 183.

Which Disk Partition to Use

If you use the first partition on a disk as a raw Oracle partition, then you will lose the disk's label. If you are lucky, you can recover this loss by using the "search for backup labels" option of the `format` command, but you should put a file system, swap space, Solstice DiskSuite state database, or small, unused partition at the start of the disk.

On modern disks, the first part of the disk is the fastest, so, for best performance, I recommend a tiny first partition followed by a database partition covering the first half of the disk. See "Zoned Bit Rate (ZBR) Disk Drives" on page 205 for more details and an explanation.

The Effect of Indices

When you look up an item in a database, your request must be matched against all the entries in a (potentially large) table. Without an index, a full table scan must be performed, and the database reads the entire table from disk in order to search every entry. If there is an index on the table, then the database looks up the request in the index and knows which entries in the table need to be read from disk. Some well-chosen indexes can dramatically reduce the amount of disk I/O and CPU time required to perform a query. Poorly designed or untuned databases are often underindexed. The problem with indexes is that when an indexed table is updated, the index must be updated as well, so peak database write performance can be reduced.

How to Configure for a Large Number of Users

One configuration scenario is for the users to interact with the database through an ASCII forms-based interface. The forms' front end is usually created by means of high-level, application-builder techniques and in some cases can consume a large amount of CPU. This forms front end inputs and echoes characters one at a time from the user over a direct serial connection or via telnet from a terminal server. Output tends to be in large blocks of text. The operating system overhead of handling one character at a time over telnet is quite high, and when hundreds of users are connected to a single machine, the Unix kernel consumes a lot of CPU power moving these characters around one at a time. In Solaris 2.5, the telnet and rlogin processing was moved into the kernel by means of streams modules. The old implementation uses a pair of daemon processes, one for each direction of each connection; the in-kernel version still has a single daemon for handling the protocol, but data traffic does not flow through the daemon. This configuration has been tested with up to 3,000 direct connections. Higher numbers are normally configured by a Transaction Processing Monitor, such as Tuxedo.

The most scalable form of client-server configuration is for each user to have a workstation or a PC running the forms-based application and generating SQL calls directly to the backend server. Even more users can be connected this way because they do not login to the database server and only a socket connection is made.

Database Tuning Summary

When you are tuning databases, it is useful to realize that in many cases the sizing rules that have been developed by database software vendors in the past do not scale well to today's systems. In the mainframe and minicomputer worlds, disk I/O capacity is large, processors are slow, and RAM is expensive. With today's systems, the disk I/O capacity, CPU power, and typical RAM sizes are all huge, but the latency for a single disk read is still very slow in comparison. It is worth trading off a little extra CPU overhead and extra RAM usage for a reduction in I/O requirements, so don't be afraid to experiment with database buffer sizes that are much larger than those recommended in the database vendors' documentation.

The next chapter examines the reasons why disk I/O is often the problem.

Disks 8

The art of tuning modern computer systems is becoming more and more dependent on disk I/O tuning. This chapter shows how to measure and interpret the disk utilization figures and suggests ways of improving I/O throughput. The chapter describes many different types of disks and controllers found on Sun systems and also talks about tuning file systems and combining disks into stripes and mirrors.

Disk Workloads

There are six different basic access patterns. Read, write, and update operations can either be sequential or randomly distributed. Sequential read and write occur when files are copied and created or when large amounts of data are being processed. Random read and write can occur in indexed database reads or can be due to page-in or page-out to a file. Update consists of a read-modify-write sequence and can be caused by a database system committing a sequence of transactions in either a sequential or random pattern. When you are working to understand or improve the performance of your disk subsystem, spend some time working out which of these categories you expect to be most important.

You cannot automatically tell which processes are causing disk activity; the kernel does not collect this information. You may be able to work out where the workload comes from by looking at how an application was installed, but often you must resort to using truss on a process or the TNF tracing system. See "Tracing Applications" on page 155. The use of TNF to trace disk activity is covered in "The Solaris 2.5 Trace Capability" on page 188. I would like to see a way of getting I/O activity on a per-file descriptor basis added to Solaris, but until that happens, application-specific instrumentation is all you have. Databases such as Oracle can collect and report data on a per-tablespace basis, so if you can map the tablespaces to physical disks, you can tell what is going on programmatically. This kind of collection and analysis is performed by the BGS Best/1 performance modeling tool, so that changes in disk workload can be modeled.

Sequential versus Random Access

Some people are surprised when they read that a disk is capable of several megabytes per second but they see a disk at 100 percent capacity providing only a few hundred kilobytes per second for their application. Most disks used on NFS or database servers spend their time serving the needs of many users, and the access patterns are essentially random. The time taken to service a disk access is taken up by seeking to the correct cylinder and waiting for the disk to go around. In sequential access, the disk can be read at full speed for a complete cylinder, but in random access, the average seek time quoted for the disk and the average rotational latency should be allowed for between each disk access. The random data rate is thus very dependent on how much data is read on each random access. For file systems, 8 Kbytes is a common block size, but for databases on raw disk partitions, 2 Kbytes is a common block size. Sybase always issues 2-Kbyte reads, but Oracle tries to cluster 2-Kbyte accesses together whenever possible to get a larger transfer size.

For example, a 5400 rpm disk takes 11 ms for a random seek, waits on average 5.6 ms for the disk to rotate to the right sector, and takes about 0.5 ms for a 2-Kbyte transfer and 2 ms for an 8-Kbyte transfer (ignoring other SCSI bus transfers and software overhead). If the disk has a sequential data rate of 4168 Kbytes/s, then the data rate in Kbytes/s for a random seek and a single transfer is thus:

$$throughput = \frac{transfersize}{seektime + rotatetime + transfertime}$$

$$throughput = \frac{transfersize}{seektime + \dfrac{60}{rpmx2} + \dfrac{transfersize}{datarate}}$$

$$throughput\ for\ 2\text{-Kbyte transfers} = \frac{2}{0.011 + 0.0056 + \dfrac{2}{4168}} = \frac{2}{0.017} = 118 Kbytes/s\ @\ 17ms$$

$$throughput\ for\ 8\text{-Kbyte transfers} = \frac{8}{0.011 + 0.0056 + \dfrac{8}{4168}} = \frac{8}{0.019} = 432 Kbytes/s\ @\ 19ms$$

$$throughput\ for\ 56\text{-Kbyte transfers} = \frac{56}{0.011 + 0.0056 + \dfrac{56}{4168}} = \frac{56}{0.030} = 1864 Kbytes/s\ @\ 30ms$$

$$throughput\ for\ 1024\text{-Kbyte transfers} = \frac{1024}{0.011 + 0.0056 + \dfrac{1024}{4168}} = \frac{1024}{0.262} = 2834 KBbytes/s\ @\ 262ms$$

The service time for each access is the denominator, and in milliseconds you can see that it increases from 17 ms for a 2-Kbyte I/O to 262 ms for a 1024-Kbyte I/O. The optimum size appears to be around 64 to 128 Kbytes because the throughput is high, but the service time is still quite reasonable.

These calculations do not include time spent processing the disk request and filesystem code in the operating system (under a millisecond); the time spent waiting in a queue for other accesses to be processed and sent over the SCSI bus; and the time spent inside the disk's on-board controller waiting for other accesses to be processed.

Anything that can be done to turn random access into sequential access or to increase the transfer size will have a significant effect on the performance of a system. *This is one of the most profitable areas for performance tuning.* You can greatly increase the throughput of your disk subsystem by increasing I/O size and reducing the number of seeks.

Disk Reads and Read Caching

A disk read is normally synchronous. The application stops running until the read is complete. In some cases, a thread block or an asynchronous read (aioread(3)) call is used, and a read may be caused by a prefetch for information that has not been requested yet, but these are not the normal cases. The perceived performance of a system is often critically dependent on how quickly reads complete. When the system reads data for the first time, the system should cache that data in case it is needed again. This caching should use the shared memory area for a database using raw disk or should use the file system cache in main memory. That way, if the data is needed again, no read need occur. *It is pointless putting large amounts of memory inside a hardware RAID controller and trying to cache reads with it*; the first read will miss the cache, and subsequent references to the data in main memory will never involve the disk subsystem. Data that is needed quickly but infrequently will be purged from all the caches between accesses. An application can avoid this purge by telling the database to keep the data resident or telling the kernel to lock the file in memory, but there is no way for an application to tell a disk subsystem what data should be cached for reads. The size of the cache for reads should be limited to what is needed to prefetch data for sequential accesses. Modern SCSI disks contain 512 Kbytes to 2 Mbytes of RAM each and perform read prefetch automatically.

Disk subsystems from vendors such as EMC and Encore (now a Sun product) with gigabytes of NVRAM have been developed in the mainframe marketplace, where memory prices are high and memory capacities are (relatively) low. Disk subsystems have also been sold with Unix systems that have had limited memory capacity, such as IBM AIX and HP's HP-UX. Until late 1997, AIX and HP-UX were limited to less than 4 Gbytes of total main memory. This problem does not apply to SPARC systems running Solaris 2. Sun's largest server systems shipped with 5 Gbytes of RAM in 1993, 30 Gbytes in 1996, and 64 Gbytes in 1997, and these systems use it all automatically as a file cache. Sun also has comparable or lower costs per gigabyte of RAM compared to disk subsystem caches. With the Solaris 2.6, 32-bit address space limitation, multiple 4-Gbyte processes can coexist with unlimited amounts of cached file data. Database shared memory is limited in Solaris 2.6 to 3.75 Gbytes, but with a 64-bit address space version of Solaris due in 1998, much more can be configured.

If you are trying to decide whether to put an extra few gigabytes of RAM in main memory or into a big disk subsystem controller, I would always recommend that you put it into main memory. You will be able to read the RAM with submicrosecond latency and far higher throughput. You will reduce the total number of reads issued, saving on CPU time, interrupt rates, and I/O bus loadings. And it will probably cost less.

The best disk subsystem for reads is therefore the one with the lowest latency for initial reads of uncached data and highest throughput for sequential transfers. With care taken to cache data effectively in a large main memory, the directly connected Sun A5000 FC-AL disk subsystem meets these criteria.

Disk Writes and the UFS Write Throttle

Disk writes are a mixture of synchronous and asynchronous operations. Asynchronous writes occur during writes to a local file system. Data is written to memory and is flushed out to the file 30 seconds later by the fsflush daemon. Applications can ask for a file to be flushed by calling fsync(3C); closing the file causes a synchronous flush of the file. When a process exits, all of its open files are closed and flushed; this procedure can take a while and may cause a lot of disk activity if many processes exit at the same time.

There is also a limit to the amount of unflushed data that can be written to a file. This limitation is implemented by the UFS write throttle algorithm, which tries to prevent too much memory from being consumed by pending write data. For each file, between 256 Kbytes and 384 Kbytes of data can be pending. When there are less than 256 Kbytes (the low-water mark ufs_LW), it is left to fsflush to write the data. If there are between 256 Kbytes and 384 Kbytes (the high-water mark ufs_HW), writes are scheduled to flush the data to disk. If more than 384 Kbytes are pending, then when the process attempts to write more, it is suspended until the amount of pending data drops below the low-water mark. So, at high data rates, writes change from being asynchronous to synchronous, and this change slows down applications. The limitation is per-process, per-file.

When you want to write quickly to a file and the underlying disk subsystem can cope with the data rate, you may find that it is impossible to drive the disk to maximum throughput because the write throttle kicks in too early. An application that performs large writes at well-spaced intervals will also be affected, and if the writes are too big for the write throttle, the process will be suspended while the data is written. The high- and low-water marks are global, tunable values that apply to the whole system, but, if necessary, they can be increased. To experiment with different levels without rebooting between trials, you can change the values online with immediate effect by using adb, but take care to increase the high-water mark first, so that it is always greater than the low-water mark. Then, add modified values to /etc/system so that they take effect after a reboot; for example, to increase them by a factor of four, use the entries shown in Figure 8-1. A side effect of this change is that a larger number of I/O requests will be queued for a busy file. This technique can increase throughput, particularly when a wide disk stripe is being used, but it also increases the average I/O response time because the queue length increases. Don't increase the thresholds too far or disable the write throttle completely, and remember that more RAM will be used by every process that is writing data, so don't increase the thresholds unless you can spare the extra memory required.

Figure 8-1   Example Tunable Settings for the UFS Write Throttle

```
set ufs:ufs_HW=1572864
set ufs:ufs_LW=1048576
```

A simple way to see the effect of this change is to time the mkfile command—I use the Solaris 2.5 and later - ptime(1) command because its precision is higher than that of the usual time(1) command—and watch how long it takes to write a 1-Mbyte file (to a fairly slow disk) with the default write throttle, compared to one where the low-water mark is changed to 1 Mbyte. The effect is that the total CPU time used is the same, but the elapsed time is greatly reduced—from 0.588s to 0.238s.

```
# /usr/proc/bin/ptime mkfile 1M JUNK ; rm JUNK

real        0.588
user        0.020
sys         0.155
# adb -kw
physmem3e39
ufs_HW/W0t1572864
ufs_HW:0x60000=0x180000
ufs_LW/W0t1048576
ufs_LW:0x40000=0x100000
^D
# /usr/proc/bin/ptime mkfile 1M JUNK ; rm JUNK

real        0.238
user        0.020
sys         0.156
```

Disk Write Caching

A large proportion of disk write activity is synchronous. This synchronicity delays application processes in cases where the writes are to raw disk partitions, are file system metadata such as UFS inodes and directory entries, are to files opened explicitly for synchronous writes, are incoming NFS write requests, and in cases where the UFS write throttle has cut in. In many cases, the same disk block is rewritten over and over again, as in inode or directory updates. In other cases, many small sequential writes to the same file are performed. Synchronous writes are used because they safely commit the data to disk, ensuring the integrity of log files, databases, and file systems against data loss in the event of a power outage or system crash.

To get good performance, we need a way to safely commit writes to NVRAM, where they can be coalesced into fewer and larger writes and don't cause applications to wait, rather than doing all the writes to disk. Nonvolatile RAM can be placed in the memory system, on an I/O bus, or in the disk subsystem controller. For simplicity and speed, the best place for the NVRAM is in the main memory system. This is an option on the SPARCstation 20 and SPARCserver 1000/SPARCcenter2000 generation of systems, using the Prestoserve software and NVSIMM hardware. In the current product range, the Netra NFS 1.2 is a packaged, high-performance, NFS server option. It uses a 32-Mbyte NVRAM card that fits in the I/O bus (initially SBus, but PCI eventually) to accelerate a modified version of Solstice DiskSuite. The problem with these solutions is that if the system goes down, the cached data is held inside the system. With the move to large, clustered, high-availability solutions, it is important to provide shared access to the NVRAM from multiple systems, so it must be placed in a multiply connected disk subsystem. This placement incurs the penalty of a SCSI operation for each write, but since the write is stored in NVRAM and immediately acknowledged, this solution is still around ten times faster than a write to disk.

The biggest benefit of disk array controllers comes from enabling fast writes and coalescing writes to reduce the number of physical disk writes. The amount of NVRAM required to perform write caching effectively is quite small. If sufficient throughput is available to drain the NVRAM to the underlying disks, a few megabytes are enough. The first-generation SPARCstorage Array only has 4 Mbytes of NVRAM but provides good fast-write performance. The second generation with 16 Mbytes has plenty. The Sun RSM2000 hardware RAID subsystem needs 64 to 128 Mbytes so that it can cache complete stripes to optimize RAID5 writes effectively. There is no need for more memory than this to act as a write cache. There is also no point in keeping the written data in the array controller to act as a read cache because a copy of the data is likely to still be in the main memory system, which is a far more effective read cache.

If you do not have any NVRAM in your configuration, a reasonable substitute is a completely dedicated log disk, using Solstice DiskSuite's metatrans option with UFS, or the Veritas VxFS file system. A dedicated log disk with a log file that spans only a few cylinders (100 Mbyes at most) will always have very short seeks, and you can lower write times to very few milliseconds, even for mirrored log disks, as long as you resist the temptation to put something on the unused parts of the log disks.

The best disk subsystem for write-intensive workloads is the RSM2000 with its hardware RAID controller. An array controller with NVRAM is promised as a future option for the A5000 FC-AL array; until then, you will need to use log-based file systems with the A5000, so make sure you have a couple of disks dedicated to making a small mirrored log—*with no other activity at all on those disks.* The best option is to configure a mixture of the two disk subsystems, so that you can have the fastest reads and the fastest writes as appropriate.

Physical Disk Combinations

It is easy to overload a single disk with too many accesses. When some disks have much higher loads than others, this situation is known as *high I/O skew.* The solution is to spread the accesses over several disks. There are many ways to do this.

- Functionally split the usage of the disk, moving some kinds of data or tablespaces to another disk. This approach works well only if the workload is very stable and repeatable. It is often used in benchmarks but is not useful in the real world.

- Split usage by users, perhaps on a mail server, locating mail files on different disks according to the user name. This approach again assumes a stable average workload.

- Allocate data space on a round-robin basis over a number of disks as it is requested. Subsequent accesses will spread the load. This is the way that Solaris 2 handles multiple swap space files. The approach is crude but works well enough with application-specific support.

- Concatenate several disks so that data is spread over all the disks. Accesses to "hot" data tend to overload just one of the concatenated disks. This situation occurs when a file system is grown online by addition of extra space at the end.

- Interlace disks in a stripe, so that the "hot" data is spread over several disks. The optimal size of the interlace is application dependent. If the interlace size is too large, then the stripe accesses will not be balanced and one disk may become much busier than the others. If the interlace size is too small, then a single small access will need data from more than one disk, and this is slower than a single read. Start at 128 Kbytes (it is often a happy medium); then, if you want to experiment, try both larger and smaller interlace values. A disadvantage of stripes is that they cannot be grown online. Another stripe must be concatenated on the end. Also, if a disk fails, the whole stripe fails.

- Stripe with mirrored protection so that all the data is stored in two places. This approach has a small additional performance impact on writes: two writes must be issued and both must complete, so the slowest disk determines the performance. This is known as RAID 1+0, or RAID 10. It is the fastest safe storage configuration.

- Stripe with parity protection. Parity distributed over all the disks is known as RAID5. It uses fewer disks but is either far slower than mirroring or uses an expensive hardware RAID5 controller that may cost more than the extra disks that mirroring would require!

If the controller is busy talking to one disk, then another disk has to wait; the resulting contention increases the latency for all the disks on that controller. As the data rate of one disk approaches the bus bandwidth, the number of disks you should configure on each bus is reduced. Fiber channel transfers data independently in both directions at the same time and so handles higher loads with less contention.

For sequential accesses, there is an obvious limit on the aggregate bandwidth that can be sustained by a number of disks. For random accesses, the bandwidth of the SCSI bus is much greater than the aggregate bandwidth of the transfers, but queuing effects increase the latency of each access as more disks are added to each SCSI bus. If you have too many disks on the bus, you will tend to see high `wait` values in `iostat -x` output. The commands queue in the device driver as they wait to be sent over the SCSI bus to the disk.

RAID and Disk Arrays

Disks can be logically combined in several ways. You can use hardware controllers and two different software packages.

The SPARCstorage Array appears to the system as 30 disks on a single controller that are then combined by means of software. Other disk array subsystems combine their disks, using a fixed-configuration hardware controller so the disk combination appears as fewer very big disks.

The term RAID stands for *Redundant Array of Inexpensive Disks,* and several levels have been defined to cover the possible configurations. The parity-based RAID configurations are a solution to the problem of low cost, high availability, but do not give as good performance as lots of independent mirrored disks. Here is a useful quote:

> *Fast, cheap, safe; pick any two.*

This book is about performance, so if I start with *fast*, then to be *fast and cheap*, I just use lots of disks; and to be *fast and safe*, I use twice as many and mirror them. If performance is not the main concern, then a RAID5 combination is *cheap and safe*.

Hardware RAID controllers containing large amounts of NVRAM, such as Sun's RSM2000 product, are in themselves fairly expensive items, but they can be used to create fast and safe combinations. The best performance comes when most operations occur to or from NVRAM. Sustained high throughput usually saturates the controller itself, internal buses, or the connection from the system to the hardware RAID unit. One approach is to increase the amount of NVRAM in the RAID controller. This approach increases the ability to cope with short-term bursts, but diminishing returns soon set in. For the write caching and coalescing required to make RAID5 operations efficient, the 64–128 Mbytes provided by the RSM2000 are plenty. Read caching is best handled elsewhere. If you need to cache a few gigabytes of data for reads, you should add extra memory to the system itself, where it can be accessed at full speed and where the operating system and applications can decide what should be cached. Don't put the extra memory in the RAID controller where there is no control over what gets cached and where a relatively slow SCSI bus is in the way.

Large disk arrays such as the EMC and the Sun/Encore SP-40 units are configured with many connections to the system. This configuration helps throughput, but the basic latency of a SCSI request is the same and is hundreds of times slower than a main memory request. Smaller arrays like the RSM2000 have two 40-Mbyte/s connections to the server, and many RSM2000 arrays can be connected to a system, increasing throughput and write cache proportionally as disk capacity is added. Much higher performance can be obtained from multiple RSM2000 subsystems than from a single larger system with the same disk capacity.

The EMC Symmetrix has become quite common on big Sun server configurations. The Encore SP40 is a similar product on a feature-by-feature basis but is less well known due to the smaller market presence of Encore. This situation is about to change—Sun has purchased the storage business of Encore and will soon be selling the SP40 in direct competition with EMC. Since benchmarks have shown that a single RSM2000 is capable of higher performance than an EMC (and probably also an SP40), it is clear that the attraction of these disk subsystems is not primarily performance driven. Their feature set is oriented toward high serviceability, automatically dialing out to report a problem, and heterogeneous connectivity, linking simultaneously to mainframes and multiple Unix systems. Where a lot of sharing is going on, there is a case for putting a larger cache in the disk subsystem so that writes from one system can be cached for read by another system. This form of read caching is much slower than host-based caching but does centralize the cache. This class of system typically supports up to 4 Gbytes of cache.

A new naming scheme from Sun refers to the RSM2000 as the A3000, the new FC-AL subsystem as the A5000, and the SP40 as the A7000. All three disk subsystems will eventually have 100 Mbyte/s fiber channel capability and can be connected via fiber channel switches into an "enterprise networked storage subsystem." Clustered systems that need to share access to the same disk subsystem to run parallel databases can use these switches to have many systems in the cluster.

Disk Configuration Trade-off

Let's say you're setting up a large server that replaces several smaller ones so it will handle a bit of everything: NFS, a couple of large databases, home directories, number crunching, intranet home pages. Do you just make one big file system and throw the lot in, or do you need to set up lots of different collections of disks?

Several trade-offs need to be made, and there is no one solution. The main factors to balance are the administrative complexity, resilience to disk failure, and the performance requirements of each workload component.

There are two underlying factors to take into account: the filesystem type and whether the access pattern is primarily random or sequential access. I've shown these factors as a two-by-two table, with the typical workloads for each combination shown (see Table 8-1). I would combine NFS, home directories, and intranet home pages into the random access filesystem category. Databases have less overhead and less interaction with other workloads if they use separate raw disks. Databases that don't use raw should be given their own filesystem setup, as should number-crunching applications that read/write large files.

Table 8-1   Workload Characteristics

Workloads	Random	Sequential
Raw disk	Database indexes	Database table scans
File system	Home directories	Number crunching

We need to make a trade-off between performance and complexity. The best solution is to configure a small number of separate disk spaces, each optimized for a type of workload. You can get more performance by increasing the number of separate disk spaces, but if you have fewer, it is easier to be able to share the spare capacity and add more disks in the future without having to go through a major reorganization. Another trade-off is between cost, performance, and availability. You can be fast, cheap, or safe; pick one, balance two, but you can't have all three. One thing about combining disks into an stripe is that the more disks you have, the more likely it is that one will fail and take out the whole stripe.

If each disk has a mean time between failure (MTBF) of 1,000,000 hours, then 100 disks have a combined MTBF of only 10,000 hours (about 60 weeks). If you have 1,000 disks, you can expect to have a failure every six weeks *on average*. Also note that the very latest, fastest disks are much more likely to fail than disks that have been well debugged over an extended period, regardless of the MTBF quoted on the specification sheet. Most Sun disks have an MTBF of around 1,000,000 hours. Failure rates in the installed base are monitored and, in most cases, improve on the quoted MTBF. Problems sometimes occur when there is a bad batch of disks. A particular customer may have several disks from the bad batch and experience multiple failures, while many other customers have very few failures. Bad batches and systematic problems are caught during testing, and Sun's Enterprise Test Center normally contains around 50 terabytes of disk undergoing maximum system configuration tests. For example, prior to the launch of the A5000, which has FC-AL connections all the way to a new kind of disk, tens of terabytes of FC-AL disks were running in the Enterprise Test Center for many months.

There are two consequences of failure: one is loss of data, the other is downtime. In some cases, data can be regenerated (from database indexes, number-crunching output, or backup tapes), so if you can afford the time it takes to restore the data and system failure is unlikely to happen often, there is no need to provide a resilient disk subsystem. In that case, you can configure for the highest performance. If data integrity or high availability is important, there are two common approaches: mirroring and parity (typically RAID5). Mirroring affords the highest performance, especially for write-intensive workloads but requires twice as many disks for its implementation. Parity uses one extra disk in each stripe to hold the redundant information required to reconstruct data after a failure. Writes require read-modify-write operations, and there is the extra overhead of calculating the parity. Sometimes, the cost of a high-performance RAID5 array controller exceeds the cost of the extra disks you would need to do simple mirroring. To achieve high performance, these controllers use nonvolatile memory to perform write-behind safely and to coalesce adjacent writes into single operations. Implementing RAID5 without nonvolatile memory will give you *very* poor write performance. The other problem with parity-based arrays is that when a disk has failed, extra work is needed to reconstruct the missing data and performance is seriously degraded.

Choosing Between Solstice DiskSuite and Veritas VxVM

Small configurations and ones that do not have any NVRAM in the disk subsystem should use Solstice DiskSuite. It is bundled with the server licence for Solaris, and it has the metatrans logging filesystem option that substitutes for NVRAM. It is also simpler to use for small configurations.

Large configurations and those that have NVRAM in the disk subsystem should use VxVM. It is bundled with the SPARCstorage Array, and it is easier to use and has fewer limitations for large configurations. To get a logging file system, you must also use the optional VxFS file system, although NVRAM provides a high-performance log for database raw disk accesses. VxFS is better than UFS for very large files, large directories, high throughput, and features like snapshot backup.

It is quite possible to use both volume managers on the same system, with DiskSuite handling logging for UFS file systems, and VxVM handling large raw database tables.

Setting Up a Disk for Home, NFS, and the Web

I assume that the file system dedicated to home directories, NFS, and web server home pages is mostly read intensive and that some kind of array controller is available (a SPARCstorage Array or RSM2000) that has nonvolatile memory configured and enabled. Note that SPARCstorage Arrays default to having NVRAM disabled. You use the ssaadm command to turn on fast writes. The nonvolatile fast writes greatly speed up NFS response times for writes, and, as long as high throughput applications do not saturate this file system, it is a good candidate for a RAID5 configuration. The extra resilience saves you from data loss and keeps the end users happy, without wasting disk space on mirroring. The default UFS filesystem parameters should be tuned slightly, inasmuch as there is no need to waste 10% on free space and almost as much on inodes. I would configure 1% or 2% free space (default is 10%) and 8-Kbyte average file size per inode (default is 2 Kbytes) unless you are configuring a file system that is under 1 Gbyte in size. The latest Solaris release automatically reduces the free space percentage when large file systems are created.

```
# newfs -i 8192 -m 1 /dev/raw_big_disk_device
```

You create the `raw_big_disk_device` itself by combining groups of disks, using the RSM2000's RM6 configuration tool or Veritas VxVM, into RAID5 protected arrays, then concatenating the arrays to make the final file system. To extend the filesystem size in the future, make up a new group of disks into a RAID5 array and extend the file system onto it. You can grow a file system online if necessary, so there is no need to rebuild the whole array and restore it from backup tapes. Each RAID5 array should contain between 5 and 30 disks. I've personally used a 25-disk RAID5 setup on a SPARCstorage Array. For highest performance, keep the setup to the lower end of this range and concatenate more smaller arrays. We have found that a 128-Kbyte interlace is optimal for this largely random access workload. Solstice DiskSuite (SDS) cannot concatenate or extend RAID5 arrays, so if you are using SDS, make one big RAID5 array and save/restore the data if the array needs to grow.

Another issue to consider is the filesystem check required on reboot. If the system shut down cleanly, `fsck` can tell that it is safe to skip the check. If the system went down in a power outage or crash, tens of minutes to an hour or more could be required to check a really huge file system. The solution is to use a logging file system, where a separate disk stores all the changes. On reboot, `fsck` reads the log in just a few seconds, and the checking is done. With SDS, this method is set up by means of a "metatrans" device and the normal UFS. In fact, a preexisting SDS-hosted file system can have the metatrans log added without any disruption to the data. With the Veritas Volume Manager, you must use the Veritas file system, VxFS, because the logging hooks in UFS are SDS specific. For good performance, put the log on a dedicated disk, and, for resilience, mirror the log. In extreme cases, the log disk might saturate and require striping over more than one disk. In very low usage cases, you can situate the log in a small partition at the start of a data disk, but this solution can hurt performance a lot because the disk heads seek between the log and the data.

An example end result is shown in Table 8-2. To extend the capacity, you would make up another array of disks and concatenate it. There is nothing to prevent you making each array a different size, either. Unless the log disk maxes out, a mirrored pair of log disks should not need to be extended.

Table 8-2   Concatenated RAID5 Configuration Example

Log 1	Log 2

Array 1	Array 1	Array 1	Array 1	Array 1	Array 1	Array 1	Array 1	Array 1	Array 1
Array 2	Array 2	Array 2	Array 2	Array 2	Array 2	Array 2	Array 2	Array 2	Array 2
Array 3	Array 3	Array 3	Array 3	Array 3	Array 3	Array 3	Array 3	Array 3	Array 3

Setting Up a Disk for High-Performance Number Crunching

High-throughput applications like number crunching that do large, high-speed, sequential reads and writes should be set up to use a completely separate collection of disks on their own controllers. In most cases, data can be regenerated if there is a disk failure, or occasional snapshots of the data can be compressed and archived into the home directory space. The key thing is to off-load frequent I/O-intensive activity from the home directories into this high-performance "scratch pad" area. Configure as many fast-wide (20 MB/s) or Ultra-SCSI (40 MB/s) disk controllers as you can. Each disk should be able to stream sequential data at between 5 and 10 Mbytes/s, so don't put too many controllers on each bus. Nonvolatile memory in array controllers may help in some cases, but it may also get in the way. The cost may also tempt you to use too few controllers. A large number of SBus SCSI interfaces is a better investment for this particular workload.

If you need to run at sustained rates of more than 20–30 Mbytes/s of sequential activity on a single file, you will run into problems with the default UFS file system. The UFS indirect block structure and data layout strategy work well for general-purpose accesses like the home directories but cause too many random seeks for high-speed, sequential performance. The Veritas VxFS file system is an extent-based structure, which avoids the indirect block problem. It also allows individual files to be designated as "direct" for raw unbuffered access. This designation bypasses the problems caused by UFS trying to cache all files in RAM, which is inappropriate for large sequential access files and stresses the pager. It is possible to get close to the theoretical limit of the I/O buses and backplane of a machine with a carefully setup VxFS configuration and a *lot* of fast disks.

Sun's HPC 2.0 software comes with a high-performance, parallel, distributed file system called PFS. The programming interface to PFS is via the Message Passing Interface I/O (MPI-IO) library, or the High Performance Fortran (HPF) language, which allows large data arrays to be distributed and written in parallel over a cluster. PFS uses its own on-disk format that is optimized for this purpose.

A log-based file system may slow down high-speed sequential operations by limiting them to the throughput of the log. It should log only synchronous updates, like directory changes and file creation/deletion, and it is unlikely to be overloaded, so use a log to keep reboot times down.

Setting Up a Disk for Databases

Database workloads are very different again. Reads may be done in small random blocks (when looking up indexes) or large sequential blocks (when doing a full table scan). Writes are normally synchronous for safe commits of new data. On a mixed workload system, running databases through the file system can cause virtual memory "churning" because of the high levels of paging and scanning associated with filesystem I/O. This activity can affect other applications adversely, so where possible, use raw disks or direct unbuffered I/O on a file system that supports it, such as UFS (a new feature for Solaris 2.6) and VxFS.

Both Oracle and Sybase default to a 2-Kbyte block size. A small block size keeps the disk service time low for random lookups of indexes and small amounts of data. When a full table scan occurs, the database may read multiple blocks in one operation, causing larger I/O sizes and sequential patterns.

Databases have two characteristics that are greatly assisted by an array controller that contains nonvolatile RAM. One characteristic is that a large proportion of the writes are synchronous and are on the critical path for user-response times. The service time for a 2-Kbyte write is often reduced from about 10–15 ms to 1–2 ms. The other characteristic is that synchronous sequential writes often occur as a stream of small blocks, typically of only 2 Kbytes at a time. The array controller can coalesce multiple adjacent writes into a smaller number of much larger operations, and that group can be written to disk far faster. Throughput can increase by as much as three to four times on a per-disk basis.

Data integrity is important, but some sections of a database can be regenerated after a failure. You can trade off performance against availability by making temporary tablespaces and perhaps indexes out of wide, unprotected stripes of disks. Tables that are largely read-only or that are not on the critical performance path can be assigned to RAID5 stripes. Safe, high-performance writes should be handled by mirrored stripes.

The same basic techniques described in previous sections can be used to configure the arrays. Use concatenations of stripes—unprotected, RAID5, or mirrored—with a 128-Kbyte interlace.

A Last Word

I have scratched the surface of a large and possibly contentious subject here. I hope this information gives you the basis for a solution. The important thing is that I divided the problem into subproblems by separating the workloads according to their performance characteristics. Next, I proposed a solution for each, based upon an appropriate balance of performance, cost, and availability. FInally, I implemented distinct blocks of disks configured to support each workload.

Disk Load Monitoring

If a system is under a heavy I/O load, then the load should be spread across as many disks and disk controllers as possible. To see what the load looks like, use the iostat command or one of the SE toolkit variants.

Output Formats and Options for iostat

The iostat command produces output in many forms. The iostat -x variant provides extended statistics and is easier to read when a large number of disks are being reported, since each disk is summarized on a separate line (see Figure 8-2). The values reported are the number of transfers and kilobytes per second, with read and write shown separately; the average number of commands waiting in the queue; the average number of commands actively being processed by the drive; the I/O service time; and the percentages of the time that commands were waiting in the queue; and commands that were active on the drive.

Figure 8-2   iostat -x Output

```
% iostat -txc 5
                          extended disk statistics       tty          cpu
disk   r/s  w/s   Kr/s   Kw/s wait actv  svc_t  %w  %b  tin tout us sy wt id
fd0    0.0  0.0   0.0    0.0  0.0  0.0    0.0   0   0    0   77 42  9  9 39
sd0    0.0  3.5   0.0   21.2  0.0  0.1   41.6   0  14
sd1    0.0  0.0   0.0    0.0  0.0  0.0    0.0   0   0
sd3    0.0  0.0   0.0    0.0  0.0  0.0    0.0   0   0
                          extended disk statistics       tty          cpu
disk   r/s  w/s   Kr/s   Kw/s wait actv  svc_t  %w  %b  tin tout us sy wt id
fd0    0.0  0.0   0.0    0.0  0.0  0.0    0.0   0   0    0   84 37 17 45  1
sd0    0.0 16.8   0.0  102.4  0.0  0.7   43.1   2  61
sd1    0.0  0.0   0.0    0.0  0.0  0.0    0.0   0   0
sd3    0.0  1.0   0.0    8.0  0.0  0.1  114.3   2   4
```

Disk configurations have become extremely large and complex on big server systems. The maximum configuration E10000 supports several thousand disk drives, but dealing with even a few hundred is a problem. When large numbers of disks are configured, the overall failure rate also increases. It can be hard to keep an inventory of all the disks, and tools like Solstice Symon depend upon parsing messages from syslog to see if any faults are reported. The size of each disk is also growing. When more than one type of data is stored on a disk, it becomes hard to work out which disk partition is active. A series of new features has been introduced in Solaris 2.6 to help solve these problems.

- Per-partition data identical to existing per-disk data. It is now possible to separate out root, swap, and home directory activity even if they are all on the same disk.

- New "error and identity" data per disk, so there is no longer a need to scan syslog for errors. Full data is saved from the first SCSI probe to a disk. This data includes Vendor, Product, Revision, Serial number, RPM, heads, and size. Soft, hard, and transport error counter categories sum up any problems. The detail option adds Media Error, Device not ready, No device, Recoverable, Illegal request, and Predictive failure analysis. Dead or missing disks can still be identified because there is no need to send them another SCSI probe.

- New `iostat` options are provided to present these metrics. One option (`iostat -M`) shows throughput in Mbytes/s rather than Kbytes/s for high-performance systems. Another option (`-n`) translates disk names into a much more useful form, so you don't have to deal with the sd43b format—instead, you get c1t2d5s1. This feature makes it much easier to keep track of per-controller load levels in large configurations.

Fast tapes now match the performance impact of disks. We recently ran a tape backup benchmark to see if there were any scalability or throughput limits in Solaris, and we were pleased to find that the only real limit is the speed of the tape drives. The final result was a backup rate of an Oracle database at 1 terabyte/hour. This result works out at about 350 Mbytes/s, which was as fast as the disk subsystem we had configured could go. To sustain this rate, we used every tape drive we could lay our hands on, including 24 StorageTEK Redwood tape transports, which run at around 15 Mbytes/s each. We ran this test using Solaris 2.5.1, but there are no measurements of tape drive throughput in Solaris 2.5.1. Tape metrics have now been added to Solaris 2.6, and you can see which tape drive is active, the throughput, average transfer size, and service time for each tape drive.

Tapes are instrumented the same way as disks; they appear in `sar` and `iostat` automatically. Tape read/write operations are instrumented with all the same measures that are used for disks. Rewind and scan/seek are omitted from the service time.

The output format and options of `sar(1)` are fixed by the generic Unix standard SVID3, but the format and options for `iostat` can be changed. In Solaris 2.6, existing `iostat` options are unchanged, and apart from extra entries that appear for tape drives and NFS mount points (described later), anyone storing `iostat` data from a mixture of Solaris 2 systems will get a consistent format. New options that extend `iostat` are as follows:

    -E   full error statistics
    -e   error summary statistics
    -n   disk name and NFS mount point translation, extended service time

-M MB/s instead of KB/s
-P partitions only
-p disks and partitions

Here are examples of some of the new `iostat` formats.

```
% iostat -xp
                                  extended device statistics
device    r/s  w/s    kr/s    kw/s wait actv   svc_t  %w  %b
sd106     0.0  0.0    0.0     0.0  0.0  0.0     0.0    0   0
sd106,a   0.0  0.0    0.0     0.0  0.0  0.0     0.0    0   0
sd106,b   0.0  0.0    0.0     0.0  0.0  0.0     0.0    0   0
sd106,c   0.0  0.0    0.0     0.0  0.0  0.0     0.0    0   0
st47      0.0  0.0    0.0     0.0  0.0  0.0     0.0    0   0
```

```
% iostat -xe
                              extended device statistics ---- errors ----
device    r/s  w/s    kr/s    kw/s wait actv   svc_t  %w  %b s/w h/w trn tot
sd106     0.0  0.0    0.0     0.0  0.0  0.0     0.0    0   0   0   0   0   0
st47      0.0  0.0    0.0     0.0  0.0  0.0     0.0    0   0   0   0   0   0
```

```
% iostat -E

sd106    Soft Errors: 0 Hard Errors: 0 Transport Errors: 0
Vendor: SEAGATE   Product: ST15230W SUN4.2G Revision: 0626 Serial No:
00193749
RPM: 7200 Heads: 16 Size: 4.29GB <4292075520 bytes>
Media Error: 0 Device Not Ready: 0 No Device: 0 Recoverable: 0
Illegal Request: 0 Predictive Failure Analysis: 0

st47     Soft Errors: 0 Hard Errors: 0 Transport Errors: 0
Vendor: EXABYTE   Product: EXB-8505SMBANSH2 Revision: 0793 Serial No:
```

New NFS Metrics

Local disk and NFS usage are functionally interchangeable, so Solaris 2.6 was changed to instrument NFS client mount points like disks! NFS mounts are *always* shown by `iostat` and `sar`. With automounted directories coming and going more often than disks coming online, that change may cause problems for performance tools that don't expect the number of `iostat` or `sar` records to change often. We had to do some work on the SE toolkit to handle dynamic configuration changes properly.

The full instrumentation includes the wait queue for commands in the client (biod wait) that have not yet been sent to the server. The active queue measures commands currently in the server. Utilization (%busy) indicates the server mount-point activity level. Note that unlike the case with disks, *100% busy does NOT indicate that the server itself is saturated*; it just indicates that the client always has outstanding requests to that server. An NFS server is much more complex than a disk drive and can handle many more simultaneous requests than a single disk drive can.

The example shows off the new -xnP option, although NFS mounts appear in all formats. Note that the P option suppresses disks and shows only disk partitions. The xn option breaks down the response time, svc_t, into wait and active times and puts the device name at the end of the line so that long names don't mess up the columns. The vold entry automounts floppy and CD-ROM devices.

```
% iostat -xnP
                                 extended device statistics
   r/s  w/s   kr/s   kw/s wait actv wsvc_t asvc_t  %w  %b device
   0.0  0.0    0.0    0.0  0.0  0.0    0.0    0.0   0   0 crun:vold(pid363)
   0.0  0.0    0.0    0.0  0.0  0.0    0.0    0.0   0   0 servdist:/usr/dist
   0.0  0.5    0.0    7.9  0.0  0.0    0.0   20.7   0   1
servhome:/export/home2/adrianc
   0.0  0.0    0.0    0.0  0.0  0.0    0.0    0.0   0   0 servmail:/var/mail
   0.0  1.3    0.0   10.4  0.0  0.2    0.0  128.0   0   2 c0t2d0s0
   0.0  0.0    0.0    0.0  0.0  0.0    0.0    0.0   0   0 c0t2d0s2
```

Idle Disks and Long Service Times

Disks can behave in puzzling ways. The only way to find out what is really happening is to delve beneath the averages shown by iostat. Solaris 2.5 and later releases include a trace system that lets you see each individual disk access. As an example, I'll track down an odd behavior in iostat that has been bugging people for years.

I keep seeing disks that are lightly used but have extremely large service times. Disks are supposed to have an average seek time of about 10–20 ms, so why do they often report over 100 ms when they can't possibly be overloaded? Why does this happen? Is it a sign of a problem?

					extended disk statistics			
disk	r/s	w/s	Kr/s	Kw/s	wait	actv	svc_t	%w	%b
sd2	1.3	0.3	11.7	3.3	0.1	0.1	146.6	0	3
sd3	0.0	0.1	0.1	0.7	0.0	0.0	131.0	0	0

This is one of those recurring questions that everyone seems to ask at one time or another, The short answer is that the apparent overload can safely be ignored because the disks are so lightly used that they don't make a difference to the performance of the system. This answer is rather unsatisfying because it doesn't explain why the large service times occur in the first place. Several theories are circulating:

Is it a bug?

This theory can be dismissed. The problem has been seen for many years and has even been reported as a bug and investigated. The calculations in `iostat` are well tested and correct.

Is it caused by rounding error at low activity levels?

This is what I thought the problem was for many years. It was only when I used I/O tracing to look at near-idle disks that I found out what was really going on. Rounding errors cannot explain the high service times we see.

Is it caused by energy star and thermal recalibration?

Modern disks have a mind of their own. If you stop using them for a while, they power off their circuitry and can even be programmed to spin down completely. Even when they are in use, they go through a recalibration sequence every now and again. This recalibration keeps the heads perfectly aligned even when temperature changes cause thermal expansion. While it's true that these activities will increase service times, they should be relatively infrequent. We might be able to find this kind of access in an I/O trace. It should appear as an isolated, short-distance seek that takes a long time.

Is it something to do with the file system?

If your system has disks that are used raw by a database such as Sybase or Oracle, then you may notice that service times are much shorter overall. Even when activity levels are low, the service time stays low. This observation seems to rule out recalibration and energy star as the cause. Perhaps the filesystem layout is a problem? Inodes, indirect blocks, and data blocks may be scattered all over the disk. The extra long-distance seeks required to find the inode, get the indirect block, and, finally, read or write data probably explain why filesystem service times are generally higher than raw disk service times. At low usage levels, though, they still don't explain why we see such long seek times.

Is it the filesystem flush process?

The `fsflush` process (pid 3) keeps the data on disk in sync with the data in memory at regular intervals. It normally runs every 5 seconds to flush data and does additional work to flush inodes every 30 seconds. This frequency is enough to be a good candidate for the problem. It also explains why the problem is not seen on raw disks. The only way to settle this question is to trace each individual access to see which process initiated the I/O, how long it took, and what else is happening at the same time. Solaris 2.5 introduced a new tracing capability that we can use, so I'll start by explaining how it works, then use it to capture the I/O trace.

The Solaris 2.5 Trace Capability

Unix systems have had a kernel trace capability for many years. It was designed for development and debugging, not for end users. The production kernel is normally built without the trace capability for performance reasons. One of the first production kernels to include tracing was IBM's AIX kernel on the RS/6000 range. They left it turned on during early releases to assist in debugging, then decided that tracing was useful enough to pay its way and the overhead was quite low, so it is now a permanent feature. SunSoft also recognized the value of trace information but decided to extend the trace capability to make it more generally useful and to implement it alongside the existing kernel trace system. It was introduced in Solaris 2.5 and consists of the following features.

- A self-describing trace output format, called Trace Normal Form (TNF), allows data structures to be embedded in the trace file without the need for an external definition of their types and contents.

- A set of libraries allows user-level programs to generate trace data. In particular, this trace data helps analyze and debug multithreaded applications.

- A well-defined set of kernel probe points covering most important events was implemented.

- A program prex(1) controls probe execution for both user and kernel traces.

- A program tnfxtract(1) reads out the kernel trace buffer, and tnfdump(1) displays TNF data in human-readable ASCII.

- There are manual pages for all the commands and library calls. The set of implemented kernel probes is documented in tnf_probes(4).

A few things about kernel probes are inconvenient. While user-level probes can write to trace files, the kernel probes write to a ring buffer. This buffer is not a single global ring; it is a buffer per kernel thread. This buffer scheme avoids any need to lock the data structures, so there is no performance loss or contention on multiprocessor systems. You cannot easily tell how big the buffer needs to be, and one highly active probe point may loop right round its buffer while others have hardly started. If you are trying to capture every single probe, make the buffer as big as you can. In general, it is best to work with low event rate probes or rely on sampling and put up with missing probes. The tnfxtract routine just takes a snapshot of the buffer, so a second snapshot will include anything left over from the first one. The tnfdump program does quite a lot of work to sort the probe events into time order.

More TNF information, including a free but unsupported GUI Trace browser, can be found at the http://opcom.sun.ca web site.

I/O Trace: Commands and Features

The command sequence to initiate an I/O trace is quite simple. You run the commands as root, and you need a directory to hold the output. I find it easiest to have two windows open: one to run `prex`, and the other to go through a cycle of extracting, dumping, and viewing the data as required. The command sequence for `prex` is to first allocate a buffer (the default is 384 Kbytes; you can make it bigger), enable the `io` group of probes, make them trace accesses, then turn on the global flag that enables all kernel tracing.

```
# prex -k
Type "help" for help ...
prex> buffer alloc
Buffer of size 393216 bytes allocated
prex> enable io
prex> trace io
prex> ktrace on
```

Now, wait a while or run the program you want to trace. In this case, I ran `iostat -x 10` in another window, didn't try to cause any activity, and waited for some slow service time to appear. After a minute or so, I stopped collecting.

```
prex> ktrace off
```

In the other window I extracted the data and dumped it to take a look.

```
# mkdir /tmp/tnf
# cd /tmp/tnf
# tnfxtract io.tnf
# tnfdump io.tnf | more
```

The first section identifies the three probes that were enabled because they have the key "io." The "strategy" probe records an I/O being issued; "biodone" records an I/O completing. The other mechanism that may cause I/O is the pageout scanner, and this is also being probed. The location of the probe in the Solaris source code is printed for kernel developers to refer to. These probes include the time taken to allocate pages of memory to hold the results of the I/O request. Being short on memory can slightly delay an I/O.

```
probe    tnf_name: "strategy" tnf_string: "keys io blockio;file
../../common/os/driver.c;line 358;"
probe    tnf_name: "pageout" tnf_string: "keys vm pageio io;file
../../common/vm/vm_pvn.c;line 511;"
probe    tnf_name: "biodone" tnf_string: "keys io blockio;file
../../common/os/bio.c;line 935;"
```

The next section is a table of probe events in time order. When a user process was scheduling the I/O, its PID was recorded. Events caused by interrupts or kernel activity were recorded as PID 0. This trace was measured on a dual CPU SPARCstation 10, so you can see a mixture of CPU 0 and CPU 2. I've listed the first few records, then skipped through, looking for something interesting.

Elapsed (ms)	Delta (ms)	PID LWPID	TID	CPU Probe Name	Data / Description
0.00000	0.00000	632	1 0xf61a1d80	0 strategy	device: 8388632 block: 795344 size: 8192 buf: 0xf5afdb40 flags: 9
108.450	108.450	0	0 0xfbf6aec0	2 biodone	device: 8388632 block: 795344 buf: 0xf5afdb40
108.977	0.52700	632	1 0xf61a1d80	0 strategy	device: 8388632 block: 795086 size: 1024 buf: 0xf610a358 flags: 524569
121.557	12.5800	0	0 0xfbf6aec0	2 biodone	device: 8388632 block: 795086 buf: 0xf610a358
121.755	0.17900	632	1 0xf61a1d80	0 pageout	vnode: 0xf61d0a48 pages_pageout: 0 pages_freed: 0 pages_reclaimed 0

The first strategy routine is an 8-Kbyte write (flags bit 0x40 is set for reads) to block 795344. To decode the device, 8388632 = 0x800018, 0x18 = 24, and running `ls -lL` on `/dev/dsk` shows that `c0t3d0s0` is minor device 24, which is mounted as `/export/home`. It's an old Sun 424-Mbyte drive, so valid blocks are from 0 to 828719. This a seek to right at the end of the disk, and it takes 108 ms. It is followed by a 1-Kbyte write to a nearby block and takes only 12.58 ms. The pageout scanner runs but finds nothing to do, so it reports no pages paged out, freed, or reclaimed this time. After 8 seconds everything goes quiet, then there is a very interesting burst of activity around the 22-second mark that is all initiated by PID 3, the `fsflush` process.

Elapsed (ms)	Delta (ms)	PID	TID	CPU Probe Name	Data / Description
8034.21800	0.019000	0	0 0xfbf6aec0	2 biodone	device: 8388632 block: 796976 buf: 0xf610a538
21862.0155	13827.72	3	1 0xf5d8cc80	2 strategy	device: 8388632 block: 240 size: 2048 buf: 0xf5e71158 flags: 9
21897.7560	35.74050	0	0 0xfbf6aec0	2 biodone	device: 8388632 block: 240 buf: 0xf5e71158
21897.9440	0.188000	3	1 0xf5d8cc80	0 strategy	device: 8388632 block: 16 ize: 2048 buf: 0xf5adadc0 flags: 524809
21907.1305	9.186500	0	0 0xfbf6aec0	2 biodone	device: 8388632 block: 16 buf: 0xf5adadc0

We start by seeking from block 796976 to 240 with a 36-ms write, followed by block 16 with a 9-ms write. This write is probably the filesystem superblock being updated. The following set of writes are issued extremely close together, 14 of them in about 1.5 ms, and they refer to two different devices. The set starts with device 8388624, which maps to c0t2d0s0, which is a Sun 1.05-GB disk holding the root file system, then also accesses /export/home briefly during the sequence. For brevity, I have trimmed this output to just the root disk and removed data that is the same as the first trace record.

Elapsed (ms)	Delta (ms)	PID	TID	CPU Probe Name	Data / Description
21934.5060	27.3755	3	1 0xf5d8cc80	0 strategy	device: 8388624 block: 32544 size: 8192 buf: 0xf5afd780 flags: 1033
21934.7320	0.2260	3	1 0xf5d8cc80	0 strategy	block: 64896 buf: 0xf5e71a40
21934.9490	0.2170	3	1 0xf5d8cc80	0 strategy	block: 887696 buf: 0xf5e71ef0
21935.0420	0.0930	3	1 0xf5d8cc80	0 strategy	block: 855296 buf: 0xf5e70e10

21935.1290	0.0870	3	1 0xf5d8cc80	0 strategy	block: 855248
					buf: 0xf5e70438
21935.3265	0.1280	3	1 0xf5d8cc80	0 strategy	block: 678272
					buf: 0xf5afd000
21935.4935	0.0825	3	1 0xf5d8cc80	0 strategy	block: 887664
					buf: 0xf5aff760
21935.5805	0.0870	3	1 0xf5d8cc80	0 strategy	block: 194560
					buf: 0xf5afdc30
21935.7530	0.0770	3	1 0xf5d8cc80	0 strategy	block: 32480
					buf: 0xf5afe4a0
21935.8330	0.0800	3	1 0xf5d8cc80	0 strategy	block: 887680
					buf: 0xf5afe6f8
21935.9115	0.0785	3	1 0xf5d8cc80	0 strategy	block: 1629440
					buf: 0xf5afd078

The requested seek order on root is blocks 32544, 64896, 887696, 855296, 855248, 678272, 887644, 194560, 32480, 887680, 1629440. That's pretty random! None of the requests complete until after the last one is issued. Here are the completions.

Elapsed (ms)	Delta (ms)	PID	TID	CPU Probe Name	Data / Description
21964.1510	28.2395	0	0 0xfbe1cec0	0 biodone	device: 8388624
					block: 32544
					buf: 0xf5afd780
21980.0535	8.2955	0	0 0xfbf6aec0	2 biodone	block: 64896
					buf: 0xf5e71a40
21994.0765	6.0985	0	0 0xfbe1cec0	0 biodone	block: 887696
					buf: 0xf5e71ef0
22009.2190	13.9775	0	0 0xfbf6aec0	2 biodone	block: 855296
					buf: 0xf5e70e10
22023.8295	14.6105	0	0 0xfbe1cec0	0 biodone	block: 855248
					buf: 0xf5e70438
22037.5215	13.6920	0	0 0xfbf6aec0	2 biodone	block: 678272
					buf: 0xf5afd000
22055.0835	17.5620	0	0 0xfbe1cec0	0 biodone	block: 887664
					buf: 0xf5aff760
22077.5950	22.5115	0	0 0xfbf6aec0	2 biodone	block: 194560
					buf: 0xf5afdc30
22099.4810	21.8860	0	0 0xfbe1cec0	0 biodone	block: 32480
					buf: 0xf5afe4a0
22125.7145	26.2335	0	0 0xfbf6aec0	2 biodone	block: 887680
					buf: 0xf5afe6f8
22146.7055	20.9910	0	0 0xfbe1cec0	0 biodone	block: 1629440
					buf: 0xf5afd078

The order of completion for this disk is the same as the order of issue because the firmware in this old, Sun 1.05-Gbyte disk is not intelligent enough to reorder seeks. More recent disks would reorder the operations, and responses would be seen out of order. There are about 1,000 blocks per cylinder on this disk, so we can approximate the number of tracks per seek. Remember that disks are variable geometry nowadays, so it's probably more than 1,000 blocks per cylinder near block 0 and progressively less at higher block numbers. For the root disk only, the delay and seek distances are shown in Table 8-3.

Table 8-3   Trace-Derived Sequence of Disk Service Times

Block	Seek Cylinders	Service Time	Response Time
32544	1333	29.65 ms	29.65 ms
64896	32	15.67 ms	45.32 ms
887696	822	13.81 ms	59.13 ms
855296	back 32	15.05 ms	74.18 ms
855248	0	14.52 ms	88.70 ms
678272	back 177	13.50 ms	102.2 ms
887644	209	17.39 ms	119.59 ms
194560	back 693	22.42 ms	142.01 ms
32480	back 162	21.72 ms	163.73 ms
887680	855	26.15 ms	189.88 ms
1629440	742	20.91 ms	210.79 ms
Average		**19.16 ms**	**111.38 ms**

What we see is that 11 writes of 8 Kbytes were fired off in one go, randomly spread over the disk, and that they completed sequentially, taking on average 19 ms each (not that bad, and accesses to the other disk may have slowed it down a bit). The later accesses were delayed by the earlier ones sufficiently that this burst (which took only 210 ms to complete) would report an average response time of 111 ms in iostat. Measured over a 10-second interval and if there was *no other disk activity*, we would see something like this:

```
% iostat -x 10
...
                              extended disk statistics
disk      r/s  w/s   Kr/s   Kw/s wait actv  svc_t  %w   %b
sd2       0.0  1.1    0.0    8.8  0.0  0.0  111.4   0    2
```

Now, that output looks very familiar. It seems that we have found the culprit! `fsflush` is causing large service-time reports by kicking off a burst of activity. In most cases, applications generate access patterns that are either sequential bursts (large transfers) or separate random accesses in a sequence over time. In this case, a long, completely random sequence is being generated in such a short time that a queue forms. It is all over with very quickly and occurs only every 30 seconds or so, but random sequence generation is quite likely to happen on any disk that contains a file system. The trace data shown was taken at the first attempt, so it isn't hard to find this situation occurring.

I hope you are also inspired to start using TNF. It can illuminate all kinds of situations for you and, at user level, is a great way of embedding timing points into applications. A dormant probe point is extremely lightweight, so there is little penalty, and probes can be left in production code.

How `iostat` Uses the Underlying Disk Measurements

To really understand the data being presented by `iostat`, `sar`, and other tools, you need to look at the raw data being collected by the kernel, remember some history, and do some simple mathematics.

In the old days, disk controllers really did control the disks directly. If you still remember the old Sun machines with SMD disks and Xylogics controllers, you may know what I mean. All the intelligence was in the controller, which was a large VMEbus card inside the system cabinet. The disk heads were directly connected to the controller, and the device driver knew exactly which track the disk was reading. As each bit was read from disk, it was buffered in the controller until a whole disk block was ready to be passed to the device driver.

The device driver maintained a queue of waiting requests, which were serviced one at a time by the disk. From this, the system could report the service time directly as milliseconds-per-seek. The throughput in transfers per second was also reported, as was the percentage of the time that the disk was busy, the utilization. The terms *utilization*, *service time*, *wait time*, *throughput*, and *wait queue length* have well-defined meanings in this scenario. A set of simple equations from queuing theory can be used to derive these values from underlying measurements. The original version of `iostat` in SunOS 3.X and SunOS 4.X was basically the same as in BSD Unix.

Over time, disk technology moved on. Nowadays, a standard disk is SCSI based and has an embedded controller. The disk drive contains a small microprocessor and about 1 Mbyte of RAM. It can typically handle up to 64 outstanding requests via SCSI tagged-command queuing. The system uses a SCSI Host Bus Adaptor (HBA) to talk to the disk. In large systems, there is another level of intelligence and buffering in a hardware RAID controller. The simple model of a disk used by `iostat` and its terminology have become confused.

In the old days, once the device driver sent the disk a request, it knew that the disk would do nothing else until the request was complete. The time it took was the service time, and the average service time was a property of the disk itself. Disks that spin faster and seek faster have lower (better) service times. With today's systems, the device driver issues a request, that request is queued internally by the RAID controller and the disk drive, and several more requests can be sent before the first one comes back. The service time, as measured by the device driver, varies according to the load level and queue length and is not directly comparable to the old-style service time of a simple disk drive.

The instrumentation provided in Solaris 2 takes account of this change by explicitly measuring a two-stage queue: one queue, called the wait queue, in the device driver; and one queue, called the active queue, in the device itself. A read or write command is issued to the device driver and sits in the wait queue until the SCSI bus and disk are both ready. When the command is sent to the disk device, it moves to the active queue until the disk sends its response. The problem with iostat is that it tries to report the new measurements in some of the original terminology. The "wait service time" is actually the time spent in the "wait" queue. This is not the right definition of service time in any case, and the word "wait" is being used to mean two different things. To sort out what we really do have, we need to move on to do some mathematics.

Let's start with the actual measurements made by the kernel. For each disk drive (and each disk partition, tape drive, and NFS mount in Solaris 2.6), a small set of counters is updated. An annotated copy of the kstat(3K)-based data structure that the SE toolkit uses is shown in Figure 8-3.

Figure 8-3   Kernel Disk Information Statistics Data Structure

```
struct ks_disks {
    long        number$;    /* linear disk number */
    string      name$;      /* name of the device */

    ulonglong nread;        /* number of bytes read */
    ulonglong nwritten;     /* number of bytes written */
    ulong       reads;      /* number of reads */
    ulong       writes;     /* number of writes */
    longlong    wtime;      /* wait queue - time spent waiting */
    longlong    wlentime;   /* wait queue - sum of queue length multiplied
by time at that length */
    longlong    wlastupdate;/* wait queue - time of last update */
    longlong rtime;     /* active/run queue - time spent active/running */
    longlong rlentime;   /* active/run queue - sum of queue length * time
at that length */
    longlong    rlastupdate;/* active/run queue - time of last update */
    ulong       wcnt;       /* wait queue - current queue length */
    ulong       rcnt;       /* active/run queue - current queue length */
};
```

None of these values are printed out directly by `iostat`, so this is where the basic arithmetic starts. The first thing to realize is that the underlying metrics are cumulative counters or instantaneous values. The values printed by `iostat` are averages over a time interval. We need to take two copies of the above data structure together with a high resolution *timestamp* for each and do some subtraction. We then get the average values between the *start* and *end* times. I'll write it out as plainly as possible, with pseudocode that assumes an array of two values for each measure, indexed by *start* and *end*. T_{hires} is in units of nanoseconds, so we divide to get seconds as T.

$$T_{hires} = \text{hires elapsed time} = EndTime - StartTime = timestamp[end] - timestamp[start]$$

$$T = \frac{T_{hires}}{100000000}$$

$$B_{wait} = \text{hires busy time for wait queue} = wtime[end] - wtime[start]$$

$$B_{run} = \text{hires busy time for run queue} = rtime[end] - rtime[start]$$

$$QB_{wait} = \text{wait queue length} * \text{time} = wlentime[end] - wlentime[start]$$

$$QB_{run} = \text{run queue length} * \text{time} = rlentime[end] - rlentime[start]$$

Now, we assume that all disk commands complete fairly quickly, so the arrival and completion rates are the same in a steady state average, and the throughput of both queues is the same. I'll use completions below because it seems more intuitive in this case.

$$C_{read} = \text{completed reads} = reads[end] - reads[start]$$

$$X_{read} = \text{read throughput} = \text{iostat rps} = \frac{C_{read}}{T}$$

$$C_{write} = \text{completed writes} = writes[end] - writes[start]$$

$$X_{write} = \text{write throughput} = \text{iostat wps} = \frac{C_{write}}{T}$$

$$C = \text{total commands completed} = C_{read} + C_{write}$$

$$X = \text{throughput in commands per second} = \text{iostat tps} = \frac{C}{T} = X_{read} + X_{write}$$

A similar calculation gets us the data rate in kilobytes per second.

K_{read} = Kbytes read in the interval = $\dfrac{nread[end] - nread[start]}{1024}$

X_{kread} = read Kbytes throughput = iostat Kr/s = $\dfrac{K_{read}}{T}$

K_{write} = Kbytes written in the interval = $\dfrac{nwritten[end] - nwritten[start]}{1024}$

X_{kwrite} = write Kbytes throughput = iostat Kw/s = $\dfrac{K_{write}}{T}$

X_k = total data rate in Kbytes per second = iostat Kps = $X_{kread} + X_{kwrite}$

Next, we can obtain the utilization—the busy time as a percentage of the total time.

U_{wait} = wait queue utilization = iostat %w = $\dfrac{100 \times B_{wait}}{T_{hires}}$

U_{run} = run queue utilization = iostat %b = $\dfrac{100 \times B_{run}}{T_{hires}}$

Now, we get to something called service time, but it is *not* what `iostat` prints out and calls service time. This is the real thing!

S_{wait} = average wait queue service time in milliseconds = $\dfrac{B_{wait}}{C \times 100000}$

S_{run} = average run queue service time in milliseconds = $\dfrac{B_{run}}{C \times 100000}$

The meaning of S_{run} is as close as you can get to the old-style disk service time. Remember that the disk can run more than one command at a time and can return them in a different order than they were issued, and it becomes clear that it cannot be the same thing.

The data structure contains an instantaneous measure of queue length, but we want the average over the time interval. We get this from that strange "length time" product by dividing it by the busy time.

$$Q_{wait} = \text{average wait queue length} = \text{iostat wait} = \frac{QB_{wait}}{B_{wait}}$$

$$Q_{run} = \text{average run queue length} = \text{iostat actv} = \frac{QB_{run}}{B_{run}}$$

Finally, we can get the number that `iostat` calls service time. It is defined as the queue length divided by the throughput, but it is actually the residence or response time and includes all queuing effects. The real definition of service time is the time taken for the first command in line to be processed, and its value is not printed out by `iostat`. Thanks to the SE toolkit, this deficiency is easily fixed. A "corrected" version of `iostat` written in SE prints out the data, using the format shown in Figure 8-4. This new format is used by several scripts in SE release 3.0.

Figure 8-4   SE-Based Rewrite of `iostat` to Show Service Time Correctly

```
% se siostat.se 10
03:42:50  ------throughput------ -----wait queue----- ----active queue----
disk      r/s  w/s   Kr/s   Kw/s qlen res_t svc_t %ut qlen res_t svc_t %ut
c0t2d0s0  0.0  0.2   0.0    1.2 0.00  0.02  0.02   0 0.00 22.87 22.87    0
03:43:00  ------throughput------ -----wait queue----- ----active queue----
disk      r/s  w/s   Kr/s   Kw/s qlen res_t svc_t %ut qlen res_t svc_t %ut
c0t2d0s0  0.0  3.2   0.0   23.1 0.00  0.01  0.01   0 0.72 225.45 16.20    5
```

The Solaris 2 disk instrumentation is complete and accurate. Now that it has been extended to tapes, partitions, and client NFS mount points, there is a lot more that can be done with it. It's a pity that the naming conventions used by `iostat` are so confusing and that `sar -d` mangles the data so much for display. We asked if `sar` could be fixed, but its output format and options are largely constrained by cross-platform Unix standards. We tried to get `iostat` fixed, but it was felt that the current naming convention was what users expected to see, so changing the header or data too much would confuse existing users. Hopefully, this translation of existing practice into the correct terminology will help reduce the confusion somewhat.

Filesystem Tuning

The UFS filesystem code includes an I/O clustering algorithm, which groups successive reads or writes into a single, large command to transfer up to 56 Kbytes rather than lots of 8-Kbyte transfers. This grouping allows the filesystem layout to be tuned to avoid sector interleaving and allows filesystem I/O on sequential files to get close to its theoretical maximum.

The UFS filesystem layout parameters can be modified by means of `tunefs`[1]. By default, these parameters are set to provide maximum overall throughput for all combinations of read, write, and update operations in both random and sequential access patterns. For a single disk, the gains that can be made by optimizing disk layout parameters with `tunefs` for one kind of operation over another are small.

The clustering algorithm is controlled by the `tunefs` parameters, `rotdelay` and `maxcontig`. The default `rotdelay` parameter is zero, meaning that files are stored in contiguous sectors. Any other value disables clustering. The default `maxcontig` parameter is 7; this is the maximum transfer size supported on all machines, and it gives a good compromise for performance with various access patterns.

Higher values can be configured and can be useful when you are working with large sequential accesses.

You can free extra capacity in file systems that contain larger than average files by creating the file system with a higher number of bytes per inode. File system creation time is also greatly reduced. The default is 2048 bytes per inode. I often use `newfs -i 8192`.

Eagle DiskPak

A product from Eagle Software, Inc., called DiskPak™, has some novel features that can improve throughput for heavily used file systems. The product reorganizes the layout of data blocks for each file on the disk to make all files sequential and contiguous and to optimize the placement of the UFS partial block fragments that occur at the end of files. It also has a filesystem browser utility that gives a visual representation of the block layout and free space distribution of a file system. The most useful capability of this product is that it can sort files on the basis of several criteria, to minimize disk seek time. The main criteria are access time, modification time, and size. If a subset of the files is accessed most often, then it helps to group them together on the disk. Sorting by size helps separate a few large files from more commonly accessed small files. According to the

---

1. See the manual page and *The Design and Implementation of the 4.3BSD UNIX Operating System* by Leffler, McKusick, Karels, and Quarterman for details of the filesystem implementation.

vendor, speedups of 20 percent have been measured for a mixed workload. DiskPak is available for both SunOS 4.X and Solaris 2.X. You can download trial software from http://www.eaglesoft.com.

Disk Specifications

Disk specifications are sometimes reported according to a "best case" approach, which is disk-format independent. Some parameters are quoted in the same way by both disk manufacturers and computer system vendors, an approach that can confuse you because they are not measuring the same thing. Sun uses disks from many different suppliers, including Seagate, IBM, Fujitsu, and Quantum. For example, the Seagate web site, http://www.seagate.com, contains complete specifications for all their recent disks. The system may call the disk a SUN2.1G, but if you use the format command to make an enquiry, as shown in Figure 8-5, or use the new iostat -E option in Solaris 2.6, you can find out the vendor and model of the disk.

Figure 8-5   How to Identify the Exact Disk Type and Vendor by Using format

```
# format
Searching for disks...done

AVAILABLE DISK SELECTIONS:
       0. c0t0d0 <SUN2.1G cyl 2733 alt 2 hd 19 sec 80>
          /sbus@1f,0/SUNW,fas@e,8800000/sd@0,0
Specify disk (enter its number): 0
selecting c0t0d0
[disk formatted]
Warning: Current Disk has mounted partitions.

FORMAT MENU:
       disk       - select a disk
... text omitted ....
       inquiry    - show vendor, product and revision
       quit
format> inquiry
Vendor:   SEAGATE
Product:  ST32171W SUN2.1G
Revision: 7462
format> quit
#
```

In this case, on an Ultra 1/170E, the vendor and disk are Seagate ST32171W. Visiting the Seagate web site, I found a data sheet that quoted this file: ftp://ftp.seagate.com/techsuppt/scsi/st32171w.txt. Excerpts are shown in Figure 8-6.

Figure 8-6   Example Vendor Disk Specification Sheet

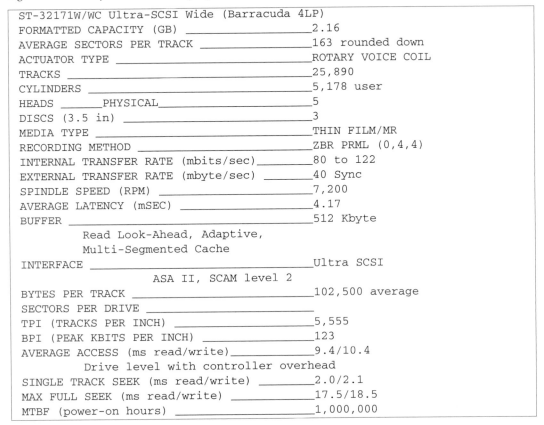

```
ST-32171W/WC Ultra-SCSI Wide (Barracuda 4LP)
FORMATTED CAPACITY (GB) _____2.16
AVERAGE SECTORS PER TRACK _____163 rounded down
ACTUATOR TYPE _____ROTARY VOICE COIL
TRACKS _____25,890
CYLINDERS _____5,178 user
HEADS _____PHYSICAL_____5
DISCS (3.5 in) _____3
MEDIA TYPE _____THIN FILM/MR
RECORDING METHOD _____ZBR PRML (0,4,4)
INTERNAL TRANSFER RATE (mbits/sec)_____80 to 122
EXTERNAL TRANSFER RATE (mbyte/sec) _____40 Sync
SPINDLE SPEED (RPM) _____7,200
AVERAGE LATENCY (mSEC) _____4.17
BUFFER _____512 Kbyte
         Read Look-Ahead, Adaptive,
         Multi-Segmented Cache
INTERFACE _____Ultra SCSI
              ASA II, SCAM level 2
BYTES PER TRACK _____102,500 average
SECTORS PER DRIVE _____
TPI (TRACKS PER INCH) _____5,555
BPI (PEAK KBITS PER INCH) _____123
AVERAGE ACCESS (ms read/write)_____9.4/10.4
         Drive level with controller overhead
SINGLE TRACK SEEK (ms read/write) _____2.0/2.1
MAX FULL SEEK (ms read/write) _____17.5/18.5
MTBF (power-on hours) _____1,000,000
```

This excerpt includes the basic information that we need.

What the Disk Makers Specify

The disk manufacturers specify certain parameters for a drive.

- Rotational speed in revolutions per minute (rpm)
- The number of tracks or cylinders on the disk
- The number of heads or surfaces in each cylinder
- The rate at which data is read and written (millions of bytes/s)
- The disk controller interface used (IDE, SCSI, Wide SCSI, Ultra SCSI, FC-AL)

- The *capacity* of the drive (millions of bytes)
- The average *access time* and single track and maximum *seek time* of the disk

When disk makers build the read/write heads, the speed of data transfer is measured in megahertz (MHz), which is converted into megabytes by division by eight. All the tracks that can be accessed without moving the heads form a cylinder. The single cylinder seek time is the time taken to move the heads to the next cylinder. On many high-performance drives, the head assembly is accelerated for the first half of the seek and decelerated for the second half. In this way, a seek of several cylinders in one attempt takes less time than many short steps with stops along the way. The average cylinder-to-cylinder seek time is usually calculated by accounting for all possible seek distances. To get to a particular sector on the disk, the disk must rotate until it comes past the heads, so another component of overall access time is the rotational latency of the disk. The average rotational latency is usually quoted as the time taken for half a rotation.

The average access time quoted by the manufacturer is the average seek and rotate time. The disk quoted above is about 10 ms. The average rotational latency for 7200 rpm drives is 4.1 ms, and the seek time varies from 2 ms to 18 ms, as shown in Figure 8-7.

Figure 8-7   Average Disk Seek and Rotation Components

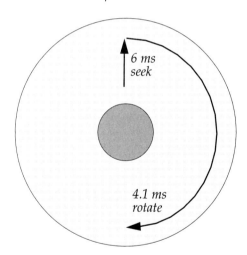

What the System Vendors Specify

The system vendors need to deal with the disk in terms of sectors, each typically containing 512 bytes of data and many bytes of header, preamble, and intersector gap. Spare sectors and spare cylinders are also allocated, so that bad sectors can be substituted. This allocation reduces the unformatted capacity to what is known as the *formatted capacity*. For example, the disk shown in Figure 8-6 has an unformatted capacity of 102,500 bytes per track and 25,890 tracks, making a total of 2.65 Gbytes. It has a formatted capacity of 163 sectors per track using 512 byte sectors, making a capacity of 2.16 Gbytes. In recent years, vendors seem to have become more consistent about quoting the formatted capacity for drives. The formatted capacity of the drive is measured in units of Mbytes = 10^6 = 1,000,000, whereas RAM sizes are measured in units of Mbytes = 2^{20} = 1,048,576. Confused? You will be! It is very easy to mix these up and make calculations that have a built-in error of 4.8 percent in the time taken to write a block of memory to disk.

Many of Sun's disks are multiply sourced to a common specification. Each vendor's disk has to meet or exceed that specification, so Sun's own published performance data may be a little bit more conservative. You should also be cautious about the data. I have come across inconsistencies in the speeds, seek times, and other details. I've also found disks advertising via SCSI inquiry that they are a completely different specification from that on the data sheet for that model.

What You Can Work Out for Yourself

For some old disks, you can work out, using information from /etc/format.dat, the real peak throughput and size in Kbytes (1024) of your disk. The entry for a typical disk is shown in Figure 8-8. In Solaris 2.3 and later releases, the format information is read directly from SCSI disk drives by the format command. The /etc/format.dat file entry is no longer required for SCSI disks.

Figure 8-8   /etc/format.dat Entry for Sun 669-Mbyte Disk

```
disk_type= "SUN0669" \
        : ctlr= MD21: fmt_time= 4 \
        : trks_zone= 15: asect= 5: atrks= 30 \
        : ncyl=  1614: acyl= 2: pcyl= 1632: nhead= 15: nsect= 54 \
        : rpm= 3600 : bpt= 31410
```

The values to note are:

- rpm = 3600, so the disk spins at 3600 rpm
- nsect = 54, so there are 54 sectors of 512 bytes per track
- nhead = 15, so there are 15 tracks per cylinder
- ncyl = 1614, so there are 1614 cylinders per disk

Since we know that there are 512 bytes per sector, 54 sectors per track and that a track will pass by the head 3,600 times per minute, we can work out the peak sustained data rate and size of the disk.

data rate (bytes/sec) = (nsect * 512 * rpm) / 60 = 1,658,880 bytes/s

size (bytes) = nsect * 512 * nhead * ncyl = 669,358,080 bytes

If we define that 1 Kbyte is 1024 bytes, then the data rate is 1620 Kbytes/s.

Standardizing on 1 Kbyte = 1024 is convenient since this is what the disk-monitoring utilities assume; since sectors are 512 bytes and pages are 4,096 bytes and the UFS file system uses 8,192 byte blocks, the standard 1 Kbyte = 1024 is more useful than 1K = 1000.

The Seagate data sheet does not give us the formatted data rate, but it does indicate that there are 168 sectors per track on average. At 7200 rpm, this data works out as:

data rate = 168 * 512 * 7200 / 60 = 10,080 Kbytes/s

This result shows the progress in disk performance that has been made over seven years or so. Random access rates have doubled as the disks spin twice as fast, but sequential data rates are up by a factor of six.

Some Sun disks are listed in Table 8-4, with Kbyte = 2^{10} = 1024. The data rate for ZBR drives cannot be calculated simply since the `format.dat` nsect entry is not the real value. Instead, I have provided an average value for sequential reads based on the quoted average number of sectors per track for an equivalent Seagate model.

Table 8-4   Common Disk Specifications

Disk Type	Bus	MB/s	RPM	Access	Capacity	Avg Data Rate
Sun 207 3.5″	5 MB/s SCSI	1.6	3600	16 ms	203148 KB	1080 KB/s
Sun 424 3.5″	5 MB/s SCSI	2.5-3.0	4400	14 ms	414360 KB	2584 KB/s ZBR
Sun 535 3.5x1″	10 MB/s SCSI	2.9-5.1	5400	11 ms	522480 KB	3608 KB/s ZBR
Sun 669 5.25″	5 MB/s SCSI	1.8	3600	16 ms	653670 KB	1620 KB/s
Sun 1.05G 3.5x1.6″	10 MB/s SCSI	2.9-5.0	5400	11 ms	1026144 KB	3840 KB/s ZBR
Sun 1.05G 3.5x1″	20 MB/s SCSI	2.9-5.0	5400	11 ms	1026144 KB	3968 KB/s ZBR
Sun 1.3G 5.25″	5 MB/s SCSI	3.0-4.5	5400	11 ms	1336200 KB	3288 KB/s ZBR
Sun 1.3G 5.25″	6 MB/s IPI	3.0-4.5	5400	11 ms	1255059 KB	2610-3510 KB/s
Sun 2.1G 5.25″	10 MB/s DSCSI	3.8-5.0	5400	11 ms	2077080 KB	3952 KB/s ZBR
Sun 2.1G 3.5x1.6″	10 MB/s SCSI	3.7-5.2	5400	11 ms	2077080 KB	3735 KB/s ZBR
Sun 2.1G 3.5x1″	20 MB/s SCSI	6.2-9.0	7200	8.5 ms	2077080 KB	6480 KB/s ZBR
Sun 2.1G 3.5x1″	40 MB/s SCSI	10-15	7200	8.5 ms	2077080 KB	10080 KB/s ZBR
Sun 2.9G 5.25″	20 MB/s DSCSI	4.4-6.5	5400	11 ms	2841993 KB	4455 KB/s ZBR
Sun 4.2G 3.5x1.6″	20 MB/s SCSI	4.2-7.8	5400	10 ms	4248046 KB	4950 KB/s ZBR
Sun 4.2G 3.5x1″	40 MB/s SCSI	10-15.2	7200	10 ms	4248046 KB	9840 KB/s ZBR
Sun 9.1G 5″	20 MB/s DSCSI	5.5-8.1	5400	11.5 ms	8876953 KB	5985 KB/s ZBR
Sun 9.1G 3.5x1.6″	40 MB/s SCSI	10-15.2	7200	8.5 ms	8876953 KB	10080 KB/s ZBR
Sun 9.1G 3.5x1″	100 MB/s FC	10-15.2	7200	8.5 ms	8876953 KB	10080 KB/s ZBR

Zoned Bit Rate (ZBR) Disk Drives

ZBR drives vary, depending on which cylinder is accessed. The disk is divided into zones with different bit rates; the outer part of the drive is faster and has more sectors per track than does the inner part of the drive. This scheme allows the data to be recorded with a constant linear density along the track (bits per inch). In other drives, the peak number of bits per inch that can be made to work reliably is set up for the innermost track, but density is too low on the outermost track, so capacity is wasted. In a ZBR drive, more data is stored on the outer tracks, so greater capacity and higher data rates are possible. The drive zones provide peak performance from the first third of the disk. The next third falls off slightly, but the last third of the disk may be as much as 25 percent slower. Table 8-5 summarizes performance for a 1.3-Gbyte ZBR disk drive.

Note – When partitioning a ZBR disk, remember that partition "a" or slice 0 will be faster than partition "h" or slice 7.

Table 8-5   1.3-Gbyte IPI ZBR Disk Zone Map

Zone	Start Cylinder	Sectors per Track	Data Rate in Kbytes/s
0	0	78	3510
1	626	78	3510
2	701	76	3420
3	801	74	3330
4	926	72	3240
5	1051	72	3240
6	1176	70	3150
7	1301	68	3060
8	1401	66	2970
9	1501	64	2880
10	1601	62	2790
11	1801	60	2700
12	1901	58	2610
13	2001	58	2610

The `format.dat` entry assumes constant geometry, so it has a fixed idea about sectors per track, and the number of cylinders in `format.dat` is reduced to compensate. The number of sectors per track is set to make sure partitions start on multiples of 16 blocks and does not accurately reflect the geometry of the outer zone. The 1.3-Gbyte IPI drive outer zone happens to match `format.dat`, but the other ZBR drives have more sectors than `format.dat` states.

IPI Disk Controllers

As long as IPI disks enjoyed a performance advantage over SCSI disks, the extra cost of low-volume, IPI-specific disks could be justified. Now that SCSI disks are higher capacity, faster, cheaper, and more intelligent, IPI subsystems have become obsolete. Each SCSI disk nowadays contains about as much intelligence and RAM buffer as the entire IPI controller from a few years ago.

An SBus IPI controller is available from Genroco, Inc., so that old disk subsystems can be migrated to current generation servers.

SCSI Disk Controllers

SCSI controllers can be divided into five generic classes. Very old ones support only *Asynchronous SCSI*, old controllers support *Synchronous SCSI*, most recent ones support *Fast Synchronous SCSI*; the latest two types to appear are *Fast and Wide Synchronous SCSI*, and *Ultra SCSI*. In addition, there are now two kinds of fiber channel that carry the SCSI protocol. Working out which type you have on your Sun is not that simple. The main differences between interface types are in the number of disks that can be supported on a SCSI bus before the bus becomes saturated and the maximum effective cable length allowed.

SCSI Interface Types

The original asynchronous and synchronous SCSI interfaces support data rates up to 5 Mbytes/s on a 6 meter effective cable length. The speed of asynchronous SCSI drops off sharply as the cable length increases, so keep the bus as short as possible.

Fast SCSI increases the maximum data rate from 5 Mbytes/s to 10 Mbytes/s and halves the cable length from 6 meters to 3 meters. By use of the latest type of very high quality SCSI cables and active termination plugs from Sun, fast SCSI can be made to work reliably at up to 6 meters.

Fast and Wide SCSI uses a special cable with extra signals (68 rather than 50 pins) to carry 16 bits of data rather than 8 bits in each clock cycle. This usage doubles the data rate to 20 Mbytes/s and provides 8 more drive select lines, and so can support 15 target devices.

Ultra SCSI doubles the clock rate again to 20 MHz on the same cabling and connectors as fast-wide SCSI, hence providing a 40 Mbyte/s bandwidth. Cable lengths are halved as a consequence, severely limiting the number of devices that can be connected. Ultra SCSI is most commonly used to connect to a hardware RAID controller if a large number of devices need to be configured. There is also an Ultra2 SCSI that runs at 40 MHz, providing 80 Mbytes/s bandwidth, but there are serious cabling problems at this data rate and Sun has moved on to fiber interfaces instead.

Differential signaling can be used with Fast SCSI, Fast/Wide SCSI, and Ultra SCSI to increase the cable length to 25 meters (12 meters for UltraSCSI), but it uses incompatible electrical signals and a different connector and so can only be used with devices that have purpose-built differential interfaces. The principle is that instead of a single electrical signal varying between 0V and +5V, the transmitter generates two signals varying between +5V and -5V, where one is the inverse of the other. Any noise pickup along the cable tends to be added to both signals; however, in the receiver, the difference between the two signals is used, so the noise cancels out and the signal comes through clearly.

Sun's original Fiber Channel SCSI uses a high-speed, optical fiber interconnect to carry the SCSI protocol to a disk array. It runs at about 25 Mbytes/s in each direction simultaneously for a 1,000 meters or more. This is actually quarter-speed fiber.

The latest type of fiber channel is full speed at 100 Mbytes/s in both directions. The very latest standard forms a loop of fiber that connects to individual disk drives that have been fitted with their own fiber interfaces. This is called Fiber Channel Arbitrated Loop, or FC-AL (often pronounced eff-cal); a double loop is used for redundancy and even higher throughput. Sun's A5000 FC-AL array can sustain 180 Mbytes/s over its dual FC-AL loops that go directly to every disk in the package.

The SCSI disks shown in Table 8-5 on page 205 transfer data at a much slower rate than that of the FC-AL array. They do, however, have a buffer built into the SCSI drive that collects data at the slower rate and can then pass data over the bus at a higher rate. With Asynchronous SCSI, the data is transferred by means of a handshake protocol that slows down as the SCSI bus gets longer. For fast devices on a very short bus, the SCSI bus can achieve full speed, but as devices are added and the bus length and capacitance increases, the transfers slow down. For Synchronous SCSI, the devices on the bus negotiate a transfer rate that will slow down if the bus is long, but by avoidance of the need to send handshakes, more data can be sent in its place and throughput is less dependent on the bus length.

Tagged Command Queuing Optimizations

TCQ provides optimizations similar to those implemented on IPI controllers, but the buffer and optimization occur in each drive rather than in the controller for a string of disks. TCQ is implemented in Solaris 2 only and is supported on the disks listed in Table 8-6. Sun spent a lot of time debugging the TCQ firmware in the disks when it was first used. Since few other vendors used this feature at first, it may be wise to disable TCQ if old, third-party disks are configured on a system. Some old, third-party drives, when probed, indicate that they support TCQ but fail when it is used. This may be an issue when upgrading from SunOS 4 (which never tries to use TCQ) to Solaris 2, but is not likely to be an issue on recent systems. In Solaris 2, TCQ is disabled by clearing a `scsi_options` bit, as described in the next section.

Table 8-6   Advanced SCSI Disk Specifications

Disk Type	Tagged Commands	On-board Cache
Sun 424 3.5″	None	64 KB
Sun 535 thin 3.5″	64	256 KB
Sun 1.05G 3.5″	64	256 KB
Sun 1.05G thin 3.5″	64	256 KB
Sun 2.1G 5.25″	16	256 KB
Sun 2.1G 3.5″ 5400rpm	64	256 KB
Sun 2.9G 5.25″	64	512 KB
Most recent disks	64	512 – 2048 KB

Setting the SCSI Options Variable

A kernel variable called *scsi_options* globally enables or disables several SCSI features. To see the option values, look at the values defined in the file (for Solaris 2) `/usr/include/sys/scsi/conf/autoconf.h`. The default value for the kernel variable *scsi_options* is 0x3F8, which enables all options. To disable tagged command queuing, set *scsi_options* to 0x378. If wide SCSI disks are being used with Solaris 2.3, then `/etc/system` should have the command `set scsi_options=0x3F8` added. The command is set by default in later releases. Table 8-7 lists the *scsi_options* values.

Table 8-7   SCSI Options Bit Definitions

`#define SCSI_OPTIONS_DR`	`0x8`	Global disconnect/reconnect
`#define SCSI_OPTIONS_LINK`	`0x10`	Global linked commands
`#define SCSI_OPTIONS_SYNC`	`0x20`	Global synchronous xfer capability
`#define SCSI_OPTIONS_PARITY`	`0x40`	Global parity support
`#define SCSI_OPTIONS_TAG`	`0x80`	Global tagged command support
`#define SCSI_OPTIONS_FAST`	`0x100`	Global FAST scsi support
`#define SCSI_OPTIONS_WIDE`	`0x200`	Global WIDE scsi support

Sun's SCSI Controller Products

The original SPARCstation 1 and the VME-hosted SCSI controller used by the SPARCserver 470 do not support Synchronous SCSI. In the case of the SPARCstation 1, this nonsupport is due to SCSI bus noise problems that were solved for the SPARCstation 1+ and subsequent machines. If noise occurs during a Synchronous SCSI transfer, then a SCSI reset happens, and, although disks will retry, tapes will abort. In versions of SunOS before SunOS 4.1.1, the SPARCstation 1+, IPC, and SLC have Synchronous SCSI disabled as well. The VME SCSI controller supports a maximum of 1.2 Mbytes/s, whereas the original SBus SCSI supports 2.5 Mbytes/s because it shares its unbuffered DMA controller bandwidth with the Ethernet.

The SPARCstation 2, IPX, and ELC use a higher-performance, buffered-SBus DMA chip than in the SPARCstation 1, 1+, SLC, and IPC, and they can drive sustained SCSI bus transfers at 5.0 Mbytes/s. The original SBus SCSI add-on cards and the built-in SCSI controller on the SPARCstation 330 and the original SPARCserver 600 series are also capable of this speed. The SPARCserver 600 spawned the first combined SCSI/Buffered Ethernet card, the SBE/S; one is integrated into the CPU board.

The SPARCstation 10 introduced the first fast SCSI implementation from Sun, together with a combined fast SCSI/Buffered Ethernet SBus card, the FSBE/S. The SPARCserver 600 series was upgraded to have the fast SCSI controller built in at this time.

A differential version of the fast SCSI controller with buffered Ethernet, the DSBE/S, was then introduced to replace the IPI controller in the high-end, rack-based systems. The DSBE/S is used together with differential fast SCSI drives, which come in rack-mount packages. All the above SCSI controllers are relatively simple DMA bus master devices that are all supported by the esp driver in Solaris 2.

The replacement for the DSBE/S is the DWI/S, which is a differential, wide SCSI interface with no Ethernet added. The wide SCSI interface runs at twice the speed and can support twice as many SCSI target addresses, so the controller can connect to two trays of disks. The DWI/S is a much more intelligent SCSI controller and has a new isp device driver. The isp driver is much more efficient than the esp driver and uses fewer interrupts and less CPU power to do an I/O operation. More recently, the UltraSPARC-based generation of systems mostly uses an interface, called fas, that lies between the esp and isp in its features. It supports fast SCSI but is less efficient and costs less than the isp controller. The latest PCI bus-based version of fas includes Ultra SCSI support.

Table 8-8 summarizes the specifications. Real throughput is somewhat less than the speed quoted, in the range 27,000-33,000 Kbytes/s for a "40MB/s" UltraSCSI connection.

Table 8-8   SCSI Controller Specifications

Controller	Bus Interface	Speed	Type
Sun SCSI-II	VME	1.2 MB/s	Asynchronous
SPARCserver 330	Built-in	5.0 MB/s	Synchronous
SPARCstation 1	Built-in SBus	2.5 MB/s	Asynchronous
SPARCstation 1+ SPARCstation IPC SPARCstation SLC	Built-in SBus	2.5 MB/s	Synchronous

Table 8-8   SCSI Controller Specifications (Continued)

Controller	Bus Interface	Speed	Type
SPARCstation 2 SPARCstation ELC SPARCstation IPX	Built-in SBus	5.0 MB/s	Synchronous
SBus SCSI X1055	SBus Add-on	5.0 MB/s	Synchronous
Early SPARCserver 600	Built-in SBus	5.0 MB/s	Synchronous
SBE/S X1054	Sbus Add-on	5.0 MB/s	Synchronous
SPARCstation 10 SPARCclassic SPARCstation LX SPARCstation 5 SPARCstation 20 Ultra 1/140, 170	Built-in SBus (esp)	10.0 MB/s	Fast
Late model SPARCserver 600	Built-in SBus (esp)	10.0 MB/s	Fast
Ultra 1/140E, 170E, 200E Ultra 2 E3000, E4000, E5000, E6000	Built-in Sbus (fas)	20.0MB/s	Fast and wide
Ultra 30 E450	PCI Bus	40MB/s	Ultra-SCSI 20MHz wide
FSBE/S X1053	SBus Add-on	10.0 MB/s	Fast
DSBE/S X1052	SBus Add-on	10.0 MB/s	Differential fast
SPARCserver 1000	Built-in SBus	10.0 MB/s	Fast
DWI/S X1062	SBus Add-on	20.0 MB/s	Differential wide
RSM2000 UltraSCSI	SBus Add-on	40.0 MB/s	Differential
SPARCstorage Array SOC	SBus Add-on	25+25MB/s	2 x Fiber Channel
SPARCstorage Array Internal	Built-in SBus (isp)	20.0 MB/s	Wide
Array5000 SOC+	Sbus Add-on	100+100MB/s	Fiber Channel Arbitrated Loop

The SPARCstorage Disk Array

The first fiber-based interface from Sun was the SPARCstorage Disk Array. The architecture of this subsystem is shown in Figure 8-9. The subsystem connects to a system by means of the SCSI protocol over a fiber channel link. A single SBus Fiber Channel card (the SBus Optical Channel) supports two separate connections, so that two disk arrays can be connected to a single SBus slot.

Figure 8-9   SPARCstorage Disk Array Architecture

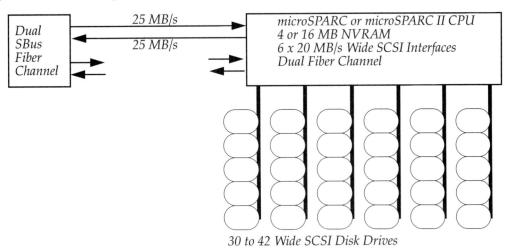

Several components make up the product in several combinations, as summarized in Table 8-9. The product name is a three-digit code such as 102 or 214.

- The first digit indicates the physical package. The 100 package is a compact unit the same size as a SPARCserver 1000; the unit takes thirty 1-inch high 3.5-inch drives that are hot pluggable in trays of 10. The 200 package is a rack-mounted cabinet that uses six of the old-style differential SCSI trays with six 5.25-inch disks—36 in total. The 210RSM package uses six of the RSM trays, which take seven individually hot-pluggable 3.5-inch disks each—42 in total.

- The middle digit in the product code indicates the controller. The original controller with 4 Mbytes of NVRAM is used in the 100 and 200 packages. The updated controller with 16 Mbytes of NVRAM is used in the 110 and 210 packages. The early models were just called the Model 100 and Model 200.

- For later models, the third digit indicates the size of the disk in gigabytes. The model 100 was mainly shipped with 1.05 Gbyte and 2.1 Gbyte disks as models 100 and 112. The original model 200 can be connected to existing trays of 2.9 Gbyte disks, but is most often used with trays of six 9.1 Gbyte disks, for a total of 648 Gbytes per SBus slot in high-capacity installations. The RSM trays are normally used with 4.2-Gbyte or 9-Gbyte disks for a total of 756 Gbytes per SBus slot.

Table 8-9   Common SPARCstorage Array Configurations

Product Name	Controller	Disk	Total
Model 100	4 Mbytes NVRAM	30 x 1.05 Gbytes	31 Gbytes
Model 112	16 Mbytes NVRAM	30 x 2.1 Gbytes	63 Gbytes
Model 114	16 Mbytes NVRAM	30 x 4.2 Gbytes	126 Gbytes
Model 200	4 Mbytes NVRAM	36 x 9.1 Gbytes	328 Gbytes
Model 214RSM	16 Mbytes NVRAM	42 x 4.2 Gbytes	176 Gbytes
Model 219RSM	16 Mbytes NVRAM	42 x 9.1 Gbytes	382 Gbytes

Each fiber channel interface contains two fibers that carry signals in opposite directions at up to 25 Mbytes/s. This is unlike normal SCSI where the same set of wires is used in both directions, and it allows concurrent transfer of data in both directions. Within the SPARCstorage Disk Array, a microSPARC processor connects to a dual fiber channel interface, allowing two systems to share a single array for high-availability configurations. A 4- or 16-Mbyte nonvolatile RAM buffer stores data that is on its way to disk. Since the NVRAM buffer has a battery backup, writes can safely be acknowledged as soon as they are received, before the data is actually written to disk. The microSPARC processor also controls six separate Fast and Wide SCSI channels, each connected to five, six, or seven disks at 20 Mbytes/s. The combination of software and hardware supports any mixture of mirroring, disk striping, and RAID5 across the drives. The SPARCstorage Array controller can sustain over 2,000 I/O operations per second (IOPS).

The fiber channel interface is faster than most SCSI controller interfaces and supports simultaneous transfer in both directions, unlike a conventional SCSI bus. The NVRAM store provides a very fast turnaround for writes. Read latency is not quite as good as a directly connected wide SCSI disk, and the ultimate throughput for sequential access is limited by the fiber capacity. These characteristics are ideally suited to general-purpose NFS service and on-line transaction processing (OLTP) workloads such as TPC-C, which are dominated by small random accesses and require fast writes for good interactive performance. The Veritas Volume Manager-derived SPARCstorage Manager software provided with the array has a GUI that helps keep track of all the disks, monitors performance, and makes it easy to allocate space within the array. Figure 8-10 and Figure 8-11 illustrate the graphical user interface.

Figure 8-10 SPARCstorage Array Manager Configuration Display

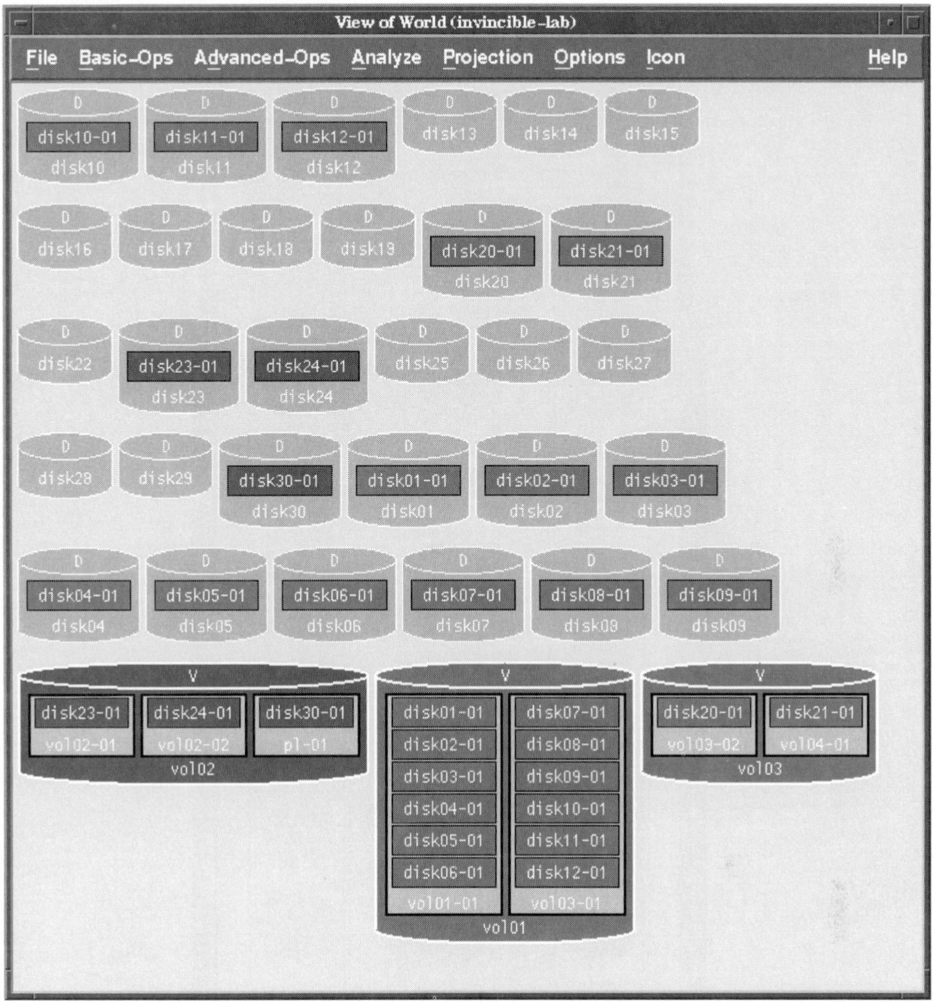

Figure 8-11   SPARCstorage Array Monitoring Display Screen Shot

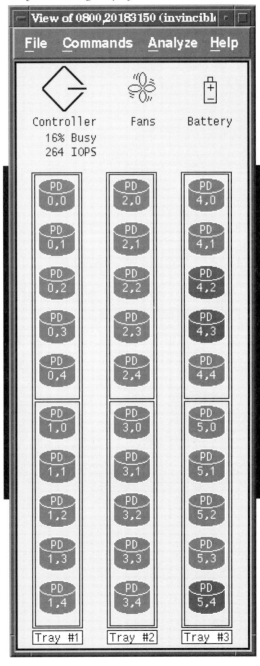

The RSM2000, A1000 and A3000 Hardware RAID Subsystems

The RSM2000 was renamed as the A3000 in early 1998. The A1000 is a small RAID subsystem using a single controller, while the A3000 uses dual controllers with higher capacity packaging. The controller is based on a hardware RAID controller design from Symbios. Sun worked with Symbios to upgrade the product, packaged it into Sun disk subsystems, and developed firmware and device drivers for Solaris. The A3000 design is fully redundant, with no single point of failure and very high performance in RAID5 mode. It has two Ultra SCSI connections to the host system and can sustain 66 Mbytes/s. In the event of a failure, it can continue to work with a single Ultra-SCSI connection. This mechanism is handled by means of a special rdac device driver that makes the two Ultra SCSI buses look like a single connection. A 100 Mbyte/s fiber channel connection in place of each Ultra SCSI to the host is an obvious upgrade to this product. The A1000 in a smaller package with a single controller provides an entry-level, high-performance RAID5 solution. Figure 8-12 illustrates the architecture. The RSM disk tray is superseded by a new package that includes an internal controller in the A1000, and direct connection to an external pair of controllers in the A3000.

Figure 8-12 RSM2000/A3000 Disk Array Architecture

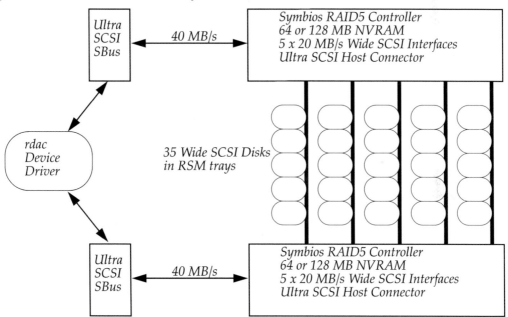

≡ 8

The Enterprise Network Array 5000: A5000 FC-AL Subsystem

The A5000 is a building block, used to construct a fiber-based storage fabric, that is very well suited to access from clusters of systems. The package is fully redundant and hot pluggable, with dynamic multipath connections, dual power supplies, and so on. The FC-AL loop goes right through the drives with no separate controller. The high bandwidth and lack of contention at the drive level allows each disk to support a 5%-10% higher random access rate—perhaps 115 IOPS rather than 105 on a comparable 7200 rpm disk. It also provides the lowest latency for reads and the highest bandwidth for streaming sequential reads and writes. Lack of NVRAM in the basic product can be compensated for by use of dedicated log disks to accelerate writes. It is best used in a mirrored configuration, inasmuch as there is no NVRAM for RAID5 acceleration in the initial product. Figure 8-13 illustrates the architecture.

Figure 8-13 56" Rack-Mounted A5000 Disk Array Architecture

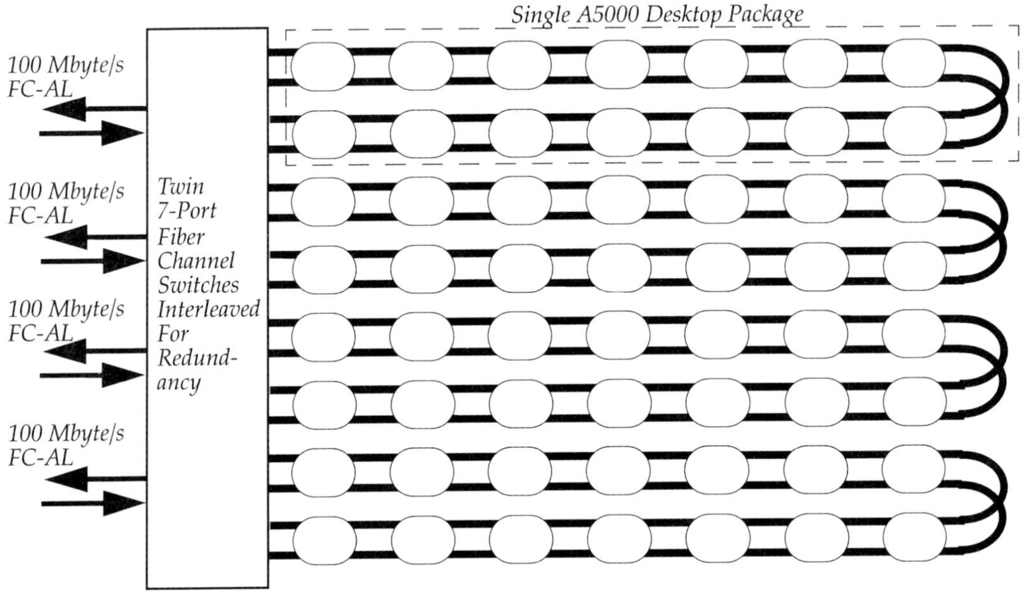

There are two packaging options: The desktop package contains 14 disks with twin loop interfaces; the rack-mounted server option contains four of the desktop packages combined with two 7-port fiber channel switches, so that no single point of failure can prevent access to all the disks. The dual loops from each package of 14 disks go to separate switches. The host interface has four loops, and fully redundant, high-bandwidth connections can be made between loops of hosts and disks in clustered configurations. When configured with 9.1-Gbyte disks, a 56-disk rack adds up to 510

Gbytes of disk with sustainable sequential throughput of about 360 Mbytes/s. These characteristics are ideal for data warehouse and high-performance computing applications in particular.

The A7000 High-End Disk Subsystem

In late 1997 Sun acquired the storage business of Encore corporation, and the Encore SP-40 product was renamed the Sun A7000 as the high end of Sun's new StorEdge product line. The A7000 is equally at home connected over an ESCON channel to a mainframe system or connected to Unix systems over SCSI. Uniquely, the same on-disk data can be accessed by both types of system concurrently. This avoids any copying overhead if mainframe data is being accessed for data warehousing applications on Unix systems. The A7000 also supports wide-area remote data copy at the storage subsystem level, which can be used to implement distributed disaster-resilient configurations. Unlike other Sun disk subsystems, the A7000 is configured to order by Sun personnel, contains "phone home" modem connections for automated remote diagnostics, and is designed with flexibility and availability as its primary characteristics. With up to 4 Gbytes of mirrored cache memory and over 1 terabyte per unit, the A7000 is a direct competitor to the EMC Symmetrix product line. It is also the first Sun disk subsystem supported on non-Sun servers (mainframe, Unix, and NT), although it is planned for the rest of Sun's disk subsystem products to be supported on HP-UX and NT platforms.

Networks

The subject of network configuration and performance has been extensively covered by other writers[1]. For that reason, this chapter concentrates on Sun-specific networking issues, such as the performance characteristics of the many network adapters and operating system releases.

New NFS Metrics

Local disk usage and NFS usage are functionally interchangeable, so Solaris 2.6 was changed to instrument NFS client mount points as if they were disks! NFS mounts are *always* shown by `iostat` and `sar`. Automounted directories coming and going more often than disks coming online may be an issue for performance tools that don't expect the number of `iostat` or `sar` records to change often.

The full instrumentation includes the wait queue for commands in the client (`biod wait`) that have not yet been sent to the server; the active queue for commands currently in the server; and utilization (%busy) for the server mount point activity level. Note that unlike the case with disks, 100% busy does *not* indicate that the server itself is saturated, it just indicates that the client always has outstanding requests to that server. An NFS server is much more complex than a disk drive and can handle a lot more simultaneous requests than a single disk drive can.

Figure 9-1 shows the new `-xnP` option, although NFS mounts appear in all formats. Note that the `P` option suppresses disks and shows only disk partitions. The `xn` option breaks down the response time, `svc_t`, into wait and active times and puts the expanded device name at the end of the line so that long names don't mess up the columns. The `vold` entry is used to mount floppy and CD-ROM devices.

---

1. In particular, see *Managing NFS and NIS* by Hal Stern.

Figure 9-1   Example iostat *Output Showing NFS Mount Points*

```
crun% iostat -xnP
                                   extended device statistics
   r/s   w/s    kr/s    kw/s wait actv wsvc_t asvc_t  %w %b device
   0.0   0.0     0.0     0.0  0.0  0.0    0.0    0.0    0  0 crun:vold(pid363)
   0.0   0.0     0.0     0.0  0.0  0.0    0.0    0.0    0  0 servdist:/usr/dist
   0.0   0.5     0.0     7.9  0.0  0.0    0.0   20.7    0  1
servhome:/export/home/adrianc
   0.0   0.0     0.0     0.0  0.0  0.0    0.0    0.0    0  0 servhome:/var/mail
   0.0   1.3     0.0    10.4  0.0  0.2    0.0  128.0    0  2 c0t2d0s0
   0.0   0.0     0.0     0.0  0.0  0.0    0.0    0.0    0  0 c0t2d0s2
```

New Network Metrics

The standard SNMP network management MIB for a network interface is supposed to contain IfInOctets and IfOutOctets counters that report the number of bytes input and output on the interface. These were not measured by network devices for Solaris 2, so the MIB always reported zero. Brian Wong and I filed bugs against all the different interfaces a few years ago, and bugs were filed more recently against the SNMP implementation. The result is that these counters have been added to the "le" and "hme" interfaces in Solaris 2.6, and the fix has been backported in patches for Solaris 2.5.1, as 103903-03 (le) and 104212-04 (hme).

The new counters added were:

* rbytes, obytes — read and output byte counts
* multircv, multixmt — multicast receive and transmit byte counts
* brdcstrcv, brdcstxmt — broadcast byte counts
* norcvbuf, noxmtbuf — buffer allocation failure counts

The full set of data collected for each interface can be obtained as described in "The Solaris 2 "kstat" Interface" on page 387. An SE script, called dumpkstats.se, prints out all of the available data, and an undocumented option, netstat -k, prints out the data. In Solaris 2.6, netstat -k takes an optional kstat name, as shown in Figure 9-2, so you don't have to search through the reams of data to find what you want.

Figure 9-2   Solaris 2.6 Example of netstat *-k to See Network Interface Data in Detail*

```
% netstat -k le0
le0:
ipackets 0 ierrors 0 opackets 0 oerrors 5 collisions 0
defer 0 framing 0 crc 0 oflo 0 uflo 0 missed 0 late_collisions 0
retry_error 0 nocarrier 2 inits 11 notmds 0 notbufs 0 norbufs 0
nocanput 0 allocbfail 0 rbytes 0 obytes 0 multircv 0 multixmt 0
brdcstrcv 0 brdcstxmt 5 norcvbuf 0 noxmtbuf 0
```

Virtual IP Addresses

You can configure more than one IP address on each interface, as shown in Figure 9-3. This is one way that a large machine can pretend to be many smaller machines consolidated together. It is also used in high-availability failover situations. In earlier releases, up to 256 addresses could be configured on each interface. Some large virtual web sites found this limiting, and now a new ndd tunable in Solaris 2.6 can be used to increase that limit. Up to about 8,000 addresses on a single interface have been tested. Some work was also done to speed up ifconfig of large numbers of interfaces. You configure a virtual IP address by using ifconfig on the interface, with the number separated by a colon. Solaris 2.6 also allows groups of interfaces to feed several ports on a network switch on the same network to get higher bandwidth.

Figure 9-3   Configuring More Than 256 IP Addresses Per Interface

```
# ndd /dev/ip -set ip_addrs_per_if 300
# ifconfig hme0:283 ...
```

Network Interface Types

There are many interface types in use on Sun systems. In this section, I discuss some of their distinguishing features.

10-Mbit SBus Interfaces — "le" and "qe"

The "le" interface is used on many SPARC desktop machines. The built-in Ethernet interface shares its direct memory access (DMA) connection to the SBus with the SCSI interface but has higher priority, so heavy Ethernet activity can reduce disk throughput. This can be a problem with the original DMA controller used in the SPARCstation 1, 1+, SLC, and IPC, but subsequent machines have enough DMA bandwidth to support both.

The add-on SBus Ethernet card uses exactly the same interface as the built-in Ethernet but has an SBus DMA controller to itself. The more recent buffered Ethernet interfaces used in the SPARCserver 600, the SBE/S, the FSBE/S, and the DSBE/S have a 256-Kbyte buffer to provide a low-latency source and sink for the Ethernet. This buffer cuts down on dropped packets, especially when many Ethernets are configured in a system that also has multiple CPUs consuming the memory bandwidth. The disadvantage is increased CPU utilization as data is copied between the buffer and main memory. The most recent and efficient "qe" Ethernet interface uses a buffer but has a DMA mechanism to transfer data between the buffer and memory. This interface is found in the SQEC/S qe quadruple 10-Mbit Ethernet SBus card and the 100-Mbit "be" Ethernet interface SBus card.

100-Mbit Interfaces — "be" and "hme"

The 100baseT standard takes the approach of requiring shorter and higher-quality, shielded, twisted pair cables, then running the normal Ethernet standard at ten times the speed. Performance is similar to FDDI, but with the Ethernet characteristic of collisions under heavy load. It is most useful to connect a server to a hub, which converts the 100baseT signal into many conventional 10baseT signals for the client workstations.

FDDI Interfaces

Two FDDI interfaces have been produced by Sun, and several third-party PCIbus and SBus options are available as well. FDDI runs at 100 Mbits/s and so has ten times the bandwidth of standard Ethernet. The SBus FDDI/S 2.0 "bf" interface is the original Sun SBus FDDI board and driver. It is a single-width SBus card that provides single-attach only. The SBus FDDI/S 3.0, 4.0, 5.0 "nf" software supports a range of SBus FDDI cards, including both single- and dual-attach types. These are OEM products from Network Peripherals Inc. The nf_stat command provided in /opt/SUNWconn/SUNWnf may be useful for monitoring the interface.

SBus ATM 155-Mbit Asynchronous Transfer Mode Cards

There are two versions of the SBus ATM 155-Mbit Asynchronous Transfer Mode card: one version uses a fiber interface, the other uses twisted pair cables like the 100baseT card. The ATM standard allows isochronous connections to be set up (so audio and video data can be piped at a constant rate), but the AAL5 standard used to carry IP protocol data makes it behave like a slightly faster FDDI or 100baseT interface for general-purpose use. You can connect systems back-to-back with just a pair of ATM cards and no switch if you only need a high-speed link between two systems. ATM configures a 9-Kbyte segment size for TCP, which is much more efficient than Ethernet's 1.5-Kbyte segment.

622-Mbit ATM Interface

The 622-Mbit ATM interface is one of the few cards that comes close to saturating an SBus. Over 500 Mbits/s of TCP traffic have been measured on a dual CPU Ultra 2/2200. The PCIbus version has a few refinements and a higher bandwidth bus interface, so runs a little more efficiently. It was used for the SPECweb96 benchmark results when the Enterprise 450 server was announced. The four-CPU E450 needed two 622-Mbit ATM interfaces to deliver maximum web server throughput. See "SPECweb96 Performance Results" on page 83.

Gigabit Ethernet Interfaces—vge

Gigabit Ethernet is the latest development. With the initial release, a single interface cannot completely fill the network, but this will be improved over time. If a server is feeding multiple 100-Mbit switches, then a gigabit interface may be useful because all the packets are the same 1.5-Kbyte size. Overall, Gigabit Ethernet is less efficient than ATM and slower than ATM622 because of its small packet sizes and relative immaturity as a technology. If the ATM interface was going to be feeding many Ethernet networks, ATM's large segment size would not be used, so Gigabit Ethernet may be a better choice for integrating into existing Ethernet networks.

Using NFS Effectively

The NFS protocol itself limits throughput to about 3 Mbytes/s per active client-side process because it has limited prefetch and small block sizes. The NFS version 3 protocol allows larger block sizes and other changes that improve performance on high-speed networks. This limit doesn't apply to the aggregate throughput if you have many active client processes on a machine.

First, some references:

- *Managing NFS and NIS* by Hal Stern (O'Reilly)—essential reading!

- *SMCC NFS Server Performance and Tuning Guide*

  The *SMCC NFS Server Performance and Tuning Guide* is part of the SMCC hardware-specific manual set. It contains a good overview of how to size an NFS server configuration. It is updated with each Solaris release, and I think you will find it very useful.

How Many NFS Server Threads?

In SunOS 4, the NFS daemon nfsd services requests from the network, and a number of nfsd daemons are started so that a number of outstanding requests can be processed in parallel. Each nfsd takes one request off the network and passes it to the I/O subsystem. To cope with bursts of NFS traffic, you should configure a large number of nfsds, even on low-end machines. All the nfsds run in the kernel and do not context switch in the same way as user-level processes do, so the number of hardware contexts is not a limiting factor (despite folklore to the contrary!). If you want to "throttle back" the NFS load on a server so that it can do other things, you can reduce the number. If you configure too many nfsds, some may not be used, but it is unlikely that there will be any adverse side effects as long as you don't run out of process table entries. Take the highest number you get by applying the following three rules:

- Two NFS threads per active client process

- Sixty-four NFS threads per SuperSPARC processor, 200 per UltraSPARC

- Sixteen NFS threads per Ethernet, 160 per 100-Mbit network

What Is a Typical NFS Operation Mix?

There are characteristic NFS operation mixes for each environment. The SPECsfs mix is based on the load generated by slow diskless workstations with a small amount of memory that are doing intensive software development. It has a large proportion of writes compared to the typical load mix from a modern workstation. If workstations are using the cachefs option, then many reads will be avoided, so the total load is less, but the percentage of writes is more like the SPECsfs mix. Table 9-1 summarizes the

Table 9-1   The LADDIS NFS Operation Mix

NFS Operation	Mix	Comment (Possible Client Command)
getattr	13%	Get file attributes (ls -1)
setattr	1%	Set file attributes (chmod)
lookup	34%	Search directory for a file and return handle (open)
readlink	8%	Follow a symbolic link on the server (ls)
read	22%	Read an 8-KB block of data
write	15%	Write an 8-KB block of data
create	2%	Create a file
remove	1%	Remove a file (rm)
readdir	3%	Read a directory entry (ls)
fsstat	1%	Get filesystem information (df)

information.

The nfsstat Command

The nfsstat -s command shows operation counts for the components of the NFS mix. This section is based upon the *Solaris 2.4 SMCC NFS Server Performance and Tuning Guide*. Figure 9-4 illustrates the results of an nfsstat -s command.

Figure 9-4   NFS Server Operation Counts

```
% nfsstat -s

Server rpc:
calls       badcalls    nullrecv    badlen      xdrcall
```

```
2104792    0              0            0            0

Server nfs:
calls        badcalls
2104792      5
null         getattr     setattr     root        lookup       readlink    read
10779   1%   966412 46%  13165  1%   0   0%      207574 10%   572  0%     686477 33%
wrcache      write       create      remove      rename       link        symlink
0   0%       179582  9%  5348  0%    9562  0%    557  0%      579  0%     32   0%
mkdir        rmdir       readdir     statfs
120   0%     386  0%     12650   1%  10997  1%
```

The meaning and interpretation of the measurements are as follows:

- calls — The total number of remote procedure (RPC) calls received. NFS is just one RPC application.

- badcalls — The total number of RPC calls rejected, the sum of badlen and xdrcall. If this value is non-zero, then RPC requests are being rejected. Reasons include having a user in too many groups, attempts to access an unexported file system, or an improper secure RPC configuration.

- nullrecv — The number of times an RPC call was not there when one was thought to be received.

- badlen — The number of calls with length shorter than the RPC minimum.

- xdrcall — The number of RPC calls whose header could not be decoded by the external data representation (XDR) translation.

- readlink — If this value is more than 10 percent of the mix, then client machines are making excessive use of symbolic links on NFS-exported file systems. Replace the link with a directory, perhaps using a loopback mount on both server and clients.

- getattr — If this value is more than 60 percent of the mix, then check that the attribute cache value on the NFS clients is set correctly. It may have been reduced or set to zero. See the mount_nfs command and the actimo option.

- null — If this value is more than 1 percent, then the automounter time-out values are set too short. Null calls are made by the automounter to locate a server for the file system.

- writes — If this value is more than 5 percent, then configure a Prestoserve option, NVRAM in the disk subsystem, or a logging file system on the server.

9

NFS Clients

On each client machine, use nfsstat -c to see the mix, as shown in Figure 9-5; for Solaris 2.6 or later clients, use iostat -xnP to see the response times.

Figure 9-5   NFS Client Operation Counts (Solaris 2.4 Version)

```
% nfsstat -c

Client rpc:
calls      badcalls   retrans   badxids   timeouts  waits      newcreds
1121626    61         464       15        518       0          0
badverfs   timers     toobig    nomem     cantsend  bufulocks
0          442        0         0         0         0


Client nfs:
calls      badcalls   clgets    cltoomany
1109675    6          1109607   0
Version 2: (1109678 calls)
null       getattr    setattr   root      lookup    readlink   read
0 0%       345948 31% 4097 0%   0 0%      375991 33% 214 0%     227031 20%
wrcache    write      create    remove    rename    link       symlink
0 0%       112821 10% 3525 0%   3120 0%   290 0%    54 0%      0 0%
mkdir      rmdir      readdir   statfs
370 0%     45 0%      10112 0%  26060 2%
```

- calls — The total number of calls sent.

- badcalls — The total number of calls rejected by RPC.

- retrans — The total number of retransmissions.

- badxid — The number of times that a duplicate acknowledgment was received for a single NFS request. If it is approximately equal to timeout and above 5 percent, then look for a server bottleneck.

- timeout —The number of calls that timed out waiting for a reply from the server. If the value is more than 5 percent, then RPC requests are timing out. A badxid value of less than 5 percent indicates that the network is dropping parts of the requests or replies. Check that intervening networks and routers are working properly; consider reducing the NFS buffer size parameters (see mount_nfs rsize and wsize), but reducing the parameters will reduce peak throughput.

- wait — The number of times a call had to wait because no client handle was available.

- newcred — The number of times authentication information had to be refreshed.

- null — If this value is above zero by a nontrivial amount, then increase the automount timeout parameter timeo.

You can also view each UDP-based mount point by using the `nfsstat -m` command on a client, as shown in Figure 9-6. TCP-based NFS mounts do not use these timers.

Figure 9-6   NFS Operation Response Times Measured by Client

```
% nfsstat -m
/home/username from server:/export/home3/username
 Flags:    vers=2,hard,intr,down,dynamic,rsize=8192,wsize=8192,retrans=5
 Lookups: srtt=7 (17ms), dev=4 (20ms), cur=2 (40ms)
 Reads:    srtt=16 (40ms), dev=8 (40ms), cur=6 (120ms)
 Writes:   srtt=15 (37ms), dev=3 (15ms), cur=3 (60ms)
 All:      srtt=15 (37ms), dev=8 (40ms), cur=5 (100ms)
/var/mail from server:/var/mail
 Flags:    vers=2,hard,intr,dynamic,rsize=8192,wsize=8192,retrans=5
 Lookups: srtt=8 (20ms), dev=3 (15ms), cur=2 (40ms)
 Reads:    srtt=18 (45ms), dev=6 (30ms), cur=5 (100ms)
 Writes:   srtt=9 (22ms), dev=5 (25ms), cur=3 (60ms)
 All:      srtt=8 (20ms), dev=3 (15ms), cur=2 (40ms)
```

This output shows the smoothed round-trip times (srtt), the deviation or variability of this measure (dev), and the current time-out level for retransmission (cur). Values are converted into milliseconds and are quoted separately for read, write, lookup, and all types of calls.

The system will seem slow if any of the round trip times exceeds 50 ms. If you find a problem, watch the `iostat -x` measures on the server for the disks that export the slow file system, as described in "How `iostat` Uses the Underlying Disk Measurements" on page 194. If the write operations are much slower than the other operations, you may need a Prestoserve, assuming that writes are an important part of your mix.

NFS Server Not Responding

If you see the "not responding" message on clients and the server has been running without any coincident downtime, then you have a serious problem. Either the network connections or the network routing is having problems, or the NFS server is completely overloaded.

The **netstat** Command

Several options to the netstat command show various parts of the TCP/IP protocol parameters and counters. The most useful options are the basic netstat command, which monitors a single interface, and the netstat -i command, which summarizes all the interfaces. Figure 9-7 shows an output from the iostat -i command.

Figure 9-7   netstat -i Output Showing Multiple Network Interfaces

```
% netstat -i
Name  Mtu  Net/Dest      Address        Ipkts   Ierrs Opkts   Oerrs Collis Queue
lo0   8232 loopback      localhost      1247105 0     1247105 0     0      0
bf0   4352 labnet-fddi   testsys-fddi   5605601 0     1266263 0     0      0
le1   1500 labnet-71     testsys-71      738403 0      442941 0     11485  0
le2   1500 labnet        testsys-lab    4001566 1     3141510 0     47094  0
le3   1500 labnet-tpt    testsys        4140495 2     6121934 0     70169  0
```

From a single measurement, you can calculate the collision rate since boot time; from noting the difference in the packet and collision counts over time, you can calculate the ongoing collision rates as Collis * 100 / Opkts for each device. In this case, lo0 is the internal loopback device, bf0 is an FDDI so has no collisions, le1 has a 2.6 percent collision rate, le2 has 1.5 percent, and le3 has 1.2 percent.

For more useful network performance summaries, see the network commands of the SE toolkit, as described starting with "net.se" on page 486.

Processors

Previous chapters have looked at the disk and network components of a system. This chapter covers the processor component. The details of particular processors are dealt with later. This chapter explains the measurements that each version of Solaris makes on a per processor basis. It also discusses the trade-offs made by different multiprocessor architectures.

Monitoring Processors

This section lists the most important commands that you should know and explains where their data comes from.

CPU Control Commands — `psrinfo`, `psradm`, and `psrset`

`psrinfo` tells you which CPUs are in use and when they were last enabled or disabled. `psradm` actually controls the CPUs. Note that in server systems, interrupts are bound to specific CPUs to improve the cache hit rate, and clock interrupts always go to CPU 0. Even if a CPU is disabled, it still receives interrupts. The `psrset` command manages processor sets in Solaris 2.6.

The Load Average

The load average is the sum of the run queue length and the number of jobs currently running on CPUs. The three figures given are averages over the last 1, 5, and 15 minutes. They can be used as an average run queue length indicator to see if more CPU power is required.

```
% uptime
  11:40pm  up 7 day(s),   3:54,   1 user,   load average: 0.27, 0.22, 0.24
```

The Data Behind `vmstat` and `mpstat` Output

What do all those columns of data in `vmstat` mean? How do they relate to the data from `mpstat`, and where does it all come from?

First, let's look at Figure 10-1 to remind ourselves what vmstat itself looks like.

Figure 10-1 Example vmstat Output

```
% vmstat 5
 procs      memory            page                disk           faults        cpu
 r b w   swap  free  re  mf pi po fr de sr f0 s0 s2 s3   in   sy   cs us sy id
 0 0 0  72724 25348   0   2  3  1  1  0  0  0  0  1  0   63  362   85  1  1 98
 0 0 0  64724 25184   0  24 56  0  0  0  0  0 19  0  311 1112  356  2  4 94
 0 0 0 .64724 24796   0   5 38  0  0  0  0  0 15  0   92  325  212  0  1 99
 0 0 0  64680 24584   0  12 106 0  0  0  0  0 41  0  574 1094  340  2  5 93
 0 1 0  64632 23736   0   0 195 0  0  0  0  0 66  0  612  870  270  1  7 92
 0 0 0  64628 22796   0   0 144 0  0  0  0  0 59  0  398  764  222  1  8 91
 0 0 0  64620 22796   0   0 79  0  0  0  0  0 50  0  255 1383  136  2 18 80
```

The command prints the first line of data immediately, then every five seconds prints a new line that gives the average rates over the five-second interval. The first line is also the average rate over the interval that started when the system was booted because the numbers are stored by the system as counts of the number of times each event has happened. To average over a time interval, you measure the counters at the start and end and divide the difference by the time interval. For the very first measure, there are zero counters to subtract, so you automatically get the count since boot, divided by the time since boot. The absolute counters themselves can be seen with another option to vmstat, as shown in Figure 10-2.

Figure 10-2 Example vmstat −s Raw Counters Output

```
% vmstat -s
        0 swap ins
        0 swap outs
        0 pages swapped in
        0 pages swapped out
   208724 total address trans. faults taken
    45821 page ins
     3385 page outs
    61800 pages paged in
    27132 pages paged out
      712 total reclaims
      712 reclaims from free list
        0 micro (hat) faults
   208724 minor (as) faults
    44636 major faults
    34020 copy-on-write faults
    77883 zero fill page faults
     9098 pages examined by the clock daemon
        1 revolutions of the clock hand
    27748 pages freed by the clock daemon
```

Figure 10-2 Example `vmstat  -s` *Raw Counters Output (Continued)*

```
      1333 forks
       187 vforks
      1589 execs
   6730851 cpu context switches
  12848989 device interrupts
    340014 traps
  28393796 system calls
    285638 total name lookups (cache hits 91%)
       108 toolong
    159288 user    cpu
    123409 system  cpu
  15185004 idle    cpu
    192794 wait    cpu
```

The other closely related command is `mpstat`, which shows basically the same data but on a per-CPU basis. Figure 10-3 shows some output on a dual CPU system.

Figure 10-3 Example `mpstat` *Output*

```
% mpstat 5
CPU minf mjf xcal  intr ithr  csw icsw migr smtx  srw syscl  usr sys  wt idl
  0    1   0    4    82   17   43    0    5    1    0   182    1   1    1  97
  2    1   0    3    81   17   42    0    5    2    0   181    1   1    1  97
CPU minf mjf xcal  intr ithr  csw icsw migr smtx  srw syscl  usr sys  wt idl
  0    2   0   39   156  106   42    0    5   21    0    30    0   2   61  37
  2    0   0    0   158  106  103    5    4    8    0  1704    3  36   61   0
CPU minf mjf xcal  intr ithr  csw icsw migr smtx  srw syscl  usr sys  wt idl
  0    0  19   28   194  142   96    1    4   18    0   342    1   8   76  16
  2    0   6   11   193  141   62    4    4   10    0   683    5  15   74   6
CPU minf mjf xcal  intr ithr  csw icsw migr smtx  srw syscl  usr sys  wt idl
  0    0  22   33   215  163   87    0    7    0    0   287    1   4   90   5
  2    0  22   29   214  164   88    2    8    1    0   304    2   5   89   4
```

The Sources of **vmstat** Data

The data is read from the kernel statistics interface that is described in "The Solaris 2 "kstat" Interface" on page 387. Most of the data is maintained on a per-CPU basis by the kernel and is combined into the overall summaries by the commands themselves. The same `kstat`(3K) programming interface that is used to get at the per-disk statistics is used. It is very lightweight—it takes only a few microseconds to retrieve each data structure. The data structures are based on those described in the file `/usr/include/sys/sysinfo.h`, the system information header file. Of course, all the raw `kstat` data is directly available to the SE toolkit, which contains customized scripts; see "vmstat.se" on page 500 and "mpvmstat.se" on page 485.

Process Queues

As we follow through the fields of vmstat, we see that the first one is labeled procs, r, b, w. This field is derived from the sysinfo data, and there is a single global kstat with the same form as the sysinfo structure shown in Figure 10-4.

Figure 10-4 The sysinfo Process Queue Data Structure

```
typedef struct sysinfo {          /* (update freq) update action          */
        ulong   updates;          /* (1 sec) ++                           */
        ulong   runque;           /* (1 sec) += num runnable procs        */
        ulong   runocc;           /* (1 sec) ++ if num runnable procs > 0 */
        ulong   swpque;           /* (1 sec) += num swapped procs         */
        ulong   swpocc;           /* (1 sec) ++ if num swapped procs > 0  */
        ulong   waiting;          /* (1 sec) += jobs waiting for I/O      */
} sysinfo_t;
```

As the comments indicate, the field is updated once per second. The run queue counts the number of runnable processes that are not running. The extra data values, called runocc and swpocc, are displayed by sar -q and show the occupancy of the queues. Solaris 2 counts the total number of swapped-out *idle* processes, so if you see any swapped jobs registered in swpque, don't be alarmed. sar -q is strange: If the number to be displayed is zero, sar -q displays nothing at all, just white space. If you add the number of processes actually running on CPUs in the system, then you get the same measure on which the load average is based. waiting counts how many processes are waiting for a block device transfer (a disk I/O) to complete. It shows up as the b field in vmstat.

Virtual Memory Counters

The next part of vmstat lists the free swap space and memory. This information is obtained as a kstat from a single global vminfo structure, as shown in Figure 10-5.

Figure 10-5 The vminfo Memory Usage Data Structure

```
typedef struct vminfo {            /* (update freq) update action          */
      longlong_t freemem;          /* (1 sec) += freemem in pages          */
      longlong_t swap_resv;        /* (1 sec) += reserved swap in pages    */
      longlong_t swap_alloc;       /* (1 sec) += allocated swap in pages   */
      longlong_t swap_avail;       /* (1 sec) += unreserved swap in pages  */
      longlong_t swap_free;        /* (1 sec) += unallocated swap in pages */
} vminfo_t;
```

The only swap number shown by vmstat is swap_avail, which is the most important one. If this number ever goes to zero, your system will hang up and be unable to start more processes! For some strange reason, sar -r reports swap_free instead and converts the data into useless units of 512-byte blocks. The bizarre state of the sar command is one reason why we were motivated to create and develop the SE toolkit in the first place!

These measures are accumulated, so you calculate an average level by taking the values at two points in time and dividing the difference by the number of updates.

Paging Counters

The paging counters shown in Figure 10-6 are maintained on a per-cpu basis; it's also clear that vmstat and sar don't show all of the available information. The states and state transitions being counted are described in detail in "The Life Cycle of a Typical Physical Memory Page" on page 326.

Figure 10-6 The cpu_vminfo Per CPU Paging Counters Structure

```
typedef struct cpu_vminfo {
        ulong   pgrec;          /* page reclaims (includes page-out)    */
        ulong   pgfrec;         /* page reclaims from free list     */
        ulong   pgin;           /* page-ins                 */
        ulong   pgpgin;         /* pages paged in           */
        ulong   pgout;          /* page-outs                */
        ulong   pgpgout;        /* pages paged out          */
        ulong   swapin;         /* swap-ins                 */
        ulong   pgswapin;       /* pages swapped in         */
        ulong   swapout;        /* swap-outs                */
        ulong   pgswapout;      /* pages swapped out        */
        ulong   zfod;           /* pages zero filled on demand      */
        ulong   dfree;          /* pages freed by daemon or auto        */
        ulong   scan;           /* pages examined by page-out daemon    */
        ulong   rev;            /* revolutions of the page daemon hand  */
        ulong   hat_fault;      /* minor page faults via hat_fault()    */
        ulong   as_fault;       /* minor page faults via as_fault()     */
        ulong   maj_fault;      /* major page faults        */
        ulong   cow_fault;      /* copy-on-write faults     */
        ulong   prot_fault;     /* protection faults        */
        ulong   softlock;       /* faults due to software locking req   */
        ulong   kernel_asflt;   /* as_fault()s in kernel addr space     */
        ulong   pgrrun;         /* times pager scheduled    */
} cpu_vminfo_t;
```

A few of these might need some extra explanation. Protection faults occur when a program tries to access memory it shouldn't, gets a segmentation violation signal, and dumps a core file. Hat faults occur only on systems that have a software-managed memory management unit (sun4c and sun4u). *Hat* stands for hardware address translation.

10

I'll skip the disk counters because `vmstat` is just reading the same `kstat` data as `iostat` and providing a crude count of the number of operations for the first four disks.

CPU Usage and Event Counters

Let's remind ourselves again what `vmstat` looks like.

```
% vmstat 5
 procs     memory            page            disk          faults      cpu
 r b w   swap  free  re  mf pi po fr de sr f0 s0 s2 s3   in   sy   cs us sy id
 0 0 0  72724 25348   0   2  3  1  1  0  0  0  1  0   63  362   85  1  1 98
```

The last six columns show the interrupt rate, system call rate, context switch rate, and CPU user, system, and idle time. The per-cpu structure from which these are derived is the biggest structure yet, with about 60 values. Some of them are summarized by `sar`, but a lot of interesting stuff here is being carefully recorded by the kernel, is read by `vmstat`, and is then just thrown away. Look down the comments in Figure 10-7, and at the end I'll point out some nonobvious and interesting values. The cpu and wait states are arrays holding the four CPU states—usr/sys/idle/wait—and three wait states, io/swap/pio. Only the io wait state is implemented, so this measurement is superfluous. (I made the `mpvmstat.se` script print out the wait states before I realized that they were always zero.)

Figure 10-7 The cpu_sysinfo Per-CPU System Information Structure

```
typedef struct cpu_sysinfo {
        ulong   cpu[CPU_STATES]; /* CPU utilization               */
        ulong   wait[W_STATES];  /* CPU wait time breakdown       */
        ulong   bread;           /* physical block reads          */
        ulong   bwrite;          /* physical block writes (sync+async)  */
        ulong   lread;           /* logical block reads           */
        ulong   lwrite;          /* logical block writes          */
        ulong   phread;          /* raw I/O reads                 */
        ulong   phwrite;         /* raw I/O writes                */
        ulong   pswitch;         /* context switches              */
        ulong   trap;            /* traps                         */
        ulong   intr;            /* device interrupts             */
        ulong   syscall;         /* system calls                  */
        ulong   sysread;         /* read() + readv() system calls */
        ulong   syswrite;        /* write() + writev() system calls  */
        ulong   sysfork;         /* forks                         */
        ulong   sysvfork;        /* vforks                        */
        ulong   sysexec;         /* execs                         */
        ulong   readch;          /* bytes read by rdwr()          */
        ulong   writech;         /* bytes written by rdwr()       */
        ulong   rcvint;          /* XXX: UNUSED                   */
```

```
        ulong   xmtint;         /* XXX: UNUSED                          */
        ulong   mdmint;         /* XXX: UNUSED                          */
        ulong   rawch;          /* terminal input characters           */
        ulong   canch;          /* chars handled in canonical mode     */
        ulong   outch;          /* terminal output characters          */
        ulong   msg;            /* msg count (msgrcv()+msgsnd() calls)  */
        ulong   sema;           /* semaphore ops count (semop() calls)  */
        ulong   namei;          /* pathname lookups                    */
        ulong   ufsiget;        /* ufs_iget() calls                    */
        ulong   ufsdirblk;      /* directory blocks read               */
        ulong   ufsipage;       /* inodes taken with attached pages    */
        ulong   ufsinopage;     /* inodes taken with no attached pages */
        ulong   inodeovf;       /* inode table overflows               */
        ulong   fileovf;        /* file table overflows                */
        ulong   procovf;        /* proc table overflows                */
        ulong   intrthread;     /* interrupts as threads (below clock) */
        ulong   intrblk;        /* intrs blkd/preempted/released (swtch) */
        ulong   idlethread;     /* times idle thread scheduled         */
        ulong   inv_swtch;      /* involuntary context switches        */
        ulong   nthreads;       /* thread_create()s                    */
        ulong   cpumigrate;     /* cpu migrations by threads           */
        ulong   xcalls;         /* xcalls to other cpus                */
        ulong   mutex_adenters; /* failed mutex enters (adaptive)      */
        ulong   rw_rdfails;     /* rw reader failures                  */
        ulong   rw_wrfails;     /* rw writer failures                  */
        ulong   modload;        /* times loadable module loaded        */
        ulong   modunload;      /* times loadable module unloaded      */
        ulong   bawrite;        /* physical block writes (async)       */
/* Following are gathered only under #ifdef STATISTICS in source       */
        ulong   rw_enters;      /* tries to acquire rw lock            */
        ulong   win_uo_cnt;     /* reg window user overflows           */
        ulong   win_uu_cnt;     /* reg window user underflows          */
        ulong   win_so_cnt;     /* reg window system overflows         */
        ulong   win_su_cnt;     /* reg window system underflows        */
        ulong   win_suo_cnt;    /* reg window system user overflows    */
} cpu_sysinfo_t;
```

Some of the numbers printed by mpstat are visible here. The smtx value used to watch for kernel contention is mutex_adenters. The srw value is the sum of the failures to obtain a readers/writer lock. The term xcalls is shorthand for cross-calls. A cross-call occurs when one CPU wakes up another CPU by interrupting it.

vmstat prints out 22 columns of numbers, summarizing over a hundred underlying measures (even more on a multiprocessor). It's good to have a lot of different things summarized in one place, but the layout of vmstat (and sar) is as much a result of their long history as it is by design. Could you do better?

I'm afraid I'm going to end up plugging the SE toolkit again. It's just so easy to get at this data and do things with it. All the structures can be read by any user, with no need to be setuid root. (This is a key advantage of Solaris 2; other Unix systems read the kernel directly, so you would have to obtain root permissions.)

If you want to customize your very own vmstat, you could either write one from scratch in C, using the kstat library as described in "The Solaris 2 "kstat" Interface" on page 387, or you could load the SE toolkit and spend a few seconds modifying a trivial script. Either way, if you come up with something that you think is an improvement, while staying with the basic concept of one line of output that fits in 80 columns, send it to me, and we'll add it to the next version of SE.

If you are curious about how some of these numbers behave but can't be bothered to write your own SE scripts, you should try out the GUI front end to the raw kstat data that is provided in the SE toolkit as infotool.se. A sample snapshot is shown in Figure 16-12 on page 480.

Use of mpstat to Monitor Interrupts and Mutexes

The mpstat output shown below was measured on a 16-CPU SPARCcenter 2000 running Solaris 2.4 and with about 500 active time-shared database users. One of the key measures is smtx, the number of times the CPU failed to obtain a mutex immediately. If the number is more than about 200 per CPU, then usually system time begins to climb. The exception is the master CPU that is taking the 100 Hz clock interrupt, normally CPU 0 but in this case CPU 4. It has a larger number (1,000 or more) of very short mutex stalls that don't hurt performance. Higher-performance CPUs can cope with higher smtx values before they start to have a problem; more recent releases of Solaris 2 are tuned to remove sources of mutex contention. The best way to solve high levels of mutex contention is to upgrade to at least Solaris 2.6, then use the lockstat command to find which mutexes are suffering from contention, as described in "Monitoring Solaris 2.6 Lock Statistics" on page 239.

Figure 10-8 Monitoring All the CPUs with mpstat

CPU	minf	mjf	xcal	intr	ithr	csw	icsw	migr	smtx	srw	syscl	usr	sys	wt	idl
0	45	1	0	232	0	780	234	106	201	0	950	72	28	0	0
1	29	1	0	243	0	810	243	115	186	0	1045	69	31	0	0
2	27	1	0	235	0	827	243	110	199	0	1000	75	25	0	0
3	26	0	0	217	0	794	227	120	189	0	925	70	30	0	0
4	9	0	0	234	92	403	94	84	1157	0	625	66	34	0	0
5	30	1	0	510	304	764	213	119	176	0	977	69	31	0	0
6	35	1	0	296	75	786	224	114	184	0	1030	68	32	0	0
7	29	1	0	300	96	754	213	116	190	0	982	69	31	0	0
9	41	0	0	356	126	905	231	109	226	0	1078	69	31	0	0
11	26	0	0	231	2	805	235	120	199	0	1047	71	29	0	0

CPU	minf	mjf	xcal	intr	ithr	csw	icsw	migr	smtx	srw	syscl	usr	sys	wt	idl
12	29	0	0	405	164	793	238	117	183	0	879	66	34	0	0
15	31	0	0	288	71	784	223	121	200	0	1049	66	34	0	0
16	71	0	0	263	55	746	213	115	196	0	983	69	31	0	0
17	34	0	0	206	0	743	212	115	194	0	969	69	31	0	0

Cache Affinity Algorithms

When a system that has multiple caches is in use, a process may run on a CPU and load part of itself into that cache, then stop running for a while. When it resumes, the Unix scheduler must decide which CPU to run it on. To reduce cache traffic, the process must preferentially be allocated to its original CPU, but that CPU may be in use or the cache may have been cleaned out by another process in the meantime.

The cost of migrating a process to a new CPU depends on the time since it last ran, the size of the cache, and the speed of the central bus. To strike a delicate balance, a general-purpose algorithm that adapts to all kinds of workloads was developed. In the case of the E10000, this algorithm manages up to 256 Mbytes of cache and has a significant effect on performance. The algorithm works by moving jobs to a private run queue for each CPU. The job stays on a CPU's run queue unless another CPU becomes idle, looks at all the queues, finds a job that hasn't run for a while on another queue, and migrates the job to its own run queue. A cache will be overwritten very quickly, so there is little benefit from binding a process very tightly to a CPU.

There is also a surprising amount of low-level background activity from various daemons and dormant applications. Although this activity does not add up to a significant amount of CPU time used, it is enough to cause a large, CPU-bound job to stall long enough for it to migrate to a different CPU. The time-share scheduler ensures that CPU-bound jobs get a long time slice but a low priority. Daemons get a short time slice and a high priority, because they wake up only briefly. The average time slice for a process can be calculated from the number of context switches and the CPU time used (available from the PRUSAGE call described in "Process Data Sources" on page 416). The SE Toolkit calculates and displays this data with an example script; see "pea.se" on page 488.

Unix on Shared Memory Multiprocessors

The Unix kernel has many critical regions, or sections of code, where a data structure is being created or updated. These regions must not be interrupted by a higher-priority interrupt service routine. A uniprocessor Unix kernel manages these regions by setting the interrupt mask to a high value while executing in the region. On a multiprocessor, there are other processors with their own interrupt masks, so a different technique must be used to manage critical regions.

The Spin Lock or Mutex

One key capability in shared memory, multiprocessor systems is the ability to perform interprocessor synchronization by means of atomic load/store or swap instructions. All SPARC chips have an instruction called LDSTUB, which means load-store-unsigned-byte. The instruction reads a byte from memory into a register, then writes 0xFF into memory in a single, indivisible operation. The value in the register can then be examined to see if it was already 0xFF, which means that another processor got there first, or if it was 0x00, which means that this processor is in charge. This instruction is used to make *mutual exclusion locks* (known as mutexes) that make sure only one processor at a time can hold the lock. The lock is acquired through LDSTUB and cleared by storing 0x00 back to memory.

If a processor does not get the lock, then it may decide to *spin* by sitting in a loop and testing the lock until it becomes available. By checking with a normal load instruction in a loop before issuing an LDSTUB, the processor performs the spin within the cache, and the bus snooping logic watches for the lock being cleared. In this way, spinning causes no bus traffic, so processors that are waiting do not slow down those that are working. A spin lock is appropriate when the wait is expected to be short. If a long wait is expected, the process should sleep for a while so that a different job can be scheduled onto the CPU. The extra SPARC V9 instructions introduced with UltraSPARC include an atomic compare-and-swap operation, which is used by the UltraSPARC-specific version of the kernel to make locking more efficient.

Code Locking

The simplest way to convert a Unix kernel that is using interrupt levels to control critical regions for use with multiprocessors is to replace the call that sets interrupt levels high with a call to acquire a mutex lock. At the point where the interrupt level was lowered, the lock is cleared. In this way, the same regions of code are locked for exclusive access. This method has been used to a greater or lesser extent by most MP Unix implementations, including SunOS 4 on the SPARCserver 600MP machines. The amount of actual concurrency that can take place in the kernel is controlled by the number and position of the locks.

In SunOS 4 there is effectively a single lock around the entire kernel. The reason for using a single lock is to make these MP systems totally compatible with user programs and device drivers written for uniprocessor systems. User programs can take advantage of the extra CPUs, but only one of the CPUs can be executing kernel code at a time.

When code locking is used, there are a fixed number of locks in the system; this number can be used to characterize how much concurrency is available. On a very busy, highly configured system, the code locks are likely to become bottlenecks, so that adding extra processors will not help performance and may actually reduce performance.

Data Locking and Solaris 2

The problem with code locks is that different processors often want to use the same code to work on different data. To allow this use, locks must be placed in data structures rather than in code. Unfortunately, this solution requires an extensive rewrite of the kernel—one reason why Solaris 2 took several years to create. The result is that the kernel has a lot of concurrency available and can be tuned to scale well with large numbers of processors. The same kernel is used on uniprocessors and multiprocessors, so that all device drivers and user programs must be written to work in the same environment and there is no need to constrain concurrency for compatibility with uniprocessor systems. The locks are still needed in a uniprocessor because the kernel can switch between kernel threads at any time to service an interrupt.

With data locking, there is a lock for each instance of a data structure. Since table sizes vary dynamically, the total number of locks grows as the tables grow, and the amount of concurrency that is available to exploit is greater on a very busy, highly configured system. Adding extra processors to such a system is likely to be beneficial. Solaris 2 has hundreds of different data locks and multiplied by the number of instances of the data, there will typically be many thousand locks in existence on a running system. As Solaris 2 is tuned for more concurrency, some of the remaining code locks are turned into data locks, and "large" locks are broken down into finer-grained locks. There is a trade-off between having lots of mutexes for good MP scalability and few mutexes for reduced CPU overhead on uniprocessors.

Monitoring Solaris 2.6 Lock Statistics

In Solaris 2.6, the lockstat(1) command offers a kernel lock monitoring capability that is very powerful and easy to use. The kernel can dynamically change its locks to start collecting information and return to the normal, highly optimized lock code when the collection is complete. There is some extra overhead while the locks are instrumented, but useful measurements can be taken in a few seconds without disruption of the work on production machines. Data is presented clearly with several options for how it is summarized, but you still must have a very good understanding of Unix kernel architecture and Solaris 2, in particular, to really understand what is happening.

You should read the lockstat(1) manual page to see all its options, but in normal operation, it is run by the root user for the duration of a process for which you want to monitor the effects. If you want to run it for an interval, use the sleep command. I had trouble finding an example that would cause lock contention in Solaris 2.6. Eventually, I found that putting a C shell into an infinite loop, as shown below, generates 120,000 or more system calls per second duplicating and shutting file descriptors. When two shells are run at the same time on a dual CPU system, mpstat shows that hundreds of mutex spins/second occur on each CPU. This test is not intended to be serious! The system call mix was monitored with `truss -c`, as shown in Figure 10-9. With `truss` running, the system call rate dropped to about 12,000 calls per second, so I ran `lockstat` separately from `truss`.

```
% while 1
? end
```

Figure 10-9   System Call Mix for C Shell Loop

```
% truss -c -p 351
^C
syscall         seconds    calls  errors
open                .26     2868
close               .43    17209
getpid              .44    17208
dup                 .31    14341
sigprocmask         .65    28690
                   ----     ---     ---
sys totals:        2.09    80316       0
usr time:           .39
elapsed:           6.51
```

The intention was to see what system calls were causing the contention, and it appears to be a combination of `dup` and `close`, possibly `sigprocmask` as well. Although there are a lot of calls to `getpid`, they should not cause any contention.

The example output shows that there were 3,318 adaptive mutex spins in 5 seconds, which is 663 mutex stalls per second in total and which matches the data reported by `mpstat`. The locks and callers are shown; the top lock seems to be `flock_lock`, which is a file-related lock. Some other locks that are not named in this display may be members of hashed lock groups. Several of the calling routines mention file or filesystem operations and `sigprocmask`, which ties up with the system call trace.

If you see high levels of mutex contention, you need to identify both the locks that are being contended on and the component of the workload that is causing the contention, for example, system calls or a network protocol stack. You can then try to change the workload to avoid the problem, and you should make a service call to Sun to report the contention. As Sun pushes multiprocessor scalability to 64 processors and beyond, there are bound to be new workloads and new areas of contention that do not occur on smaller configurations. Each new release of Solaris 2 further reduces contention to allow even higher scalability and new workloads. There is no point reporting high mutex contention levels in anything but the latest release of Solaris 2.

Figure 10-10 Example `lockstat` *Output*

```
# lockstat sleep 5


Adaptive mutex spin: 3318 events

Count indv cuml rcnt     spin Lock                     Caller
------------------------------------------------------------------------
  601  18%  18% 1.00        1 flock_lock               cleanlocks+0x10
  302   9%  27% 1.00        7 0xf597aab0               dev_get_dev_info+0x4c
  251   8%  35% 1.00        1 0xf597aab0               mod_rele_dev_by_major+0x2c
  245   7%  42% 1.00        3 0xf597aab0               cdev_size+0x74
  160   5%  47% 1.00        7 0xf5b3c738               ddi_prop_search_common+0x50
  157   5%  52% 1.00        1 0xf597aab0               ddi_hold_installed_driver+0x2c
  141   4%  56% 1.00        2 0xf5c138e8               dnlc_lookup+0x9c
  129   4%  60% 1.00        6 0xf5b1a790               ufs_readlink+0x120
  128   4%  64% 1.00        1 0xf5c46910               cleanlocks+0x50
  118   4%  67% 1.00        7 0xf5b1a790               ufs_readlink+0xbc
  117   4%  71% 1.00        6 stable_lock              specvp+0x8c
  111   3%  74% 1.00        1 0xf5c732a8               spec_open+0x54
  107   3%  77% 1.00        3 stable_lock              stillreferenced+0x8
   97   3%  80% 1.00        1 0xf5b1af00               vn_rele+0x24
   92   3%  83% 1.00       19 0xf5c732a8               spec_close+0x104
   84   3%  86% 1.00        1 0xf5b0711c               sfind+0xc8
   57   2%  87% 1.00        1 0xf5c99338               vn_rele+0x24
   53   2%  89% 1.00       54 0xf5b5b2f8               sigprocmask+0xa0
   46   1%  90% 1.00        1 0xf5b1af00               dnlc_lookup+0x12c
   38   1%  91% 1.00        1 0xf5b1af00               lookuppn+0xbc
   30   1%  92% 1.00        2 0xf5c18478               dnlc_lookup+0x9c
   28   1%  93% 1.00       33 0xf5b5b4a0               sigprocmask+0xa0
   24   1%  94% 1.00        4 0xf5c120b8               dnlc_lookup+0x9c
   20   1%  95% 1.00        1 0xf5915c58               vn_rele+0x24
   19   1%  95% 1.00        1 0xf5af1e58               ufs_lockfs_begin+0x38
   16   0%  96% 1.00        1 0xf5915c58               dnlc_lookup+0x12c
   16   0%  96% 1.00        1 0xf5c732a8               spec_close+0x7c
   15   0%  97% 1.00        1 0xf5915b08               vn_rele+0x24
   15   0%  97% 1.00       17 kmem_async_lock          kmem_async_dispatch+0xc
   15   0%  97% 1.00        1 0xf5af1e58               ufs_lockfs_end+0x24
   12   0%  98% 1.00        1 0xf5c99338               dnlc_lookup+0x12c
   11   0%  98% 1.00        1 0xf5c8ab10               vn_rele+0x24
    9   0%  98% 1.00        1 0xf5b0711c               vn_rele+0x24
    8   0%  99% 1.00        3 0xf5c0c268               dnlc_lookup+0x9c
    8   0%  99% 1.00        5 kmem_async_lock          kmem_async_thread+0x290
    7   0%  99% 1.00        2 0xf5c11128               dnlc_lookup+0x9c
    7   0%  99% 1.00        1 0xf5b1a720               vn_rele+0x24
    5   0%  99% 1.00        2 0xf5b5b2f8               clock+0x308
    5   0% 100% 1.00        1 0xf5b1a720               dnlc_lookup+0x12c
    3   0% 100% 1.00        1 0xf5915b08               dnlc_lookup+0x12c
    2   0% 100% 1.00        1 0xf5b5b4a0               clock+0x308
```

Figure 10-10 Example `lockstat` *Output (Continued)*

```
    2    0% 100% 1.00        1 0xf5c149b8           dnlc_lookup+0x9c
    2    0% 100% 1.00        1 0xf5c8ab10           dnlc_lookup+0x12c
    1    0% 100% 1.00        1 0xf5b183d0           esp_poll_loop+0xcc
    1    0% 100% 1.00        1 plocks+0x110         polldel+0x28
    1    0% 100% 1.00        2 kmem_async_lock      kmem_async_thread+0x1ec
    1    0% 100% 1.00        6 mml_table+0x18       srmmu_mlist_enter+0x18
    1    0% 100% 1.00        3 mml_table+0x10       srmmu_mlist_enter+0x18
-------------------------------------------------------------------------


Adaptive mutex block: 24 events

Count indv cuml rcnt     nsec Lock                 Caller
-------------------------------------------------------------------------
    3   12%  12% 1.00    90333 0xf5b3c738           ddi_prop_search_common+0x50
    3   12%  25% 1.00   235500 flock_lock           cleanlocks+0x10
    2    8%  33% 1.00   112250 0xf5c138e8           dnlc_lookup+0x9c
    2    8%  42% 1.00   281250 stable_lock          specvp+0x8c
    2    8%  50% 1.00   107000 0xf597aab0           ddi_hold_installed_driver+0x2c
    2    8%  58% 1.00    89750 0xf5b5b2f8           clock+0x308
    1    4%  63% 1.00    92000 0xf5c120b8           dnlc_lookup+0x9c
    1    4%  67% 1.00   174000 0xf5b0711c           sfind+0xc8
    1    4%  71% 1.00   238500 stable_lock          stillreferenced+0x8
    1    4%  75% 1.00   143500 0xf5b17ab8           esp_poll_loop+0x8c
    1    4%  79% 1.00    44500 0xf5b183d0           esp_poll_loop+0xcc
    1    4%  83% 1.00    81000 0xf5c18478           dnlc_lookup+0x9c
    1    4%  88% 1.00   413000 0xf5c0c268           dnlc_lookup+0x9c
    1    4%  92% 1.00  1167000 0xf5c46910           cleanlocks+0x50
    1    4%  96% 1.00    98500 0xf5c732a8           spec_close+0x7c
    1    4% 100% 1.00    94000 0xf5b5b4a0           clock+0x308
-------------------------------------------------------------------------


Spin lock spin: 254 events

Count indv cuml rcnt     spin Lock                 Caller
-------------------------------------------------------------------------
   48   19%  19% 1.00        3 atomic_lock+0x29e    rw_exit+0x34
   45   18%  37% 1.00       25 atomic_lock+0x24e    rw_exit+0x34
   44   17%  54% 1.00        1 atomic_lock+0x29d    rw_exit+0x34
   35   14%  68% 1.00        1 atomic_lock+0x24e    rw_enter+0x34
   32   13%  80% 1.00       19 cpus+0x44            disp+0x78
   22    9%  89% 1.00        1 atomic_lock+0x29d    rw_enter+0x34
   17    7%  96% 1.00       52 cpu[2]+0x44          disp+0x78
    6    2%  98% 1.00       10 cpu[2]+0x44          setbackdq+0x15c
    5    2% 100% 1.00        1 atomic_lock+0x29e    rw_enter+0x34
-------------------------------------------------------------------------


Thread lock spin: 3 events
```

Figure 10-10 Example `lockstat` *Output (Continued)*

```
Count indv cuml rcnt     spin Lock                  Caller
-------------------------------------------------------------------------
    3 100% 100% 1.00      19 0xf68ecf5b             ts_tick+0x8
-------------------------------------------------------------------------
```

Multiprocessor Hardware Configurations

At any point in time, there exist CPU designs that represent the best performance that can be obtained with current technology at a reasonable price. The cost and technical difficulty of pushing the technology further means that the most cost-effective way of increasing computer power is to use several processors. There have been many attempts to harness multiple CPUs and, today, there are many different machines on the market. Software has been the problem for these machines. It is hard to design software that will be portable across a large range of machines and that will scale up well when large number of CPUs are configured. Over many years, Sun has shipped high unit volumes of large-scale multiprocessor machines and has built up a large portfolio of well-tuned applications that are optimized for the Sun architecture.

The most common applications that can use multiprocessors are time-shared systems and database servers. These have been joined by multithreaded versions of CPU-intensive programs like MCAD finite element solvers, EDA circuit simulation packages, and other High Performance Computing (HPC) applications. For graphics-intensive applications where the X server uses a lot of the CPU power on a desktop machine, configuring a dual CPU system will help—the X protocol allows buffering and batched commands with few commands needing acknowledgments. In most cases, the application sends X commands to the X server and continues to run without waiting for them to complete. One CPU runs the application, and the other runs the X server and drives the display hardware.

Two classes of multiprocessor machines have some possibility of software compatibility, and both have SPARC-based implementations. For illustrations of these two classes, see Figure 10-11 and Figure 10-12.

Distributed Memory Multiprocessors

Distributed memory multiprocessors, also known as Massively Parallel Processors (MPP), can be thought of as a network of uniprocessors. Each processor has its own memory, and data must be explicitly copied over the network to another processor before it can be used. The benefit of this approach is that there is no contention for memory bandwidth to limit the number of processors. Moreover, if the network is made up of point-to-point links, then the network throughput increases as the number of processors increases. There is no theoretical limit to the number of processors that can be used in a system of this type, but there are problems with the high latency of the point-to-point links, and it is hard to find algorithms that scale with large numbers of processors.

Figure 10-11 Typical Distributed Memory Multiprocessor with Mesh Network

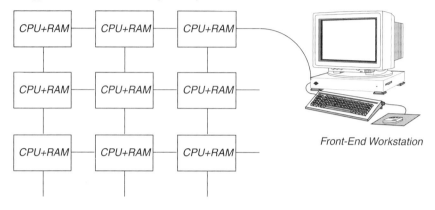

Shared Memory Multiprocessors

A shared memory multiprocessor is much more tightly integrated than a distributed memory multiprocessor and consists of a fairly conventional starting point of CPU, memory, and I/O subsystem, with extra CPUs added onto the central bus.

Figure 10-12 Typical Small-Scale, Shared Memory Multiprocessor

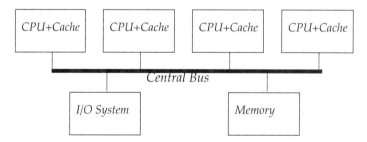

This configuration multiplies the load on the memory system by the number of processors, and the shared bus becomes a bottleneck. To reduce the load, caches are always used and very fast memory systems and buses are built. If more and faster processors are added to the design, the cache size must increase, the memory system must be improved, and the bus throughput must be increased. Most small-scale MP machines support up to four processors. Larger ones support a few tens of processors. With some workloads, the bus or memory system will saturate before the maximum number of processors has been configured.

Special circuitry snoops activity on the bus at all times so that all the caches can be kept coherent. If the current copy of some data is in more than one of the caches, then it will be marked as being shared. If it is updated in one cache, then the copies in the other caches are either invalidated or updated automatically. From a software point of view, there is never any need to explicitly copy data from one processor to another, and shared memory locations are used to communicate values among CPUs. The cache-to-cache transfers still occur when two CPUs use data in the same cache line, so such transfers must be considered from a performance point of view, but the software does not have to worry about it.

There are many examples of shared memory mainframes and minicomputers. SPARC-based Unix multiprocessors range from the dual-processor Ultra 2 and the 4-processor E450, to the 30-processor E6000 and the 64-processor E10000.

The high-end machines normally have multiple I/O subsystems and multiple memory subsystems connected to a much wider central bus, allowing more CPUs to be configured without causing bottlenecks in the I/O and memory systems. The E10000 goes one step further by using a crossbar switch as its interconnect. Multiple transfers occur between CPU, memory, and I/O on separate point-to-point data paths that all transfer data concurrently. This mechanism provides higher throughput, low contention, and low latency.

An unavoidable fact of life is that the memory latency increases as more CPUs are handled by a system design. Even with the same CPU module configuration, an Ultra 2 or E450 has lower main memory latency than does an E6000, which is in turn lower latency than an E10000. The performance of a single uniprocessor job is therefore higher on a smaller machine. The latency of a system increases at high load levels, and this load-dependent increase is more of an issue on a smaller machine. When comparing the E6000 and E10000, it seems that the E6000 has an advantage up to 20 CPUs, and the E10000 is usually faster for loads that consume 24–28 CPUs. The E10000 is the only option from 30–64 CPUs, and it maintains a lower latency under heavy load than any other system. So, from purely a performance point of view, it is far faster to have a row of four CPU E450s than to use an E10000 that is divided into many, separate, four-CPU domains.

Clusters of Shared Memory Machines

In any situation, the most efficient configuration is to use the smallest number of the fastest CPUs communicating over the lowest latency interconnect. This configuration minimizes contention and maximizes scalability. It is often necessary to compromise for practical or cost reasons, but it is clear that the best approach to building a large-scale system is to use the largest shared memory systems you can get, then cluster them together with the smallest number of nodes. The performance of a cluster is often limited by activities that are too hard to distribute, and so performance degrades to the performance of a single node for some of the time. If that node is as large as possible, then the overall efficiency is much higher.

Shared/Distributed Memory Multiprocessors

Although the two types of MP machines started out as very different approaches, the most recent examples of these types have converged.

The shared memory machines all have large caches for each CPU. For good performance, it is essential for the working set of data and instructions to be present in the cache. The cache is now analogous to the private memory of a distributed memory machine, and many algorithms that have been developed to partition data for a distributed memory machine are applicable to a cache-based, shared memory machine.

The latest distributed memory machines have moved from a software- or DMA-driven point-to-point link to an MMU-driven, cache-line-based implementation of distributed shared memory. With this system, the hardware is instructed to share a region of address space with another processor, and cache coherence is maintained over a point-to-point link. As the speed of these links approaches the speed of a shared memory backplane, the distributed memory system can be used to run shared memory algorithms more efficiently. Link speeds are comparable to the low end of shared memory backplane speeds, although they typically have much higher latency. The extra latency is due to the physical distances involved and the use of complex switching systems to interconnect large numbers of processors. Large distributed memory systems have higher latency than do smaller ones.

NUMA Multiprocessors

The hybrid that has emerged is known as nonuniform memory access, or NUMA. NUMAs are shared memory, multiprocessor machines where the memory latency varies. If the access is to memory in the local node, then access is fast; if the access request has to travel over one or more communication links, then access becomes progressively slower. The node itself is often a single-board SMP with two to four CPUs. The SGI Origin 2000 system uses a twin-CPU node; the various Intel Pentium-based systems from Sequent, Data General, and others use a 4-CPU node. However, it makes far more sense when building NUMA systems to use an entire high-end server as a node, with 20 or more CPUs. The bulk of high-end server system requirements are for 10 to 30 or so CPUs, and customers like to buy a half-configured system to allow for future expansion. For Sun this requirement can be satisfied by an SMP such as the E6000 or E10000, so Sun had no need to develop a NUMA-based system for the 1996–1998 generation. NUMA-based competitors must configure multiple nodes to satisfy today's requirements, and users of these systems are suffering from the new problems that come with this technology.

Benchmarks such as the TCP-D data warehouse test—see http://www.tpc.org—have shown that Sun's SMP machines do beat the NUMA machines on price and performance over the whole range of database sizes. This benchmark is ideally suited to NUMA because the query structures are well understood and the data layout can be optimized to keep the NUMA nodes well balanced. In real life, data warehouse queries are often constructed ad hoc, and it is not possible to optimize data placement in advance. The TPC-D benchmark is substantially overstating the performance of NUMA machines as data warehouse engines because of this effect. Data placement is not an issue in one large SMP node. In general, the workload on a system is not constant; it can vary from one query to the next or from one day to the next. In a benchmark situation, a NUMA machine can be optimized for the fixed benchmark workload but would need to be continuously reoptimized for real-world workloads.

A technique used to speed up NUMA systems is data replication. The same data can be replicated in every node so that it is always available at a short memory latency. This technique has been overused by some vendors in benchmarks, with hundreds of Mbytes of data duplicated over all the nodes. The effect is that a large amount of RAM is wasted because there are many nodes over which to duplicate the data. In a 32-CPU system made up of 2-way or 4-way nodes, you might need to configure extra memory to hold 16 or 8 copies of the data. On a 32-CPU SMP system, there is a single copy. If there are any writes to this data, the NUMA machines must synchronize all their writes, a significant extra load.

For all these reasons, the best MPP or NUMA configuration should be built by clustering the smallest number of the largest possible SMP nodes.

CPU Caches

Performance can vary even among machines that have the same CPU and clock rate if they have different memory systems. The interaction between caches and algorithms can cause performance problems, and an algorithm change may be called for to work around the problem. This section provides information on the CPU caches and memory management unit designs of various SPARC platforms so that application developers can understand the implications of differing memory systems[1]. This section may also be useful to compiler writers.

---

1. *High Performance Computing* by Keith Dowd covers this subject very well.

CPU Cache History

Historically, the memory systems on Sun machines provided equal access times for all memory locations. This was true on the Sun-2™ machines and was true for data accesses on the Sun-3/50™ and Sun-3/60 machines.

Equal access was achieved by running the entire memory system as fast as the processor could access it. On Motorola 68010 and 68020 processors, four clock cycles were required for each memory access. On a 10 MHz Sun-2, the memory ran at a 400 ns cycle time; on a 20 MHz Sun-3/60, it ran at a 200 ns cycle time, so the CPU never had to wait for memory to be ready.

SPARC processors run at higher clock rates and want to access memory in a single cycle. Main memory cycle times have improved a little, and very wide memory systems can transfer a 32- or 64-byte block almost as quickly as a single word. The CPU cache is designed to cope with the mismatch between the way DRAM can handle blocks of memory efficiently and the way that the CPU wants to access one word at a time at much higher speed.

The CPU cache is an area of fast memory made from *static* RAM, or SRAM. The cache transfers data from main DRAM memory using page mode in a block of 16, 32, or 64 bytes at a time. Hardware keeps track of the data in the cache and copies data into the cache when required.

More advanced caches have multiple levels and can be split so that instructions and data use separate caches. The UltraSPARC CPU has a 16-Kbyte instruction cache and separate 16-Kbyte data cache, which are loaded from a second-level 512-Kbyte to 4-Mbyte combined cache that loads from the memory system. We first examine simple caches before we look at the implications of more advanced configurations.

Cache Line and Size Effects

A SPARCstation 2 is a very simple design with clearly predictable behavior. More recent CPU designs are extremely complicated, so I'll start with a simple example. The SPARCstation 2 has its 64 Kbytes of cache organized as 2048 blocks of 32 bytes each. When the CPU accesses an address, the cache controller checks to see if the right data is in the cache; if it is, then the CPU loads it without stalling. If the data needs to be fetched from main memory, then the CPU clock is effectively stopped for 24 or 25 cycles while the cache block is loaded. The implications for performance tuning are obvious. If your application is accessing memory very widely and its accesses are *missing t*he cache rather than *hitting* the cache, then the CPU may spend a lot of its time stopped. By changing the application, you may be able to improve the *hit rate* and achieve a worthwhile performance gain. The 25-cycle delay is known as the *miss cost*, and the effective performance of an application is reduced by a large miss cost and a low hit rate. The effect of context switches is to further reduce the cache hit rate because after a context switch the contents of the cache will need to be replaced with instructions and data for the new process.

Applications access memory on almost every cycle. Most instructions take a single cycle to execute, and the instructions must be read from memory; data accesses typically occur on 20–30 percent of the cycles. The effect of changes in hit rate for a 25-cycle miss cost are shown in Table 10-1 and Figure 10-13 in both tabular and graphical forms. A 25-cycle miss cost implies that a hit takes 1 cycle and a miss takes 26 cycles.

Table 10-1 Application Speed Changes as Hit Rate Varies with a 25-Cycle Miss Cost

Hit Rate	Hit Time	Miss Time	Total Time	Performance
100%	100%	0%	100%	100%
99%	99%	26%	125%	80%
98%	98%	52%	150%	66%
96%	96%	104%	200%	50%

Figure 10-13 Application Speed Changes as Hit Rate Varies with a 25-Cycle Miss Cost

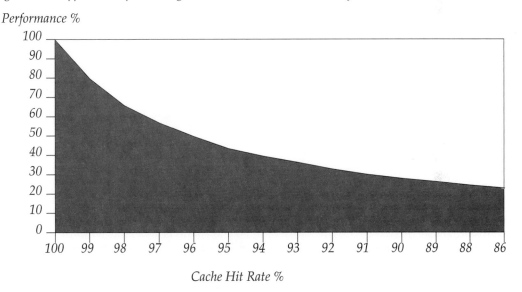

The execution time increases dramatically as the hit rate drops. Although a 96 percent hit rate sounds quite high, you can see that the program will be running at half speed. Many small benchmarks like Dhrystone run at 100 percent hit rate; real applications such as databases are moving data around and following linked lists and so have a poor hit rate. It isn't that difficult to do things that are bad for the cache, so it is a common cause of reduced performance.

A complex processor such as UltraSPARC I does not have fixed cache miss costs; the cost depends upon the exact instruction sequencing, and in many cases the effective miss cost is reduced by complex hardware pipelining and compiler optimizations. The on-chip, 16-Kbyte data cache takes 1 cycle, the external cache between 1 and 7 clock cycles (it can supply a word of data in every cycle but may stall the CPU for up to 7 cycles if the data is used immediately), and main memory between 40 and 50 cycles, depending upon the CPU and system clock rates. With the cache hit rate varying in a two-level cache, we can't draw a simple performance curve, but relatively, performance is better than the curve shown in Figure 10-13 when the system is running inside the large second-level cache, and worse when running from main memory.

A Problem with Linked Lists

Applications that traverse large linked lists cause problems with caches. Let's look at this in detail on a simple SPARCstation 2 architecture and assume that the list has 5,000 entries. Each block on the list contains some data and a link to the next block. If we assume that the link is located at the start of the block and that the data is in the middle of a 100-byte block, as shown in Figure 10-14, then we can deduce the effect on the memory system of chaining down the list.

Figure 10-14 Linked List Example

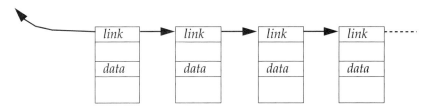

The code to perform the search is a tight loop, shown in Figure 10-15. This code fits in seven words, one or two cache lines at worst, so the cache is working well for code accesses. Data accesses occur when the link and data locations are read. If the code is simply looking for a particular data value, then these data accesses will occur every few cycles. They will never be in the same cache line, so every data access will cause a 25-cycle miss that reads in 32 bytes of data when only 4 bytes were wanted. Also, with a 64-Kbyte cache, only 2,048 cache lines are available, so after 1,024 blocks have been read in, the cache lines must be reused. This means that a second attempt to search the list will find that the start of the list is no longer in the cache.

The only solution to this problem is an algorithmic change. The problem will occur on any of the current generation of computer systems. In fact, the problem gets worse as the processor gets faster since the miss cost tends to increase because of the difference in speed between the CPU and cache clock rate and the main memory speed. With more recent processors, it may be possible to cache a larger linked list in external cache, but the on-chip cache is smaller than 64 Kbytes. What may happen is that the first time through the list, each cache miss costs 50 cycles, and on subsequent passes it costs 8 cycles.

Figure 10-15 Linked List Search Code in C

```
/* C code to search a linked list for a value and miss the cache a lot */

struct block {
        struct block *link;             /* link to next block */
        int pad1[11];
        int data;                       /* data item to check for */
        int pad2[12];
        } blocks[5000];

struct block *find(pb,value)
        struct block *pb;
        int value;
        {
        while(pb)                       /* check for end of linked list */
                {
                if (pb->data == value) /* check for value match */
                        return pb;      /* return matching block */
                pb = pb->link;          /* follow link to next block */
                }
        return (struct block *)0; /* return null if no match */
        }
```

The `while` loop compiles with optimization to just seven instructions, including two loads, two tests, two branches, and a no-op, as shown in Figure 10-16. Note that the instruction after a branch is always executed on a SPARC processor. This loop executes in 9 cycles (225 ns) on a SPARCstation 2 if it hits the cache, and in 59 cycles (1,475 ns) if both loads miss. On a 200 MHz UltraSPARC, the loop would run in approximately 5 cycles (25 ns) if it hit the on-chip cache, 20 cycles (100 ns) in the off-chip cache, and 100 cycles (500 ns) from main memory the first time through.

The memory latency test in Larry McVoy's `lmbench` set of benchmarks is based on this situation. It gives a worst-case situation of unrelated back-to-back loads but is very common in real application code. See also "The Cache-Aligned Block Copy Problem" on page 265 for a description of another cache problem.

Figure 10-16 Linked List Search Loop in Assembler

```
LY1:                              /* loop setup code omitted */
        cmp     %o2,%o1           /* see if data == value */
        be      L77016            /* and exit loop if matched */
        nop                       /* pad branch delay slot */
        ld      [%o0],%o0         /* follow link to next block */
        tst     %o0               /* check for end of linked list */
        bne,a   LY1               /* branch back to start of loop */
        ld      [%o0+48],%o2      /* load data in branch delay slot */
```

For detailed information on specific cache architectures, see "SPARC CPU Cache Architectures" on page 258. Chapter 12, "Caches," on page 299 provides a more detailed explanation of the way in which caches in general work.

System Architectures 11

This chapter describes the architecture of recent SPARC-based systems and explores the performance trade-offs that are made throughout the range. The appropriate SPEC benchmarks are listed for each machine. I first describe the uniprocessor SPARC machines, then I describe in detail the multiprocessor machines. Subsequent chapters describe in more depth the components that make up these systems.

SPARC Architecture and Implementation

The SPARC architecture defines everything that is required to ensure application-level portability across varying SPARC implementations. It intentionally avoids defining some things, like how many cycles an instruction takes, to allow maximum freedom within the architecture to vary implementation details. This is the basis of SPARC's scalability from very low cost to very high performance systems. Implementation differences are handled by kernel code only, so that the instruction set and system call interface are the same on all SPARC systems. The SPARC Compliance Definition, controlled by the independent SPARC International organization, specifies this interface. Within this standard there is no specification of the performance of a compliant system, only its correctness. The performance depends on the chip set used (i.e., the implementation) and the clock rate at which the chip set runs. To avoid confusion, some terms need to be defined.

Instruction Set Architecture (ISA)

The ISA is defined by the SPARC Architecture Manual. SPARC International has published Version 7, Version 8, and Version 9, and the IEEE has produced a standard based on Version 8, IEEE 1754. Version 9 defines major extensions including 64-bit addressing in an upward-compatible manner for user-mode programs. Prentice Hall has published both the Version 8 and Version 9 SPARC Architecture manuals.

SPARC Implementation

A chip-level specification, the SPARC implementation defines how many cycles each instruction takes and other details. Some chip sets define only the integer unit (IU) and floating-point unit (FPU); others define the memory management unit (MMU) and cache design and may include the whole lot on a single chip.

System Architecture

System architecture defines a board-level specification of everything the kernel has to deal with on a particular machine. It includes internal and I/O bus types, address space uses, and built-in I/O functions. This level of information is documented in the SPARCengine™ User Guides that are produced for the bare-board versions of Sun's workstation products. The information needed to port a real-time operating system to the board and physically mount the board for an embedded application is provided.

Kernel Architecture

A number of similar systems may be parameterized so that a single GENERIC kernel image can be run on them. This grouping is known as a kernel architecture. Sun has one kernel architecture for VME-based SPARC machines (Sun-4™), one for SBus-based SPARC machines (Sun-4c), one for the VME and SBus combined 6U eurocard machines (Sun-4e), one for MBus-based machines and machines that use the SPARC reference MMU (Sun-4m), and one for XDBus-based machines (Sun-4d). These are listed in Table 11-1 on page 256.

Register Windows and Different SPARC CPUs

SPARC defines an instruction set that uses 32 integer registers in a conventional way but has many sets of these registers arranged in overlapping *register windows*. A single instruction is used to switch in a new set of registers very quickly. The overlap means that 8 of the registers from the previous window are part of the new window, and these are used for fast parameter passing between subroutines. A further 8 global registers are always the same; of the 24 that make up a register window, 8 are passed in from the previous window, 8 are local, and 8 will be passed out to the next window. This usage is described further in *The SPARC Architecture Manual Version 8* and *Version 9* both published as books by Prentice Hall.

Some SPARC implementations have seven overlapping sets of register windows, and some have eight. One window is always reserved for taking traps or interrupts since these will need a new set of registers; the others can be thought of as a stack cache for six or seven levels of procedure calls with up to six parameters per call passed in registers. The other two registers hold the return address and the old stack frame pointer. If there are more than six parameters to a call, then the extra ones are passed on the external stack as in a conventional architecture. You can see that the register windows architecture allows much faster subroutine calls and returns and faster interrupt handling than in conventional architectures that copy parameters out to a stack, make the call, then copy the parameters back into registers. Programs typically spend most of their time calling up and down a few levels of subroutines; however, when the register windows have all been used, a special trap takes place, and one window (16 registers) is copied to the stack in main memory. On average, register windows seem to cut down the number of loads and stores required by 10–30 percent and provide a speedup of 5–15 percent. Programmers must be careful to avoid writing code that makes a large number of recursive or deeply nested calls and keeps returning to the top level. If very little work is done at each level and very few parameters are being passed, then the program may generate a large number of save and restore traps. The SunPro™ SPARCompiler optimizer performs tail recursion elimination and leaf routine optimization to reduce the depth of the calls.

If an application performs a certain number of procedure calls and causes a certain number of window traps, the benefit of reducing the number of loads and stores must be balanced against the cost of the traps. The overflow trap cost is very dependent on the time taken to store eight double-words to memory. On systems with write-through caches and small write buffers, like the SPARCstation 1, a large number of write stalls occur and the cost is relatively high. The SPARCstation 2 has a larger write buffer of two double-words, which is still not enough. The SuperSPARC chip in write-through mode has an 8-double-word write buffer, so will not stall; other systems with write-back caches will not stall (unless a cache line needs to be updated).

The SPARC V9 architecture supports a new, multiple-level, trap architecture. This architecture greatly reduces the administrative overhead of register window traps since the main trap handler no longer has to check for page faults. This feature increases the relative performance boost of register windows by reducing the trap time.

The Effect of Context Switches and Interrupts

When a program is running on a SPARC chip, the register windows act as a stack cache and provide a performance boost. Subroutine calls tend to occur every few microseconds on average in integer code but may be infrequent in vectorizable floating-point code. Whenever a context switch occurs, the register windows are flushed to memory and the stack cache starts again in the new context. Context switches tend to occur every few milliseconds on average, and a ratio of several hundred subroutine calls per context switch is a good one—there is time to take advantage of the register windows before they are flushed again. When the new context starts up, it loads in the register windows one at a time, so programs that do not make many subroutine calls do not load registers that they will not need. Note that a special trap is provided that can be called to flush the register windows; this trap is needed if you wish to switch to a different stack as part of a user written co-routine or threads library. When SunOS is running, a context switch rate of 1000 per second on each CPU is considered fast, so there are rarely any problems. There may be more concern about this ratio when real-time operating systems are running on SPARC machines, but there are alternative ways of configuring the register windows that are more suitable for real-time systems. These systems often run entirely in kernel mode and can perform special tricks to control the register windows.

The register window context switch time is a small fraction of the total context-switch time. On machines with virtual write-back caches, a cache flush is also required on some context switches. Systems have varying amounts of support for fast cache flush in hardware. The original SunOS 4.0 release mapped the kernel u-area at the same address for all processes, and the u-area flush gave the Sun-4/260 with SunOS 4.0 (the first SPARC machine) a bad reputation for poor context-switch performance that some people mistakenly blamed on the register windows.

Identifying Different SPARC CPUs

You can use Table 11-1 to find which SPARC CPU each machine has. In some cases, the CPU MHz shown is the actual clock rate rather than the nominal one used in product literature. Some UltraSPARC systems use a programmable clock generator that goes up in steps of 8 MHz; hence, 248 MHz is used rather than 250 MHz.

Table 11-1 Which SPARC IU and FPU Does Your System Have?

System (Kernel Architecture)	CPU MHz	CPU Type
Sun-4/110 and Sun4/150 (sun4)	14	Fujitsu MB86901
Sun-4/260 and Sun4/280 (sun4)	16	Fujitsu MB86901
SPARCserver 300 series (sun4)	25	Cypress 601
SPARCserver 400 series (sun4)	33	Cypress 601
SPARCstation 1 and SLC (sun4c)	20	LSI/Fujisu L64911
SPARCstation 1+ and IPC (sun4c)	25	LSI/Fujitsu L64911
Tadpole SPARCbook 1 (sun4m)	25	Cypress 601
SPARCstation ELC (sun4c)	33	Fujitsu MB86903
SPARCstation IPX (sun4c)	40	Fujitsu MB86903
Tadpole SPARCbook 2 (sun4m)	40	Fujitsu MB86903
SPARCstation 2 (sun4c)	40	Cypress 601
SPARC PowerUP - SS2 and IPX upgrade (sun4c)	80	Weitek
SPARCserver 600 Model 120/140 (sun4m)	40	Cypress 601
SPARCstation 10 & SPARCstation 20 (sun4m)	33–60	SuperSPARC - TI390Z50
SPARCstation 20 (sun4m)	75	SuperSPARC II - TI390Z50
Cray SuperServer CS6400 (sun4d)	60–85	SuperSPARC - TI390Z50
SPARCclassic & SPARCstation LX (sun4m)	50	microSPARC
SPARCcenter 1000 & 2000 (sun4d)	50–60	SuperSPARC - TI390Z50
SPARCcenter 1000E & 2000E (sun4d)	85	SuperSPARC II - TI390Z50
Cray S-MP & FPS 500EA (sun4)	66	BIT B5000
SPARCstation Voyager (sun4m)	65	microSPARC II
SPARCstation 4 and SPARCstation 5 (sun4m)	70–110	microSPARC II
Tadpole SPARCbook 3 (sun4m)	85–110	microSPARC II

Table 11-1 Which SPARC IU and FPU Does Your System Have? (Continued)

System (Kernel Architecture)	CPU MHz	CPU Type
SPARCstation 5 (sun4m)	170	Fujitsu TurboSPARC
Tadpole SPARCbook 3XT & 3000 (sun4m)	170	Fujitsu TurboSPARC
Ultra 1 (sun4u)	144–200	UltraSPARC I
Ultra 2 (sun4u)	168–200	UltraSPARC I
Ultra 2 (sun4u)	296	UltraSPARC II
Ultra 30 and Ultra Enterprise 450 (sun4u)	248–296	UltraSPARC II
Ultra Enterprise 3000, 4000, 5000, 6000 (sun4u)	168	UltraSPARC I
Ultra Enterprise 3002, 4002, 5002, 6002, 10000 (sun4u)	248	UltraSPARC II
Integrated Ultra II, DRAM control and PCI bus	266–300	UltraSPARC IIi
Next generation chip announced 1997	600	UltraSPARC III

SuperSPARC

The SuperSPARC can issue three instructions in one clock cycle; just about the only instructions that cannot be issued continuously are integer multiply and divide, floating-point divide, and square root. A set of rules controls how many instructions are grouped for issue in each cycle. The main ones are that instructions are executed strictly in order and subject to the following conditions:

- Three instructions in a group
- One load or store anywhere in a group
- A control transfer (branch or call) ends a group at that point
- One floating point operation anywhere in a group
- Two integer-word results or one double-word result (including loads) per group
- One shift can cascade into another operation, but not vice versa

Dependent compare-and-branch is allowed, and simple ALU cascades are allowed (a + b + c). Floating-point load and a dependent operation are allowed, but dependent integer operations have to wait for the next cycle after a load.

Cypress/Fujitsu Ross HyperSPARC

The HyperSPARC design can issue two instructions in one clock cycle. The combinations allowed are more restrictive than with SuperSPARC, but the simpler design allows a higher clock rate to compensate. The overall performance of a 66 MHz HyperSPARC is comparable to that of a 50 MHz SuperSPARC, but electronic design simulations run much faster on HyperSPARC, and database servers run much faster on SuperSPARC.

UltraSPARC

UltraSPARC implements the 64-bit SPARC V9 architecture, but a hybrid specification called SPARC V8plus is used as an extended 32-bit subset. A version of Solaris that supports the 64-bit V9 address space should be available during 1998. UltraSPARC issues up to four instructions per clock cycle: one load/store, one floating point, and two integer. It also contains an extended set of operations called the Visual Instruction Set or VIS. VIS mostly consists of pixel-based operations for graphics and image processing, but it also includes cache-line-oriented block move operations. These are used to accelerate large block-copy and block-zero operations by the kernel and by user programs that dynamically link to the bcopy(3C) and memcpy(3C) routines. See also "When Does "64 Bits" Mean More Performance?" on page 134 and "UltraSPARC Compiler Tuning" on page 146.

SPARC CPU Cache Architectures

Since the hardware details vary from one machine implementation to another and the details are sometimes hard to obtain, the cache architectures of some common machines are described below, divided into four main groups: virtually and physically addressed caches with write-back algorithms, virtual write-through caches, and on-chip caches. For more details of the hardware implementation of older systems, read *Multiprocessor System Architectures*, by Ben Catanzaro (SunSoft Press). For up-to-date information on SPARC, detailed datasheets and white papers are available from Sun Microelectronics via http://www.sun.com/sparc.

Virtual Write-through Caches

Most older desktop SPARCstations from Sun and the deskside SPARC system 300 series use virtual write-through caches. The virtual write-through cache works by using virtual addresses to decide the location in the cache that has the required data in it. This technique avoids the need to perform an MMU address translation except when there is a cache miss.

Data is read into the cache a block at a time, but writes go through the cache into main memory as individual words. This approach avoids the problem of data in the cache being different from data in main memory but may be slower since single word writes are less efficient than block writes would be. An optimization is for a buffer to be provided so that the word can be put into the buffer; then, the CPU can continue immediately while the buffer is written to memory. The depth (one or two words) and width (32 or 64 bits) of the write buffer vary. If a number of words are written back-to-back, then the write buffer may fill up and the processor will stall until the slow memory cycle has completed. A double-word write on a SPARCstation 1 (and similar machines) will always cause a write-buffer overflow stall that takes 4 cycles.

On the machines listed in Table 11-2, the processor waits until the entire cache block has been loaded before continuing.

The SBus used for memory accesses on the SS2, IPX, and ELC machines runs at half the CPU clock rate. This speed difference may give rise to an extra cycle on the miss cost to synchronize the two buses and the extra cycle occurs half of the time on average.

Table 11-2 Virtual Write-through Cache Details

Machine	Clock	Size	Line	Read Miss	WB size	WB Full Cost
SS1, SLC	20 MHz	64 KB	16 B	12 cycles	1 word	2 cycles (4 dbl)
SS1+, IPC	25 MHz	64 KB	16 B	13 cycles	1 word	2 cycles (4 dbl)
SS330, 370, 390	25 MHz	128 KB	16 B	18 cycles	1 double	2 cycles
ELC	33 MHz	64 KB	32 B	24–25 cycles	2 doubles	4–5 cycles
SS2, IPX	40 MHz	64 KB	32 B	24–25 cycles	2 doubles	4–5 cycles

Virtual Write-back Caches

The larger desk-side SPARCservers use virtual write-back caches. The cache uses virtual addresses as described above. The difference is that data written to the cache is not written through to main memory. This reduces memory traffic and allows efficient back-to-back writes to occur. The penalty is that a cache line must be written back to main memory before it can be reused, so there may be an increase in the miss cost. The line is written efficiently as a block transfer, then the new line is loaded as a block transfer. Most systems have a buffer that stores the outgoing cache line while the incoming cache line is loaded, then the outgoing line is passed to memory while the CPU continues.

The SPARCsystem 400 backplane is 64 bits wide and runs at 33 MHz, synchronized with the CPU. The SPARCsystem 600 uses a 64-bit MBus and takes data from the MBus at full speed into a buffer; the cache itself is 32 bits wide and takes extra cycles to pass data from the buffer in the cache controller to the cache itself. The cache coherency mechanisms required for a multiprocessor machine also introduce extra cycles. There is a difference between the number of MBus cycles taken for a cache miss (the bus occupancy) and the number of cycles that the CPU stalls for. A lower bus occupancy means that more CPUs can be used on the bus. Table 11-3 summarizes the details of the cache.

Table 11-3 Virtual Write-back Cache Details

Machine	Size	Line	Miss Cost	CPU Clock Rate
Sun-4/200 series	128 Kb	16 bytes	7 cycles	16 MHz
SPARCserver 400	128 Kb	32 bytes	12 cycles	33 MHz
SPARCserver 600 model 120	64 Kb	32 bytes	30 cycles	40 MHz

Physical Write-back Caches: SuperSPARC and UltraSPARC

All SuperSPARC- and UltraSPARC-based systems use physical write-back caches for their second-level cache. The first-level cache is described in "On-chip Caches" on page 261.

The MMU translations occur on every CPU access before the address reaches the cache logic. The cache uses the physical address of the data in main memory to determine where in the cache it should be located. In other respects, this type is the same as the virtual write-back cache described above.

The SuperSPARC SuperCache™ controller implements sub-blocking in its 1 Mbyte cache. The cache line is actually 128 bytes but is loaded as four separate, contiguous, 32-byte lines. This approach cuts the number of cache tags required at the expense of needing an extra three valid bits in each tag. In XDBus mode for the SPARCserver 1000, the same chip set switches to two 64-byte blocks. The SPARCcenter 2000 takes advantage of this switch to use four 64-byte blocks per 256-byte line, for a total of 2 Mbytes of cache on a special module. This module cannot be used in any other systems since it requires the twin XDBus BusWatchers that hold duplicate tags for 1 Mbyte of cache each. In XDBus mode, the cache request and response are handled as separate transactions on the bus, and other bus traffic can interleave for better throughput but delayed response. The larger cache line takes longer to transfer, but the memory system is in multiple, independent banks, accessed over two interleaved buses on the SPARCcenter 2000. When many CPUs access memory at once, the single MBus memory system bottlenecks more quickly than with the XDBus.

The UltraSPARC external cache controller is an integrated part of the design, and this integration greatly reduces latency. The miss cost measured in CPU clock cycles is similar to that of SuperSPARC, but since the clock rate is three to four times higher, the actual latency measured in nanoseconds is far lower. The SuperSPARC-based design is asynchronous, with the CPU and cache running from a different clock to the system backplane. UltraSPARC is synchronous, with a central clock source; this arrangement reduces latency because there is never a need to wait for clocks to synchronize to transfer data around the system. The extra performance is traded off against convenience of upgrades. It is not possible to mix different speed UltraSPARC processors in the same system. It was possible to do this with SuperSPARC, but it was never fully tested and supported. It was also possible to have smaller clock rate increments with SuperSPARC without changing the system bus clock rate. With UltraSPARC, the CPU clock rate must be an exact multiple of the system bus clock rate, often a multiple of 83 or 100 MHz.

The two-level cache architecture is so complex that a single cache miss cost cannot be quoted. It can range from about 25 cycles in the ideal case, through about 40 cycles in a typical case, to over 100 cycles in the worst case. The worst-case situation involves a read miss that victimizes a full but dirty cache line. Up to four blocks must be written back to main memory before the read data can be loaded.

On-chip Caches

Highly integrated SPARC chip sets like SuperSPARC, microSPARC, and UltraSPARC use on-chip caches. The Fujitsu/Ross HyperSPARC uses a hybrid on-chip instruction cache with off-chip unified cache. The microSPARC II has four times the cache size of the original microSPARC and has other performance improvements. One other development is the Weitek PowerUP, which is a plug-in replacement for the SS2 and IPX CPU chip that adds on-chip caches and doubles the clock rate. UltraSPARC requires the second-level cache to be present as well.

Since the entire first-level cache is on chip, complete with its control logic, a different set of trade-offs applies to cache design. The size of the cache is limited, but the complexity of the cache control logic can be enhanced more easily. On-chip caches may be *associative* in that a line can exist in the cache in several possible locations. If there are four possible locations for a line, then the cache is known as a *four-way, set-associative cache*. It is hard to build off-chip caches that are associative, so they tend to be *direct mapped*, where each memory location maps directly to a single cache line.

On-chip caches also tend to be split into separate instruction and data caches since this division allows both caches to transfer during a single clock cycle, thus speeding up load and store instructions. This optimization is not often done with off-chip caches because the chip would need an extra set of pins and more chips would be needed on the circuit board.

Intelligent cache controllers can reduce the miss cost by passing the memory location that missed as the first word in the cache block, rather than starting with the first word of the cache line. The processor can then be allowed to continue as soon as this word arrives, before the rest of the cache line has been loaded. If the miss occurred in a data cache and the processor can continue to fetch instructions from a separate instruction cache, then this continuation will reduce the miss cost. In contrast, with a combined instruction and data cache, the cache load operation keeps the cache busy until it has finished, so the processor cannot fetch another instruction anyway. SuperSPARC, microSPARC, and UltraSPARC do implement this optimization.

The microSPARC design uses page-mode DRAM to reduce its miss cost. The first miss to a 1-Kbyte region takes 9 cycles for a data miss; consecutive accesses to the same region avoid some DRAM setup time and complete in 4 cycles.

The SuperSPARC processor implements sub-blocking in its instruction cache. The cache line is actually 64 bytes but is loaded as two separate, contiguous, 32-byte lines. If the on-chip cache is connected directly to main memory, it has a 10-cycle effective miss cost; if it is used with a SuperCache, it can transfer data from the SuperCache to the on-chip cache with a 5-cycle cost. These details are summarized in Table 11-4.

Table 11-4 On-chip Cache Details

Processor	I-Size	I-line	I-Assoc	D-Size	D-line	D-Assoc	D-Miss
MB86930	2 KB	16	2	2 KB	16	2	N/A
microSPARC	4 KB	32	1	2 KB	16	1	4–9 cycles
microSPARC II	16 KB	32	1	8 KB	16	1	N/A
PowerUP	16 KB	32	1	8 KB	32	1	N/A
HyperSPARC	8 KB	32	1	256 KB[1]	32	1	10 cycles
SuperSPARC	20 KB	64 (32)	5	16 KB	32	4	5–10 cycles
UltraSPARC	16 KB	32	2	16KB	16+16	1	7–10 cycles

1. This is a combined external instruction and data cache.

The SuperSPARC with SuperCache Two-Level Cache Architecture

As previously described, the SuperSPARC processor has two sophisticated and relatively large on-chip caches and an optional 1-Mbyte external cache, known as SuperCache or MXCC (for MBus XBus Cache Controller)[1]. It can be used without the external cache, and, for transfers, the on-chip caches work directly over the MBus in write-back mode. For multiprocessor snooping to work correctly and efficiently, the on-chip caches work in write-through mode when the external cache is used. This technique guarantees that the on-chip caches contain a subset of the external cache so that snooping is required only on the external cache. An 8-double-word (64-byte) write buffer flushes through to the external cache.

Cache Block Prefetch

A mode bit can be toggled (see Figure 11-1) in the SuperCache to cause cache blocks to be fetched during idle time. If a cache line has invalid sub-blocks but a valid address tag, then the missing sub-blocks will be prefetched. This mode is turned on by default in Solaris 2.2. It is off by default (but switchable) in Solaris 2.3 and later because database and SPEC benchmarks run better without it in most cases.

1. See "The SuperSPARC Microprocessor Technical White Paper."

Figure 11-1 Setting SuperCache Prefetch Mode

Figure 11-1 Setting SuperCache Prefetch Mode

```
* Control the prefetch performance bit
* on SuperSPARC/MXCC machines. Ignored on non-SuperSPARC machines.
* Valid values are boolean: non-zero means yes, zero means no.
* "use_mxcc_prefetch" controls whether sub-blocks are prefetched
* by MXCC. E-cache miss rates may improve, albeit at higher
* memory latency. Improvement depends on workload.
SET use_mxcc_prefetch = 1
```

Efficient Register Window-Overflow Handling

One common case in SPARC systems is a register window overflow trap, which involves eight consecutive double-word writes to save the registers. All eight writes can fit in the SuperSPARC and UltraSPARC write buffers, and they can be written to the second-level cache in a burst transfer.

UltraSPARC Two-Level Cache Architecture

UltraSPARC configures each of its on-chip caches differently. The instruction cache is associative using 32 byte lines, whereas the data cache is direct mapped using two 16 byte sub-blocks per line. The on-chip caches are virtual so that they can be accessed without first going through the MMU translation, to save time on loads and stores. In the event of a level-one cache miss, the MMU translation is performed before the second-level, physically indexed cache is accessed. The UltraSPARC I design operates with the fastest external SRAM cache at up to 200 MHz with the external cache also operating at 200 MHz. UltraSPARC II operates too quickly for the external cache, so it pipelines the access differently and cycles the external cache at half the CPU clock rate. The UltraSPARC I at 167 MHz takes 7 clock cycles, 42 ns to load from the external cache. The UltraSPARC II at 300 MHz takes 10 clock cycles, 30 ns to perform the same load. These are worst case latency figures, and pipelining allows independent cache transfer to start every three or four cycles.

I/O Caches

If an I/O device is performing a DVMA transfer—for example, a disk controller is writing data into memory—the CPU can continue other operations while the data is transferred. Care must be taken to ensure that the data written to by the I/O device is not also in the cache, otherwise inconsistencies can occur. On older Sun systems and the 4/260 and SPARC system 300, every word of I/O is passed through the cache. A lot of I/O activity slows down the CPU because the CPU cannot access the cache for a cycle. The SPARC system 400 has an I/O cache that holds 128 lines of 32 bytes and checks its validity with the CPU cache once for each line. The interruption to the CPU is reduced from once every

4 bytes to once every 32 bytes. The other benefit is that single-cycle VMEbus transfers are converted by the I/O cache into cache-line-sized block transfers to main memory, which is much more efficient[2]. The SPARCserver 600 has a similar I/O cache on its VMEbus-to-SBus interface but has 1,024 lines rather than 128. The SBus-to-MBus interface can use block transfers for all I/O, so it does not need an I/O cache. However, it does have its own I/O MMU, and I/O is performed in a cache-coherent manner on the MBus in the SPARCserver 10 and SPARCserver 600 machines, on the XDBus in the SPARCserver 1000 and SPARCcenter 2000 machines, and over the UPA in the UltraSPARC-based machines.

Block Copy Support

The kernel spends a large proportion of its time copying or zeroing blocks of data. These blocks may be internal buffers or data structures, but a common operation involves zeroing or copying a page of memory, which is 4 Kbytes or 8 Kbytes. The data is not often used again immediately, so it does not need to be cached. In fact, the data being copied or zeroed will normally remove useful data from the cache. The standard C library routines for this operation are called `bcopy` and `memcpy`; they handle arbitrary alignments and lengths of copies.

Software Page Copies

The most efficient way to copy a page on a system with a write-back cache is to read a cache line, then write it as a block, using two bus transactions. The sequence of operations for a software copy loop is actually the following:

1. Load the first word of the source, causing a cache miss.

2. Fetch the entire cache line from the source.

3. Write the first word to the destination, causing a cache miss.

4. Fetch the entire cache line from the destination (the system cannot tell that you are going to overwrite all the old values in the line).

5. Copy the rest of the source cache line to the destination cache line.

6. Go back to the first stage in the sequence, using the next cache line for the source and destination until the transfer is completed.

7. At some later stage, when the destination cache line is reused by another read, the destination cache line will be flushed back to memory.

---

2. See "A Cached System Architecture Dedicated for the System IO Activity on a CPU Board," by Hseih, Wei, and Loo.

This sequence is fairly efficient but involves three bus transactions; since the source data is read, the destination data is read unnecessarily, and the destination data is written. There is also a delay between the bus transactions while the cache line is copied, and the copy cycles through the whole cache overwriting any preexisting data.

The Cache-Aligned Block Copy Problem

There is a well-known cache-busting problem with direct mapped caches. It occurs when the buffers are aligned in such a way that the source and destination address are separated by an exact multiple of the cache size. Both the source and destination use the same cache line, and a software loop doing 4-byte loads and stores with a 32-byte cache line would cause eight read misses and eight write misses for each cache line copied, instead of two read misses and one write miss. This case is desperately inefficient and can be caused by simplistic coding like that shown in Figure 11-2.

Figure 11-2 Cache-Busting Block-Copy Code

```
#define BUFSIZE 0x10000/* 64Kbytes matches SS2 cache size */
char source[BUFSIZE], destination[BUFSIZE];
for(i=0; i < BUFSIZE; i++)
    destination[i] = source[i];
```

The compiler will allocate both arrays adjacently in memory, so they will be aligned and the copy will run very slowly. The library `bcopy` routine unrolls the loop to read for one cache line then write, which avoids the problem.

Block Copy Acceleration Hardware

The SPARCserver 400 series machines, the SuperSPARC SuperCache controller, and the UltraSPARC Visual Instruction Set (VIS) extensions implement hardware block copy acceleration. For SuperSPARC, block copy is controlled by commands sent to special cache controller circuitry. The commands use privileged instructions (Address Space Identifier, or ASI, loads and stores) that cannot be used by normal programs but are used by the kernel to control the memory management unit and cache controller in all SPARC machines. The SPARCserver 400 and SuperCache have extra hardware that uses a special cache line buffer within the cache controller, and they use special ASI load and store addresses to control the buffer. A single ASI load causes a complete line load into the buffer from memory; a single ASI write causes a write of the buffer to memory. The data never enters the main cache, so none of the existing cached data is overwritten. The ideal pair of bus transactions occur back-to-back with minimal delays between occurrences and use all the available memory bandwidth. An extra ASI store that writes values into the buffer is defined, so that block zero can be implemented by writing zero to the buffer and performing block writes of zero at full memory speed without also filling the cache with zeroes. Physical addresses are used, so the kernel has to look up the virtual-to-physical address translation before it uses the ASI commands. The size of the block transfer is examined to see if the setup overhead is worth the cost, and small copies are done in software.

The VIS instruction set implemented by the UltraSPARC processor includes block copy instructions for use by both kernel- and user-mode block copy. It takes virtual addresses and loads or stores 64 bytes to or from the floating-point register set, bypassing the caches but remaining consistent with any data that happens to be in the cache already. This is the most efficient mechanism possible; it has very low setup overhead and is used by both bcopy and memcpy on UltraSPARC systems.

Memory Management Unit Designs

Unlike many other processor architectures, the memory management unit is not specified as part of the SPARC architecture. This permits great flexibility of implementation, and over the years several very different MMU designs have been implemented. These designs vary depending upon the cost, level of integration, and functionality required for the system design.

The Sun-4 MMU: sun4, sun4c, sun4e Kernel Architectures

Older Sun machines use a "Sun-4™" hardware memory management unit that acts as a large cache for memory translations. It is much larger than the MMU translation cache found on more recent systems, but the entries in the cache, known as PMEGs, are larger and take longer to load. A PMEG is a Page Map Entry Group, a contiguous chunk of virtual memory made up of 32 or 64 physical 8-Kbyte or 4-Kbyte page translations. A SPARCstation 1 has a cache containing 128 PMEGs, so a total of 32 Mbytes of virtual memory can be cached. Note that a program can still use 500 Mbytes or more of virtual memory on these machines; it is the size of the translation cache, which affects performance, that varies. The number of PMEGs on each type of Sun machine is shown in Table 11-5.

Table 11-5 Sun-4 MMU Characteristics

Processor Type	Page Size	Pages/PMEG	PMEGS	Total VM	Contexts
SS1(+), SLC, IPC	4 KB	64	128	32 MB	8
ELC	4 KB	64	128	32 MB	8
SPARCengine 1E	8 KB	32	256	64 MB	8
IPX	4 KB	64	256	64 MB	8
SS2	4 KB	64	256	64 MB	16
Sun 4/110, 150	8 KB	32	256	64 MB	16

Table 11-5 Sun-4 MMU Characteristics (Continued)

Processor Type	Page Size	Pages/PMEG	PMEGS	Total VM	Contexts
Sun 4/260, 280	8 KB	32	512	128 MB	16
SPARCsystem 300	8 KB	32	256	64 MB	16
SPARCsystem 400	8 KB	32	1024	256 MB	64

Contexts in the Sun-4 MMU

Table 11-5 shows the number of hardware contexts built into each machine. A hardware context can be thought of as a tag on each PMEG entry in the MMU that indicates which process that translation is valid for. The tag allows the MMU to keep track of the mappings for 8, 16, or 64 processes in the MMU, depending on the machine. When a context switch occurs, if the new process is already assigned to one of the hardware contexts, then some of its mappings may still be in the MMU and a very fast context switch can take place. For up to the number of hardware contexts available, this scheme is more efficient than that for a more conventional TLB-based MMU. When the number of processes trying to run exceeds the number of hardware contexts, the kernel has to choose one of the hardware contexts to be reused, has to invalidate all the PMEGs for that context, and has to load some PMEGs for the new context. The context-switch time starts to degrade gradually and probably becomes worse than that in a TLB-based system when there are more than twice as many active processes as contexts.

Monitoring the Sun-4 MMU

The number of various MMU-related cache flushes can be monitored by means of vmstat -c.

```
% vmstat -c
flush statistics: (totals)
    usr    ctx    rgn    seg     pag    par
    821    960      0      0  123835     97
```

For Solaris 2, the required information can be obtained from the kernel statistics interface, with the undocumented netstat -k option to dump out the virtual memory hardware address translation statistics (the vmhatstat section).

```
vmhatstat:
vh_ctxfree 650 vh_ctxstealclean 274 vh_ctxstealflush 209 vh_ctxmappings
4507
vh_pmgallocfree 4298 vh_pmgallocsteal 9 vh_pmgmap 0 vh_pmgldfree 3951
vh_pmgldnoctx 885 vh_pmgldcleanctx 182 vh_pmgldflush 0 vh_pmgldnomap 0
vh_faultmap 0 vh_faultload 711 vh_faultinhw 27667 vh_faultnopmg 3193
```

```
vmhatstat:
vh_faultctx 388 vh_smgfree 0 vh_smgnoctx 0 vh_smgcleanctx 0
vh_smgflush 0 vh_pmgallochas 123790 vh_pmsalloc 4 vh_pmsfree 0
vh_pmsallocfail 0
```

This output is very cryptic, and I haven't been able to work out any rules for which variables might indicate a problem. The Sun-4 MMU is uninteresting because the systems that use it are obsolete.

The SPARC Reference MMU: sun4m and sun4d Kernel Architectures

Many Sun machines use the SPARC Reference MMU, which has an architecture that is similar to that of many other MMUs in the rest of the industry. Table 11-6 lists the characteristics.

Table 11-6 SPARC Reference MMU Characteristics

Processor Types	Page Sizes	TLB	Contexts	Mappable
Cypress SPARC/MBus chip set, e.g., SPARCserver 600 -120 and -140 & Tadpole SPARCbook	4 KB	64	4096	256 KB
SuperSPARC e.g., SPARCserver 600 -41 SPARCstation 10, 20 models 30 to 61 SPARCserver 1000 and SC2000 to 60 MHz	4 KB	64	65536	256 KB
SuperSPARC II e.g., SPARCstation 20 model 71 SPARCserver 1000E and 2000E - 85 MHz	4 KB	16 I and 64 D	65536	256 KB
Fujitsu SPARClite embedded CPU	4 KB	32	256	128 KB
microSPARC e.g., SPARCclassic and SPARCstation LX	4 KB	32	64	128 KB
microSPARC II e.g., SPARCstation Voyager, SS4, SS5	4 KB	64	256	256 KB

A detailed description of the hardware involved can be found in *Multiprocessor System Architectures*, by Ben Catanzaro. Datasheets are available at http://www.sun.com/microelectronics.

There are four common implementations: the Cypress uniprocessor 604 and multiprocessor 605 MMU chips, the MMU that is integrated into the SuperSPARC chip, the Fujitsu SPARClite, and the highly integrated microSPARC.

Unlike the case with the Sun-4 MMU, there is a small, fully associative cache for address translations (a translation lookaside buffer or TLB), which typically has 64 entries that map one contiguous area of virtual memory each. These areas are usually a single

4-Kbyte page, but larger segments are used for mapping the SX frame buffer. This process requires contiguous and aligned physical memory for each mapping, which is hard to allocate except for special cases. Each of the 64 entries has a tag that indicates the context to which the entry belongs. This means that the MMU does not have to be flushed on a context switch. The tag is 12 bits on the Cypress/Ross MMU and 16 bits on the SuperSPARC MMU, giving rise to a much larger number of hardware contexts than in the Sun-4 MMU, so that MMU performance is not a problem when very large numbers of users or processes are present. The total mappable memory is the page size multiplied by the number of TLB entries. When this size is exceeded, the CPU will stall while TLB entries are replaced. This control is done completely in hardware, but it takes several cycles to load the new TLB entry.

The SPARC Reference MMU Table-Walk Operation

The primary difference of the SPARC MMU from the Sun-4 MMU is that TLB entries are loaded automatically by table-walking hardware in the MMU. The CPU stalls for a few cycles, waiting for the MMU, but unlike many other TLB-based MMUs or the Sun-4 MMU, the CPU does not trap to use software to reload the entries itself. The kernel builds in memory a table that contains all the valid virtual memory mappings and loads the address of the table into the MMU once at boot time. The MMU then does a table walk by indexing and following linked lists to find the right page translation to load into the TLB, as shown in Figure 11-3.

The table walk is optimized by the MMU hardware, which keeps the last accessed context, region, and segment values in registers, so that the only operation needed is to index into the page table with the address supplied and load a page table entry. For the larger page sizes, the table walk stops with a special PTE at the region or segment level.

Figure 11-3 SPARC Reference MMU Table Walk

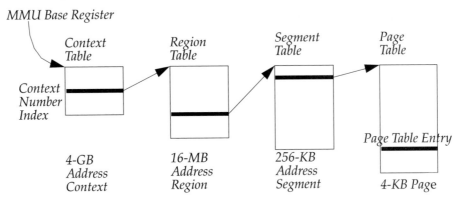

The Sun-4 MMU-based systems can cache sufficient virtual memory translations to run programs many megabytes in size with no MMU reloads. Exceeding the MMU limits results in a large overhead. The SPARC Reference MMU caches only 64 pages of 4 Kbytes at a time in normal use, for a total of 256 Kbytes of simultaneously mapped virtual memory. The SRMMU is reloading continuously as the CPU uses more than this small set of pages, but it has an exceptionally fast reload, so there is a low overhead.

The UltraSPARC MMU Architecture

The SPARC Version 9 UltraSPARC architecture is a compatible, pure superset of previous SPARC designs in user mode but is very different from previous SPARC designs when in kernel mode. The MMU architecture is implemented partly in hardware and partly in software; the table-walk operation is performed by a nested fast trap in software. This trap can occur even during other trap routines since SPARC V9 defines several sets of registers to support nested traps efficiently. The flexible MMU support is designed to handle both 32-bit and 64-bit address spaces efficiently, and different sizes from the SRMMU were chosen for the region, segment, and page levels, as shown in Figure 11-4. UltraSPARC has a completely separate kernel context, which is mapped by means of a 4-Gbyte context TLB entry for code and data. In Solaris 2.6, intimate shared memory (ISM) is implemented with 4-Mbyte regions. These optimizations greatly reduce the number of TLB miss traps that occur in normal operation.

Figure 11-4   UltraSPARC MMU Table Walk

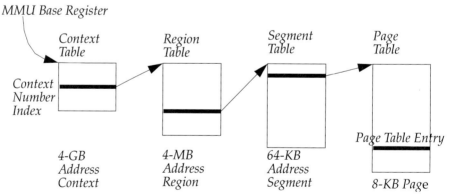

In the `vmhatstat` structure, the kernel maintains detailed statistics on the MMU operation; you can read them by using the SE toolkit, or you can dump them out by using `netstat -k`, as shown in Figure 11-5.

Figure 11-5   Example UltraSPARC MMU Statistics

```
% netstat -k | more
...
vmhatstat:
```

Figure 11-5   Example UltraSPARC MMU Statistics   (Continued)

```
vh_ctxfree 98546 vh_ctxdirty 12 vh_ctxsteal 21 vh_tteload 20329401 vh_hblk_hit
20220550
vh_hblk8_nalloc 1957 vh_hblk8_dalloc 28672 vh_hblk8_dfree 23962 vh_hblk1_nalloc 308
vh_hblk1_dalloc 5687 vh_hblk1_dfree 4536 vh_hblk8_startup_use 302
vh_pgcolor_conflict 85883 vh_uncache_conflict 30 vh_unload_conflict 4
vh_mlist_enter 0 vh_mlist_exit 0 vh_pagesync 117242342 vh_pagesync_invalid 0
vh_itlb_misses 0 vh_dtlb_misses 0 vh_utsb_misses 0 vh_ktsb_misses 0
vh_tsb_hits 0 vh_umod_faults 0 vh_kmod_faults 0 vh_slow_tsbmiss 2458310
vh_pagefaults 0 vh_uhash_searches 0 vh_uhash_links 0 vh_khash_searches 0
vh_khash_links 0 vh_steal_count 0 vh_kernel_xcalls 3141911 vh_user_xcalls 3882838
```

11

Early SPARC System Architectures

The earliest SPARC systems are relatively simple. In this section, I group them into six generations of system designs. I have included benchmark results for early systems; the benchmarks are now obsolete and may be hard to find. More recent systems have benchmark results that can be obtained from the http://www.specbench.org web site.

SPARC Uniprocessor VMEbus Systems

At the time SPARC was introduced, it was positioned at the high end of the product line. These systems were built with many components on large-format VMEbus cards. Each member of this family implemented different variations on a common theme, with a single CPU, 128-Kbyte cache to hold both data and instructions (apart from the Sun-4/100), Sun-4 MMU, single large memory system, some on-board I/O devices, and a single VMEbus for expansion. These entities formed the "sun4" kernel architecture, and a single version of the kernel code could run on any of these systems. The Sun-4 range is now obsolete, and relatively small volumes were produced; their many variations are not discussed in great detail, but Table 11-7 summarizes their benchmark results.

Table 11-7 SPEC89 Benchmark Results for SPARC Uniprocessor VMEbus Systems

Machine	MHz	SPECmark89	Compiler
Sun4/110 and Sun4/150	14	6.1 (est)	SunPro 1.0
Sun4/260 and Sun4/280	16.6	8.1	SunPro 1.0
Sun4/330, Sun4/370 and Sun4/390	25	13.4	SunPro 1.0
Sun4/470 and Sun4/490	33	19.4	SunPro 1.0

The First Generation of SPARC Uniprocessor Desktop Systems

This family of systems conforms to a set of kernel-to-hardware interfaces known as the "sun4c" kernel architecture. The key design goal was to keep the cost down, so all main memory accesses and I/O were carried by a single 32-bit SBus. A small set of very highly integrated chips was used to implement these machines, so they all share a great many architectural details. Compared to the earlier Sun-4 machines, they have a smaller 64-Kbyte cache, a simplified version of the Sun-4 MMU, and a smaller main memory system. The I/O bus changes from VME to SBus, and unlike previous systems, the SBus is also used to carry all the CPU-to-memory system traffic. The CPU boards are much smaller than before, despite the inclusion of more I/O options as standard; see Figure 11-6.

In earlier machines (the SS1, 1+, IPC, and SLC), there was a single clock rate for the whole system, and main memory could provide data only at half-speed, so there was a wait cycle on the SBus between each cycle of data transfer from memory. The SBus DMA interface on these machines performed only single-word transfers on the SBus, and the overhead of acquiring the bus and sending the address for every word severely limited DMA transfer rates.]

In later machines (the SS2, IPX, ELC), the CPU Integer Unit (IU), Floating-Point Unit (FPU), Memory Management Unit (MMU), and cache were clocked at twice the speed of the SBus, and the memory system used faster DRAM to transfer data on every cycle. A newer version of the SBus DMA, called DMA+, transferred up to four words at a time on the Sbus, for much better performance.

Figure 11-6 The SPARCstation 1, 1+, IPC, SLC, 2, IPX, and ELC Family System Architecture

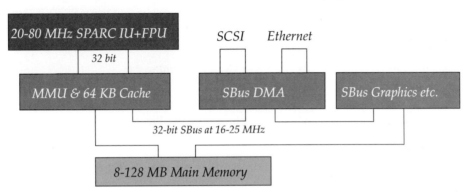

An upgrade for the SPARCstation IPX and SPARCstation 2, called the PowerUP, is available from Weitek. It consists of a plug-in replacement CPU chip that runs at 80 MHz internally, using a 16-Kbyte instruction cache and an 8-Kbyte data cache. It uses the external 64-Kbyte cache as a second level. Generally, the rest of the system hardware and software doesn't need to know that anything is different, so it is quite compatible and substantially faster.

I have had to provide two sets of benchmark results for these machines, shown in Table 11-8 and Table 11-9, because published results for the early machines ensued from the use of SPEC89 only. Later published results reflected the use of SPEC92 as well.

Table 11-8 SPEC89 Benchmark Results for First-Generation SPARC Desktops

Machine	MHz	SPECmark89	Compiler
SPARCstation 1	20	8.8	SunPro 1.0[1]
SPARCstation SLC	20	8.8	SunPro 1.0
SPARCstation 1+ (old compiler)	25	11.8	SunPro 1.0
SPARCstation 1+ (new compiler)	25	13.5	SunPro 2.0[2]
SPARCstation IPC	25	13.5	SunPro 2.0

Table 11-8 SPEC89 Benchmark Results for First-Generation SPARC Desktops (Continued)

Machine	MHz	SPECmark89	Compiler
SPARCstation ELC	33	20.3	SunPro 2.0
SPARCstation IPX	40	24.4	SunPro 2.0
SPARCstation 2	40	25.0	SunPro 2.0

1. The SunPro 1.0 code generator was used by C 1.1 and F77 1.4.

2. The SunPro 2.0 code generator was used by C 2.0 and F77 2.0

Table 11-9 SPEC92 Benchmark Results for First-Generation SPARC Desktops

Machine	MHz	SPECint92	Compiler	SPECfp92	Compiler
SPARCstation 1	20	N/A		N/A	
SPARCstation SLC	20	N/A		N/A	
SPARCstation 1+	25	13.8	SunPro 2.0	11.1	SunPro 2.0
SPARCstation IPC	25	13.8	SunPro 2.0	11.1	SunPro 2.0
SPARCstation ELC	33	18.2	SunPro 2.0	17.9	SunPro 2.0
SPARCstation IPX	40	21.8	SunPro 2.0	21.5	SunPro 2.0
SPARCstation 2	40	21.8	SunPro 2.0	22.7	SunPro 2.0
SPARCstation 2 PowerUP	80	32.2	SunPro 2.0	31.1	SunPro 2.0

Second-Generation Uniprocessor Desktop SPARC Systems

The design goal was to provide performance comparable to that of the SPARCstation 2, but at the lowest possible cost, using the highest levels of integration. The resulting pair of machines were the SPARCclassic™ and the SPARCstation LX. A large number of chips from the previous designs were combined, and the highly integrated microSPARC CPU was used. microSPARC has a much smaller cache than does the SPARCstation 2 but compensates with a higher clock frequency and a faster memory system to get slightly higher overall performance. The 6-Kbyte cache is split into a 4-Kbyte instruction cache and a 2-Kbyte data cache. Unlike previous designs, the sun4m kernel architecture is used along with a SPARC Reference Memory Management Unit (SRMMU). The memory bus is 64-bits wide rather than 32, and main memory traffic does not use the same data path as SBus I/O traffic, which improves performance for both memory-intensive and I/O-intensive applications. The SBus DMA controller is integrated along with SCSI, Ethernet, and high-speed parallel ports into a single chip. The difference between the two machines is that the SPARCstation LX adds a GX graphics accelerator, ISDN interface, and CD quality audio to the basic SPARCclassic design. Figure 11-6 illustrates the architecture; Table 11-10 summarizes the benchmark results.

Figure 11-7   The SPARCstation LX and SPARCclassic Family System Architecture

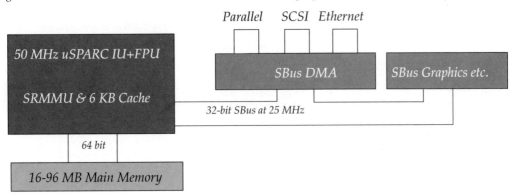

Table 11-10 SPEC Benchmark Results for Second-Generation SPARC Desktops

Machine	MHz	SPECint92	Compiler	SPECfp92	Compiler
SPARCclassic	50	26.3	SunPro 3.0	20.9	Apogee 0.82
SPARCstation LX	50	26.3	SunPro 3.0	20.9	Apogee 0.82

Third-Generation Uniprocessor Desktop SPARC Systems

Following the SPARCclassic and the SPARCstation LX, a much faster version of the microSPARC processor, called microSPARC II, was developed and is used in the SPARCstation 4, SPARCstation 5, and SPARCstation™ Voyager™. The main differences are that microSPARC II has a much larger cache, runs at higher clock rates, and has a special graphics interface on the memory bus to augment the usual SBus graphics cards. As in the original microSPARC, the sun4m kernel architecture is used along with the SPARC Reference MMU. The SPARCstation 4 came later than the SPARCstation 5 and is a heavily cost-reduced design. Most of the cost was saved in the packaging restrictions, and architecturally it is the same as a SPARCstation 5. The SPARCstation™ Voyager™ is a nomadic system, and it has an integrated driver for a large LCD, flat-screen display, power management hardware, and a PCMCIA bus interface via the SBus. The speed of the SBus is either one-third, one-fourth, or one-fifth of the processor speed since the SBus standard specifies a maximum of 25 MHz. These speeds give rise to some odd SBus rates at the clock rates used in the various versions of the SPARCstation 5. The final version of the SPARCstation 5/170 uses a new CPU design called TurboSPARC. It is derived from microSPARC II but has a 256-Kbyte external, level-two cache as well as a much higher clock rate, at 170 MHz. Figure 11-6 illustrates the architecture; Table 11-11 summarizes the benchmark results.

Figure 11-8   The SPARCstation Voyager and SPARCstation 4 and 5 Family System Architecture

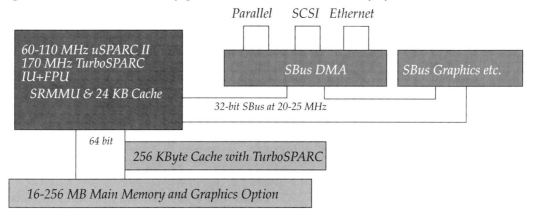

Table 11-11 SPEC Benchmark Results for Third-Generation SPARC Desktops

Machine	MHz	SPECint92	Compiler	SPECfp92	Compiler
SPARCstation Voyager	60	47.5	Apogee 2.951	40.3	Apogee 2.951
SPARCstation 4/70 5/70	70	57.0	Apogee 2.951	47.3	Apogee 2.951
SPARCstation 4/85 5/85	85	64.1	Apogee 2.951	54.6	Apogee 2.951
SPARCstation 4/110 5/110	110	N/A		N/A	
SPARCstation 5/170	170	N/A		N/A	

Entry-Level Multiprocessor-Capable Desktop

The SPARCstation 10 and SPARCstation 20 are often used as uniprocessors, particularly since SunOS 4 is not supported on multiprocessor configurations. These machines are multiprocessor capable since the SPARC modules can be upgraded and a second module can be added. The diagram shown in Figure 11-9 is rather complex, but later sections will refer to this diagram as the details are explained. The entry-level models do not include the 1-Mbyte SuperCache, so the processor is directly connected to the MBus and takes its clock signal from the bus. The SX option shown in the diagram is supported only on the SPARCstation 10SX and all SPARCstation 20 models. These models also have a 64-bit SBus interface, although it is not supported until Solaris 2.4. Table 11-12 summarizes the benchmarks for these models.

Figure 11-9   SPARCstation 10 Model 30, 40, and SPARCstation 20 Model 50 Organization

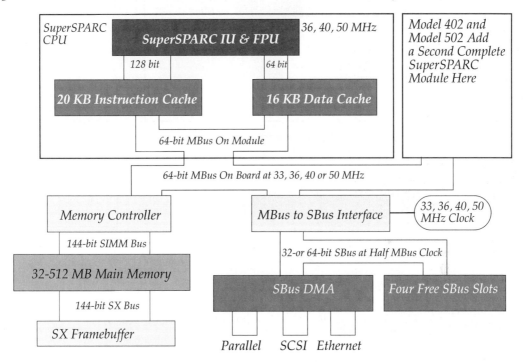

Table 11-12 SPEC Benchmark Results for Entry-Level MP-Capable Desktops

Machine	MHz	SPECint92	Compiler	SPECfp92	Compiler
SPARCstation 10 Model 30	36	45.2	SunPro 3.0α	54.0	Apogee 1.059
SPARCstation 10 Model 40	40	50.2	SunPro 3.0α	60.2	Apogee 1.059
SPARCstation 20 Model 50	50	69.2	Apogee 2.3	78.8	Apogee 2.3

Multiprocessor-Capable Desktop and Server

The SPARCserver 600 was the first Sun machine to use multiprocessor-capable architecture. It has a VMEbus interface coming off the SBus, as shown in Figure 11-10. It also uses a different memory controller and SIMM type that gives more RAM capacity by using extra boards; there is no SX interface or parallel port. The SPARCstation 10 and 20 are as described in the previous section except for the addition of a SuperCache controller and 1 Mbyte of cache RAM. There are now two clocks in the machine, the SPARC module clock and the system clock. In the performance table, both are shown as module/system. Benchmarks are summarized in Table 11-13.

Figure 11-10 SPARCsystem 10, 20, and 600 Model 41, 51, and 61 Organization

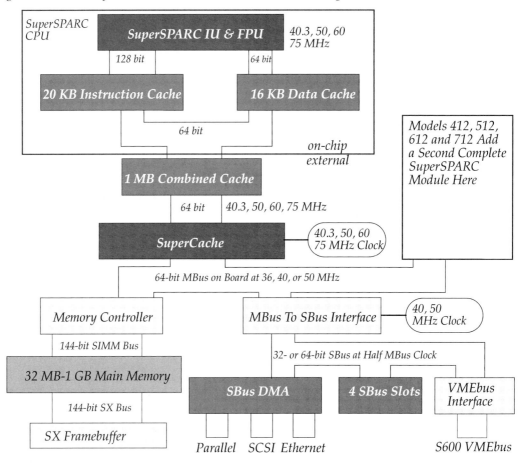

Table 11-13 SPEC Benchmark Results for High-end MP-Capable Desktops and Servers

Machine	MHz	SPECint92	Compiler	SPECfp92	Compiler
SPARCserver 600 Model 41	40.33/40	53.2	Sun 3.0α	67.8	Apogee 1.059
SPARCstation 10 Model 41	40.33/40	53.2	Sun 3.0α	67.8	Apogee 1.059
SPARCstation 10 Model 51	50/40	65.0	Sun 3.0α	83.0	Apogee 2.3
SPARCstation 20 Model 51	50/40	73.6	Apogee 2.3	84.8	Apogee 2.3
SPARCstation 20 Model 61	60/50	88.9	Apogee 2.3	102.8	Apogee 2.3
SPARCstation 20 Model 71	75/50	N/A		N/A	

Adding More Processors

In the SPARCstation 10 Model 402MP and the SPARCstation 20 Model 502MP, two SuperSPARC+ processors are directly connected to the memory, as shown in Figure 11-11. If one processor is running a program that doesn't fit well in the on-chip caches and it makes heavy use of main memory, then the second processor will have to wait longer for its memory accesses to complete and will not run at full speed. This diagram has been simplified to show only the SPARC modules and the memory system; the symbol "$" is used, as is common, as an abbreviation for the word "cache" (cash).

Figure 11-11 SPARCstation 10 Model 402MP and SPARCstation 20 Model 502MP Cache Organization

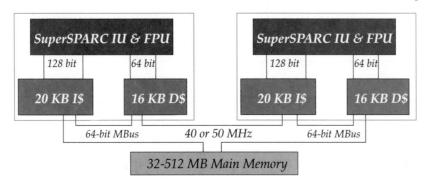

In the Model 412MP, Model 512MP, Model 612MP, Model 712MP, and Model 514MP, each processor has its own SuperCache, as shown in Figure 11-12. This reduces the number of references to main memory from each processor so that there is less contention for the available memory bandwidth. The 60 MHz processors run hotter than the 50 MHz ones, and cooling limits in the package prevent a Model 614MP from being configured. When the 50 MHz parts are used in the SPARCstation 20, it automatically senses and reduces its MBus clock rate from 50 MHz to 40 MHz; this technique maintains the clock rate difference required for synchronization, but it is unfortunate that the system that needs the fastest possible MBus doesn't get it.

Figure 11-12 The SPARCsystem 10, 20, and 600 Model 514MP Cache Organization

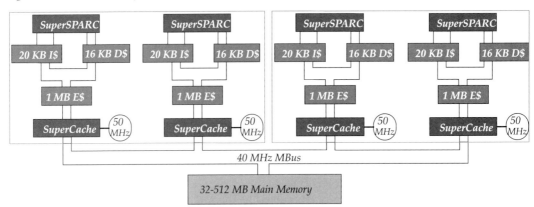

SuperSPARC-Based Multiprocessor Hardware

Several classes of multiprocessor machines are based on SPARC architecture: 1- to 4-processor, MBus-based systems; high-end systems with up to 8, 20, or 64 SuperSPARC processors; 1- to 4-processor UltraSPARC-based systems; and high-end UltraSPARC servers with up to 30 and up to 64 processors. Their system architectures are quite different and all are quite complex. I'll start by discussing bus architectures in general, then look at the implementations of systems based on SuperSPARC. Then, I'll describe the bus architectures and implementations used by UltraSPARC.

Bus Architectures Overview

There are two things to consider about bus performance. The peak data rate is easily quoted, but the ability of the devices on the bus to source or sink data at that rate for more than a few cycles is the real limit to performance. The second consideration is whether the bus protocol includes cycles that do not transfer data, thus reducing the sustained data throughput.

Older buses like VMEbus usually transfer one word at a time, so each bus cycle includes the overhead of deciding which device will access the bus next (arbitration) as well as setting up the address and transferring the data. This procedure is rather inefficient, so more recent buses like SBus, MBus, and UPA transfer data in blocks. Arbitration can take place once per block; then, a single address is set up and multiple cycles of data are transferred. The protocol gives better throughput if more data is transferred in each bus transaction. For example, SPARCserver 600MP systems are optimized for a standard transaction size of 32 bytes by providing 32-byte buffers in all the devices that access the bus and by using a 32-byte cache line. The SPARCcenter 2000 and UltraSPARC-based systems are optimized for 64-byte transactions, and UltraSPARC overlaps the address setup and arbitration to occur in parallel with data transfers.

MP Cache Issues

In systems that have more than one cache on the bus, a problem arises when the same data is stored in more than one cache and the data is modified. A cache coherency protocol and special cache tag information are needed to keep track of the data. The basic solution is for all the caches to include logic that watches the transactions on the bus (known as snooping the bus) and looks for transactions that use data that is being held by that cache. The I/O subsystem on Sun's multiprocessor machines has its own MMU and cache, so that full bus snooping support is provided for DVMA[3] I/O transfers. The coherency protocol uses invalidate transactions that are sent from the cache that owns the data when the data is modified. This technique invalidates any other copies of that data in the rest of the system. When a cache tries to read some data, the data is provided by the owner of that data, which may not be the memory system, so cache-to-cache transfers occur.

Circuit-switched Bus Protocols

One class of bus protocols effectively opens a circuit between the source and destination of the transaction and holds on to the bus until the transaction has finished and the circuit is closed. This protocol is simple to implement, but when a transfer from a slow device like main memory to a fast device like a CPU cache (a cache read) occurs, there must be a number of wait states to let the main memory DRAM access complete in the interval between sending the address to memory and the data returning. These wait states reduce cache read throughput, and nothing else can happen while the circuit is open. The faster the CPU clock rate, the more clock cycles are wasted. On a uniprocessor, this wait time just adds to the cache miss time, but on a multiprocessor the number of CPUs that a bus can handle is drastically reduced by the wait time. Note that a fast device like a cache can write data with no delays to the memory system write buffer. MBus uses this type of protocol and is suitable for up to four CPUs.

---

3. DVMA stands for Direct Virtual Memory Access. It is used by intelligent I/O devices that write data directly into memory, using virtual addresses, for example, the disk and network interfaces.

11

Packet-switched Bus Protocols

To make use of the wait time, a bus transaction must be split into a request packet and a response packet. This protocol is hard to implement because the response must contain some identification and a device, such as the memory system, on the bus may have to queue up additional requests coming in while it is trying to respond to the first one.

A protocol called XBus extends the basic MBus interface to implement a packet-switched protocol in the SuperCache controller chip used with SuperSPARC. This extension provides more than twice the throughput of MBus and is designed to be used in larger multiprocessor machines that have more than four CPUs on the bus. The SPARCcenter 2000 uses XBus within each CPU board and multiple, interleaved XBuses on its inter-board backplane. The backplane bus is called XDBus. The SPARCserver 1000 has a single XDBus, and the SPARCcenter 2000 has a twin XDBus. The Cray SuperServer CS6400 has a quadruple XDBus running at a higher clock rate.

Table 11-14 SuperSPARC Multiprocessor Bus Characteristics

Bus Name	Clock	Peak Bandwidth	Read Throughput	Write Throughput
MBus	40 MHz	320 Mbytes/s	90 Mbytes/s	200 Mbytes/s
XBus	40 MHz	320 Mbytes/s	250 Mbytes/s	250 Mbytes/s
Single XDBus	40 MHz	320 Mbytes/s	250 Mbytes/s	250 Mbytes/s
Dual XDBus	40 MHz	640 Mbytes/s	500 Mbytes/s	500 Mbytes/s
Quad XDBus	55 MHz	1760 Mbytes/s	1375 Mbytes/s	1375 Mbytes/s

SuperSPARC XDBus Server Architecture

The SuperSPARC server architecture was the first Sun product range to address the high end of the server marketplace. Two packages deliver the architecture: one low-cost package that can sit on or beside a desk in an office environment, and one package that maximizes expansion capacity, for the data center. These two packages contain scaled versions of the same architecture, and the investment in IC designs and operating system porting and tuning is shared by both machines. The same architecture was used by Cray Research SuperServers, Inc., in their much larger CS6400 package. This division of Cray was purchased by Sun during 1996.

A key theme of the SuperSPARC server architecture is that it is built from a small number of highly integrated components that are replicated to produce the required configuration. Several of these components, including processor modules and SBus I/O cards, are identical to those used in the high-volume workstation product line, which reduces per-processor costs and provides a wide choice of I/O options. The system design that connects processors, I/O, and memory over multiple, high-speed buses is implemented in a small number of complex application-specific integrated circuits (ASICs); this implementation reduces the number of components on each board, easing manufacture, reducing cost, and increasing reliability.

Compared to an MBus system with one to four processors connected to one memory bank and one SBus, the additional throughput of the SPARCserver 1000 and SPARCcenter 2000 comes from the use of many more processors interconnected via substantially faster buses to multiple, independent memory banks and multiple SBuses, as summarized in Table 11-15.

Table 11-15 SPARCserver System Expansion Comparisons

Machine	SS 10, 20	SS 1000	SC 2000	CS6400
SuperSPARC Clock Rate	40,50,60,75 MHz	50,60,85 MHz	50,60,85 MHz	60,85 MHz
CPU External Cache	Optional 1 MB	1 MB	1 MB or 2 MB	2 MB
Max Number of CPUs	4	8	20	64
Total Memory	32–512 MB	32–2048 MB	64–5120 MB	128 MB–16 GB
Memory Banks	1 512 MB	4 x 512 MB	20 x 256 MB	64 x 256 MB
SBus I/O Slots	4 at 20–25 MHz	12 at 20 MHz	40 at 20 MHz	64 at 25 MHz
Independent SBuses	1@40–100 MB/s	4@50 MB/s	10@50 MB/s	16@60 MB/s
Interconnect	MBus	XDBus	2 x XDBus	4 x XDBus
Speed and Width	40, 50 MHz, 64 bits	40, 50 MHz, 64 bits	40, 50 MHz, 64 bits	55 MHz, 64 bits
Interconnect Throughput	100-130 MB/s	250-310 MB/s	500-620 MB/s	1500 MB/s

SuperSPARC Server Architectural Overview

The SuperSPARC server architecture is based on a small number of building blocks that are combined in three configurations to produce the SPARCserver 1000, SPARCcenter 2000, and CS6400.

SPARCserver 1000 System Implementation Overview

The design objective for the SPARCserver 1000 was to take the architecture into an office environment and to introduce a low-cost entry point into the range. This goal was achieved by use of a very compact package, about the same size as an office laser printer, that can be put on a desktop, stacked on the floor, or rack-mounted.

The SPARCserver 1000 system board contains twin CPU blocks sharing a single BootBus, a single SBus I/O block, including an integrated FSBE/S interface, and a single memory bank on one XDBus. The backplane accepts up to four system boards for a total of 8 CPUs, 16 SBus slots, and 2048 Mbytes of RAM. Figure 11-13 illustrates the configuration.

Figure 11-13 SPARCserver 1000 Configuration

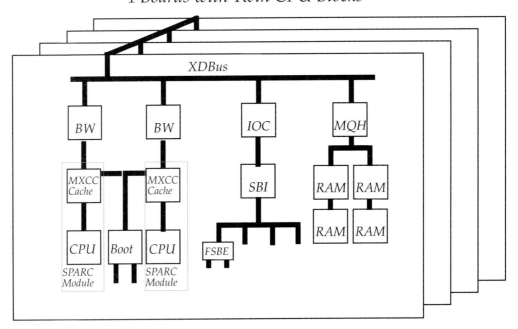

SPARCcenter 2000 System Implementation Overview

Taking the three basic building blocks already described, the SPARCcenter 2000 system board contains a dual CPU block sharing a single BootBus, a single SBus I/O block and a single memory bank on each XDBus. The entire system board contains only 19 highly integrated ASICs: 9 large 100-K gate ASICs and 10 much smaller chips. The backplane accepts up to 10 system boards for a total of 20 CPUs, 40 SBus slots, and 5120 Mbytes of RAM. The SPARCcenter 2000 uses a modified form of the Sun rack-mount server packaging that was used on the previous generation SPARCserver 690. Figure 11-14 illustrates the configuration.

Figure 11-14 SPARCcenter 2000 System Board Configuration

Ten Boards with Twin CPUs

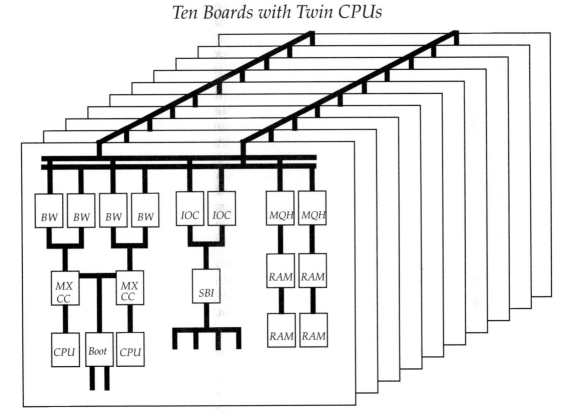

≡ 11

Interrupt Distribution Tuning

On the SPARCserver 1000 and SPARCcenter 2000, there are up to 10 independent SBuses, and there is hardware support for steering the interrupts from each SBus to a specific processor.

The algorithm used in Solaris 2.2 permanently assigns the clock interrupt to a CPU to obtain good cache hit rates in a single cache. The clock presents a relatively light and fixed load at 100 Hz, so this load does not significantly unbalance the system. To balance the load across all the other CPUs, a round-robin system is used, whereby all interrupts are directed to one CPU at a time. When the CPU takes the first interrupt, it sends a special broadcast command over the XDBus to all the SBus controllers to direct the next interrupt to the next CPU. This scheme balances the load, but when there is a heavy interrupt load from a particular device, it is less efficient from the point of view of cache hit rate.

The algorithm can be switched to a static interrupt distribution, whereby each SBus device is assigned to a different CPU. For some I/O-intensive workloads, this scheme has given better performance, and it is the default in Solaris 2.3 and later releases.

A kernel variable, do_robin, controls interrupt distribution and defaults to 1 in the sun4d kernel architecture of Solaris 2.2, and to 0 in 2.3 and later releases. If it is set to 0 in /etc/system, then the static interrupt distribution algorithm is used.

Console Terminal and Clock Interrupt Issues

Since Solaris expects to have a single console terminal, the board to which the console is connected is designated as the master CPU during the first power-on boot. One of the CPUs on this board always takes the 100 Hz clock interrupt. If the system ever finds it has no master at boot time, then it selects the lowest numbered board that has a working CPU. It is best to keep this as board zero because the file /etc/iu.ap only has autopush stream entries for the ports on this board and the installation is hard to use on a raw stream device. The commands to manually push streams (if you find that you have no echo on the console in single-user boot mode) are shown in Figure 11-15. The first line must be typed blind with a control-J terminator. This sounds obscure, but it took me ages to work out why an SC2000 with the console on board two did this, so it is worth sharing!

Figure 11-15 How to Manually Push Streams on an Alternative Console Port

```
# strchg -h ldterm^J
# strchg -h ttcompat
```

Using `prtdiag` to Show the Configuration

The system configuration can be seen on SPARCserver1000 and SPARCcenter2000 machines with the `/usr/kvm/prtdiag` or `/usr/platform/sun4d/sbin/prtdiag` command; see "The Openboot Device Tree — `prtconf` and `prtdiag`" on page 438. The following output shows the configuration of an 8-processor SPARCserver 1000 with 384 Mbytes of RAM and a 4-Mbyte bank of NVSIMM. The NVSIMM is incorrectly sensed as 8 Mbytes by the configuration software, but this does not cause any problems in operation. A substantial number of disk and network interfaces are configured on this system. The SCSI bus cards are a mixture of normal `esp` interfaces and wide SCSI `isp` interfaces. The network cards are a mixture of several buffered Ethernet `le` and an FDDI `bf`. To help identify each card, the vendor identity and part number are given for each one. Table 11-16 provides an example.

Table 11-16Example Output from `Prtdiag` for a SPARCserver 1000

```
% prtdiag
System Configuration:  Sun Microsystems  sun4d SPARCserver 1000
System clock frequency: 40 MHz
Memory size: 392Mb
Number of XDBuses: 1
        CPU Units: Frequency Cache-Size      Memory Units: Group Size
            A: MHz MB    B: MHz MB         0: MB   1: MB   2: MB   3: MB
            ---------    ---------         -----   -----   -----   -----
Board0:      50 1.0       50 1.0            32      32      32      32
Board1:      50 1.0       50 1.0            32      32      32      32
Board2:      50 1.0       50 1.0            32      32      32      32
Board3:      50 1.0       50 1.0             8       0       0       0
=====================SBus Cards=========================================
Board0:          0: dma/esp(scsi)          'SUNW,500-2015'
                    lebuffer/le(network)   'SUNW,500-2015'
                 1: <empty>
                 2: bf                      'SUNW,501-1732'
                 3: QLGC,isp/sd(block)      'QLGC,ISP1000'
Board1:          0: dma/esp(scsi)          'SUNW,500-2015'
                    lebuffer/le(network)   'SUNW,500-2015'
                 1: dma/esp(scsi)          'SUNW,500-2015'
                    lebuffer/le(network)   'SUNW,500-2015'
                 2: <empty>
                 3: <empty>
Board2:          0: dma/esp(scsi)          'SUNW,500-2015'
                    lebuffer/le(network)   'SUNW,500-2015'
                 1: <empty>
                 2: QLGC,isp/sd(block)      'QLGC,ISP1000'
                 3: <empty>
Board3:          0: dma/esp(scsi)          'SUNW,500-2015'
```

Table 11-16 Example Output from `Prtdiag` *for a SPARCserver 1000 (Continued)*

```
                     lebuffer/le(network)    'SUNW,500-2015'
             1: <empty>
             2: <empty>
             3: <empty>

No failures found in System
============================
```

UltraSPARC Interconnect Architectures

The UltraSPARC I and UltraSPARC II processors have far higher bandwidth requirements than do the previous generation SuperSPARC systems. A completely new approach to interconnect technologies was developed to support them. In this section, I first describe the interconnect architectures, followed by the system implementations and packaging.

The UltraSPARC Port Architecture Switched Interconnect

Bus architectures like MBus (and many other buses in use today) use each wire to carry data and address information from every device on the bus. This use makes the wire long and makes the protocol complex. It also reduces data bandwidth because the wire has to carry address information in between the data transfers. The bandwidth required by different types of bus device is also compromised. Memory and CPU devices need a very wide bus, and I/O devices that do not need as much bandwidth have to implement a full-width bus interface, and this requirement pushes up costs. The UltraSPARC Port Architecture (UPA), shown in Figure 11-17 on page 293, is a very neat solution to all these problems.

In the networking arena, shared Ethernets have been replaced by switched Ethernet, with some ports on the switch at 10 Mbit/s and some at 100 Mbit/s. The move from a shared bus architecture to the UPA switch has the same benefits. Low-speed devices can use a low-cost UPA port, and all devices have their own dedicated wire to the switch, so there is less contention and shorter wire lengths. Shorter wires can be clocked faster, so the UPA clock rate of 83 MHz to 100 MHz is easier to achieve. Unlike a network switch, the UPA separates the addresses and data. Addresses are fed to a system controller so that cache coherency can be maintained, and the system controller manages a queue of requests and sequences the data switch. All ports on the UPA operate at the same clock rate but have different widths. Some *master ports* such as CPUs and I/O controllers can initiate a transfer, whereas *slave ports* such as memory and framebuffer devices only need to respond and are simpler to implement. All ports connect to 64-byte, cache-line-sized buffers in the data switch. Several external transfers may be needed to fill a buffer from a narrow port. When the buffer is full, it is switched to the destination port in a single cycle. In each UPA cycle (at 83 or 100 MHz), 16 bytes can be switched from one port's output buffer to another port's input buffer, so four cycles are used to transfer a 64-byte cache line. The next four cycles can be used to transfer a different cache line. The overall data bandwidth is 16 bytes at 100 MHz or 1.6 Gbytes/s. All data carries error correction bits, so the switch is really 144 bits wide rather than 128 bits.

Unlike the case with most other buses, there are no dead cycles between transfers and no address transfers to get in the way. All address transfers occur in parallel on separate wires. All signals are either error corrected or parity protected. There is one address transfer for every four data transfers, and the system design is really limited by the rate at which addresses can be issued and arbitrated (25 million addresses/s). Each device has its own dedicated connection to a port, so slow devices do not interfere with fast devices, and all these buses can be transferring at once. There is very little contention under heavy load, so the latency of the UPA stays low longer than bus-based alternatives.

The Gigaplane Ultra Enterprise Server Backplane

The Ultra Enterprise Server range is a configurable, multiple-board-based system. It uses a passive backplane to keep the package and entry-level configuration costs down. The Gigaplane bus connects the boards with a 256-bit-wide data path and a separate address path. It is a remarkably efficient design that has no wasted clock cycles and approaches the limits set by the laws of physics. Gigaplane is a distributed extension of the techniques used by the UPA design.

Each address is broadcast to the entire system in one clock cycle, and the snoop results are returned in the next cycle. A 64-byte cache line is also transferred over the data path in two cycles. Again, there are no dead cycles on the bus, even when the direction of transfer is changed. Two-cycle arbitration with no dead cycles is a very aggressive implementation (some competing systems take five cycles and need a dead cycle between each phase before the bus is driven in the opposite direction). The result is a capacity of 41 million addresses/s at 82 MHz. This is a key measure for large SMP systems, known as the coherency bandwidth. The data bandwidth is the coherency bandwidth multiplied by the cache line size of 64 bytes, which is 2,624,000,000 bytes/s. Data rates of over 2500 Mbytes/s have been measured on these systems.

The Gigaplane also has some special optimizations that make memory sharing and spin locks more efficient for the E3000, E4000, E5000, and E6000.

The Gigaplane XB Crossbar

The E10000 Starfire is also a configurable, multiple-board-based system, but it has an active backplane. This means that the entry-level configuration includes the full cost of the complex circuitry that implements the crossbar interconnect. This design decision is one of the key differentiators between the two server architectures. The active backplane adds to the throughput and flexibility of the design and, unfortunately, also adds to the system cost and memory latency.

In some ways, Gigaplane XB is more like the entry-level UPA design, in that it uses point-to-point 128-bit-wide buses, all connected to ports on a central switch. The essential difference is that while UPA transfers one block of data in each clock cycle between any pair of ports, Gigaplane XB moves eight blocks of data at the same time between pairs of ports, using a 16-port crossbar switch rather than the single switch of UPA. At the same clock rate, the data bandwidth of Gigaplane XB is eight times that of the entry-level UPA-based systems, and four times that of the Gigaplane. Since it uses short point-to-point wiring, there is also more headroom in the design (it is easier to achieve high clock rates) and better fault isolation. The entire system was designed to run at 100 MHz, but it shares its CPU modules with the rest of the enterprise server range and operates at a nominal clock rate of 83 MHz with the 250 MHz module.

A challenge for Gigaplane XB is to obtain enough address bus coherence bandwidth to keep its crossbar busy. It does this by using four interleaved global address buses with two-cycle arbitration. This approach matches the cache line transfer rate, which takes four cycles, with eight occurring in parallel. It thus has four times the bandwidth of the Gigaplane, at 167 million addresses/s at 83 MHz. With 64-byte cache lines, this bandwidth works out to 10.6 million bytes/s. When converting to megabytes and gigabytes, take care that you are using consistent definitions as either a power of 10 or a power of 2 throughout your calculations. Exact clock rates for your system can be obtained from `prtconf`, as described in "The Openboot Device Tree — `prtconf` and `prtdiag`" on page 438. Table 11-17 shows exact measured rates taken from `prtdiag`, rather than the nominal rates, and approximate latency.

Table 11-17 UltraSPARC Multiprocessor Bus Characteristics

Bus Name	Bus Clock	CPU Clock	Addresses	Data bytes/s	Latency
UPA	84.0 MHz	168 MHz	21 MHz	1,344,000,000	170 ns
UPA	82.0 MHz	248 MHz	20.5 MHz	1,312,000,000	170 ns
UPA	100.0 MHz	200, 300 MHz	25 MHz	1,600,000,000	160 ns
Gigaplane	82 MHz	248	41 MHz	2,624,000,000	270 ns
Gigaplane XB	83,294,357 Hz	249,883,071 Hz	166,588,714 Hz	10,661,677,696	400 ns
Gigaplane XB	100 MHz	N/A	200 MHz	12,800,000,000	N/A

Main memory latency for a cache miss is about 400 ns with the Gigaplane XB. It is higher than for the Gigaplane because there is an extra level of switching circuitry to pass through. The Gigaplane XB data path is 144 bits wide, rather than 288 bits wide as for Gigaplane, so transfers take four rather than two cycles. The Gigaplane spin lock optimizations are not used by the E10000, which was designed by the Cray SuperServers team before Sun acquired their organization. In effect, when running within the bandwidth limitations of the Gigaplane, the Gigaplane is higher performance than the Gigaplane XB. The full bandwidth of the Gigaplane XB is available only in a maximum configuration. It increases as pairs of boards are added to a domain, as shown in Table 11-18. An odd number of boards does not add any bandwidth, as the odd board has nothing to communicate with. Comparing with the Gigaplane, you can see that up to 20 CPUs, Gigaplane should have a performance advantage; above 20 CPUs, Gigaplane XB has significantly higher bandwidth. As described "The E10000 Starfire Implementation" on page 297, the E10000 also adds more I/O capability on each board, whereas Gigaplane-based systems have to reduce the number of I/O boards to fit in more CPUs. If you are interested in an E10000 for its ultimate performance, you should configure it into a single large domain. If you want flexibility in a single rack, the performance of a small domain is very good, but you need to take into account that it will be lower than a dedicated system with the same number of CPUs.

Table 11-18 Data Bandwidth Variation with Domain Size

Domain Size	CPU Count	Data Bandwidth Mbyte/s
UPA	1-4	1600
Gigaplane	1 to 30	2624
Gigaplane XB 1 to 3 boards	1-12	1333
Gigaplane XB 4 to 5 boards	13-20	2666
Gigaplane XB 6 to 7 boards	21-28	4000
Gigaplane XB 8 to 9 boards	29-36	5331
Gigaplane XB 10 to 11 boards	37-44	6664
Gigaplane XB 12 to 13 boards	45-52	7997
Gigaplane XB 14 to 15 boards	53-60	9330
Gigaplane XB 16 boards	61-64	10662

UltraSPARC III Interconnect Considerations

The first details about UltraSPARC III were disclosed at the Microprocessor Forum event in October 1997. The press release, available on Sun's web site, contains the following details: the target CPU clock rate is 600 MHz, and the per-CPU bandwidth is 2.4 Gbytes/s, with performance two to three times higher than that of UltraSPARC II.

None of the above interconnects can interface to a CPU with this much bandwidth. In the meantime, with higher-performance UltraSPARC II CPU modules and excellent SMP scalability to large numbers of processors, there is plenty of room for growth in the current product range.

UltraSPARC System Implementations

There are five UltraSPARC I- and UltraSPARC II-based system implementations to discuss. The most recent and simplest is the highly integrated uniprocessor UltraSPARC IIi, a successor to the microSPARC. The initial UltraSPARC workstations are based on a simple UPA configuration. An expanded UPA configuration is used in the workgroup server systems. The Enterprise Server range uses a Gigaplane bus to link large numbers of CPUs and I/O buses. The E10000 Starfire uses an active backplane crossbar to support the very biggest configurations.

The Ultra 5 and Ultra 10

The UltraSPARC IIi provides a highly integrated design for building low-cost systems in the same way as its microSPARC predecessor. The CPU chip includes a complete memory controller, external cache controller, I/O bus controller (32-bit PCIbus this time) and a UPA slave interface for Creator graphics options. Figure 11-16 illustrates the architecture.

Figure 11-16 UltraSPARC IIi-Based, Entry-Level Ultra 5, Ultra 10 System Architecture

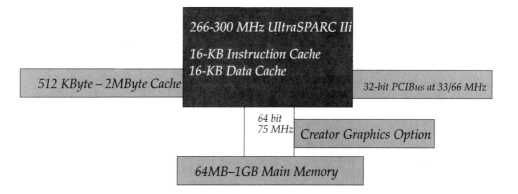

The Ultra 1, Ultra 2 and Ultra 30, Ultra 60

The UPA configuration of these systems is shown in Figure 11-17. The address connections are omitted, leaving just the data paths through the port. ECC adds to the real width of each port, making the sizes 72, 144, and 288 bits, to carry 64, 128, and 256 bits of data.

Memory is a problem because DRAM is slow to respond, compared to other devices. It is given a double-width port, which is loaded at half the rate (i.e., 50 MHz) from a pair of memory modules. Since a full cache line is 64 bytes, or 576 bits including ECC, a second pair of memory modules is set up to transfer immediately afterward in the dual-CPU,

Ultra 2 version of this design. This interleaving reduces latency in case the other CPU wishes to access the memory port immediately. The Ultra 30 and Ultra 60 support a second UPA graphics interface for Creator or Elite graphics options. These systems benefit from the low latency of the UPA but do not come close to using up its bandwidth. The design is limited by memory bandwidth to around 300–500 Mbytes/s. Main memory latency in this configuration is 28 cycles (168 ns) for a 167 MHz CPU with 83 MHz UPA. Latency in nanoseconds is a little better with a 100 MHz UPA, but the number of clock cycles gets worse as the CPU speed increases—approximately 30 cycles at 200 MHz, 40 at 250 MHz, and 50 at 300 MHz.

The Ultra 30 is packaged as a PCIbus tower system, closer to a PC configuration than to the traditional Sun "pizza box" used in the Ultra 1 and Ultra 2. The Ultra 60 is a dual-CPU version of the Ultra 30. Their architecture is the same as that of the Ultra 2 but with the substitution of a PCIbus controller for the SBus controller used in previous designs. This UPA-to-PCI controller is used in many UltraSPARC systems. It has two PCIbuses: one is a high-speed, 64-bit @ 66 MHz bus with a single slot; the other is a 32/64-bit @ 33 MHz bus that can support several slots.

Figure 11-17 The UltraSPARC Port Architecture (UPA) Ultra 1, 2, and 30 Implementation

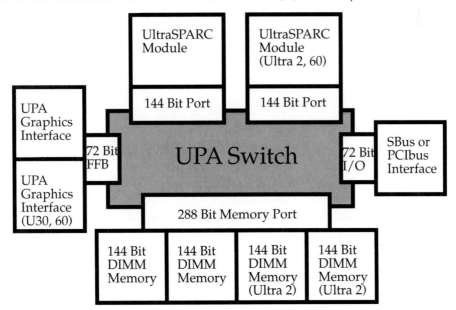

Larger UPA-Based Systems: The Enterprise 450

To extend the design to cope with the demands of the four-processor Enterprise 45, a more complex switch was developed with twice as many ports, as shown in Figure 11-18. The configuration includes not only four processor ports but also two independent memory ports, two graphics ports, and two I/O bus ports, each supporting dual PCI buses for a total of four. This design represents the largest balanced configuration that can be built on a single motherboard, yet it still does not saturate the throughput capabilities of the UPA switch. It retains the low latency of the entry level designs, while providing twice the CPU power and twice the memory and I/O bandwidth.

Figure 11-18 The E450 UltraSPARC Port Architecture (UPA) Switched Interconnect

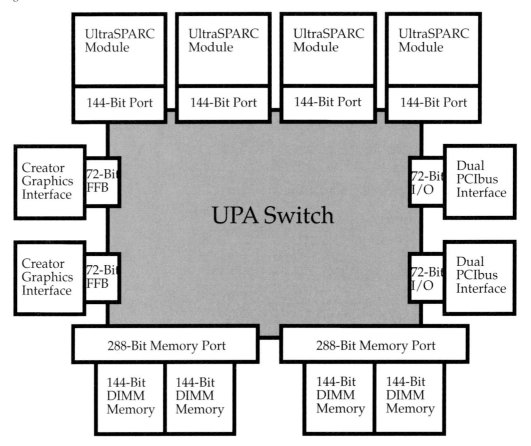

Memory is accessed four DIMMs at a time, and additional performance comes from interleaving the four banks of four DIMMs. The interleaving rules are very restrictive, and for best performance, the simple rule is to always use the same size DIMM throughout. A mixture of DIMM capacities will prevent interleaving. Two banks of identical DIMMS, with two empty banks, will be two-way interleaved. Four banks of identical DIMMs will be four-way interleaved. Any other combination prevents any interleaving. This is unlikely to be an issue on systems with less than four CPUs, but a high-end configuration that is heavily loaded should at least have two-way interleaving, and preferably four.

The low latency of the E450 gives it significantly higher performance than a four-CPU Enterprise Server at substantially lower cost. The scope for expansion is limited, however, so next we will look at the multiboard Ultra Enterprise Server Architecture.

The Ultra Enterprise Server Architecture

Boards come in two types, CPU+Memory and I/O+Framebuffer. The CPU+Memory board shown in Figure 11-19 allows memory to be added to the system in proportion to the CPU power configured. Some competing designs use separate CPU and memory boards and suffer from having to trade off CPU for memory in big configurations.

Figure 11-19 The Ultra Enterprise Server CPU+Memory Board Implementation

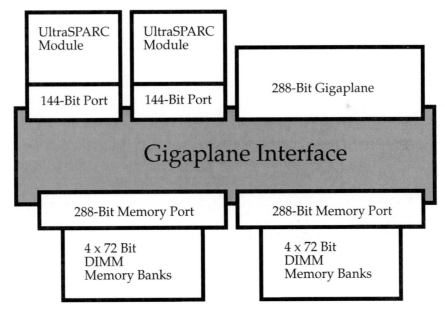

The three different designs of separate I/O+Framebuffer board shown in Figure 11-20 allow systems to be configured for CPU-intensive or I/O-intensive workloads and also allow a mixture of I/O types (SBus, PCIbus, and SBus+Creator Framebuffer) to be configured as needed.

Figure 11-20 The Ultra Enterprise Server I/O Board Implementation

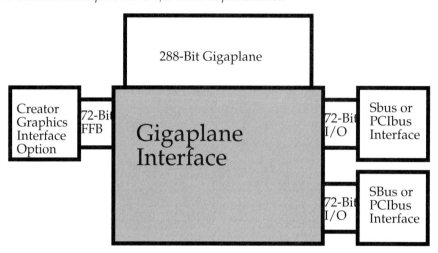

These two board types are combined into three basic packages: the four-board E3000; the eight-board E4000, which is called the E5000 when rack-mounted; and the sixteen-board E6000. The larger systems use a centerplane, with boards plugging in horizontally from both the front and back of the chassis, as shown in Figure 11-21. The E3000 has boards numbered 1, 3, 5, 7 only, the E4000 has boards numbered 0 to 7 inclusive, and the E6000 has boards numbered 0–15.

Figure 11-21 Enterprise Server Board Configuration: Side View with Numbering

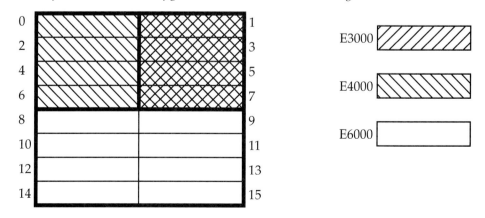

The E10000 Starfire Implementation

The E10000 uses a single, large-format board type, with removable daughter cards that can configure SBus or PCIbus options for I/O. Each board includes four CPU modules, four memory banks, and two I/O buses, as shown in Figure 11-22. The packaging takes up to sixteen boards, connected as described in "The Gigaplane XB Crossbar" on page 289. More information is available from the "Ultra Enterprise 10000 System Overview White Paper" and other papers at http://www.sun.com/servers/ultra_enterprise/10000/wp.

Figure 11-22 The E10000 Starfire Implementation

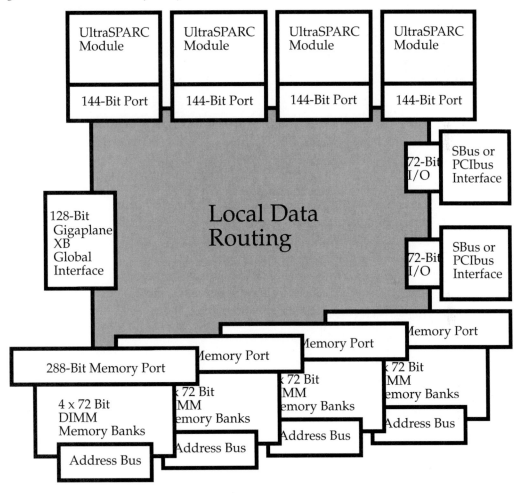

The four memory banks are interleaved. Each memory bank has its own global address bus that maintains coherency with that bank on other boards.

Each board can function independently, and single boards or groups of boards can be configured into domains. (Domain memory bandwidth is described in Table 11-18 on page 291.) The system can boot multiple copies of Solaris, one per domain. The crossbar switch is configured so that data transfers between boards in one domain do not affect the performance of any other domain. There is also very good fault isolation between domains. Hardware failures are not propagated. Domains can be changed on line via dynamic reconfiguration.

Caches

Caches store a small amount of information for repeated fast access. Many types of caches occur throughout computer hardware and software systems. We'll take a look at the common principles, with examples of CPU cache, directory name lookup cache (DNLC), and name service cache. Then, we'll discuss some caches used with local disks and caches used with networks.

Cache Principles

Caches work on two basic principles that should be quite familiar to you from everyday life. The first is that if you spend a long time going to get something and you think you may need it again soon, you keep it nearby. For example, if you are working on your car, you find a 15 mm spanner in your tool box, then crawl under the car. If you then need a 10 mm spanner, you don't put the 15 mm back in the tool box, you leave it under the car. When you have finished, there is a *cache* of tools in a pile under the car that make up your *working set*. If you allowed only one tool at a time under the car, you would waste a lot of time going back to the tool box. However, if the pile of tools gets too large, you may decide to put away a few tools that you think you won't need any more.

The second principle is that when you get something, you can save time by getting a few extra things that you think you might need soon. In the car example, you could grab a handful of spanners each time, thus saving yourself from having to make a few trips. You find that the pile under the car gets bigger much more quickly, you never use some tools, and it takes you longer to pick up and put down a handful of tools on each trip to the tool box.

The first principle, called "temporal locality," depends on reusing the same things over time. The second principle, called "spacial locality," depends on using things at the same time that are located near each other. Caches work well only if there is good locality in what you are doing.

Another good example is the "cache" of groceries that you keep in your house that saves you a trip to the supermarket every time you want a bite to eat. To take this analogy a bit further, let's say you are the kind of person who hates shopping and lives off tinned and frozen food that you buy once a month. You have a very efficient cache, with few shopping trips, and you can spend all your spare time browsing the Internet. Now, let's say that your mother comes to stay and tells you that you need a diet of fresh fruit and salad instead. You can't buy in bulk as these items don't freeze or keep, and you need to visit the shops almost every day. You now waste all your spare time shopping. You notice one day that your local shop is now also on the Internet, and you can use your browser to place orders for delivery. Now you can surf the Internet all the time, keep a good diet, and never go grocery shopping again! In cache terms, this is an asynchronous prefetch of stuff that you know you will need soon, but, by requesting it in advance, you never have to stop and wait for it to arrive.

This analogy illustrates that some sequences of behavior work very efficiently with a cache, and others make little or no use of the cache. In some cases, "cache busting" behavior can be fixed by changing the system to work in a different way that bypasses the normal cache fetch. These alternative methods usually require extra hardware or software support in a computer system.

Before going on to a specific kind of cache, let's look at some generic terms and measurements that parameterize caches. When the cache is used to hold some kind of information, a read from the cache is very different from writing new information, so we'll take a look at cache reads first, then look at writes.

Cache Reads That Succeed

Many kinds of information can be cached: the value of a memory location, the location of a file, or the network address of another system. When the information is needed, the system first looks for it in the cache. This approach requires that each item in the cache has a unique name or tag associated with the information. When a cache lookup occurs, the first thing that happens is a search during which the system tries to match the name you gave it with one of the tags. If the search succeeds, the associated data is returned; this case is called a *read hit*. This situation is the best case, as it is both quick and successful. The two measures of interest are the *read hit rate* and the *read hit cost*. The read hit rate is the number of read hits that occur per second; the read hit cost is the time it takes to search the cache and return the data.

CPU Cache Example

For a CPU's primary data cache, an address is used as the tag. Millions of read hits occur each second; the cost is known as the *load use delay,* a constant small number of CPU clock cycles. When the CPU issues a load instruction to move data from memory to a register, it has to wait a few cycles before it can use the register. A good compiler will try to optimize code by moving load instructions forward and filling in the load use delay with other work. It is hard to measure (and understand) what is going on in the CPU cache.

Directory Name Lookup Cache Example

For the directory name lookup cache (DNLC), an open system call causes a pathname string, e.g., "export," to be looked up to find its inode. The rate at which this lookup occurs is reported by sar -a as *namei/s*; it can reach a few thousand per second on a busy file server. The read hit cost is relatively low and consumes only CPU time. An efficient hashed search is used, so the size of the search is not an issue.

Name Service Cache Example

The name service cache is implemented as a multithreaded daemon process (nscd). It caches password and group information for users, and the host IP address information for systems. For example, a call to gethostbyname(3N) would ordinarily involve a search through the local /etc/hosts file, a call to a local NIS or NIS+ server, and perhaps a DNS lookup, as specified in /etc/nsswitch.conf. The nscd provides a systemwide cache for the results of these searches, and gethostbyname accesses it through a very fast, new, interprocess call mechanism known as a *door call*. The read hit cost is only a few tens of microseconds, depending on your CPU speed.

Cache Reads That Miss the Cache

If the search fails and the data is not in the cache, the case is called a *read miss*. The rate at which this situation occurs is called the *read miss rate*, and the time taken is called the *read miss cost*. A read miss corresponds to the work that would be needed if the cache did not exist, plus the added overhead of checking the cache. Read misses are slow, and the read miss cost can be unpredictable, although it is usually possible to figure out the best case, the worst case, and the average.

CPU Cache Example

CPU caches come in many configurations. The most common setup is to have two separate primary caches built into the CPU chip, one to hold instructions and one to hold data, and often holding about 16 Kbytes each. These caches then refer to an external level-2 cache holding between 256 Kbytes and 4 Mbytes of data. A read miss in the small primary cache may result in a hit or a miss in the level-2 cache. A level-2 hit takes a few cycles longer than a level-1 hit but is still very efficient. A level-2 miss involves a main memory reference, and in a multiprocessor system, the system must access the backplane and check every CPU cache in the system as well. If the backplane is already very busy, there may be a considerable extra delay. This approach explains why heavily loaded multiprocessor servers run faster and scale better with the reduced number of read misses that come with larger CPU caches. For example, Sun currently offers a choice of

512-Kbyte, 1-Mbyte, 2-Mbyte, and 4-Mbyte caches on the UltraSPARC range. The 4-Mbyte cache choice is always faster, but it will have a proportionately greater benefit on performance and scalability of a 24-CPU E6000 than on a 4-CPU E3000.

An anomaly can arise in some cases. It takes time to search the cache and to load new data into it, and these processes slow down the fetch operation. If you normally operate in a cache-busting mode, you actually go faster if there is no cache at all. Since caches add to the cost of a system (extra memory used or extra hardware), they may not be present on a simpler or cheaper system. The anomaly is that a cheaper system may be faster than a more expensive one for some kinds of work. The microSPARC processor used in the 110 MHz SPARCstation 5 is very simple: it has a high cache miss rate but a low cache miss cost. The SuperSPARC processor used in the SPARCstation 20 has much bigger caches, a far lower cache miss rate, but a much higher cache miss cost. For a commercial database workload, the large cache works well, and the SPARCstation 20 is much faster. For a large Verilog EDA simulation, the caches are all too small to help, and the low latency to access memory makes the SPARCstation 5 an extremely fast machine. The lessons learned from this experience were incorporated in the UltraSPARC design, which also has very low latency to access memory. To get the low latency, the latest, fastest cache memory and very fast, wide system buses are needed.

Directory Name Lookup Cache Example

If we consider our other examples, the DNLC is caching a file name. If the system cannot find out the corresponding inode number from the DNLC, it has to read through the directory structures of the file system. This procedure may involve a linear search through a UFS directory structure or a series of `readdir` calls over NFS to an NFS server. There is some additional caching of blocks of directory data and NFS attributes that may save time, but often the search has to sleep for many milliseconds while waiting for several disk reads or network requests to complete. You can monitor the number of directory blocks read per second with `sar  -a` as *dirbk/s*; you can also look at the number of NFS2 `readdir` calls and NFS3 `readdirplus` calls. NFS2 reads a single entry with each `readdir` call, whereas NFS3 adds the `readdirplus` call that reads a series of entries in one go for greater efficiency (but longer latency).

To summarize the effects of a DNLC miss: A little extra CPU is consumed during the search, but a lot of sleeping—waiting for the disk and network—dominates the miss cost. DNLC hit rates (the number of read hits as a proportion of all lookups) are often in the 80%–100% range. If you run the `find` command, which walks through the directory structure, you will discover that the hit rate drops to perhaps 30%–40%. My rule for the DNLC hit rate is a bit too simple. It tells you to increase tne DNLC size if it is fairly small, the hit rate drops below 80%, and the reference rate is above 100/s. In some cases, a lot of new files are being created or a `find`-like operation is needed, and there is no point having a big DNLC.

Name Service Cache Example

A read miss on the name service cache causes a sequence of lookups by the nscd; the sequence is controlled by the /etc/nsswitch.conf file. If the file contains the entry:

```
hosts: files nisplus dns
```

then the nscd first lookup uses the standard files "backend" to look in /etc/hosts. In recent releases of Solaris 2, the files backend itself caches the file and does a hashed lookup into it; so, very long host and passwd files are searched efficiently, and the read miss could be quite quick and CPU bound with no waiting. A NIS or NIS+ lookup involves a call over the network to a name server and so incurs at least a few milliseconds of delay. If the lookup is eventually passed up a hierarchy of DNS servers across the Internet, the lookup could take several seconds. The worst case is a lookup in a remote DNS domain for a hostname that does not exist. Unfortunately, some applications repeat the same lookup several times in quick succession, so a novel feature of the nscd is that it supports *negative caching*. It remembers that a lookup failed and tells you immediately that the host does not exist if you ask a second time. There is a five second time-out for negative entries by default. The full output from nscd -g (on a recently booted Solaris 2.5 system) is shown Figure 12-1.

Figure 12-1 Example Name Service Cache Daemon (nscd) Configuration

```
% nscd -g
nscd configuration:

        0   server debug level
"/dev/null"   is server log file

passwd cache:

       Yes   cache is enabled
       507   cache hits on positive entries
         0   cache hits on negative entries
        55   cache misses on positive entries
         2   cache misses on negative entries
       89%   cache hit rate
         0   queries deferred
        16   total entries
       211   suggested size
       600   seconds time to live for positive entries
         5   seconds time to live for negative entries
        20   most active entries to be kept valid
       Yes   check /etc/{passwd,group,hosts} file for changes
        No   use possibly stale data rather than waiting for refresh
```

Figure 12-1 Example Name Service Cache Daemon (nscd) Configuration (Continued)

```
group cache:

         Yes  cache is enabled
          27  cache hits on positive entries
           0  cache hits on negative entries
          11  cache misses on positive entries
           0  cache misses on negative entries
         71% cache hit rate
           0  queries deferred
           5  total entries
         211  suggested size
        3600  seconds time to live for positive entries
           5  seconds time to live for negative entries
          20  most active entries to be kept valid
         Yes  check /etc/{passwd,group,hosts} file for changes
          No  use possibly stale data rather than waiting for refresh

hosts cache:

         Yes  cache is enabled
          22  cache hits on positive entries
           3  cache hits on negative entries
           7  cache misses on positive entries
           3  cache misses on negative entries
         71% cache hit rate
           0  queries deferred
           4  total entries
         211  suggested size
        3600  seconds time to live for positive entries
           5  seconds time to live for negative entries
          20  most active entries to be kept valid
         Yes  check /etc/{passwd,group,hosts} file for changes
          No  use possibly stale data rather than waiting for refresh
```

Cache Replacement Policies

So far, we have assumed that there is always some spare room in the cache. In practice, the cache will fill up and at some point cache entries will need to be reused. The *cache replacement policy* varies, but the general principle is that you want to get rid of entries that you will not need again soon. Unfortunately, the "won't need soon" cache policy is hard to implement unless you have a very structured and predictable workload or you can predict the future! In its place, you will often find caches that use "least recently used" (LRU) or "not recently used" (NRU) policies, in the hope that your accesses have good temporal locality. CPU caches tend to use "direct mapping"—where there is no choice, the address in memory is used to fix an address in cache. For small, on-chip caches, there may be "n-way associative mapping"—where there are "n" choices of location for each cache line, usually two or four, and an LRU or random choice implemented in hardware.

Random replacement (RR) policies seem to offend some of the engineering purists among us, as they can never work optimally, but I like them because the converse is true, and they rarely work badly either! Caches work well if the access pattern is somewhat random with some locality or if it has been carefully constructed to work with a particular cache policy (an example is SunSoft Performance WorkShop's highly tuned math library). Unfortunately, many workloads have structured access patterns that work against the normal policies. Random replacement policies can be fast, don't need any extra storage to remember the usage history, and can avoid some nasty interactions.

Cache Writes and Purges

So far, we have looked only at what is involved in reading existing information through a cache. When new information is created or old information is overwritten or deleted, there are extra problems to deal with.

The first issue to consider is that a memory-based cache contains a copy of some information and the official master copy is kept somewhere else. When we want to change the information, we have several choices. We could update the copy in the cache only, which is very fast, but that copy now differs from the master copy. We could update both copies immediately, which may be slow, or we could throw away the cached copy and just update the master (if the *cache write cost* is high).

Another issue to consider is that the cache may contain a large block of information and we want to update only a small part of it. Do we have to copy the whole block back to update the master copy? And what if there are several caches for the same data, as in a CPU with several levels of cache and other CPUs in a multiprocessor? There are many possibilities, so I'll just look at the examples we have discussed already.

The CPU cache is optimized for speed by hardware that implements relatively simple functions with a lot of the operations overlapped so they all happen at once. On an UltraSPARC, a cache block contains 64 bytes of data. A write will change between 1 and 8 bytes at a time. Each block contains some extra flags that indicate whether the data is shared with another CPU cache and whether the data has been written to. A write updates both the internal level-1 and the external level-2 caches. It is not written out to memory, but the first time a shared block in a multiprocessor system is written to, a special signal, invalidating any copies of the data that other CPUs hold, is sent to all the other CPUs. The flags are then changed from shared/clean to private/dirty. If another CPU then tries to reread that data, it is provided directly in a cache-to-cache transfer and becomes shared/dirty. The data is eventually written back to main memory only when that cache block is needed to hold different data by a read. In this case, the read operation is held in an input buffer while the dirty cache block is copied to an output buffer, then the read from memory completes, and finally the dirty cache line write completes.

Another situation to consider is the case of a context switch or a process exiting. If an address space is no longer valid, the cache tags may also be invalid. For systems that store a virtual address in the cache tag, all the invalid addresses must be purged; for systems that store only a physical address in the cache tag, there is no such need. Older SPARC systems, the HyperSPARC range, and some other systems such as HP-PA use virtual caches. SuperSPARC and UltraSPARC use physical caches. In general, a virtual cache can be faster for uniprocessor systems and scientific workloads, and a physical cache scales much better on multiprocessor systems and commercial workloads that have lots of context switches.

There are a lot more ways to implement caches. If you are interested, I recommend you read *Computer Architecture — A Quantitative Approach* by Hennessy and Patterson, published by Morgan Kaufmann.

Returning to our consideration of the DNLC: When a file is created or deleted, the new directory entry is written to disk or sent over NFS immediately, so it is a slow operation. The extra overhead of updating or purging the DNLC is very small in comparison.

The name service cache does not get involved in updates. If someone changes data in the name service, the nscd relies on time-outs and watching the modification dates on files to register the change.

Cache Efficiency

A cache works well if there are a lot more reads than writes, and the reads or writes of the same or nearby data occur close together in time. An efficient cache has a low reference rate (doesn't make unnecessary lookups), a very short cache hit time, a high hit ratio, the minimum possible cache miss time, and an efficient way of handling writes and purges.

Some trade-offs can be made. A small, fast cache may have a lower hit ratio but can compensate by having a low miss cost. A big, slower cache can compensate for the extra miss cost by missing much less often.

Beware of looking at hit ratios alone. A system may be running more efficiently by referencing the cache less often. If there are multiple levels of cache and the first level is working well, the second level will tend to see a higher proportion of misses but a low reference rate. It is actually the miss rate (in misses/second) multiplied by the miss cost (to give a total time delay) that matters more than the ratio of hits or misses as a percentage of the total references

Generic Cache Behavior Summary

I've tried to illustrate some of the generic behavior of caches with examples that show what is similar and what is different. Computer systems are constructed from a large number of hardware and software caches of many types, and there can be huge differences in performance between a workload that works with a cache and one that works against a cache. Usually, all we can tune is the cache size for software caches like the DNLC. This tuning has some effect, but it is much more effective to change your workload (don't run the find command any more often that you have to!) to work within the cache you have. Your computer is spending more time stalled, waiting for some kind of cache miss to complete, than you think.

File Access Caching with Local Disk

Accessing a file on disk or over a network is hundreds of times slower than reading a cached copy from memory. Many types of cache exist to speed up file accesses. Changing your workload to make it more "cache friendly" can result in very significant performance benefits.

We'll start by looking at the simplest configuration, the open, fstat, read, write, and mmap operations on a local disk with the default UFS file system, as shown in Figure 12-2.

Figure 12-2 File Access Caches for Local Disk Access

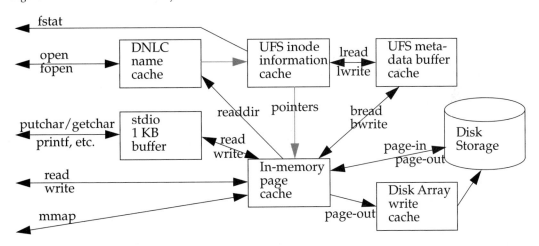

There are a lot of interrelated caches. They are systemwide caches, shared by all users and all processes. The activity of one cache-busting process can mess up the caching of other well-behaved processes. Conversely, a group of cache-friendly processes working on similar data at similar times help each other by prefilling the caches for each other. The diagram in Figure 12-2 shows the main data flows and relationships.

Directory Name Lookup Cache

The directory name lookup cache (DNLC) is a cache of directory information. A directory is a special kind of file that contains names and inode number pairs. The DNLC holds the name and a pointer to an inode cache entry. If an inode cache entry is discarded, any corresponding DNLC entries must also be purged. When a file is opened, the DNLC figures out the right inode from the file name given. If the name is in the cache, the system does a fast hashed lookup if directories need not be scanned.

The UFS directory file structure is a sequence of variable length entries requiring a linear search. Each DNLC entry is a fixed size, so there is only space for a pathname component of up to 30 characters. Longer components are not cached (many older systems like SunOS 4 cache only up to 14 characters). Directories that have thousands of entries can take a long time to search, so a good DNLC hit rate is important if files are being opened frequently and very large directories are in use. In practice, file opening is not usually frequent enough to be a serious problem. NFS clients hold a file handle that includes the inode number for each open file, so each NFS operation can avoid the DNLC and go directly to the inode.

The maximum tested size of the DNLC is 34906, corresponding to the maximum allowed `maxusers` setting of 2048. The largest size the DNLC will reach with no tuning is 17498, on systems with over 1 Gbyte of RAM. The size defaults to (`maxusers` * 17) + 90, and `maxusers` is set to just under the number of megabytes of RAM in the system, with a default limit of 1024.

I find that people are overeager in tuning `ncsize`; it really only needs to be increased manually on small-memory (512 Mbytes or less) NFS servers, and even then, any performance increase is unlikely to be measurable unless you are running the SPECsfs NFS stress test benchmark.

Inode Cache

The `fstat` call returns the inode information about a file. This information includes file size and datestamps, as well as the device and inode numbers that uniquely identify the file. Every concurrently open file corresponds to an active entry in the inode cache, so if a file is kept open, its information is locked in the inode cache and is immediately available. A number (set by the tunable `ufs_ninode`) of inactive inode entries are also kept. `ufs_ninode` is set, using the same calculation as that for `ncsize` above, but the total size of the inode cache will be bigger because ufs_ninode limits only the inactive entries. ufs_ninode doesn't normally need tuning, but if the DNLC is increased, make ncsize and ufs_ninode the same.

Inactive files are files that were opened at some time in the past and that may be opened again in the future. If the number of inactive entries grows too large, entries that have not been used recently are discarded. Stateless NFS clients do not keep the inode active, so the pool of inactive inodes caches the inode data for files that are opened by NFS clients. The inode cache entry also provides the location of every data block on disk and the location of every page of file data in memory. If an inactive inode is discarded, all of its file data in memory is also discarded, and the memory is freed for reuse. The percentage of inode cache entries that had pages when they were freed, causing cached file data to be discarded, is reported by sar -g as %ufs_ipf. My inode cache rule described in "Inode Rule" on page 460 warns when non-zero values of %ufs_ipf are seen.

The inode cache hit rate is often 90 percent or more, meaning that most files are accessed several times in a short period of time. If you run a cache-busting command, like find or ls -R, that looks at many files once only, you will see a much lower DNLC and inode cache hit rate. An inode cache hit is quick because a hashed lookup finds the entry efficiently. An inode cache miss varies because the inode may be found in the UFS metadata buffer cache or because a disk read may be needed to get the right block of inodes into the UFS metadata buffer cache.

UFS Metadata Buffer Cache

This cache is often just referred to as "the buffer cache," but there has been so much confusion about its use that I like to specifically mention metadata. Historically, Unix systems used a "buffer cache" to cache all disk data, assigning about 10 percent of total memory to this job. This changed in about 1988, when SunOS 4.0 came out with a combined virtual memory and I/O setup. This setup was later included in System V Release 4, and variants of it are used in most recent Unix releases. The buffer cache itself was left intact, but it was bypassed for all data transfers, changing it from a key role to a mostly inconsequential role. The sar -b command still reports on its activity, but I can't remember the buffer cache itself being a performance bottleneck for many years. As the title says, this cache holds only UFS metadata. This includes disk blocks full of inodes (a disk block is 8 Kbytes, an inode is about 300 bytes), indirect blocks (used as inode extensions to keep track of large files), and cylinder group information (which records the way the disk space is divided up between inodes and data). The buffer cache sizes itself dynamically, hits are quick, and misses involve a disk access.

In-memory Page Cache

When we talk about memory usage and demand on a system, it is actually the behavior of the in-memory page cache that is the issue. This cache contains all data that is held in memory, including the files that make up executable code and normal data files, without making any distinction between them. A large proportion of the total memory in the system is used by this cache because it holds all the pages that make up the current working set of the system as a whole. All page-in and page-out operations occur between this cache and the underlying file systems on disk (or over NFS). Individual pages in the cache may currently be unmapped (e.g., a data file) or may be mapped into the address space of many processes (e.g., the pages that make up the libc.so.1 shared library). Some pages do not correspond to a named file (e.g., the stack space of a process); these anonymous pages have swap space reserved for them so that they can be written to disk if required. The vmstat and sar -pg commands monitor the activity of this cache.

The cache is made up of 4-Kbyte or 8-Kbyte *page frames*. Each page of data may be located on disk as a file system or swap space data block, or in memory in a page frame. Some page frames are ready for reuse or empty and are kept on the free list (reported as free by vmstat).

A cache hit occurs when a needed page is already in memory; this hit may be recorded as an attach to an existing page or as a reclaim if the page was on the free list. A cache miss occurs when the page needs to be created from scratch (zero fill fault), duplicated (copy on write), or read in from disk (page-in). Apart from the page-in, these operations are all quite quick, and all misses take a page frame from the free list and overwrite it.

Consider a naive file-reading benchmark that opens a small file, then reads it to "see how fast the disk goes." If the file was recently created, then all of the file may be in memory. Otherwise, the first read-through will load it into memory. Subsequent runs may be fully cached with a 100% hit rate and no page-ins from disk at all. The benchmark ends up measuring memory speed, not disk speed. The best way to make the benchmark measure disk speed is to invalidate the cache entries by unmounting and remounting the file system between each run of the test.

The complexities of the entire virtual memory system and paging algorithm are beyond the scope of this book. The key thing to understand is that data is evicted from the cache only if the free memory list gets too small. The data that is evicted is any page that has not been referenced recently, where *recently* can means a few seconds to a few minutes. Page-out operations occur whenever files are written and also when data is reclaimed for the free list because of a memory shortage. Page-outs occur to all file systems but are often concentrated on the swap space.

Disk Array Write Cache

Disk array units, such as Sun's SPARCstorage Array, or "Hardware RAID" subsystems, such as the RSM2000, contain their own cache RAM. This cache is so small in comparison to the amount of disk space in the array that it is not very useful as a read cache. If there is a lot of data to read and reread, it would be better to add large amounts of RAM to the main system than to add it to the disk subsystem. The in-memory page cache is a faster and more useful place to cache data. A common setup is to make reads bypass the disk array cache and to save all the space to speed up writes. If there is a lot of idle time and memory in the array, then the array controller may also look for sequential read patterns and prefetch some read data, but in a busy array, this practice can get in the way. The OS generates its own prefetch reads in any case, further reducing the need to do additional prefetch in the controller. Three main situations, described below, are helped by the write cache.

When a lot of data is being written to a single file, it is often sent to the disk array in small blocks, perhaps 2 Kbytes to 8 Kbytes in size. The array can use its cache to coalesce adjacent blocks, which means that the disk gets fewer larger writes to handle. The reduction in the number of seeks greatly increases performance and cuts service times dramatically. This operation is safe only if the cache has battery backup for its cache (nonvolatile RAM) because the operating system assumes that when a write completes, the data is safely on the disk. As an example, 2-Kbyte raw writes during a database load can go two to three times faster.

The simple Unix write operation is buffered by the in-memory page cache until the file is closed or data gets flushed out after 30 seconds. Some applications use synchronous writes to ensure that their data is safely on disk. Directory changes are also made synchronously. These synchronous writes are intercepted by the disk array write cache and safely stored in nonvolatile RAM. Since the application is waiting for the write to complete, this approach has a dramatic effect, often reducing the wait from as much as 20 ms to as little as 2 ms. For the SPARCstorage Array, use the ssaadm command to check that fast writes have been enabled on each controller and to see if they have been enabled for all writes or just synchronous writes. The ssaadm command defaults to off, so if someone has forgotten to enable fast writes, you could get a good speedup! Use ssaadm to check the SSA firmware revision and upgrade it first. Use the copy in /usr/lib/firmware/ssa, or get a later version from the patch database.

The final use for a disk array write cache is to accelerate the RAID5 write operations in Hardware RAID systems. This usage does not apply to the SPARCstorage Array, which uses a slower, software-based RAID5 calculation in the host system. RAID5 combines disks, using parity for protection, but during writes, the calculation of parity means that all the blocks in a stripe are needed. With a 128-Kbyte interlace and a 6-way RAID5, each full stripe cache entry would use 768 Kbytes. Each individual small write is then combined into the full stripe before the full stripe is written back later on. This method needs a much larger cache than that needed for performing RAID5 calculations at the per-write level, but it is faster because the disks see fewer larger reads and writes. The SPARCstorage Array is very competitive for use in striped, mirrored, and read-mostly RAID5 configurations, but its RAID5 write performance is slow because each element of the RAID5 data is read into main memory for the parity calculation and then written back. With only 4 Mbytes or 16 Mbytes of cache, the SPARCstorage Array doesn't have space to do hardware RAID5, although this is plenty of cache for normal use. Hardware RAID5 units have 64 Mbytes or more (sometimes much more); see "Disk Workloads" on page 169 for more on this topic.

The Standard I/O Buffer

Simple text filters in Unix process data one character at a time, using the `putchar` and `getchar` macros, `printf` and the related `stdio.h` routines. To avoid a system call for every read or write of one character, `stdio` uses a buffer to cache the data for each file. The buffer size is 1 Kbyte, so every 1024 calls of `getchar`, a `read` system call of 1 Kbyte will occur. Every 8 system calls, a filesystem block will be paged in from disk. If your application is reading and writing data in blocks of 1 Kbyte or more, there is no point in using the `stdio` library—you can save time by using the `open/read/write` calls instead of `fopen/fread/fwrite`. Conversely, if you are using `open/read/write` for a few bytes at a time, you are generating a lot of unnecessary system calls and `stdio` would be faster.

Read, Write, and Memory Mapping

When you read data, you must first allocate a buffer, then read into that buffer. The data is copied out of a page in the in-memory page cache to your buffer, so there are two copies of the data in memory. This duplication wastes memory and wastes the time it takes to do the copy. The alternative is to use `mmap` to map the page directly into your address space. Data accesses then occur directly to the page in the in-memory page cache, with no copying and no wasted space. The drawback is that `mmap` changes the address space of the process, which is a complex data structure. With a lot of memory mapped files, the data structure gets even more complex. The `mmap` call itself is more complex than a read or write, and a complex address space also slows down the fork operation. My recommendation is to use read and write for short-lived or small files. Use `mmap` for random access to large, long-lived files where the avoidance of copying and reduction in `read/write/lseek` system calls offsets the initial `mmap` overhead.

Networked File Access

Paralleling the discussion of local disk accesses, this section looks at networked access. Accessing a file over a network is hundreds of times slower than reading a cached copy from memory. Many types of cache exist to speed up file accesses. Changing your workload to make it more "cache friendly" can result in very significant performance benefits.

NFS Access Caching

Again, we'll start by looking at the simplest configuration, the open, fstat, read, write, and mmap operations on an NFS-mounted file system, as shown in Figure 12-3.

Figure 12-3 File Access Caches for NFS and Cachefs

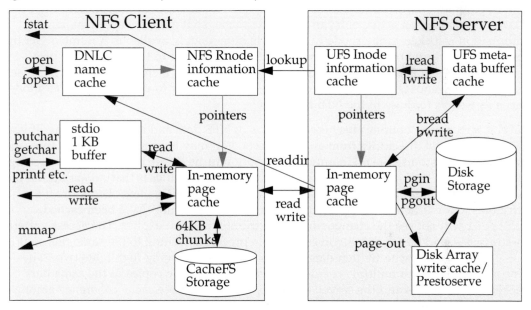

Compared with the previous diagram of UFS access caching, the diagram in Figure 12-3 has been split in the middle, pulled to each side, and divided between the two systems. Both systems contain an in-memory page cache, but the NFS file system uses an rnode (remote node) to hold information about the file. Like the UFS inode cache, the rnode keeps pointers to pages from the file that are in the local page cache. Unlike the UFS inode, it does not contain the disk block numbers; instead, it holds the NFS file handle. The handle has no meaning on the client, but on the server it is used to locate the mount point and inode number of the file so that NFS reads and writes can go directly to the right file on the server. An NFS file open on the client causes a DNLC lookup on the client; failure to find the file causes a DNLC lookup on the server that sets up both the DNLC entry and the rnode entry on the client, as shown in Figure 12-3.

There are a lot of interrelated caches. They are systemwide caches, shared by all users and all processes. The activity of one cache-busting process can mess up the caching of other well-behaved processes. Conversely, a group of cache-friendly processes working on similar data at similar times help each other by prefilling the caches for each other. The diagram in Figure 12-3 shows the main data flows and relationships.

Rnode Cache

The `lookup` NFS call returns the rnode information about a file. This information includes the file size and datestamps, as well as the NFS file handle that encodes server mount point and inode numbers that uniquely identify the file. Every concurrently open file corresponds to an active entry in the rnode cache, so if a file is kept open, its information is locked in the rnode cache and is immediately available. A number (set by the tunable `nrnode`) of rnode entries are kept. `nrnode` is set to twice the value of `ncsize`. It doesn't normally need tuning, but if the DNLC is increased, `nrnode` increases as well. DNLC entries are filesystem independent; they refer to entries in the UFS inode cache as well as to those in the NFS rnode cache.

Several NFS mount options affect the operation of NFS data and attribute caching. If you mount mail spool directories from an NFS server, you may have seen a warning message that advises you to use the `noac` option. This option turns off attribute and write caching. Why would this be a good idea? The access pattern for mail files is that `sendmail` on the server appends messages to the file. The `mailtool` on an NFS client checks the file attributes to see if new mail has been delivered. If the attributes have been cached, `mailtool` will not see the change until the attribute time-out expires. The access pattern of `sendmail` and `mailtool` involves multiple processes writing to the same file, so it is not a good idea to cache written data on the client. This warning highlights two issues. One issue is that with multiple clients, there may be multiple copies of the same data cached on the clients and the server, and NFS does not enforce cache coherency among the clients. The second is that in situations where the cache is of no benefit, it can be disabled. See the `mount_nfs`(1M) manual page for full details on the attribute cache time-out options.

In-memory Page Cache on NFS Client

When we talk about memory usage and demand on a system, it is actually the behavior of this cache that is the issue. It contains all data that is held in memory, including the files that make up executable code and normal data files, without making any distinction between them. A large proportion of the total memory in the system is used by this cache because it holds all the pages that make up the current working set of the system as a whole. All page-in and page-out operations occur between this cache and the underlying file systems on disk and over NFS. Individual pages in the cache may currently be unmapped (e.g., a data file) or may be mapped into the address space of many processes (e.g., the pages that make up the libc.so.1 shared library). Some pages do not correspond to a named file (e.g., the stack space of a process); these anonymous pages have swap space reserved for them so that they can be written to disk if required. The vmstat and sar -pg commands monitor the activity of this cache.

The cache is made up of 4-Kbyte or 8-Kbyte *page frames*. Each page of data may be located in a file system (local or NFS) or swap space data block, or in memory in a page frame. Some page frames are ready for reuse or empty and are kept on the free list (reported as free by vmstat).

A cache hit occurs when a needed page is already in memory; this hit may be recorded as an attach to an existing page or as a reclaim if the page was on the free list. A cache miss occurs when the page needs to be created from scratch (zero fill fault), duplicated (copy on write), or read in from disk or over the network (page-in). Apart from the page-in, these operations are all quite quick, and all misses take a page frame from the free list and overwrite it.

Page-out operations occur whenever data is reclaimed for the free list because of a memory shortage. Page-outs occur to all file systems, including NFS, but are often concentrated on the swap space (which may itself be an NFS-mounted file on diskless systems).

Disk Array Write Cache or Prestoserve

When the client system decides to do an NFS write, it wants to be sure that the data is safely written before continuing. With NFS V2, each 8-Kbyte NFS write is performed synchronously. On the server, the NFS write may involve several disk writes to update the inode and indirect blocks before the write is acknowledged to the client. Files that are over a few Mbytes in size will have several indirect blocks randomly spread over the disk. When the next NFS write arrives, it may make the server rewrite the same indirect blocks. The effect of this process is that writing a large sequential file over NFS V2 causes perhaps three times as many writes on the server, and those writes are randomly distributed, not sequential. The network is idle while the writes are happening. Thus, an NFS V2 write to a single disk will often show a throughput of 100 Kbytes/s or less over the network and 300 Kbytes/s of writes at the disk (about 40 random 8-Kbyte writes). And although the network is only 10% busy, the disk may be 80% busy or more, and the data rate being sustained is very poor.

There are several possible fixes for this situation. Increasing the amount of data written per NFS write increases throughput, but 8 Kbytes are the practical maximum for the UDP-based transport used by older NFS2 implementations. Providing nonvolatile memory on the server with a Prestoserve or a SPARC Storage Array greatly speeds up the responses and also coalesces the rewrites of the indirect blocks. The amount of data written to disk is no longer three times that sent over NFS, and the written data can be coalesced into large sequential writes that allow several Mbytes/s to be sustained over a 100-Mbit network.

NFS V3 and TCP/IP Improvements

In Solaris 2.5, two new NFS features were introduced. The NFS version 3 protocol uses a two-phase commit to safely avoid the bottleneck of synchronous writes at the server. Basically, the client has to buffer for a longer time the data being sent, in case the commit fails. However, the amount of outstanding write data at the server is increased to make the protocol more efficient.

As a separate feature, the transport used by NFS V2 and V3 can now be TCP as well as UDP. TCP handles segment retransmissions for NFS, so there is no need to resend the whole NFS operation if a single packet is lost. This approach allows the write to be safely increased from 8 Kbytes (6 Ethernet packets) to 32 Kbytes (20 Ethernet packets) and makes operation over lossy wide-area networks practical. The larger NFS reads and writes reduce both protocol and disk seek overhead to give much higher throughput for sequential file accesses. The mount protocol defaults to both NFS V3 and TCP/IP with 32-Kbyte blocks if they are supported by both the client and the server, although NFS V3 over UDP with 32-Kbyte blocks is a little faster on a "clean" local network where retransmissions are unlikely.

The use of larger blocks with NFS V3 assumes that there is good spacial locality. When the workload consists of small random reads, the extra size of each transfer slows down the read rate. It may be helpful to use a mount option to reduce the block size to 8 Kbytes and tune the server to allow a larger multiblock read-ahead.

The Cache File System

Cachefs was introduced in Solaris 2.3 and is normally used to reduce network traffic by caching copies of NFS-mounted data to local disk. Once a cache directory has been set up with cfsadmin(1M), file data is cached in chunks of 64 Kbytes for files of up to 3 Mbytes total size (by default). Bigger files are left uncached, although it may be worth checking the sizes of commonly used commands in your environment to make sure that large cache-mounted executables (e.g., Netscape Navigator) are not being excluded.

When new data is read, extra work must be done. The read is rounded up to a 64-Kbyte chunk and issued to the NFS server. When the data returns, it is written to the cachefs store on disk. If the data is not subsequently reread several times, a lot of extra work has gone to waste.

When data is written, any data in the cache is invalidated by default. A subsequent read is needed to reload the cachefs entry on disk. This requirement is not too bad: A copy of the data is being written in RAM in the page cache, so it is likely that subsequent reads will be satisfied from RAM in the short term.

Another issue is the relative speed and utilization of the local disk compared to the NFS server. A fast NFS server, over a lightly loaded 100-Mbit network, with striped NVRAM accelerated disks, may make cache misses faster than cache hits to a slow, busy, local disk! If the disk is also handling paging to and from a swap partition, the activity from paging and the cache may often be synchronized at the time a new application starts up. The best use for cachefs is with a busy, low-bandwidth network—a reduction in network load can dramatically improve client performance for all the users on the network.

The best file systems to cache are read-only or read-mostly. You can check the cache hit rate with the cachefsstat(1M) command that was included in Solaris 2.5. If you are running Solaris 2.3 or 2.4, you can't determine the hit rate, but I was getting between 97% and 99% hit rate on a read-only, application-distribution NFS mount. A development of cachefs is the Solstice Autoclient application (see http://www.sun.com/Solstice). This application lets you run systems with local disks as cache-only clients. The local disks run the entire operating system installation from cache, avoiding the high network loads and low performance associated with diskless systems while providing highly automated operation with low administration costs.

RAM and Virtual Memory 13

The paging algorithm manages and allocates physical memory pages to hold the active parts of the virtual address space of processes running on the system. First, the monitoring statistics are explained; then, the algorithms for paging and swap are explained. The most important reason to understand paging is that you can then tell when adding more RAM will make a difference to performance.

Memory Usage and Sizing Tools

There are four primary consumers of memory: the kernel, processes, filesystem caches, and System V shared memory. Kernel memory usage is described in "Kernel Memory Allocation" on page 365. Process memory usage is described in "Process Memory Usage Information" on page 421. Filesystem caches invisibly consume large amounts of memory; there are no measurements of this usage in Solaris 2. System V Shared Memory can be observed by means of the `ipcs` command.

The Solaris Memory System is a white paper available via http://www.sun.com/sun-on-net/performance.html, written by my colleague Richard McDougall. It explains how to measure and size memory usage. Richard has also written a loadable kernel module that instruments memory usage by processes and the file system in detail and a set of tools that view this data. The `memtool` package has also been known internally at Sun as the bunyip[1] tool for the last few years. The tools can be obtained by sending email to memtool-request@chessie.eng.sun.com. The loadable kernel module is unsupported and should not be used in production environments, although it is suitable for use in benchmarks and sizing exercises. There is a significant risk that in the future the module could interact with updated kernel patches and cause a machine to crash. At present (early 1998), modules that work reliably with current patch levels of Solaris 2.5.1 and Solaris 2.6 are provided.

The process memory usage command `/usr/proc/bin/pmap  -x` is provided only in Solaris 2.6. It is based on code written by Richard, and his `memtool` package includes this functionality for Solaris 2.5.1. Filesystem cache memory usage is instrumented in detail by `memtool`. When the process and file information is cross-referenced, it is possible to

---

1. A Bunyip is kind of Australian Loch Ness Monster that lives in a lake in the outback.

see how much of each executable file and shared library is actually in memory, as well as how much of that memory is mapped to each individual process. You can also see all the space taken up by data files and watch the page scanner reclaiming idle memory from files that are not being accessed often. These measurements consume significant amounts of CPU time, comparable to running a ps command, so should not be run continuously. They do provide a very valuable insight into memory usage, and work is in progress on extending the supported Solaris tools to add more information on memory usage in future releases.

Understanding **vmstat** and **sar** Output

The units used by the vmstat and sar commands are not consistent. Sometimes they use pages, sar tends to use blocks, where a block is 512 bytes, and vmstat tends to use Kbytes defined as 1024 bytes. Page sizes are not constant either. As described in "Memory Management Unit Designs" on page 266, the original SPARC systems used 8-Kbyte pages. Designs then switched to 4 Kbytes for a long time, the same size used by Intel x86 and other CPU designs. With UltraSPARC there was a return to 8 Kbytes. A larger page reduces MMU activity, halves the number of page faults required to load a given amount of data, and saves kernel memory by halving the size of tables used to keep track of pages. It also wastes RAM by rounding up small segments of memory to a larger minimum size, but with today's typical memory sizes, this is a very minor problem. One problem is that collected data may not tell you the page size. If you collect a sar binary file on an UltraSPARC server and display it by using sar on a SPARCstation 5, the conversion of free swap space from pages to 512 byte blocks will be wrong. You can obtain the page size on each system by calling getpagesize(3C) or running the pagesize command.

```
% pagesize
8192
```

Memory Measurements

The paging activity on a Sun can be monitored by means of vmstat or sar. sar is better for logging the information, but vmstat is more concise and crams more information into each line of text for interactive use. There is a simple correspondence between most of the values reported by sar and vmstat, as compared below. The details of some parts of vmstat and the underlying per-CPU kernel data are covered in "The Data Behind vmstat and mpstat Output" on page 229.

Swap Space: `vmstat swap,` `sar -r freeswap,` **and** `swap -s`

`vmstat swap` shows the available swap in Kbytes, `sar -r freeswap` shows the available swap in 512-byte blocks, and `swap -s` shows several measures including available swap. When *available* swap is exhausted, the system will not be able to use more memory. See "Swap Space" on page 339.

Free Memory: `vmstat free` **and** `sar -r freemem`

`vmstat` reports the free memory in Kbytes, that is, the pages of RAM that are immediately ready to be used whenever a process starts up or needs more memory. `sar` reports `freemem` in pages. The kernel variable `freemem` that they report is discussed later. The absolute value of this variable has no useful meaning. Its value relative to some other kernel thresholds is what is important.

Reclaims: `vmstat re`

Reclaims are the number of pages reclaimed from the free list. The page had been stolen from a process but had not yet been reused by a different process so it can be reclaimed by the process, thus avoiding a full page fault that would need I/O. This procedure is described in "The Life Cycle of a Typical Physical Memory Page" on page 326.

Page Fault Measurements

The `sar` paging display is shown in Figure 13-1. It includes only counters for page in operations and minor faults. The `vmstat` and `sar` measurements are compared below.

Figure 13-1 Example `sar` Paging Display

```
% sar -p 1
09:05:56  atch/s  pgin/s ppgin/s  pflt/s  vflt/s slock/s
09:05:57    0.00    0.00    0.00    7.92    3.96    0.00
```

Attaches to Existing Pages: vmstat at and sar -p atch

These commands measure the number of attaches to shared pages already in use by other processes; the reference count is incremented. The `at` data is shown only by the old SunOS 4 `vmstat`.

Pages Paged In: **vmstat pi** and **sar -p pgin, ppgin**

vmstat pi reports the number of Kbytes/s, and sar reports the number of page faults and the number of pages paged in by swap space or filesystem reads. Since the filesystem block size is 8 Kbytes, there may be two pages or 8 Kbytes, paged in per page fault on machines with 4-Kbyte pages. UltraSPARC uses 8-Kbyte pages; almost all other CPU types use 4-Kbyte pages.

Minor Faults: **vmstat mf** and **sar -p vflt**

A minor fault is caused by an address space or hardware address translation fault that can be resolved without performing a page-in. It is fast and uses only a little CPU time. Thus, the process does not have to stop and wait, as long as a page is available for use from the free list.

Other Fault Types: **sar -p pflt, slock, vmstat -s copy-on-write, zero fill**

There are many other types of page faults. Protection faults are caused by illegal accesses of the kind that produce "segmentation violation - core dumped" messages. Copy-on-write and zero-fill faults are described in "The Life Cycle of a Typical Physical Memory Page" on page 326. Protection and copy-on-write together make up sar -p pflt. Faults caused by software locks held on pages are reported by sar -p slock. The total counts of several of these fault types are reported by vmstat -s.

Page-out Measurements

The sar page-out display is shown in Figure 13-2.

Figure 13-2 Example sar *Page-out Display*

```
% sar -g 1
09:38:04  pgout/s ppgout/s pgfree/s pgscan/s %ufs_ipf
09:38:05    0.00     0.00     0.00     0.00     0.00
```

Pages Paged Out: **vmstat po** and **sar -g pgout, ppgout**

vmstat po reports the number of Kbytes/s, and sar reports the number of page-outs and the number of pages paged out to the swap space or file system. Because of the clustering that occurs on swap space writes, there may be very many pages written per page-out. "Swap Space Operations" on page 339 describes how this works.

Pages Freed: **vmstat fr** and **sar -g pgfree**

Pages freed is the rate at which memory is being put onto the free list by the page scanner daemon. vmstat fr is in Kbytes freed per second, and sar -g pgfree is in pages freed per second. Pages are usually freed by the page scanner daemon, but other mechanisms, such as processes exiting, also free pages.

The Short-Term Memory Deficit: **vmstat de**

Deficit is a paging parameter that provides some hysteresis for the page scanner when there is a period of high memory demand. If the value is non-zero, then memory was recently being consumed quickly, and extra free memory will be reclaimed in anticipation that it will be needed. This situation is described further in "Free List Performance Problems and Deficit" on page 332.

The Page Daemon Scanning Rate: **vmstat sr** and **sar -g pgscan**

These commands report the number of pages scanned by the page daemon as it looks for pages to steal from processes that aren't using them often. This number is the key memory shortage indicator if it stays above 200 pages per second for long periods.

Pages Freed by the Inode Cache

ufs_ipf measures UFS inode cache reuse, which can cause pages to be freed when an inactive inode is freed. It is the number of inodes with pages freed (ipf) as a percentage of the total number of inodes freed.

Swapping Measurements

The sar swapping display is shown in Figure 13-3. It also includes the number of process context switches per second.

Figure 13-3 Example sar Swapping Display

```
% sar -w 1
09:11:00 swpin/s bswin/s swpot/s bswot/s pswch/s
09:11:01    0.00     0.0    0.00     0.0     186
```

Pages Swapped In: **vmstat -S si** and **sar -w swpin, bswin**

vmstat -S si reports the number of Kbytes/s swapped in, sar -w swpin reports the number of swap-in operations, and sar -w bswin reports the number of 512-byte blocks swapped in.

Pages Swapped Out: `vmstat so` and `sar -w swpot, bswot`

`vmstat -S so` reports the number of Kbytes/s swapped out, `sar -w swpot` reports the number of swap-out operations, and `sar -w bswot` reports the number of 512-byte blocks swapped out.

Example `vmstat` Output Walk-through

To illustrate the dynamics of `vmstat` output, Figure 13-4 presents an annotated `vmstat` log taken at 5-second intervals. It was taken during an Empower RTE-driven 200 user test on a SPARCserver 1000 configured with Solaris 2.2, 128 Mbytes of RAM, and four CPUs. Emulated users logged in at 5-second intervals and ran an intense, student-style, software-development workload, that is, edit, compile, run, core dump, debug, look at man pages, and so forth. I have highlighted in bold type the numbers in the `vmstat` output that I take note of as the test progresses. Long sequences of output have been replaced by comments to reduce the log to a manageable length. As is often the case with Empower-driven workloads, the emulation of 200 dedicated users who never stop to think for more than a few seconds at a time provides a much higher load than 200 real-life students.

Figure 13-4   Example Vmstat 5 *Output for a SPARCserver 1000 with 200 Users*

```
 procs       memory              page                   disk            faults         cpu
 r b w    swap  free   re  mf pi po fr de  sr s0 s1 s2 s3   in   sy   cs us sy id
 0 0 0 330252 80708    0    2  0  0  0  0   0  0  0  0  1   18  107  113  0  1 99
 0 0 0 330252 80708    0    0  0  0  0  0   0  0  0  0  0   14   87   78  0  0 99
...users begin to log in to the system
 4 0 0 320436 71448    0  349  7  0  0  0   0  2  1  0 12  144 4732  316 65 35  0
 6 0 0 318820 69860    0  279 25  0  0  0   0  0  0  0  2   54 5055  253 66 34  0
 7 0 0 317832 68972    0  275  3  0  0  0   0  1  0  0  1   48 4920  278 64 36  0
...lots of minor faults are caused by processes starting up
50 0 0 258716 14040    0  311  2  0  0  0   0  1  0  0  1  447 4822  306 59 41  0
51 0 0 256864 12620    0  266  2  0  0  0   0  3  1  0 12  543 3686  341 66 34  0
...at this point the free list drops below 8MB and the pager starts to scan
56 0 0 251620  8352    0  321  4  1  1  0   0  1  1  0  1  461 4837  342 57 43  0
60 0 0 238280  5340    5  596  1 371 1200 0 4804  0  0  0  6  472 3883  313 48 52  0
59 0 0 234624 10756   97  172  0 1527 1744 0 390  0  0  0 14  507 4582  233 59 41  0
60 0 0 233668 10660    9  297  2  0  0  0   0  4  2  0 12  539 5223  272 57 43  0
61 0 0 232232  8564    2  225  0 75 86  0  87  0  0  0  2  441 3697  217 71 29  0
62 0 0 231216  8248    2  334 11 500 547 0 258  1  0  0  7  484 5482  292 52 48  0
...some large processes exit, freeing up RAM and swap space
91 0 0 196868  7836    0  227  8 511 852 0 278  1  7  0  5  504 5278  298 50 50  0
91 1 0 196368  8184    1  158  3 1634 2095 0 652 0 37  0  5  674 3930  325 50 50  0
92 0 0 200932 14024    0  293 85 496 579 0  42  0 17  0 21  654 4416  435 47 53  0
93 0 0 208584 21768    1  329  9  0  0  0   0  0  0  0  3  459 3971  315 62 38  0
92 1 0 208388 20964    0  328 12  0  0  0   0  3  3  0 14  564 5079  376 53 47  0
```

```
procs      memory              page             disk           faults        cpu
r b w    swap  free   re  mf pi po  fr de  sr  s0 s1 s2 s3   in    sy    cs us sy id
...it was steady like this for a long time. RAM is OK, need more CPUs
189 0 0 41136 8816   3   99 32 243 276 0 168  1  1  0  9   500  3804   235 67 33  0
190 0 0 40328 8380   6   65 76  0   0  0   0  3  2  0 19   541  3666   178 71 29  0
190 0 0 40052 7976   1   56 102 58 65  0  32  0  1  0 15   457  3415   158 72 28  0
...users exit causing an I/O block as closing files flushes changes to disk
57 14 0 224600 55896 5  114 284  0   0  0   0  0  1  0 69   843   368   436 84 16  0
39 10 0 251456 61136 37 117 246  0   0  0   0  1  4  0 70   875   212   435 81 19  0
19 15 0 278080 65920 46 129 299  0   0  0   0  0  1  0 74   890   223   454 82 18  0
3 5 0 303768 70288   23  88 248  0   0  0   0  0  1  0 59   783   324   392 60 11 29
0 1 0 314012 71104    0  47 327  0   0  0   0  0  3  0 47   696   542   279 12  5 83
```

Virtual Memory Address Space Segments

All the RAM in a system is managed in terms of pages; these are used to hold the *physical address space* of a process. The kernel manages the *virtual address space* of a process by maintaining a complex set of data structures. Each process has a single-address space structure, with any number of segment data structures to map each contiguous segment of memory to a backing device, which holds the pages when they are not in RAM. The segment keeps track of the pages that are currently in memory, and from this information, the system can produce the PMEG or PTE data structures that each kind of MMU reads directly to do the virtual-to-physical translations. The machine-independent routines that do this are called the *hat* (hardware address translation) layer. This architecture is generic to SunOS 4, SVR4, and Solaris 2. Figure 13-5 illustrates the concept. This diagram has been greatly simplified. In practice, there are many more segments than are shown here!

The code segment contains executable instructions, and the data segment contains pre-initialized data, such as constants and strings. BSS stands for Block Starting with Symbol and holds uninitialized data that will be zero to begin with. In this diagram, the kernel is shown at the top of the address space. This placement is true for older systems, but UltraSPARC uses a completely separate address space for the kernel.

Figure 13-5 Simplified Virtual Memory Address Space and File Mappings

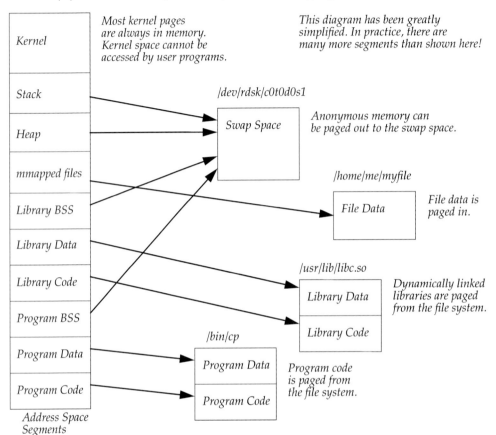

The Life Cycle of a Typical Physical Memory Page

This section provides additional insight into the way memory is used and makes the following sections easier to understand. The sequence described is an example of some common uses of pages; there are many other possibilities.

1. **Initialization — A Page Is Born**
   When the system boots, all free memory is formed into pages, and a kernel data structure is allocated to hold the state of every page in the system.

2. **Free — An Untouched Virgin Page**
   All the memory is put onto the free list to start with. At this stage, the content of the page is undefined.

3. ZFOD — Joining a BSS Segment

When a program accesses a BSS segment for the very first time, a minor page fault occurs and a Zero Fill On Demand (ZFOD) operation takes place. The page is taken from the free list, block-cleared to contain all zeroes, and added to the list of anonymous pages for the BSS segment. The program then reads and writes data to the page.

4. Scanned — The `pagedaemon` Awakes

When the free list gets below a certain size, the pagedaemon starts to look for memory pages to steal from processes. It looks at every page in physical memory order; when it gets to this page, the page is synchronized with the MMU and a reference bit is cleared.

5. Waiting — Is the Program Really Using This Page Right Now?

There is a delay that varies depending upon how quickly the pagedaemon scans through memory. If the program references the page during this period, the MMU reference bit is set.

6. Page-out Time — Saving the Contents

The pageout daemon returns and checks the MMU reference bit to find that the program has not used the page, so it can be stolen for reuse. The page is checked to see if anything had been written to it since it does contain data in this case; a page-out occurs. The page is moved to the page-out queue and marked as I/O pending. The swapfs code clusters the page together with other pages on the queue and writes the cluster to the swap space. The page is then free and is put on the free list again. It remembers that it still contains the program data.

7. Reclaim — Give Me Back My Page!

Belatedly, the program tries to read the page and takes a page fault. If the page had been reused by someone else in the meantime, a major fault would occur and the data would be read from the swap space into a new page taken from the free list. In this case, the page is still waiting to be reused, so a minor fault occurs, and the page is moved back from the free list to the program's BSS segment.

8. Program Exit — Free Again

The program finishes running and exits. The BSS segments are private to that particular instance of the program (unlike the shared code segments), so all the pages in the BSS segment are marked as undefined and put onto the free list. This is the same as Step 2.

9. Page-in — A Shared Code Segment

A page fault occurs in the code segment of a window system shared library. The page is taken off the free list, and a read from the file system is scheduled to get the code. The process that caused the page fault sleeps until the data arrives. The page is attached to the vnode of the file, and the segments reference the vnode.

10. Attach — A Popular Page

Another process using the same shared library page faults in the same place. It discovers that the page is already in memory and attaches to the page, increasing its vnode reference count by one.

11. COW — Making a Private Copy

If one of the processes sharing the page tries to write to it, a copy-on-write (COW) page fault occurs. Another page is grabbed from the free list, and a copy of the original is made. This new page becomes part of a privately mapped segment backed by anonymous storage (swap space) so it can be changed, but the original page is unchanged and can still be shared. Shared libraries contain jump tables in the code that are patched, using COW as part of the dynamic linking process.

12. File Cache — Not Free

The entire window system exits, and both processes go away. This time the page stays in use, attached to the vnode of the shared library file. The vnode is now inactive but will stay in its cache until it is reused, and the pages act as a file cache in case the user is about to restart the window system again.[2]

13. Fsflush — Flushed by the Sync

Every 30 seconds, all the pages in the system are examined in physical page order to see which ones contain modified data and are attached to a vnode. Any modified pages will be written back to the file system, and the pages will be marked as clean.

This example sequence can continue from Step 4 or Step 9 with minor variations. The `fsflush` process occurs every 30 seconds by default for all pages, and whenever the free list size drops below a certain value, the `pagedaemon` scanner wakes up and reclaims some pages.

Free Memory—The Memory-Go-Round

Pages of physical memory circulate through the system via "free memory"; the concept seems to confuse a lot of people. This section explains the basic memory flows and describes the latest changes in the algorithm. The section also provides some guidance on when free memory may need tuning and what to change.

---

2. This subject was covered in "Vnodes, Inodes, and Rnodes" on page 360. The file system could be UFS or NFS.

First, let's look at some vmstat output again.

```
% vmstat 5
 procs     memory              page               disk           faults        cpu
 r b w   swap   free  re  mf pi po fr de sr s0 s1 s5 --   in   sy   cs us sy id
 0 0 0 480528 68056   0   3  5  2  2  0  0 65 12  9  0  165  968  101  2  2 95
 0 0 0 476936 85768   0  15 107 0  0  0  0  3  4  7  0  465 1709  231  6  3 91
 0 0 0 476832 85160   0  31 144 0  0  0  0  7  0  9  0  597 3558  367  8  6 87
 0 0 0 476568 83840   0   7 168 0  0  0  0  4  1  6  0  320  796  155  6  1 93
 0 0 0 476544 83368   0   0 28  0  0  0  0  1  2  0  0  172 1739  166 10  5 85
```

The first thing to remember is that vmstat prints out averaged rates, based on the difference between two snapshots of a number of kernel counters. The first line of output is printed immediately; hence, it is the difference between the current value of the counters and zero. This value works out to be the average since the system was booted. Second, if you run vmstat with a small time interval, you tend to catch all the short-term peaks and get results that are much more variable from one line to the next. I typically use five or ten seconds but may use one second to try and catch peaks or as much as 30 to 60 seconds to just "keep an eye" on a system. vmstat is a useful summary of what is happening on a system. The units of swap, free, pi, po, fr, and de are in Kbytes, and re, mf, and sr are in pages.

The Role of the Free List

Memory is one of the main resources in the system. There are four main consumers of memory, and when memory is needed, they all obtain it from the free list. Figure 13-6 shows these consumers and how they relate to the free list. When memory is needed, it is taken from the head of the free list. When memory is put back on the free list, there are two choices. If the page still contains valid data, it is put on the tail of the list so it will not be reused for as long as possible. If the page has no useful content, it is put at the head of the list for immediate reuse. The kernel keeps track of valid pages in the free list so that they can be reclaimed if their content is requested, thereby saving a disk I/O.

The vmstat reclaim counter is two-edged. On one hand, it is good that a page fault was serviced by a reclaim, rather than a page-in that would cause a disk read. On the other hand, you don't want active pages to be stolen and end up on the free list in the first place. The vmstat free value is simply the size of the free list, in Kbytes. The way the size varies is what tends to confuse people. The most important value reported by vmstat is the scan rate - sr. If it is zero or close to zero, then you can be sure that the system does have sufficient memory. If it is always high (hundreds to thousands of pages/second), then adding more memory is likely to help.

Figure 13-6 The Memory-Go-Round

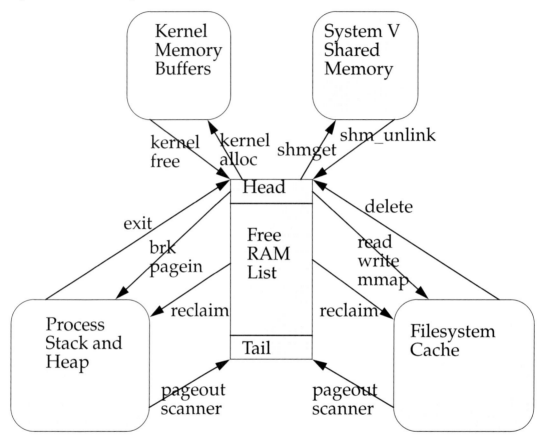

Kernel Memory

At the start of the boot process, the kernel takes two or three megabytes of initial memory and puts all the rest on the free list. As the kernel dynamically sizes itself and loads device drivers and file systems, it takes memory from the free list. Kernel memory is normally locked and cannot be paged out in a memory shortage, but the kernel does free memory if there is a lot of demand for it. Unused device drivers will be unloaded, and unused slabs of kernel memory data structures will be freed. I notice that sometimes during heavy paging there is a pop from the speaker on a desktop system. This occurs when the audio device driver is unloaded. If you run a program that keeps the device open, that program cannot be unloaded.

One problem that can occur is reported as a kernel memory allocation error by `sar -k` and by the kernel rule in the SE toolkit. There is a limit on the size of kernel memory, but at 3.75 Gbytes on UltraSPARC systems, this limit is unlikely to be reached. The most common cause of this problem is that the kernel tried to get some memory while the free list was completely empty. Since the kernel cannot always wait, this attempt may cause operations to fail rather than be delayed. The streams subsystem cannot wait, and I have seen remote logins fail due to this issue when a large number of users try to log in at the same time. In Solaris 2.5.1 and the current kernel jumbo patch for Solaris 2.3, 2.4, and 2.5, changes were made to make the free list larger on big systems and to try and prevent it from ever being completely empty.

Filesystem Cache

The second consumer of memory is files. For a file to be read or written, memory must be obtained to hold the data for the I/O. While the I/O is happening, the pages are temporarily locked in memory. After the I/O is complete, the pages are unlocked but are retained in case the contents of the file are needed again. The filesystem cache is often one of the biggest users of memory in a system. Note that in all versions of Solaris 1 and Solaris 2, the data in the filesystem cache is separate from kernel memory. It does not appear in any address space, so there is no limit on its size. If you want to cache many gigabytes of filesystem data in memory, you just need to buy a 30-Gbyte E6000 or a 64-Gbyte E10000. We cached an entire 9-Gbyte database on a 16-Gbyte E6000 once, just to show it could be done, and read-intensive queries ran 350 times faster than reading from disk. SPARC-based systems use either a 36-bit (SuperSPARC) or 41-bit (UltraSPARC) physical address, unlike many other systems that limit both virtual and physical to 32 bits and so stop at 4 Gbytes. A 64-bit virtual address space will be supported on UltraSPARC systems via the next major Solaris release during 1998.

If you delete or truncate a file, the cached data becomes invalid, so it is returned to the head of the free list. If the kernel decides to stop caching the inode for a file, any pages of cached data attached to that inode are also freed.

For most files, the only way they become uncached is by having inactive pages stolen by the pageout scanner. The scanner runs only when the free list shrinks below a threshold (`lotsfree` in pages, usually set at a few Mbytes), so eventually most of the memory in the system ends up in the filesystem cache. When there is a new, large demand for memory, the scanner will steal most of the required pages from the inactive files in the filesystem cache. These files include executable program code files as well as data files. Anything that is currently inactive and not locked in memory will be taken.

Files are also mapped directly by processes using mmap. This command maps in the code and shared libraries for a process. Pages may have multiple references from several processes while also being resident in the filesystem cache. A recent optimization is that pages with eight or more references are skipped by the scanner, even if they are inactive. This feature helps shared libraries and multiprocess server code stay resident in memory.

Process Private Memory

Processes also have private memory to hold their stack space, modified data areas, and heap. Stack and heap memory is always initialized to zero before it is given to the process. The stack grows dynamically as required; the heap is grown by the brk system call, usually when the malloc library routine needs some more space. Data and code areas are initialized by mapping from a file, but as soon as they are written to, a private copy of the page is made. The only way to see how much resident memory is used by private or shared pages is to use the /usr/proc/bin/pmap -x command in Solaris 2.6, or memtool, described in "Memory Usage and Sizing Tools" on page 319. All that is normally reported is the total number of resident mapped pages, as the RSS field in some forms of ps output (e.g., /usr/ucb/ps uax). The SIZE or SZ field indicates the total size of the address space, which includes memory mapped devices like framebuffers as well as pages that are not resident. SIZE really indicates how much virtual memory the process needs and is more closely related to swap space requirements.

When a process first starts up, it consumes memory very rapidly until it reaches its working set. If it is a user-driven tool, it may also need to grab a lot more memory to perform operations like opening a new window or processing an input file. In some cases, the response time to the user request is affected by how long it takes to obtain a large amount of memory. If the process needs more than is currently in the free list, it goes to sleep until the pageout scanner has obtained more memory for it. In many cases, additional memory is requested one page at a time, and on a uniprocessor the process will eventually be interrupted by the scanner as it wakes up to replenish the free list.

Free List Performance Problems and Deficit

The memory reclaim algorithm can cause problematic behavior. After a reboot, the free list is very large, and memory-intensive programs have a good response time. After a while, the free list is consumed by the file cache, and the page scanner cuts in. At that point, the response time may worsen because large amounts of memory are not immediately available. System administrators may watch this happening with vmstat and see that free memory decreases, and see that when free memory gets low, paging starts and performance worsens. An initial reaction is to add some more RAM to the system, but this response does not usually solve the problem. It may postpone the problem, but it may also make paging more intense because some paging parameters are scaled up as you add RAM. The kernel tries to counteract this effect by calculating running averages of the memory demand over 5-second and 30-second periods. If the average demand is high, the kernel expects that more memory will be needed in the future, so it sets up a deficit, which makes the target size of the free list up to twice as big as normal. This is the de column reported by vmstat. The deficit decays over a few seconds back to zero, so you often see a large deficit suddenly appear, then decay away again. With the latest kernel code, the target size of the free list (set by lotsfree) increases on big memory systems, and since the deficit is limited to the same value, you should expect to see larger peak values of de on large-memory systems.

The real problem is that the free list is too small, and it is being replenished too aggressively, too late. The simplest fix is to increase lotsfree, but remember that the free list is unused memory. If you make it too big, you are wasting RAM. If you think that the scanner is being too aggressive, you can also try reducing fastscan, which is the maximum page scanner rate in pages/s. By default, fastscan is limited to a maximum of 64 Mbytes/s: either 16,384 or 8,192 pages/s, depending upon the page size. By increasing lotsfree, you also increase the maximum value of the deficit. You also have to let the system stabilize for a while after the first time that the page scanner cuts in. It needs to go right round the whole of memory once or twice before it settles down. (vmstat -s tells you the number of revolutions it has done). It should then run on a "little and often" basis. As long as you always have enough free RAM to handle the short-term demand and don't have to scan hard all the time, performance should be good.

System V Shared Memory

There are a few applications that make trivial use of System V shared memory, but the big important applications are the database servers. Databases benefit from very large shared caches of data in some cases, and use System V shared memory to allocate as much as 3.75 Gbytes of RAM. By default, applications such as Oracle, Informix, and Sybase use a special flag to specify that they want intimate shared memory (ISM). In this case, two special changes are made. First, all the memory is locked and cannot be paged out. Second, the memory management data structures that are normally created on a per-process basis are created once, then shared by every process. In Solaris 2.6, a further optimization takes place as the kernel tries to find 4-Mbyte contiguous blocks of physical memory that can be used as large pages to map the shared memory. This process greatly reduces memory management unit overhead. See "Shared Memory Tunables" on page 344.

Filesystem Flush

Unlike SunOS 4 where the update process does a full sync of memory to disk every 30 seconds, Solaris 2 uses the fsflush daemon to spread out the sync workload. autoup is set to 30 seconds by default, and this value is the maximum age of any memory-resident pages that have been modified. fsflush wakes up every 5 seconds (set by tune_t_fsflushr) and checks a portion of memory on each invocation (5/30 = one-sixth of total RAM by default). The pages are queued on the same list that the pageout daemon uses and are formed into clustered sequential writes. During each invocation, every tune_t_fsflushr seconds, fsflush also flushes modified entries from inode caches to disk. This process occurs for all relevant filesystem types and can be disabled by setting doiflush to zero.

On systems with very large amounts of RAM, fsflush has a lot of work to do on each invocation. Since Solaris 2.4, a special algorithm monitors and limits CPU usage of fsflush. The workload can be reduced if necessary. fsflush should still always wake up every few seconds, but autoup can be increased from 30 seconds to a few hundred seconds if required. In many cases, files that are being written are closed before fsflush gets around to them. For NFS servers, all writes are synchronous, so fsflush is hardly needed at all. For database servers using raw disk partitions, fsflush will have little useful effect, but its fixed overhead increases as memory size increases. The biggest use of fsflush comes on time-shared systems and systems that do a lot of local filesystem I/O without using direct I/O or synchronous writes. Note the time and the CPU usage of fsflush, then watch it later and see if its CPU usage is more than 5%. If it is, increase autoup, as shown in Figure 13-7, or disable page flushing completely by setting dopageflush to zero.

Figure 13-7 Reducing fsflush *CPU Usage by Increasing* autoup *in* /etc/system

```
set autoup=240
```

Local files are flushed when they are closed, but long-lived log files may be truncated in a crash if page flushing is completely disabled. Figure 13-8 shows commands for evaluating fsflush.

Figure 13-8 Measuring fsflush *CPU Usage*

```
# prtconf | head -2
System Configuration: Sun Microsystems sun4u
Memory size: 21248 Megabytes
# /usr/ucb/ps 3
   PID TT       S  TIME COMMAND
     3 ?        S 23:00 fsflush
# uptime
 12:42pm  up 4:44,  1 user,  load average: 0.03, 0.04, 0.04
# /opt/RICHPse/bin/se pwatch.se
fsflush has used 1382.1 seconds of CPU time since boot
fsflush used 8.3 %CPU, 8.3 %CPU average so far
fsflush used 8.3 %CPU, 8.3 %CPU average so far
```

Since boot on this 20-Gbyte E10000, `fsflush` has used 1366 seconds of CPU time, which is 8.3% of a CPU. This usage is not unreasonable, but the system is idle and `fsflush` CPU usage will increase when it gets busy. Systems with less memory will show proportionally less CPU usage.

Scan Rate Threshold Indicating a Memory Shortage

By default, `fsflush` makes sure that any modified page is flushed to its backing store after 30 seconds. The pageout scanner is also scanning memory looking for inactive pages at a variable rate. If that rate corresponds to more than 30 seconds, then `fsflush` will have got there first and flushed the page. If the page is inactive, it can be freed immediately. If the scan rate corresponds to less than 30 seconds, then many inactive pages will still be modified and unflushed and will need a page-out operation to flush them before they can be put on the free list. The system will run better if the page-out scan rate is slower than the `fsflush` scan rate because freed pages will be available immediately. My SE toolkit rule for memory shortage, described in "RAM Rule" on page 456, divides the average scan rate into the value of `handspreadpages` to obtain the idle page residence time. The thresholds used are 40 seconds as an amber warning level, and 20 seconds as a red problem level. The rate at which `fsflush` works, given by `autoup` and defaulting to 30 seconds, is the unflushed page delay time. If there is a memory shortage on a system with a small amount of memory, it may be a good idea to try reducing `autoup` to 10 or 20 seconds.

The value of `handspreadpages` is clamped at 64 Mbytes, or a quarter of all memory. For UltraSPARC systems with 256 Mbytes or more of memory, the value will be fixed at 8192. This value gives a simpler threshold to watch for—a scan rate of above 300 pages per second indicates a memory shortage.

$$\text{scan rate threshold} = \frac{\text{handspreadpages}}{\text{residence time}} = \frac{8192}{30} = 273$$

The 30-second memory residence time threshold is not just based on the interaction with `fsflush`. It is a generally accepted threshold for sizing disk caches on mainframe systems, for example. If `autoup` has been increased on a system because `fsflush` is not necessary, then the scan rate residence time should still be 30 seconds. In the case of NFS servers and database servers, writes are synchronous, so most filesystem pages in memory should be unmodified and can be freed immediately.

Kernel Values, Tunables, and Defaults

In this section I describe the most important kernel variables that can be used to tune the virtual memory system. They are normally set in the /etc/system file. Figure 13-9 illustrates the relationship between the parameters that control page scanning.

Figure 13-9   Parameters to Control Page Scanning Rate and Onset of Swapping

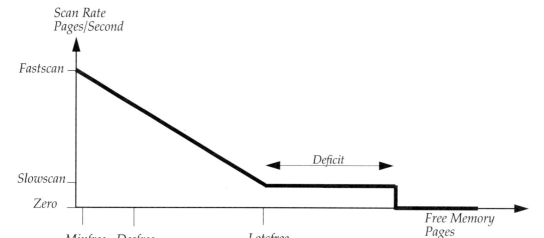

fastscan

> The fastest scan rate, corresponding to an empty free list. It can be reduced if lotsfree has been increased, but it must be more than slowscan. fastscan can be changed on line. fastscan is set to (physmem/2) in Solaris 2.1 through 2.3 and (physmem/4) with a limit of 64 Mbytes (8,192 or 16,384 pages) since Solaris 2.4.

slowscan

> The initial scan rate at the point where scanning first starts. It defaults to 100, but some recent tests seem to indicate that refixing it at around 500 is beneficial. The idea of a minimum is that it is only worth waking up the scanner if it has a reasonable amount of work to do. Higher values of slowscan cause the pager to run less often and do more work each time. slowscan can be changed on line.

physmem

Set to the number of pages of usable physical memory. The maxusers calculation is based upon physmem, as described in "Parameters Derived from maxusers" on page 359. If you are investigating system performance and want to run tests with reduced memory on a system, you can set physmem in /etc/system and reboot to prevent a machine from using all its RAM. The unused memory still uses some kernel resources, and the page scanner still scans it, so if the reduced memory system does a lot of paging, the effect will not be exactly the same as physically removing the RAM.

lotsfree

The target size of the free list in pages. Set to physmem/16 in Solaris 2.3, it was too large and memory was being wasted. It was originally fixed at 128 pages on desktop machines, and 256 pages on servers (sun4d) in Solaris 2.4 and 2.5. This allocation turned out to be too small. For Solaris 2.5.1, it is scaled again, to physmem/64 (with a minimum of 512 Kbytes), and there are many other changes to make the algorithm more robust. This code has been backported to all the current kernel jumbo patches for previous releases. lotsfree can be changed on line with immediate effect if you know what you are doing and are careful. During the 100 Hz clock routine, the kernel tests four times a second to see if freemem is less than lotsfree. If so, a wakeup is sent to the pageout daemon.

desfree

The desperation threshold. It is set to half the value of lotsfree. desfree is used for the following purposes:
- If a 30-second average of free memory is less than desfree, then inactive processes will be swapped out.
- At the point where pages are taken from the free list, if freemem is less than desfree, then an immediate wakeup call is sent to the pageout daemon, rather than waiting for pageout to be awakened by the clock interrupt.

minfree

The minimum threshold. It is set to half of the value of desfree. minfree is used for the following purposes:
- If the short-term (5-second) average free memory is less than minfree, then processes will be swapped out.
- When exec is running on a small program (under 280 Kbytes), the entire program is loaded in at one time rather than being paged in piecemeal, as long as doing so would not reduce freemem below minfree.

throttlefree

Suspends processes that are trying to consume memory too quickly. It is set the same as minfree by default and must be less than desfree. throttlefree penalizes processes that are consuming additional memory and favors existing processes that are having memory stolen from them. If freemem reaches throttlefree, any process that tries to get another page is suspended until memory goes back above desfree.

handspreadpages

Set to (physmem/4) but is increased during initialization to be at least as big as fastscan, which makes it (physmem/2) for Solaris 2.1 through 2.3. It is usually set to the same value as fastscan. In Solaris 2, it is limited to 64 Mbytes, like fastscan. Note that the definition of this variable changed from handspread, measured in bytes in SunOS 4, to handspreadpages, measured in pages in Solaris 2.

max_page_get

Set to half the number of pages in the system. It limits the maximum number of pages that can be allocated in a single operation. In some circumstances, a machine may be sized to run a single, very large program that has a data area or single malloc space of more than half the total RAM. It will be necessary to increase max_page_get in that circumstance. If max_page_get is increased too far and reaches total_pages (a little less than physmem), then deadlock can occur and the system will hang trying to allocate more pages than exist.

maxpgio

The maximum number of page-out I/O operations per second that the system will schedule. The default is 40 in older releases, which is set to avoid saturating random access to a single 3600 rpm (60 rps) disk at two-thirds of the rotation rate. maxpgio is set to 60 for sun4d kernels only; it should be increased if more or faster disks are being used for the swap space. Many systems now have 7200 rpm (120 rps) disks, so maxpgio should be set to about 100 times the number of swap disks in use. See Table 8-4 on page 204 for disk specifications. The value is divided by four during system initialization since the pageout daemon runs four times per second; the resulting value is the limit on the number of page-outs that the pageout daemon will add to the page-out queue in each invocation. Note that in addition to the clock-based invocations, an additional invocation will occur whenever more memory is allocated and freemem is less than desfree, so more than maxpgio pages can be queued per second when a lot of memory is allocated in a short time period. Changes to `maxpgio` only take effect after a reboot, so it cannot be tweaked on a running system.

`tune_t_fsflushr` and `autoup`

Described in "Filesystem Flush" on page 333.

`tune_t_gpgslo`

A feature derived from Unix System V.3. Since Solaris 2.4, it is no longer used.

Swap Space

For all practical purposes, swapping can be ignored in Solaris 2. The time-based soft swapouts that occur in SunOS 4 are no longer implemented. `vmstat -s` will report total numbers of swap-ins and swap-outs, which are almost always zero. Prolonged memory shortages can trigger swap-outs of inactive processes. Swapping out idle processes helps performance of machines with less than 32 Mbytes of RAM. The number of *idle* swapped-out processes is reported as the swap queue length by `vmstat`. This measurement is not explained properly in the manual page since that measure used to be the number of *active* swapped-out processes waiting to be swapped back in. As soon as a swapped-out process wakes up again, it will swap its basic data structures back into the kernel and page in its code and data as they are accessed. This activity requires so little memory that it can always happen immediately.

Figure 13-10 Example `vmstat` Output Highlighting Swap Queue

```
% vmstat 5
 procs     memory            page            disk          faults      cpu
 r b w   swap  free  re  mf pi po fr de sr f0 s0 s1 s5   in   sy  cs us sy id
 . . .
 0 0 4 314064  5728   0   7  2  1  1  0  0  0 177 91 22 132  514   94  1  0 98
```

If you come across a system with a non-zero swap queue reported by `vmstat`, it is a sign that at some time in the past, free memory stayed low for long enough to trigger swapping out of idle processes. This is the only useful conclusion you can draw from his measure.

Swap Space Operations

Swap space is really a misnomer of what really is the paging space. Almost all the accesses are page related rather than being whole-process swapping.

Swap space is allocated from spare RAM and from swap disk. The measures provided are based on two sets of underlying numbers. One set relates to physical swap disk, the other set relates to RAM used as swap space by pages in memory.

Swap space is used in two stages. When memory is requested (for example, via a `malloc` call) swap is reserved and a mapping is made against the `/dev/zero` device. Reservations are made against available disk-based swap to start with. When that is all gone, RAM is reserved instead. When these pages are first accessed, physical pages are obtained from the free list and filled with zeros, and pages of swap become allocated rather than reserved. In effect, reservations are initially taken out of disk-based swap, but allocations are initially taken out of RAM-based swap. When a page of anonymous RAM is stolen by the page scanner, the data is written out to the swap space, i.e., the swap allocation is moved from memory to disk, and the memory is freed.

Memory space that is mapped but never used stays in the reserved state, and the reservation consumes swap space. This behavior is common for large database systems and is the reason why large amounts of swap disk must be configured to run applications like Oracle and SAP R/3, even though they are unlikely to allocate all the reserved space.

The first swap partition allocated is also used as the system dump space to store a kernel crash dump into. It is a good idea to have plenty of disk space set aside in `/var/crash` and to enable `savecore` by uncommenting the commands in `/etc/rc2.d/S20sysetup`. If you forget and think that there may have been an unsaved crash dump, you can try running `savecore` long after the system has rebooted. The crash dump is stored at the very end of the swap partition, and the `savecore` command can tell if it has been overwritten yet.

Swap Space Calculations

Please refer to Jim Mauro's Inside Solaris columns in SunWorld Online December 1997 and January 1998 for a detailed explanation of how swap space works. See http://www.sun.com/sunworldonline/swol-01-1998/swol-01-insidesolaris.html.

Disk space used for swap is listed by the `swap -l` command. All swap space segments must be 2 Gbytes or less in size. Any extra space is ignored. The `anoninfo` structure in the kernel keeps track of anonymous memory. In Solaris 2.6 this structure changed its name to `k_anoninfo`, but these three values are the same. This illustrates why it is best to rely on the more stable `kstat` interface rather than the raw kernel data. In this case, the data provided is so confusing that I felt I had to see how the `kstat` data is derived.

> `anoninfo.ani_max` is the total amount of disk-based swap space.

> `anoninfo.ani_resv` is the amount reserved thus far from both disk and RAM.

> `anoninfo.ani_free` is the amount of unallocated physical space plus the amount of reserved unallocated RAM.

If `ani_resv` is greater than `ani_max`, then we have reserved all the disk and reserved some RAM-based swap. Otherwise, the amount of disk-resident swap space available to be reserved is `ani_max` minus `ani_resv`.

> `swapfs_minfree` is set to `physmem`/8 (with a minimum of 3.5 Mbytes) and acts as a limit on the amount of memory used to hold anonymous data.

> `availrmem` is the amount of resident, unswappable memory in the system. It varies and can be read from the `system_pages` kstat shown in Figure 13-11.

The amount of swap space that can be reserved from memory is `availrmem` minus `swapfs_minfree`.

The total amount available for reservation is thus MAX(`ani_max` - `ani_resv`, 0) + (`availrmem` - `swapfs_minfree`). A reservation failure will prevent a process from starting or growing. Allocations are not really interesting.

The counters provided by the kernel to commands such as `vmstat` and `sar` are part of the `vminfo` kstat structure. These counters accumulate once per second, so average swap usage over a measurement interval can be determined. The `swap -s` command reads the kernel directly to obtain a snapshot of the current `anoninfo` values, so the numbers will never match exactly. Also, the simple act of running a program changes the values, so you cannot get an exact match. The `vminfo` calculations are:

`swap_resv` += `ani_resv`

`swap_alloc` += MAX(`ani_resv`, `ani_max`) - `ani_free`

`swap_avail` += MAX(`ani_max` - `ani_resv`, 0) + (`availrmem` - `swapfs_minfree`)

`swap_free` += `ani_free` + (`availrmem` - `swapfs_minfree`)

Figure 13-11 Example `system_pages` kstat Output from `netstat -k`

```
system_pages:
physmem 15778 nalloc 7745990 nfree 5600412 nalloc_calls 2962 nfree_calls 2047
kernelbase 268461504 econtig 279511040 freemem 4608 availrmem 13849 lotsfree 256
desfree 100 minfree 61 fastscan 7884 slowscan 500 nscan 0 desscan 125
pp_kernel 1920 pagesfree 4608 pageslocked 1929 pagesio 0 pagestotal 15769
```

To figure out how the numbers really do add up, I wrote a short program in SE and compared it to the example data shown in Figure 13-12. To get the numbers to match, I needed some odd combinations for `sar` and `swap -s`. In summary, the only useful measure is `swap_available`, as printed by `swap -s`, `vmstat`, and `sar -r` (although `sar` labels it `freeswap` and before Solaris 2.5 `sar` actually displayed `swap_free` rather than `swap_avail`). The other measures are mislabeled and confusing. The code for the SE program in Figure 13-13 shows how the data is calculated and suggests a more useful display that is also simpler to calculate.

Figure 13-12 Example Swap Data Calculations

```
# se swap.se
ani_max 54814  ani_resv 19429  ani_free 37981  availrmem 13859  swapfs_minfree 1972
ramres 11887  swap_resv 19429  swap_alloc 16833  swap_avail 47272  swap_free 49868

Misleading data printed by swap -s
134664 K allocated + 20768 K reserved = 155432 K used, 378176 K available
Corrected labels:
134664 K allocated + 20768 K unallocated = 155432 K reserved, 378176 K available

Mislabelled sar -r 1
freeswap (really swap available) 756352 blocks

Useful swap data: Total swap 520 M
available 369 M  reserved 151 M  Total disk 428 M  Total RAM 92 M
# swap -s
total: 134056k bytes allocated + 20800k reserved = 154856k used, 378752k available
# sar -r 1
18:40:51 freemem freeswap
18:40:52    4152    756912
```

The only thing you need to know about SE to read this code is that reading kvm$name causes the current value of the kernel variable `name` to be read.

Figure 13-13 SE Code to Read Swap Measures and Display Correctly Labeled Data

```
/* extract all the swap data and generate the numbers */
/* must be run as root to read kvm variables */

struct anon {
    int ani_max;
    int ani_free;
    int ani_resv;
    };

int max(int a, int b) {
    if (a > b) {
    return a;
    } else {
    return b;
    }
}

main() {
#if MINOR_RELEASE < 60
    anon kvm$anoninfo;
```

Sun Performance and Tuning

Figure 13-13 SE Code to Read Swap Measures and Display Correctly Labeled Data (Continued)

```
#else
    anon kvm$k_anoninfo;
#endif
    anon tmpa;
    int  kvm$availrmem;
    int  availrmem;
    int  kvm$swapfs_minfree;
    int  swapfs_minfree;
    int  ramres;
    int  swap_alloc;
    int  swap_avail;
    int  swap_free;
    int  kvm$pagesize;
    int  ptok = kvm$pagesize/1024;
    int  res_but_not_alloc;
#if MINOR_RELEASE < 60
    tmpa = kvm$anoninfo;
#else
    tmpa = kvm$k_anoninfo;
#endif
    availrmem = kvm$availrmem;
    swapfs_minfree = kvm$swapfs_minfree;

    ramres = availrmem - swapfs_minfree;
    swap_alloc = max(tmpa.ani_resv, tmpa.ani_max) - tmpa.ani_free;
    swap_avail =  max(tmpa.ani_max - tmpa.ani_resv, 0) + ramres;
    swap_free = tmpa.ani_free + ramres;
    res_but_not_alloc = tmpa.ani_resv - swap_alloc;

    printf("ani_max %d  ani_resv %d  ani_free %d  availrmem %d  swapfs_minfree %d\n",
    tmpa.ani_max, tmpa.ani_resv, tmpa.ani_free,
    availrmem, swapfs_minfree);
    printf("ramres %d  swap_resv %d  swap_alloc %d  swap_avail %d  swap_free %d\n",
    ramres, tmpa.ani_resv, swap_alloc, swap_avail, swap_free);

    printf("\nMisleading data printed by swap -s\n");
    printf("%d K allocated + %d K reserved = %d K used, %d K available\n",
    swap_alloc * ptok, res_but_not_alloc * ptok,
    tmpa.ani_resv * ptok, swap_avail * ptok);
    printf("Corrected labels:\n");
    printf("%d K allocated + %d K unallocated = %d K reserved, %d K available\n",
    swap_alloc * ptok, res_but_not_alloc * ptok,
    tmpa.ani_resv * ptok, swap_avail * ptok);

    printf("\nMislabelled sar -r 1\n");
    printf("freeswap (really swap available) %d blocks\n",
    swap_avail * ptok * 2);

    printf("\nUseful swap data: Total swap %d M\n",
```

Figure 13-13 SE Code to Read Swap Measures and Display Correctly Labeled Data (Continued)

```
        swap_avail * ptok / 1024 + tmpa.ani_resv * ptok / 1024);
        printf("available %d M  reserved %d M  Total disk %d M  Total RAM %d M\n",
        swap_avail * ptok / 1024, tmpa.ani_resv * ptok / 1024,
        tmpa.ani_max * ptok /1024, ramres * ptok / 1024);
        }
```

Over the years, many people have struggled to understand the Solaris 2 swap system. When people try to add up the numbers from the commands, they get even more confused. It's not their fault. It really is confusing, and the numbers don't add up unless you know how they were calculated in the first place!

System V Shared Memory, Semaphores, and Message Queues

I'm listing these interprocess communication tunables all together because they are often set up together in /etc/system. This set of descriptions is based on a listing put together by Jim Mauro. The default and maximum values are tabulated in Table A-7 on page 559.

Shared Memory Tunables

As described in "System V Shared Memory" on page 333, System V shared memory is mostly used by database applications.

shmmax

The maximum size of a shared memory segment. The largest value a program can use in a call to shmget(2). Setting this tunable to a high value doesn't impact anything because kernel resources are not preallocated with this value.

shmmin

The smallest possible size of a shared memory segment. It is the smallest value that a program can use in a call to shmget(2). The default is 1 byte; there should never be any reason to change shmmin.

shmmni

The maximum number of shared memory identifiers that can exist in the system at any point in time. Every shared segment has an identifier associated with it, and this is what shmget(2) returns. The number of shared memory identifiers you need depends on the application. How many shared segments do we need? Setting shmmni too high has some fallout since the system uses this value during initialization to allocate kernel resources. Specifically, a shmid_ds structure is created for each possible shmmni: thus, the kernel memory allocated equals `shmmni` times `sizeof(struct shmid_ds)`. A `shmid_ds` structure is 112 bytes; you can do the arithmetic and determine the initial overhead in making this value large.

shmseg

The maximum number of segments per process. We don't allocate resources based on this value; we simply keep a per-process count of the number of shared segments the process is attached to, and we check that value to ensure it is less than `shmseg` before we allow another attach to complete. The maximum value should be the current value of `shmmni`, since setting it greater than `shmni` is pointless, and it should always be less than 65535. It is application dependent. Ask yourself, "How many shared memory segments do the processes running my application need to be attached to at any point in time?"

Semaphores

Semaphore tunables are not as easy to understand as those of shared segments because of the complex features of semaphores, such as the ability to use a single semaphore, or several semaphores in a set.

semmap

The number of entries in the semaphore map. The memory space given to the creation of semaphores is taken from the semaphore map, which is initialized with a fixed number of map entries based on the value of `semmap`. The implementation of allocation maps is generic within SVR4, supported with a standard set of kernel routines (`rmalloc()`, `rmfree()`, etc.). The use of allocations maps by the semaphore subsystem is just one example of their use. They prevent the kernel from having to deal with mapping additional kernel memory as semaphore use grows. By initializing and using allocation maps, kernel memory is allocated up front, and map entries are allocated and freed dynamically from the `semmap` allocation maps. `semmap` should never be larger than `semmni`. If the number of semaphores per semaphore set used by the application is known and we call that number "n," then you can use:

$semmap = ((semmni + n - 1) / n) + 1$

If you make `semmap` too small for the application, you'll get: "`WARNING: rmfree map overflow`" messages on the console. Set it higher and reboot.

semmni

The maximum number of semaphore sets, systemwide; the number of semaphore identifiers. Every semaphore set in the system has a unique identifier and control structure. During initialization, the system allocates kernel memory for `semmni` control structures. Each control structure is 84 bytes, so you can calculate the result of making `semmni` large.

semmns

The maximum number of semaphores in the system. A semaphore set may have more than one semaphore associated with it, and each semaphore has a `sem` structure. During initialization the system allocates `semmns * sizeof(struct sem)` out of kernel memory. Each `sem` structure is only 16 bytes. You should set `semmns` to `semmni` times `semmsl`.

semmnu

The systemwide maximum number of undo structures. It seems intuitive to make this equal to `semmni`; doing so would provide for an undo structure for every semaphore set. Semaphore operations performed via `semop(2)` can be undone if the process should terminate for whatever reason. An undo structure is required to guarantee this operation.

semmsl

The maximum number of semaphores, per unique identifier. As mentioned previously, each semaphore set may have one or more semaphores associated with it. This tunable defines what the maximum number is per set.

semopm

The maximum number of semaphore operations that can be performed per `semop(2)` call.

semume

The maximum per process undo structures. See if the application sets the SEM_UNDO flag when it gets a semaphore. If not, you don't need undo structures. `semume` should be less than `semmnu` but sufficient for the application. Set it equal to `semopm` times the average number of processes that will be doing semaphore operations at any time.

semusz

Although listed as the size in bytes of the undo structure, in reality `semusz` is the number of bytes required for the maximum configured per-process undo structures. During initialization, it gets set to `semume` * (1 + `sizeof`(undo)), so setting it in `/etc/system` is pointless. It should be removed as a tunable.

semvmx

The maximum value of a semaphore. Because of the interaction with undo structures (and `semaem`), this tunable should not exceed a max of its default value of 32767 unless you can guarantee that `SEM_UNDO` is never being used.

semaem

The maximum adjust-on-exit value. A signed short, because semaphore operations can increase or decrease the value of a semaphore, even though the actual value of a semaphore can never be negative. `semaem` needs to represent the range of changes possible in a single semaphore operation, which limits `semvmx`, as described above. We should not be tweaking either `semvmx` or `semaem` unless we *really* understand how the applications will be using summaries. And even then, leave `semvmx` as the default.

Message Queues

System V message queues provide a standardized message-passing system that is used by some large commercial applications.

msgmap

The number of entries in the msg map. See `semmap` above. The same implementation of preallocation of kernel space by use of resource maps applies.

msgmax

The maximum size of a message.

msgmnb

The maximum number of bytes on the message queue.

msgmni

The number of message queue identifiers.

msgssz

The message segment size.

msgtql

The number of system message headers.

msgseg

The number of message segments.

Kernel Algorithms and Tuning 14 ≣

This chapter explains some of the inner workings of the kernel. This chapter also describes buffer sizes and variables that can be changed by a system administrator when tuning a kernel. "Tunables Quick Reference" on page 557 contains a quick summary of what can safely be changed.

The kernel algorithms are noted as being based on System V Release 4 (SVR4) if they are generic and as Solaris 2-based if Solaris 2 is different from generic SVR4. Later releases of SunOS 4 have Solaris 1 names, which I have avoided for clarity (although this is not considered the correct use of the terms). The kernel part of Solaris 2 is known as SunOS 5.

There are no "magic silver bullet" tunable values that will make a big difference to performance. If you look at the relative balance of user and system CPU time, and user CPU time is much higher than system time, then kernel tuning can have little or no effect.

Kernel Tuning

Tuning the kernel is a hard subject to deal with. Some tunables are well known and easy to explain. Others are more complex or change from one release to the next. The settings in use are often based on out-of-date folklore. This chapter identifies and explains some of the variables that are safe to tune. If you also use other versions of Unix, you may be accustomed to having a long list of tunable parameters to set up when you rebuild the kernel. You are probably looking for the equivalent list for Solaris 2, so I will compare tunables with other Unix implementations to identify the ones that size automatically in Solaris 2 and don't need tuning.

A fundamental issue is the distinction between interfaces, implementations, and behaviors.

Interfaces

Interfaces are designed to stay the same over many releases of the product. This way, users or programmers have time to figure out how to use the interface. A good analogy is that the controls used to drive a car are an interface that stays relatively constant. The basic controls for stop, go, steer are always in the same place. You don't need to know how many cylinders there are in the engine before you can drive the car.

Implementations

The implementation hides behind the interface and does the actual work. Bug fixes, performance enhancements, and underlying hardware differences are handled by changes in the implementation. There are often changes from one release of the product to the next, or even from one system to another running the same software release. If a car engine starts to misfire and you need to lift the hood and change the spark plugs, you are suddenly confronted with a lot of implementation details. Outwardly identical cars might have a four-, a six-, or an eight-cylinder engine and many other detailed differences that change year by year as well.

Behaviors

Even with no knowledge of the implementation details, the behavior of a system changes from one implementation to the next. For example, Solaris 2.6 on an Ultra 1 has the same set of interfaces as Solaris 2.4 on a SPARCstation 5. The behavior is quite different because Solaris has been tuned in several ways and the hardware implementation's performance is much higher. To take the car analogy again, a BMW 518i and a BMW 540i look very similar, but one has a 1.8-liter four-cylinder engine, and the other has a 4.0-liter eight-cylinder engine. They don't sound the same, and they don't behave the same way when you push the accelerator pedal!

Self-Tuning Systems

In normal use there is no need to tune the Solaris 2 kernel; it dynamically adapts itself to the hardware configuration and the application workload. If it isn't working properly, you may have a configuration error, a hardware failure, or a software bug. To fix a problem, you check the configuration, make sure all the hardware is OK, and load the latest software patches.

Documented Configuration Tunables

The tunable parameters that are mentioned in the Solaris 2 AnswerBook Performance Section configure the sizes or limits of some data structures. The size of these data structures has no effect on performance, but if they are set too low, an application might not run at all. Configuring shared memory allocations for databases falls into this category.

Kernel configuration and tuning variables are normally edited into the /etc/system file by hand. Unfortunately, any kernel data that has a symbol can be set via this file at boot time, whether or not it is a documented tunable. The kernel is supplied as many separate modules (type % `ls /kernel/*` to see some of them). To set a variable in a module or device driver when it is loaded, prefix the variable name by the module name and a colon. For example:

```
set pt_cnt = 1000
set shmsys:shminfo_shmmax = 0x20000000
```

The History of Kernel Tuning

So why is there so much emphasis on kernel tuning? And why are there such high expectations of the performance boost available from kernel tweaks? I think the reasons are historical, and I'll return to my car analogy to explain it.

Compare a 1970s car with a 1998 car. The older car has a carburetor, needs regular tune-ups, and is likely to be temperamental at best. The 1998 car has computerized fuel injection, self-adjusting engine components, and is easier to live with, consistent and reliable. If the old car won't start reliably, you get out the workshop manual and tinker with a large number of fine adjustments. The 1998 car's computerized ignition and fuel injection systems have no user serviceable components.

Unix started out in an environment where the end users had source code and did their own tuning and support. If you like this way of working, you probably already run the free Unix clone, Linux, on your PC at home. As Unix became a commercial platform for running applications, the end users changed. Commercial users just want to run their application, and tinkering with the operating system is a distraction. SunSoft engineers have put a lot of effort into automating the tuning for Solaris 2. It adaptively scales according to the hardware capabilities and the workload it is running. The self-tuning nature of modern cars is now a major selling point. The self-configuring and tuning nature of Solaris contributes to its ease of use and greatly reduces the gains from tweaking it yourself. Each successive version of Solaris 2 has removed tuning variables by converting hand-adjusted values into adaptively managed limits.

If SunSoft can describe a tunable variable and when it should be tuned in detail, they could either document this in the manual or implement the tuning automatically. In most cases, automatic tuning has been implemented. The tuning manual should really tell you which things don't need to be tuned any more, but it doesn't. This is one of my complaints about the manual, which is really in need of a complete rewrite. It is too closely based on the original Unix System V manual from many years ago when things did need tuning.

14

Tuning to Incorporate Extra Information

An adaptively managed kernel can react only to the workload it sees. If you know enough about the workload, you may be able to use the extra information to effectively preconfigure the algorithms. In most cases, the gains are minor. Increasing the size of the name caches on NFS servers falls into this category. One problem is that the administrator often knows enough to be dangerous, but not enough to be useful.

Tuning During Development

The primary reason why there are so many obscure "folkloric" kernel tunables is that they are used to provide options and allow tuning during the development process. Kernel developers can read the source code and try things out under controlled conditions. When the final product ships, the tunables are often still there. Each bug fix and new version of the product potentially changes the meaning of the tunables. This is the biggest danger for an end user, who is guessing what a tunable does from its name or from knowledge of an older Unix implementation.

Tuning to Solve Problems

When a bug or performance problem is being fixed, the engineer tries to find an easy workaround that can be implemented immediately. It takes much longer to rewrite and test the code to eliminate the problem, and the proper fix will be part of a patch or turn up in the next release of the operating system. There may be a kernel tunable that can be changed to provide a partial workaround, and this information will be provided to the end user. The problem is that these "point patch" fixes sometimes become part of the folklore and are propagated indiscriminately, where they may cause problems.

In one real-life case, a large SPARCcenter 2000 configuration was running very slowly. The problem turned out to be a setting in /etc/system that had been supplied to fix a problem on a small SPARCstation 2 several years before. The administrator had carefully added it during installation to every machine at his site. Instead of increasing the size of a dynamically configured kernel table on a machine with 32 Mbytes of RAM, it was drastically reducing its size on a machine with 1 Gbyte of RAM. The underlying problem did not even exist in the version of Solaris 2 that was currently being used at the site!

The message is, clean out your /etc/system when you upgrade.

The Placebo Effect

You may be convinced that setting a tunable has a profound effect on your system when it is truly doing nothing. In one case, an administrator was adamant that a bogus setting could not be removed from /etc/system without causing serious performance problems. When the "variable not found" error message that displayed during boot was pointed out, it still took a while to convince him that this meant that the variable no longer existed in this release, and so it could not be having any effect.

Tunable Parameters

The kernel tunable values listed in this book include *the main tunables that are worth worrying about*. A huge number of global values are defined in the kernel; if you hear of a tweak that is not listed here or in "Tunables Quick Reference" on page 557, think twice before using it. The algorithms, default values, and existence of many of these variables vary from one release to the next. Do not assume that an undocumented tweak that works well for one kernel will apply to other releases, other kernel architectures of the same release, or even a different patch level.

The Ones That Went Away

I looked at HP-UX 9.0 on an HP9000 server; the sam utility provides an interface for kernel configuration. Like Solaris 1/SunOS 4, the HP-UX kernel must be recompiled and relinked if it is tuned and drivers and subsystems are added. In Solaris 2, file systems, drivers, and modules are loaded into memory when they are used, and the memory is returned if the module is no longer needed. Rather than a GUI being provided, the whole process is made transparent. There are 50 or more tunable values listed in sam. Some of them are familiar or map to dynamically managed Solaris 2 parameters. There is a maxusers parameter that must be set manually, and the size of several other parameters is based upon maxusers in a way similar to sizing in Solaris 2. Of the tunables that I can identify, the Solaris 2 equivalents are either unnecessary or listed in "Tunables Quick Reference" on page 557.

Dynamic Kernel Tables in Solaris 2

Solaris 2 dynamically manages the memory used by the open file table, the lock table (in 2.5), the callout queue, the streams subsystem, the process table, and the inode cache. Unlike other Unix implementations that statically allocate a full-size array of data structures, wasting a lot of precious memory, Solaris 2 allocates memory as it goes along. Some of the old tunables that are used to size the statically allocated memory in other Unixes still exist. They are now used as limits to prevent too many data structures from being allocated. This dynamic allocation approach is one reason why it is safe to let maxusers scale automatically to very high levels. In Solaris 1 or HP-UX 9, setting maxusers to 1024 and rebuilding the kernel would result in a huge kernel (which might not be able to boot) and a huge waste of memory. In Solaris 2, the relatively small directory name lookup cache is the only statically sized table derived from maxusers.

Take a look at your own `/etc/system` file. If there are things there that are not listed in this book and that you don't understand, you have a problem. There should be a large comment next to each setting that explains why it is there and how its setting was derived. You could even divide the file into sections for configuration, extra information, development experiments, problem fixes, and placebos.

I hope I have convinced you that there are very few Solaris tunables that should be documented and supported for general use. Why worry about tweaking a cranky and out-of-date Unix system, when you can use one that takes care of itself?

SunOS and Solaris Release Overview

The number of fixed-size tables in the kernel has been reduced in each release of Solaris. Most are now dynamically sized or are linked to the `maxusers` calculation, which is now also sized automatically. There is no need for general-purpose tuning in recent Solaris releases; the main performance improvements come from keeping patch levels up to date. Specific situations may require tuning for configuration or performance reasons that are later. My own personal recommendations for each release vary, as summarized in Table 14-1.

Table 14-1 Tuning SunOS Releases

Release	Recommendations
Older releases	Upgrade to a more recent release
SunOS 5.4/Solaris 2.4	Add kernel patch to fix pager, add TCP/IP and year2000 patches
SunOS 5.5/Solaris 2.5	Add kernel patch to fix pager, add TCP/IP and year2000 patches
SunOS 5.5.1/Solaris 2.5.1	Add kernel patch, TCP/IP and year2000 patches, `hme` patch
SunOS 5.6/Solaris 2.6	Add TCP/IP patch

Solaris 2 Performance Tuning Manuals

There is a manual section called *Administering Security, Performance, and Accounting in Solaris 2*. The manual was revised and corrected for Solaris 2.4 but has not changed significantly since and so is not very useful. The *SMCC NFS Server Performance and Tuning Guide* is kept up to date in each release and contains useful information. Parts of the NFS guide were originally written by Brian Wong and me, along with NFS engineering staff. The first of these manuals is part of the *SunSoft System Software AnswerBook*, the second is part of the *Sun Microsystems Computer Corporation Hardware AnswerBook*. Both can be read via the online documentation service at http://docs.sun.com.

Using `/etc/system` to Modify Kernel Variables in Solaris 2

In SunOS 4, the kernel must be recompiled after values in `param.c` or `conf.c` are tweaked to increase table sizes. In Solaris 2, there is no need to recompile the kernel; it is modified by changing `/etc/system` and rebooting. `/etc/system` is read by the kernel at startup. It configures the search path for loadable kernel modules and allows kernel variables to be set. See the manual page for `system`(4) for the full syntax.[1]

Be very careful with `set` commands in `/etc/system`; they cause arbitrary, unchecked, and automatic changes to variables in the kernel, so there is plenty of opportunity to break your system. If your machine will not boot and you suspect a problem with `/etc/system`, use the `boot -a` option. With this option, the system prompts (with defaults) for its boot parameters. One of these parameters is the configuration file `/etc/system`. Either enter the name of a backup copy of the original `/etc/system` file or enter `/dev/null`. Fix the file and reboot the machine immediately to check that it is again working properly.

Watch for messages at boot time. If an error is detected or a variable name is misspelled or doesn't exist, then a message is displayed on the console during boot.

General Solaris 2 Performance Improvements

The changes in Solaris 2.4 focus on improving interactive performance in small memory configurations, improving overall efficiency, and providing better support for large numbers of connected time-sharing users with high-end multiprocessor machines.

Some of the changes that improve performance on the latest processor types and improve high-end multiprocessor scalability could cause a slight reduction in performance on earlier processor types and on uniprocessors. Trade-offs like this are carefully assessed; in most cases, when changes to part of the system are made, an improvement must be demonstrated on all configurations.

In some areas, internationalization and stricter conformance to standards from the SVID, POSIX, and X/Open cause higher overhead compared to that of SunOS 4.1.3.

The base Solaris 2 operating system contains support for international locales that require 16-bit characters, whereas the base SunOS 4 is always 8-bit. The internationalized and localized versions of SunOS 4 were recoded and released much later than the base version. Solaris 2 releases have a much simpler localization process. One side effect of this

---

1. The command to use is `man -s 4 system`, since there are other things called "system" in the manual.

simplification is that Solaris 2 commands such as `sort` deal with 16-bit characters and localized collation ordering, which slows them down. The standard sort algorithm taken from SVR4 is also very inefficient and uses small buffers. If you use `sort` a lot, then it would be worth getting a copy of a substitute from the GNU archives. Heavy-duty commercial sorting should be done with a commercial package such as SyncSort.

Using Solaris 2 with Large Numbers of Active Users

To connect large numbers of users into a system, Ethernet terminal servers using the Telnet protocol are normally used. Characters typed by several users at one terminal server cannot be multiplexed into a single Ethernet packet; a separate packet must be sent for any activity on each Telnet session. The system calls involved include `poll`, which is implemented with single-threaded code in releases before Solaris 2.4. This call prevents raw CPU power from being used to solve this problem—the effect in Solaris 2.3 and earlier releases is that a lot of CPU time is wasted in the kernel contending on `poll`, and adding another CPU has no useful effect. In Solaris 2.4, `poll` is fully multithreaded; so, with sufficient CPU power, Telnet no longer limits the number of users, and kernel CPU time stays low to 500 users and beyond. Now that the Telnet and `poll` limit have gone, any subsequent limit is much more application dependent. Tests on a 16-processor SPARCcenter 2000 failed to find any significant kernel-related limits before the machine ran out of CPU power.

Solaris 2.5 further increased efficiency for network-connected users. The `telnet` and `rlogin` daemons are not in the normal path; a single daemon remains to handle the protocol itself, but the regular character data that is sent backward and forward is processed entirely within the kernel, using new streams modules that take the characters directly from the TCP/IP stack and put them directly into the pseudoterminal. This technique makes the whole process much more efficient and, since the `poll` system call is no longer called, also bypasses the contention problems.

The underlying efficiency of the network protocol is part of the problem, and one solution is to abandon the Telnet protocol completely. There are two good options, but both have the disadvantage of using a proprietary protocol. The terminal server that Sun supplies is made by Xylogics, Inc. Xylogics has developed a multiplexed protocol that takes all the characters from all the ports on their terminal server and sends them as a single large packet to Solaris. A new protocol streams driver that Xylogics supplies for Solaris demultiplexes the packet and writes the correct characters to the correct pseudoterminal. Another possible alternative is to use the DECnet LAT protocol, which addresses the same issues. Many terminal servers support LAT because of its widespread use in DEC sites. There are several implementations of LAT for Solaris; for example, Meridian does one that is implemented as a stream module and so should be quite efficient.

Directly connected terminals also work well, but the Sun-supplied SBus SPC 8-port serial card is very inefficient and should be avoided. A far better alternative is a SCSI-connected serial port multiplexer. This choice saves valuable SBus slots for other things, and large servers usually have spare SCSIbus slots that can be used.

The Performance Implications of Patches

Every release has a set of patches for the various subsystems. The patches generally fall into three categories: security-related patches, reliability-related patches, and performance-related patches. In some cases, the patches are derived from the ongoing development work on the next release, where changes have been backported to previous releases for immediate availability. Some patches are also labeled as recommended patches, particularly for server systems. Some of the reliability-related patches are for fairly obscure problems and may reduce the performance of your system. If you are benchmarking, try to get benchmark results with and without patches so that you can see the difference.

Solaris 2.6 Performance Improvements

Solaris 2.6 is a different kind of release from Solaris 2.5 and Solaris 2.5.1. Those releases were tied to very important hardware launches: UltraSPARC support in Solaris 2.5 and Ultra Enterprise Server support in Solaris 2.5.1. With a hard deadline, you have to keep functionality improvements under control, so there were relatively few new features. Solaris 2.6 is not tied to any hardware launch; new systems released in early 1998 all run an updated version of 2.5.1 as well as Solaris 2.6. The current exception is the Enterprise 10000 (Starfire), which was not a Sun product early enough (Sun brought in the development team from Cray during 1996) to have Solaris 2.6 support at first release. During 1998, an update release of Solaris 2.6 will include support for the E10000. Because Solaris 2.6 had a more flexible release schedule and fewer hardware dependencies, it was possible to take longer over the development and add far more new functionality. Some of the projects that weren't quite ready for Solaris 2.5 (like large-file support) ended up in Solaris 2.6. Other projects, like the integration of Java 1.1, were important enough to delay the release of Solaris 2.6 for a few months. Several documents on www.sun.com describe the new features, so I'll concentrate on explaining some of the performance tuning that was done for Solaris 2.6 and tell you about some small but useful changes to the performance measurements that sneaked into Solaris 2.6. Some of them were filed as Requests For Enhancements (RFEs) by Brian Wong and me over the last few years.

14

Web Server Performance

The most dramatic performance change in Solaris 2.6 is to web servers. The published SPECweb96 results show that Solaris 2.6 is far faster than Solaris 2.5.1. The message should be obvious. Upgrade busy web servers to Solaris 2.6 as soon as you can. The details are discussed in "Internet Servers" on page 57.

Database Server Performance

Database server performance was already very good and scales well with Solaris 2.5.1. There is always room for improvement though, and several changes have been made to increase efficiency and scalability even further in Solaris 2.6. A few features are worth mentioning.

The first new feature is a transparent increase in efficiency on UltraSPARC systems. The intimate shared memory segment used by most databases is now mapped by 4-Mbyte pages, rather than by lots of 8-Kbyte pages.

The second new feature is direct I/O. This feature enables a database table that is resident in a file system to bypass the filesystem buffering and behave more like a piece of raw disk. See "Direct I/O Access" on page 161.

New and Improved Performance Measurements

A collection of Requests For Enhancement (RFE) had built up over several years, asking for better measurements in the operating system and improvements for the tools that display the metrics. Brian Wong and I filed some of them, while others came from database engineering and from customers. These RFEs have now been implemented—so I'm having to think up some new ones! You should be aware that Sun's bug-tracking tool has three kinds of bug in it: problem bugs, RFEs, and Ease Of Use (EOU) issues. If you have an idea for an improvement or think that something should be easier to use, you can help everyone by taking the trouble to ask Sun Service to register your suggestion. It may take a long time to appear in a release, but it will take even longer if you don't tell anyone!

The improvements we got this time include new disk metrics, new `iostat` options, tape metrics, client-side NFS mount point metrics, network byte counter, and accurate process memory usage measurements.

Parameters Derived from `maxusers`

When BSD Unix was originally developed, its designers addressed the problem of scaling the size of several kernel tables and buffers by creating a single sizing variable. The scaling needed was related to the number of time-sharing terminal users the system could support, so the variable was named `maxusers`. Nowadays, so much has changed that there is no direct relationship between the number of users a system supports and the value of `maxusers`. Increases in memory size and more complex applications require much larger kernel tables and buffers for the same number of users.

The calculation of parameters derived from `maxusers` is shown in Table 14-2. The inode and name cache are described in more detail in "Directory Name Lookup Cache" on page 308. The other variables are not performance related.

Table 14-2 Default Settings for Kernel Parameters

Kernel Resource	Variable	Default Setting
Processes	`max_nprocs`	10 + 16 * maxusers
Inode Cache	`ufs_ninode`	max_nprocs + 16 + maxusers + 64
Name Cache	`ncsize`	max_nprocs + 16 + maxusers + 64
Quota Table	`ndquot`	(maxusers * NMOUNT)/4 + max_nprocs
User Process Limit	`maxuprc`	max_nprocs - 5

Changing `maxusers` and Pseudo-ttys in Solaris 2

The variable that really limits the number of user logins on the system is `pt_cnt`. It may be necessary to set the number of pseudo-ttys higher than the default of 48, especially in a time-sharing system that uses Telnet-from-Ethernet terminal servers to connect users to the system. If you are configuring a time-shared multiuser system with more than a hundred active users, make sure you have first read "Using Solaris 2 with Large Numbers of Active Users" on page 356. A practical limit is imposed by the format of the `utmp` file entry to 62*62 = 3844 Telnets and another 3844 rlogins; until this limit is changed, keep `pt_cnt` under 3000.

To actually create the `/dev/pts` entries, run `boot -r` after you set `pt_cnt`; see Figure 14-1.

Figure 14-1 Example Pseudo-tty Count Setting in `/etc/system`

```
set pt_cnt = 1000
```

Autoconfiguration of `maxusers` in Solaris 2.3 Through Solaris 2.6

The `maxusers` setting in Solaris 2 is automatically set via the `physmem` variable to be approximately equal to the number of Mbytes of RAM configured into the system. `maxusers` is usually set to 2 or 3 Mbytes less than the total RAM in the system. The minimum limit is 8 and the maximum automatic limit is 1024, corresponding to systems with 1 Gbyte or more of RAM. `maxusers` can still be set manually in `/etc/system`, but the manual setting is checked and limited to a maximum of 2048. This setting was tested on all kernel architectures but could waste kernel memory. In most cases, you should not need to set `maxusers` explicitly.

Filesystem Name and Attribute Caching

This section provides a simplified view of how the kernel algorithms work. Some of the details are skipped, as the intent is to understand the measurements provided by `sar`. This topic has already been covered in some detail in "File Access Caching with Local Disk" on page 307.

Vnodes, Inodes, and Rnodes

Unix traditionally uses inodes to hold the information required to access files, such as the size, owner, permissions, modification date and the location of the data blocks for the file. SunOS 4, SVR4, and Solaris 2 all use a higher-level abstraction called a virtual node, or vnode. This scheme allows all filesystem types to be implemented in the same way since the kernel works in terms of vnodes and each vnode contains some kind of inode that matches the filesystem type. For UFS, these structures are still called inodes. For NFS, they are called rnodes.

Directory Name Lookup Cache

The directory name lookup cache (DNLC) is used whenever a file is opened. The DNLC associates the name of a file with a vnode. Since the file system forms a hierarchy, many directories need to be traversed to get at a typical, deeply nested, user file. Short file names are cached, and names that are too long to be cached are looked up the slow way by reading the directory. The number of name lookups per second is reported as `namei/s` by the `sar -a` command; see Figure 14-2.

Figure 14-2 Example `sar` *Command to Monitor Attribute Cache Rates*

```
% sar -a 1
SunOS hostname 5.4 sun4m    06/19/94
09:00:00  iget/s namei/s dirbk/s
09:00:01       4       9       2
```

For SunOS 4, names up to 14 characters long are cached. For Solaris 2, names of up to 30 characters are cached. A cache miss or oversized entry means that more kernel CPU time and perhaps a disk I/O may be needed to read the directory. The number of directory blocks read per second is reported as `dirbk/s` by `sar -a`. It is good policy to keep heavily used directory and symbolic link names down to 14 or 30 characters.

The DNLC is sized to a default value based on `maxusers` and a large cache size (`ncsize` in Table 14-2) significantly helps NFS servers that have a lot of clients. The command `vmstat -s` shows the DNLC hit rate since boot. A hit rate of less than 90 percent will need attention. Every entry in the DNLC cache points to an entry in the inode or rnode cache (only NFS clients have an rnode cache).

The only limit to the size of the DNLC cache is available kernel memory. For NFS server benchmarks, the limit has been set as high as 16,000; for the maximum `maxusers` value of 2048, the limit would be set at 34,906. Each DNLC cache entry is quite small; it basically just holds the 14 or 30 character name and a vnode reference. Increase it to at least 8000 on a busy NFS server that has 512 Mbytes or less RAM by adding the line below to `/etc/system`. Figure 14-3 illustrates DNLC operation.

```
set ncsize = 8000
```

Figure 14-3 The Directory Name Lookup Cache and Attribute Information Flows

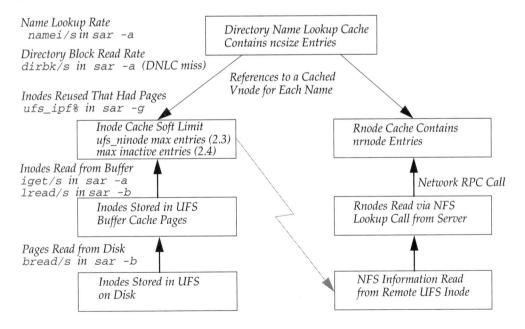

The Inode Cache and File Data Caching

UFS stores inodes on the disk; the inode must be read into memory whenever an operation is performed on an entity in UFS. The number of inodes read per second is reported as `iget/s` by the `sar  -a` command. The inode read from disk is cached in case it is needed again, and the number of inodes that the system will cache is influenced by a kernel tunable called `ufs_ninode`. The inodes are kept on a linked list rather than in a fixed-size table. A UFS file is read or written by paging from the file system. All pages that are part of the file and are in memory will be attached to the inode cache entry for that file. When a file is not in use, its data is cached in memory by an inactive inode cache entry. When an inactive inode cache entry that has pages attached is reused, the pages are put on the free list; this case is shown by `sar  -g` as `%ufs_ipf`. This number is the percentage of UFS inodes that were overwritten in the inode cache by `iget` and that had reusable pages associated with them. These pages are flushed and cannot be reclaimed by processes. Thus, this number is the percentage of `igets` with page flushes. Any non-zero values reported by `sar  -g` indicate that the inode cache is too small for the current workload.

In Solaris 2.4, the inode algorithm was reimplemented. A reuse list is maintained of blank inodes for instant use. The number of active inodes is no longer constrained, and the number of idle inodes (inactive but cached in case they are needed again) are kept between `ufs_ninode` and 75 percent of `ufs_ninode` by a kernel thread that scavenges the inodes to free them and maintains entries on the reuse list. If you use `sar  -v` to look at the inode cache, you may see a larger number of existing inodes than the reported "size."

The only upper limit is the amount of kernel memory used by the inodes. The tested upper limit in Solaris 2 corresponds to `maxusers = 2048`, which is the same as `ncsize` at 34906. Use `sar  -k` to report the size of the kernel memory allocation; each inode uses about 300 bytes of kernel memory. Since it is just a limit, `ufs_ninode` can be tweaked with `adb` on a running system with immediate effect. On later Solaris 2 releases, you can see inode cache statistics by using `netstat  -k` to dump out the raw kernel statistics information, as shown in Figure 14-4.

Figure 14-4 Example `netstat` Output to Show Inode Statistics

```
% netstat -k
inode_cache:
size 1200 maxsize 1200 hits 722 misses 2605 mallocs 1200 frees 0
maxsize_reached 1200
puts_at_frontlist 924 puts_at_backlist 1289 dnlc_looks 0 dnlc_purges 0
```

If the `maxsize_reached` value is higher than the `maxsize` (this variable is equal to `ufs_ninode`), then the number of `active` inodes has exceeded the cache size at some point in the past, so you should increase `ufs_ninode`. Set it on a busy NFS server by editing `param.c` and rebuilding the kernel in SunOS 4 and by adding the following line to `/etc/system` for Solaris 2.

```
set ufs_ninode=10000          For Solaris 2.2 and 2.3 only
set ufs_ninode=5000           For Solaris 2.4 only
```

Rnode Cache

A similar cache, the rnode cache, is maintained on NFS clients to hold information about files in NFS. The data is read by NFS `getattr` calls to the NFS server, which keeps the information in a vnode of its own. The default rnode cache size is twice the DNLC size and should not need to be changed.

Buffer Cache

The buffer cache is used to cache all UFS disk I/O in SunOS 3 and BSD Unix. In SunOS 4, generic SVR4, and Solaris 2, it is used to cache inode-, indirect block-, and cylinder group-related disk I/O only.

In Solaris 2, nbuf keeps track of how many page-sized buffers have been allocated, and a new variable called p_nbuf (default value 100) defines how many new buffers are allocated in one go. A variable called `bufhwm` controls the maximum amount of memory allocated to the buffer and is specified in Kbytes. The default value of `bufhwm` allows up to two percent of system memory to be used. On SPARCcenter 2000 systems that have a large amount of memory, two percent of the memory is too much and the buffer cache can cause kernel memory starvation, as described in "Kernel Memory Allocation" on page 365. The `bufhwm` tunable can be used to fix this case by limiting the buffer cache to a few Mbytes, as shown below.

```
set bufhwm = 8000
```

In Solaris 2, the buffer cache can be monitored by `sar -b`, which reports a read and a write hit rate for the buffer cache, as shown in Figure 14-5. "Administering Security, Performance, and Accounting in Solaris 2" contains unreliable information about tuning the buffer cache.

Figure 14-5 Example sar *Output to Show Buffer Cache Statistics*

```
# sar -b 5 10
SunOS hostname 5.2 Generic sun4c    08/06/93
23:43:39 bread/s lread/s %rcache bwrit/s lwrit/s %wcache pread/s pwrit/s
...
Average         0      25     100       3      22      88       0       0
```

An alternative look at the buffer cache hit rate can be calculated from part of the output of netstat -k, as shown in Figure 14-6.

Figure 14-6 Example netstat *Output to Show Buffer Cache Statistics*

```
% netstat -k
biostats:
buffer cache lookups 9705 buffer cache hits 9285 new buffer requests 0
waits for buffer allocs 0 buffers locked by someone 3 duplicate buffers
found 0
```

Comparing buffer cache hits with lookups (9285/9705) shows a 96 percent hit rate since reboot in this example, which seems to be high enough.

Measuring the Kernel

This section explains how you can use the tools provided to monitor the algorithms described earlier in this chapter.

The sar utility has a huge number of options and some very powerful capabilities. One of its best features is that you can log its full output in date-stamped binary form to a file. You can even look at a few selected measures interactively, then go back to look at all the other measures if you need to. sar generates average values automatically and can be used to produce averages between specified start and end times from a binary file. Many of the sar options have already been described in "Vnodes, Inodes, and Rnodes" on page 360 and "Understanding vmstat and sar Output" on page 320.

One particularly useful facility is that the system is already set up to capture binary sar records at 20-minute intervals and to maintain one-month's worth of past records in /var/adm/sa. This feature can easily be enabled, as discussed in "Collecting Measurements" on page 48.

Using **sar** to Examine Table Sizes

sar likes to average sizes over time, so sar -v 1 tells sar to make one measure over a one-second period. The file table is no longer a fixed-size data structure in Solaris 2, so its size is given as zero. The examples in Figure 14-7 were taken on a 128-Mbyte desktop machine with maxusers set at the default value of 123.

Figure 14-7   Example sar Output to See Table Sizes in Solaris 2

```
% sar -v 1
SunOS hostname 5.5.1 Generic_103640-14 sun4u     01/19/98
11:22:51  proc-sz    ov  inod-sz    ov  file-sz    ov  lock-sz
11:22:52    72/1978    0 3794/3794    0  526/526     0    0/0
```

Kernel Memory Allocation

The kernel is probably using more memory than you expect. Kernel memory usage increases as you add RAM, CPUs, and processes to a system. You need to monitor usage on very large active systems because it is possible for the kernel to reach its kernelmap limit. This is a problem on SPARCcenter 2000 systems, which have a 512-Mbyte limit for the whole kernel address space. UltraSPARC-based systems have a separate 4-Gbyte address space for the kernel; this limit is plenty and avoids any problems. In the future, the 64-bit Solaris kernel will not have even this limit.

A completely new kernel memory allocation system is implemented in Solaris 2.4. It has less CPU overhead and allocates packed data structures in a way that saves space and improves CPU cache hit rates. On desktop workstations, this allocation frees up a megabyte or more and helps bring the memory requirements closer to SunOS 4 levels. The allocation statistics are summarized in groups for reporting via sar -k, but the details of the allocations at each block size can be seen via part of the crash kmastat command output, as shown in Figure 14-8 in cut-down form. As you can see, the memory allocator contains special support for individual types of data, and it can be interesting to monitor the memory usage of each kernel subsystem in this way. Nonspecific memory allocations are made by means of the kmem_alloc_*xxxx* pools. The kmem_magazine concept was introduced in Solaris 2.5. It forms CPU-specific subpools for the commonest data types. This approach avoids multiprocessor locking overhead and improves cache hit rates in a multiprocessor system. This highly sophisticated kernel memory allocator is one of the key reasons why Solaris 2 scales efficiently, better than other operating systems, to large numbers of CPUs.

Figure 14-8   Example Output from crash kmastat

```
# crash
dumpfile = /dev/mem, namelist = /dev/ksyms, outfile = stdout
> kmastat
```

cache name	buf size	buf avail	buf total	memory in use	#allocations succeed	fail
kmem_magazine_1	8	923	1020	8192	1370	0
kmem_magazine_3	16	397	510	8192	1931	0
kmem_magazine_7	32	394	510	16384	6394	0
....						
kmem_alloc_12288	12288	3	14	172032	1849	0
kmem_alloc_16384	16384	2	12	196608	261	0
sfmmu8_cache	232	1663	5304	1277952	27313	0
sfmmu1_cache	64	811	1582	114688	5503	0
seg_cache	28	852	2805	90112	2511092	0
ddi_callback_cache	24	0	0	0	0	0
thread_cache	288	77	168	49152	80659	0
lwp_cache	472	45	136	65536	407	0
cred_cache	96	58	85	8192	245144	0
file_cache	40	256	850	40960	7550686	0
streams_msg_40	112	244	884	106496	28563463	0
streams_msg_88	160	290	336	57344	15292360	0
...						
streams_msg_4024	4096	2	2	8192	3485	0
streams_msg_9464	9536	54	54	516096	44775	0
streams_msg_dup	72	88	102	8192	367729	0
streams_msg_esb	72	0	0	0	2516	0
stream_head_cache	152	72	408	65536	21523	0
flk_edges	24	0	0	0	0	0
snode_cache	128	90	660	90112	3530706	0
...						
ufs_inode_cache	320	1059	5520	1884160	974640	0
fas0_cache	188	156	168	32768	619863	0
prnode_cache	108	65	72	8192	4746459	0
fnode_cache	160	31	42	8192	278	0
pipe_cache	288	34	75	24576	4456	0
rnode_cache	384	15	21	8192	95	0
lm_vnode	84	0	0	0	0	0
lm_xprt	16	0	0	0	0	0
lm_sysid	96	0	0	0	0	0
lm_client	40	0	0	0	0	0
lm_async	24	0	0	0	0	0
lm_sleep	64	0	0	0	0	0
lm_config	56	143	145	8192	2	0
----------						
permanent	–	–	–	409600	3100	0
oversize	–	–	–	2809856	10185	0

Total	–	–	–	14606336	128754134	0

Kernel Lock Profiling with `lockstat` in Solaris 2.6

The use of this tool is described in "Monitoring Solaris 2.6 Lock Statistics" on page 239.

Kernel Clock Tick Resolution

Many measurements in the kernel occur during the 100 Hz clock tick interrupt. This parameter sets a limit on the time resolution of events. As CPU speed increases, the amount of work done in 10 milliseconds increases greatly. Increasing the clock tick rate for all systems would just add overhead, so a new option in Solaris 2.6 allows the clock tick to be set to 1000 Hz, as shown below. This option is most useful for real-time processing. It increases the resolution of CPU time measurements, but it is better to use microstate accounting, described in "Process Data Sources" on page 416, to obtain really accurate measurements.

```
set hires_tick=1
```

Setting Default Limits

The default limits are shown by the `sysdef -i` command, which lists the values in hexadecimal, as shown in Figure 14-9.

Figure 14-9 Example Systemwide Resource Limits Shown by `sysdef`

```
% sysdef -i
...
    Soft:Hard           Resource
Infinity:Infinity       cpu time
Infinity:Infinity       file size
1fefe000:1fefe000       heap size
  800000: ff00000       stack size
Infinity:Infinity       core file size
     40:     400        file descriptors
Infinity:Infinity       mapped memory
```

The hard limits for data size and stack size vary. Some older machines with the Sun-4 MMU can map only 1 Gbyte of virtual address space, so stack size is restricted to 256 Mbytes and data size is restricted to 512 Mbytes. For machines with the SPARC Reference MMU, the maximums are 2 Gbytes each.

To increase the default number of file descriptors per process, you can set the kernel tunables `rlim_fd_cur` and `rlim_fd_max` in `/etc/system`.

The definition of FILE for the stdio library can handle only 256 open files at most, but raw read/write will work above that limit. The select system call uses a fixed-size bitfield that can only cope with 1024 file descriptors; the alternative is to use poll, which has no limit.

It is dangerous to set rlim_fd_cur to more than 256. Programs that need more file descriptors should either call setrlimit directly or have their own limit set in a wrapper script. If you need to use many file descriptors to open a large number of sockets or other raw files, it is best to force all of them to file descriptors numbered above 256. This lets system functions such as name services, which depend upon stdio file operations, continue to operate using the low-numbered file descriptors.

Mapping Device Nicknames to Full Names in Solaris 2

The boot sequence builds a tree in memory of the hardware devices present in the system; the tree is passed to the kernel and can be viewed with the prtconf command, as described in "The Openboot Device Tree — prtconf and prtdiag" on page 438. This tree is mirrored in the /devices and /dev directories; after hardware changes are made to the system, these directories must be reconfigured with the drvconfig, tapes, and disks commands that are run automatically whenever you do a boot -r. The file /etc/path_to_inst maps hardware addresses to symbolic device names. An extract from a simple configuration with the symbolic names added is shown in Figure 14-10.

When a large number of disks are configured, it is important to know this mapping so that iostat and related commands can be related to the output from df. In Solaris 2.6 and later, this mapping is done for you by the -n option to iostat. For earlier releases, you need to do it yourself or use the SE toolkit disks.se command described in "disks.se" on page 479. The sbus@1 part tells you which SBus is used (an E10000 can have up to 32 separate SBuses); the esp@0 part tells you which SBus slot the esp controller (one of the many types of SCSI controller) is in. The sd@0 part tells you that this is SCSI target address 0. The /dev/dsk/c0t0d0s2 device name indicates SCSI target 0 on SCSI controller 0 and is a symbolic link to a hardware specification similar to that found in /etc/path_to_inst. The extra :c at the end of the name in /devices corresponds to the s2 at the end of the name in /dev. Slice s0 is partition :a, s1 is :b, s2 is :c, and so forth.

Figure 14-10 Mapping Solaris 2 Device Nicknames into Full Names

```
% more /etc/path_to_inst
. . .
"/fd@1,f7200000" 0                               fd0
"/sbus@1,f8000000/esp@0,800000/sd@3,0" 3         sd3
"/sbus@1,f8000000/esp@0,800000/sd@0,0" 0         sd0
"/sbus@1,f8000000/esp@0,800000/sd@1,0" 1         sd1
```

```
% iostat -x
                               extended disk statistics
disk    r/s  w/s   Kr/s    Kw/s wait actv  svc_t   %w   %b
fd0     0.0  0.0   0.0     0.0  0.0  0.0    0.0     0    0
sd0     0.1  0.1   0.4     0.8  0.0  0.0    49.3    0    1
sd1     0.1  0.0   0.8     0.1  0.0  0.0    49.0    0    0
sd3     0.1  0.1   0.6     0.8  0.0  0.0    75.7    0    1
```

```
% df -k
Filesystem           kbytes    used    avail capacity  Mounted on
/dev/dsk/c0t3d0s0     19107    13753    3444    80%     /            sd3
/dev/dsk/c0t3d0s6     56431    46491    4300    92%     /usr         sd3
/proc                    0        0       0     0%      /proc
fd                       0        0       0     0%      /dev/fd¹
swap                  2140       32    2108     1%      /tmp
/dev/dsk/c0t3d0s5     19737    17643     124    99%     /opt         sd3
/dev/dsk/c0t1d0s6     95421    71221   14660    83%  /usr/openwin    sd1
/dev/dsk/c0t0d0s2    308619   276235    1524    99%     /export      sd0
```

1. /dev/fd is a file descriptor filesystem type, nothing to do with floppy disks!

```
% ls -l /dev/dsk/c0t0d0s2
lrwxrwxrwx   1 root               51 Jun   6 15:59 /dev/dsk/c0t0d0s2 ->
../../devices/sbus@1,f8000000/esp@0,800000/sd@0,0:c
```

A Command Script to Do It for You

The csh/nawk script presented in Figure 14-11 can be used to print out the device-to-nickname mappings. Enter it with three long command lines starting with set, if, and nawk— it doesn't work if you try to use multiple lines or backslash continuation.

Figure 14-11 Whatdev: *Device to Nickname Mapping Script*

```
#!/bin/csh
# print out the drive name - st0 or sd0 - given the /dev entry
# first get something like "/iommu/.../.../sd@0,0"
set dev = `/bin/ls -l $1 | nawk '{ n = split($11, a, "/");
split(a[n],b,":"); for(i = 4; i < n; i++) printf("/%s",a[i]);
printf("/%s\n", b[1]) }'`
if ( $dev == "" ) exit
# then get the instance number and concatenate with the "sd"
nawk -v dev=$dev '$1 ~ dev { n = split(dev, a, "/"); split(a[n], \
b, "@"); printf("%s%s\n", b[1], $2) }' /etc/path_to_inst
```

An example of its use:

```
% foreach device (/dev/dsk/c*t*d*s2)
> echo -n $device " ---- "
> whatdev $device
> end
/dev/dsk/c0t3d0s2  ---- sd3
/dev/dsk/c0t5d0s2  ---- sd5
```

Metric Collection Interfaces 15

There are many sources of performance information in Solaris; this chapter gives detailed examples that show how to get at all the available data.

Standards and Implementations

There are well-defined, portable standards for the many Unix programming interfaces. The System V Interface Definition, POSIX, and X/Open Unix95 all tie down various aspects of the system so that application programs can be moved among systems by recompilation. Beneath these interfaces lie implementations that have a common ancestry but that are diverging rapidly as each Unix vendor seeks to gain a feature, performance, or scalability advantage. Although the interface is well defined, the performance-oriented behavior and limitations are not closely defined. For management of the performance of an implementation, implementation-specific metrics are collected and provided to performance management tools. Some of these metrics, especially those rooted in physical operations like network packet counts, are well defined and portable. Other metrics vary according to the underlying hardware, for example, collision counts, which are under-reported by some Ethernet interfaces and don't exist for FDDI. Some metrics monitor software abstractions, such as transmit buffer availability, that can vary from one operating system to another or from one release of Solaris to the next.

By their nature, performance management applications must be aware of the metrics and behavior of the underlying implementation. This necessity forces performance management applications to be among the least portable of all software packages. The problem is compounded by lack of standardization of the metric collection interfaces and common metric definitions. On top of all that, each vendor of performance tools collects a different subset of the available metrics and stores them in a proprietary format. It is very hard to use one vendor's tool to analyze or browse data collected with a different vendor's tool.

15

The X/Open Universal Measurement Architecture Standard

The X/Open UMA standard attempts to define a commonality for metrics measurements: the UMA Data Pool Definition (DPD), a common set of metrics; the UMA Data Capture Interface (DCI), a common collection interface; and the UMA Measurement Layer Interface (MLI), a common way for applications to read data.

I personally worked on the DPD to make sure that it contains portable, well-defined, and useful metrics. However, I think the DPD metrics are too low level, based mainly on the raw kernel counters; it would be better to collect and store per-second rates for many metrics together with higher-level health and status indicators that would be far more portable. Still, if you ever decide to build a tool from scratch, the Data Pool Definition does summarize what is common across all Unix implementations and a set of extensions to raise the bar somewhat. The nearest thing to a full implementation of the final Data Pool Definition is a prototype for Solaris written in SE, which Graham Hazel wrote for me.

I am less keen on the two interfaces—they seem more complex than they should be. While there are reference implementations of both, the reference DCI is implemented on a Hitachi version of OSF/1, which does not have an MLI to go with it, and the reference MLI is implemented in the Amdahl AUMA product, which does not use a DCI interface and is based on a prerelease of the standard. I personally think that an interface based on a Java Remote Method Invocation (RMI) would be more portable and useful than the DCI and MLI.

In the end, though, there has not been enough interest or demand to give vendors a good business case to make the difficult move from their own formats and interfaces.

The Application Resource Measurement Standard

The ARM standard aims to instrument application response times. The hope is that by tagging each ARM call with a transaction identifier and tracking these transactions as they move from system to system, we can measure end-to-end response time. When a user transaction slows down for whatever reason, the system in the end-to-end chain of measurements that shows the biggest increase in response time can be pinpointed.

This plan sounds very useful, and there is both good news and bad news about ARM. The good news is that all vendors support the one standard, and several implementations exist, from HP and Tivoli (who jointly invented the standard) and, more recently, BGS. The bad news is that to measure user response time, application code must be instrumented and sophisticated tools are needed to handle the problems of distributed transaction tracking. There does seem to be some interest from the application vendors, and over time, more measurements will become available.

To encourage this effort, tell your application and database vendors that you want them to instrument their code according to ARM so that you can manage user response times more effectively.

Solaris 2 Native Metric Interfaces

Solaris 2 provides many interfaces to supply performance and status metrics. The SE Toolkit provides a convenient way to get at the data and use it, but if you want to implement your own measurement code, you need to know how to program to the interfaces directly from C code. Richard Pettit, the author of the SE language, contributed the following sections that explain how to program to the "kvm," "kstat," "mib", and "ndd" interfaces used by SE. I added information on processes, trace probes, the rstat protocol, and configuration information.

The Traditional Kernel Memory Interface

The kvm library is the legacy interface for accessing kernel data in SunOS. Although it was available in SunOS 4.x, it is still not a library widely used by other Unix operating systems. The name stands for "kernel virtual memory," which provides the data on which the library operates. This data takes the form of variables that provide feedback regarding the state of the operating system. From this data, you can extrapolate information regarding the relative performance of the computer. Performance analysis applications such as vmstat originally used this interface.

The kvm library provides a robust interface to accessing data within the address space of an operating system. This access includes a running operating system or the disk image of a dump of a running kernel, such as the result of a system crash. The files from which this data is read include the "core file" and the "swap file"; these files accommodate the situations when data to be read is no longer present in physical memory but has been written to the swap file, as is the case when the user area (u-area) of an application program is read—one of the capabilities of the kvm library.

On a system without a kvm library, you can create a simplified version of the library by opening the file /dev/kmem, which is a character special file that provides user-level access to kernel memory. You can retrieve symbols and their addresses within kernel memory by searching the name list of the operating system. Then, you can use the address of a variable as an offset to the lseek system call once /dev/kmem has been opened. The value of the variable can then be retrieved by the read system call. Data can also be written by means of the write system call, although this capability is quite dangerous and you should avoid using it. Instead, use system utilities that are designed specifically for modifying tunable parameters in the kernel.

An application program needs to know about the type and size of the variable being read from the kernel. Thus, this type of program is nonportable—not only to other Unix systems but even between releases of Solaris. The specifics of the internals of the operating system are not guaranteed to remain the same between releases. Only the documented interfaces such as the Device Driver Interface and Driver Kernel Interface (DDI/DKI) are obliged to remain consistent across releases.

The "kvm" interface exposes the kernel data types to the application. When a 64-bit address space capability is added to Solaris, the kernel data types will include 64-bit addresses, and applications that still want to access kvm in this environment will have to be compiled in 64-bit mode. These applications include many performance tool data collectors.

Symbols

Variables in the kernel are the same as those in an application program. They have a type, a size, and an address within the memory of the running program, this program being the operating system. The library call for extracting this information from a binary is nlist. The declaration for nlist from nlist.h is

```
extern int nlist(const char *namelist, struct nlist *nl);
```

The first parameter is the path name of a binary to be searched for symbols. The second parameter is an array of struct nlist, which contains the names of the symbols to be searched for. This array is terminated with a name value of zero.

Figure 15-1 shows the declaration of the nlist structure from nlist.h. Figure 15-2 is an example declaration of an array of nlist structures to be passed to the nlist library call.

Figure 15-1 The nlist Structure Declaration

```
struct nlist {
        char            *n_name;        /* symbol name */
        long            n_value;        /* value of symbol */
        short           n_scnum;        /* section number */
        unsigned short  n_type;         /* type and derived type */
        char            n_sclass;       /* storage class */
        char            n_numaux;       /* number of aux. entries */
};
```

Note that in Figure 15-2, the only member of the aggregate that has an initialization value is the n_name member. This is the only a priori value and is all that is required for the library call to do its job.

Figure 15-2 Example Declaration Ready for nlist Call

```
static struct nlist nl[] = {
        {"maxusers"},
        { 0            }
};
```

Once the call to nlist is successful, the n_value member will contain the address of the variable that can be used as the offset value to the lseek system call. Figure 15-3 shows the example call to nlist.

Figure 15-3 Call to nlist

```
if (nlist("/dev/ksyms", nl) == -1) {
        perror("nlist");
        exit(1);
}
```

In Figure 15-3, the name of the binary specified is actually a character special file that allows access to an ELF (executable and linking format) memory image containing the symbol and string table of the running kernel. This interface allows access to symbols of loadable device drivers whose symbols would not appear in the /kernel/genunix binary but are present in the running kernel. To illustrate, create a local version of the kernel symbols by copying with dd and inspect the resulting binary (this example used Solaris x86) by using the file and nm commands.

```
# dd if=/dev/ksyms of=ksyms.dump bs=8192
# file ksyms.dump
ksyms.dump: ELF 32-bit LSB executable 80386 Version 1, statically linked,
not stripped
# /usr/ccs/bin/nm ksyms.dump | egrep '(Shndx|maxusers)'
[Index]   Value       Size     Type  Bind  Other Shndx    Name
[6705]  |0xe0518174|0x00000004|OBJT |GLOB |0    |ABS     |maxusers
```

The value field of 0xe0518174 represents the address of the maxusers variable and the offset value passed to lseek. You will see this again in the complete example program.

15

Extracting the Values

We have laid the foundation for retrieving the data from kernel memory, and now we can undertake the business of seeking and reading. First, we need a file descriptor. Opening /dev/kmem is not for the average user, though. This character special file is readable only by root or the group sys. And only root may write to /dev/kmem. Figure 15-4 shows the complete demo program.

Figure 15-4 Accessing Kernel Data Without the kvm Library

```
/* compile with -lelf */

#include <stdio.h>
#include <stdlib.h>
#include <unistd.h>
#include <fcntl.h>
#include <nlist.h>

main()
{
int fd;
int maxusers;
static struct nlist nl[] = {
    { "maxusers" },
    { 0          }
};

/* retrieve symbols from the kernel */
if (nlist("/dev/ksyms", nl) == -1) {
    perror("nlist");
    exit(1);
}
/* open kernel memory, read-only */
fd = open("/dev/kmem", O_RDONLY);
if (fd == -1) {
    perror("open");
    exit(1);
}
/* seek to the specified kernel address */
if (lseek(fd, nl[0].n_value, 0) == -1) {
    perror("lseek");
    exit(1);
}
/* read the value from kernel memory */
if (read(fd, &maxusers, sizeof maxusers) == -1) {
    perror("read");
    exit(1);
```

Figure 15-4 Accessing Kernel Data Without the kvm Library (Continued)

```
    }
    /* print and done */
    printf("maxusers(0x%x) = %d\n", nl[0].n_value, maxusers);
    close(fd);
    exit(0);
    }
```

The read system call provides the address of the maxusers local variable as the buffer into which the value of kernel variable is read. The size provided is the size of the variable itself. When this program is compiled and run, the output is:

```
    maxusers(0xe0518174) = 16
```

Once again, the address 0xe0518174 appears. This value is the same as that provided by the nm command when it is searching the local ksyms file.

Now we can translate the logic followed by this program into the equivalent functionality by using the kvm library.

Using libkvm

The facilities presented in the previous example program are the low-level mechanisms for accessing data within the running kernel. This same code can be used on other Unix systems to retrieve data from the running kernel, although the kernel variables will obviously be different. The kvm library removes some of the system knowledge from the application program, so the coding of /dev/ksyms and /dev/kmem into the program are not necessary. The library also has all of the necessary character special files open and kept within the kvm "cookie" so that all necessary accesses can be accomplished by passing this cookie to the kvm functions.

The initial step is to call the open function, kvm_open. This function can be passed a number of null values for path names. When null values are passed, kvm_open will use default values that represent the currently running system. Remember that the kvm library can also be used to examine crash dumps, so you can specify a kmem image, such as a crash dump image, instead of the running system image in /dev/kmem. The prototype for the kvm_open function with parameter names and comments added is:

```
extern kvm_t *kvm_open(char *namelist, // e.g., /dev/ksyms
   char *corefile, // e.g., /dev/kmem
   char *swapfile, // the current swap file
   int flag,       // O_RDONLY or O_RDWR
   char *errstr);  // error prefix string
```

The `swapfile` parameter is useful only when you are examining a running system and then only if the `kvm_getu` function is used to examine the u-area of a process.

An example of the use of `kvm_open` with the default values is shown in Figure 15-5.

Figure 15-5 Example Use of kvm_open with Default Values

```
        kvm_t    *kd;

        /* open kvm */
        kd = kvm_open(0, 0, 0, O_RDONLY, 0);
        if (kd == 0) {
                perror("kvm_open");
                exit(1);
        }
```

With this usage, the values for the running system become implementation dependent and are not included in the application program. The cookie returned by `kvm_open` is reused for all of the kvm library functions, and among the data it contains are file descriptors for the core file and swap file.

The `kvm_nlist` function looks the same as the `nlist` function with the exception that it uses the kvm cookie instead of a file descriptor. The return value is the same and the resulting `nlist` structure is the same. Figure 15-6 shows the call to `kvm_nlist`.

Figure 15-6 Call to kvm_nlist

```
        /* use the kvm interface for nlist */
        if (kvm_nlist(kd, nl) == -1) {
                perror("kvm_nlist");
                exit(1);
        }
```

The final step is the use of `kvm_kread`. This example differs from the non-kvm example program in that it involves no explicit seek. Instead, the address of the kernel variable is included as a parameter to the `kvm_kread` call. `kvm_kread` is responsible for seeking to the correct offset and reading the data of the specified size. Figure 15-7 shows the call to `kvm_kread`, and Figure 15-8 shows the example program in its entirety.

Figure 15-7 Call to kvm_kread

```
        /* a read from the kernel */
        if (kvm_kread(kd, nl[0].n_value,
                        (char *) &maxusers, sizeof maxusers) == -1) {
                perror("kvm_kread");
                exit(1);
        }
```

Figure 15-8 Simple Application That Uses the kvm Library

```
/* compile with -lkvm -lelf */

#include <stdio.h>
#include <stdlib.h>
#include <fcntl.h>
#include <kvm.h>

main()
{
kvm_t*kd;
int maxusers;
static struct nlist nl[] = {
    { "maxusers" },
    { 0            }
};

/* open kvm */
kd = kvm_open(0, 0, 0, O_RDONLY, 0);
if (kd == 0) {
    perror("kvm_open");
    exit(1);
}
/* use the kvm interface for nlist */
if (kvm_nlist(kd, nl) == -1) {
    perror("kvm_nlist");
    exit(1);
}
    /* a read from the kernel */
if (kvm_kread(kd, nl[0].n_value,
        (char *) &maxusers, sizeof maxusers) == -1) {
    perror("kvm_kread");
    exit(1);
}
    /* print and done */
printf("maxusers(0x%x) = %d\n", nl[0].n_value, maxusers);
kvm_close(kd);
exit(0);
}
```

As expected, the output of this program is the same as that of the previous one. Running truss on this program will show some extra work being done because the kvm library assumes that any of the kvm functions may be called and a search of the swap file may be required. Nonetheless, this example, although still desperately lacking in portability because of the low-level nature of the subject matter, is more portable across releases of Solaris since the details of interfacing to the operating system are left to the library.

Procs and U-Areas

The reason the kvm library opens the swap area is so user application images can be accessed as well as the kernel image. The kernel cannot be swapped out, but the user-level applications can. If an application does get swapped out, the kvm library can find the image in the swap area.

The second example program used the kvm_kread call to read the kernel memory. You can use the kvm_uread call to read user memory. In order for this command to work, make a call to the kvm_getu function so that the kvm library knows what u-area to read from. The kvm_getu function needs a struct proc * as an argument, so call the kvm_getproc function first. The prototypes for these functions are:

```
extern struct proc *kvm_getproc(kvm_t *kd, int pid);
extern struct user *kvm_getu(kvm_t *kd, struct proc *procp);
```

The third example program uses a combination of calls from the first two programs as well as the kvm_getproc and kvm_getu functions. The example shows how to read the address space of a user application, using the kvm library.

Since the address space of a user application rather than the kernel will be read from, we cannot use the kvm_nlist function since it searches the name list of the kernel. The name list of the user application needs to be searched, so we use the nlist function directly. Figure 15-9 shows the third example.

Figure 15-9 Use of the kvm_getproc and kvm_getu Functions

```
/* compile with -lkvm -lelf */

#include <stdio.h>
#include <stdlib.h>
#include <fcntl.h>
#include <kvm.h>
#include <sys/proc.h>
#include <sys/user.h>

intglobal_value = 0xBEEFFACE;

main()
{
int local_value;
kvm_t*kd;
```

Figure 15-9 Use of the kvm_getproc and kvm_getu Functions (Continued)

```
      pid_tpid = getpid();
      struct proc *proc;
      struct user *u;
      static struct nlist nl[] = {
          { "global_value" },
          { 0                 }
      };

      /* open kvm */
      kd = kvm_open(0, 0, 0, O_RDONLY, 0);
      if (kd == 0) {
          perror("kvm_open");
          exit(1);
      }
      /* use nlist to retrieve symbols from the a.out binary */
      if (nlist("a.out", nl) == -1) {
          perror("nlist");
          exit(1);
      }
      /* get the proc structure for this process id */
      proc = kvm_getproc(kd, pid);
      if (proc == 0) {
          perror("kvm_getproc");
          exit(1);
      }
      /* get the u-area */
      u = kvm_getu(kd, proc);
      if (u == 0) {
          perror("kvm_getu");
          exit(1);
      }
      /* read from the u-area */
      if (kvm_uread(kd, nl[0].n_value,
          (char *) &local_value, sizeof local_value) == -1) {
          perror("kvm_uread");
          exit(1);
      }
      /* print and done */
      printf("global_value(0x%x) = 0x%X\n",
          nl[0].n_value, local_value);
      kvm_close(kd);
      exit(0);
      }
```

The output of the program is

```
global_value(0x8049bbc) = 0xBEEFFACE
```

For further verification of the value, we use the nm command to look up the value of global_value in the a.out file, yielding

```
[Index]    Value          Size    Type  Bind  Other Shndx Name
[56]    |0x08049bbc|0x00000004|OBJT  |GLOB |0     |17    |global_value
```

which shows the value field as 0x08049bbc, the same as printed out by the example program.

Other Functions

The remaining functions in the kvm library concern the traversal and viewing of information about processes on the system. The process traversal functions are kvm_setproc and get_nextproc. kvm_getproc is also in this category but has been covered specifically by the third example program. Prototypes for these functions are:

```
extern int kvm_setproc(kvm_t *kd);
extern struct proc *kvm_nextproc(kvm_t *kd);
extern int kvm_getcmd(kvm_t *kd, struct proc *procp, struct user *up, char
***argp, char ***envp);
```

The kvm_setproc function acts as a rewind function for setting the logical "pointer" to the beginning of the list of processes. The kvm_nextproc function simply retrieves the next process on this logical list.

The function kvm_getcmd retrieves the calling arguments and the environment strings for the process specified by the parameters to the function.

These functions can be used together to build an application that works much like the ps command. The fourth example in Figure 15-10 shows how to do this.

Figure 15-10 Use of kvm_nextproc and kvm_getcmd

```
/* compile with -D_KMEMUSER -lkvm -lelf */

#include <stdio.h>
#include <stdlib.h>
#include <fcntl.h>
#include <kvm.h>
#include <sys/proc.h>
#include <sys/user.h>
```

Figure 15-10 Use of `kvm_nextproc` *and* `kvm_getcmd` *(Continued)*

```
main()
{
char**argv = 0;
char**env = 0;
int i;
kvm_t*kd;
struct pid pid;
struct proc *proc;
struct user *u;

/* open kvm */
kd = kvm_open(0, 0, 0, O_RDONLY, 0);
if (kd == 0) {
    perror("kvm_open");
    exit(1);
}
/* "rewind" the get-process "pointer" */
if (kvm_setproc(kd) == -1) {
    perror("kvm_setproc");
    exit(1);
}
/* get the next proc structure */
while((proc = kvm_nextproc(kd)) != 0) {
    /* kvm_kread the pid structure */
    if (kvm_kread(kd, (unsigned long) proc->p_pidp,
            (char *) &pid, sizeof pid) == -1) {
        perror("kvm_kread");
        exit(1);
    }
    /* reassign with the user space version */
    proc->p_pidp = &pid;

    /* get the u-area for this process */
    u = kvm_getu(kd, proc);
    if (u == 0) {
        /* zombie */
        if (proc->p_stat == SZOMB)
        printf("%6d <defunct>\n",
            proc->p_pidp->pid_id);
        continue;
    }
    /* read the command line info */
    if (kvm_getcmd(kd, proc, u, &argv, &env) == -1) {
        /* insufficient permission */
        printf("%6d %s\n",
```

Figure 15-10 Use of `kvm_nextproc` *and* `kvm_getcmd` *(Continued)*

```
                proc->p_pidp->pid_id, u->u_comm);
                continue;
        }
        /* got what we need, now print it out */
        printf("%6d ", proc->p_pidp->pid_id);
        for(i=0; argv && argv[i]; i++)
            printf("%s ", argv[i]);
        /* need to free this value, malloc'ed by kvm_getcmd */
        free(argv);
        argv = 0;

        /* now print the environment strings */
        for(i=0; env && env[i]; i++)
            printf("%s ", env[i]);
        /* need to free this value, malloc'ed by kvm_getcmd */
        free(env);
        env = 0;
        putchar('\n');
    }
    /* done */
    kvm_close(kd);
    exit(0);
    }
```

Caveats

Extracting data from a running kernel can present problems that may not be evident to the uninitiated. Here are some of the issues that may arise during use of the kvm library.

- Permission

  The files that need to be opened within the kvm library have permissions that permit only specific users to access them. If the kvm_open call fails with "permission denied," you've run into this situation.

- 64-bit pointers in future releases

  If the kernel is using 64-bit pointers, so must a user of the kvm library. See "64-bit Addressing" on page 138.

- Concurrency

  Since the SunOS 5.x kernel is a multithreaded operating system, data structures within the kernel have locks associated with them to prevent the modification of an area of memory in parallel by two or more threads. This locking is in contrast to the monolithic operating system architecture that used elevated or masked processor interrupt levels to protect critical regions.

  This issue illuminates a shortcoming of accessing kernel memory from the user space as demonstrated by these examples. There is no mechanism whereby a user-level application can lock a data structure in the kernel so that it is not changed while being accessed and thereby cause the read to yield inaccurate data. This is, of course, a necessary precaution since a user-level application could lock a kernel data structure indefinitely and cause deadlock or starvation.

- Pointers within data

  A common error in reading kernel data with kvm is to assume when reading structures with kvm_kread that all associated data has been read with it. If the structure read with kvm_kread contains a pointer, the data that it points at is not read. It must be read with another call to kvm_kread. This problem will manifest itself quickly with a segmentation violation. Figure 15-11 shows how to read the platform name from the root node of the devinfo tree.

Figure 15-11 Reading Pointers Within Pointers

```
/* compile with -lkvm -lelf */

#include <stdio.h>
#include <stdlib.h>
#include <fcntl.h>
#include <kvm.h>
#include <nlist.h>
#include <sys/dditypes.h>
#include <sys/ddidmareq.h>
#include <sys/ddi_impldefs.h>

main()
{
char    name_buf[BUFSIZ];
kvm_t   *kd;
caddr_t top_devinfo;
struct dev_inforoot_node;
static struct nlist nl[] = {
    { "top_devinfo" },
    { 0              }
};
```

Figure 15-11 Reading Pointers Within Pointers (Continued)

```
    /* open kvm */
    kd = kvm_open(0, 0, 0, O_RDONLY, 0);
    if (kd == 0) {
        perror("kvm_open");
        exit(1);
    }
    /* get the address of top_devinfo */
    if (kvm_nlist(kd, nl) == -1) {
        perror("kvm_nlist");
        exit(1);
    }
    /* read the top_devinfo value, which is an address */
    if (kvm_kread(kd, nl[0].n_value,
        (char *) &top_devinfo, sizeof top_devinfo) == -1) {
        perror("kvm_kread: top_devinfo");
        exit(1);
    }
    /* use this address to read the root node of the devinfo tree */
    if (kvm_kread(kd, (unsigned long) top_devinfo,
        (char *) &root_node, sizeof root_node) == -1) {
        perror("kvm_kread: root_node");
        exit(1);
    }
    /* the devinfo structure contains a pointer to a string */
    if (kvm_kread(kd, (unsigned long) root_node.devi_binding_name,
        name_buf, sizeof name_buf) == -1) {
        perror("kvm_kread: devi_binding_name");
        exit(1);
    }
    /* finally! */
    puts(name_buf);
    kvm_close(kd);
    exit(0);
    }
```

Summary

We have laid out all the necessary tools for accessing kernel data. The remaining piece is knowing what data is useful for extraction. This information changes between different Unix systems and, for many cases, between releases of Solaris. The header files in /usr/include/sys define many of the data structures and variables in the kernel, but it is generally a bad idea to use kvm nowadays. There is a far better alternative, which we describe next.

The Solaris 2 "`kstat`" Interface

The `kstat` library is a collection of functions for accessing data stored within user-level data structures that are copies of similar structures in the kernel. The nature of this data concerns the functioning of the operating system, specifically in the areas of performance metrics, device configuration, and capacity measurement. The name *kstat* means "kernel statistics" to denote this role.

The collection of structures, both in user space and in the kernel, is referred to as the `kstat` chain. This chain is a linked list of structures. The user chain is accessible through the `kstat` library, and the kernel chain is accessible through the `/dev/kstat` character special file. The sum of the components is referred to as the `kstat` framework.

The `kstat` framework, shown in Figure 15-12, consists of the kernel chain, a loadable device driver that acts as the liaison between the kernel chain and the user chain, the user chain, and the `kstat` library, which acts as the liaison between the user chain and the application program.

Figure 15-12 The `kstat` Framework

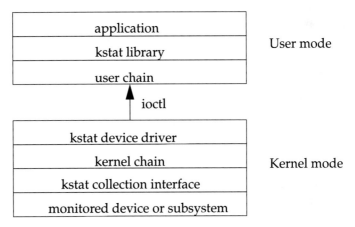

The library and driver within the kernel are tightly coupled. When the `kstat` library sends an `ioctl` request to the driver to read `kstat` data, the driver can lock the appropriate data structures to ensure consistency of the data being read. This point is important since the reading of data that is being written simultaneously by another kernel thread could result in incorrect data being transmitted to the user space.

☰ 15

Link Structure

Each link in the `kstat` chain represents a functional component such as inode cache statistics. A link is identified by three values:

- Module — A functional area such as a class or category.

- Instance number — A numerical occurrence of this module.

- Name — The text name for the link; an example of the names of two Lance Ethernet devices on a machine is:
  - le.0.le0
  - le.1.le1

The dots connecting the parts are for notational convenience and do not have any relation to the full name. In this case, the category is `le`, the instance numbers are 0 and 1, and the names are the concatenation of the module and instance, `le0` and `le1`. The juxtaposition of the module and instance to form the name is neither uniform nor mandatory.

`kstat` Data Types

Each link in the chain has a pointer to the data for that link. The pointer does not point to one uniform structure. A type field within the link describes what the pointer is pointing at. The types and the type of data being pointed to are one of five different types:

- `KSTAT_TYPE_RAW` — Points to a C structure that is cast to the appropriate structure pointer type and indirected as a structure pointer.

- `KSTAT_TYPE_NAMED` — Points to an array of structures that contain a name and polymorphic value represented by a union and type flag. The supported types for the union in releases prior to Solaris 2.6 are:

  KSTAT_DATA_CHAR 1-byte integer signed

  KSTAT_DATA_LONG 4-byte integer signed

  KSTAT_DATA_ULONG 4-byte integer unsigned

  KSTAT_DATA_LONGLONG 8-byte integer signed

  KSTAT_DATA_ULONGLONG 8-byte integer unsigned

  KSTAT_DATA_FLOAT 4-byte floating point

  KSTAT_DATA_DOUBLE 8-byte floating point

The types in Solaris 2.6 and later releases are:

KSTAT_DATA_CHAR1-byte integer signed

KSTAT_DATA_INT324-byte integer signed

KSTAT_DATA_UINT324-byte integer unsigned

KSTAT_DATA_INT648-byte integer signed

KSTAT_DATA_UINT648-byte integer unsigned

The LONG, ULONG, LONGLONG, and ULONGLONG names are maintained for portability but are obsolete. Since the FLOAT and DOUBLE types were never used, they have been deleted. These new values are explicitly portable between 32-bit and 64-bit kernel implementations.

- KSTAT_TYPE_INTR — Points to a structure containing information pertaining to interrupts.

- KSTAT_TYPE_IO — Points to a structure containing information pertaining to I/O devices, disks, and, in Solaris 2.6, disk partitions, tape drives, and NFS client mount points. Also, with Solstice DiskSuite version 4.1 and later, metadevices will appear here.

- KSTAT_TYPE_TIMER — The representation of this type is the same as that for KSTAT_TYPE_NAMED.

A visual representation of the aforementioned `le` devices is shown in Figure 15-13.

Figure 15-13 `kstat` Chain Structure Example

```
ks_module   = "le"
  ks_instance = 0
  ks_name     = "le0"
  ks_type     = KSTAT_TYPE_NAMED
  ks_data     = {     /* array of structures */
                  {  /* first element of the array */
                    name      = "ipackets"
                    data_type = KSTAT_DATA_ULONG
                    value.ul  = 1112729
                  }
                  {  /* second element of the array */
                    name      = "ierrors"
                    data_type = KSTAT_DATA_ULONG
                    value.ul  = 10
                  }
              ... and so forth for the remaining members
                }
  ks_next
```

```
ks_module   = "le"
  ks_instance = 1
  ks_name     = "le1"
  ks_type     = KSTAT_TYPE_NAMED
  ks_data     = {
                  {
                    name      = "ipackets"
                    data_type = KSTAT_DATA_ULONG
                    value.ul  = 10224
                  }
                  {
                    name      = "ierrors"
                    data_type = KSTAT_DATA_ULONG
                    value.ul  = 0
                  }
              ... and so forth for the remaining members
                }
  ks_next    /* points to the next link in the chain */
```

The **kstat** Library

The programming model for accessing `kstat` data is:

- Open
- Traverse the `kstat` chain, reading any links of interest
- Close

Manual pages are available for the `kstat` library functions, starting with SunOS 5.4. The minimal set of `kstat` functions necessary for accessing `kstat` data from the chain are as follows.

The initial call to initialize the library, open the `/dev/kstat` device, and build the user chain:

```
extern kstat_ctl_t *kstat_open(void);
```

To read a link in the chain:.

```
extern kid_t kstat_read(kstat_ctl_t *kc, kstat_t *ksp, void *buf);
```

Reciprocal of `kstat_open`: to terminate `kstat` functions, release heap memory, and close the `/dev/kstat` device:

```
extern int kstat_close(kstat_ctl_t *kc);
```

Additional functions for accessing `kstat` data are the lookup functions.

To look up a specific link in the chain:

```
extern kstat_t *kstat_lookup(kstat_ctl_t *kc, char *ks_module, int
ks_instance, char *ks_name);
```

To look up a symbolic name within a `KSTAT_TYPE_NAMED` link.

```
extern void *kstat_data_lookup(kstat_t *ksp, char *name);
```

To synchronize the user chain with the kernel chain:.

```
extern kid_t kstat_chain_update(kstat_ctl_t *kc);
```

To write the `kstat` link back to the kernel, if possible:

```
extern kid_t kstat_write(kstat_ctl_t *kc, kstat_t *kp, void *buf);
```

You can use the `kstat_lookup` function to look up links in the chain by their explicit name. Use this function when access to a unique link is required. If the link being sought was `ufs.0.inode_cache`, this function would be convenient to use instead of writing the code to traverse the chain. In the case of a link representing a resource with multiple instances, such as network interfaces or disks, it is necessary to traverse the chain manually, searching for the module name of interest.

Use the function `kstat_data_lookup` to look up the name of a member of a `KSTAT_TYPE_NAMED` structure. The `KSTAT_TYPE_NAMED` links have a `kstat_data` member that points to an array of structures that represent the members of a structure. This function traverses the array, finds the structure with that name, and returns a pointer to it.

A minimal program for traversing the `kstat` chain is shown in Figure 15-14.

Figure 15-14 A Simple Program for Traversing the `kstat` Chain

```
/* compile with cc ex1.c -lkstat */

#include <stdio.h>
#include <stdlib.h>
#include <kstat.h>

main()
{
kstat_ctl_t*kc;
kstat_t *kp;
static char*type_names[] = { /* map ints to strings */
    "KSTAT_TYPE_RAW",
    "KSTAT_TYPE_NAMED",
    "KSTAT_TYPE_INTR",
    "KSTAT_TYPE_IO",
    "KSTAT_TYPE_TIMER"
};

/* initialize the kstat interface */
kc = kstat_open();
if (kc == 0) {
    perror("kstat_open");
    exit(1);
}
/* traverse the chain */
for (kp = kc->kc_chain; kp; kp = kp->ks_next)
    printf("%-16.16s %s.%d.%s\n", type_names[kp->ks_type],
        kp->ks_module, kp->ks_instance, kp->ks_name);
/* done */
kstat_close(kc);
return 0;
}
```

Reading the **kstat** Chain

By itself, `kstat_open` will construct the entire chain without reading the data for the individual links. If you need the data associated with a link, use `kstat_read` to read that data. Figure 15-17 uses `kstat_lookup`, `kstat_read`, and `kstat_data_lookup` to find the inode cache data and display the cache hit rate. Figure 15-18 shows the use of kstat_read and kstat_data_lookup to display the statistics of the le interfaces on the system.

Figure 15-15 Use of kstat_lookup and kstat_data_lookup

```
/* compile with cc ex2.c -lkstat */

#include <stdio.h>
#include <stdlib.h>
#include <kstat.h>

static ulong_t *get_named_member(kstat_t *, char *);

main()
{
kstat_ctl_t*kc;
kstat_t *kp;
ulong_t *hits;
ulong_t *misses;
ulong_t total;

/* initialize the kstat interface */
kc = kstat_open();
if (kc == 0) {
    perror("kstat_open");
    exit(1);
}
/* find the inode cache link */
kp = kstat_lookup(kc, "ufs", 0, "inode_cache");
if (kp == 0) {
    fputs("Cannot find ufs.0.inode_cache\n", stderr);
    exit(1);
}
/* read the ks_data */
if (kstat_read(kc, kp, 0) == -1) {
    perror("kstat_read");
    exit(1);
}
/* get pointers to the hits and misses values */
hits   = get_named_member(kp, "hits");
misses = get_named_member(kp, "misses");
total = *hits + *misses;

/* print the hit rate percentage */
printf("inode cache hit rate: %5.2f %%\n",
    ((double) *hits * 100.0) / (double) total);
```

Figure 15-15 Use of `kstat_lookup` *and* `kstat_data_lookup` *(Continued)*

```
    /* done */
    kstat_close(kc);
    return 0;
    }



    /* return a pointer to the value inside the kstat_named_t structure */
    static ulong_t *
    get_named_member(kstat_t *kp, char *name)
    {
    kstat_named_t*kn;

    kn = (kstat_named_t * ) kstat_data_lookup(kp, name);
    if (kn == 0) {
        fprintf(stderr, "Cannot find member: %s\n", name);
        exit(1);
    }
    return &kn->value.ul;
    }
```

Figure 15-16 Traversing the Chain, Looking for "`le`*" Devices*

```
    /* compile with cc ex3.c -lkstat */

    #include <stdio.h>
    #include <stdlib.h>
    #include <string.h>
    #include <kstat.h>

    static ulong_t *get_named_member(kstat_t *, char *);

    main()
    {
    ulong_t *ipackets;
    ulong_t *opackets;
    ulong_t *ierrors;
    ulong_t *oerrors;
    ulong_t *collisions;
    double  collision_rate;
    kstat_ctl_t*kc;
    kstat_t *kp;

    /* initialize the kstat interface */
    kc = kstat_open();
    if (kc == 0) {
```

Figure 15-16 Traversing the Chain, Looking for "le" Devices (Continued)

```
        perror("kstat_open");
        exit(1);
    }
    /* print the header */
    printf("%-8.8s %-10.10s %-10.10s %-10.10s %-10.10s %-10.10s %s\n",
        "Name", "Ipkts", "Ierrs",
        "Opkts", "Oerrs", "Collis", "Collis-Rate");

    /* traverse the chain looking for "module" name "le" */
    for (kp = kc->kc_chain; kp; kp = kp->ks_next) {
        /* only interested in named types */
        if (kp->ks_type != KSTAT_TYPE_NAMED)
            continue;
        /* only interested in "le" module names */
        if (strcmp(kp->ks_module, "le") != 0)
            continue;
        /* read ks_data */
        if (kstat_read(kc, kp, 0) == -1) {
            perror("kstat_read");
            exit(1);
        }
        /* get pointers to members of interest */
        ipackets   = get_named_member(kp, "ipackets");
        opackets   = get_named_member(kp, "opackets");
        ierrors    = get_named_member(kp, "ierrors");
        oerrors    = get_named_member(kp, "oerrors");
        collisions = get_named_member(kp, "collisions");

        /* compute and print */
        if (*opackets)
            collision_rate = (*collisions * 100) / *opackets;
        else
            collision_rate = 0.0;
        printf("%-8.8s %-10d %-10d %-10d %-10d %-10d %-5.2f %%\n",
            kp->ks_name, *ipackets, *ierrors,
            *opackets, *oerrors, *collisions, collision_rate);
    }

    /* done */
    kstat_close(kc);
    return 0;
    }

    /* return a pointer to the value inside the kstat_named_t structure */
    static ulong_t *
```

Figure 15-16 Traversing the Chain, Looking for "le" Devices (Continued)

```
get_named_member(kstat_t *kp, char *name)
{
kstat_named_t*kn;

kn = (kstat_named_t *) kstat_data_lookup(kp, name);
if (kn == 0) {
    fprintf(stderr, "Cannot find member: %s\n", name);
    exit(1);
}
return & kn->value.ul;
}
```

Figure 15-17 Use of `kstat_lookup` *and* `kstat_data_lookup`

```
/* compile with cc ex2.c -lkstat */

#include <stdio.h>
#include <stdlib.h>
#include <kstat.h>

static ulong_t *get_named_member(kstat_t *, char *);

main()
{
kstat_ctl_t*kc;
kstat_t *kp;
ulong_t *hits;
ulong_t *misses;
ulong_t total;

/* initialize the kstat interface */
kc = kstat_open();
if (kc == 0) {
    perror("kstat_open");
    exit(1);
}
/* find the inode cache link */
kp = kstat_lookup(kc, "ufs", 0, "inode_cache");
if (kp == 0) {
    fputs("Cannot find ufs.0.inode_cache\n", stderr);
    exit(1);
}
/* read the ks_data */
if (kstat_read(kc, kp, 0) == -1) {
    perror("kstat_read");
```

Figure 15-17 Use of `kstat_lookup` *and* `kstat_data_lookup` *(Continued)*

```
        exit(1);
    }
    /* get pointers to the hits and misses values */
    hits   = get_named_member(kp, "hits");
    misses = get_named_member(kp, "misses");
    total = *hits + *misses;

    /* print the hit rate percentage */
    printf("inode cache hit rate: %5.2f %%\n",
        ((double) *hits * 100.0) / (double) total);

    /* done */
    kstat_close(kc);
    return 0;
    }


    /* return a pointer to the value inside the kstat_named_t structure */
    static ulong_t *
    get_named_member(kstat_t *kp, char *name)
    {
    kstat_named_t*kn;

    kn = (kstat_named_t * ) kstat_data_lookup(kp, name);
    if (kn == 0) {
        fprintf(stderr, "Cannot find member: %s\n", name);
        exit(1);
    }
    return &kn->value.ul;
    }
```

Figure 15-18 Traversing the Chain, Looking for "1e" Devices

```
    /* compile with cc ex3.c -lkstat */

    #include <stdio.h>
    #include <stdlib.h>
    #include <string.h>
    #include <kstat.h>

    static ulong_t *get_named_member(kstat_t *, char *);

    main()
    {
    ulong_t *ipackets;
```

Figure 15-18 Traversing the Chain, Looking for "le" Devices (Continued)

```
    ulong_t *opackets;
    ulong_t *ierrors;
    ulong_t *oerrors;
    ulong_t *collisions;
    double  collision_rate;
    kstat_ctl_t*kc;
    kstat_t *kp;

    /* initialize the kstat interface */
    kc = kstat_open();
    if (kc == 0) {
        perror("kstat_open");
        exit(1);
    }
    /* print the header */
    printf("%-8.8s %-10.10s %-10.10s %-10.10s %-10.10s %-10.10s %s\n",
        "Name", "Ipkts", "Ierrs",
        "Opkts", "Oerrs", "Collis", "Collis-Rate");

    /* traverse the chain looking for "module" name "le" */
    for (kp = kc->kc_chain; kp; kp = kp->ks_next) {
        /* only interested in named types */
        if (kp->ks_type != KSTAT_TYPE_NAMED)
            continue;
        /* only interested in "le" module names */
        if (strcmp(kp->ks_module, "le") != 0)
            continue;
        /* read ks_data */
        if (kstat_read(kc, kp, 0) == -1) {
            perror("kstat_read");
            exit(1);
        }
        /* get pointers to members of interest */
        ipackets   = get_named_member(kp, "ipackets");
        opackets   = get_named_member(kp, "opackets");
        ierrors    = get_named_member(kp, "ierrors");
        oerrors    = get_named_member(kp, "oerrors");
        collisions = get_named_member(kp, "collisions");

        /* compute and print */
        if (*opackets)
            collision_rate = (*collisions * 100) / *opackets;
        else
            collision_rate = 0.0;
        printf("%-8.8s %-10d %-10d %-10d %-10d %-10d %-5.2f %%\n",
```

Figure 15-18 Traversing the Chain, Looking for "1e" Devices (Continued)

```
                kp->ks_name, *ipackets, *ierrors,
                *opackets, *oerrors, *collisions, collision_rate);
    }

    /* done */
    kstat_close(kc);
    return 0;
    }

    /* return a pointer to the value inside the kstat_named_t structure */
    static ulong_t *
    get_named_member(kstat_t *kp, char *name)
    {
    kstat_named_t*kn;

    kn = (kstat_named_t *) kstat_data_lookup(kp, name);
    if (kn == 0) {
        fprintf(stderr, "Cannot find member: %s\n", name);
        exit(1);
    }
    return & kn->value.ul;
    }
```

The above examples show how to obtain a link in the kstat chain, read it, look up values, and display information regarding the kstat data. But this sequence of operations is done only once. In the case of programs such as vmstat, iostat, and mpstat, the output is continually displayed on a regular interval. When this regular display is done, the function kstat_chain_update must be called before every access to ensure that the user chain matches the kernel chain. Since these examples use pointers to values inside of a structure of type kstat_named_t, it is possible that the pointer references a value inside a structure that is no longer valid since the user chain may have changed in response to the modified kernel chain. When this situation happens, the pointers must be reinitialized to reflect the new user chain. Figure 15-19 demonstrates the use of kstat_chain_update.

Figure 15-19 Use of kstat_chain_update

```
    /* compile with -lkstat */

    #include <stdio.h>
    #include <unistd.h>
    #include <stdlib.h>
    #include <kstat.h>
```

Figure 15-19 Use of `kstat_chain_update` *(Continued)*

```
#define MINUTES    60
#define HOURS     (60 * MINUTES)
#define DAYS      (24 * HOURS)

static kstat_t *build_kstats(kstat_ctl_t *);
static ulong_t *get_named_member(kstat_t *, char *);

main()
{
int     i;
ulong_t *clk_intr;
ulong_t hz = sysconf(_SC_CLK_TCK);
ulong_t days;
ulong_t hours;
ulong_t minutes;
ulong_t seconds;
kstat_ctl_t *kc;
kstat_t *kp;

/* initialize the kstat interface */
kc = kstat_open();
if (kc == 0) {
    perror("kstat_open");
    exit(1);
}

/* get the link and read it in */
kp = build_kstats(kc);

/* get a pointer to the clk_intr member */
clk_intr = get_named_member(kp, "clk_intr");

/* do forever */
for (;;) {
    /* loop until kstat_chain_update returns zero */
    for (; (i = kstat_chain_update(kc)) != 0; ) {
        switch (i) {
        case -1:
        perror("kstat_chain_update");
        exit(1);
        default:
        /* state change, rebuild and reread */
        puts("<<<<<< STATE CHANGE >>>>>>");
        kp = build_kstats(kc);
        clk_intr = get_named_member(kp, "clk_intr");
```

Figure 15-19 Use of `kstat_chain_update` *(Continued)*

```
            break;
            }
        }
        /* compute and print */
        seconds = *clk_intr / hz;
        days = seconds / DAYS;
        seconds -= (days * DAYS);
        hours = seconds / HOURS;
        seconds -= (hours * HOURS);
        minutes = seconds / MINUTES;
        seconds -= (minutes * MINUTES);
        printf(
          "System up for %4d days %2d hours %2d minutes %2d seconds\r",
            days, hours, minutes, seconds);
        fflush(stdout);

        /* pause a second */
        sleep(1);

        /* update the link */
        if (kstat_read(kc, kp, 0) == -1) {
            perror("kstat_read");
            exit(1);
        }
    }
}

/* look up the link and read ks_data */
static kstat_t *
build_kstats(kstat_ctl_t *kc)
{
kstat_t*kp;

kp = kstat_lookup(kc, "unix", 0, "system_misc");
if (kp == 0) {
    fputs("Cannot find unix.0.system_misc\n", stderr);
    exit(1);
}
if (kstat_read(kc, kp, 0) == -1) {
    perror("kstat_read");
    exit(1);
}
return kp;
}
```

Figure 15-19 Use of `kstat_chain_update` *(Continued)*

```
/* return a pointer to the value inside the kstat_named_t structure */
static ulong_t *
get_named_member(kstat_t *kp, char *name)
{
kstat_named_t*kn;

kn = (kstat_named_t *) kstat_data_lookup(kp, name);
if (kn == 0) {
    fprintf(stderr, "Cannot find member: %s\n", name);
    exit(1);
}
return &kn->value.ul;
}
```

Figure 15-19 continually displays how long the computer has been up by retrieving the `clk_intr` (clock interrupts) member from the `unix.0.system_misc` link. This code also uses the `sysconf` function to retrieve the value of `hz`, which is the number of times per second a clock interrupt is received by the operating system. By dividing `clk_intr` by `hz`, you can compute the number of seconds the system has been up.

Writing the `kstat` Chain

Since the user chain is a copy of the kernel chain, you can modify a link and write it back to the kernel. However, some factors determine whether the data will actually be written. The first determining factor is whether the writing process has the correct permissions Only the superuser can write data back to the kernel. The second factor is that the individual subsystem in the kernel holding the `kstat` data within that link must determine whether the data will actually be copied back to kernel space. Many of the subsystems that contribute data to the `kstat` chain do not allow data to be written back. One subsystem that does is NFS. The `nfsstat` command has a `-z` option that specifies reinitialization of the counters within NFS and RPC by means of the `kstat_write` command.

Caveats

The `kstat` library is not very complex at the user level. Here are some minor issues that you should know about.

- Permission

    The only `kstat` call that requires any level of permissions is `kstat_write`. Modification of kernel structures should not be taken lightly, and therefore, root permission is required. An advantage to `kstat_write` over similar methods using the kvm library is that the data is bounded. The subsystem holding the kstat values being written will receive the values to be written and put them away in an orderly fashion. kvm_kwrite, on the other hand, will allow arbitrary writes to any valid memory address.

- KSTAT_TYPE_RAW data structures

  The KSTAT_TYPE_RAW data type provides a pointer to a data structure in its binary form. There is an indication of the size of the data structure, but resolving what data structure is actually pointed to is up to the programmer.

- Chain updates

  Calling kstat_chain_update to synchronize the user and kernel chains can result in an indication to the application that the chain has changed. Be careful to discontinue using any prestored pointers into the old chain. If a referencing mechanism has been built around the chain, then if the call to kstat_chain_update indicates a change, the old referencing structure must be torn down and a new one built using the new chain.

Summary

The kstat library provides a lightweight and uniform method for accessing performance data in the Solaris 2, SunOS 5.x kernel. It is specific to SunOS but is provided on both platform-specific releases of SunOS: SPARC and Intel.

Network Protocol (MIB) Statistics via Streams

MIB data is information about a device on a network. MIB stands for management information base. This information provides feedback regarding the operation of a device, primarily throughput information but also more detailed information regarding the overall state of a device. It is the MIB data that is delivered through SNMP (Simple Network Management Protocol).

The purpose of this section is not to articulate how to read SNMP and disseminate it but to describe how the MIB data is retrieved by a process in a streams-based environment. Specifically, the Solaris implementation is covered, although in theory, this code should work on any streams-based Unix system. In effect, this is how an SNMP daemon for Solaris obtains its data.

The Streams Mechanism

Starting with Unix System 5, Release 3 (SVR3), the operating system contains a *streams* mechanism. This mechanism is a capability within the operating system whereby *modules* representing functional components are associated with each other within a stack data structure. Modules are pushed onto this stack, and when the stack of modules is built, data is passed to the module on the top of the stack; that module passes the data to the module under it. In turn, that module passes the data to the module under it, and so forth until the data reaches the first module that was pushed onto the stack. This stack of modules within the kernel is called a stream.

When data is sent from an application into the kernel to travel through a stream, the data is flowing *downstream*. Data flowing from the kernel back to user space is traveling *upstream*.

Since network protocols are also stack based, the streams model is an appropriate implementation vehicle. Data flows through each module of the network stack until it reaches either the device driver or the application.

As an example, Figure 15-20 shows the layering of the RSTATD protocol.

Figure 15-20 The RSTATD Protocol Stack

Layer	Protocol	Address Space
Application Session	RSTATD RPC	User Space
Transport Network	UDP IP	Kernel Space
Device Driver		

In this example, the first module pushed onto the stream would be the IP module, followed by the UPD module. When data is written onto this stream by the `rpc.rstatd` application, it will first go through the internals of the RPC library, which exists in user space. Then, it will enter kernel space to flow through the UDP module and then through the IP module. The IP module will hand off the data to the device driver for the Network Interface Card (NIC). This procedure is how the packet is built and encapsulated as it travels downstream. Figure 15-21 demonstrates the creation of a stream and the pushing and popping of several modules onto the stream.

Figure 15-21 Pushing, Popping, and Identifying Streams Modules

```
#include <stdio.h>
#include <fcntl.h>
#include <sys/stropts.h>
```

Figure 15-21 Pushing, Popping, and Identifying Streams Modules (Continued)

```c
#define DEV_TCP     "/dev/tcp"  /* use /dev/tcp, /dev/ip is 660 mode */
#define ARP_MODULE  "arp"
#define TCP_MODULE  "tcp"
#define UDP_MODULE  "udp"

static void
fatal(char *f, char *p)
{
charbuf[BUFSIZ];

sprintf(buf, f, p);
perror(buf);
exit(1);
}

main()
{
charbuf[BUFSIZ];
int mib_sd;

mib_sd = open(DEV_TCP, O_RDWR);
if (mib_sd == -1)
    fatal("cannot open %s", DEV_TCP);

/* empty the stream */
while (ioctl(mib_sd, I_POP, 0) != -1)    ;

/* load up the stream with all these modules */
if (ioctl(mib_sd, I_PUSH, ARP_MODULE) == -1)
    fatal("cannot push %s module", ARP_MODULE);
if (ioctl(mib_sd, I_PUSH, TCP_MODULE) == -1)
    fatal("cannot push %s module", TCP_MODULE);
if (ioctl(mib_sd, I_PUSH, UDP_MODULE) == -1)
    fatal("cannot push %s module", UDP_MODULE);

/* now unload them and print them out */
while (ioctl(mib_sd, I_LOOK, buf) != -1) {
    puts(buf);
    if (ioctl(mib_sd, I_POP, 0) == -1)
        fatal("ioctl(%s)", "I_POP");
}
close(mib_sd);
exit(0);
}
```

When this program is run, the output is:

```
% pushpop
udp
tcp
arp
```

This order is the reverse of how the modules were pushed, showing the last-in, first-out (LIFO) nature of the stream structure.

Option Management Requests

In addition to data that is to be written out to the network, control messages can be sent downstream to alter the way the modules in the stream do their job or to retrieve information from the modules. Control messages are general-purpose structures for sending arbitrary data to streams modules. A process sends a control message, and an acknowledgment is sent back to the process from the modules.

One of the control messages that can be sent downstream to the modules is an option management request. This type of control message is an informational packet to be delivered to specific modules in the stream. In the case of retrieving MIB data from the streams module, only a "get all" type of message is supported. Therefore, the control message for a "get" of MIB data is sent to all modules in the stream regardless of the type of MIB data requested.

When each module in the stream receives the MIB get request, it constructs a reply in the respective structure defined above for each protocol and sends the data back in an acknowledgment message. Hence, when a MIB get operation is performed, one write to the stream is performed, but N reads are performed, where N is the number of modules in the stream that can respond to this type of request. In the case of the NFS stack, there will be two responses, one from IP and the other from TCP or UDP. Usually, a stack is constructed for the single purpose of extracting MIB data from the modules that are maintaining a MIB structure.

MIB Structures in Solaris

The include file `/usr/include/inet/mib2.h` defines many structures that define the MIB in Solaris. Each structure is specific to a particular protocol and, in the streams sense, a streams module. The MIB structures currently defined are as follows.

For IP:

`mib2_ip`Throughput and operation

`mib2_ipAddrEntry`Addressing information

`mib2_ipRouteEntry`Routing table entries

`mib2_ipNetToMediaEntry`Logical to physical address mappings

For ICMP:

`mib2_icmp`Throughput and operation

For TCP:

`mib2_tcp`Throughput and operation

`mib2_tcpConnEntry`Table of TCP connections

For UDP:

`mib2_udp`Throughput and operation

`mib2_udpEntry`UDP endpoints in the "listen" state

For performance analysis, the structures defined for "throughput and operation" are of the most interest. The remaining structures are bookkeeping structures and are of use in some cases for performance analysis, but in most cases, not. Figure 15-22 demonstrates the retrieval of the `mib2_ip`, `mib2_icmp`, `mib2_tcp`, and `mib2_udp` structures.

Figure 15-22 Extracting MIB Structures from Streams Modules

```
#include <stdio.h>
#include <stdlib.h>
#include <unistd.h>
#include <stdarg.h>
#include <string.h>
#include <stropts.h>
#include <fcntl.h>
#include <errno.h>

#include <sys/stream.h>
#include <sys/stropts.h>
#include <sys/socket.h>

#include <sys/tihdr.h>
#include <sys/tiuser.h>

#include <inet/led.h>
#include <inet/mib2.h>
#include <netinet/igmp_var.h>

/* 260 refers to Solaris 2.6.0 */
#if SOLARIS_VERSION >= 260
# include <sys/tpicommon.h>
```

Figure 15-22 Extracting MIB Structures from Streams Modules (Continued)

```
#endif

#define DEV_TCP      "/dev/tcp"
#define ARP_MODULE   "arp"
#define TCP_MODULE   "tcp"
#define UDP_MODULE   "udp"

static void    fatal(char *format, ...);

void
get_mib_data(mib2_ip_t   *ip_struct,
mib2_icmp_t *icmp_struct,
mib2_tcp_t  *tcp_struct,
mib2_udp_t  *udp_struct)
{
char    *trash = 0;
char    buf[BUFSIZ];
int     trash_size = 0;
int     mib_sd;
int     flags;
int     n;
void    *p;
struct strbuf control;
struct strbuf data;
struct T_optmgmt_req *req_opt = (struct T_optmgmt_req *) buf;
struct T_optmgmt_ack *ack_opt = (struct T_optmgmt_ack *) buf;
struct T_error_ack *err_opt = (struct T_error_ack *)   buf;
struct opthdr *req_hdr;

/* open the stream and set up the streams modules */
mib_sd = open(DEV_TCP, O_RDWR);
if (mib_sd == -1)
    fatal("open of %s failed", DEV_TCP);

while (ioctl(mib_sd, I_POP, &n) != -1)    ;
if (ioctl(mib_sd, I_PUSH, ARP_MODULE) == -1)
    fatal("cannot push %s module", ARP_MODULE);
if (ioctl(mib_sd, I_PUSH, TCP_MODULE) == -1)
    fatal("cannot push %s module", TCP_MODULE);
if (ioctl(mib_sd, I_PUSH, UDP_MODULE) == -1)
    fatal("cannot push %s module", UDP_MODULE);

/* setup the request options */
req_opt->PRIM_type = T_OPTMGMT_REQ;
req_opt->OPT_offset = sizeof(struct T_optmgmt_req );
```

Figure 15-22 Extracting MIB Structures from Streams Modules (Continued)

```
req_opt->OPT_length = sizeof(struct opthdr );
#if SOLARIS_VERSION >= 260
req_opt->MGMT_flags = T_CURRENT;
#else
req_opt->MGMT_flags = MI_T_CURRENT;
#endif

/* set up the request header */
req_hdr = (struct opthdr *) & req_opt[1];
req_hdr->level = MIB2_IP;
req_hdr->name  = 0;
req_hdr->len   = 0;

/* set up the control message */
control.buf = buf;
control.len = req_opt->OPT_length + req_opt->OPT_offset;

/* send the message downstream */
if (putmsg(mib_sd, &control, 0, 0) == -1)
    fatal("cannot send control message");

/* set up for the getmsg */
req_hdr = (struct opthdr *) & ack_opt[1];
control.maxlen = sizeof buf;

for (;;) {
    /* start reading the response */
    flags = 0;
    n = getmsg(mib_sd, &control, 0, &flags);
    if (n == -1)
        fatal("cannot read control message");

    /* end of data? */
    if ((n == 0) &&
        (control.len >= sizeof(struct T_optmgmt_ack )) &&
        (ack_opt->PRIM_type == T_OPTMGMT_ACK) &&
        (ack_opt->MGMT_flags == T_SUCCESS) &&
        (req_hdr->len == 0))
        break;

    /* if an error message was sent back */
    if ((control.len >= sizeof(struct T_error_ack )) &&
        err_opt->PRIM_type == T_ERROR_ACK)
        fatal("error reading control message");
```

Figure 15-22 Extracting MIB Structures from Streams Modules (Continued)

```
        /* check for valid response */
        if ((n != MOREDATA) ||
            (control.len < sizeof(struct T_optmgmt_ack )) ||
            (ack_opt->PRIM_type != T_OPTMGMT_ACK) ||
            (ack_opt->MGMT_flags != T_SUCCESS))
            fatal("invalid control message received");

        /* cause the default case to happen */
        if (req_hdr->name != 0)
            req_hdr->level = -1;

        switch (req_hdr->level) {
        case MIB2_IP:
            p = ip_struct;
            break;
        case MIB2_ICMP:
            p = icmp_struct;
            break;
        case MIB2_TCP:
            p = tcp_struct;
            break;
        case MIB2_UDP:
            p = udp_struct;
            break;
        default:
            if ((trash == 0) ||
                (req_hdr->len > trash_size)) {
            if (trash)
                free(trash);
            trash = (char *) malloc(req_hdr->len);
            if (trash == 0)
                fatal("out of memory");
            trash_size = req_hdr->len;
            }
            p = trash;
            break;
        }

        /* read the data from the stream */
        data.maxlen = req_hdr->len;
        data.buf    = (char *) p;
        data.len    = 0;
        flags = 0;

        n = getmsg(mib_sd, 0, &data, &flags);
```

Figure 15-22 Extracting MIB Structures from Streams Modules (Continued)

```
        if (n != 0)
            fatal("error reading data");
    }

    if (trash)
        free(trash);
    close(mib_sd);
    }

    static void
    fatal(char *format, ...)
    {
    va_list args;

    va_start(args, format);
    vfprintf(stderr, format, args);
    putc('\n', stderr);
    exit(1);
    }


    main()
    {
    mib2_ip_t    ip_struct;
    mib2_icmp_t  icmp_struct;
    mib2_tcp_t   tcp_struct;
    mib2_udp_t   udp_struct;

    get_mib_data(&ip_struct, &icmp_struct,
            &tcp_struct, &udp_struct);

    /* carry on with your newly acquired MIB data */

    puts  ("udp_struct = {");
    printf(" udpInDatagrams  = %u\n", udp_struct.udpInDatagrams);
    printf(" udpInErrors     = %u\n", udp_struct.udpInErrors);
    printf(" udpOutDatagrams = %u\n", udp_struct.udpOutDatagrams);
    printf(" udpEntrySize    = %u\n", udp_struct.udpEntrySize);
    puts  ("}");

    return 0;
    }
```

Data sent upstream as a result of the control message is sent in single blocks representing the entire mib2 structure as defined in the `mib2.h` include file. Individual values cannot be queried. Once the control message is sent, the drivers in the stream will send the entire corresponding structure.

An interesting note is that the mib2 structures contain not only the data as defined by RFC 1213, "Management Information Base for Network Management of TCP/IP-based internets: MIB-II," but also other data that is of interest to applications that query the state of the network code in the kernel. Many of the values contained in these mib2 structures, including the values not defined by RFC 1213, are shown in the output of the `netstat -s` command. The TCP section is described in "Introduction to TCP" on page 57. References to books that are relevant to this section include "Computer Networks" on page 566, "Internetworking with TCP/IP Volume II" on page 567, and "The Magic Garden Explained" on page 567.

The Network Device Driver Interface

The Network Device Driver (NDD) interface gets and sets tunable parameters that control drivers, specifically, the network stack drivers. These drivers include the IP, TCP, UDP, ICMP, and ARP drivers, and network interfaces such as `hme`.

In previous versions of Unix, including SunOS, the variables that were available for tuning were not clearly defined, and modifying them was a complex task of installing `adb` commands in system boot files. With the NDD interface comes the `ndd` command for interacting with the drivers and viewing and setting the available variables. This command must also be placed in system boot files for modifying the driver parameters upon boot but is more user friendly than `adb`.

The programming interface for interacting with the drivers to access the NDD variables is not as complex as that for the MIB structures. Accessing the MIB structures required building a stream containing the appropriate streams modules. You can access the NDD variables by opening the character special device representing the network driver in question and using the `ioctl()` system call to pass requests to the driver.

Unlike the MIB structures, the NDD variables can be written to as well as read. The same `ioctl()` interface is used to set variables as to read them, except that a different flag is used within the `ioctl()` request structure.

Figure 15-23 demonstrates how to read all NDD variables from all the protocol drivers.

In this example, you can see that by querying the value of an NDD variable with the name of `?`, you get a response from the drivers that specifies the names of all of the variables available for that driver and whether the variable is mode read-only, read/write, or write-only.

NDD read requests differ from MIB in that MIB reads return the entire MIB structure for the device in question. With NDD, only one variable at a time can be read or written unless the special value ? has been supplied in a read request.

As always, be careful what you tune kernel variables to. Improper tuning could lead to disastrous results or just very poor performance.

Figure 15-23 Dump All the Variables Available Through NDD

```
#include <stdio.h>
#include <stdlib.h>
#include <unistd.h>
#include <string.h>
#include <errno.h>
#include <fcntl.h>
#include <sys/stropts.h>
#include <inet/nd.h>

/*
 * big enough to hold tcp_status */
 * (hey it's "virtual" memory, right? :-))
 */
static charndd_buf[65536];

typedef enum {
VAR_INT_T,
VAR_STRING_T

} var_type_t;

typedef struct {
char    *var_name;
var_type_tvar_type;
union {
    int var_int;
    char*var_string;
} var_un;
} var_t;

typedef struct {
char*ndd_dev_name;
int ndd_sd;
} ndd_dev_t;

static int
ndd_name_io(ndd_dev_t *np, int cmd, var_t *vp)
{
```

Figure 15-23 Dump All the Variables Available Through NDD (Continued)

```
    char*p;
    int i;
    struct strioctl str_cmd;

    /* open the device if not open already */
    if (np->ndd_sd == 0) {
        np->ndd_sd = open(np->ndd_dev_name, O_RDWR);
        if (np->ndd_sd == -1) {
            perror(np->ndd_dev_name);
            return - 1;
        }
    }

    /* clear the buffer */
    memset(ndd_buf, '\0', sizeof ndd_buf);

    /* set up the stream cmd */
    str_cmd.ic_cmd = cmd;
    str_cmd.ic_timout = 0;
    str_cmd.ic_dp = ndd_buf;
    str_cmd.ic_len = sizeof ndd_buf;

    /* set up the buffer according to whether it's a read or write */
    switch (cmd) {
    case ND_GET:
        strcpy(ndd_buf, vp->var_name);
        break;
    case ND_SET:
        switch (vp->var_type) {
        case VAR_INT_T:
            sprintf(ndd_buf, "%s%c%d", vp->var_name,
            '\0', vp->var_un.var_int);
            break;
        case VAR_STRING_T:
            sprintf(ndd_buf, "%s%c%s", vp->var_name,
            '\0', vp->var_un.var_string);
            break;
        default:
            /* ? */
            return - 1;
        }
        break;
    default:
        /* ? */
        return - 1;
```

Figure 15-23 Dump All the Variables Available Through NDD (Continued)

```
    }

    /* retrieve the data via ioctl() */
    if (ioctl(np->ndd_sd, I_STR, &str_cmd) == -1) {
        perror("ioctl");
        return - 1;
    }

    /* if it's a read, put it back into the var_t structure */
    if (cmd == ND_GET) {
        switch (vp->var_type) {
        case VAR_INT_T:
            vp->var_un.var_int = atoi(ndd_buf);
            break;
        case VAR_STRING_T:
            for (i=0, p=ndd_buf; i<str_cmd.ic_len-1; i++, p++)
            if (*p == '\0')
                *p = '\n';
            if (vp->var_un.var_string)
            free(vp->var_un.var_string);
            vp->var_un.var_string = strdup(ndd_buf);
            break;
        default:
            /* ? */
            return - 1;
        }
    }
    return 0;
}


main()
{
static ndd_dev_t dev_names[] = {
        { "/dev/ip", 0  },
        { "/dev/tcp", 0  },
        { "/dev/udp", 0  },
        { "/dev/arp", 0  },
        { "/dev/icmp", 0  },
        { 0, 0  } };
ndd_dev_t * np;
static var_t var = {
    "tcp_status", VAR_STRING_T, 0
};
```

Figure 15-23 Dump All the Variables Available Through NDD (Continued)

```
/* traverse all the devices and dump the variables' names */
for (np = dev_names; np->ndd_dev_name; np++) {
    if (ndd_name_io(np, ND_GET, &var) != -1)
        printf("For %s\n\n%s\n", np->ndd_dev_name,
        var.var_un.var_string);
}
return 0;
}
```

Process Data Sources

Most people know about the ps command. It gives a high-level summary of the status of processes on a system. It has many options, but using it is a relatively crude way to figure out what processes are doing.

Of all the available options, the best performance-related summary comes from the BSD version /usr/ucb/ps uax, which collects all the process data in one go, sorts the output by recent CPU usage, then displays the result. The unsorted versions of ps loop through the processes, printing as they go. This approach spreads out the time at which the processes are measured, and the last line process measured is significantly later than the first. By being collected in one go, the sorted versions give a more consistent view of the system. A quick look at the most active processes can be obtained easily with this command:

```
% /usr/ucb/ps uax | head
USER       PID %CPU %MEM    SZ  RSS TT       S    START  TIME COMMAND
adrianc    333  1.0  8.2 8372 5120 console  S 09:28:38  0:29 /usr/openwin/bin/X
root       483  0.4  1.4 1016  872 pts/1    O 09:56:36  0:00 /usr/ucb/ps uax
adrianc    433  0.3 15.812492 9832 ?        S 09:31:47  0:26 /export/framemaker
root       240  0.3  5.3 3688 3260 ?        S 09:27:22  0:07 /opt/RICHPse/bin/
adrianc    367  0.2  4.2 3472 2620 ??       S 09:28:56  0:00 cmdtool -Wp 603 49
adrianc    484  0.1  0.9  724  540 pts/1    S 09:56:36  0:00 head
root         3  0.1  0.0    0    0 ?        S 09:25:17  0:02 fsflush
adrianc    370  0.1  1.4  980  824 pts/1    S 09:28:57  0:00 /bin/csh
adrianc    358  0.1  2.6 2088 1616 console  S 09:28:54  0:00 olwm -syncpid 357
```

This summary immediately tells you who is running the most active processes. The %CPU measure is a time-decayed average of recent CPU usage. %MEM tells you the proportion of the total RAM in your system that is in use by each process (it won't add up to 100 percent because some RAM is shared by several processes and some by none). SZ is the size of the process address space. It's a good indicator of how much swap space the process needs. In some cases, it includes memory mapped devices, so don't be surprised if the X process appears to be huge on an Ultra 1 with Creator frame buffer. RSS is the basis for %MEM; it's the amount of RAM in use by the process, based on the number of pages mapped. TT shows you which "teletype" the user is logged in on. S shows the status: S means sleeping, O means on-cpu or running, R means runnable and waiting for a CPU to become free. START is the time the process started up, and TIME is the total amount of CPU time it has used so far. COMMAND shows which command is being measured. To see more of the command in a wider window, use /usr/ucb/ps uaxw. To display the BSD version of the ps manual page, use man -s1b ps.

The same basic information is displayed by the well-known freeware utilities top (http://opcom.sun.ca/pub/binaries/top.Z) and the GUI-based proctool (ftp://sunsite.unc.edu/pub/sun-info/mde/proctool). Symon and most commercial performance tools also display this data.

Where Does the Data Come From?

I'm sure you have noticed the strange entry that pops up in df when you are checking how much disk space is left.

```
% df -k
Filesystem          kbytes    used    avail  capacity  Mounted on
/dev/dsk/c0t2d0s0   963662  782001   85301     91%     /
/proc                    0       0       0      0%     /proc
fd                       0       0       0      0%     /dev/fd
/dev/dsk/c0t3d0s0   406854  290066   96448     76%     /export/home
```

It seems that there is a file system called /proc. If you look at it, you find a list of numbers that correspond to the processes on your system.

```
% ls /proc
00000   00140   00197   00237   00309   00333   00358   00379   00586
00001   00149   00207   00239   00312   00334   00359   00382
00002   00152   00216   00240   00313   00342   00367   00385
00003   00154   00217   00258   00318   00349   00370   00388
```

Using ls -ld, you see the owner and size.

```
% /usr/ucb/ps uax | head - 2
USER       PID %CPU %MEM   SZ  RSS TT        S     START   TIME COMMAND
adrianc    333  0.6  8.0 8380 4984 console  S 09:28:38  1:16 /usr/openwin/bin/X
% ls -ld /proc/333
-rw-------    1 adrianc   staff      8581120 Jul 26 09:28 /proc/333
```

The units in ps are Kbytes, and 8581120/1024 = 8380 as expected. The owner and permissions of entries in /proc control access to the processes. The ps command has to be setuid root to provide permission for anyone to view the status of all processes. You can debug or trace only the processes for which you have permissions.

Process Information in Solaris 2.6

A new /proc/pid/metric structure in Solaris 2.6 allows you to use open/read/close rather than open/ioctl/close to read data from /proc. Use ls to view the data. The entries you see in the example below are all the data structures that can be read to return detailed raw information about the process.

```
% ls /proc/333
./          cred        lpsinfo     map         rmap        usage
../         ctl         lstatus     object/     root@       watch
as          cwd@        lusage      pagedata    sigact      xmap
auxv        fd/         lwp/        psinfo      status
```

As you might expect, there is a manual page for /proc, and if you are running Solaris 2.5, you will discover another manual page. A whole bunch of commands that use /proc are documented under the proc(1) manual page. The /proc programming interface is described in proc(4). Let's take a look at these commands, which reside in /usr/proc/bin. Here's an excerpt from the manual page, to save you looking it up.

```
SunOS 5.5             Last change: 9 Nov 1994            ·             1

proc(1)                       User Commands                      proc(1)

NAME
     proc, pflags, pcred, pmap, pldd, psig, pstack, pfiles, pwdx,
     pstop, prun, pwait, ptree, ptime - proc tools

DESCRIPTION
     The proc tools are utilities which exercise features of
     /proc (see proc(4)). Most of them take a list of process-
     ids (pid); those that do also accept /proc/nnn as a
     process-id, so the shell expansion /proc/* can be used to
     specify all processes in the system.

     pflags                  print the /proc tracing flags, the pend-
                             ing and held signals, and other /proc
                             status information for each lwp in each
                             process.

     pcred                   print the credentials (effective, real
```

	and saved UID's and GID's) of each process.
pmap	print the address space map of each process.
pldd	list the dynamic libraries linked into each process, including shared objects explicitly attached using dlopen(3X). (See also ldd(1).)
psig	list the signal actions of each process (See signal(5).)
pstack	print a hex+symbolic stack trace for each lwp in each process.
pfiles	report fstat(2) and fcntl(2) information for all open files in each process.
pwdx	print the current working directory of each process.
pstop	stop each process (PR_REQUESTED stop).
prun	set each process running (inverse of pstop).
pwait	wait for all of the specified processes to terminate.
ptree	print the process trees containing the specified pid's or users, with child processes indented from their respective parent processes. An argument of all digits is taken to be a process-id, otherwise it is assumed to be a user login name. Default is all processes.
ptime	time a command, such as the time(1) command, but using microstate accounting for reproducible precision.

That's already opened up a lot more possibilities. The /proc interface is designed to support the process debugging and analyzing tools in Sun's WorkShop development tools. There are a few tantalizing hints here. Look at the description of pflags: it mentions tracing. And ptime: what is microstate accounting? A way to get higher precision measurements? We need to dig further into the programming interface to find out, but first we'll take a look at a bundled tool that uses /proc to trace the system calls made by a process.

Tracing Process System Calls

The /usr/bin/truss command has many useful features not found in the SunOS 4 trace command. It can trace child processes, and it can count and time system calls and signals. Other options allow named system calls to be excluded or focused on, and data structures can be printed out in full. Here are excerpts showing a fragment of truss output with the –v option to set verbose mode for data structures, and an example of truss –c showing the system call counts.

```
% truss -v all cp NewDocument Tuning
execve("/usr/bin/cp", 0xEFFFFB28, 0xEFFFFB38)  argc = 3
open("/usr/lib/libintl.so.1", O_RDONLY, 035737561304) = 3
mmap(0x00000000, 4096, PROT_READ, MAP_SHARED, 3, 0) = 0xEF7B0000
fstat(3, 0xEFFFF768)= 0
    d=0x0080001E i=29585 m=0100755 l=1  u=2     g=2      sz=14512
    at = Apr 27 11:30:14 PDT 1993  [ 735935414 ]
    mt = Mar 12 18:35:36 PST 1993  [ 731990136 ]
    ct = Mar 29 11:49:11 PST 1993  [ 733434551 ]
    bsz=8192  blks=30     fs=ufs
....

% truss -c cp NewDocument Tuning
syscall         seconds    calls  errors
_exit              .00        1
write              .00        1
open               .00       10       4
close              .01        7
creat              .01        1
chmod              .01        1
stat               .02        2       1
lseek              .00        1
fstat              .00        4
execve             .00        1
mmap               .01       18
munmap             .00        9
memcntl            .01        1
                  ----      ---     ---
```

```
sys totals:      .07       57        5
usr time:        .02
elapsed:         .43
```

I use `truss` a great deal to find out what a process is doing and which files are being read/written. And with `truss -c`, you can see how long system calls take to execute on average and where your system CPU time is coming from. In Solaris 2.6, you can obtain trace information from calls to shared libraries with `sotruss`, as described in "Interposition and Profiling" on page 144.

Process Memory Usage Information

The memory map data has been extended in Solaris 2.6. Mappings now show how much memory a process is really using and how much is resident, shared, and private for each segment. This feature provides an excellent way to figure out memory sizing. If you want to run 100 copies of a process, you can look at one copy and figure out how much private memory you need to multiply by 100. This facility is based on work done by Richard McDougall, who started working alongside Brian Wong and me during 1997 and who specializes in memory-related issues and tools.

```
% /usr/proc/bin/pmap -x 5436
5436:    /bin/csh
Address    Kbytes Resident Shared Private Permissions       Mapped File
00010000      140      140    132       8 read/exec          csh
00042000       20       20      4      16 read/write/exec    csh
00047000      164       68      -      68 read/write/exec     [ heap ]
EF6C0000      588      524    488      36 read/exec          libc.so.1
EF762000       24       24      4      20 read/write/exec    libc.so.1
EF768000        8        4      -       4 read/write/exec     [ anon ]
EF790000        4        4      -       4 read/exec          libmapmalloc.so.1
EF7A0000        8        8      -       8 read/write/exec    libmapmalloc.so.1
EF7B0000        4        4      4       - read/exec/shared   libdl.so.1
EF7C0000        4        -      -       - read/write/exec     [ anon ]
EF7D0000      112      112    112       - read/exec          ld.so.1
EF7FB000        8        8      4       4 read/write/exec    ld.so.1
EFFF5000       44       24      -      24 read/write/exec     [ stack ]
--------   ------   ------ ------  ------
total Kb     1128      940    748     192
```

Who Ran What, When, and How Much Resource Was Used? Accounting!

Many processes have very short life spans. You cannot see such processes with ps, but they may be so frequent that they dominate the load on your system. The only way to catch them is to ask the system to keep a record of every process that has run, who ran it, what was it, when it started and ended, and how much resource it used. The answers come from the system accounting subsystem. For some reason, many administrators seem to have hang-ups about accounting. Perhaps it has connotations of "big brother is watching you," or they fear additional overhead. In truth, if someone complains that his system is too slow and the accounting records show that he spends all his time playing Doom, you should not be too sympathetic! The overhead of collecting accounting data is *always present and is insignificant.* When you turn on accounting, you are just enabling storage of a few bytes of useful data when a process exits.

Accounting data is most useful when measured over a long period of time. This temporal information can be useful on a network of workstations as well as on a single, time-shared server. From this information, you can identify how often programs run, how much CPU time, I/O, and memory each program uses, and what work patterns throughout the week look like. To enable accounting to start immediately, enter the three commands shown below. Check out the section "Administering Security, Performance, and Accounting in Solaris 2" in the *Solaris System Administration Answerbook* and see the acctcom command. You should also add some crontab entries to summarize and checkpoint the accounting logs. Collecting and checkpointing the accounting data itself puts a negligible additional load onto the system, but the summary scripts that run once a day or once a week can have a noticeable effect, so schedule them to run out of hours.

```
# ln /etc/init.d/acct /etc/rc0.d/K22acct
# ln /etc/init.d/acct /etc/rc2.d/S22acct
# /etc/init.d/acct start
Starting process accounting
```

This is what your crontab file for the adm user should contain.

```
# crontab -1 adm
#ident    "@(#)adm         1.5      92/07/14 SMI"    /* SVr4.0 1.2    */
#min      hour     day      month    weekday
0         *        *        *        *        /usr/lib/acct/ckpacct
30        2        *        *        *        /usr/lib/acct/runacct 2>
/var/adm/acct/nite/fd2log
30        9        *        *        5        /usr/lib/acct/monacct
```

You get a daily accounting summary, but the one I like to keep track of is the monthly one stored in /var/adm/acct/fiscal. Here is an excerpt from fiscrpt07 on my home system.

```
Jul 26 09:30 1996                      TOTAL COMMAND SUMMARY FOR FISCAL 07 Page 1


                   TOTAL COMMAND SUMMARY
  COMMAND NUMBER        TOTAL    TOTAL       TOTAL      MEAN      MEAN      HOG         CHARS  BLOCKS
     NAME    CMDS    KCOREMIN  CPU-MIN    REAL-MIN    SIZE-K  CPU-MIN   FACTOR        TRNSFD    READ
```

TOTALS	26488	16062007.75	3960.11	494612.41	4055.95	0.15	0.01	17427899648	39944
mae	36	7142887.25	1501.73	2128.50	4756.45	41.71	0.71	2059814144	1653
sundgado	16	3668645.19	964.83	1074.34	3802.36	60.30	0.90	139549181	76
Xsun	29	1342108.55	251.32	9991.62	5340.18	8.67	0.03	2784769024	1295
xlock	32	1027099.38	726.87	4253.34	1413.04	22.71	0.17	4009349888	15
fountain	2	803036.25	165.11	333.65	4863.71	82.55	0.49	378388	1
netscape	22	489512.97	72.39	3647.61	6762.19	3.29	0.02	887353080	2649
maker4X.	10	426182.31	43.77	5004.30	9736.27	4.38	0.01	803267592	3434
wabiprog	53	355574.99	44.32	972.44	8022.87	0.84	0.05	355871360	570
imagetoo	21	257617.08	15.65	688.46	16456.60	0.75	0.02	64291840	387
java	235	203963.64	37.96	346.35	5373.76	0.16	0.11	155950720	240
aviator	2	101012.82	22.93	29.26	4406.20	11.46	0.78	2335744	40
se.sparc	18	46793.09	19.30	6535.43	2424.47	1.07	0.00	631756294	20
xv	3	40930.98	5.58	46.37	7337.93	1.86	0.12	109690880	28

It looks as if my children were using it to play games during the day! The commands reported are sorted by KCOREMIN, which is the product of the amount of CPU time used and the amount of RAM used while the command was active. CPU-MIN is the number of minutes of CPU time. REAL_MIN is the elapsed time for the commands. SIZE-K is an average value for the RSS over the active lifetime of the process; it does not include times when the process was not actually running. In Solaris 2.4 and earlier releases, a bug causes this measure to be garbage. HOG FACTOR is the ratio of CPU-MIN to REAL-MIN; a high factor means that this command hogs the CPU whenever it is running. CHARS TRNSFD counts the number of characters read and written. BLOCKS READ counts data read from block devices (basically, local disk filesystem reads and writes). The underlying data that is collected can be seen in the `acct(4)` manual page. The data structure looks like that shown below: it's very compact—around 40 bytes.

```
DESCRIPTION
      Files produced as a result of calling acct(2) have records
      in the form defined by <sys/acct.h>, whose contents are:

      typedef ushort  comp_t;     /* pseudo "floating point" representation
*/
                                  /* 3-bit base-8 exponent in the high */
                                  /* order bits, and a 13-bit fraction */
                                  /* in the low order bits. */

      struct  acct
      {
              char    ac_flag;    /* Accounting flag */
              char    ac_stat;    /* Exit status */
              uid_t   ac_uid;     /* Accounting user ID */
              gid_t   ac_gid;     /* Accounting group ID */
              dev_t   ac_tty;     /* control tty */
              time_t  ac_btime;   /* Beginning time */
              comp_t  ac_utime;   /* accounting user time in clock */
```

```
                                        /* ticks */
            comp_t  ac_stime;     /* accounting system time in clock */
                                        /* ticks */
        comp_t  ac_etime;    /* accounting total elapsed time in clock */
                                        /* ticks */
            comp_t  ac_mem;       /* memory usage in clicks (pages) */
            comp_t  ac_io;        /* chars transferred by read/write */
            comp_t  ac_rw;        /* number of block reads/writes */
            char    ac_comm[8];   /* command name */
    };
```

Process Data Structures

There isn't a great deal of data in the accounting record. Let's see what is available from a process that is still running. Actually, a neat trick is to open an entry in /proc and wait until the process has exited. The fact that the /proc entry is still open means that you can still get the data described below. When you close the /proc "file," the zombie process will disappear.

These data structures are described in full in the proc(4) manual page. They are also available in the SE toolkit, so if you want to obtain the data and play around with it, you should look at the code for ps-ax.se and msacct.se.

The interface to /proc involves sending ioctl commands. The one that ps uses is called PIOCPSINFO, and this is what you get back.

```
proc(4)                     File Formats                      proc(4)


   PIOCPSINFO
      This returns miscellaneous process information such as that
      reported by ps(1). p is a pointer to a prpsinfo structure
      containing at least the following fields:

      typedef struct prpsinfo {
        char         pr_state;    /* numeric process state (see pr_sname) */
        char       pr_sname;    /* printable character representing pr_state */
        char       pr_zomb;    /* !=0: process terminated but not waited for */
         char        pr_nice;     /* nice for cpu usage */
         u_long      pr_flag;     /* process flags */
         int         pr_wstat;    /* if zombie, the wait() status */
         uid_t       pr_uid;      /* real user id */
         uid_t       pr_euid;     /* effective user id */
         gid_t       pr_gid;      /* real group id */
         gid_t       pr_egid;     /* effective group id */
         pid_t       pr_pid;      /* process id */
         pid_t       pr_ppid;     /* process id of parent */
```

```
      pid_t        pr_pgrp;     /* pid of process group leader */
      pid_t        pr_sid;      /* session id */
      caddr_t      pr_addr;     /* physical address of process */
      long         pr_size;     /* size of process image in pages */
      long         pr_rssize;   /* resident set size in pages */
      u_long       pr_bysize;   /* size of process image in bytes */
      u_long       pr_byrssize; /* resident set size in bytes */
      caddr_t      pr_wchan;    /* wait addr for sleeping process */
     short       pr_syscall;  /* system call number (if in syscall) */
     id_t        pr_aslwpid;  /* lwp id of the aslwp; zero if no aslwp */
   timestruc_t pr_start;    /* process start time, sec+nsec since epoch */
    timestruc_t pr_time;    /* usr+sys cpu time for this process */
    timestruc_t pr_ctime;   /* usr+sys cpu time for reaped children */
     long       pr_pri;      /* priority, high value is high priority */
     char       pr_oldpri;   /* pre-SVR4, low value is high priority */
     char       pr_cpu;      /* pre-SVR4, cpu usage for scheduling */
     u_short    pr_pctcpu;   /* % of recent cpu time, one or all lwps */
     u_short    pr_pctmem;   /* % of system memory used by the process */
    dev_t       pr_ttydev;   /* controlling tty device (PRNODEV if none) */
     char       pr_clname[PRCLSZ]; /* scheduling class name */
    char      pr_fname[PRFNSZ]; /* last component of exec()ed pathname */
     char       pr_psargs[PRARGSZ];/* initial characters of arg list */
     int        pr_argc;     /* initial argument count */
     char       **pr_argv;   /* initial argument vector */
     char       **pr_envp;   /* initial environment vector */
   } prpsinfo_t;
```

For a multithreaded process, you can get the data for each lightweight process separately. There's a lot more useful-looking information there, but no sign of the high-resolution microstate accounting that /usr/proc/bin/ptime (and msacct.se) display. They use a separate ioctl, PIOCUSAGE.

```
proc(4)                     File Formats                      proc(4)

  PIOCUSAGE
    When applied to the process file descriptor, PIOCUSAGE
    returns the process usage information; when applied to an
    lwp file descriptor, it returns usage information for the
    specific lwp.   p points to a prusage structure which is
    filled by the operation. The prusage structure contains at
    least the following fields:

    typedef struct prusage {
         id_t            pr_lwpid;    /* lwp id.  0: process or defunct */
         u_long          pr_count;    /* number of contributing lwps */
         timestruc_t     pr_tstamp;   /* current time stamp */
```

```
         timestruc_t    pr_create;    /* process/lwp creation time stamp */
         timestruc_t    pr_term;      /* process/lwp termination timestamp */
          timestruc_t    pr_rtime;     /* total lwp real (elapsed) time */
          timestruc_t    pr_utime;     /* user level CPU time */
          timestruc_t    pr_stime;     /* system call CPU time */
          timestruc_t    pr_ttime;     /* other system trap CPU time */
          timestruc_t    pr_tftime;    /* text page fault sleep time */
          timestruc_t    pr_dftime;    /* data page fault sleep time */
          timestruc_t    pr_kftime;    /* kernel page fault sleep time */
          timestruc_t    pr_ltime;     /* user lock wait sleep time *
          timestruc_t    pr_slptime;   /* all other sleep time */
          timestruc_t    pr_wtime;     /* wait-cpu (latency) time */
          timestruc_t    pr_stoptime;  /* stopped time */
          u_long         pr_minf;      /* minor page faults */
          u_long         pr_majf;      /* major page faults */
          u_long         pr_nswap;     /* swaps */
          u_long         pr_inblk;     /* input blocks */
          u_long         pr_oublk;     /* output blocks */
          u_long         pr_msnd;      /* messages sent */
          u_long         pr_mrcv;      /* messages received */
          u_long         pr_sigs;      /* signals received */
          u_long         pr_vctx;      /* voluntary context switches */
          u_long         pr_ictx;      /* involuntary context switches */
          u_long         pr_sysc;      /* system calls */
          u_long         pr_ioch;      /* chars read and written */
     } prusage_t;

     PIOCUSAGE can be applied to a zombie  process   (see
     PIOCPSINFO).

     Applying PIOCUSAGE to a process that does not have micro-
     state accounting enabled will enable microstate accounting
     and return an estimate of times spent in the various states
     up to this point.   Further invocations of PIOCUSAGE will
     yield accurate microstate time accounting from this point.
     To disable microstate accounting, use PIOCRESET with the
     PR_MSACCT flag.
```

There is a lot of useful data here. The time spent waiting for various events is a key measure. I summarize it in `msacct.se` like this:

```
Elapsed time         3:20:50.049  Current time Fri Jul 26 12:49:28 1996
User CPU time            2:11.723  System call time          1:54.890
System trap time            0.006  Text pfault sleep            0.000
```

Data pfault sleep	0.023	Kernel pfault sleep	0.000
User lock sleep	0.000	Other sleep time	3:16:43.022
Wait for CPU time	0.382	Stopped time	0.000

The other thing to notice is that microstate accounting is not turned on by default. It slows the system down very slightly; although it was on by default up to Solaris 2.3, from Solaris 2.4 on, it is enabled the first time you read the data. The way CPU time is normally measured is to sample, 100 times a second, the state of all the CPUs from the clock interrupt. Here's how microstate accounting works: A high-resolution timestamp is taken on every state change, every system call, every page fault, every scheduler change. Microstate accounting doesn't miss anything, and the results are much more accurate than those from sampled measurements. The normal measures of CPU user and system time made by sampling can be wrong by 20 percent or more because the sample is biased, not random. Process scheduling uses the same clock interrupt used to measure CPU usage, and this approach leads to systematic errors in the sampled data. The microstate-measured CPU usage data does not suffer from those errors.

A lot more things can be done with /proc, but I hope I have opened your eyes to some of the most useful performance information available in Solaris 2.

The TNF Kernel Trace Probes

I described how to use TNF to collect a disk trace in "The Solaris 2.5 Trace Capability" on page 188. Here, for convenience, I list all the available kernel probes via a cut-down copy of the Solaris 2.5.1 tnf_probes(4) manual page; the manual page was renamed tnf_kernel_probes(4) in Solaris 2.6.

NAME

tnf_probes – TNF kernel probes

DESCRIPTION

The set of probes (trace instrumentation points) available in the standard kernel. The probes log trace data to a kernel trace buffer in Trace Normal Form (TNF). Kernel probes are controlled by **prex**(1). A snapshot of the kernel trace buffer can be made using **tnfxtract**(1) and examined using **tnfdump**(1).

Each probe has a *name* and is associated with a set of symbolic *keys*, or *categories*. These are used to select and control probes from **prex**(1). A probe that is enabled for tracing generates a TNF record, called an *eventrecord*. An event record contains two common members and may contain other probe-specific data members.

Common Members
tag
encodes TNF references to two other records:
tag
describes the layout of the event record
schedule

identifies the writing thread and also contains a 64-bit base time in nanoseconds.
time_delta
a 32-bit time offset from the base time; the sum of the two times is the actual time of the event.

Threads

thread_create

Thread creation event.
tid
the thread identifier for the new thread
pid
the process identifier for the new thread
start_pc
the kernel address of its start routine.

thread_state

Thread microstate transition events.
tid
optional; if it is absent, the event is for the writing thread; otherwise, the event is for the specified thread.
state
indicates the thread state:
• running in user mode
• running in system mode
• asleep waiting for a user-mode lock
• asleep on a kernel object,
• runnable (waiting for a cpu)
• stopped.

The values of this member are defined in **<sys/msacct.h>**. Note that to reduce trace output, transitions between the *system* and *user* microstates that are induced by system calls are not traced. This information is implicit in the system call entry and exit events.

thread_exit

Thread termination event for writing thread. This probe has no data members other than the common members.

Scheduling

thread_queue

Thread scheduling events. These are triggered when a runnable thread is placed on a dispatch queue.
cpuid
specifies the cpu to which the queue is attached.
priority
the (global) dispatch priority of the thread.
queue_length
the current length of the cpu's dispatch queue.

Blocking

thread_block

Thread blockage event. This probe captures a partial stack backtrace when the current thread blocks.

reason
> the address of the object on which the thread is blocking.

symbols
> references a TNF array of kernel addresses representing the PCs on the stack at the time the thread blocks.

System Calls

syscall_start

System call entry event.

sysnum
> the system call number. The writing thread implicitly enters the *system* microstate with this event.

syscall_end

System call exit event.

rval1
rval2
> the two return values of the system call

errno
> the error return.

The writing thread implicitly enters the *user* microstate with this event.

Page Faults

address_fault

Address-space fault event.

address
> gives the faulting virtual address.

fault_type
> gives the fault type: invalid page, protection fault, software requested locking or unlocking.

access
> gives the desired access protection: read, write, execute or create.
> The values for these two members are defined in **<vm/seg_enum.h>**.

major_fault

Major page fault event. The faulting page is mapped to the file given by the *vnode* member, at the given *offset* into the file. (The faulting virtual address is in the most recent **address_fault** event for the writing thread.)

anon_private

Copy-on-write page fault event.
address
> the virtual address at which the new page is mapped.

anon_zero

Zero-fill page fault event.
address
> the virtual address at which the new page is mapped.

page_unmap

Page unmapping event. This probe marks the unmapping of a file system page from the system.
vnode and *offset*
> identifies the file and offset of the page being unmapped.

Pageins and Pageouts

pagein

Pagein start event. This event signals the initiation of pagein I/O.
vnode and *offset*
> identifies the file and offset to be paged in.
size
> specifies the number of bytes to be paged in.

pageout

Pageout completion event. This event signals the completion of pageout I/O.
vnode
> identifies the file of the pageout request.
pages_pageout
> the number of pages written out.
pages_freed
> the number of pages freed after being written out.
pages_reclaimed
> the number of pages reclaimed after being written out.

Page Daemon (Page Stealer)

pageout_scan_start

Page daemon scan start event. This event signals the beginning of one iteration of the page daemon.
pages_free
> the number of free pages in the system.
pages_needed
> the number of pages desired free.

pageout_scan_end

Page daemon scan end event. This event signals the end of one iteration of the page daemon.
pages_free
> the number of free pages in the system.
pages_scanned
> the number of pages examined by the page daemon. (Potentially more pages will be freed when any queued pageout requests complete.)

Swapper

swapout_process

Address space swapout event. This event marks the swapping out of a process address space.
pid
    identifies the process.
page_count
    reports the number of pages either freed or queued for pageout.

swapout_lwp

Lightweight process swapout event. This event marks the swapping out of an LWP and its stack.
pid
    the LWP's process identifier
lwpid
    the LWP identifier
tid member
    the LWP's kernel thread identifier.
page_count
    the number of pages swapped out.

swapin_lwp

Lightweight process swapin event. This event marks the swapping in of an LWP and its stack.
pid
    the LWP's process identifier
lwpid
    the LWP identifier
tid
    the LWP's kernel thread identifier.
page_count
    the number of pages swapped in.

Local I/O

strategy

Block I/O strategy event. This event marks a call to the **strategy**(9E) routine of a block device driver.
device
    contains the major and minor numbers of the device.
block
    the logical block number to be accessed on the device.
size
    the size of the I/O request.
buf
    the kernel address of the **buf**(9S) structure associated with the transfer.
flags
    the **buf**(9S) flags associated with the transfer.

biodone

Buffered I/O completion event. This event marks calls to the **biodone**(9F) routine.
device
    contains the major and minor numbers of the device.

block
>   the logical block number accessed on the device.

buf
>   the kernel address of the **buf**(9S) structure associated with the transfer.

physio_start

Raw I/O start event. This event marks entry into the **physio**(9F) routine which performs unbuffered I/O.

device
>   contains the major and minor numbers of the device of the transfer.

offset
>   the logical offset on the device for the transfer.

size
>   the number of bytes to be transferred.

rw
>   the direction of the transfer: read or write (see **buf**(9S)).

physio_end

Raw I/O end event. This event marks exit from the **physio**(9F) routine.

device
>   the major and minor numbers of the device of the transfer.

SEE ALSO
>   **prex**(1), **tnfdump**(1), **tnfxtract**(1), **TNF_PROBE**(3X), **strategy**(9E), **biodone**(9F), **physio**(9F), **buf**(9S)

Trace data is incredibly useful in the diagnosis of exactly what is happening in the system. It is best used to capture a problem for detailed analysis. It is not useful for long-term monitoring of the system. The biggest problem with trace data is that a busy system can generate too many trace records to be analyzed easily. tnfview is a free graphical tool that you can use to browse trace data; it is available from http://opcom.sun.ca.

The RPC Remote Statistics Daemon and `perfmeter`

The rpc.rstatd daemon is an RPC server that obtains some performance data by using kstat and returns that data in an RPC message. The rup(1) and perfmeter(1) commands monitor local and remote system activity by using the rstatd interface. SunNet Manager also uses rpc.rstatd to monitor host performance. Two versions of the protocol are currently defined in /usr/include/rpcsvc/rstat.x. The latest, version 4, allows a variable number of CPU states and a variable number of disks to be defined, as shown in Figure 15-24. Version 3 is used by SunOS 4. The information returned is the CPU user, system, wait, idle counters, the total number of operations on each disk, pages paged in and out, pages swapped in and out, the number of interrupts, total packet, error and collision counts summed across all interfaces, context switch count, average run queue lengths for 1-, 5-, and 15-minute averages (each value is shifted by 8 bits, so divide by 256.0 and report it in floating point), and a microsecond resolution timestamp for the current time and the time the system was booted.

Figure 15-24 RPC `rstatd` *Returned Data Structure*

```
struct statsvar {
        struct {
                u_int cp_time_len;
                int *cp_time_val;
        } cp_time;
        struct {
                u_int dk_xfer_len;
                int *dk_xfer_val;
        } dk_xfer;
        u_int v_pgpgin;
        u_int v_pgpgout;
        u_int v_pswpin;
        u_int v_pswpout;
        u_int v_intr;
        int if_ipackets;
        int if_ierrors;
        int if_opackets;
        int if_oerrors;
        int if_collisions;
        u_int v_swtch;
        long avenrun[3];
        rstat_timeval boottime;
        rstat_timeval curtime;
};
```

You can generate example code that collects this data, and you can use rpcgen(1) to generate a Makefile.

```
% cp /usr/include/rpcsvc/rstat.x .
% rpcgen -a rstat.x
% ls *rstat*
makefile.rstat   rstat.x          rstat_clnt.c      rstat_svc.c
rstat.h          rstat_client.c   rstat_server.c    rstat_xdr.c
% make -f makefile.rstat rstat_client
```

You now have a program that gets the data from the system you specify but does nothing with it. We need to modify the main program in rstat_client.c, as shown in Figure 15-25, to do something with the returned data structure so that we can see the results. I deleted code for handling older versions of the `rstat` protocol and added `printf` statements, as shown by the highlighted code below. Everything else was generated by `rpcgen`.

Figure 15-25 Sample `rstat_client.c` *Code for Obtaining* `rpc.rstatd` *Data*

```
/*
 * This is sample code generated by rpcgen.
 * These are only templates and you can use them
 * as a guideline for developing your own functions.
 */

#include "rstat.h"
#include <stdio.h>
#include <stdlib.h> /* getenv, exit */

/*
 * Copyright (c) 1985, 1990, 1991 by Sun Microsystems, Inc.
 */
/* from rstat.x */

void
rstatprog_4(host)
    char *host;
{
    int i;
    CLIENT *clnt;
    statsvar  *rs;
    char *  rstatproc_stats_4_arg;
    u_int  *result_2;
    char *  rstatproc_havedisk_4_arg;

#ifndefDEBUG
    clnt = clnt_create(host, RSTATPROG, RSTATVERS_VAR, "netpath");
    if (clnt == (CLIENT *) NULL) {
      clnt_pcreateerror(host);
      exit(1);
    }
#endif/* DEBUG */

    rs = rstatproc_stats_4((void *)&rstatproc_stats_4_arg, clnt);
    if (rs == (statsvar *) NULL) {
      clnt_perror(clnt, "call failed");
    }
```

Figure 15-25 Sample `rstat_client.c` *Code for Obtaining* `rpc.rstatd` *Data (Continued)*

```
    result_2 = rstatproc_havedisk_4((void *)&rstatproc_havedisk_4_arg,
clnt);
    if (result_2 == (u_int *) NULL) {
      clnt_perror(clnt, "call failed");
    }
    printf("rstat information from %s at: %s", host,
              ctime(&rs->curtime.tv_sec));
    printf("booted at %s",
      ctime(&rs->boottime.tv_sec));
    printf("pgpgin: %d  pgpgout: %d  pswpin: %d  pswpout: %d\n",
      rs->v_pgpgin, rs->v_pgpgout, rs->v_pswpin, rs->v_pswpout);
    printf("intr: %d  swtch: %d  avenrun: %3.1f %3.1f %3.1f\n",
      rs->v_intr, rs->v_swtch, rs->avenrun[0]/256.0,
      rs->avenrun[1]/256.0, rs->avenrun[2]/256.0);
    printf("ipackets: %d  ierrors: %d  opackets: %d  oerrors: %d \
collisions: %d\n",
      rs->if_ipackets, rs->if_ierrors, rs->if_opackets,
      rs->if_oerrors, rs->if_collisions);
    /* CPU states are 0=USER 1=WAIT 2=KERNEL 3=IDLE - weird... */
    printf("usr: %d  sys: %d  wio: %d  idle: %d\n",
      rs->cp_time.cp_time_val[0],
      rs->cp_time.cp_time_val[2],
      rs->cp_time.cp_time_val[1],
      rs->cp_time.cp_time_val[3]);
    for(i=0; i < rs->dk_xfer.dk_xfer_len; i++) {
        printf("disk: %d  xfers: %d\n", i, rs->dk_xfer.dk_xfer_val[i]);
    }
#ifndefDEBUG
    clnt_destroy(clnt);
#endif/* DEBUG */
}


main(argc, argv)
    int argc;
    char *argv[];
{
    char *host;

    if (argc < 2) {
      printf("usage:  %s server_host\n", argv[0]);
      exit(1);
    }
```

Figure 15-25 Sample `rstat_client.c` *Code for Obtaining* `rpc.rstatd` *Data (Continued)*

```
        host = argv[1];
        rstatprog_4(host);
}
```

Figure 15-26 shows the raw data printout. The values are counters, so to get per-second rates, you would have to take measurements twice and use the differences over a time interval. The current time does include a microsecond resolution component, so accurate time differences are available. Some counters may wrap round, as `intr` has in the example, but differences will still be valid. The disk data is hard to map to named disk devices. I compared it with counters obtained from `iostat` to check; Figure 15-27 shows that the order is the same.

Figure 15-26 Example Output from `rstat_client`

```
% rstat_client localhost
rstat information from localhost at: Fri Dec 19 09:21:53 1997
booted at Sat Nov 29 11:42:36 1997
pgpgin: 186806  pgpgout: 105086  pswpin: 24  pswpout: 145
intr: -25232137  swtch: 56685160  avenrun: 0.0 0.0 0.0
ipackets: 694345  ierrors: 0  opackets: 736283  oerrors: 0  collisions: 1
usr: 1184180  sys: 351773  wio: 280473  idle: 127491765
disk: 0  xfers: 1
disk: 1  xfers: 225406
disk: 2  xfers: 162365
disk: 3  xfers: 37496
```

Figure 15-27 Counters from `iostat` *for Comparison*

```
% iostat -xI
                              extended disk statistics
disk        r/i       w/i       Kr/i       Kw/i wait actv  svc_t  %w   %b
fd0         1.0       0.0        0.0        0.0  0.0  0.0    7.8   0    0
sd0    118384.0 108737.0 841384.5 1344148.0  0.2  0.1  477.7   0    1
sd1     94500.0  68373.0 615959.5  742512.0  0.0  0.0   53.1   0    1
sd5     28362.0   9144.0 155954.5   78172.0  0.0  0.0   40.8   0    0
```

The data shown by `perfmeter` in Figure 15-28 summarizes all this information by adding together CPU user and system time, all paging activity, packets in and out, and all disk I/O counters. `perfmeter` can log data to a file and has more options than most users realize, so read the manual page.

Figure 15-28 Example `perfmeter` Output

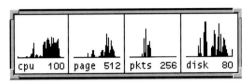

I also created a shared library that acts as a rstat client, and used it to interface to the SE toolkit. The resulting class provides this data in a more usable form and a remote vmstat-like command was developed as a test program. See my SunWorld Online February 1998 column at http://www.sun.com/sunworldonline/swol-02-1998/swol-02-perf.html.

System Configuration Information

Systems are becoming more complex, and many of the performance problems that occur can be solved by changing the configuration. Commercially available performance management tools do not do a good job of obtaining and presenting configuration information. Most tools attempt to be portable across products from multiple vendors, and it is very hard to keep track of many vendors, all continuously releasing new products. A notable exception is Sun's Solstice Symon product. This product is built by part of the same team that built the hardware, so they have inside information ahead of time and can track the new hardware as it is released. They also attempt to track only Sun hardware. The interfaces and tools provided by Solaris and Sun hardware are described here, so that other tools can make better use of configuration information.

System Identity and Basic Configuration

The uname(2) system call returns operating system information, `sysinfo`(2) gets some hardware-related information, and `sysconf`(3C), returns the values of some configurable system variables. The uname command uses the uname and `sysinfo` calls.

```
% uname -a
SunOS hostname 5.5.1 Generic_103640-14 sun4u sparc SUNW,Ultra-2
```

Useful information obtainable from `sysconf` includes the clock tick rate, page size, total number of pages of RAM, number of processors configured, and number of processors currently on line. The clock tick rate is normally 100 Hz, but starting in Solaris 2.6, it can be set to 1000 Hz when higher resolution event timing is needed for real-time work.

The Openboot Device Tree — `prtconf` and `prtdiag`

When a system powers up, the boot prom code probes the hardware to see what it can find and builds a device tree structure in memory. When Solaris starts, it picks up this device tree and configures device drivers for the components it sees. You can program to the openprom(7D) interface yourself, but it is quite hard to match the device tree entries with the Solaris devices. The file /etc/path_to_inst contains this mapping. The standard Solaris 2 command for displaying the device tree is /usr/sbin/prtconf. The full device tree is rather verbose and cryptic but contains useful information, as shown in Figure 15-29, which lists the system and CPU nodes on an Ultra 2.

Figure 15-29 Excerpt from `prtconf` Showing Device Information

```
% /usr/sbin/prtconf -pv | more
System Configuration:  Sun Microsystems   sun4u
Memory size: 128 Megabytes
System Peripherals (PROM Nodes):

Node 0xf002958c
    idprom:
01800800.2080ef75.00000000.80ef75a9.00000000.00000000.00000000.00000000
    reset-reason:  'B-POR'
    breakpoint-trap:  0000007f
    #size-cells:  00000002
    energystar-v2:
    model:  'SUNW,501-3132'
    name:  'SUNW,Ultra-2'
    clock-frequency:  05e188aa
    banner-name:  'Sun Ultra 2 UPA/SBus (2 X UltraSPARC-II 296MHz)'
    device_type:  'upa'
.....
Node 0xf0071264
        manufacturer#:  00000017
        implementation#:  00000011
        mask#:  00000011
        sparc-version:  00000009
        ecache-associativity:  00000001
        ecache-line-size:  00000040
        ecache-size:  00200000
        #dtlb-entries:  00000040
        dcache-associativity:  00000001
```

Figure 15-29 Excerpt from `prtconf` *Showing Device Information (Continued)*

```
            dcache-line-size:  00000020
            dcache-size:  00004000
            #itlb-entries:  00000040
            icache-associativity:  00000002
            icache-line-size:  00000020
            icache-size:  00004000
            upa-portid:  00000000
            clock-frequency:  11a49a00
            reg:  000001c0.00000000.00000000.00000008
            device_type:  'cpu'
            name:  'SUNW,UltraSPARC-II'
```

A more user friendly derivative is the platform-specific `prtdiag` command. It is located in the `/usr/platform` directory, and you have to specify the kernel architecture of the system you are on, using the `arch -k` command to obtain `sun4u`, `sun4m`, or whatever to get the output like that shown in Figure 15-30.

Figure 15-30 Example `prtdiag` *Output*

```
% /usr/platform/`arch -k`/sbin/prtdiag
System Configuration:  Sun Microsystems  sun4u Sun Ultra 2 UPA/SBus (2 X
UltraSPARC-II 296MHz)
System clock frequency: 99 MHz
Memory size: 128 Megabytes
        CPU Units: Frequency Cache-Size Version
            A: MHz  MB  Impl. Mask  B: MHz  MB  Impl. Mask
            ----------  ----- ----  ----------  ----- ----
            296 2.0   11    1.1     296 2.0   11    1.1
=====================IO Cards=========================================
            SBus clock frequency: 25 MHz
            2: SUNW,rtvc              'SUNW,501-2232-06REV50'
            FFB:          Double Buffered


No failures found in System
===========================
ASIC Revisions:
---------------
SBus: sbus Rev 1
FEPS: SUNW,hme Rev 22


FFB Hardware Configuration:
---------------------------
    Board: rev 3
    FBC: version 0x1
    DAC: Brooktree 9068, version 4
```

Figure 15-30 Example `prtdiag` *Output (Continued)*

```
     3DRAM: Mitsubishi 1308, version 5

 System PROM revisions:
 ---------------------
   OBP 3.7.0 1997/01/09 13:06   POST 3.2.1 1996/12/20 03:01
```

The Symon Configuration Daemon

`prtdiag` is more readable than `prtconf`, but it would be nice to have something that a program could use to obtain detailed configuration information at a high level. The configuration daemon, `sm_configd`, was built to solve this problem for Sun's Symon system monitoring product. Here is the manual page, in case you don't have Symon installed.

```
% setenv MANPATH /opt/SUNWsymon/man:$MANPATH
% man sm_configd

sm_configd(1M)          Maintenance Commands          sm_configd(1M)

NAME
     sm_configd - Solstice SyMON configuration reader

SYNOPSIS
     /opt/SUNWsymon/sbin/sm_configd [ -D debug-value ] [ -T  file
     ] [ -i interval ]

AVAILABILITY
     SUNWsymon

DESCRIPTION
     Monitors the physical configuration of a machine and reports
     on the status of components. For further details, please
     see the Solstice SyMON User's Guide.

OPTIONS
     -D        Set a debug option for AIL.

     -T        Run the configuration from a file; for testing
               purposes.

     -i        Set the polling interval for the Config Reader.

FILES
     cfg_sun4d.so.1
```

```
       cfg_sun4u.so.1

       cfg_sun4uI.so.1

SEE ALSO
       symon(1),   sm_confsymon(1M),   sm_control(1M),   sm_egd(1M),
       sm_krd(1M),          sm_logscand(1M),          sm_symond(1M),
       verify_rules(1M),    auth_checker.tcl(4),    auth_list.tcl(4),
       event_gen.tcl(4),        logscan.tcl(4),        rules.tcl(4),
       sm_symond.conf(4)
```

Symon is provided free of charge with Solaris 2.5.1 and later releases on the SMCC Hardware CD-ROM that comes with the Solaris release. Symon is supported only on server platforms, which include the sun4d and sun4u architectures and the sun4uI variant that is used by the E10000 system. Symon actually works on all Sun Ultra models, as well as on the older SPARCserver 1000 and SPARCcenter 2000. If it is run on a desktop workstation, it will report the name of the equivalent server that uses the same CPU board. Symon does not work on sun4c or sun4m kernels, as used by the SPARCstation 2 and SPARCstation 20, for example. All kernel architectures are listed in Table 11-1 on page 256.

The output is designed to be parsed easily and contains a lot of very useful information. A lot of extra knowledge about the hardware is embedded in this tool; it would be hard to build it yourself from scratch. There are actually two configuration commands, although only one has a manual page. The /opt/SUNWsymon/sbin/sm_configd command runs as a daemon, while the /opt/SUNWsymon/bin/configd command has no manual page and seems to be a test program. They both must be run as root.

Figure 15-31 shows configd output for the same machine that was used for the previous examples. On a large server, the output would be far more complex.

Figure 15-31 Example Output from Symon Configuration Daemon

```
# /opt/SUNWsymon/bin/configd | more

#------------------------------------
system OS="SunOS 5.5.1" OS_version="Generic_103640-14" \
        System_clock_frequency="98 MHz" architecture="sparc" \
        hostname="hostname" image_name="chassis" machine="sun4u" \
        platform="Ultra-Enterprise-2" sample#="1" \
        serial_number="2155933557" timestamp="Fri Dec 19 10:50:47 1997" \
        timestamp_raw="882528647" total_disks="3" total_memory="128 Mb" \
        total_processors="2" total_tape_devices="1" \
        view_points="front rear side top"
```

Figure 15-31 Example Output from Symon Configuration Daemon (Continued)

```
system-board board-num="1" fru="yes" image_name="-" memory_size="128 Mb" \
          state="active" type="<unknown>" type-int="-1"
  SUNW,Ultra-2 device_type="upa" image_name="-" model="SUNW,501-3132"
   SUNW,ffb(0) device_type="display" image_name="ffb" instance="0" \
          model="SUNW,501-3129" pdistr="ffb-slot" reg="508,0" \
          upa-portid="30"
   cpu-unit(0) clock-frequency="296 MHz" cpu-type="sparc" \
          dcache-size="16.0 KB" device_type="cpu" ecache-size="2.0 MB" \
          fru="yes" icache-size="16.0 KB" image_name="cpu-unit" \
          model="SUNW,UltraSPARC-II" pdistr="cpu-unit-A" \
          processor-id="0" reg="448,0" status="online" unit="A" \
          upa-portid="0" view_points="front"
   cpu-unit(1) clock-frequency="296 MHz" cpu-type="sparc" \
          dcache-size="16.0 KB" device_type="cpu" ecache-size="2.0 MB" \
          fru="yes" icache-size="16.0 KB" image_name="cpu-unit" \
          model="SUNW,UltraSPARC-II" pdistr="cpu-unit-B" \
          processor-id="1" reg="450,0" status="online" unit="B" \
          upa-portid="1" view_points="front"
   memory image_name="-" reg="0,0"
    simm(0) board_reference_number="U0701" fru="yes" image_name="simm" \
          pdistr="simm-0" size="32 Mb" slot="0" type="dram"
    simm(1) board_reference_number="U0601" fru="yes" image_name="simm" \
          pdistr="simm-1" size="32 Mb" slot="1" type="dram"
    simm(2) board_reference_number="U0501" fru="yes" image_name="simm" \
          pdistr="simm-2" size="32 Mb" slot="2" type="dram"
    simm(3) board_reference_number="U0401" fru="yes" image_name="simm" \
          pdistr="simm-3" size="32 Mb" slot="3" type="dram"
   sbus(0) device_type="sbus" image_name="-" instance="0" \
          model="SUNW,sysio" network_count="1" reg="510,0" \
          upa-portid="31" version#="1"
    SUNW,CS4231(0) device_type="audio" instance="0" reg="13,201326592"
    SUNW,bpp(0) instance="0" reg="14,209715200"
    SUNW,fas(0) device_type="scsi" disk_count="3" image_name="-" \
          instance="0" reg="14,142606336" tape_count="1"
     cdrom0(6) device_type="CD-ROM" fru="yes" image_name="cd-drive" \
          instance="6" mounted_partitions="0" name="c0t6d0" \
          pdistr="cd-drive" pv_parent="system"
     sd(0) device_type="disk" fru="yes" image_name="disk" instance="0" \
          mounted_partitions="1" name="c0t0d0" pdistr="disk-0" \
          pv_parent="system"
      / avail_bytes="81 mbytes" device_type="partition" name="c0t0d0s0" \
          percent_used="93%" total_bytes="1504 mbytes" \
          used_bytes="1272 mbytes"
     sd(1) device_type="disk" fru="yes" image_name="disk" instance="1" \
          mounted_partitions="1" name="c0t1d0" pdistr="disk-1" \
```

Figure 15-31 Example Output from Symon Configuration Daemon (Continued)

```
               pv_parent="system"
   /export/home/adrianc avail_bytes="50 mbytes" device_type="partition"
\
               name="c0t1d0s0" percent_used="97%" \
               total_bytes="1994 mbytes" used_bytes="1944 mbytes"
    sd(5) device_type="disk" fru="yes" instance="5" \
            mounted_partitions="1" name="c0t5d0"
     /export/home5 avail_bytes="16 mbytes" device_type="partition" \
           name="c0t5d0s2" percent_used="98%" total_bytes="941 mbytes" \
            used_bytes="830 mbytes"
   st(4) device_type="tape drive" fru="yes" instance="4" \
           model="Archive Python 4mm Helical Scan" name="/dev/rmt/0n" \
            status="OK"
   SUNW,fdtwo(0) device_type="block" fru="yes" image_name="floppy-drive"
\
            instance="0" pdistr="floppy-drive" pv_parent="system" \
            reg="15,20971520"
   SUNW,hme(0) device_type="network" ether="8:0:20:80:ef:75" \
            inet="129.1.1.1" instance="0" name="hme0" \
            reg="14,146800640" symbol="hostname"
   sbus-slot(2) image_name="-" slot-num="2"
    sbus-board(2) board-num="2" fru="yes" image_name="sbus-board" \
            model="SUNW,501-2232-06REV50" pdistr="sbus-slot-2" \
            state="active" type="<unknown>"
     SUNW,rtvc(0) instance="0" model="SUNW,501-2232-06REV50" reg="2,0"
    zs(0) device_type="serial" instance="0" reg="15,17825792"
    zs(1) device_type="serial" instance="1" reg="15,16777216"
```

The SunVTS Diagnostic Test System

You can use SunVTS to stress test a system, component by component. It is used within Sun as part of the system and component testing process. You can invoke SunVTS from the Symon GUI to test a component that is reporting errors. Once you have set up SunVTS, use the vtsprobe command to obtain detailed hardware configuration information. The SunVTS and Symon documentation is provided in AnswerBook format on the Solaris 2.x SMCC Hardware CD-ROM, along with the tools themselves.

SCSI Device Information

SCSI device information is covered in "Output Formats and Options for iostat" on page 183 and "Disk Specifications" on page 200.

☰ 15

Logical Volume Issues

In the simple case, a single disk is partitioned and file systems are placed on a partition. Everything is easy to figure out. It is now much more common to use logical volumes, with striped, mirrored, or RAID5 combinations of many disks. Tools need to know how to track usage of these logical volumes.

Solstice Disk Suite Configuration

You can obtain the Solstice Disk Suite configuration by using the `/usr/opt/SUNWmd/sbin/metastat` command. With the `-a` option, the command uses a format that can easily be parsed programmatically.

```
% /usr/opt/SUNWmd/sbin/metastat -a
d0 -t d1 d100
d1 -m d2 d3 1
d2 1 3 c0t0d0s2 c0t0d1s2 c0t0d2s2 -i 128b
d3 1 3 c0t0d3s2 c0t0d4s2 c0t0d6s2 -i 128b
d10 -t d11 d110
d11 -m d13 1
d13 1 1 c2t0d1s2 -h hsp000
d20 -t d21 d120
d21 -r c0t4d0s2 c0t4d1s2 c0t4d2s2 c0t4d3s2 c0t4d4s2 c0t4d5s2 c0t5d0s2
c0t5d1s2 c0t5d2s2 c2t0d2s2 c2t1d0s2 c2t1d1s2 c2t1d2s2 c2t2d0s2 c2t2d1s2
c2t2d2s2 c2t3d0s2 c2t3d1s2 -k -i 128b -h hsp000
d30 -t d31 d110
d31 -r c0t2d0s2 c0t2d1s2 c0t2d3s2 c0t2d4s2 c0t2d5s2 -k -i 128b
...
hsp000 c0t5d4s2 c0t5d5s2 c2t4d0s2 c2t4d1s2 c2t4d2s2 c2t5d0s2 c2t5d1s2
c2t5d2s2
```

Veritas Volume Manager Configuration

You can obtain the Veritas Volume Manager configuration by using the `vxprint` command. With the `-a` option, the command also uses a parsable format, but it is much more complex than DiskSuite. In the following output, I cut out a lot of the uninteresting details.

```
% vxprint -a
Disk group: rootdg

dg   rootdg tutil0=" tutil1=" tutil2=" import_id=0.1 real_name=rootdg
comment=" putil0=" putil1=" putil2=" dgid=881857902.1025.moan rid=0.1025
update_tid=0.1047 disabled=off noautoimport=off nconfig=default
nlog=default base_minor=0
```

```
dm    disk01 tutil0=" tutil1=" tutil2=" da_name=c1t12d0s2
device_tag=c1t12d0 da_type=sliced pub_bpath="/dev/dsk/c1t12d0s4 ...
dm    disk02 tutil0=" tutil1=" tutil2=" da_name=c1t13d0s2
device_tag=c1t13d0 da_type=sliced pub_bpath="/dev/dsk/c1t13d0s4 ...
sd    disk01-01 tutil0=" tutil1=" tutil2=" dev=32/1052 busy=on devopen=off
enabled=on detach=off writeonly=off nodevice=off removed=off is_log=off
da_name=c1t12d0s2 device_tag=c1t12d0 dm_name=disk01
path="/dev/dsk/c1t12d0s4 pl_name=vol01-01 ...
sd    disk02-01 tutil0=" tutil1=" tutil2=" dev=32/1060 busy=on devopen=off
enabled=on detach=off writeonly=off nodevice=off removed=off is_log=off
da_name=c1t13d0s2 device_tag=c1t13d0 dm_name=disk02
path="/dev/dsk/c1t13d0s4 pl_name=vol01-01 ...
vol   vol01 tutil0=" tutil1=" tutil2=" kstate=ENABLED r_all=GEN_DET_SPARSE
r_some=GEN_DET_SPARSE w_all=GEN_DET_SPARSE w_some=GEN_DET_SPARSE
lasterr=0 use_type=fsgen fstype=" comment=" putil0=" putil1=" putil2="
state="ACTIVE writeback=on writecopy=off specify_writecopy=off
logging=off has_logs=off devopen=on log_serial_lo=0 log_serial_hi=0
node_bdev=140/5 node_cdev=140/5 iosize=512 pl_num=1 pref_name=vol01-01
start_opts=" read_pol=SELECT current_read_pol=PREFER minor=5 user=root
group=root mode=0600 log_type=REGION len=16609280 log_len=0
update_tid=0.1152 rid=0.1124 pref_plex_rid=0.1126 detach_tid=0.0
active=off forceminor=off badlog=off recover=off krecover=off invalid=off
recover_checkpoint=0 lasterr_tid=0.0 sd_num=0 sdnum=0 dirty=off busy=on
degraded=off unusable=off kdetach=off storage=off applrecov=off
recover_seqno=0 app_dirty=off plex=vol01-01
```

RSM2000 Hardware RAID Configuration

Hardware RAID controllers hide details of their configuration behind pseudo-disk devices. Each disk that Solaris sees maps to a combination of striped, mirrored, or RAID5 disks and RAM buffer. The reported behavior is quite different from that of a single disk. Compounding this problem, some RAID controllers support multiple attachments to host systems for redundant access. There are two controllers and two SCSI buses or fiber channel ports that reach the same disk device. For the RSM2000, a pseudo-device that maps to the two underlying disk controllers is created and uses the Redundant Disk Array Controller (RDAC) interface.

To explore an RSM2000 configuration, you use commands located in /usr/sbin/osa. First, list the array devices with the lad(1M) command. Then, you can find the information shown in Figure 15-32: the individual drives in the whole array or individual devices, using `drivutil`(1M); the redundant access path RDAC Configuration information, using the `rdacutil`(1M) command; and the RAID configuration, using `raidutil`(1M).

Figure 15-32 Configuration Information Command Examples for RSM2000 Disk Subsystem

```
# lad
c1t5d0s0 1T71017828 LUNS: 0 2 4 6
c2t5d0s0 1T70614616 LUNS: 0 2 4 6
c4t4d1s0 1T70917291 LUNS: 1 3 5
c5t4d1s0 1T63350913 LUNS: 1 3 5
c6t5d0s0 1T63852670 LUNS: 0 2 4 6
c7t5d0s0 1T63852694 LUNS: 0 2 4 6
c8t4d1s0 1T63852856 LUNS: 1 3 5
c9t4d1s0 1T63852762 LUNS: 1 3 5
c10t4d1s0 1T70917132 LUNS: 1 3 5
c11t4d1s0 1T71321825 LUNS: 1 3 5
c12t5d0s0 1T70815597 LUNS: 0 2 4 6
c13t4d1s0 1T63852877 LUNS: 1 3 5
c14t5d0s0 1T63852862 LUNS: 0 2 4 6
c15t5d0s0 1T63852796 LUNS: 0 2 4 6


# drvutil -l c1t5d0s0
Logical Unit Information for stardcr-RM03

   LUN        Group       Device         RAID      Capacity     Status
                          Name           Level     (MB)

    0          1          c1t5d0s0         5         34541      Optimal
    1          2          c4t4d1s0         5         34541      Optimal
    2          3          c1t5d2s0         5         34541      Optimal
    3          4          c4t4d3s0         5         34541      Optimal
    4          5          c1t5d4s0         5         34541      Optimal
    5          6          c4t4d5s0         5         34541      Optimal
    6          7          c1t5d6s0         5         34541      Optimal

drivutil succeeded!
# drivutil -d c1t5d0s0

Drives in Group for stardcr-RM03

   Group           Drive List   [Channel,Id]

 Group  1:        [1,8]; [2,8]; [3,8]; [4,8]; [5,8];
 Group  2:        [1,9]; [2,9]; [3,9]; [4,9]; [5,9];
 Group  3:        [1,10]; [2,10]; [3,10]; [4,10]; [5,10];
 Group  4:        [1,11]; [2,11]; [3,11]; [4,11]; [5,11];
```

Figure 15-32 Configuration Information Command Examples for RSM2000 Disk Subsystem (Continued)

```
Group  5:      [1,12]; [2,12]; [3,12]; [4,12]; [5,12];
Group  6:      [1,13]; [2,13]; [3,13]; [4,13]; [5,13];
Group  7:      [1,14]; [2,14]; [3,14]; [4,14]; [5,14];

drivutil succeeded!
stardcr# drivutil -i c1t5d0s0

Drive Information for stardcr-RM03

Location  Capacity  Status        Vendor  Product         Firmware Serial
          (MB)                            ID              Version  Number
[1,8]     8637      Optimal       FUJITSU M2949ESP SUN9.0G 2848     000301
[2,8]     8637      Optimal       FUJITSU M2949ESP SUN9.0G 2848     000358
[3,8]     8637      Optimal       FUJITSU M2949ESP SUN9.0G 2848     000367
[4,8]     8637      Optimal       FUJITSU M2949ESP SUN9.0G 2848     000367
[5,8]     8637      Optimal       FUJITSU M2949ESP SUN9.0G 2848     000360
[1,9]     8637      Optimal       FUJITSU M2949ESP SUN9.0G 2848     000284
[2,9]     8637      Optimal       FUJITSU M2949ESP SUN9.0G 2848     000371
[3,9]     8637      Optimal       FUJITSU M2949ESP SUN9.0G 2848     000372
[4,9]     8637      Optimal       FUJITSU M2949ESP SUN9.0G 2848     000370
[5,9]     8637      Optimal       FUJITSU M2949ESP SUN9.0G 2848     000365
[1,10]    8637      Optimal       FUJITSU M2949ESP SUN9.0G 2848     000309
[2,10]    8637      Optimal       FUJITSU M2949ESP SUN9.0G 2848     000324
[3,10]    8637      Optimal       FUJITSU M2949ESP SUN9.0G 2848     000364
[4,10]    8637      Optimal       FUJITSU M2949ESP SUN9.0G 2848     000370
[5,10]    8637      Optimal       FUJITSU M2949ESP SUN9.0G 2848     000377
[1,11]    8637      Optimal       FUJITSU M2949ESP SUN9.0G 2848     000320
[2,11]    8637      Optimal       FUJITSU M2949ESP SUN9.0G 2848     000362
[3,11]    8637      Optimal       FUJITSU M2949ESP SUN9.0G 2848     000335
[4,11]    8637      Optimal       FUJITSU M2949ESP SUN9.0G 2848     000361
[5,11]    8637      Optimal       FUJITSU M2949ESP SUN9.0G 2848     000365
[1,12]    8637      Optimal       FUJITSU M2949ESP SUN9.0G 2848     000370
[2,12]    8637      Optimal       FUJITSU M2949ESP SUN9.0G 2848     000288
[3,12]    8637      Optimal       FUJITSU M2949ESP SUN9.0G 2848     000357
[4,12]    8637      Optimal       FUJITSU M2949ESP SUN9.0G 2848     000364
[5,12]    8637      Optimal       FUJITSU M2949ESP SUN9.0G 2848     000353
[1,13]    8637      Optimal       FUJITSU M2949ESP SUN9.0G 2848     000368
[2,13]    8637      Optimal       FUJITSU M2949ESP SUN9.0G 2848     000381
[3,13]    8637      Optimal       FUJITSU M2949ESP SUN9.0G 2848     000101
[4,13]    8637      Optimal       FUJITSU M2949ESP SUN9.0G 2848     000315
[5,13]    8637      Optimal       FUJITSU M2949ESP SUN9.0G 2848     000381
[1,14]    8637      Optimal       FUJITSU M2949ESP SUN9.0G 2848     000381
[2,14]    8637      Optimal       FUJITSU M2949ESP SUN9.0G 2848     000365
[3,14]    8637      Optimal       FUJITSU M2949ESP SUN9.0G 2848     000368
[4,14]    8637      Optimal       FUJITSU M2949ESP SUN9.0G 2848     000380
```

Figure 15-32 Configuration Information Command Examples for RSM2000 Disk Subsystem (Continued)

```
 [5,14]     8637        Optimal        FUJITSU M2949ESP SUN9.0G 2848   000364

drivutil succeeded!

# rdacutil -i c1t5d0s0

stardcr-RM03:   dual-active
     Active    controller a (c1t5d0s0)            units:    0 2 4 6
     Active    controller b (c4t4d1s0)            units:    1 3 5

rdacutil succeeded!

# raidutil -c c1t5d0s0 -i
LUNs found on c1t5d0s0.
  LUN 0     RAID 5    34541 MB
  LUN 2     RAID 5    34541 MB
  LUN 4     RAID 5    34541 MB
  LUN 6     RAID 5    34541 MB

Vendor ID          SYMBIOS
ProductID          RSM Array 2000
Product Revision   0204
Boot Level         02.04.04.00
Boot Level Date    07/24/97
Firmware Level     02.04.04.01
Firmware Date      09/15/97
raidutil program successful.
```

Monitoring and configuration interfaces for RAID controllers have not been standardized, although the issue has been recognized and work is in progress to improve the situation. The X/Open UMA standard does define a way to capture and report on the configuration and performance of complex disk subsystems; this definition may be a useful starting point for the data to be reported by a common interface.

The SymbEL Example Tools   16

The toolkit is continuously being developed and upgraded. We decided that it was not a good idea to put a copy on a disk and include it with this book. It is much better to use the Internet to download the packages, which are about 1 megabyte in total. One problem is that Internet addresses change over time, as web sites are reorganized, and the location may change over time. The best way to get the latest information on SE is to read my latest SunWorld Online performance Q&A column. There is always a link to the SE download area at the end in the "Resources" section. SunWorld Online is located at http://www.sun.com/sunworldonline. The SE3.0 release described in this book can be found at http://www.sun.com/sun-on-net/performance/se3.

Installing and Using SE3.0

SE is provided as three packages. Two are largely by Richard Pettit and contain the interpreter and basic examples (RICHPse) and the SE Graphical Extension libraries (RICHPsex). The third is largely by Adrian Cockcroft and contains rules and related tools (ANCrules). There is a dependency on an optional Solaris package SUNWsprot, which contains the /usr/ccs/lib/cpp command and is part of the standard Solaris 2 distribution. If you have a full installation of Solaris 2, it will be present, but users often get confused, and think—incorrectly—that this package has something to do with a compiler product. The three packages are provided in compressed tar format (see Figure 16-1). You can use pkgchk to see if an SE release is already installed and use pkgrm to remove the packages if they are there. The packages must be uncompressed and extracted into their installable format; pkginfo is used to check that they are ready to be loaded, then pkgadd is used to load them, specifying the current directory. The only question you are asked during installation of RICHPse and RICHPsex is whether you would like to let us know that you installed SE by sending an email that specifies the organization you work for.

Figure 16-1 SE Installation Example

```
# pkginfo SUNWsprot RICHPse RICHPsex ANCrules
system       SUNWsprot       Solaris Bundled tools
ERROR: information for "RICHPse" was not found
ERROR: information for "RICHPsex" was not found
ERROR: information for "ANCrules" was not found
```

Figure 16-1 SE Installation Example (Continued)

```
# zcat RICHPse.tar.Z | tar xf -
# zcat RICHPsex.tar.Z | tar xf -
# zcat ANCrules.tar.Z | tar xf -
# pkginfo -d .
application ANCrules        Adrian's Rules & Tools
application RICHPse         The SymbEL Interpreter
application RICHPsex        The SE eXtensions Package
# pkgadd -d . RICHPse RICHPsex ANCrules
```

During ANCrules installation, you are asked if you want to install scripts in
/etc/rc2.d and /etc/rc3.d so that SE monitoring tools are started automatically at
boot time. The first time you try this out, you should answer "n". You can then try out the
scripts by hand as a regular user to build up your confidence in them, then try them as
root. If all seems well, enable the auto-startup next time you add ANCrules via pkgadd
on a system.

Add /opt/RICHPse/bin to your path, as shown in Figure 16-2. Unlike the case in
previous releases, scripts are now run via the se command, rather than directly. This
allows the SE toolkit to be mounted from a server and avoids the need to specify the
location of SE in the heading of every script. The se command is a shell script that uses
the environment variable SEPATH to find scripts to run. By default SEPATH contains the
examples directory followed by the current directory. If you define your own SEPATH, it
is prepended. The se script also figures out what kind of hardware and Solaris release
you are using and starts the right interpreter binary.

Figure 16-2 Running SE Example Tools

```
% set path=($path /opt/RICHPse/bin)
% se vmstat.se 5
   procs            memory        page                       faults           cpu
  r  b  w      swap      free  pi  po  sr  rt    in   sy    cs   mx  us  sy  id
  0  0  0    446992     38536   0   0   0 999   184  108    64    0   0   0 100
  0  0  0    446984     38400   0   0   0 999   145 2083   171   23   0   0  96
```

System Performance Monitoring with SE

A basic reason why we monitor the performance of a system is to define the overall state
of the machine ("it's OK" or "it's slow," etc.). This monitoring breaks down into the states
of the main components of a system such as disks, nets, RAM, and so on. I have produced
a set of performance rules that you can use to find out what state you are in. These were
originally described in Appendix A of the first edition of this book, but it was hard to

obtain the data and follow the rules by hand. I have coded all the rules in SE and no longer attempt to describe them the way I did before. The SE rules code defines the rules unambiguously, and you can test them by running monitoring scripts that use the rules.

Monitoring Your System with `zoom.se`

It's too much work to manually apply all the rules mentioned in this book. Luckily, you don't have to! I have coded each rule as a reusable object, using the SE toolkit, and there is a GUI front end to the rules, so you can just run `zoom.se` and see the state of the system. A typical display is shown in Figure 16-3. The overall system state is amber because two disks are at the amber warning level and RAM is getting short. If you click on any part of the window, you pop up a display that gives you more detail.

Figure 16-3 Example Display of `zoom.se`

The usual convention is to define color-coded states based on green, amber, and red. I have extended these states a little; the full set I use is as follows.

- White state — Completely idle, untouched, inactive
- Blue state — Imbalance, idle while other instances of the resource are overloaded

- Green state — No problems, normal active operating state
- Amber state — Warning condition for problems that don't need immediate action
- Red state — Overloaded or problem detected, action needed to fix it
- Black state— Error conditions that indicate component or system failure

Long-Term Monitoring with Calendar Manager

When you install the SE toolkit, an option you get is to start up some scripts automatically at boot time. One of these is called `mon_cm.se`; it wakes up every 15 minutes, runs the rules, and if there are any amber, red, or black states, it creates a calendar appointment, indicating the problem, for the root user. You can browse the calendar at any time, and using multibrowse, you can view several machines at once. Some example output is shown in Figure 16-4. In this case, you can see that for the 15-minute period from 5:59 p.m., the overall state is red. There are no rules in the black state, the Nets rule is in the red state, and there are no rules in the amber state. You can also see the list of times and states for the whole day.

Figure 16-4 Calendar Manager Performance Appointment

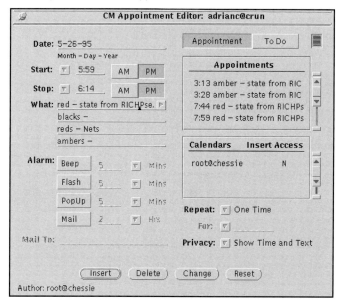

In Figure 16-5 I used multibrowse to look at both an NFS server (chessie) and a client (crun) at the same time. Chessie has a lot of entries, and crun has a few that overlap and are shown as darker bars. You can see the pattern through the working week. This output includes some activity at about 3:15 a.m. that corresponds to the `nfsfind` command run by cron.

Figure 16-5   Calendar Manager Multibrowse Performance

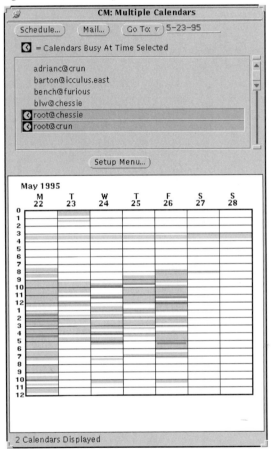

Actions Explained for the Performance Rules

The SE toolkit contains a set of 11 coded rules that generate status codes and action strings. The actions are quite terse, and I am sometimes asked what the actions mean or what to do about them. Some rules also have an explanation string that gathers together multiple actions. This section lists every action setting of every rule from SE3.0. There are two generic action strings. "No activity" is used when the subsystem being monitored is inactive or there are not enough samples to obtain a consistent average value for a measurement. Previous versions of SE use "No problem" to indicate that the subsystem is active and working well. During a trip to Australia in 1995, I decided to localize this message to "No worries, mate." I'd welcome additional localizations or translations of the messages. Send them to me, and I'll include them in a future release.

Disk Rule

The rule for disks is quite complex because there are many disks on a system, and I chose to implement a rule that complains about an imbalance in the usage of the disks. I also pick out two special cases and recognize the presence of a single floppy disk and a single CD-ROM drive as much slower devices. I'm looking for disks that are more than 20% busy and have service times of more than 30–50 ms.

The action strings are quite easy to understand. If you see a sustained problem state, do what it says!

"Move load from busy disks to idle disks"

"No activity"

"No worries, mate"

"Don't add more load to disks"

"Reduce load on disks or add more disks"

You can reduce load by several means. If the RAM rule is also showing a problem, adding RAM may help reduce swap space and filesystem paging activity on the disk subsystem. If there is a lot of write activity, adding NVRAM to the I/O subsystem or enabling fast writes on a SPARCstorage Array will coalesce writes and reduce the disk load. You may also be able to tune an application, perhaps adding an index to a database to reduce full table scans. If all else fails, rearrange the disk partitions, making wider stripes for the busiest data. If a stripe is unbalanced, it may have too large an interlace; an interlace of 128 Kbytes is reasonable for most purposes.

Network Rule

The network rule looks at all the Ethernets in the system in one go. I don't have any rules for other network types. I have recently uprated the rule to look for deferred transmissions rather than collisions as the main indicator of a slow interface. I also look for IP-level discards and errors on the interface. With the latest patches in Solaris 2.5. and in Solaris 2.6, we can see how many bytes are being transferred on some interfaces, but this data is not yet used by the rule. I increased the default packet rate and collision rate thresholds to reduce false alarms. All network interfaces are monitored, whether or not the interface is plumbed and in use. This monitoring tends to cause the rule to nag at you about any unused interfaces that could in theory be used to share the load. In practice, you may not have the right network configuration to take advantage of them easily.

"Move load from busy ethernets to idle Ethernets"

"No activity"

"No worries, mate"

"Don't add more load to Ethernets"

"Add more or faster nets"

"Problem: network failure"

If more than one problem occurs at the same time, a multiline explanation is constructed containing all the warnings and problems.

"Error seen, check hardware and cables"

"Errors seen, fix hardware or cables"

"IP dropped incoming packet"

"IP dropping incoming packets"

"Defer rate warning, output slowed"

"Defer rate excessive, output slow"

"Collision rate warning"

"Collision rate excessive"

In some cases, the RAM and network rules together may indicate that a lot of paging over NFS is a problem that could be fixed with more RAM. In most cases, you will find that a 10-Mbit network is just not enough capacity. If you ever get the chance to run a 100-Mbit network from your desktop to the server, you will realize just how much performance is being thrown away due to lack of network capacity. The latest systems can easily overload a 100-Mbit network! Network errors can be hard to eliminate: Check cables and other hardware and look for other systems on the network that may be transmitting bad packets. I suspect that many errors are overlooked, so this rule is going to highlight a lot of latent problems. You can get more detail by using `netstat -k` to check the individual error counters.

NFS Rule

The NFS client activity is monitored by looking at the client-side RPC counters for time-outs and duplicate packets. A minimum NFS call rate is needed before a problem is reported.

"No client NFS/RPC activity"

"No worries, mate"

"Packets lost, fix network"

"Server slow, increase time-out"

Explanations add some more detail.

"Packets being lost, fix bad network or reduce NFS/RPC packet sizes"

"Duplicate replies seen, speedup NFS/RPC server or increase client time-out"

Sometime routers drop part of a sequence of packets, so reducing the NFS read and write sizes decreases the chance of a buffer overflow. If the system can tell that the server is accessed through a router, the transfer size is automatically reduced.

Duplicate replies can occur if the server is so slow that the client retransmits the request and the server eventually answers both requests.

Swap Space Rule

The swap space rule is not really a performance rule, but if you run out of swap space, the system will stop working properly. This rule keeps an eye on available swap space (note that "available" swap reported by `vmstat` and used by the rule is not the same as "free" swap reported by `sar`!), so you can see when it starts to get low. Hopefully, you will be warned soon enough to add some more swap space or kill overlarge processes.

"There is a lot of unused swap space"

"No worries, mate"

"Not much swap left, perhaps add some more"

"Swap space shortage, add some more now"

"Dangerous swap space shortage, add more immediately"

The last action is associated with one of the few "black" states. If you have less than 1 Mbyte of available swap space, things will fail and the system will eventually become unusable.

RAM Rule

The virtual memory system indicates that it needs more memory when it scans looking for idle pages to reclaim for other uses. My first attempt at this rule put a threshold on the scan rate itself, as continuous high scanning is a sign of RAM demand. I found that this rule worked but did not scale well. Machines with very little memory would tend to show a paging disk overload but not a high enough scan rate. I came up with an approximation to idle page residence time instead. This is the time duration that an idle page will stay in memory. It is obtained by dividing the scan rate into a quarter of the memory size in pages (the default value of the kernel variable `handspreadpages`). This approach could result in a divide by zero condition, so the residence time is reported at the upper threshold of 600 seconds by the toolkit code if zero scan rate is seen.

In previous releases of SE, the value of `handspreadpages` was estimated incorrectly on large memory systems. It is clamped to a 64-Mbyte limit in recent Solaris releases.

"RAM available"

"No worries, mate"

"RAM shortage"

"Severe RAM shortage"

Matching explanations are a little more verbose.

"Page scanner is inactive, no RAM being reclaimed"

"Page scanner gently reclaiming unused RAM"

"Getting short on RAM, page residence time low"

"Very short on RAM, active pages being stolen"

Make sure you avoid the common mistakes of worrying about paging rates or free RAM. If this rule doesn't show a problem, there is no point adding more RAM to a system—folklore and `vmstat` notwithstanding!

Kernel Memory Rule

I have had no end of queries about this rule. Like the swap rule, it is not really a performance rule, it is just a nice thing to have the toolkit keep an eye on for you. We went through a phase with Solaris 2.4 and 2.5 where the kernel could try to grab some memory only to find that the free list was temporarily empty. This situation causes an allocation error. In some cases, the subsystem manages to retry and recover from the problem. In other cases, a seemingly unrelated operation could fail—perhaps a login attempt would die with a streams allocation error. A fix included in Solaris 2.5.1 was backported to earlier releases, so if you see this problem, make sure you have an up-to-date kernel patch installed. The rule latches into amber if it has ever seen a problem since the time the rule initialized. You can get rid of the amber state only by restarting the rule.

"No worries, mate"

"Allocation errors since startup"

"New allocation errors"

"Kernel failed to get memory at some time in the past, check kernel size and increase lotsfree, check kernel patch level"

"Kernel failed to get memory, either free list too small or kernel address space limit reached, upgrade kernel patch level"

"Kernel failed to get memory, free list too small, upgrade kernel patch level"

If you see transient allocation errors, you should increase the free list size and make the system a little more aggressive at reclaiming memory. Do this by increasing `slowscan` to 500 and multiplying the base `lotsfree` and `desfree` by the number of CPUs configured. This tuning is performed automatically if necessary when you run `virtual_adrian.se` as root.

If you see continuous allocation errors when the free list is not exhausted, then the kernel may have exceeded its address space. This case is most likely to occur on very highly configured systems with maximum RAM, disk, and CPU configurations, and large numbers of processes. The kernel runs out of space to keep track of all this. The sun4d kernel (e.g., SPARCserver 1000) has twice as much `kmap` as the sun4m kernel (e.g., SPARCstation 20). The sun4u kernel (UltraSPARC systems) avoids this problem by having a separate address space with seven or eight times the `kmap` space of a sun4d.

CPU Rule

The CPU rule does not know how fast your CPU is or how fast you want your program to run. It does not complain if one job is using 100% of the CPU. It only complains if you try to run too many things at once. Large run queue and load average levels increase interactive response times to unacceptable levels. You may still want a faster CPU if you need more throughput, but this rule has no way to measure throughput.

"CPU idling"

"No worries, mate"

"CPU busy"

"CPU overload"

Matching explanations:

"There is more CPU power configured than you need right now"

"CPU busy, more or faster CPUs would help"

"CPU overload, add more or faster CPUs, or reduce workload"

Kernel Mutex Rule

The kernel mutex rule is another rule that causes a lot of questions. Mutex contention is hard to explain. Basically, the kernel maintains locks on many resources. It is carefully designed so that there are enough locks to allow lots of CPUs to get their work done at once. If a lot of CPUs try to get the same lock at the same time, all but one CPU will stall for a while. The number of stalls on mutual exclusion locks is reported by the mpstat command as "smtx." A high level of contention will waste CPU time (it appears as extra "sys" time) and limit multiprocessor scaling.

"No worries, mate"

"Possible MP kernel overload"

"MP Kernel overloaded"

Matching explanations:

"High mutex contention rate, multiprocessor kernel is becoming overloaded, faster CPUs should help, more CPUs may make it worse"

"Serious mutex contention, multiprocessor kernel overloaded, use lockstats command to identify overloaded kernel subsystem, faster CPUs will help, more CPUs will make it worse"

Each release of Solaris is better than the previous one. The best thing to do if the rule shows a problem is to upgrade to the latest release. If you are already running the latest release, you should try to identify which component of your workload is causing the contention. Solaris 2.6 includes a supported lockstats command that can be used to discover which locks are causing contention. Call your local Sun Answer Center to describe your problem and the application. It may be possible to work around it or get it fixed in a future release. If you complain about contention in an old release of Solaris, you won't get much sympathy.

One other workaround is to use fewer, faster CPUs. If you have contention problems with an eight-way 85 MHz SPARCserver 1000, an upgrade to a four-way 250 MHz E4000 will help.

DNLC Rule

The directory name lookup cache (DNLC) speeds up directory accesses by caching the file names and makes opening a file faster. If the cache is too small, extra disk reads will be needed and NFS server response time and throughput will be worse. NFS is stateless, so a sequence of NFS reads on a file will reopen the same file for each read, unlike local file accesses where the file is opened once.

If you are monitoring an NFS server, this rule is important. For most other systems, it is much less significant. In SE2.5 and later, `virtual_adrian.se` limits its size recommendation to 34000; older releases would keep telling you to double it without limit whenever anyone ran something like `find` on the system. This is one reason why the state only ever reports "amber" at worst.

> "No activity"

> "No worries, mate"

> "Poor DNLC hitrate"

If you have a small NFS server, the DNLC is likely to be too small. If you have less than 256 Mbytes of RAM, set `ncsize=5000` in `/etc/system`. You will find that `virtual_adrian.se` gives some tuning advice when run as root, but it cannot dynamically change `ncsize`.

Inode Rule

The UFS inode cache is related to the DNLC. Rather than storing the name of a file, it stores the information about a file in the local (UFS) file system. There are two kinds of entries. Active entries are for open files; they must remain in memory while the file is open, and they contain the locations in memory of the pages that cache file data. Inactive entries are for files that are not currently open. The current algorithm only limits the number of inactive entries to the value of `ufs_ninode` (by default, the same as `ncsize`). Remember that NFS opens and closes the file for each NFS read to a file, causing the inode to keep returning to the inactive state. If the inode cache is too small, it may be discarded, causing extra overhead for the next NFS read of that file.

> "No activity"

> "No worries, mate"

> "Poor inode cache hitrate"

You will see this message if you run `find`, and you can ignore it unless you see poor performance on an NFS server.

> "Inodes with pages being stolen, increase ufs_ninode"

This message indicates that cached file data is being discarded because the inactive inode for the file was discarded. If the file is opened again, there will be extra work to get at its data.

TCP/IP Rule

The TCP stack is monitored using the data that is normally obtained via the `netstat -s` command or SNMP. SE can read this data directly from the kernel and runs five separate rules, which are summarized into the overall TCP state.

"Low TCP activity"

"No worries, mate"

"Problems: retransmit, listen queue, resets, attempts, all seen"

The action may consist of one of the following messages or may use the line above to indicate multiple problems. The explanation concatenates all the problems, including the state code for each problem (amber or red). Some of the actions depend upon the TCP patch level and Solaris release in use.

"Moderate retransmissions"

"High retransmissions, check TCP patch level"

"High retransmissions, fix network"

"Listen queue dropout warning"

"Listen HalfOpenDrops, possible SYN denial attack"

"Listen queue dropouts, speedup accept processing"

"Multiple ListenDrops, update TCP patch"

"Incoming connection refused: invalid port, RST sent"

"Incoming connections refused: port scanner (Satan?) attack"

"Attempt failures: can't connect to remote application"

Outgoing retransmissions can be high unless the TCP patch is installed. The listen queue is described in "TCP/IP Patches and the Listen Queue Fix" on page 59. Incoming connections to invalid port numbers are noted, and if they occur at a high rate, it is possible that someone is using a port scanner program, such as Satan, to look for security flaws in your system. It could also indicate that a service has failed on your server; for example, if the web server is not running, connections to port 80 will fail. If you are monitoring the client rather than the server, attempt failures occur when your system tries to connect to a server and it rejects the connection.

Look Out, There's a Guru About

Sys Admin: "What's wrong with this system? Can you tune it please? Here's the root password."

Performance Guru: "I've tuned a few kernel variables, but it looks pretty idle to me right now."

Sys Admin: "Yes, but it gets really, really busy some of the time....."

Performance Guru: "You should start collecting some data. Call me again when you have some logs of when it was busy."

Have you ever found that your most troublesome system is idle, or behaves perfectly, when you call in the consultants and performance gurus? Then, when you collect data that shows the problem, the guru wants some extra data that you didn't bother to collect!

The SE toolkit provides a way to capture and distribute the expertise of a performance specialist. I have used the toolkit to build a personalized performance monitoring and tuning tool called `virtual_adrian.se`. It starts up when the system boots, does some simple tuning, and every 30 seconds it takes a look at the state of the system. When run with superuser permissions, it can monitor more of the system than `zoom.se`. It can also make immediate changes to some kernel tunables.

When you run `virtual_adrian.se`, it keeps quiet until it sees a problem. It then complains and shows the data that caused the complaint. For example, if it keeps complaining about a slow disk, then you should find a way to reduce the load on that disk. Unlike a real performance guru, the virtual guru can look at lots of data very quickly and never gets bored or falls asleep. Most performance problems occur over and over again. The script picks out a number of "obvious" problems. (Obvious to a guru!).

If you disagree with my rules (they are a bit crude in places) or want to add your own rules, it is easy to modify the script and rename it `virtual_kimberley.se` or whatever.

The `virtual_adrian.se` Performance Tuner And Monitor

The core of `virtual_adrian.se` is the same set of rules that are used by `ruletool.se`. There is an initial check and tune of the system, and there are a few extra rules that require superuser permissions. If you run it as a regular user, it runs with functionality equivalent to `ruletool.se` writing to a logfile.

Check and Tune the System

I'm always asked for the "magic bullet"—the secret tweak to a kernel variable that will miraculously make the whole machine run much faster. I'm sorry, but tuning the kernel should be the last thing you try. It is very rare for a change to make a difference that can be reliably measured *at all*. That said, there are a small number of common kernel tuning variables that I like to tune. I generally bring older releases in line with later ones, so most tweaks are for Solaris 2.3 and are not needed for Solaris 2.4 or 2.5.

The usual method is to set variables in /etc/system. The problem is that these variables may be set incorrectly because of folklore. They may also be unnecessary or harmful in later releases, and the /etc/system file is often propagated intact to very different systems. Deciding when a tweak is useful and what the value should be for a particular release is complex. Your motto should be, if in doubt, do without!

My solution is to remove everything from /etc/system that doesn't have a big comment that explains why it is there and how its value was derived. The well-known maxusers tunable automatically scales as you add memory, so you don't need to set it unless you have several gigabytes of RAM and are short on kernel memory. I implement a check-and-tune routine in virtual_adrian.se that checks and tunes some values directly. It tells you what it does and tells you to set variables in /etc/system for the next reboot if they cannot be set on line. The check is performed once only at startup and is implemented by a routine called static_check(). Note that the current value of each tunable is checked by my script. Please do not blindly set all these values in your own /etc/system file because you may decrease something that you thought you were increasing.

The tuning actions performed for Solaris 2.3 are:

- Reduce slowscan to 100, to make memory reclaims less aggressive, and reduce fastscan to 16000. These are the maxima in Solaris 2.4.

- Increase inode cache size by setting ufs_ninode to 10000. Request that the DNLC size be increased to 5000 by adding set ncsize=5000 in /etc/system. If the values are already this big, leave them alone.

If you have a patched Solaris 2.3 kernel (patch 101318-45 or later), the Solaris 2.4 inode cache algorithm was added to the patch. It's not necessary to make the inode cache limit so big, but it doesn't hurt. I don't have code to figure out the patch level!

The tuning actions performed for Solaris 2.4 and 2.5 are:

- Increase the free list threshold lotsfree as CPUs are added, to 128 pages per CPU. This has no effect on uniprocessor systems, which default to 128. A larger free list helps prevent transient kernel memory allocation failures. If the free list is at zero when the kernel needs memory and can't wait, then kmem errors will be reported by the kmem error rule.

- Increase inactive inode cache size by setting ufs_ninode to 5000. Request that the DNLC size be increased to 5000 by adding set ncsize=5000 in /etc/system. If the values are already this big, leave them alone.

File System Flush Process Monitor

The `fsflush` process is responsible for flushing modified filesystem data to disk. It usually flushes anything that has been resident for 30 seconds (`autoup`); and runs every 5 seconds (`tune_t_fsflushr`). `fsflush` checks each page of memory in turn. Systems with a lot of memory can waste CPU time. If you are running a raw disk resident database, `fsflush` does not need to run often. In `virtual_adrian.se`, a configurable process monitor watches a single process and complains if the process uses too much CPU. By default, process id 3 (`fsflush`) is monitored, and a complaint occurs if it takes more than 5% of one CPU.

NFS Mount Point Service Time Monitor

The NFS protocol maintains retransmit timers for client-side requests when it is run over the UDP/IP protocol. These timers can be viewed with `nfsstat -m` on the NFS clients. Note that Solaris 2.5 supports NFS over TCP/IP; the timers are not needed and are reported as zero in this case. The timers can only be read when the program is running as root, which is the main reason this check is not part of `ruletool.se`. I check that the overall smoothed round-trip time is under 50 ms (srtt for All:). This practice is similar in concept to checking that disk I/O service time is better than 50 ms in the disk rule.

Figure 16-6   Example Output from `nfsstat -m`

```
/home/username from server:/export/home3/username
 Flags:    vers=2,hard,intr,down,dynamic,rsize=8192,wsize=8192,retrans=5
 Lookups:  srtt=7 (17ms), dev=4 (20ms), cur=2 (40ms)
 Reads:    srtt=16 (40ms), dev=8 (40ms), cur=6 (120ms)
 Writes:   srtt=19 (47ms), dev=3 (15ms), cur=6 (120ms)
 All:      srtt=15 (37ms), dev=8 (40ms), cur=5 (100ms)
```

Sample Output from `virtual_adrian.se`

When you install the SE toolkit, you are asked if you want to set up `virtual_adrian.se` to run automatically at boot time. If you say yes, then output is sent to the console and logged to `/var/adm/sa/monitor.log`. Let's take a look at the output from running it by hand.

```
% se virtual_adrian.se
Warning: Cannot init kvm: Permission denied
Warning: Kvm not initialized: Variables will have invalid values
Adrian is monitoring your system starting at: Sun Nov 30 15:12:36 1997

Warning: Cannot get info for pid 3.
superuser permissions are needed to access every process
Using predefined rules for disk, net, rpcc, swap, ram, kmem,
```

```
cpu, mutex, dnlc, inode, and tcp

Checking the system every 30 seconds...
```

The warning about kvm (the raw kernel data interface) can be ignored because the script does not attempt to use any kvm data unless it runs as root. When you run it as root, you see some kernel tuning (this is a dual CPU Solaris 2.5.1 system) and the extra rules are configured.

```
# /opt/RICHPse/bin/se virtual_adrian.se
Adrian is monitoring your system starting at: Sun Nov 30 15:19:01 1997

Setting lotsfree to 128 * ncpus = 256
Setting desfree to 50 * ncpus = 100
Increasing slowscan to 500 pages/s to reduce kvm alloc problems
Process watcher pid set to 3, process name fsflush, max CPU usage  5.0%
NFS client threshold set at All: srtt=20 (50ms) max NFS round trip
Minimum client NFS ops/sec considered active 2.00/s
Using predefined rules for disk, net, rpcc, swap, ram, kmem,
cpu, mutex, dnlc, inode, and tcp

Checking the system every 30 seconds...
```

I ran the command

```
% find / -ls >/dev/null
```

which makes the disk and the name caches rather busy, and got this output.

```
Adrian detected slow disk(s) red: Sun Nov 30 15:16:06 1997
Move load from busy disks to idle disks
State       ------throughput------ -----wait queue----- -----active queue---
  disk      r/s w/s   Kr/s   Kw/s qlen res_t svc_t %ut qlen  res_t svc_t %ut
R c0t1d0    59.6 15.5  203.2  123.7 0.05  0.60  0.60   5 8.33 110.89  8.97  67

Adrian detected heavy Directory Name Cache activity (amber): Sun Nov 30
15:16:06 1997
Poor DNLC hitrate
DNLC hitrate 56.3%, reference rate 1484.70/s

Adrian detected Inode Cache problem (amber): Sun Nov 30 15:16:06 1997
Poor inode cache hitrate
Inode hitrate 10.5%, reference rate 632.77/s
```

As you can see, the output is somewhat verbose and is based on extended versions of familiar command output where appropriate.

The whole point of the SE toolkit is that you can customize the tools very easily. To encourage you to do this, the rest of this chapter is a tour of the SE language and toolkit classes.

Features of the SE Language

The SE language is based on a subset of the C language. It is much easier to learn a dialect of an existing language than it is to learn a brand-new language.

- Scripts are passed through the standard C preprocessor before being executed.
- C statement types are all implemented, apart from `goto`.
- C operators are all implemented, apart from a few unary and ternary operators.
- Most C data types are implemented, including floating point, but there are no pointers in the language. A new type called string is added. Some common C library routines are redefined to avoid pointer arguments.
- Arrays, structures, and initialized structures are implemented.
- A mechanism for defining entry points into the standard, dynamically linked C libraries is provided. This mechanism avoids the need to supply more than a basic set of built-in functions in the interpreter.
- A large set of header files is provided. These files define structures that map onto the many kernel data structures that provide performance information.
- The most significant extension to the language is a simple object-oriented class, which is just a structure definition that has a function definition embedded in it. A variable of this type can be defined so that whenever an element of the structure is accessed, the function is executed first.
- Classes that map onto the kernel data sources are defined, so that each time the classes are read, the current values of each metric are provided.
- The code required to provide data in ready-to-use formats is also embedded in classes. For example, an `iostat` class provides the per-second rates for each disk as floating-point values in a data structure.

A typical script includes a whole bunch of header files that define the functions and classes to be used, then handles command-line arguments and loops, reading a class variable and printing out the values.

`iostat` Written in SE

The SE language comes with a collection of scripts that clone the common Unix performance utilities like `iostat` and `vmstat`. The code for an `iostat  -x` clone called `xiostat.se` is very simple and easy to understand. See Figure 16-7.

Figure 16-7 Code for `xiostat.se`

```
#include <stdio.se>
```

```
#include <stdlib.se>
#include <unistd.se>
#include <string.se>
#include <kstat.se>
#include <sysdepend.se>
#include <time.se>
#include <dirent.se>
#include <diskinfo.se>
#include <p_iostat_class.se>

#define SAMPLE_INTERVAL    1
#define LOTS             10000

main(int argc, string argv[3])
{
  p_iostat p_iostat$disk;
  p_iostat tmp_disk;
  int i;
  int interval = SAMPLE_INTERVAL;
  int iterations = LOTS;
  int ndisks;

  switch(argc) {
  case 1:
    break;
  case 2:
    interval = atoi(argv[1]);
    break;
  case 3:
    interval = atoi(argv[1]);
    iterations = atoi(argv[2]);
    break;
  default:
    printf("use: %s [interval] [count]\n", argv[0]);
    exit(1);
  }
  ndisks = p_iostat$disk.disk_count;
  for(; iterations > 0; iterations--) {
    sleep(interval);
    print_header();
    for(i=0; i<ndisks; i++) {
      p_iostat$disk.number$ = i;
      tmp_disk = p_iostat$disk;
     printf("%-8.8s %4.1f %4.1f %6.1f %6.1f %4.1f %4.1f %6.1f %3.0f %3.0f\n",
        tmp_disk.info.long_name,
        tmp_disk.reads, tmp_disk.writes,
```

```
        tmp_disk.kreads, tmp_disk.kwrites,
        tmp_disk.avg_wait, tmp_disk.avg_run,
        tmp_disk.service,
        tmp_disk.wait_percent, tmp_disk.run_percent);
    }
  }
}

print_header()
{
  printf("                                extended disk statistics\n");
  printf("disk       r/s  w/s   Kr/s   Kw/s wait actv  svc_t  %%w  %%b\n");
}
```

To illustrate the language, we'll walk through this script.

1. The `#include` lines bring in the definitions and the code that does the real work.

2. The definitions in `main()` define two copies of the per-disk `iostat` class. One has the special prefix `p_iostat$` that matches the function name defined in the class. This is an active variable. By convention, dollar signs are embedded in active variables to indicate that the variables are special. The other is just a regular data structure of the same storage type. It is used to hold a temporary snapshot copy of the data. Internally, a snapshot of the kernel's disk counters is made as the class initializes itself.

3. Simple command-line processing allows the measurement interval to be specified.

4. The first read of the class picks out how many disks there are.

5. The script loops forever until it is interrupted. It sleeps to start with, so that the first measurement is made over the specified interval.

6. After printing the headers, the script loops through the disks. For each disk, you need to write the index into the class to tell the class which disk you want data for.

7. A structure-to-structure copy takes a snapshot of all the data for a single disk. Before the data is read from the class, the kernel counters are read, differenced from the previous measurements, and processed into floating-point values.

8. All that remains is to print out the data in the right format. The output matches the regular `iostat -x` command, but more useful disk names are substituted.

```
% se iostat.se
                                extended disk statistics
disk       r/s  w/s   Kr/s   Kw/s wait actv  svc_t  %w  %b
c0t0d0     0.0  0.0    0.0    0.0  0.0  0.0    0.0   0   0
```

cOt1d0	0.0	27.0	0.0	380.0	0.0	1.2	44.4	0	32
cOt5d0	0.0	0.0	0.0	0.0	0.0	0.0	0.0	0	0
fd0	0.0	0.0	0.0	0.0	0.0	0.0	0.0	0	0

Rule Construction

It is easy to define and use your own performance rules. In just a few hours you can build a complete customized virtual guru of your own. If you would like to share your work, send it to se-feedback@chessie.eng.sun.com, and we will try to add it to the next release of the SE Performance Toolkit.

States and Actions

As a reminder, here are the possible states that can be reported.

- White state — Completely idle, untouched
- Blue state — Imbalance, idle while other instances of the resource are overloaded
- Green state — No problems, normal operating state
- Amber state — Warning condition
- Red state — Overloaded or problem detected
- Black state — Critical problem that may cause processes or the whole system to fail

Associated with each state is an action string, which indicates the nature of the problem, and if possible, what to do about it.

Rules as Objects

I used the object-oriented class mechanism of the language to implement the rules. This approach has several benefits:

- It provides a way to package each rule.
- It offers a common interface based on a data structure.
- The implementation is hidden in the class function.
- Changes to the rule can be made without changing the interface, as long as the input data is the same.
- Rules become reusable components stored in a header file.
- Existing rules provide templates for the creation of new rules.
- Common operations like setting custom thresholds can be performed using generic functions.

Pure Rule Objects

I built what I called "pure rules." These rules are provided with input data to evaluate, by writing to elements of the class. They are evaluated by reading the rule, and examining the state code and action string that are always provided as elements of the class. These rules make no assumptions about where the data came from. They could be given simulated data, provided with historical data samples, or fed with live data.

Live Rule Objects

The next set of rule classes produced were called "live rules." These package up the code needed to:

- Read data from the current system
- Feed it to a copy of the pure rule
- Pass on the state code and action string
- Pass on derived data that was used to determine the state and action

In addition, globally available copies of the complete vmstat, iostat, and netstat classes are maintained.

A live rule is completely trivial to use in a script. It is self-initializing and self-updating. You just declare an instance of the class, and each time you read it, you get the current state and action string.

```
lr_disk_t lr_disk$dr;
lr_disk_t tmp_dr;
/* use the live disk rule */
tmp_dr = lr_disk$dr;
if ( tmp_dr.state > ST_GREEN) {
  printf("The disks are in the %s state: %s\n",
      state_string(tmp_dr.state), tmp_dr.action);
}
```

The CPU Power Rule Explained in Detail

The CPU power rule is a relatively simple rule, so it will be explained in detail. The full implementation of all the rules is too complex to explain here, but you can browse the `pure_rules.se`, `live_rules.se`, and `tcp_rules.se` header files.

CPU Pure Rule Code

Each pure rule has a series of threshold values that have defaults and that can be set via environment variables. To describe each threshold, an initialized data structure is declared. This data structure is used by a number of standard functions that get or print the threshold. Each structure contains the environment variable name, the default value, the units of the value (e.g., pages or milliseconds), precision values for formatting the value with `printf`, and a descriptive string. Thresholds can be integer, double precision floating point, or string types. The code is shown in Figure 16-8.

Figure 16-8 Code for Pure CPU Rule

```
/* CPU Power Rule */
rule_thresh_dbl cpu_runq_idle = {"RUNQ_IDLE", 1.0, "", 4, 1,
        "Spare CPU capacity" };
rule_thresh_dbl cpu_runq_busy = {"RUNQ_BUSY", 2.0, "", 4, 1,
        "OK up to this level" };
rule_thresh_dbl cpu_runq_overload = {"RUNQ_OVERLOAD", 5.0, "", 4, 1,
        "Warning up to this level" };

print_pr_cpu(ulong f) {
    print_thresh_dbl(f, cpu_runq_idle);
    print_thresh_dbl(f, cpu_runq_busy);
    print_thresh_dbl(f, cpu_runq_overload);
}

class pr_cpu_t {
  /* output variables */
  int state;
  string action;
  string explanation;
  /* input variables */
  ulong timestamp;                /* one-second resolution */
  int runque;         /* i.e., p_vmstat.runque load level */
  int ncpus;/* i.e. sysconf(_SC_NPROCESSORS_ONLN) */
  /* threshold variables */
  double cpu_idle;
  double cpu_busy;
  double cpu_overload;

  pr_cpu$()
  {
    double cpu_load;
    ulong lasttime;               /* previous timestamp */
    if (timestamp == 0) {         /* reset defaults */
      cpu_idle = get_thresh_dbl(cpu_runq_idle);
      cpu_busy = get_thresh_dbl(cpu_runq_busy);
      cpu_overload = get_thresh_dbl(cpu_runq_overload);
      return;
    }
    if (timestamp != lasttime) {
      cpu_load = runque; cpu_load /= ncpus; /* promote to double */
```

```
   if (cpu_load < cpu_idle)
      {
      state = ST_WHITE;
      action = "CPU idling";
 explanation = "There is more CPU power configured than you need right now";
      }
   else
      {
      if (cpu_load < cpu_busy)
         {
         state = ST_GREEN;
         action = "No worries, mate";
         explanation = action;
         }
      else
         {
         if (cpu_load < cpu_overload)
            {
            state = ST_AMBER;
            action = "CPU busy";
            explanation = "CPU busy, more or faster CPUs would help";
            }
         else
            {
            state = ST_RED;
            action = "CPU overload";
   explanation = "CPU overload, add more or faster CPUs, or reduce workload";
            }
         }
      }
   lasttime = timestamp;
   }
 }
};
```

The code defines three threshold structures and a function to print them to a file descriptor. The function is provided for convenience use in scripts.

The CPU rule itself is defined as a class. The first part is just like a regular C structure definition. By convention, output variables for the state and action are always defined. Input variables are used to provide the information needed by the rule (runque and ncpus) and to timestamp each invocation of the rule. Threshold variables hold the current values of the thresholds.

The final element of the class is the block of code that is executed when the class is declared and whenever its data is read. The function name used ends in a "$" and must be used exactly as the prefix for the name of any active instances of the class.

Some local variables are defined. By convention, the timestamp is used in two special ways. A zero timestamp causes rule initialization code to be executed. In this case, the thresholds are set by means of a function that checks the environment variable and, if not defined, uses the default. If the timestamp is unchanged from the last invocation of the rule, then the code is not executed. This technique prevents unnecessary evaluations of the rule. I use a one-second resolution timestamp, which I judged was sufficient for my purpose.

Finally, the per-CPU run queue length is calculated and is compared with the thresholds to determine the state code and action string.

The rule is used by setting the input variables, updating the timestamp, and reading the output variables. This usage is shown in the definition of the live rule.

CPU Live Rule Code

The live rule wraps up the code needed to read the current values of the required input variables, with the pure rule. As shown in Figure 16-9, the definition is simpler than that of the pure rule. The only data items defined are a state code and action string. Again, the class function name is used as a prefix for active variables. An active instance of the pure rule is defined along with a temporary copy that just holds the defined data.

The live rule initializes itself when it is first declared, i.e., before the script starts to run, by reading the time, updating the global copy of the vmstat class data, setting the number of CPUs correctly in the pure rule, then resetting the pure rule while initializing the temporary copy. The state code and action string are set up.

The first time the live rule is actually read, it again updates the global copy of the vmstat class, then sets the run queue and timestamp in the pure rule and invokes it by reading it into the temporary copy. The state code and action string are propagated unchanged up to the live rule values.

Figure 16-9 Code for Live CPU Rule

```
/* CPU power - live rule */
class lr_cpu_t {
  /* output variables */
  int state;
  string action;
  string explanation;

  lr_cpu$()
  {
    ulong lasttime = 0;                 /* previous timestamp */
    ulong timestamp = 0;
    pr_cpu_t pr_cpu$cpu;
```

```
pr_cpu_t tmp_cpu;

if (timestamp == 0) {
  timestamp = time(0);
  pvm_update(timestamp);
  pr_cpu$cpu.ncpus = GLOBAL_pvm_ncpus;
  pr_cpu$cpu.timestamp = 0;
  tmp_cpu = pr_cpu$cpu; /* reset pure rule */
  action = uninit;
  explanation = action;
  state = ST_WHITE;
  lasttime = timestamp;
  return;
}
timestamp = time(0);
if (timestamp == lasttime) {
  return;   /* wait at least a second between rule invocations */
}
/* use the rule */
pvm_update(timestamp);
pr_cpu$cpu.runque = GLOBAL_pvm[0].runque;
pr_cpu$cpu.timestamp = timestamp;
tmp_cpu = pr_cpu$cpu;
state = tmp_cpu.state;
action = tmp_cpu.action;
explanation = tmp_cpu.explanation;
lasttime = timestamp;
  }
};
```

This example is one of the simplest live rules, but it is used in the same way as the most complex ones. Simply define an instance of the live rule class, then read it whenever you want to know what state the CPU is in.

Example Program Descriptions

The SE Toolkit comes with over 40 example tools. They are all provided as source code scripts written in the SE dialect of the C language. The programs are mostly located in the directory /opt/RICHPse/examples, with some additional contributed code in /opt/RICHPse/contrib. They are classified by function in Table 16-1.

Table 16-1 Example SE Programs Grouped by Function

Function	Example SE Programs		
Rule Monitors	cpg.se	monlog.se	mon_cm.se
	live_test.se	percollator.se	zoom.se
	virtual_adrian.se	virtual_adrian_lite.se	
Disk Monitors	siostat.se	xio.se	xiostat.se
	iomonitor.se	iost.se	xit.se
	disks.se		
CPU Monitors	cpu_meter.se	vmmonitor.se	mpvmstat.se
Process Monitors	msacct.se	pea.se	ps-ax.se
	ps-p.se	pwatch.se	
Network Monitors	net.se	tcp_monitor.se	netmonitor.se
	netstatx.se	nx.se	nfsmonitor.se
Clones	iostat.se	uname.se	vmstat.se
	nfsstat-m.se	perfmeter.se	xload.se
Data browsers	aw.se	infotool.se	multi_meter.se
Contributed Code	anasa	dfstats	kview
	systune	watch	
Test Programs	syslog.se	cpus.se	pure_test.se
	collisions.se	uptime.se	dumpkstats.se
	net_example	nproc.se	kvmname.se

If you are inspired to write something, send it to se-feedback@chessie.eng.sun.com, and we will consider it for a future release.

anasa.se

The anasa.se program is located in /opt/RICHPse/contrib/anasa. It is named after the Indian Anasazi tribe of Arizona, and it writes a general-purpose performance log file. Thanks to Jim Davis of the University of Arizona.

Use: anasa.se interval logfile

Here is an example of a logfile record. Read the code to work out which number is which.

```
date Fri Nov 28 21:04:39 1997
nusers 5
nprocs 61
loadaves 0.03 0.07 0.09
cpu 0 0 0 0 0 0 0 0 204 18 11 0 0 0 0 0 100 454464 10496
cpu 1 0 0 0 0 0 0 0 0 50 11 0 0 0 0 0 100
disk sd0 0.0 0.0 0.0
disk sd1 0.0 0.0 0.0
disk sd5 0.0 0.0 0.0
disk fd0 0.0 0.0 0.0
net hme0 2176 0 394 0 0
etad
```

aw.se

The `aw.se` program is an application wrapper for finding out what's up on the system while a command runs. It uses just about every class provided.

Use: `aw.se [-abcdefghijlmnopqrstuxy] [-[w|z] interval] command [args]`

-a	All info
-b	Miscellaneous system info
-c	CPU system info
-d	CPU VM info
-e	Disk info
-f	Network info
-g	RPC client info
-h	RPC server info
-i	NFS client info
-j	NFS server info
-l	Segment map info
-m	Buffer cache info
-n	Inode cache info
-o	Interrupt info
-p	Process info
-q	Memory info
-r	VM HAT info
-s	DNLC info
-t	VAC flush info
-u	System variables info
-v	Generate continuous running info
-w	Pause for interval seconds when running

-x	Give totals
-y	Don't prompt for input
-z	Snapshot for interval seconds

collisions.se

The `collisions.se` program prints out the collision rate for each Ethernet interface on the system. It is a test program for the `netif.se` class.

```
% se collisions.se
Collision rate for le0: 0.00 %
```

cpg.se

The `cpg.se` program is the Capacity Planning Guide script written in SymbEL

Use: `cpg.se [-c] [-s count] [-i interval]`

-c	Continuous mode
-s *count*	Sample count
-i *interval*	Sleep time between samples

```
% se cpg.se
----------------- Sun May 18 23:53:30 BST 1997 --------------------------
Gathering information........ok
Checking paging/swapping...
Checking disk saturation...
Checking DNLC hit rate...
Checking CPU times...
Checking network condition...
Errors on interface: le0 (ierrors = 0 oerrors = 5)
```

cpu_meter.se

The cpu_meter.se program is a basic meter showing usr/sys/wait/idle CPU as separate bars, using the SE graphics extensions library.

Figure 16-10 Example cpu_meter.se *Screenshot*

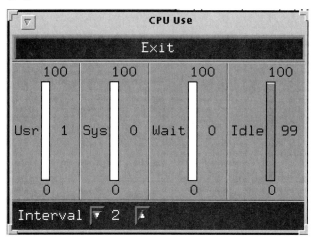

cpus.se

The cpus.se program prints out the CPUs and clock rates, like psrinfo does.

```
% se cpus.se
cpu:  0 state: online  clock: 85 MHz
```

df_stats.se

The `df_stats.se` program is located in `/opt/RICHPse/contrib/dfstats`. It is a GUI display of disk space usage statistics for read/write UFS file systems. It also provides a filesystem class and an example clone of the `df` command. Thanks to Peter Samuel of Uniq, Australia.

Figure 16-11 Example Display from `df_stats.se`

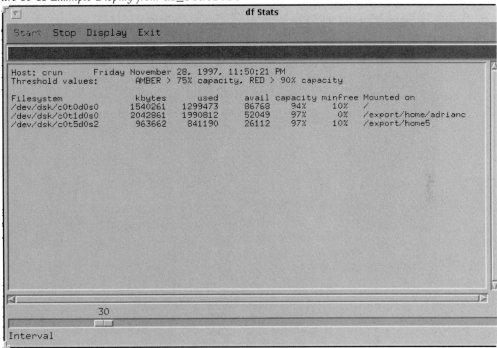

disks.se

The `disks.se` program prints out the disk instance to controller/target mappings and partition usage. The functionality was rewritten in SE3.0 so that `inst_to_path` mappings are always generated and stored with the disk data by the `p_iostat_class` code. There is no separate need to invoke `inst_to_path_class`, which simplifies code. Unbundled old SE scripts will need to be modified to work with the new `p_iostat_class`.

```
% se disks.se
kernel    -> path_to_inst -> /dev/dsk part_count [fstype mount]
sd3       -> sd3          -> c0t3d0       2
                             c0t3d0s0            ufs  /
                             c0t3d0s1            swap swap
```

infotool.se

The `infotool.se` program is a neat GUI-based tool that shows you the most interesting sets of data that the system can read via kstat. It shows totals since boot, or updates over a time period based on a slider setting, as shown in Figure 16-12. It is related to the `aw.se` program described above.

Figure 16-12 Example `infotool.se` *Screenshot*

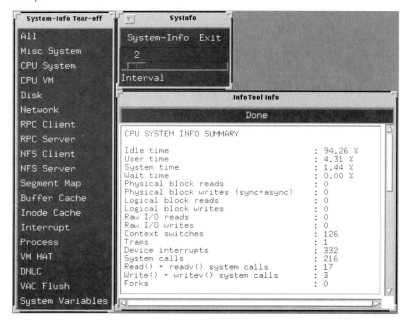

iomonitor.se

The `iomonitor.se` program is like `iostat -x` but doesn't print anything unless it sees a slow disk When it sees such a disk, it tries to sound an alarm and prints out a timestamped complaint based on `iostat -x`. The additional column headed "delay" prints out the total number of I/O's multiplied by the service time for the interval. This is an aggregate measure of the amount of waiting for I/O that is happening due to that disk on a per-second basis. High values could be cause by a few very slow I/O's or many fast ones. The disk name is converted to a more useful form, and the "slow" thresholds can be set using environment variables.

Use: /opt/RICHPse/examples/iomonitor.se [interval] [-|command]
with environment IOSLOW (default 50.0) and IOMINBUSY (default 20.0)

```
% se iomonitor.se
iomonitor.se thresholds set at 50.0 ms service time and 20.0 %busy
```

```
iomonitor.se detected slow disk(s): Tue Mar 21 21:22:24 1995
disk      r/s  w/s   Kr/s   Kw/s wait actv  svc_t  %w  %b  delay
c0t5d0    0.3 21.7    0.9 1026.5  1.9  1.8  170.1  57  61 3736.0
```

iost.se

The iost.se program is iostat -x output that is trimmed to *not* show inactive disks. The bottom line shows totals of I/O activity in reads and writes per second and Kbytes read and written. The default is to skip 0.0% busy, but the threshold can be set on the command line.

Use: iost.se [interval] [min busy to disp]

% **se iost.se**

```
                              extended disk statistics
disk       r/s  w/s   Kr/s   Kw/s wait actv  svc_t  %w  %b
c0t1d0    13.5  0.0  108.0    0.0  0.0  0.3   25.8   0  35
c0t2d0    14.0  0.0  112.0    0.0  0.0  0.3   23.1   0  32
TOTAL w/s       0.0          0.0
     r/s  27.5         220.0
```

iostat.se

The iostat.se program is a clone of the iostat -D format.

% **se iostat.se**

```
         sd3              sd5
 rps wps util    rps wps util
 0.0 0.0  0.0    0.0 0.0  0.0
 0.0 0.0  0.0    0.0 0.0  0.0
```

kviewx.se

The kviewx.se tool is located at /opt/RICHPse/contrib/kview/kviewx.se. It is an interactive monitor for kernel variables and must be run as root to read the kvm data. You can specify kernel variables that you want to monitor by name; the program then updates their values in the display at a frequency set by the slider, as shown in Figure 16-13. Thanks to Madhusudhan Talluri of Sun Labs.

Figure 16-13 Example Display for kviewx.se

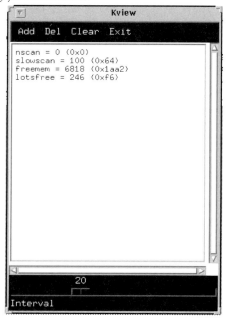

kvmname.se

The kvmname.se program is a test program for devinfo using kvm. Must be run as root.

```
# /opt/RICHPse/bin/se kvmname.se
SUNW,Ultra-2
```

live_test.se

The live_test.se program tests and displays everything in live_rules.se. It also provides a text-based system monitor output with a 30-second default interval. It can be useful as a substitute for zoom.se when no X display is available.

Use: live_test.se [interval] [-|command]

```
% se live_test.se
```

```
live_test.se Version 1.0: Started monitoring at Sun Nov 30 13:08:41 1997
Live rule specific thresholds:
LR_DISK_SLOW_FD     default=10.0x    getenv=10.0x    derate slow floppys
LR_DISK_SLOW_CD     default=10.0x    getenv=10.0x    derate slow CDs
LR_DISK_FLOPPY      default=  fd0    getenv=  fd0    default floppy device
LR_DISK_CDROM       default=c0t6d0   getenv=c0t6d0   default CD device
TCP_ACTIVE       default= 2.0KB/s getenv= 2.0KB/s ignore if no output activity
TCP_RETRANS_WARN    default=15.0%    getenv=15.0%    moderate retransmissions
TCP_RETRANS_PROBLEM default=25.0%    getenv=25.0%    excessive retransmissions
TCP_LISTEN_WARN     default=0.00/s   getenv=0.00/s   look out for listen drops
TCP_LISTEN_PROBLEM  default=0.50/s   getenv=0.50/s   excessive listen drops
TCP_HALFOPEN_PROBLEM default=2.00/s getenv=2.00/s excessive dubious SYNs
TCP_OUT_RSTS        default=0.50/s   getenv=0.50/s   moderate RSTs generated
TCP_OUT_RSTS        default=2.00/s   getenv=2.00/s   excessive RSTs generated
TCP_ATTEMPT_FAILS   default=2.00/s   getenv=2.00/s   excessive connect failures
TCP_DUP_WARN     default=15.0%   getenv=15.0%   moderate dups (remote retran)
TCP_DUP_PROBLEM     default=25.0%    getenv=25.0%    excessive dups (remote
retran)
```

```
Overall current state is green at: Sun Nov 30 13:09:11 1997
Subsystem   State Action
Disk        white No activity
    c0t0d0 white    c0t1d0 white     c0t5d0 white
Networks    white No activity
     hme0 white
NFS client white No client NFS/RPC activity
Swap space white There is a lot of unused swap space
RAM demand green No worries, mate
Kernel mem white No worries, mate
CPU power  white CPU idling
Mutex      green No worries, mate
DNLC       white No activity
Inode      white No activity
TCP        white No activity
```

mon_cm.se

Use: `mon_cm.se [interval] [calendar]`

The `mon_cm.se` program runs the live rules over a 15-minute period. Then, if any rule gives an amber or worse state, it uses `cm_insert` to create a calendar entry for that time period in `user@nodename`, indicating the rule states. For example,

```
  ** Calendar Appointment **
```

```
Date: 5/15/95
Start:  3:05am
End:  3:20am
Repeat: One Time
What: amber - state from RICHPse.mon_cm
blacks -
reds -
ambers - Disks DNLC
```

In this case, both the Disk and DNLC rules are amber; all other rules are white, blue, or green and are not shown. This data fits neatly in the calendar manager display.

The default interval is 900 seconds. To set a different calendar, use

```
% se mon_cm.se 900 username@server
```

This command can be useful to centralize calendar files on a server machine, although either a different user should be specified for each client system or the script should be changed to add the hostname to each entry. Insert permissions will be needed for the calendar specified.

You can browse remotely by using cm, and you can view multiple machines on a weekly basis by using the multibrowse capability of cm. You must run /usr/openwin/bin/cm one time as that user, to create the initial calendar. If mon_cm.se is started at boot time, it runs as root and the root calendar must be created. There is no need to restart mon_cm if it is running and failing to add the calendar entry. Just create the calendar, and mon_cm.se will add an entry next time it tries.

This technique is a very low overhead way to keep track of a large number of systems and browse their condition over long time spans, looking for periods of peak activity.

monlog.se

The monlog.se program runs the 11 predefined rules and logs state changes to syslog at 2-minute intervals. The syslog identifier can be set; it defaults to a parseable proposed syslog message standard. Loghost can be set to send syslog messages to a central logging machine.

Use: monlog.se [interval] [identifier]

```
Mar 21 20:30:59 bloodnok ID[RICHPse.monlog.2000]: Disk state white entered,
Action: No activity
```

mpvmstat.se

The `mpvmstate.se` program provides a modified `vmstat`-like display. It prints out a line per CPU, including mutex enter failures (`smtx`) and a wait time breakdown (which is always zero for `sw` and `pio`).

Use: `mpvmstat.se [interval] [count]`

```
% se mpvmstat.se
mpvmstat.se  1 second intervals starting at Tue Mar 21 21:54:34 1995
cpu r  b  w  pi po  sr smtx  in   sy   cs  us  sy  io  sw pio  id   swap   free
 0  0  0  0   0  0   0  20  191  182  155   2   0   0   0   0  98  52940   1552
 1  0  0  0   0  0   0  23  142  172  139   2   0   0   0   0  98
```

msacct.se

The `msacct.se` program uses a little-known performance measurement called microstate accounting to show the detailed sleep time and causes for a process. For Solaris 2.3, this data is always collected. For Solaris 2.4 and later, the data starts to be collected after the first measurement and will be collected until the process exits or the microstate accounting process flag is cleared via an `ioctl` to `/proc`.

Use: `msacct.se pid [interval]`

```
Elapsed time        3:29:26.344  Current time Tue May 23 01:54:57 1995
User CPU time             5.003  System call time             1.170
System trap time          0.004  Text pfault sleep            0.245
Data pfault sleep         0.000  Kernel pfault sleep          0.000
User lock sleep           0.000  Other sleep time           9:09.717
Wait for CPU time         1.596  Stopped time                 0.000
```

multi_meter.se

The `multi_meter.se` program is a useful tool that shows a total of eight measurements as horizontal bars in a gui meter. The display includes CPU system time and context switches, inode cache and DNLC hit rates, VM scan rate and pager runs, and mutex and system call rates. It also includes an interval widget to set the update rate interactively.

Figure 16-14 Example `multi_meter.se` *Screenshot*

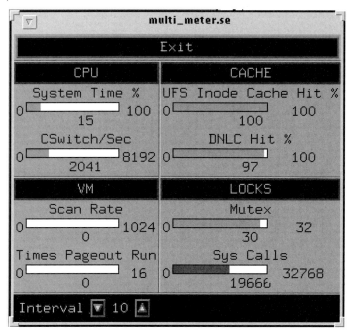

net.se

The `net.se` program is a test program for `netif` class; its output is like that of `netstat -i` plus collision percentage.

```
% net.se
Name      Ipkts    Ierrs    Opkts    Oerrs    Colls    Coll-Rate
le0           0        0        0        6        0        0.00 %
```

net_example

The `net_example` program is an example that shows how to build a distributed client/server tool with SE. An unresolved problem is that the client and server configuration environment is different. So, the number of disks that SE thinks it deals with on the client does not match the server. Careful coding is needed to work around this issue.

netmonitor.se

The `netmonitor.se` program, which embodies the same concept as `iomonitor.se`, waits for a slow network, then prints out same basic data as `netstatx.se`. It uses `p_netstat_class`, which gives per-second rates, whereas the `netif` class gives counts since boot time.

Use: `netmonitor.se [interval] [-|command]`
with environment NETACTIVE (default `10.0`) and NETMAXCOLL (default `2.0`)

```
% se netmonitor.se
netmonitor.se thresholds set at 10.0 packets/s and  2.0% collisions
```

netstatx.se

The `netstatx.se` program is like `iostat  -x` in format. It shows per-second rates like the basic `netstat` does but formats the data like `netstat  -i` does. It's a good example of how a very useful command can be simply built to fill a hole in the standard Solaris offerings. It uses `p_netstat_class` and also uses the `ndd` class to check the TCP/IP time-out, shows the total bytes sent, and retransmits using the `mib` class.

```
% se netstatx.se
Current tcp minimum retransmit timeout is 200   Mon May 19 01:09:17 1997
Name  Ipkt/s Ierr/s Opkt/s Oerr/s Coll/s  Coll%  tcpIn  tcpOut DupAck %Retran
le0      0.0    0.0    0.0    0.4    0.0   0.00      0       0      0    0.00
```

nfsmonitor.se

The `nfsmonitor.se` program is the same as `nfsstat-m.se` except that it is built as a monitor. It prints out only slow NFS client mount points, ignoring the ones that are OK. It runs only as root. For Solaris 2.5, `nfsmonitor.se` reliably reports data only for NFS V2. For NFS V3, it always reports zeroes (as does the regular `nfsstat  -m`).

nfsstat-m.se

The `nfsstate-m.se` program is a clone of the `nfsstat -m` command, testing the `nfs_class` that provides per-NFS mount point information. The program runs only as root. For Solaris 2.5, it reliably reports data only for NFS V2. For NFS V3, it always reports zeroes (as does the regular `nfsstat -m`).

nproc.se

The `nproce.se` program is a simple test program for the `first_proc/next_proc` built-in calls that get per-process data.

```
% se nproc.se
There are 56 processes on the system
```

nx.se

The `nx.se` script prints out `netstat` and `tcp` class information. "NoCP" means nocanput, which is a packet discarded because it lacks IP-level buffering on input. It can cause a TCP connection to time out and retransmit the packet from the other end. "Defr" is defers, an Ethernet metric that counts the rate at which output packets are delayed before transmission. The second interface shown is a PPP modem connection.

```
% se netstat.se
Current tcp RtoMin is 200, interval 5, start Mon May 19 01:10:40 1997
Name  Ipkt/s Opkt/s  Err/s  Coll% NoCP/s Defr/s  tcpIn  tcpOut Conn/s %Retran
le0      0.0    0.0   0.20   0.00   0.00   0.00      0       0   0.00    0.00
ipdptp0  0.0    0.0   0.00   0.00   0.00   0.00
```

pea.se

```
Usage: se [-DWIDE] pea.se [interval]
```

The `pea.se` script is an extended process monitor that acts as a test program for the `process_class` and displays very useful information that is not extracted by any standard tool. It is based on the microstate accounting information described in "Process Data Sources" on page 416. The script runs continuously and reports on the average data for each active process in the measured interval. This reporting is very different from tools such as `top` or `ps`, which print the current data only. There are two display modes: by default `pea.se` fits into an 80-column format, but the wide mode has much more information. The initial data display includes all processes and shows their average data since the process was created. Any new processes that appear are also treated this way. When a process is measured a second time, if it has consumed some CPU time, then its averages for the measured interval are displayed. Idle processes are ignored. The output is generated every ten seconds by default. It can report only on processes that it has permission to access, so it must be run as root to see everything.

```
% se pea.se
```

09:34:06 name	lwp	pid	ppid	uid	usr%	sys%	wait%	chld%	size	rss	pf
olwm	1	322	299	9506	0.01	0.01	0.03	0.00	2328	1032	0.0
maker5X.exe	1	21508	1	9506	0.55	0.33	0.04	0.00	29696	19000	0.0
perfmeter	1	348	1	9506	0.04	0.02	0.00	0.00	3776	1040	0.0
cmdtool	1	351	1	9506	0.01	0.00	0.03	0.00	3616	960	0.0
cmdtool	1	22815	322	9506	0.08	0.03	2.28	0.00	3616	1552	2.2
xterm	1	22011	9180	9506	0.04	0.03	0.30	0.00	2840	1000	0.0
se.sparc.5.5.1	1	23089	22818	9506	1.92	0.07	0.00	0.00	1744	1608	0.0
fa.htmllite	1	21559	1	9506	0.00	0.00	0.00	0.00	1832	88	0.0
fa.tooltalk	1	21574	1	9506	0.00	0.00	0.00	0.00	2904	1208	0.0

```
nproc 31  newproc 0  deadproc 0
```

I'm afraid I had to reduce the font size a long way to fit this in.

```
% se -DWIDE pea.se
```

09:34:51 name	lwp	pid	ppid	uid	usr%	sys%	wait%	chld%	size	rss	pf	inblk	outblk	chario	sysc	vctx	ictx	msps
maker5X.exe	1	21508	1	9506	0.86	0.36	0.10	0.00	29696	19088	0.0	0.00	0.00	5811	380	60.03	0.30	0.20
perfmeter	1	348	1	9506	0.03	0.02	0.00	0.00	3776	1040	0.0	0.00	0.00	263	12	1.39	0.20	0.29
cmdtool	1	22815	322	9506	0.04	0.00	0.04	0.00	3624	1928	0.0	0.00	0.00	229	2	0.20	0.30	0.96
se.sparc.5.5.1	1	3792	341	9506	0.12	0.01	0.00	0.00	9832	3376	0.0	0.00	0.00	2	9	0.20	0.10	4.55
se.sparc.5.5.1	1	23097	22818	9506	0.75	0.06	0.00	0.00	1752	1616	0.0	0.00	0.00	119	19	0.10	0.30	20.45
fa.htmllite	1	21559	1	9506	0.00	0.00	0.00	0.00	1832	88	0.0	0.00	0.00	0	0	0.10	0.00	0.06

```
nproc 31  newproc 0  deadproc 0
```

The pea.se script is a simple printf in a loop. The real work is done in process_class.se and can be used by any other script. The default data shown by pea.se consists of:

- Current time and process name
- Number of lwp's for the process, so you can see which are multithreaded
- Process ID, parent process ID, and user ID
- User and system CPU percentage measured accurately by microstate accounting
- Process time percentage spent waiting in the run queue or for page faults to complete
- CPU percentage accumulated from child processes that have exited
- Virtual address space size and resident set size, in Kbytes
- Page fault per second rate for the process over this interval

When the command is run in wide mode, the following data is added:

- Input and output blocks/second—I'm still not sure what this actually counts
- Characters transferred by read and write calls
- System call per second rate over this interval
- Voluntary context switches, where the process slept for a reason
- Involuntary context switches where the process was interrupted by higher priority work or exceeded its time slice

- Milliseconds per slice—the calculated average amount of CPU time consumed between each context switch

`percollator.se` and `/etc/rc3.d/S99percol`

The `percollator.se` script is a performance collator. It collects data from all sources, including the access logfile from a web server. It can easily be modified to handle special logfile formats and is set up for the common logfile format by default, with a customized Netscape proxy log format parser as an option. The ideas behind `percollator.se` are described in "The SE Toolkit Web Server Performance Collator, `percollator.se`" on page 88, and the proxy logfile format is described in "Configuring and Monitoring the Netscape 2.5 Proxy Cache" on page 98.

Percollator stores measurements in output files that are created daily with the file name `percol-YYYY-MM-DD`. These files contain regular columns of data, a header line identifies the column, and one line is written at each interval. The interval defaults to 300 seconds, although an inner loop in `percollator.se` checks the access logfile every 5 seconds. If the `OUTDIR` environment variable is not set, then data is written to stdout at the end of each interval. *No file is opened and nothing is output until the end of the first interval.* The output file format can be imported into a spreadsheet or viewed by means of the GPercollator Java browser. The file format is several hundred characters wide, so I have broken it down into sections in the explanations below.

The startup file `/etc/rc3.d/S99percol` is automatically installed. It sets up environment variables to configure percollator and the rule set, then starts collecting. It is enabled only if the file `/opt/RICHPse/etc/start_wl` exists.

```
use: se percollator.se [interval]
setenv NCSAHTTPLOG /ns-home/httpd-80/logs/access
setenv GATEWAY some.where.com    special address to monitor
setenv OUTDIR /ns-home/docs/percollator/logs - default stdout
use: se -DPROXY percollator.se [interval] to process proxy server log
```

Figure 16-15 shows `percollator.se` being invoked interactively with the proxy cache option set. The proxy cache option causes additional logfile processing and extra columns of output. The first column contains a Unix timestamp in seconds. The second column contains the local time of day. The third is a compressed form of the 11 generic rule states. Each rule reports its color code as w (white), g (green), A (amber), R (red), B (black). The rules order is given in the header as D (Disks), N (Networks), n (nfs), s (swap), r (ram), k (kernel memory), c (cpu), m (mutex contention), d (dnlc), i (inode), and t (TCP}. The next two columns report the overall CPU usage, and the last two shown contain the utilization of the busiest disk, peak disk busy (pdb); and the utilization averaged over all the disks, mean disk busy (mdb).

Figure 16-15 Example Output from `percollator.se` *— Time, Rules, CPU, and Disk*

% **se -DPROXY percollator.se 10**						
timestamp	locltime	DNnsrkcmdit	usr	sys	pdb	mdb
880460808	12:26:48	Awwwwwwgwww	4	2	6	6
880460818	12:26:58	wwwwwwwgwww	9	0	0	0

Figure 16-16 shows overall network packet rates, collision rate, TCP input and output data rates in bytes, and the TCP retransmission percentage.

Figure 16-16 Example Output from `percollator.se` *— Network and TCP Data*

Ipkt/s	Opkt/s	Coll%	tcpIn/s	tcpOut/s	Retran%
0.0	0.0	0.0	0	0	0.000
0.0	0.0	0.0	0	0	0.000

Figure 16-17 shows the incoming and outgoing TCP connection rate, a snapshot of the current number of established TCP connections, the HTTP operation rate, and the peak HTTP operation rate measured over a 5-second interval.

Figure 16-17 Example Output from `percollator.se` *— Connection and HTTP Rates*

conIn/s	conOut/s	conEstab	httpop/s	http/p5s
0.000	0.000	12	0.00	0.00
0.000	0.000	12	0.00	0.00

Figure 16-18 shows the conditional get rate (a header only was returned), the search rate, the `cgi-bin` script invocation rate, the HTTP error rate, and the HTTP data rate as calculated from the access log.

Figure 16-18 Example Output from `percollator.se` *— HTTP Protocol Mixture*

cndget/s	srch/s	cgi/s	htErr/s	httpb/s
0.00	0.000	0.000	0.000	0
0.00	0.000	0.000	0.000	0

Figure 16-19 shows the percentage size mix, up to 1 Kbyte, 1–10 Kbytes, 10–100 Kbytes, 100 Kbytes–1 Mbyte, and over 1 Mbyte. If the GATEWAY environment variable is set, then the rate at which connections are received from the specified Internet address is given. If GATEWAY is undefined, then the header prints not.set; otherwise, it shows its value.

Figure 16-19 Example Output from `percollator.se` *— HTTP Size Distribution*

%to1KB	%to10KB	%to100KB	%to1MB	%ov1MB	not.set
0.00	0.00	0.00	0.00	0.00	0.00
0.00	0.00	0.00	0.00	0.00	

Figure 16-20 shows proxy cache-specific information, the percentage of lookups that have to make an indirect trip through a gateway to the Internet, the cache hit rate, the percentage that caused data to be written to the cache, the percentage of uncacheable data, and the average total transfer time.

Figure 16-20 Example Output from `percollator.se` *— Proxy Cache Mixture and Transfer Time*

%indir	%cch_hit	%cch_wrt	%cch_unc	xfr_t
0.00	0.00	0.00	0.00	0.00
0.00	0.00	0.00	0.00	0.00

Figure 16-21 shows a breakdown of transfer time according to transfer size. The average time for transfers up to 1 Kbyte, 1–10 Kbytes, 10–100 Kbytes, 100 Kbytes–1 Mbyte, and over 1 Mbyte are recorded.

Figure 16-21 Example Output from `percollator.se` *— Proxy Cache Transfer Time by Size*

xfr1_t	xfr10_t	xfr100_t	xfr1M_t	xfroM_t
0.00	0.00	0.00	0.00	0.00
0.00	0.00	0.00	0.00	0.00

GPercollator Java Browser

The GPercollator program is written in Java 1.1 and runs as an applet or as a stand-alone program. If percollator.se output files are written to a browseable directory, then they can be viewed over the web, using GPercollator. This program is also used as an example in "Java Tuning" on page 125.

GPercollator is Java1.1-based, and it uses the new event model feature, so it doesn't work with older versions of Java. This means that you cannot run it using Netscape Navigator (at least up to version 4.02) or Microsoft Internet Explorer. It does work in HotJava 1.0 (the version provided with Solaris 2.6) and the JDK1.1.3 appletviewer also provided with Solaris 2.6. It also runs as a program from the command line, using JDK1.1.3. By default,

Java WorkShop builds in the code wrappers that allow generated programs to be run as applets *and as applications* without any changes. As full Java1.1 support rolls out, it will be easier to use `GPercollator` as an applet.

I appended several days of data, cloned the sequence twice and picked http operations/second, the peak 5-second rate, and the status code display, as shown in Figure 16-22. This display looks nicer in color, and you could then see that the solid bars across the bottom of the display are almost completely green.

Figure 16-22 Example Display for `GPercollator` *Java Viewer*

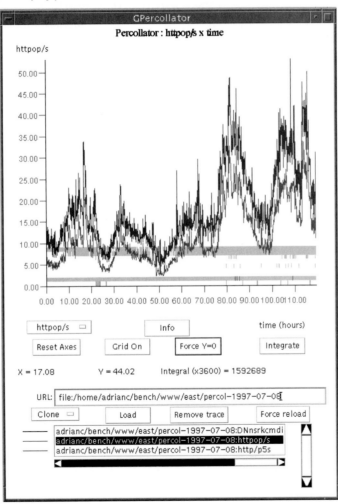

ps-ax.se

The `ps-ax.se` program is a `/usr/ucb/ps ax` clone written as a script, testing `first_proc, next_proc`. The program monitors only processes that you own. It can easily be extended to print out any combination of process data.

```
% se ps-ax.se
  PID TT        S   TIME COMMAND
  563 pts/1     S   6:02 roam
  218 console   S   0:00 -csh
  240 console   S   0:00 sh /usr/openwin/lib/Xinitrc
  316 pts/2     S 21:32 /export/home/framemaker,v5.1/bin/sunxm.s5.sparc/maker
  245 console   S   0:00 fbconsole
  258 console   S   0:16 olvwm -syncpid 257
```

ps-p.se

The `ps-p.se` program is a `/bin/ps -p` clone (using UCB output format) written as a script, testing `get_proc`. The program monitors only processes that you own.

```
% se ps-p.se 550
  PID TT        S   TIME COMMAND
  550 pts/1     S   1:16 roam
```

pure_test.se

The `pure_test.se` program is a test program for `pure_rules.se`. It shows all the thresholds, then drives the rules directly. When creating a new rule, first create it in `pure_rules.se`, use `pure_test.se` to exercise it, and then figure out how to get the data it needs. Next, build a live rule to feed it and test that, using `live_rules.se`. In the case shown in Figure 16-23, an unconnected Ethernet interface is giving errors, which shows up as a "black" failure state, and the system is showing a "red" state for RAM, as it was scanning fast over the short 10-second interval used.

Figure 16-23 Example Output for `pure_test.se`

```
use: pure_test.se [interval] [-|command]
pure_test.se Version 1.1: Started monitoring at Tue Nov 25 12:44:17 1997
DISK_BUSY_WARNING  default= 5.0%   getenv= 5.0%    ignore less than this
DISK_BUSY_PROBLEM  default=20.0%   getenv=20.0%
DISK_SVC_T_WARNING default=30.0ms  getenv=30.0ms
DISK_SVC_T_PROBLEM default=50.0ms  getenv=50.0ms
ENET_INUSE         default=50.0/s  getenv=50.0/s   ignore fewer output packets/s
ENET_COLL_WARNING  default=15.0%   getenv=15.0%
ENET_COLL_PROBLEM  default=30.0%   getenv=30.0%
ENET_ERROR_PROBLEM default=0.050/s getenv=0.050/s
ENET_DEFER_WARNING default=2.00%   getenv=2.00%    some delayed output packets
```

Figure 16-23 Example Output for `pure_test.se` *(Continued)*

```
ENET_DEFER_WARNING default=10.00%   getenv=10.00%   too many delayed output packets
ENET_NOCANPUT_PROBLEM default=1.000/s getenv=1.000/s incoming packet dropped by IP
RPCCLIENT_MINCALLS default= 0.1/s  getenv= 0.1/s  calls per sec for idle
RPCCLIENT_TIMEOUT  default= 5.0%   getenv= 5.0%   calls that timeout
RPCCLIENT_BADXID   default= 0.0%   getenv= 0.0%   timeouts with badxid
SWAP_WASTE         default=100000KB getenv=200000KB  more may be a waste
SWAP_LOTS          default= 10000KB getenv= 50000KB  more is lots
SWAP_LOW           default=  4000KB getenv= 10000KB  warning LOW to LOTS
SWAP_NONE          default=  1000KB getenv=  4000KB  danger LOW-NONE, crisis
RESTIME_LONG       default=600s   getenv=600s   No scanning - long res time
RESTIME_OK         default= 40s   getenv= 40s   residence time of unref pages
RESTIME_PROBLEM    default= 20s   getenv= 20s   pages stolen too quickly
KMEM_FREEMEM_LOW   default= 64pg  getenv= 64pg  few pages for kernel to use
RUNQ_IDLE          default= 1.0   getenv= 1.0   Spare CPU capacity
RUNQ_BUSY          default= 2.0   getenv= 2.0   OK up to this level
RUNQ_OVERLOAD      default= 5.0   getenv= 5.0   Warning up to this level
MUTEX_BUSY         default=200.0/s getenv=200.0/s OK up to this level per-CPU
MUTEX_OVERLOAD     default=500.0/s getenv=500.0/s Warning up to this level
DNLC_ACTIVE        default=100.0/s getenv=100.0/s minimum activity
DNLC_WARNING       default=80.0%  getenv=80.0%   warning missrate
INODE_ACTIVE       default=100.0/s getenv=100.0/s minimum activity
INODE_WARNING      default=80.0%  getenv=80.0%   warning missrate
INODE_IPF          default= 0.0%  getenv= 0.0%   stolen inodes w/pages frac

Overall current state is black at: Tue Nov 25 12:44:27 1997
Subsystem   State Action
Disk        white No activity
Ethernet    black Problem: network failure
NFS client  green No worries, mate
Swap space  white There is a lot of unused swap space
RAM demand   red Severe RAM shortage
Kernel mem  white No worries, mate
CPU power   white CPU idling
Mutex       green No worries, mate
DNLC hits   white No activity
DNLC hitrate 90.0%, reference rate 0.00/s
Inode hits white No activity
Inode hitrate 55.0%, reference rate 0.00/s
```

pwatch.se

The `pwatch.se` program watches a process as it consumes CPU time. It defaults to process id 3 to watch the system process `fsflush`. It monitors only processes that you own.

```
# /opt/RICHPse/bin/se pwatch.se
fsflush has used 24.4 seconds of CPU time since boot
fsflush used 0.1 %CPU, 0.1 %CPU average so far
```

siostat.se

The `siostate.se` program is a version of `iostat` that shows service times and uses correct terminology. It is described in detail in "How `iostat` Uses the Underlying Disk Measurements" on page 194.

Use: `siostat.se [interval] [count]`

```
% se siostat.se 30
13:02:25   ------throughput------ -----wait queue----- ----active queue----
disk       r/s  w/s   Kr/s    Kw/s qlen res_t svc_t %ut qlen res_t svc_t %ut
c0t3d0     0.4  6.3    1.9    73.4 0.24 36.30  2.43    2 0.16 23.63 15.92  11
13:02:55   ------throughput------ -----wait queue----- ----active queue----
disk       r/s  w/s   Kr/s    Kw/s qlen res_t svc_t %ut qlen res_t svc_t %ut
c0t3d0     7.8  3.6   46.2    26.9 0.08  6.91  0.78    1 0.21 18.42 15.40  17
13:03:25   ------throughput------ -----wait queue----- ----active queue----
disk       r/s  w/s   Kr/s    Kw/s qlen res_t svc_t %ut qlen res_t svc_t %ut
c0t3d0     0.2  7.1    0.9   148.8 0.02  2.33  1.45    1 0.23 31.05 20.18  15
```

syslog.se

The `syslog.se` program tests the syslog interface by submitting a test message.

systune.se

The `systune.se` program is a GUI front end to some of the tools provided in the release, an excellent way to explore the toolkit. Thanks to Tim Gledhill of The University of Hertfordshire, UK.

Figure 16-24 Example Display for `systune.se`

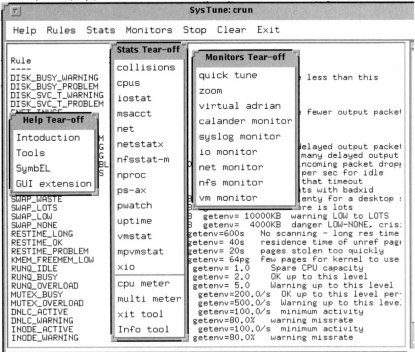

tcp_monitor.se

The `tcp_monitor.se` program was written by Mike Bennett. It is a GUI that monitors TCP and also has a set of sliders that allow you to tune some of the parameters if you run as root. You can see an example screenshot in Figure 4-1 on page 68.

uname.se

The `uname.se` program is a clone of the regular `uname` command.

```
% se uname.se -a
SunOS nodename 5.5 Generic sun4m sparc
```

uptime.se

The `uptime.se` program provides a continuous display as each second of uptime occurs.

```
% se uptime.se
 System up for:    3 days  5 hours 19 minutes 27 seconds
```

virtual_adrian.se and /etc/rc2.d/S90va_monitor

Running this script is like having Adrian actually watching over your machine for you, whining about anything that doesn't look well tuned. If it is not run as root, then it cannot perform all its checks, but it does the basic rules. See the main description earlier in this chapter "Look Out, There's a Guru About" on page 461.

During install it can be set up to run automatically from `/etc/rc2.d/S90va_monitor`, logging output to the console and to `/var/adm/sa/monitor.log`. To enable startup, the file `/opt/RICHPse/etc/start_va` must exist.

You control the thresholds by setting environment variables. The first three are specific to this script, but the rest are the generic ones used whenever the pure rules initialize themselves. Set them once in a shell window or in `/etc/rc2.d/S90va_monitor`, and they will persist for any commands that use the rules.

Figure 16-25 Usage and Configuration of `virtual_adrian.se`

```
 use: virtual_adrian.se [interval] [command]
 with environment variables:
 PWPID (default 3 is fsflush)
 PWMAXCPU (default  5.0% max CPU usage)
 NFSRTALLSLOW (default 50ms max NFS round trip time)
 NFSCACTIVE (default 2.00 minimum client NFS ops/sec)
 DISK_BUSY_WARNING  default= 5.0%    getenv= 5.0%    ignore less than this
 DISK_BUSY_PROBLEM  default=20.0%    getenv=20.0%
 DISK_SVC_T_WARNING default=30.0ms   getenv=30.0ms
 DISK_SVC_T_PROBLEM default=50.0ms   getenv=50.0ms
 LR_DISK_SLOW_FD    default=10.0x    getenv=10.0x    derate slow floppys
 LR_DISK_SLOW_CD    default=10.0x    getenv=10.0x    derate slow CDs
 LR_DISK_FLOPPY     default=   fd0   getenv=   fd0   default floppy device
 LR_DISK_CDROM      default=c0t6d0   getenv=c0t6d0   default CD device
 ENET_INUSE         default=50.0/s   getenv=50.0/s   ignore fewer output packets/s
 ENET_COLL_WARNING  default=15.0%    getenv=15.0%
 ENET_COLL_PROBLEM  default=30.0%    getenv=30.0%
 ENET_ERROR_PROBLEM default=0.050/s getenv=0.050/s
 ENET_DEFER_WARNING default=2.00%    getenv=2.00% some delayed output packets
 ENET_DEFER_WARNING default=10.00%   getenv=10.00% too many delayed output packets
 ENET_NOCANPUT_PROBLEM default=1.000/s getenv=1.000/s incoming packet dropped by IP
 RPCCLIENT_MINCALLS default= 0.1/s   getenv= 0.1/s   calls per sec for idle
 RPCCLIENT_TIMEOUT  default= 5.0%    getenv= 5.0%    calls that timeout
 RPCCLIENT_BADXID   default= 0.0%    getenv= 0.0%    timeouts with badxid
```

Figure 16-25 Usage and Configuration of `virtual_adrian.se` *(Continued)*

```
SWAP_WASTE            default=200000KB getenv=200000KB  plenty for a desktop system
SWAP_LOTS             default= 50000KB getenv= 50000KB  more is lots
SWAP_LOW              default= 10000KB getenv= 10000KB  warning LOW to LOTS
SWAP_NONE             default=  4000KB getenv=  4000KB  danger LOW-NONE, crisis
RESTIME_LONG          default=600s     getenv=600s      No scanning - long res time
RESTIME_OK            default= 40s     getenv= 40s      residence time of unref pages
RESTIME_PROBLEM       default= 20s     getenv= 20s      pages stolen too quickly
KMEM_FREEMEM_LOW      default= 64pg    getenv= 64pg     few pages for kernel to use
RUNQ_IDLE             default= 1.0     getenv= 1.0      Spare CPU capacity
RUNQ_BUSY             default= 2.0     getenv= 2.0      OK up to this level
RUNQ_OVERLOAD         default= 5.0     getenv= 5.0      Warning up to this level
MUTEX_BUSY            default=200.0/s getenv=200.0/s OK up to this level per-CPU
MUTEX_OVERLOAD        default=500.0/s getenv=500.0/s Warning up to this level
DNLC_ACTIVE           default=100.0/s getenv=100.0/s minimum activity
DNLC_WARNING          default=80.0%    getenv=80.0%    warning missrate
INODE_ACTIVE          default=100.0/s getenv=100.0/s minimum activity
INODE_WARNING         default=80.0%    getenv=80.0%    warning missrate
INODE_IPF             default= 0.0%    getenv= 0.0%    stolen inodes w/pages frac
TCP_ACTIVE            default=2.0KB/s getenv=2.0KB/s ignore if no output activity
TCP_RETRANS_WARN      default=15.0%    getenv=15.0%    moderate retransmissions
TCP_RETRANS_PROBLEM default=25.0%    getenv=25.0%    excessive retransmissions
TCP_LISTEN_WARN       default=0.00/s  getenv=0.00/s  look out for listen drops
TCP_LISTEN_PROBLEM default=0.50/s  getenv=0.50/s  excessive listen drops
TCP_HALFOPEN_PROBLEM default=2.00/s getenv=2.00/s excessive dubious SYNs
TCP_OUT_RSTS          default=0.50/s  getenv=0.50/s  moderate RSTs generated
TCP_OUT_RSTS          default=2.00/s  getenv=2.00/s  excessive RSTs generated
TCP_ATTEMPT_FAILS     default=2.00/s  getenv=2.00/s  excessive connect failures
TCP_DUP_WARN          default=15.0%    getenv=15.0%    moderate dups (remote retran)
TCP_DUP_PROBLEM       default=25.0%    getenv=25.0%    excessive dups (remote retran)
```

virtual_adrian_lite.se

The `virtual_adrian_lite.se` program started life as `iomonitor.se`, `vmmonitor.se`, and `netmonitor.se`, all combined so that one script would watch everything. It now includes the functionality of `pwatch.se` as well, and the latest version includes `nfsmonitor.se`. In addition, it makes a static check to see what the system parameters are set to when it starts. If it runs as root, it can read the parameters and will recommend changes or directly modify well-known kernel parameters in safe ways.

If there is insufficient RAM (under 24 Mbytes), the program exits because it will only make the system slower. If it sees swap space get very low, it also exits. This behavior guards against memory leaks.

This older version of `virtual_adrian.se` is provided because it is simpler and smaller and hence uses less RAM and CPU. At 30-second intervals, you don't save much CPU, even on an old SS2 or IPX because all the scripts are pretty lightweight. If it is not run as root, you get the error messages from kvm, as shown below. You can ignore the messages because the code checks and doesn't attempt to use the kvm interface unless it is running as root.

Use: `virtual_adrian_lite.se [interval] [-|command]`
with environment variables:

```
IOSLOW (default 50.0 ms)
IOMINBUSY (default 20.0% busy)
VMMINSWAP (default   4000 KB)
VMMAXSCAN (default 200 pages/s)
CPUMAXRUN (default 4.00 processes/CPU in run queue)
NETACTIVE (default 10.0 packets/sec)
NETMAXCOLL (default   5.0% collisions)
NETMAXERR (default   1.0 errors/sec)
PWPID (default 3 is fsflush)
PWMAXCPU (default   5.0% max CPU usage)
NFSRTALLSLOW (default 50ms max NFS round trip time)
```

% se virtual_adrian_lite.se
```
Warning: Cannot init kvm: Permission denied
Warning: Kvm not initialized: Variables will have invalid values
Adrian is monitoring your system starting at: Tue Nov 25 13:15:46 1997

Warning: Cannot get info for pid 3.
superuser permissions are needed to access every process
I/O thresholds set at 50.0 ms service time and 20.0 %busy
VM thresholds set at 4000KB min swap space or 200 pages/s max scan rate
CPU max load threshold set at 4.00 processes/CPU in run queue
Net thresholds set at 10.0 packets/s and 1.0 errors/s or 5.0% collisions
```

vmmonitor.se

The vmmonitor.se program is an old and oversimple vmstat-based monitor script that looks for low RAM and swap.

Use: vmmonitor.se [interval] [-|command]
with environment VMMINSWAP (default 4000 KB) and VMMAXSCAN (default 200 pages/s)

vmstat.se

The vmstat.se program is a modified vmstat that shows a measure of page residence time, i.e., the approximate time a page stays in memory if it is never used again. If this becomes a small number of seconds, then active pages may become stolen.

Use: vmstat.se [interval] [count]

```
% se vmstat.se 10
    procs              memory         page                    faults             cpu
    r  b  w       swap      free   pi  po   sr   rt    in    sy    cs   mx  us  sy   id
    0  0  0     445920      2424    0  17   36  113   642  5747   476   33  11   6   82
    0  0  0     446544      3560    5 107    0  999   341  2210   256   13   2   1   74
    0  0  0     446608      3704    0   0    0  999   112   856    80    7   0   0  100
```

watch.se

The watch.se program is located in /opt/RICHPse/contrib/watch/watch.se. It is an improved process watcher. Thanks to Holger Mai in Germany.

Use: watch.se [-f statfile][-d delay][-n name [params]|-p pid]

```
% se watch.se -p 2027
TIME    ABS_TIME    MEM
00:00   0:09:25    6720
00:01   0:09:26    6720
00:00   0:09:26    6720
00:01   0:09:27    6720
00:00   0:09:27    6720
00:01   0:09:28    6720
```

xio.se

The xio.se program is a modified xiostat.se that tries to work out whether accesses are mostly random or sequential by looking at the transfer size and typical disk access time values. Based on the expected service time for a single random access read of the average size, results above 100% indicate random access, and under 100% indicate sequential access.

Use: xio.se [interval] [count]

```
% se xio.se 10
                              extended disk statistics
disk     r/s  w/s   Kr/s    Kw/s  wtq  actq  wtres  actres  %w  %b  svc_t %rndsvc
c0t0d0   0.0 27.0    0.0   216.0  0.0   2.6    0.0    95.2   0   17   6.3    40.8
c0t1d0   0.0  1.0    0.0     8.0  0.0   0.0    0.0     4.8   0    0   4.8    31.3
c0t5d0   0.0  0.0    0.0     0.0  0.0   0.0    0.0     0.0   0    0   0.0     0.0
fd0      0.0  0.0    0.0     0.0  0.0   0.0    0.0     0.0   0    0   0.0     0.0
```

xiostat.se

The xio.stat.se program is a basic iostat -x clone that actually prints the name of each disk in a usable form rather than sdXX!

					extended disk statistics				
disk	r/s	w/s	Kr/s	Kw/s	wait	actv	svc_t	%w	%b
c0t3d0	0.0	0.0	0.0	0.0	0.0	0.0	0.0	0	0
c0t5d0	0.0	0.0	0.0	0.0	0.0	0.0	0.0	0	0
fd0	0.0	0.0	0.0	0.0	0.0	0.0	0.0	0	0

xit.se

The xit.se program is xit—the eXtended Iostat Tool. It does the same as running iostat -x in a cmdtool. But beyond that, it shows how to write a SymbEL program that sends its output to a GUI that can then display that data. It also uses a slider to interactively set the update rate and to start/stop/clear the output.

Figure 16-26 Example Display from xit.se

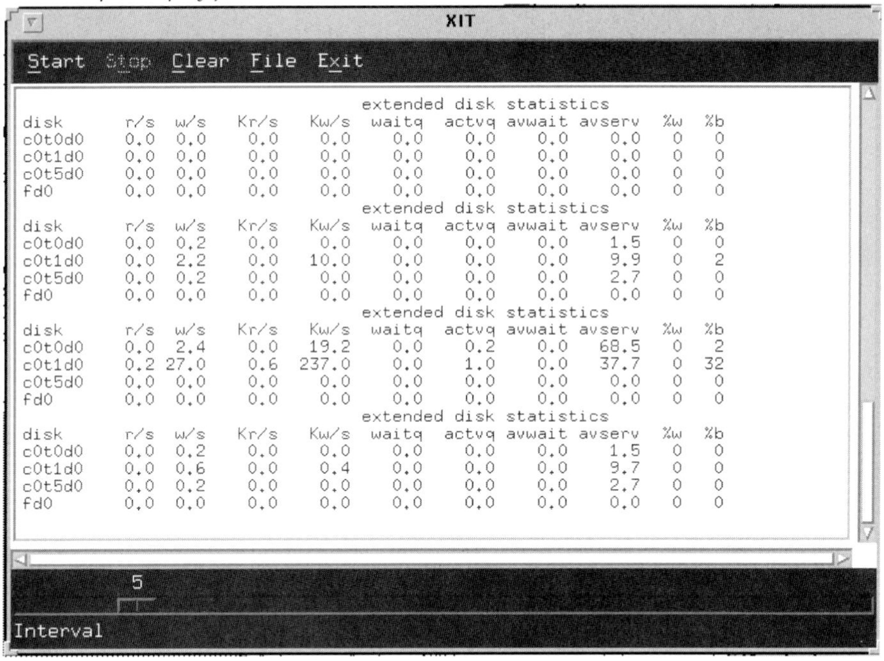

zoom.se

The zoom.se program is a GUI front end to the rules, with popup screens to show you all the background data upon which the state is based (see Figure 16-27). Probably the most functional program written in SE so far, it's a powerful tool for monitoring a system.

Click on any of the buttons to see more detail, and click on the little "face" icons to learn more about the kind of guys who write this stuff. The code for zoom.se contains detailed instructions on how to add more rules to the GUI.

Figure 16-27 Example Display for zoom.se

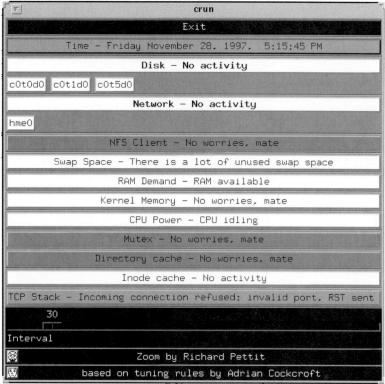

The SymbEL Language

SymbEL is an interpretive language, based on C, that was created to address the need for simplified access to data residing in the SunOS kernel. Although kernel interface API libraries have made this data more available to C application programmers, it is still out of reach by means other than writing and compiling a program. The goal was to create a language that did not need compilation to run and would allow the development of scripts that could be distributed to a large audience via e-mail without sending very large files or requiring the end user to possess a compiler.

The control and data structures of SymbEL are extensive enough to allow a complex program to be written, but the language is not burdened with superfluous syntax, and the resulting grammar is far more compact than C. The original interpreter, se, was developed under SunOS 5.2 FCS-C and tested on an MP690, SC1000, and an LC. Since then, it has been modified and tested on every subsequent release of SunOS. The latest release is SunOS 5.6, a.k.a. Solaris 2.6. The SPARC and Intel platforms are supported, and every effort has been made to support new devices and configurations for each of these hardware platforms. The se interpreter does not now, nor will it ever, run under any release of SunOS 4.x.

This chapter assumes that you are conversant in the C programming language. Expertise is not necessary, but you should be comfortable with C to best understand this chapter.

Collection of Performance Data

The first step in understanding the relevance of the collected performance data is to become familiar with the interface from which this data comes. Solaris has several such interfaces that need examination.

Tuning and Performance

Operating system performance is one of the most painful areas of system administration because it seems to involve so much magic. In fact, gaining proficiency in performance tuning is much like any other endeavor. Time and experience are the best teachers.

17

Yet for all that is known about tuning, the need to tune systems becomes more desperate because of the lack of adequate tuning tools. This lack of tools stems from the rapid advances in machine architecture and operating system design. And as the underlying technology continues to expand, the existing tools for performance tuning become insufficient to solve performance problems.

SunOS is an excellent starting place for the development of tools for tuning. The existing tools shipped with SunOS provide a wealth of data regarding the workings of the kernel in its management of the process spaces and of the underlying hardware. It is from the examination of this data that the decisions on how to tune the system are made.

Traditionally, examination of this data is a manual process: typing in commands, examining the output, and making decisions based on some preset rules. This process is time consuming and tedious, especially when you try to talk another person through it over the telephone or explain the procedure via e-mail. It also leaves the information about how to make decisions regarding system performance where it does the least good—in someone's memory.

In an attempt to translate this expertise from memory to written form, one could write C, Bourne, or Korn shell scripts to run these commands, extract the output, and compare them to known threshold values. This approach serves the purpose of making the expertise more portable and thus more accessible to the masses. It also impacts the performance of the machine under analysis enough to render the script useless as a "round the clock" diagnostician. Access to the data is needed without the overhead of the multiple applications and the shell language.

The first step toward solving this problem is to determine how the applications themselves retrieve the data from the kernel. An application programming interface (API) can then be built that performs the same actions as these applications. These APIs could extract their data from any of these sources on SunOS 5.x.

We examine these APIs:

- `kvm` — Kernel virtual memory
- `kstat` — Kernel statistics
- `mib` — Management information base
- `ndd` — Network device driver

The `kvm` Library

The `kvm` library is an API for reading the values of kernel variables from the kernel memory. Before the `kvm` library, this reading was all done manually, using `open()`, `lseek()`, and `read()`. The code for reading values from the kernel is repetitive, so the kvm library was developed. It solved this problem and provided additional functionality for reading core files and checking the validity of the addresses being read. The kvm library functions that perform the work are kvm_open(), kvm_nlist(), kvm_read(), kvm_write(), and kvm_close().

The kstat Library

A limitation of the kvm library is that the program reading values from kernel memory must have superuser permission because /dev/kmem is not readable by the world. A solution developed by Sun is the addition of a kernel framework that is accessible for read-only access by the world and write access by the privileged user. This framework is called the kstat framework. kstat also has the benefit of having low overhead and being extensible to accommodate any new kernel statistics that may be useful on future architectures.

The kstat interface, /dev/kstat, is an entry point into the kstat driver. It resides in the kernel and collects data from predefined functional areas within various subsystems and drivers. kstat collects data from I/O and VM subsystems and the HAT layer, and it also gathers various information about network interfaces and CPU activity.

The software interface to /dev/kstat is the kstat library, libkstat. It contains functions for opening and reading the kstat data from the kstat driver and for the superuser, writing data back to the kernel.

When the kstat data is copied out of the kernel, it is put into a linked list of structures. Each node in the list is a structure that contains data about a particular functional area and identifies the format of the data. The possible data formats are listed below.

KSTAT_TYPE_RAW — The data is a pointer to a structure, commonly defined in a /usr/include/sys include file.

KSTAT_TYPE_NAMED — The data is an array of structures that represent a polymorphic type. Each structure contains a textual name, a type designation, and a union of members of the supported types. The supported types are:

KSTAT_DATA_CHAR 8 bits signed or unsigned

KSTAT_DATA_INT32 32 bits signed

KSTAT_DATA_UINT32 32 bits unsigned

KSTAT_DATA_INT64 64 bits signed

KSTAT_DATA_UINT64 64 bits unsigned

KSTAT_TYPE_INTR — The data is a pointer to a structure containing an array of unsigned long values whose indices represent the type of interrupt. The types of interrupts and their index values are

KSTAT_INTR_HARD=0	From the device itself
KSTAT_INTR_SOFT=1	From the system software
KSTAT_INTR_WATCHDOG=2	Timer expiration
KSTAT_INTR_SPURIOUS=3	Entry point called with no interrupt pending
KSTAT_INTR_MULTSVC=4	Interrupt serviced prior to return from other interrupt service

KSTAT_TYPE_IO — The data is a pointer to a structure containing information relevant to I/O.

KSTAT_TYPE_TIMER — The data is a pointer to a structure containing timing information for any type of event.

The structures used by the kstat library are defined in /usr/include/sys/kstat.h. Note that the kstat framework is constantly evolving, and developing code around it is precarious because the mechanism may grow, shrink, or change at any time.

Management Information Base (MIB)

The management information base is a set of structures containing data relative to the state of the networking subsystem of the kernel. The nature, structure, and representation of this data are based on RFC 1213, *Management Information Base for Network Management of TCP/IP-based internets: MIB-II*. Specifically, data is stored regarding the performance of the kernel drivers for IP, TCP, UDP, ICMP, and IGMP. This data is contained in one structure for each driver. You can retrieve the data by building a stream containing the drivers whose MIB data is to be read, sending a control message downstream, and reading the results sent back by all modules in the stream that interpreted the message and responded.

The structures are also declared as variables in the kernel address space and therefore can be read by conventional kvm methods.

The Network Device Driver (NDD) Interface

The NDD interface is another source of data regarding the state of the networking subsystem. Whereas the MIB is a source of data that is statistical in nature, the NDD interface allows for tuning of driver variables that control the function of the driver. The NDD interface can access variables kept by the IP, TCP, UDP, ICMP, and ARP drivers.

Whereas the interface to the MIB structures is through the streams control message interface, retrieval of NDD variables is through a much simpler `ioctl()` mechanism. The structures kept by the drivers are also accessible through the kvm interface but are rather convoluted and therefore are most easily modified by use of the NDD interface.

Summary

From these sources comes a great deal of data to manage in an application when the mechanisms used to retrieve it are the conventional APIs. It is possible to distill this information into library calls so that the information is more generalized. The next step is to develop a syntactic notation for accessing the data, a language whose most significant feature is the retrieval of the necessary data from the appropriate places without the notational overhead of actually performing the read. What follows is the description of a language that was designed to remove the complication of accessing these values and to provide a framework for building applications that can make use of these values. This language is called SymbEL, the Symbol Engine Language.

Basic Structure

In response to the need for simplified access to data contained inside the SunOS kernel, the SymbEL (pronounced "symbol") language was created and the SymbEL interpreter, se, was developed. SymbEL resembles C visually and contains many similar syntactic structures. This orthogonality was done for ease of use and to leverage existing programming knowledge.

First Program

Since the best way to learn a new language is through example, let's look at an example SymbEL program.

```
main()
{
    printf("hello, world\n");
}
```

This program shows that the language structure is similar to C. This similarity does not imply that you can pick up a book on C and start writing SymbEL programs. There are a lot of differences, and the interpreter lets you know if the syntax is incorrect. This short program demonstrates some of the similarities and differences in the language. First, a SymbEL program *must* have a function called main. This is the similarity to C. The difference from C is that the `printf()` function in SymbEL is a built-in, not a library call.

To test this small program, put it in a file called `hello.se` and enter

```
se hello.se
```

and the resulting output is what you expect. The format string used in `printf()` works the same as any equivalent statement that could be used in a C program. Syntax of the `printf()` format string is not addressed in this document; you can find additional information in the `printf()` man page or in any good book on the C language.

Simple Types

The simple types available in SymbEL are scalar, floating point, and string.

Scalar

> `char`8-bit signed integer
> `uchar`8-bit unsigned integer
> `shor`16-bit signed integer
> `ushort`16-bit unsigned integer
> `int` Same as `long`
> `uint`Same as `ulong`
> `long`32-bit signed integer
> `ulong`32-bit unsigned integer
> `longlong`64- bit signed integer
> `ulonglong`64-bit unsigned integer

Floating Point

> `double`double precision floating point

String

> `string`pointer to null-terminated ASCII text

There are also structured types, which are covered later. There are no pointer types in SymbEL. This absence is also discussed in a later section.

Simple Program

The following program demonstrates some of the features of the language, although it has nothing to do with extracting data from the kernel.

```
/* print the times table for 5 */
main()
{
  // C++ style comments are also allowed
  int lower;
  int upper;
  lower = 1;    // lower limit
  upper = 10;   // upper limit
```

```
    while(lower <= upper) {
      printf("%4d\n", lower * 5);
      lower = lower + 1;
    }
  }
```

About the Program

```
  lower = 1;    // lower limit
```

Since se uses the C preprocessor to read the programs, the use of C and C++ style comments and pound-sign directives such as #define and #include is valid.

```
  while(lower <= upper) {
```

The while structure is one of the control structures supported by SymbEL.

This example requires curly braces around the two statements inside the block of the while loop. However, the syntax of SymbEL requires all sequences of statements inside control structures to be bracketed by curly braces, even sequences of just one statement. The purpose for this requirement is to ensure cleanliness of the grammar.

```
  printf("%4d\n", lower * 5);
```

The function printf() is a built-in function. Built-in functions are used for library functions that cannot be implemented as attached functions or that represent a functionality specific to the interpreter. Attached functions are discussed on page 532.

```
  lower = lower + 1;
```

This code simply increments lower by one.

Embellishing the Simple Program

Let's rewrite the program, using different constructs and techniques.

```
#define LOWER    1
#define UPPER    10
#define DIGIT    5
main()
{
  int lower;
  int upper = UPPER;
  for(lower = LOWER; lower <= upper; lower = lower + 1) {
    printf("%4d\n", lower * DIGIT);
  }
}
```

About the Program

```
#define LOWER    1
```

As pointed out before, the use of pound-sign directives is valid because the interpreter reads the program through the C preprocessor.

```
int upper = UPPER;
```

Variables can be initialized to an expression. The expression can be another variable, a constant, or an arithmetic expression. Assignment of the result of a logical expression is not allowed.

```
for(lower = LOWER; lower <= UPPER; lower = lower + 1) {
  printf("%4d\n", lower * DIGIT);
}
```

The syntax of the `for` loop in SymbEL will provide plenty of errors from the parser. It is a simple `for` loop syntax insofar as it may only have one initial assignment and one do-after statement. Multiple statements separated by commas won't work. Remember, the rule of thumb is "If you feel like being tricky, don't. It probably won't work."

This control structure is very convenient for many situations, but there are specific rules that go with it. SymbEL does not allow the flexibility of the `for` loop that C does.

Array Types

SymbEL supports single-dimension arrays. Subscripts for array types start at zero, as is the case in C. The next example is a new version of the previous example, using arrays.

A Program That Uses Arrays

```
#define LOWER    1
#define UPPER    10
#define DIGIT    5
main()
{
  int value[UPPER + 1];
  int i;
  for(i = LOWER; i <= UPPER; i++) {
    value[i] = i * DIGIT;
  }
  for(i = LOWER; i <= UPPER; i++) {
    printf("%4d\n", value[i]);
  }
}
```

About the Program

```
int value[UPPER + 1];
for(i = LOWER; i <= UPPER; i++) {
```

The size of the array is declared as UPPER + 1. You can use expressions as the size of an array in its declaration provided that the array size expression is an integral constant expression. That is, it can't contain other variables or function calls.

The size of the array must be UPPER + 1 because the for loop uses the (i <= UPPER) condition for terminating the loop. If the array were declared with a size of UPPER, then se would abort with a "subscript out of range" error during execution.

Also, instead of using the i = i + 1 notation, we used the increment notation. Prefix and postfix increment and decrement are supported by SymbEL.

Functions and Parameters

So far, only one function has been shown in the examples: main with no return type. If no return type is declared on a function, then returning values will result in an error from the parser. A function can be declared as returning a type, and the function can then return a value of that type. For example, here is a function to raise a value to a power.

A Program That Uses Functions and Parameters

```
#define BASE    2
ulong
power(int b, int p)         // raise base b to power p
{
  ulong i;
  ulong n;
  n = 1;
  for(i=1; i<=p; i++) {
    n *= b;
  }
  return n;
}
main()
{
  int i;
  for(i=0; i<=32; i++) {
    printf("%d raised to power %d = %u\n", BASE, i, power(BASE, i));
  }
}
```

About the Program

```
ulong
power(int b, int p)           /* raise base b to power p */
```

This code is the declaration of a function returning unsigned `long` and taking as parameters two integers. All parameters in SymbEL are value parameters and have the syntax of ANSI C parameters. As in local declarations, each parameter must be declared separately. The syntax does not support comma-separated lists of parameters. Parameters are treated as local variables and have all of the semantic constraints of local variables.

In this example, the `power()` function is declared before `main`. This allows the parser to obtain type information about the function's return value so that type checking can be done on the parameters to `printf()`.

```
int i;
int n;
n = 1;
```

It is important to note a semantic feature of local variables that this code demonstrates. In C, the assignment of `n` could be made part of the declaration. Although SymbEL supports the initialization of local variables, the semantics of local variables are equivalent to a `static` declaration in a C program. That is, the initialization of the local variable is done only once, upon entry to the function for the first time; it is not performed on every call. The rationale is that the overhead of maintaining automatic variables in an interpretive environment would be too high for the language to perform reasonably. One of the goals of `se` is to put as little load on the system as possible and still provide usable runtime performance.

```
for(i=1; i<=p; i++) {
    n *= b;
}
```

The `for` loop is like the one shown in the previous example; however, the statement inside the loop shows that SymbEL supports the compressed arithmetic assignment operators. These work just like the C counterparts and are supported for the operations add, subtract, multiply, divide, and modulus.

```
printf("%d raised to power %d = %u\n", BASE, i, power(BASE, i));
```

Here, the call to `power()` is part of the parameter list for `printf()`. The order of evaluation of actual parameters is from left to right.

Global Variables

SymbEL also supports global variables. These act in the same way as globals in C. They are declared outside of the block of a function and can be accessed by any function in the program. Global variables can have initial values just like local variables and are initialized before the function `main` is called.

Operators and Expressions

To help you better understand what operators are available in SymbEL and how expressions are constructed, here is an overview of the constituent parts.

Variable Names

Variable names are limited to 1,024 characters and can begin with any alphabetic character or an underscore. Characters beyond the first character can be any alphabetic character, digit, underscore, or dollar sign.

Constants

There are four types of constants: integer, floating point, character, and string. These constants can be used in expressions (except for strings), assigned to variables, and passed as parameters. For convenience, these constants can be placed into `#define` statements for expansion by the preprocessor.

Integer

An integer constant can be any integer with or without sign whose value is no more than 2 to the 32nd power minus 1. Note that a large enough value that has been negated results in sign extension. Constants of type `longlong` are not currently supported; a workaround is to add .0 to the end of the constant and assign the constant to a variable of type `double`. The `double` variable can then be assigned to a variable of type `longlong`.

Floating Point

A floating-point constant can be

{0-9} [. {0-9}] [{eE} {+-} {0-9}+]

Here are some examples of valid floating-point constants:

```
0.01
1e-2
1.0e-2
0.001E+1
```

These constants all represent the same value, 0.01.

Character

A character constant is a character enclosed in single forward quotes. As in C, the character may also be a backslash followed by another backslash (for the backslash character itself) or a character that represents a special ASCII value. The current special characters are:

```
\bBackspace
\fForm feed
\nNew line
\t Tab
\rCarriage return
\0 Null
```

The value following the backslash may also be an octal or hex value. For an octal value, use a backslash followed by a valid octal digit beginning with 0. For hex, use a backslash followed by the character x followed by a valid hex digit. Examples are:

```
\012New line in octal
\xA New line in hex
```

String

A string constant is enclosed in double quotes and can contain regular ASCII characters or any of the special characters shown above. Examples are:

```
"hello"
"hello\nworld\n"
"\thello world\xA"
```

A a special string value, `nil`, defines a pointer value of zero. String variables can be assigned `nil` and compared to it. Parameters of type `string` can also be sent `nil` as an actual parameter.

Declarations

The syntax for a variable declaration is the same for local and global variables. There may be an initialization part that is an expression. An oddity of the interpretive environment is that the initialization part of a global declaration may contain a function call. Take great care not to break your program, however.

Some example declarations are

```
char c;
int n = 5;
ulong ul = compute_it(n);
string hello = "world";
```

Note that the syntax allows only one variable per line.

Arithmetic Operators

The current operators available for performing arithmetic on numeric values are

+Addition of scalar or floating types

–Subtraction of scalar or floating types

*Multiplication of scalar or floating types

/Division of scalar or floating types

%Modulus of scalar types

These operators work the same as they do in C, and arithmetic operations between numeric variables of different types are allowed. Explicit modulus of floating-point types will be caught and disallowed by the parser; however, if the result of an expression yields a floating-point value and is used as an operand to the modulus operator, it is converted to type `longlong` first, then performed. This feature has the potential for yielding unexpected results, so be wary when using it.

In expressions that contain mixed types of scalar or scalar and floating point, the resulting expression will be of the type of the highest precedence. The order of precedence from lowest to highest is:

```
char
uchar
short
ushort
int  /  long
uint  /  ulong
```

```
longlong
ulonglong
double
```

So, in this statement—

```
int fahrenheit;
double celsius;
...
celsius = (5.0 / 9.0) * (fahrenheit - 32);
```

—the resulting value will be double. The (5.0 / 9.0) expression yields a double, while (fahrenheit - 32) yields a long (int is long internally). The multiply operator then changes the right side of the expression into a double for multiplication. Take care not to lose accuracy because SymBEL does not support type casting.

The precedence of the operators + and – is at the same level and of lower precedence than the *, /, and % operators, which are also at the same level. Parentheses can be used to create explicit precedence, as in the expression above. Without parentheses, the implicit value of the expression would be

```
celsius = (5.0 / (9.0 * fahrenheit)) - 32;
```

Logical Operators

The logical operators of SymBEL are

      <Less than

      >Greater than

      <=Less than or equal to

      >= Greater than or equal to

      !=Not equal to

      == Equal to

      =~Regular expression comparison

The logical operators are all of equal precedence because the syntax does not allow for expressions of the type a < b != c. The junctural operators for short circuit logical AND and short circuit logical OR are && and | |, respectively. They are implicitly of lower precedence than the comparators. There is no logical NOT defined by the language. You can rewrite statements without the logical NOT operation by comparing the value to zero or by using inverse comparators and/or juncturals.

The regular expression comparison operator =~ expects the regular expression on the right side of the operator. Comparisons with regular expressions on the left side of the operator will not yield the expected results.

Bitwise Operators

The bitwise operators of SymbEL are

&Bitwise AND

|Bitwise OR

^Bitwise XOR

<<Shift left

>>Shift right

Just as there is no logical NOT, there is no bitwise NOT. The addition of a bitwise NOT would add certain unwanted complexities to the parser. Working around this issue is more complex than for the logical NOT, but the problem is not insurmountable.

Increment and Decrement Operators

SymbEL supports the prefix and postfix increment and decrement operators. These operators can be used only on scalar types. Use on nonscalar variables will result in an error from the parser. Variables using these operators can appear in a stand-alone statement or as part of an expression.

Compressed Assignment Operators

The operators +=, -=, *=, /=, and %= are supported, and the semantics for these operators are the same as for the arithmetic operators and the assignment of values. Statements with these operators can be used in the "do" part of the for loop as well as in a statement by itself. For instance:

```
for(i=0; i<10; i+=2) {
   ...
}
```

The bitwise version of these compressed operators is also supported. These are the &=, |=, ^=, <<=, and >>= operators.

Address Operator

To obtain the address of a variable, use the address operator as a prefix to the variable name. This is the same as in C except that the address of a structure cannot be taken. The address operator works only with simple types and arrays of simple types. In the case of arrays, using the address operator is equivalent to taking the address of the first element of the array. The address of an array does not result in a pointer to a pointer.

The return value of the address operator is `ulong`. Since there is no pointer type in SymbEL, `ulong` satisfies the requirements for an address in that it is 32 bits in length and has no sign associated with it. An example of the use of the address operator is:

```
int int_var = 5;
ulong pointer = &int_var;
```

The address operator is useful for functions such as `scanf`.

Type Casting

SymbEL supports type casting between string and 4-byte numerics. This is useful for orthogonality when taking the address of a variable of type `string`. If the `ulong` result needs to be viewed as a string, again, you can use a type cast.

The syntax of the type cast is slightly different than in C. The entire expression must be enclosed in parentheses. This is yet another effort to keep the complexity of the grammar to a minimum. Here is an example of type casting.

```
#include <stdio.se>
#include <unistd.se>
#include <uio.se>

main()
{
  char buf[128];
  iovec_t iov[1];

  iov[0].iov_base = &buf;
  iov[0].iov_len = sizeof(buf);
  if (readv(0, iov, 1) > 0) {
    fputs(((string) iov[0].iov_base), stdout);
  }
}
```

Type casting between `string` and `double` or casts of structured types is not allowed and results in an error message from the parser.

Control Flow

Some of the control structures have already been covered. This section discusses all of the control structures in detail.

Blocks

All control statements in SymbEL must have a block associated with them. The block begins with a left curly brace, {, and ends with a right curly brace, }. This convention keeps the grammar clean and provides additional code clarity.

If-Then-Else Statement

The `if` statement can be an `if` by itself or an `if` statement and an `else` part. The structure of an `if` construct is:

```
if ( logical expression ) {
  . . .
}
```

Two points need to be made about this construct.

The first point is that the condition `if` checks on cannot be an *expression*—it must be a *logical expression*. Therefore, statements such as

```
if (running) {
  . . .
}
```

are not correct. In C, this syntax is valid. In SymbEL, it is not. The condition must be a comparison in order for it to be a logical expression. This `if` statement is correctly written as

```
if (running != 0) {
  . . .
}
```

where the condition is a *logical expression* instead of an *expression*.

The second point is that curly braces must always surround the statement blocks of the `if` and the `else` parts, even if there is only one statement. Here are some examples.

```
if (x > y) {
  printf("x is greater than y\n");
}
if (x < y) {
  printf("x is less than y\n");
} else {
```

```
      printf("x is greater than y\n");
  }
```

Take care when writing if-then-else-if-then statements. It is easy to mistakenly write

```
if (x == 2) {
  printf("x is equal to 2\n");
} else if (x == 3) {
  printf("x is equal to 3\n");
}
```

which is incorrect. The `else` part must begin with a curly brace. This code is correctly written as:

```
if (x == 2) {
  printf("x is equal to 2\n");
} else {
  if (x == 3) {
    printf("x is equal to 3\n");
  }
}
```

Conditional Expression

The ternary operator `?:`, known as a conditional expression, is supported as a value in an expression. There is a syntactic requirement on this expression type, however: the entire conditional expression must be enclosed in parentheses. The logical expression part can be any supported logical expression. The two expression parts can be any supported expression, provided their types are compatible. Here's an example that prints out the numbers from 1 to 10 and prints whether they're even or odd.

```
main()
{
  int i;
  for(i=1; i<=10; i++) {
    printf("%2d %s\n", i, ((i % 2) == 0 ? "even" : "odd"));
  }
}
```

`switch` Statement

The `switch` statement selects a value from many possible values. This statement type works exactly like the C equivalent, with an addition. The `switch` statement in SymbEL also works on strings. Here are some examples.

```
// character switch
main()
```

```
{
  char t = 'w';

  switch(t) {
  case 'a':
    printf("a - wrong\n");
    break;
  case 'b':
    printf("b - wrong\n");
    break;
  case 'c':
    printf("c - wrong\n");
    break;
  case 'w':
    printf("w - correct\n");
    break;
  default:
    printf("say what?\n");
    break;
  }
}
// string switch
main()
{
  string s = "hello";

  switch(s) {
  case "yo":
  case "hey":
  case "hi":
    printf("yo/hey/hi - wrong\n");
    break;
  case "hello":
    printf("%s, world\n", s);
    break;
  default:
    printf("say what?\n");
    break;
  }
}
```

Loops

The C language provides five mechanisms for iteration. Four of them are syntactic and the fifth is semantic. The syntactic iterators are the `while`, `for`. and `do` loops and the goto/label construct. The semantic iterator is recursion. SymbEL supports only three of these five mechanisms—the loop constructs.

While Loop

The three looping constructs in SymbEL are the `while`, `for`, and `do` loops. The structure of the while loop is:

```
while( logical expression ) {
   ...
}
```

Two points must be made about this construct.

The first point is that the condition on which the `while` checks cannot be an *expression*—it must be a *logical expression*. Therefore, loops such as

```
while(running) {
   ...
}
```

are not correct. In C, this syntax is valid. In SymbEL, it is not. The condition must be a comparison in order for it to be a logical expression. This loop is correctly written as:

```
while(running != 0) {
   ...
}
```

The second point is that curly braces must always surround the statement blocks of the `while`, `for`, and `do` statements, even if there is only one statement in the block. This requirement is consistent with the other control constructs of SymbEL.

For Loop

The structure of the `for` loop is:

```
for( assign part; while part; do part ) {
   ...
}
```

The `assign part` can be a simple assignment such as
```
i = 0
```

or a compressed assignment such as

```
i *= 2
```

or it can be omitted. The while part can be any logical expression or it can be omitted. The do part can be a simple assignment, a compressed assignment, an increment of a variable, a decrement of a variable, or it can be omitted. Some examples of valid for loops are:

```
for(i = 0; i < 10; i++) {
   ...
}
for(i *= 2; i < 10 || x != 3; i = recompute(i)) {
   ...
}
for(; i < 10; ) {
   ...
}
for(;;) {
   ...
}
```

Do Loop

The structure of the do loop is:

```
do {
   ...
} while( logical expression );
```

The rule regarding the logical expression is the same as for the while loop.

Break

The break statement can be used for exiting from a "switch" case, or exiting a while, for, or do loop. As in C, only the innermost loop is exited. This program

```
for(i=0; i<10; i++) {
   if (i == 2) {
     printf("i is 2\n");
     break;
   }
}
printf("now, i is %d\n", i);
```

yields the output

```
i is 2
now, i is 2
```

when run. The same holds true for while and do loops.

Continue

The `continue` statement is supported for `while`, `for`, and `do` loops. It works identically to the C construct and continues the innermost loop at the top of the loop. If in a `for` loop, the `do` part of the `for` loop is executed before the block is entered again.

```
while(i != 18) {
  if (i < 10) {
    continue;
  }
  i = do_something();
}
```

Goto

There is no `goto` in SymbEL.

Functions, Procedures, and Programming Notes

SymbEL supports encapsulated, scoped blocks that can return a value. These blocks are referred to as functions and procedures for notational brevity. To complete our picture, we need to make some points about these constructs.

Function Return Types

So far, the only value that functions have returned in the examples has been a scalar type, but functions can return `double` or `string` as well. More complex types, covered in later sections, can be returned as well.

Functions cannot return arrays because there is no syntactic accommodation for doing so. However, there is a way to get around this limitation for arrays of nonstructured types. See "Returning an Array of Nonstructured Type from a Function" on page 552.

Scope

Although variables may be declared local to a function, the default semantics for local variables are for them to be the C equivalent of `static`. Therefore, even though a local variable has an initialization part in a local scope, this initialization *is not* performed on each entry to the function. It is done once before the first call and never done again.

Initializing Variables

Variables can be initialized to values that are compatible with their declared type. This is the case for both simple and structured types. The only exceptional condition in initializing variables is the ability to initialize a global variable with a function call. This capability is supported, but use it with great care. In general, avoid it as bad practice.

Arrays can be given initial values through an aggregate initialization. The syntax is identical to that in C. For example:

```
int array[ARRAY_SIZE] = {
  1, 2, 3, 4, 5, -1
};
```

The size of the array must be large enough to accommodate the aggregate initialization or the parser will flag it as an error.

Notes About Arrays and Strings

The type `string` is native to SymbEL and has no equivalent in C. Since `string` is an atomic type, it is incorrect to use the subscript operator to access individual characters in the string. For this reason, we need to be able to interchange values between variables that are of type `string` and `char[]`.

Array Assignment

Although pointer types are not allowed in SymbEL, assignment of arrays is allowed provided that the size of the target variable is equal to or greater than the size of the source variable. This is not a pointer assignment, though. Consider it a value assignment where the values of the source array are being copied to the target array.

String Type and Character Arrays

Variables declared as type `string` and arrays of type `char` have interchangeable values to allow access to individual characters contained in a string. For example:

```
char tmp[8];
string s = "hello";
tmp = s;
if (tmp[0] == 'h') {
  ...
}
```

Accessing the individual characters in the string cannot be done with the s variable by itself. If a subscript was used, it would mean that the variable s was an array of strings, not an array of characters. After any modification to the variable tmp in this example is done, the value could be assigned back to s.

Assignment to String Variables

When a variable of type string is assigned a new value, the existing value of the variable is freed and a new copy of the source string is allocated and assigned to the variable. This is also the case when string variables are assigned the return value of a function that returns type string. See "Using Return Values from Attached Functions" on page 553.

Empty Arrays

When a function accepts an array as a parameter, it is not always convenient to send an array of the same size as the parameter. For this reason, the empty array declaration was added for use in parameter declarations. This is a notation where no subscript size is included in the declaration, just the [] suffix to the variable name. Here is an example.

```
print_it(int array[])
{
  int i;
  for(i=0; array[i] != -1; i++) {
    printf("%d\n", array[i]);
  }
}
main()
{
  int array[6] = { 1, 2, 3, 4, 5, -1 };
  print_it(array);
}
```

Upon entry to the function containing the empty array parameter, the parameter variable obtains a size. In this example, the array parameter is given a size of 24 (6 * 4) upon entry to the function print_it. This size will change for every array passed as an actual parameter.

Recursion

Recursion is not supported. Direct recursion is flagged as an error by the parser. Indirect recursion is silently ignored. The disallowance of recursion is due to a problem in the run time that could not be overcome in the short term and may be fixed in a future release. Examine the following program.

```
one()
{
  // remember, initialization is only done once
  int i = 0;
  i++;
  switch(i) {
  case 1:
    printf("Here I am\n");
    break;
  case 2:
    printf("Here I am again\n");
    return;
  }
  two();
}
two()
{
  one();
}
main()
{
  one();
}
```

It seems that the output of this program would be

```
Here I am
Here I am again
```

but, in fact, only the first line will be printed out. The second call to one is detected by the run time, and a return from the function is performed before anything is done. SymbEL is not the place to do recursion. Again, if you feel like being tricky, don't be. It probably won't work.

Built-in Functions

SymbEL currently supports a limited set of built-in functions. As the need arises, more built-ins will be added. Many of these built-ins work the same as or similarly to the C library version. For a complete description of those functions, see the manual page for the C function. The current built-in functions are described below.

`int fileno(int)`
> Send the return value of an fopen() or popen() to fileno() to retrieve the underlying file descriptor. This function works like the stdio macro, only it's a built-in.

int fprintf(int, string, ...)

Print a formatted string onto the file defined by the first parameter. The man page for the fprintf C library function defines the use of this function in more detail.

int sizeof(...)

Return the size of the parameter. This parameter can be a variable, a numeric value, or an expression.

string itoa(int)

Convert an integer into a string.

string sprintf(string, ...)

Return a string containing the format and data specified by the parameters. This function is like the C library function in what it does, but it does not use a buffer parameter as the first argument. The buffer is returned instead. The function is otherwise like the C function.

struct prpsinfo_t first_proc(void)

In conjunction with the next_proc() function, traverse through all of the processes in the system. All of the fields of the prpsinfo_t structure may not be filled because of permissions. With root permissions, they are filled in completely.

struct prpsinfo_t get_proc(int)

Get a process by its process ID (instead of traversing all of the processes). The same rules regarding permissions apply to this function as well as to first_proc().

struct prpsinfo_t next_proc(void)

In conjunction with first_proc(), traverse through all of the processes on the system. When the pr_pid member of the prpsinfo_t structure is -1 after a return from this function, then all of the processes have been visited.

ulong kvm_address(VAR)

Return the kernel seek value for this variable. This function works only on variables designated as special kvm variables in the declaration.

ulong kvm_declare(string)

Declare a new kvm variable while the program is running. The return value is the kvm address of the variable, used as the second parameter to kvm_cvt.

Sun Performance and Tuning

void debug_off(void)
> Turn debugging off until the next call to debug_on().

void debug_on(void)
> Turn debugging on following this statement. Debugging information is printed out until the next call to debug_off().

void kvm_cvt(VAR, ulong)
> Change the kernel seek value for this variable to the value specified by the second parameter.

void printf(string, ...)
> Print a formatted string. Internally, a call to fflush() is made after every call to printf(). This call causes a write() system call; consider the effects of this call when writing SymbEL programs.

void signal(int, string);
> Specify a signal catcher. The first parameter specifies the signal name according to the signal.se include file. The second parameter is the name of the SymbEL function to call upon receipt of the signal.

void struct_empty(STRUCT, ulong)
> Dump the contents of the structure variable passed as the first parameter into the memory location specified by the second parameter. The binary value dumped will be the same format as when used in a C program.

void struct_fill(STRUCT, ulong)
> Replace the data from the second parameter into the structure variable passed as the first parameter. This function allows C-structure-format data to be translated into the internal representation of structures used by SymbEL.

void syslog(int, fmt, ...)
> Log a message through the syslog() facility. Note that the %m string must be sent as %%m because the interpreter passes the format string through vsprintf() before passing it to syslog() internally.

Dynamic Constants

The SymbEL interpreter deals with a few physical resources that have variable quantities on each computer on which the interpreter is run. These are the disks, network interfaces, CPUs, and devices that have an interrupt-counters structure associated with the device. It is often necessary to declare arrays that are bounded by the quantity of such a resource. When this is the case, a value is required that is sufficiently large to prevent subscripting errors when the script is running. This requirement is dealt with by means of dynamic constants. These constants can be used as integer values, and the interpreter views them as such. These dynamic constants are:

- `MAX_DISK` — Maximum number of disk or disk-like resources

- `MAX_IF` — Maximum number of network interfaces

- `MAX_CPU` — Maximum number of CPUs

- `MAX_INTS` — Maximum number of devices with interrupt counters

These values are typically set to the number of discovered resources plus one. A single-CPU computer, for instance, will have a `MAX_CPU` value of 2.   Run this script on your system and see what it says.

```
main()
{
  printf("MAX_DISK = %d\n", MAX_DISK);
  printf("MAX_IF   = %d\n", MAX_IF);
  printf("MAX_CPU  = %d\n", MAX_CPU);
  printf("MAX_INTS = %d\n", MAX_INTS);
}
```

Attachable Functions

To ensure against the rampant effects of "creeping featurism" overtaking the size and complexity of the interpreter, a mechanism had to be devised so many procedures and functions could be "built in" without being a built-in.

The solution was to provide a syntactic remedy that defined a shared object that could be attached to the interpreter at run time. This declaration would include the names of functions contained in that shared object. Here is an example.

```
attach "libc.so" {
  int puts(string s);
};
main()
{
  puts("hello");
}
```

The `attach` statements are contained in the same se include files as the C counterpart in `/usr/include`. The man page for `fopen`, for instance, specifies that the file `stdio.h` should be included to obtain its declaration. In SymbEL, the include file `stdio.se` is included to obtain the declaration inside an `attach` block.

Here are some rules governing the use of attached functions:

- Only parameters that are four bytes long or less can be passed as parameters. No `longlong` types or `doubles`.

- Structures can be passed, but they are sent as pointers to structures.

  The equivalent C representation of the SymbEL structure can be declared, and the parameters should then be declared as pointers to that type. The structure pointer parameter can then be used as it normally would be used. And although the structure parameter in the C code is a pointer, it still is not a reference parameter and any changes made will not be copied back to SymbEL variable.

- Attached functions declaring a structure type as their return value are treated as if the function returns a pointer to that type.

  There is no way to declare an attached function that returns a structure, i.e., not a pointer to a structure, but a structure. The value returned is converted from the C representation into the internal SymbEL representation. No additional code is needed to convert the return value.

  Note that attached functions returning pointers to structures sometimes return zero (a null pointer) to indicate error or end-of-file conditions. Such functions should be declared as returning `ulong`, and their return value compared to zero. If a non-zero value is returned, the `struct_fill` built-in can be used to fill a structure. If an attached function is declared to return a structure and it returns zero, then a null pointer exception occurs in the program and the interpreter exits.

- No more than 12 parameters can be passed.

- Arrays passed to attached functions are passed by reference. The call

    ```
    fgets(buf, sizeof(buf), stdin);
    ```

  does exactly what it is expected to do. The `buf` parameter will be filled in by `fgets` directly because the internal representation of an array of characters is, not surprisingly, an array of characters. These semantics include passing arrays of structures. The SymbEL structure will be emptied before passing and filled upon return when sent to attached functions.

- The rules for finding the shared library in an `attach` statement are the same as those defined in the man page for `ld`.

Ellipsis Parameter

For attached functions only, you can use the ellipsis parameter (. . .) to specify that there are an indeterminate number and type of parameters to follow. Values passed up until the ellipsis argument are type checked, but everything after that is not type checked. The ellipsis parameter allows functions like `sscanf` to work and therefore makes the language more flexible. For instance, the program

```
attach "libc.so" {
   int sscanf(string buf, string format, ...);
};
main()
{
   string buf_to_parse = "hello 1:15.16 f";
   char str[32];
   int n;
   int i;
   double d;
   char c;
   n = sscanf(buf_to_parse, "%s %d:%lf %c", str, &i, &d, &c);
   printf("Found %d values: %s %d:%5.2lf %c\n", n, str, i, d, c);
}
```

yields the output

```
"Found 4 values: hello 1:15.16 f"
```

Attached Variables

Global variables contained in shared objects can be declared within an `attach` block with the keyword `extern` before the declaration. This declaration causes the values within the internal SymbEL variable to read and be written to the variable as it is used in the execution of the program.

Here is an example of the declaration of `getopt`, with its global variables `optind`, `opterr`, and `optarg` from the include file `stdlib.se`.

```
attach "libc.so" {
   int    getopt(int argc, string argv[], string optstring);
   extern int optind;
   extern int opterr;
   extern string optarg;
};
```

This code works for all types, including structures.

Built-in Variables

Although extern variables can be attached with the `extern` notation, there are three very special cases of variables that cannot be attached this way. These variables are `stdin`, `stdout`, and `stderr`. These "variables" in C are actually #define directives in the `stdio.h` include file; they reference the addresses of structure members. Since the address of structures cannot be taken in SymbEL, there is no way to represent these so-called variables. They are, therefore, provided by the interpreter as built-in variables. They can be used without any declaration or include file usage.

Parameters to **main** and Its Return Value

In C programs, the programmer can declare `main` as accepting three parameters:

- An argument count (usually `argc`)
- An argument vector (usually `argv`)
- An environment vector (usually `envp`)

Similarly, the SymbEL `main` function can be declared as accepting two of these parameters, `argc` and `argv`. Here is an example that uses these variables.

```
main(int argc, string argv[])
{
  int i;
  for(i=0; i<argc; i++) {
    printf("argv[%d] = %s\n", i, argv[i]);
  }
}
```

This example also demonstrates the use of an empty array declaration. When this program is run with the command

```
se test.se one two three four five six
```

the resulting output is

```
argv[0] = test.se
argv[1] = one
argv[2] = two
argv[3] = three
argv[4] = four
argv[5] = five
argv[6] = six
```

It is not necessary to declare these parameters to `main`. If they are not declared, then the interpreter does not send any values for them.

It is also possible to declare `main` as being an integer function. Although the `exit` function can be used to exit the application with a specific code, the value can also be returned from `main`. In this case, the previous example would be:

```
int main(int argc, string argv[])
{
    int i;
    for(i=0; i<argc; i++) {
        printf("argv[%d] = %s\n", i, argv[i]);
    }
    return 0;
}
```

The value returned by the `return` statement is the code that the interpreter exits with.

Structures

SymbEL supports the aggregate type `struct`, which is similar to the C variety, with some exceptions. An aggregate is a collection of potentially dissimilar objects collected into a single group. As it turns out, most of the SymbEL code developed will contain structures.

As an example, here is what a SymbEL password file entry might look like.

```
struct passwd {
    string pw_name;
    string pw_passwd;
    long   pw_uid;
    long   pw_gid;
    string pw_age;
    string pw_comment;
    string pw_gecos;
    string pw_dir;
    string pw_shell;
};
```

The declaration of structure variables differs from C in that the word `struct` is left out of the variable declaration. So, to declare a variable of type `struct passwd`, only `passwd` would be used.

Accessing Structure Members

You access a structure member with *dot notation*. The first part of the variable is the variable name itself, followed by a dot and then the structure member in question. To access the `pw_name` member of the `passwd` structure above, the code could look like this.

```
main()
{
```

```
    passwd pwd;
    pwd.pw_name = "richp";
     ...
  }
```

Structure members can be any type, including other structures. A structure may *not* contain a member of its own type. If it does, the parser posts an error.

Arrays of Structures

Declarations of arrays of structures is the same as for any other type, with the provision stated in the previous paragraph. Notation for accessing members of an array of structures is *name[expression].member*.

Structure Assignment

The assignment operation is available to variables of the same structure type.

Structure Comparison

Comparison of variables of structure type is not supported.

Structures as Parameters

Variables of structure type can be passed as parameters. As with other parameters, they are passed by value so the target function can access its structure parameter as a local variable.

Arrays of structures to other SymbEL functions are also passed by value. This is not the case with passing arrays of structures to attached functions (see "Attachable Functions" on page 532).

Structures as Return Values of Functions

Functions can return structure values. Assigning a variable the value of the result of a function call that returns a structure is the same as a structure assignment between two variables.

Language Classes

The preceding sections have discussed the basic structure of SymbEL. The remainder of this chapter discuss the features that make SymbEL powerful as a language for extracting, analyzing, and manipulating data from the kernel.

When generalizing a capability, the next step after creation of a library is the development of a syntactic notation which represents the capability that the library provided. The capability in question here is the retrieval of data from the sources within the kernel that provide performance tuning data. SymbEL provides a solution to this problem through the use of predefined language classes that can be used to declare the type of a variable and to designate it as being a special variable. When a variable with this special designation is accessed, the data from the source that the variable represents is extracted and placed into the variable before it is evaluated.

There are four predefined language classes in SymbEL:

- kvm — Access to any global kernel symbol

- kstat — Access to any information provided by the kstat framework

- mib — Read-only access to the MIB2 variables in the IP, ICMP, TCP, and UDP modules in the kernel

- ndd — Access to variables provided by the IP, ICMP, TCP, UDP, and ARP modules in the kernel

Variables of these language classes have the same structure as any other variable. They can be a simple type or a structured type. What needs clarification in the declaration of the variable is

- Whether the variable type is simple or structured

- Whether the variable has a predefined language class attribute

The syntax selected for this capability defines the variable with a name that is the concatenation of the language class name and a dollar sign ($). This convention allows these prefixes for variables to denote their special status.

- kvm$ kvm language class

- kstat$ kstat language class

- mib$ mib language class

- ndd$ ndd language class

Examples of variables declared with a special attribute are:

```
ks_system_misc kstat$misc;   // structured type, kstat language class
int            kvm$maxusers; // simple type,     kvm   language class
mib2_ip_t      mib$ip;       // structured type, mib   language class
ndd_tcp_t      ndd$tcp;      // structured type, ndd   language class
```

When any of these variables appear in a statement, the values that the variables represent are retrieved from the respective source before the variable is evaluated. Variables declared of the same type but not possessing the special prefix are not evaluated in the same manner. For instance, the variable

```
ks_system_misc tmp_misc;   // structured type, no language class specified
```

can be accessed without any data being read from the `kstat` framework.

Variables that use a language class prefix in their name are called *active* variables. Those that do not are called *inactive* variables.

The **kvm** Language Class

Let's look at an example of the use of a kvm variable.

```
main()
{
  int kvm$maxusers;
  printf("maxusers is set to %d\n", kvm$maxusers);
}
```

In this example, there is a local variable of type `int`. The fact that it is an `int` is not exceptional. The fact that the name of the variable begins with kvm$ *is* exceptional. It is the kvm$ prefix that flags the interpreter to look up this value in the kernel via the kvm library. The actual name of the kernel variable is whatever follows the kvm$ prefix. The program need not take special action to read the value from the kernel. Simply accessing the variable by using it as a parameter to the `printf()` statement (in this example) causes the interpreter to read the value from the kernel and place it in the variable before sending the value to `printf()`. Use of kvm variables is somewhat limiting since the effective uid of se must be superuser or the effective gid must be sys in order to successfully use the kvm library.

In this example, the variable `maxusers` is a valid variable in the kernel and when accessed is read from the kernel address space. It is possible and legal to declare a kvm$ active variable with the name of a variable that is not in the kernel address space. The value will contain the original initialized value, and refreshing of this type of variable is futile because there is no actual value in the kernel. This technique is useful when dealing with pointers, though, and an example is included in "Using kvm Variables and Functions" on page 553.

≡ 17

The **kstat** Language Class

The use of kstat variables differs from the use of kvm variables in that all of the kstat types are defined in the header file kstat.se. All kstat variables must be structures because this is how they are defined in the header file. Declaration of an active kstat variable that is not a structure results in a semantic error. Declaration of an active kstat variable that is not of a type declared in the kstat.se header file results in the variable always containing zeros unless the program manually places something else in the variable. Here is an example of using kstat variables.

```
#include <kstat.se>
main()
{
  ks_system_misc kstat$misc;
  printf("This machine has %u CPU(s) in it.\n", kstat$misc.ncpus);
}
```

Just as in the kvm example, no explicit access need be done to retrieve the data from the kstat framework. The access to the member of the active ks_system_misc variable in the parameter list of printf() causes the member to be updated by the run time.

Multiple Instances

The kstat.se header file contains many structures that have information that is unique in nature. The ks_system_misc structure is an example.

The number of CPUs on the system is unique and does not change depending on something else. However, the activity of each of the individual CPUs *does* change, depending on which CPU is in question. This is also the case for network interfaces and disks. This situation is handled by the addition to structures of two members that contain data for devices that have multiple instances. These members are name$ and number$.

The name$ member contains the name of the device as supplied by kstat. The number$ member is a linear number representing the *n*th device of this type encountered. It is *not* the device instance number. This representation allows a for loop to be written such that all of the devices of a particular type can be traversed without the need to skip over instances that are not in the system. It is not unusual, for instance, for a multiprocessor machine to contain CPUs that do not have linear instance numbers. When traversing through all the devices, the program will encounter the end of the list when the number$ member contains a -1. Here is an example of searching through multiple disk instances.

```
#include <kstat.se>
main()
{
  ks_disks kstat$disk;
  printf("Disks currently seen by the system:\n");
```

```
    for(kstat$disk.number$=0; kstat$disk.number$ != -1; kstat$disk.number$++)
{
        printf("\t%s\n", kstat$disk.name$);
    }
}
```

In this program, `kstat$disk.number$` is set initially to zero. The "while part" of the loop is then run, checking the value of `kstat$disk.number$` to see if it's -1. That comparison causes the run time to verify that there is an *n*th disk. If there is, then the `number$` member is left with its value and the body of the loop runs. When the run time evaluates the `kstat$disk.name$` value in the `printf()` statement, it reads the name of the *n*th disk and places it in the `name$` member, which is then sent to `printf()`.

Other Points About `kstat`

Here are some points about how to best use `kstat` variables in a program.

Some of the values contained in the `kstat` structures are not immediately useful by themselves. For instance, the `cpu` member of the `ks_cpu_sysinfo` structure is an array of four unsigned `long`s representing the number of clock ticks that have occurred since system boot in each of the four CPU states: idle, user, kernel, and wait. This data must be disseminated to be useful.

If a program needs to access many members of a `kstat` variable, then it is in the best interest of the performance of the program and the system to copy the values into an inactive `kstat` variable by using a structure assignment. The single structure assignment causes all of the members of the structure to be read from the `kstat` framework with one read and then copied to the inactive variable. When these values are accessed by the inactive variable, no more reads from the `kstat` framework will be initiated. The net result is a reduction in the number of system calls being performed by the run time, and therefore se does not have a significant impact on the performance of the system. Here is an example.

Example kstat Program

```
#include <unistd.se>
#include <sysdepend.se>
#include <kstat.se>

main()
{
    ks_cpu_sysinfo kstat$cpusys;    // active kstat variable
    ks_cpu_sysinfo tmp_cpusys;      // inactive kstat variable
    ks_system_misc kstat$misc;      // active kstat variable
    int ncpus = kstat$misc.ncpus;   // grab it and save it
```

```
int old_ints[MAX_CPU];
int old_cs[MAX_CPU];
int ints;
int cs;
int i;

// initialize the old values
for(i=0; i<ncpus; i++) {
  kstat$cpusys.number$ = i;        // does not cause an update
  tmp_cpusys = kstat$cpusys;        // struct assignment, update performed
  old_ints[i] = tmp_cpusys.intr;   // no update, inactive variable
  old_cs[i] = tmp_cpusys.pswitch; // no update, inactive variable
}
for(;;) {
  sleep(1);
  for(i=0; i<ncpus; i++) {
    kstat$cpusys.number$ = i;      // does not cause an update
    tmp_cpusys = kstat$cpusys;      // struct assignment, update performed
    ints = tmp_cpusys.intr - old_ints[i];
    cs = tmp_cpusys.pswitch - old_cs[i];

    printf("CPU: %d   cs/sec = %d  int/sec = %d\n", i, cs, ints);

    old_ints[i] = tmp_cpusys.intr;
    old_cs[i] = tmp_cpusys.pswitch;  // save old values
  }
}
}
```

About the Program

```
ks_cpu_sysinfo kstat$cpusys;   // active kstat variable
ks_cpu_sysinfo tmp_cpusys;     // inactive kstat variable
```

This code is the declaration of the active and inactive variable. Use of the active variable causes the run time to read the values from the kstat framework for the ks_cpu_sysinfo structure. Later accesses to the inactive variable do not cause the reads to occur.

```
ks_system_misc kstat$misc;     // active kstat variable
int ncpus = kstat$misc.ncpus;  // grab it and save it
```

Since the ncpus variable will be used extensively, it is best to put the value into a variable that does not cause continual updates.

```
int old_ints[MAX_CPU];
int old_cs[MAX_CPU];
```

Since the program computes the rate at which interrupts and context switches are occurring, the values from the previous iteration need to be saved so they can be subtracted from the values of the current iteration. They are arrays bounded by the maximum number of CPUs available on a system.

```
// initialize the old values
for(i=0; i<ncpus; i++) {
   kstat$cpusys.number$ = i;        // does not cause an update
    tmp_cpusys = kstat$cpusys;      // struct assignment, update performed
   old_ints[i] = tmp_cpusys.intr;  // no update, inactive variable
   old_cs[i] = tmp_cpusys.pswitch;  // no update, inactive variable
}
```

This code grabs the initial values that will be subtracted from the current values after the first `sleep()` is completed. For simplicity, no timers are kept, and it is assumed that only one second has elapsed between updates. In practice, the elapsed time would be computed.

```
for(i=0; i<ncpus; i++) {
   kstat$cpusys.number$ = i;        // does not cause an update
    tmp_cpusys = kstat$cpusys;      // struct assignment, update performed
```

Here, the `number$` member is set to the CPU in question, and then the contents of the entire active structure variable are copied into the inactive structure variable. This coding causes only one system call to update the `kstat` variable.

```
ints = tmp_cpusys.intr - old_ints[i];
cs = tmp_cpusys.pswitch - old_cs[i];

printf("CPU: %d   cs/sec = %d   int/sec = %d\n", i, cs, ints);

old_ints[i] = tmp_cpusys.intr;
old_cs[i] = tmp_cpusys.pswitch;  // save old values
```

This code computes the number of interrupts and context switches for the previous second and prints it out. The current values are then saved as the old values, and the loop continues.

Runtime Declaration of **kstat** Structures

The `kstat` framework is dynamic and contains information regarding devices attached to the system. These devices are built by Sun and by third-party manufacturers. The interpreter contains static definitions of many devices, and these definitions are mirrored by the `kstat.se` include file. However, it is unreasonable to assume that the interpreter will always contain all of the possible definitions for devices. To accommodate this situation, a syntactic element was needed. This is the `kstat` structure.

A `kstat` structure can define only `KSTAT_TYPE_NAMED` structures, which are the structures that define devices such as network interfaces. As an example, the following script prints out the values of a `kstat` structure that is not declared in the `kstat.se` file but has been part of the `kstat` framework since the very beginning.

```
kstat struct "kstat_types" ks_types {
   ulong raw;
   ulong "name=value";
   ulong interrupt;
   ulong "i/o";
   ulong event_timer;
};
main()
{
   ks_types kstat$t;
   ks_types tmp = kstat$t;
   printf("raw          = %d\n", tmp.raw);
   printf("name=value  = %d\n", tmp.name_value);
   printf("interrupt   = %d\n", tmp.interrupt);
   printf("i/o         = %d\n", tmp.i_o);
   printf("event_timer = %d\n", tmp.event_timer);
}
```

The `kstat` structure introduces a few new concepts:

• The structure starts with the word "kstat" to denote its significance.

• The structure also contains members that are quoted. Quoted members work only for `kstat` structures and do not work in an ordinary structure declaration. Quoted members enable programmers to declare variables that accurately reflect the name of the member within the `kstat` framework. For instance, the member `"name=value"` could not be declared without quotes since the parser would generate errors. When accessed in the `printf()` statement, special characters are translated to underscores. This is the case for any character that is recognized as a token and also for spaces. The characters that will be translated to underscores are:

    `[]{}()@|!&#;:.,+*/=-><~%? \t\n\\^`

• Members of `KSTAT_TYPE_NAMED` structures sometimes have no name. This situation will also be correctly handled by the interpreter. Any member of a structure with the name `""` is changed to `missingN` where *N* starts at 1 and increments for each occurrence of a missing member name. A declaration of

```
kstat struct "asleep" ks_zzzz {
  ulong "";  // translates into missing1
};
```

translates into

```
kstat struct "asleep" ks_zzzz {
  ulong missing1;
};
```

for the purposes of the programmer. It is a good idea to document such declarations, as shown above.

- Members with reserved words as names are also munged into another form—the prefix SYM_ is added to the name. For instance, this declaration

```
kstat struct "unnecessary" ks_complexity {
  short "short";
};
```

is munged into

```
kstat struct "unnecessary" ks_complexity {
  short SYM_short;
};
```

so you can continue.

- The quoted string following the keyword struct in the declaration represents the name of the KSTAT_TYPE_NAMED structure in the kstat framework and is an algebra unto itself. First, an introduction.

Each "link" in the kstat "chain" that composes the framework has three name elements: a module, an instance number, and a name. The "kstat_types" link, for instance, has the complete name "unix".0."kstat_types". "unix" is the module, 0 is the instance number, and "kstat_types" is the name. Here are the possible ways to specify the kstat name within this quoted string.

  - "kstat_types" — The "name" of the kstat.

  - "cpu_info:" — The "module" of the kstat. A link with the full name of "cpu_info".0."cpu_info0" would map onto this structure. However, so too would "cpu_info".1."cpu_info1", and this case brings up an issue. When a kstat structure is declared with a kstat module name, the first two members of the structure must be:

    ```
    long number$;
    string name$;
    ```

This requirement is in keeping with other kstat declarations with multiple instances. In the case of structures with multiple module names that have the same structure members, the list of names continues with colon separators, for example:

```
kstat struct "ieef:el:elx:pcelx" ks_elx_network { ...
```

- "*kmem_magazine" — The prefix of the name portion of the kstat. In the case of the kmem_magazines, the module name is always "unix", which is the module name of many other links that do not share the same structure members as the kmem_magazines. As is the case with specifying a module name, the number$ and name$ members must be present.

Note that when a dynamic kstat structure declaration replaces a static declaration inside of the interpreter, the old declaration is discarded and replaced with the new one. Therefore, if a kmem_magazine declaration were used to replace the "ks_cache" declaration from kstat.se, the only kstat links seen would be the kmem_magazine members and all of the other cache links (and there are a lot of them) would no longer be seen.

Adding New Disk Names

You can use an internal function, se_add_disk_name(*string name*), to add new disk names to the existing list internally. Therefore, if the tape drives and nfs mounts that are recorded in the KSTAT_TYPE_IO section of the kstat framework were to be added to the list of disks for display by any script that shows disk statistics, you could add these lines at the beginning of the script.

```
se_add_disk_name("st");
se_add_disk_name("nfs");
```

This function is declared in the se.se include file.

The **mib** Language Class

A lot of data regarding the network resides in the mib variables of the kernel. Unfortunately, these mib variables are not part of the kstat framework. Therefore, a new language class was created to facilitate access to this information.

Variables of the mib class have a unique feature in that they can be read, but assigning values generates a warning from the interpreter. This warning is to remind you that assigning values to the members of the mib2_* structures will *not* result in the information being placed back into the kernel. The mib variables are read-only.

mib variables do not have the permissions limitation of kvm variables. Any user can view mib variable values without special access permissions.

To view the mib information available from within SymbEL, run the command `netstat -s` from the command line. All but the IGMP information is available.

Since all `mib` variables are structures, the rules regarding structure assignment being used to cut down on the overhead of the interpreter are the same as for the `kstat` and `kvm` classes. Here is an example of using `mib` class variables.

```
#include <mib.se>
main()
{
  mib2_tcp_t mib$tcp;
  printf("Retransmitted TCP segments = %u\n", mib$tcp.tcpRetransSegs);
}
```

The ndd Language Class

SunOS 5.x provides access to variables that define the operation of the network stack through a command called ndd (see ndd(1M)). The ndd language class within SymbEL provides access to the variables within the IP, ICMP, TCP, UDP, and ARP modules. The definitions of the available variables are in the ndd.se include file. For each module, there is a structure that contains all of the variables available for that module.

Some of these variables are read-write and others are read-only. If you try to modify a variable that is read-only, the interpreter posts a warning message. Some of the read-only variables are tables that can be quite large. Note that the largest table size that can be handled is 64 kilobytes (65,536 bytes). If an ndd variable is larger than 64 kilobytes, it is truncated.

Like `kstat` and `mib` variables, all ndd variables are structures.

The following program displays the `tcp_status` variable of the TCP module. This variable is type `string` and when printed looks like a large table.

```
#include <stdio.se>
#include <ndd.se>
main()
{
  ndd_tcp_t ndd$tcp;
  puts(ndd$tcp.tcp_status);
}
```

User-Defined Classes

The four language classes provide a significant amount of data to a program for analysis. But the analysis of this data can become convoluted and make the program difficult to deal with. This is one of the problems that SymbEL hoped to clear up. Adding more language classes is a potential solution to this problem.

An example of an additional language class that would be useful is a vmstat class. This would be a structure that provided all of the information that the vmstat program provides. The problem is that such an addition would make se larger and provide functionality that didn't really require the internals of the interpreter to accomplish. All of what vmstat does can be done by a SymbEL program.

In addition to the vmstat class, it would be useful to have classes for iostat, mpstat, nfsstat, netstat, and any other "stat" program that provided this type of statistical information. What was needed to accomplish this task correctly was a language feature that allowed programmers to create their own language classes in SymbEL. This "user defined class" would be a structure and an associated block of code that was called whenever one of the members of the structure was accessed. This idea led to the development of the aggregate type class.

A class type is a structure and a block of code inside the structure that are first called when the block that contains the declaration of the class variable is entered. Thereafter, whenever a member of the class variable is accessed, the block is called. To illustrate the class construct, here is a program that continually displays how long a system has been up. The first example is without the use of a class.

```
#include <stdio.se>
#include <unistd.se>
#include <kstat.se>

#define MINUTES (60 * hz)
#define HOURS   (60 * MINUTES)
#define DAYS    (24 * HOURS)

main()
{
  ulong ticks;
  ulong days;
  ulong hours;
  ulong minutes;
  ulong seconds;
  ks_system_misc kstat$misc;
  long hz = sysconf(_SC_CLK_TCK);

  for(;;) {
```

```
        ticks = kstat$misc.clk_intr;
        days = ticks / DAYS;
        ticks -= (days * DAYS);
        hours = ticks / HOURS;
        ticks -= (hours * HOURS);
        minutes = ticks / MINUTES;
        ticks -= (minutes * MINUTES);
        seconds = ticks / hz;
        printf("System up for: %4u days %2u hours %2u minutes %2u seconds\r",
          days, hours, minutes, seconds);
        fflush(stdout);
        sleep(1);
    }
  }
```

This program continues in an infinite `for` loop, computing the uptime based on the number of clock ticks the system has received since boot. The computation is contained completely within the main program. This code can be distilled into a user-defined class, as the following code shows.

```
#include <unistd.se>
#include <kstat.se>

#define MINUTES (60 * hz)
#define HOURS   (60 * MINUTES)
#define DAYS    (24 * HOURS)

class uptime {

  ulong ticks;
  ulong days;
  ulong hours;
  ulong minutes;
  ulong seconds;

  uptime$()
  {
    ks_system_misc kstat$misc;
    long hz = sysconf(_SC_CLK_TCK);

    ticks = kstat$misc.clk_intr;    /* assign these values to the */
    days = ticks / DAYS;            /* class members              */
    ticks -= (days * DAYS);
    hours = ticks / HOURS;
    ticks -= (hours * HOURS);
    minutes = ticks / MINUTES;
    ticks -= (minutes * MINUTES);
```

```
      seconds = ticks / hz;
   }
};
```

The start of the class looks like a structure, but the final "member" of the structure is a block of code called the "class block." The name used after the `class` keyword is the type name that will be used in the declaration of the variable. The name of the class block is the prefix used in variable names to denote that the variable is active. Variables declared in a user-defined class type that do not use the prefix in the variable name are inactive.

The `main()` function of the `uptime` program would now be written to use the `uptime` class as shown in this example.

```
#include <stdio.se>
#include <unistd.se>
#include "uptime_class.se"

main()
{
  uptime uptime$value;
  uptime tmp_uptime;

  for(;;) {
    tmp_uptime = uptime$value;
    printf("System up for: %4u days %2u hours %2u minutes %2u seconds\r",
      tmp_uptime.days, tmp_uptime.hours,
      tmp_uptime.minutes, tmp_uptime.seconds);
    fflush(stdout);
    sleep(1);
  }
}
```

The previous section discussed how the assignment of entire structures cuts down on the overhead of the system because only one copy is required. Not only is this true here as well, but the structure copy also ensures that the data printed out represents the calculations of one snapshot in time, instead of printing different values for each time that the class block was called to update each member of the class that was used as a parameter to `printf()`.

Pitfalls

Here are some of the idiosyncrasies of the language that will catch programmers by surprise if they're accustomed to using a particular feature in C and assume that it will be supported in SymbEL.

- Only one variable can be declared per line. The variable names may not be a comma-separated list.

- There is no type `float`. All floating-point variables are type `double`.

- Curly braces must surround all sequences of statements in control structures, including sequences of length one.

- The comparators work with scalars, floats, and strings. Therefore, the logical comparison (`"hello" == "world"`) is valid and in this case returns `false`.

- If the result of an expression yields a floating value as an operand to the modulus operator, that value is converted to `long` before the operation takes place. This conversion occurs while the program is running.

- Assignment of the result of a logical expression is not allowed.

- The `for` loop has some limitations.
  - There can be only one assignment in the assignment part.
  - There can be only logical expressions in the `while` part.

- There can be only one assignment in the `do` part.

- All local variables have `static` semantics.

- All parameters are passed by value.

- Global variables can be assigned the value of a function call. * `while(running)` is not syntactically correct. `while(running != 0)` is correct.

- There is no recursion in SymbEL.

- Structure comparison is not supported.

- Syntax of conditional expressions is rigid: (*condition* ? do_exp : else_exp)

- Calling attached functions with incorrect values can result in a core dump and is not avoidable by the interpreter. This simple but effective script will cause a segmentation fault core dump:

```
#include <stdio.se>
main()
{
  puts(nil);
}
```

Tricks

As the creator of a programming language and the developer of the interpreter, it is much easier for me to see through the intricacies of the features to underlying functionality of the interpreter itself. This knowledge manifests itself in programming "tricks" that allow certain operations to be done that may not be obvious. Here are some that I've used. If there's something you need done and it doesn't seem to fit into any language feature, try to work around it. You may find a loophole that you didn't know existed.

Returning an Array of Nonstructured Type from a Function

Although it is not allowed to declare a function as

```
int []
not_legal()
{
  int array[ARRAY_SIZE] = { 1, 2, 3, 4, 5, -1 };
  return array;
}
```

it is still possible to return an array. Granted, this code is unattractive, but most of the tricks in this section involve something that is not very appealing from the programming standpoint. SymbEL is, after all, just a scripting language. And if it can be done at all, it's worth doing. So, here's how to return an array of nonstructured type from a function.

```
#define ARRAY_SIZE 128
ulong
it_is_legal()
{
  int array[ARRAY_SIZE] = { 1, 2, 3, 4, 5, -1 };
  return &array;
}
struct array_struct {
  int array[ARRAY_SIZE];
};
main()
{
  array_struct digits;
  ulong address;
  int i;
  address = it_is_legal();
  struct_fill(digits, address);
  for(i=0; digits.array[i] != -1; i++) {
    printf("%d\n", digits.array[i]);
  }
}
```

Using Return Values from Attached Functions

It is common to read input lines by using `fgets`, then locate the newline character with `strchr` and change it to a null character. This approach has unexpected results in SymbEL. For instance, the code segment

```
while(fgets(buf, sizeof(buf), stdin) ! = nil) {
  p = strchr(buf, '\n');
  p[0] = '\0';
  puts(buf);
}
```

would be expected to null the newline character and print the line (yes, I know this code segment will cause se to exit with a null pointer exception if a line is read with no newline character). But this is not the case because the `strchr` function will return a string that is assigned to the variable p. When this happens, a new copy of the string returned by `strchr` is allocated and assigned to p. When the `p[0] = '\0';` line is executed, the newline character in the copy is made null. The original `buf` from the `fgets` call remains intact. The way around this result (and this workaround should be done only when it is certain that the input lines contain the newline character) is:

```
while(fgets(buf, sizeof(buf), stdin) ! = nil) {
  strcpy(strchr(buf, '\n'), "");
  puts(buf);
}
```

In this case, the result of the `strchr` call is never assigned to a variable, and its return value remains uncopied before being sent to the `strcpy` function. `strcpy` then copies the string `" "` onto the newline and in doing so, changes it to the null character.

Using **kvm** Variables and Functions

Using the `kvm` functions and dealing with `kvm` variables in general is quite confusing because there are so many levels of indirection of pointers. This simple script performs the equivalent of `/bin/uname -m`.

```
#include <stdio.se>
#include <devinfo.se>

main()
{
  ulong kvm$top_devinfo;     // top_devinfo is an actual kernel variable
  dev_info_t kvm$root_node;  // root_node is not, but it needs to be active

  // The next line affects a pointer indirection. The value of top_devinfo
  // is a pointer to the root of the devinfo tree in the kernel.  This value
  // is extracted, and the root_node variable has its kernel address changed
```

```
  // to this value.  Accessing the root_node variable after this assignment
  // will cause the reading of the dev_info_t structure from the kernel
  // since root_node is an active variable.  Note that root_node is not
  // a variable in the kernel though, but it's declared active so that
  // the value will be read out *after* it's given a valid kernel address.
  // And there's no need to explicitly read the string, it's done already.
  kvm_cvt(kvm$root_node, kvm$top_devinfo);
  puts(kvm$root_node.devi_name);
}
```

Another example of extracting kvm values is with the kvm_declare function. This
function allows kernel variables to be declared while the program is running. Instead of
declaring a kvm variable for maxusers, for instance, you could do it this way:

```
main()
{
  ulong address;
  int kvm$integer_value;

  address = kvm_declare("maxusers");
  kvm_cvt(kvm$integer_value, address);
  printf("maxusers is %d\n", kvm$integer_value);
}
```

A more general way to peruse integer variables entered at the user's leisure is shown in
this example.

```
#include <stdio.se>
#include <string.se>

int main()
{
  char var_name[BUFSIZ];
  ulong address;
  int kvm$variable;

  for(;;) {
    fputs("Enter the name of an integer variable: ", stdout);
    if (fgets(var_name, sizeof(var_name), stdin) == nil) {
      return 0;
    }
    strcpy(strchr(var_name, '\n'), "");  // chop
    address = kvm_declare(var_name);     // look it up with nlist
    if (address == 0) {
      printf("variable %s is not found in the kernel space\n", var_name);
      continue;
    }
    kvm_cvt(kvm$variable, address);      // convert the address of the kvm var
```

```
   printf("%s = %u\n", var_name, kvm$variable);
   }
}
```

Using an **attach** Block to Call Interpreter Functions

The attach feature of SymbEL implements the use of the dynamic linking feature of Solaris. The dl functions allow an external library to be attached to a running process, thus making the symbols within that binary available to the program.

One of the features of dynamic linking is the ability to access symbols within the binary that is running. That is, a process can look into itself for symbols. This can also be accomplished in SymbEL by using an attach block with no name. With this trick, a script can call functions contained within the interpreter, but the author of the script has to know what functions are available. Currently, the only functions available to the user are listed in the se.se include file.

The most useful of these functions is the se_function_call function, which allows the script to call a SymbEL function indirectly. This function can be used for a callback mechanism. It's the equivalent of a pointer to a function. For example, this script calls the function "callback" indirectly.

```
#include <se.se>
main()
{
   se_function_call("callback", 3, 2, 1);
}

callback(int a, int b, int c)
{
   printf("a = %d b = %d c = %d\n", a, b, c);
}
```

The se_function_call function is declared with an ellipsis argument so any number of parameters can be passed (up to the internal limit) to the function being called. Be careful to pass the correct type and number of arguments.

An extreme example of this functionality is demonstrated below. The script calls on the interpreter to parse a function from an external file and then run the function. It's an absurd example, but it demonstrates the tangled web that can be weaved with attached functions and variables.

```
// this is the file "other_file"
some_function(int param)
{
   printf("hello there: %d\n", param);
}
```

```
// this is the demo script
#include <stdio.se>
#include <string.se>
#include <se.se>

attach "" {
  extern ulong Lex_input;
  extern int Se_errors;
  yyparse();
  se_fatal(string p);
};

int main()
{
  Lex_input = fopen("other_file", "r");
  if (Lex_input == 0) {
    perror("fopen");
    return 1;pf
  }
  yyparse();
  if (Se_errors != 0) {
    se_fatal("parse errors in other_file");
    return 1;
  }
  se_function_call("some_function", 312);
  return 0;
}
```

Tunables Quick Reference

This appendix lists the kernel variables that are tunable. The data is tabulated with references to the rest of the book for more information and explanation.

Tunable Kernel Parameters

The kernel chapter of this book explains how the main kernel algorithms work. The kernel tunable values listed in this section include *the tunables that are worth worrying about*. There are a huge number of global values defined in the kernel; if you hear of a tweak that is not listed in this book, think twice before using it. The algorithms, default values, and existence of many of these variables vary from one release to the next. Do not assume that an undocumented tweak that works well for one kernel will apply to other releases, other kernel architectures of the same release, or even a different patch level.

SunService maintain a list of tunable parameters as SunSolve Infodoc 11915.

Configuration-related parameters are shown in Table A-1.

Table A-1 Configuration Variables

Name	Default	Min	Max	Reference
hires_tick	0	0	1	"Kernel Clock Tick Resolution" on page 367
maxusers	MB available RAM (*physmem*)	8	2048	"Autoconfiguration of maxusers in Solaris 2.3 Through Solaris 2.6" on page 360
ngroups_max	32	32		Max number of supplementary groups per user
npty	48	48	3000	SunOS 4.X-compatible pty entries
pt_cnt	48	48	3000	"Changing maxusers and Pseudo-ttys in Solaris 2" on page 359
rstchown	1	0	1	See chown (1) sets value of POSIX_CHOWN_RESTRICTED
rlim_fd_cur	64	64	256	Breaks stdio if > 256
rlim_fd_max	1024	1024		Breaks select if > 1024

A

File attribute cache parameters are shown in Table A-2. These scale up automatically with memory size and have little effect on performance, except on NFS servers.

Table A-2   File Name and Attribute Cache Sizes

Name	Default	Min	Max	Reference
ncsize	(maxusers * 17) + 90	226	34906	"Directory Name Lookup Cache" on page 360
ufs_ninode	(maxusers * 17) + 90	226	34906	"The Inode Cache and File Data Caching" on page 362

Hardware-specific parameters are shown in Table A-3.

Table A-3   Hardware-Specific Configuration Tunables

Name	Default	Min	Max	Reference
use_mxcc_prefetch	0 (sun4d) 1 (sun4m)	0	1	"The SuperSPARC with SuperCache Two-Level Cache Architecture" on page 262.

Memory-related tunables are shown in Table A-4.

Table A-4   Memory-Related Tunables

Name	Default	Min	Max	Reference
autoup	30	5	240	"Filesystem Flush" on page 333
desfree	lotsfree/2			"desfree" on page 337
doiflush	1	0	1	"Filesystem Flush" on page 333
dopageflush	1	0	1	"Filesystem Flush" on page 333
fastscan	physmem/4		64 MB	"fastscan" on page 336
handspreadpages	physmem/4		64 MB	"handspreadpages" on page 338
lotsfree	physmem/64	512 KB		"lotsfree" on page 337
max_page_get	physmem/2			"max_page_get" on page 338
maxpgio	40 or 60	40		"maxpgio" on page 338
minfree	desfree/2			"minfree" on page 337
physmem	total page count			"desfree" on page 337
slowscan	fastscan/10	100		"slowscan" on page 336
throttlefree	minfree		desfree	"throttlefree" on page 338
tune_t_fsflushr	5	1	autoup	"Filesystem Flush" on page 333

Disk I/O-related and filesystem-related tunables are listed in Table A-5.

Table A-5 I/O-Related Tunables

Name	Default	Min	Max	Reference
ufs_LW	262144	262144	1048576	"Disk Writes and the UFS Write Throttle" on page 172
ufs_HW	393216	> ufs_LW	1572864	

Network-related tunables are listed in Table A-6.

Table A-6 Network-Related Tunables

Name	Default	Min	Max	Reference
tcp:tcp_conn_hash_size	256	256	262144	"Tuning the Close Wait Interval and TCP Connection Hash Table Size" on page 65

System V IPC Tunables

Shared memory parameters are usually set based on the needs of specific application programs. The maximum value can be misleading since almost all the IPC tunables are declared as an int, which has a maximum value of 2147483647. In many cases, the data item itself must fit into something smaller, such as a ushort embedded in a data structure, and this requirement reduces the theoretical maximum. The maximum listed is a technical limitation based on the data type and is not attainable in real life. The tunables listed in Table A-7 are described in "System V Shared Memory, Semaphores, and Message Queues" on page 344.

It is not really possible to provide a realistic maximum since too many other factors need to be considered, not the least of which is the amount of kernel memory required by everything besides the IPC resources.

Table A-7 Shared Memory, Semaphore, and Message Queue Tunables in Solaris 2

Name	Default	Min	Max	Reference
msgsys:msginfo_msgmap	100	100	2147482637	Number of msgmap entries
msgsys:msginfo_msgmax	2048	2048	2147482637	Max message size
msgsys:msginfo_msgmnb	4096	4096	2147482637	Max bytes on msg queue
msgsys:msginfo_msgmni	50	50	2147482637	Number of msg IDs
msgsys:msginfo_msgseg	1024	1024	32767	Number msg segments
msgsys:msginfo_msgssz	8	8	2147482637	Msg segment size
msgsys:msginfo_msgtql	40	40	2147482637	Number of msg headers

Table A-7 Shared Memory, Semaphore, and Message Queue Tunables in Solaris 2 (Continued)

Name	Default	Min	Max	Reference
semsys:seminfo_semaem	16384	16384	32767	Adjust on exit maximum value
semsys:seminfo_semmap	10	10	2147482637	Number of entries in semaphore map
semsys:seminfo_semmni	10	10	65535	Number of semaphore identifiers
semsys:seminfo_semmns	60	60	65535	Number of semaphores in system
semsys:seminfo_semmnu	30	30	2147482637	Number of undo structures in system
semsys:seminfo_semmsl	25	25	2147482637	Maximum number of semaphores per ID
semsys:seminfo_semopm	10	10	2147482637	Maximum number of operations per semop call
semsys:seminfo_semume	10	10	2147482637	Maximum number of undo entries per process
semsys:seminfo_semusz	96	96	96	Size in bytes of undo structure, derived from semume
semsys:seminfo_semvmx	32767	32767	32767	Semaphore maximum value
shmsys:shminfo_shmmax	1048576	1048576	3.75 Gbytes	Maximum request size
shmsys:shminfo_shmmin	1	1	1	Minimum request size
shmsys:shminfo_shmni	100	100	65535	Number of identifiers to preallocate
shmsys:shminfo_shmseg	6	6	65535	Maximum number of shm segments per process

References

References throughout *Sun Performance and Tuning* are collected here with a few words to indicate what is of interest in the reference and, when appropriate, where the reference can be obtained.

Internet Resources

In 1994, for the first edition of *Sun Performance and Tuning*, there were a few obscure FTP sites where PostScript copies of white papers could be found. In 1998, for the second edition, the Internet probably contains too much information! The information you want is very likely to be available on a web site, but if you search for a keyword such as "performance," you will be overwhelmed with thousands of search hits.

Sun's main web site at www.sun.com contains a lot of useful information, including performance briefs for all the current products and detailed data sheets for SPARC CPUs. I maintain a performance information area on Sun's web server at http://www.sun.com/sun-on-net/performance.html. I'd like this to become a useful starting point, with links to any other interesting performance information. Drop an email to Adrian.Cockcroft@sun.com if you find something that you think should be referenced from this location.

Performance Information

This section lists general sources of performance information.

http://www.sun.com/sun-on-net/performance.html

> The Sun performance information starting point that I maintain.

http://docs.sun.com

> The complete online documentation set for Sun products.

http://www.sun.com/sunworldonline/common/swol-backissues-columns.html#perf

My monthly column of performance questions and answers, dating back to 1995. Updated versions of some of these columns appear in this book.

http://www.sun.com/sunworldonline/common/swol-backissues-columns.html#insidesolaris

Jim Mauro's column on the internal workings of Solaris 2.

http://www.sun.com/books

The SunSoft Press book listings.

http://www.specbench.org

The SPEC benchmark site, which contains full official benchmark results for CPU, NFS server, web server, Java, and other workloads.

http://www.tpc.org

The Transaction Performance Council site contains full official benchmark results for database benchmarks such as the order-entry TPC-C and data warehouse TPC-D workloads.

Java Performance Information

This section lists general sources of Java performance information.

http://www.sun.com/solaris/java/wp-java/

This *Java On Solaris 2.6* white paper is essential reading. It is a very comprehensive and useful source of information. Many Java performance tuning techniques are described in part 6 of this paper, along with the use of TNF tracing capabilities to instrument Java programs.

http://www.cs.cmu.edu/~jch/java/optimization.html

A central reference to a large amount of information on Java optimization, maintained by Jonathan Hardwick.

http://www.sun.com/workshop/java/wp-javaio

Java I/O performance tuning white paper. This contains a more advanced example of Java tuning than the one I describe in "The Java WorkShop Performance Analyzer" on page 129, but it is the same message. This paper and my own write-up were originally written independently of each other at about the same time.

Freely Available Performance Tools

The locations of freely available performance tools are listed in this section.

http://www.sun.com/sun-on-net/performance/se3

The SE Performance Toolkit

http://www.sun.com/sun-on-net/www.sun.com/gpercol

The Java Browser for SE Toolkit `percollator` data

http://sunsolve2.sun.com/sunsolve/symon

The latest release of Symon can be downloaded from this location.

http://opcom.sun.ca

The Solaris Developer Support Center site. It contains Solaris migration tools, and TNF tools, utilities, and documentation, among other useful information.

http://www.sun.com/sunsite

There is a large collection of free software on the network of SunSite servers. `proctool` can be found at http://sunsite.unc.edu/pub/sun-info/mde/proctool.

http://playground.sun.com/psh

The packet shell for TCP/IP analysis, as described in "TCP Transfer Characteristics for Web Servers" on page 68.

Commercial Performance Tool Vendor Web Sites

These are the web sites for performance tool vendors discussed in "Performance Management Products" on page 26.

Amdahl is at http://www.amdahl.com

BGS is at http://www.bgs.com

BMC is at http://www.bmc.com

Compuware is at http://www.compuware.com

Datametrics is at http://www.datametrics.com

HP is at http://www.hp.com/openview/rpm

Landmark is at http://www.landmark.com

Metron is at http://www.metron.co.uk

Resolute is at http://www.resolute.com

SAS is at http://www.sas.com/vision/itservice

SES is at http://www.ses.com

Softway is at http://www.softway.com.au

Symon is at http://www.sun.com/products-n-solutions/hw/servers/symon.html

Teamquest is at http://www.teamquest.com

Sun Products

There is a huge amount of information that is being updated all the time. Each product usually has a collection of white papers that describe the product architecture in detail and performance results on appropriate benchmarks.

http://java.sun.com

This is the main web site for Java information.

http://www.suntest.com

Sun Test's JavaStar product allows automated Java program testing to be performed and was used to generate sizing information for Java server data in "Sizing Tests and Results" on page 115.

http://www.sun.com/servers/ultra_enterprise

Enterprise server specifications, architecture white papers, and performance briefs.

http://www.sun.com/servers/workgroup

Workgroup server specifications, architecture white papers, and performance briefs.

http://www.sun.com/products-n-solutions/hw/networking

Network interface and switch specifications and performance briefs.

http://www.sun.com/servers/hpc

Sun has recently begun to invest heavily in developing products for High-Performance Computing.

http://www.sun.com/solaris

There is a lot of useful information, including white papers and downloadable software, in this section of Sun's web site.

http://www.sun.com/sparc

Sun Microelectronics describes SPARC Processor products and the VIS accelerated multimedia libraries here.

Document Descriptions

Administering Security, Performance, and Accounting in Solaris 2

This document is the basic reference on Solaris 2 and is part of the manual set on the AnswerBook CD. It describes the tweakable parameters that can be set in `/etc/system` and provides a tutorial on how to use performance analysis tools such as `sar` and `vmstat`.

An Analysis of TCP Processing Overhead

by David Clark, Van Jacobson, John Romkey, and Howard Salwen

Describes things that can be tuned to improve TCP/IP and Ethernet throughput. IEEE Communications, June 1989.

The Art of Computer Systems Performance Analysis

by Raj Jain

This book is a comprehensive and very readable reference work covering techniques for experimental design, measurement, simulation, and modeling. Published by Wiley, ISBN 0-471-50336-3.

B

A Cached System Architecture Dedicated for the System IO Activity on a CPU Board
by Hseih, Wei, and Van Loo.
Describes the patented Sun I/O cache architecture used in the SPARCserver 490 and subsequent server designs. Proceedings of the International Conference on Computer Design, October 2 1989.

Computer Architecture — A Quantitative Approach
by John Hennessy and David Patterson
The definitive reference book on modern computer architecture. ISBN 1-55860-069-8.

Computer Networks
by Andrew S. Tanenbaum
This book is one of Rich Pettit's favorites. Second Edition, Prentice Hall, Englewood Cliffs, NJ 07632, ISBN 0-13-162959-X

Configuration and Capacity Planning for Solaris Servers
by Brian Wong
This book tells you how to think about the job of configuring a server to perform a task. It contains detailed guidelines and case studies for the configuration of NFS, database, and time-shared servers. It also contains the performance characteristics of most Sun peripheral options and an extensive section on the theory and practice of the SCSI interface. Published in 1997 by SunSoft Press/PTR Prentice Hall. ISBN 0-13-349952-9.

The Design and Implementation of the 4.3BSD UNIX Operating System
by Leffler, McKusick, Karels, and Quarterman
This book describes the internal design and algorithms used in the kernel of a very closely related operating system. SunOS 3.X was almost a pure BSD4.3; SunOS 4 redesigned the virtual memory system, and UNIX System V Release 4 is about 80 percent based on SunOS 4 with about 20 percent Unix System V.3. Solaris 2 has been further rewritten to support multiple processors. Despite the modifications to the operating system over time, this is a definitive work, and there are few other sources for insight into the kernel algorithms. ISBN 0-201-06196-1.

Extent-like Performance from a UNIX File System
by McVoy and Kleiman
This paper was presented at Usenix in Winter 1991. It describes the filesystem clustering optimization that was introduced in SunOS 4.1.1.

High Performance Computing

by Keith Dowd

This book covers the architecture of high-performance workstations, compute servers, and parallel machines. It is full of examples of the coding techniques required to get the best performance from the new architectures, and it contrasts vector machines with the latest, microprocessor-based technologies. The importance of coding with caches in mind is emphasized. The book is essential reading for FORTRAN programmers trying to make numerical codes run faster. Published by O'Reilly, ISBN 1-56592-032-5.

Internetworking with TCP/IP Volume II

by Douglas E. Comer and David L. Stevens.

Design, implementation, and internals. Prentice Hall, Englewood Cliffs, NJ 07632. ISBN 0-13-472242-6.

The Magic Garden Explained

by Berny Goodheart and James Cox

The internals of Unix System V Release 4, an open systems design. Prentice Hall, Englewood Cliffs, NJ 07632, ISBN 0-13-098138-9.

Managing NFS and NIS

by Hal Stern

Network administration and tuning is covered in depth. An essential reference published by O'Reilly, ISBN 0-937175-75-7.

Multiprocessor System Architectures

by Ben Catanzaro

This book is a reference to all the details of SuperSPARC-based system hardware. It describes all the chip sets and system board designs. Published 1994 by SunSoft Press/PTR Prentice Hall. ISBN 0-13-089137-1.

Performance Tuning an Application

This book is part of the SPARCworks online AnswerBook with the compiler products and the Teamware manuals. New tools are described that may be unfamiliar to many users doing software development.

The Practical Performance Analyst

by Neil Gunther

I have learned a lot from working with Neil. This book contains one of the most accessible treatments of the theoretical basis of performance analysis and modeling. It has practical examples of how to keep models simple enough to be immediately useful and introduces the ideas and theory of large transient behavior in computer systems. Published by McGraw-Hill, 1998, ISBN 0-07-912946-3.

Realtime Scheduling in SunOS 5.0

by Sandeep Khanna, Michael Sebrée, and John Zolnowsky
This paper was presented at Usenix Winter '92 and describes the implementation of the kernel in Solaris 2.0. It covers how kernel threads work, how real-time scheduling is performed, and the novel priority-inheritance system.

SBus /SCSI Developers Kit, Release III

A comprehensive, 4-manual set for developers creating SBus cards and SCSI device drivers. The kit includes Openboot Command Reference, The SBus Handbook, SunOS 5.3 Writing Device Drivers, and Writing FCode Programs. ISBN 0-13-107202-1, SunSoft Press/Prentice Hall.

SMCC NFS Server Performance and Tuning Guide

This guide is part of the SMCC hardware-specific manual set and AnswerBook CD. It contains a good overview of how to size an NFS server configuration and is highly recommended.

The SPARC Architecture Manual Version 8

This manual is available as a book from Prentice Hall. It is also available from the IEEE because the IEEE 1754 standard is based on SPARC version 8. ISBN 0-13-825001-4.

The SPARC Architecture Manual Version 9

This manual has also been published by Prentice Hall as a book. It includes upward-compatible extensions to version 8. A new kernel interface and 64-bit addressing modes are the main changes. ISBN: 0-13-099227-5.

Statistical Models in S

by John M. Chambers and Trevor J. Hastie
This book is specific to the S Language and the S-Plus statistical package, but because the raw statistical techniques are wrapped up in library functions, it is easier to get into than a pure statistics textbook. The book contains many examples of methods that can be used to extract patterns and relationships from large amounts of raw, incomplete, and error-prone data. Published by Wadsworth and Brooks/Cole 1992. ISBN 0-534-16764-0.

SunOS System Internals Course Notes

These notes cover the main kernel algorithms, using pseudocode and flowcharts to avoid source code licensing issues. The notes are from a 5-day course that is run occasionally by Sun.

Sybase SQL Server Performance and Tuning Guide

by Karen Paulsell

This is the place to start if you are trying to tune a Sybase system. It covers Sybase Release 11. ISBN 1-85032-883-8, 1996, Sybase Press/International Thompson Computer Press.

System Performance Tuning

by Mike Loukides

This reference book covers tuning issues for SunOS 4, BSD, System V.3, and System V.4 versions of Unix. It was written in the early 1990s and has now become quite out of date. ISBN 0-937175-60-9. Published by O'Reilly.

TCP/IP Illustrated Volumes 1, 2, 3

This is an excellent and practical introduction to how TCP/IP really works, bugs and all. Volume 1 covers the protocols. Volume 2 covers the implementation of TCP/IP, and Volume 3 covers HTTP and T/TCP.

See the updated Appendix E TCP tunables reference at http://www.kohala.com/~rstevens/tcpipiv1.html.

tmpfs: A Virtual Memory File System

by Peter Snyder

This Sun white paper discusses the design goals and implementation details of tmpfs.

Ultra Enterprise 10000 System Overview White Paper

This paper discusses the key technical features of the E10000 server, including a discussion of Gigaplane XB crossbar data interconnect, Dynamic System Domains, Reliability, Availability and Serviceability features.
http://www.sun.com/servers/ultra_enterprise/10000/wp

Unix Internals — The New Frontiers

by Uresh Vhalia

This is my favorite book on the internal operations of Unix. It is relatively up to date and explains and compares the implementations used by the major Unix variants. Published by Prentice Hall, 1996. ISBN 0-13-101908-2.

Virtual Swap Space in SunOS

by Howard Chartock and Peter Snyder

The concept of swap space in SunOS 5 has been extended by the abstraction of a virtual swap file system, which allows the system to treat main memory as if it were a backing store. Further, this abstraction allows for more intelligent choices to be made about swap space allocation.This paper contrasts the existing mechanisms and their limitations with the modifications made to implement virtual swap space. May 1992.

You and Your Compiler

by Keith Bierman

This is the definitive guide to using the compilers effectively for benchmarking or performance tuning. It has been modified as a performance tuning chapter in the manual set for FORTRAN 1.4 and later.

Index

☰ Index

☰ Index